The Editor

BIODUN JEYIFO was educated at the University of Ibadan in Nigeria and New York University. His books include *The Popular Traveling Theatre of Nigeria, The Truthful Lie, Conversations with Wole Soyinka,* and *Perspectives on Wole Soyinka: Freedom and Complexity.* He has written monographs and essays on Marxist cultural theory, colonial and postcolonial studies, and Anglophone African and Caribbean literatures. He is Professor of English at Cornell University, where he is on the graduate faculty of four departments: English, Comparative Literature, Africana Studies, and Theatre Arts.

W. W. NORTON & COMPANY, INC.
Also Publishes

ENGLISH RENAISSANCE DRAMA: A NORTON ANTHOLOGY
edited by David Bevington et al.

THE NORTON ANTHOLOGY OF AFRICAN AMERICAN LITERATURE
edited by Henry Louis Gates Jr. and Nellie Y. McKay et al.

THE NORTON ANTHOLOGY OF AMERICAN LITERATURE
edited by Nina Baym et al.

THE NORTON ANTHOLOGY OF CHILDREN'S LITERATURE
edited by Jack Zipes et al.

THE NORTON ANTHOLOGY OF ENGLISH LITERATURE
edited by M. H. Abrams and Stephen Greenblatt et al.

THE NORTON ANTHOLOGY OF LITERATURE BY WOMEN
edited by Sandra M. Gilbert and Susan Gubar

THE NORTON ANTHOLOGY OF MODERN AND CONTEMPORARY POETRY
edited by Jahan Ramazani, Richard Ellmann, and Robert O'Clair

THE NORTON ANTHOLOGY OF POETRY
edited by Margaret Ferguson, Mary Jo Salter, and Jon Stallworthy

THE NORTON ANTHOLOGY OF SHORT FICTION
edited by R. V. Cassill and Richard Bausch

THE NORTON ANTHOLOGY OF THEORY AND CRITICISM
edited by Vincent B. Leitch et al.

THE NORTON ANTHOLOGY OF WORLD LITERATURE
edited by Sarah Lawall et al.

THE NORTON FACSIMILE OF THE FIRST FOLIO OF SHAKESPEARE
prepared by Charlton Hinman

THE NORTON INTRODUCTION TO LITERATURE
edited by Alison Booth, J. Paul Hunter, and Kelly J. Mays

THE NORTON INTRODUCTION TO THE SHORT NOVEL
edited by Jerome Beaty

THE NORTON READER
edited by Linda H. Peterson and John C. Brereton

THE NORTON SAMPLER
edited by Thomas Cooley

THE NORTON SHAKESPEARE, BASED ON THE OXFORD EDITION
edited by Stephen Greenblatt et al.

For a complete list of Norton Critical Editions, visit
wwnorton.com/college/English/nce_home.htm

A NORTON CRITICAL EDITION

MODERN AFRICAN DRAMA

Authoritative Texts of

FATE OF A COCKROACH
INTELLIGENCE POWDER
SIZWE BANSI IS DEAD
DEATH AND THE KING'S HORSEMAN
COLLISION OF ALTARS
THE DILEMMA OF A GHOST
I WILL MARRY WHEN I WANT
ESU AND THE VAGABOND MINSTRELS

Backgrounds and Criticism

Edited by

BIODUN JEYIFO

CORNELL UNIVERSITY

W • W • NORTON & COMPANY • *New York* • *London*

Copyright © 2002 by W. W. Norton & Company, Inc.

The text of this book is composed in Fairfield Medium with the display set in Bernhard Modern.
Composition by PennSet, Inc.
Manufacturing by LSC Communications, Crawfordsville.
Book design by Antonina Krass.

Library of Congress Cataloging-in-Publication Data
Modern African drama : backgrounds and criticism / selected and edited by Biodun Jeyifo.
    p.   cm.—(A Norton critical edition)
Includes bibliographical references.
    Contents: The fate of a cockroach / Tawfik al Hakim—Intelligence powder / Kateb Yacine—Sizwe Bansi is dead / Athol Fugard, John Kani & Winston Nthsona—Death and the king's horseman / Wole Soyinka—A collision of altars / Tsegaye Gabre-Medhin—Dilemma of a ghost / Ama Ata Aidoo—I will marry when I want / Ngugi wa Thiong'o—Esu and the vagabond minstrels / Femi Osofisan.

ISBN 0-393-97529-0 (pbk)

    1. African drama (English)   2. African drama (English)—History and criticism.   3. Theater—Africa.   4. Africa—Drama.   I. Jeyifo, Biodun, 1946–

PR9347 .M63 2001
822.008'096—dc21

2001044667

W. W. Norton & Company, Inc., 500 Fifth Avenue, New York, N.Y. 10110
www.wwnorton.com

W. W. Norton & Company Ltd., 15 Carlisle Street,
London W1D 3BS

5 6 7 8 9 0

Contents

Preface

On February 22, 1826, in the ancient city of Oyo, the capital of the West African empire of the same name, the British explorer Hugh Clapperton and his party were treated to a theatrical performance by a Yoruba Alarinjo troupe. Clapperton's account of the event is contained in his travelogue, *Journal of a Second Exhibition Into the Interior of Africa*. From this account, it is evident that the Alafin, or monarch, of Oyo organized the event as a sort of command performance for the white visitors and their party, a performance in which the foreign guests found themselves simultaneously importuned as spectators and good-naturedly lambasted in the form of a character in the performance itself. Here is Clapperton on this double signification on his white, foreign presence at this 1826 performance in the then not yet formally colonized southern Nigeria:

> The third act consisted of the white devil. The actors having retired to some distance in the background, one of them was left in the centre, whose sack falling gradually down, exposed a white head, at which the crowd gave a shout that rent the air; they appeared indeed to enjoy this sight and the perfection of the actor's art. The whole body was at last cleared of the incumbrance of the sack, when it exhibited the appearance of a human figure cast in white wax, of the middle size, miserably thin, and starved with cold. It frequently went through the motion of taking snuff and rubbing its hands; when it walked, it was the most awkward gait, treading as the most tender-footed white man would do in walking barefooted for the first time over frozen ground. The spectators often appealed to us, as to the excellence of the performance, and entreated I would look and be attentive to what was going on. I pretended to be fully as much pleased with this caricature of a white man as they could be, and certainly the actor burlesqued the part to admiration.

We know from the considerable body of scholarly research and publications on the Alarinjo theatrical art of masked dance-mummers that Clapperton's application of terms of theatrical theory and criticism such as "the third act," "actors," "actor's art," "spectators," and "burlesque" constitutes an accurate reflection of the evolved, professional, and secular standards of this African theatrical tradition. It also appears that Clapperton, on this occasion at least, was a good sport, giving the artistry, if not the content of the performance, high praise. But while there is no reason to question the emotional truth of his negative identification with the theatrical sign semiotized in the "figure cast in white wax," Clapperton's reading of the roots of what is imitated in the performance is very fanciful. When he writes, "when it walked, it was the most awkward gait, treading as the most tender-footed white man would do in walking barefooted for the first time over frozen ground," he misses the whole point of the "burlesque," for this figure could in no way have had the bracing, wintry cold of Clapperton's temperate homeland as the source of its caricature. What we have here, it seems, is Clapperton drawing on his own cultural frame of reference and thereby misinterpreting what probably was a caricature of whites, not at home in the wilds of, say, the Yorkshire moors in the dead of winter, but in the tropical "interior of Africa" stripped of the comforts of the legendary white explorer's litter and its band of native head porters, guides, and body servants. The Alarinjo theatre tradition did evolve from sacred funerary rites, but its repertoire of masks and sketches was, and is still, rigorously based on historical events and topical civic issues; moreover, its repertoire of masks consists of stock social types. Indeed, several decades after this 1826 performance, the formal incorporation of the Oyo empire into what became the Nigerian colony of the British imperial system generated the appearance of the coupled figure of the white colonial district commissioner and his wife in the Alarinjo troupe's theatrical fare as one of the most colorful and frequently animated masks, comparable in popularity to two groups of masks. These are, respectively, the masks of "local foreigners" such as "Tapa" (the Nupe man) and "Gambari" (the Hausa man)—the Nupes and the Hausas being northern neighbors of the Yoruba with a long history of trade, warfare, and limited but significant cultural intermixture with the Yoruba—and the satirical masks of moral or social types such as "Iyawo Palo" ("Parlor Wife," i.e., the young housewife of loose sexual morals) and "Omuti Farasofo" (the perpetually inebriated drunkard). Thus, if Clapperton had given more critical significance to the fact that the burlesque of the "white devil" was only one act out of many in the total performance staged for his entertainment, he might have recognized the theatrical sign in that particular "third act" as part of a chain of signifiers whose logic of signification, like all signifying chains, was context-specific. Within the representational compass of this logic, the mask of the "white devil" in which Clapperton saw himself caricatured belongs to the same category—the category of "foreigners"—as the "Tapa" and "Gambari" masks. Within this composite category, one set of masks designates "distant" foreigners and the other set is made up of masks of close, contiguous foreigners. And both sets of masks, it might be noted, form a logic of representational difference with the "straight" and satirical masks of "insider" social types, such as "Malam" (Moslem priest), "Iyawo Palo," and "Omuti Farasofo."

This 1826 performance—and our deconstruction of Clapperton's reading of it—is emblematic of the perspectives that informed the selection of the materials assembled for this volume of plays and critical documents on modern African drama. For as with nearly every other aspect of its experience of modernity, the "modern" in African drama and theatre is the product of the complex articulation of the local with the foreign, the indigenous with the alien within the historic context of the modern migrations of peoples and cultures *within* the continent, and the waves of imperialist expansion and colonial domination that swept over the continent in a five-hundred-year span. Because the European colonization of Africa has been the single most decisive factor in Africa's experience of modernity, until very recently it has been impossible to keep this mosaic of genealogies of the modern in Africa in the purview of even the most influential practitioners and scholars of the continent's traditions of drama and theatre. Very often and quite simplistically, the modern in African drama has been apprehended in the reified polarity of native traditions versus Western influences in which the latter always supervened the former in the manner of Clapperton's inability to imagine that the theatrical sign of the "white devil" could have had sources in local history.

As some of the plays and documents assembled in this volume demonstrate, the wide-ranging legacies of the encounter of Africa with Europe in the modern period as the object of imperialist ambition and colonial domination remains a central dimension of modern African drama and theatre. But equally important, though almost always undertheorized and underspecified as a determinant of the genealogy of contemporary African drama, are two other large-scale modern experiences of African societies. These are, respectively, the migrations and population shifts of African communities across short and long distances before, during, and after formal colonial conquest and rule; and centuries of trade, religious proselytization, and slavery between the two blocs of the African continent north and south of the great Sahara desert. To illustratively refer again to the masks of the Alarinjo theatre, long before the appearance of the masks of the colonial district commissioner and his wife in that theatre's repertoire of stock characters, the Moslem priest had appeared as "Malam," not within the category of "foreigners" but as the mask of a completely assimilated "insider." Needless to say, this is the product of the Islamic penetration from North Africa and the Arab world across the Sahara in West Africa and the Indian Ocean in East Africa. Given the sheer historical and cultural weight of this factor, it should normally need no editorial justification as to why this volume of modern African drama includes entries from North Africa. That such justification is being hereby tendered is a reflection of the pervasive practice of separating Africa north and south of the Sahara in anthologies of the plays, poetry, fiction, and popular culture of the continent. It is incontestable that this practice is defensible and even productive at the level at which constructions such as "Black Africa" (as in the volume of poems edited by Wole Soyinka, *Poems of Black Africa*) and "North African" or "Maghrebian writing" refer to formations and communities of expression *within* African letters, arts, society, and culture. However, as the bloody and self-maiming civil war of the last three decades in the Sudan demonstrates, the suppression of shared histories, cultures, and ethnicities between Africa north and south of the Sahara often entails violent, tragic consequences.

If the Western impact, via colonization, on modern African drama is often overstated (or conversely, tendentiously understated in some versions of nationalist counterdiscourses on the nature and sources of contemporary African drama) while the long duration of intercultural contact between north and south across the "natural" divide of the Sahara is often blithely ignored, there is also a pervasive act of amnesia about the scope of cultural intermixing among the continent's peoples and cultures as a decisive aspect of the modern experience of the continent. This particular act of discursive amnesia is all the more surprising given the fact that the artificiality, the porousness of the colonially imposed borders of African nation-states is as tireless invoked by statesmen, writers, journalists, and foreign pundits as the anodyne invocation of Africa as the origin of the human race. The *comparative* slant of nearly all the critical documents assembled in this volume is an attempt, one hopes not too belated, to give credence and weight to this dimension of Africa's experience of modernity. Fortunately, in much of recent scholarship in diverse disciplines, due and necessary cognizance is being given this crucial historical and geopolitical fact of Africa's modern experience. Consequently, the widespread practice of treating African cultures, precolonial as well as postcolonial and in the framework of a now discredited colonialist anthropology, as bounded and fixed within thousands of separate "tribes" is gradually giving way to the recognition that Africans are as much border-crossers in culture and the arts as they are of the territorial boundaries of the nation-state.

The upshot of the foregoing observations on the thinking that shaped the selection of plays and critical documents for this volume is that what is truly modern in African drama and theatre as it has evolved in the last hundred and fifty years or so is a function both of African self-encounter and of the continent's encounter with the outside world. Both sets of encounters inevitably replicate many of the themes of both the "promise" of modernity and its horrendous discontents that have been documented elsewhere in the world. That being said, it is noteworthy that such replication of "modernizing" global currents has taken irreducibly *African* expressions. One of the most remarkable of these unique African expressions of global modernity is the incidence of the much vaster scale of Anglophone and Francophone drama and theatre in this continent than elsewhere in the formerly colonized regions of the world. This point needs careful elaboration.

The term *Anglophone* and *Francophone* are key words of cultural criticism and, more broadly, transnational, transhemispheric intellectual and cultural currents of the late modern world. Anglophone for its part now generally denotes that vast stretch of the English-speaking world that is outside Britain and North America, especially the United States. Similarly, Francophone now generally denotes a French-speaking community of writing and cultural expression outside of metropolitan France. Now, it is one of the most significant features of these Anglophone and Francophone worlds that while in poetry and fiction there are more or less equally powerful currents coming out of Asia, Africa, and the Caribbean, Francophone and Anglophone drama significantly bulk much bigger in Africa than in other parts of the non-Western English- and French-speaking worlds. True enough, world-class African Anglophone and Francophone dramatists are, so far, only a handful, but there is now in existence a considerable number of fine, sensitive dramatists in this newly emergent tradition; moreover, the sheer volume and social impact of the English- and French-language drama of Africa is, quite simply, one of the contemporary world's most significant cultural developments. What makes this such an outstanding aspect of post–World War II cultural history is the fact that the scale of Francophone and Anglophone African drama grew out of some of the much-discussed limitations of the theatrical heritage of Africa. These include the relative absence in Africa of the great professional, highly specialized, and rigidly codified theatre institutions and practices, in both written and unwritten forms, of Asian and European antiquity and the early modern period. In this case, the saying "the poor shall inherit the earth" takes on a special resonance, because unencumbered by the dead weight of these monuments of theatre tradition, African Anglophone and Francophone drama has zestfully raided a great number of the continent's "little" theatre and performance traditions in ways that Francophone and Anglophone drama elsewhere has not dared to do. These "little" traditions are, however, capacious in their range, stretching from popular festivals to the most esoteric cultic rituals, and from oral storytelling traditions to the arts of sacred and carnivalesque idioms of masqueradery, dance, and music.

The ramifications of this pattern have barely been acknowledged, let alone extensively explored. For one thing, anticolonial and postcolonial nationalism, with its resilience and pitfalls, is one of the most paradigmatic and at the same time extensively interrogated constructions of political community in the late modern world. It has been thematized and explored in Anglophone and Francophone African drama as in no other major cultural region of the world, with the possible exception of Latin America. As a corollary to this, outside of Europe and Latin America, the revolutionary potential of contemporary dramatic and theatrical theory and criticism has found no theorists or critics of the caliber of pundits that have emerged from critical discourses on African Francophone and Anglophone drama. This particular feature of contemporary African drama and theatre is amply illustrated in some of the critical documents assembled in this volume.

French and English are of course not the only languages of expression in modern African drama. To speak only of literary drama, African theatre of the last century has seen the emergence and growth of drama in other major literary languages of the continent, such as Arabic, Amharic, Yoruba, Swahili, Hausa, Twi, Gikuyu, Zulu, and Sotho. Regrettably, since this volume is an English-language publication, this richness and diversity of African drama is not immediately apparent in the content of the materials collected here. However, this richness is inscribed in subtle ways in the forms and idioms of expression explored by many of the plays, as well as in some of the theoretical speculation in the critical documents. No doubt some of these will seem strangely familiar to readers knowledgeable about the technical and stylistic armory of the Western theatrical avant-garde. Conversely, some readers wedded to a unilinear and Eurocentric view of the course of evolution of modern world drama will see in one or two of these plays modes of dramatic expression that seem to belong to earlier phases of literary drama. But in the main, many features of this confident genre-bending and form-stretching impulse of African drama will startle because they indicate fresh and radical extensions of dramatic form.

The generally affirmative tone of these observations and musings should not, finally, blind us to the present precarious condition of African drama, or indeed the toil and sacrifice that many African dramatists, theatre companies, and performers have had to bear in the course of plying their trade and craft, both in the colonial and postcolonial periods. Contemporary African drama, in its exploration of both social and existential themes, is a vigorous response to the crippling vagaries and frustrations of what some of the most prominent social theorists of the twentieth century, taking a deep, sober measure of the broken promises of independence in much of the developing world, have aptly termed "the development of underdevelopment"; it is also often a hostage to this stultifying process. The list is very long of theatre people in Africa who, in the cause of social justice and human rights, have paid small and heavy prices so that the ancient, primordial energies of the mimetic faculty that lie at the root of the dramatic enterprise may be rekindled and revitalized for our age, especially on the continent of Africa. This volume is dedicated to all such theatre people of the past, present, and future.

THE TEXTS OF THE PLAYS

TAWFIK AL-HAKIM

Fate of a Cockroach[†]

Characters

Cockroaches
KING
QUEEN
MINISTER
SAVANT
PRIEST
A SUBJECT COCKROACH

Procession of Ants

Mortals
SAMIA, a housewife
ADIL, her husband
COOK
DOCTOR

Act One—The Cockroach as King

The scene is a spacious courtyard—as viewed of course by the cockroaches. In actual fact the courtyard is nothing more than the bathroom floor in an ordinary flat. In the front part of this courtyard stands an immense wall, which is nothing but the outer wall of the bath. The time is night, though from the point of view of the cockroaches it is daytime—our bright daylight being so blinding to them that it causes them either to disappear or go to sleep. At the beginning of the play, night has not completely fallen, which is to say that the cockroaches' day is about to begin. The King is standing in sprightly fashion next to a hole in the wall, perhaps the doorway to his palace, and is calling to the Queen who is asleep inside the palace.

KING Come along—wake up! It's time for work.

QUEEN (*from inside*) The darkness of evening has not yet appeared.

KING Any moment now it will.

† From Tawfik al-Hakim, *"Fate of a Cockroach" and Other Plays*, sel. and trans. from the Arabic by Denys Johnson-Davies (Washington, D.C.: Three Continents Press, 1980). Copyright © 1996 by Lynne Rienner Publishers, Inc. Used by permission of the publisher.

QUEEN   Has the blinding light of day completely disappeared?

KING   Any moment now it will.

QUEEN   Until it disappears completely and night has completely come, let me be and don't bother me.

KING   What laziness! What laziness!

QUEEN (*making her appearance*)   I wasn't sleeping. You must remember that I have my toilet and make-up to do.

KING   Make-up and toilet! If all wives were like you, then God help all husbands!

QUEEN (*aroused to anger*)   I'm a queen! Don't forget I'm the Queen!

KING   And I'm the King!

QUEEN   I'm exactly the same as you—there's no difference between us at all.

KING   There is a difference.

QUEEN   And what, prithee, might this difference be?

KING   My whiskers.

QUEEN   Just as you have whiskers, so have I.

KING   Yes, but my whiskers are longer than yours.

QUEEN   That is a trifling difference.

KING   So it seems to you.

QUEEN   To you rather. It is your sickly imagination that always makes it appear to you that there is a difference between us.

KING   The difference exists—it can be clearly seen by anyone with eyes to see. If you don't believe me, ask the Minister, the Priest, the Savant, and all those worthy gentlemen connected with the court . . .

QUEEN (*sarcastically*)   The court!

KING   Please—no sarcasm! I have an ever-growing feeling that you're always trying to belittle my true worth.

QUEEN   Your worth?

KING   Yes, and my authority. You are always trying to diminish my authority.

QUEEN (*even more sarcastically*)   Your authority? Your authority over whom? Not over me at any rate—you are in no way better than me. You don't provide me with food or drink. Have you ever fed me? I feed myself, just as you feed yourself. Do you deny it?

KING   In the whole cockroach kingdom there is no one who feeds another. Every cockroach strives for his own daily bread.

QUEEN   Then I am free to do as I like?

KING   And who ever said you weren't?

QUEEN   Let me be then. It is I who will decide when I shall work and when be lazy, when to sleep and when to get up.

KING   Of course you are free to do as you like but, in your capacity as Queen, you must set a good example.

QUEEN   A good example to whom?

KING   To the subjects, naturally.

QUEEN   The subjects? And where might they be? In my whole life I've never seen anyone around you but those three: the Minister, the Priest, and the learned Savant.

KING   They are enough, they are the élite, the cream . . .

QUEEN   But if you are the King you should be surrounded by the people.

KING   Have you forgotten the characteristics of our species? We are not like those small creatures called 'ants', who gather together in their thousands on the slightest pretext.

QUEEN   Don't remind me of ants! A king like you claiming you have worth and authority and you don't know how to solve the ant problem!

KING   The ant problem! Ah . . . um . . .

QUEEN   Ah . . . um . . . is that all you can say?

KING   What reminded you of ants?

QUEEN   Their being a continual threat to us. A queen like me, in my position and with my beauty, elegance, and pomp, can't take a step without trembling for fear that I might slip and fall on my back— and woe to me should I fall on my back, for I would quickly become a prey to the armies of ants.

KING   Be careful, therefore, that you do not fall on your back!

QUEEN   Is that the only solution you have?

KING   Do you want, from one day to the next, a solution to a problem that is as old as time?

QUEEN   Then shut up and don't boast about the length of your whiskers!

KING   Please! Don't talk to the King in such a tone!

QUEEN   King! I would just like to ask *who* made you a king.

KING   I made myself a king.

QUEEN   And what devious means and measures brought you to the throne and placed you on the seat of kingship?

KING (*indignantly*)   Means and measures? Pardon me for saying so, but you're stupid!

QUEEN   I confess I'm stupid about this . . .

KING   What means and what measures, Madam? The question's a lot simpler than that. One morning I woke up and looked at my face in the mirror—or rather in a pool of water near the drain. You yourself know this drain well—it's the one at which we first met. Do you remember?

QUEEN   Of course I remember, but what's the connection between the drain, your face, and the throne?

KING   Have a little patience and you'll find out. I told you that I looked at my face in the mirror—something that you naturally do every day, perhaps every hour, in order to assure yourself of the beauty of your face.

QUEEN   At present we're talking about *your* face. Speak and don't get away from the subject.

KING (*rather put out by now*)   As I told you, I looked at my face in the mirror—this was of course by chance . . . that is to say by sheer accident . . . meaning that it was not intentional, I swear to you.

QUEEN   That's neither here nor there. You looked at your face in the drain—what did you discover?

KING   I discovered something that surprised me and aroused in me . . .

QUEEN   A feeling of dejection.

KING   Not at all—of admiration.

QUEEN   Admiration of what?

KING   Of the length of my whiskers. I was really delighted at the length of my whiskers. I immediately rose up and challenged all the cockroaches to compare their whiskers with mine, and that if it was apparent that mine were the longest then I should become king over them all.

QUEEN   And they accepted the challenge?

KING   No, they conceded it to me there and then, saying that they had no time for whisker-measuring.

QUEEN   And so you automatically became His Majesty!

KING   Just so.

QUEEN   And did they tell you what your privileges were to be?

KING   No.

QUEEN   And did they tell you what their duties towards you were?

KING   No. They merely said that as I was pleased with the title and rank, I could do as I pleased. So long as this cost them nothing and they were not required to feed me, then they had no objection to my calling myself what I liked. And so they left me, each going his own way in search of his daily bread.

QUEEN   Then how was it that I became Queen?

KING   By commonsense logic. As I was King and you were the female I loved and lived with, so you were of necessity Queen.

QUEEN   And your Minister? How did he become a minister?

KING   His talents nominated him for the office of Minister, just as mine did for the throne.

QUEEN   We know about your talents—the length of your whiskers. But what are your Minister's talents?

KING   His consummate concern with proposing disconcerting problems and producing unpleasant news.

QUEEN   And the Priest, what are his talents?

KING   The completely incomprehensible things he says.

QUEEN   And the learned Savant?

KING   The strange information he has about things that have no existence other than in his own head.

QUEEN   And what induced you to put up with these people?

KING   Necessity. I found no one but them wanting to be close to me. They are in need of someone to whom they can pour out their absurdities, whereas I am in need of close companions who will call me 'Your Majesty'.

QUEEN   All of which was brought upon you by your long whiskers.

KING   And am I responsible? I was born with them like this.

QUEEN   Maybe there was someone with longer whiskers than you and yet he never thought of declaring himself a king.

KING   Very likely, yet it was I who thought . . .

QUEEN   A stupid idea in any case.

KING (*indignantly*)   And who are you to say? You understand nothing!

QUEEN   I understand more than you.

KING   You're a garrulous and conceited cockroach!

QUEEN   And you're a . . .

KING   Hush! The Minister's coming.

QUEEN   Then have some self-respect in front of him and treat me with respect.

KING   To hear is to obey, Your Majesty.

QUEEN   That's better! Husbands like you are submissive only to a woman who maintains her rights.

The Minister makes his appearance, wailing.

MINISTER   My Lord King! Help, my Lord King!

KING   What is it?

MINISTER   A calamity! A great calamity, my Lord!

KING   Goodness gracious! (*aside*) I told you his hobby was to bring unpleasant news. (*loudly*) Yes? Tell us, delight our ears!

MINISTER   My son, Your Majesty—my one and only son.

KING   What's wrong with him?

MINISTER   He has been taken in the prime of youth—has died in the spring of life—he has been killed! Killed!

KING   Killed! How? Who killed him?

MINISTER   The ants.

KING   The ants again?

QUEEN   There, you see? The ants. The ants.

MINISTER   Yes, Your Majesty, the ants—none but the ants.

KING   Ah, those ants! Tell us what happened.

MINISTER   What always happens.

KING   Be more explicit.

MINISTER   My son was walking along the wall, just going for a stroll for amusement's sake, like anyone else at his age—a perfectly innocent stroll of course, for you well know what a well-behaved person he is. He's exceedingly serious, with no inclinations towards flirtations or foolhardy ventures, all those kinds of nonsensical pastimes . . .

KING (*impatiently*)   That's neither here nor there—what happened?

MINISTER   His foot slipped and he fell to the ground. Of course he fell on his back and was unable to turn on to his front and get to his feet. And then the ants spotted him. They brought along their troops and armies, surrounded him, smothered him, and carried him off to their towns and villages.

QUEEN   What a terrible thing! Truly a catastrophe!

MINISTER   A great catastrophe, Your Majesty—a national catastrophe!

KING   I share your feelings of sadness for the deceased. Don't, though, ask that I announce public mourning.

MINISTER   I have not asked for an announcement of mourning, Your Majesty.

KING   That's extremely intelligent of you.

MINISTER   I am merely announcing that it is a catastrophe for the whole of our species.

KING   The whole of our species? The death of your son?

MINISTER   I mean rather the ants' aggression against us all in this manner.

QUEEN (to the Minister)   He understands what you mean perfectly well. He merely pretends not to. He turns the matter into a personal one so that he need not bother himself about the decisive solution which everyone awaits from him.

KING   What are you saying? Are you trying to accuse me of neglecting the duties of my position?

QUEEN   I am not accusing you, I am merely drawing your attention to the necessity for finding a solution to the problem of the ants.

KING   And is the problem of the ants a new one? Speak, Minister?

MINISTER   No, Your Majesty.

KING   Then you know that it is not new, that it is old as Time itself.

MINISTER   Certainly, Your Majesty.

KING   We grew up, our fathers, our grandfathers, and our grandfathers' grandfathers grew up, with the problem of the ants there.

MINISTER   Truly, Your Majesty.

KING   Seeing that you know all that, why do you today assign me the task of solving it? Why should it be my bad luck that I, out of all those fathers and grandfathers who came before me, should alone be asked to find the solution?

QUEEN   Because before you came along there had been no one who was so delighted with the length of his whiskers that he demanded to be made king!

KING   Shut up, you . . .

QUEEN   Mind what you say!

KING (between his teeth)   Your . . . Your Majesty!

QUEEN   Yes, that's the polite way in which you should address me.

KING   And with all politeness I would like to ask you how you know that before me there was no cockroach who wanted to be king?

QUEEN   Because such ideas only occur to someone like you.

KING   Like me?

QUEEN   Yes, because you're my husband and I know you well.

KING   Kindly note that we are not alone now, also that I am now fulfilling my official functions.

QUEEN   Go ahead and fulfil your official functions!

KING   Speak, Minister.

MINISTER   Before you, Your Majesty, we lived in an age of primitive barbarism. We had neither a king nor a minister, then you came along, with your sense of organization and sound thinking, and ascended the throne.

KING   Then I have a sense of organization and sound thinking?

MINISTER   Without doubt, Your Majesty.

KING   Tell Her Majesty that!

QUEEN (sarcastically)   Her Majesty is primarily concerned with the practical results. I want to see the fruit of this thinking and organization. Come on, produce a solution to the problem of the ants!

KING (*impatiently*) Come along, Minister—suggest something!

MINISTER As you think best, Your Majesty.

KING Yes, but it's up to you first to put forward an opinion, even if it's a stupid one. I'll then look into it.

MINISTER Put forward an opinion?

KING Yes, any opinion. Speak—quickly. It's one of the duties of your position to put forward an opinion—and for me to make fun of it.

QUEEN Perhaps his opinion will be sound.

KING I don't think so—I know his opinions.

QUEEN Why, then, did you appoint him Minister?

KING I didn't appoint him. I told you so a thousand times—I never appointed anyone. It's he who appointed himself. I accepted because he had no rival.

MINISTER I volunteered to act without a salary.

KING Talk seriously, Minister, and don't waste the State's time.

MINISTER I've found it! Your Majesty, I think we could overcome the ants with the same weapon they use.

KING And what's their weapon?

MINISTER Armies. They attack us with huge armies. Now if we were able to mobilize ourselves and assemble in great numbers we'd find it easy to attack them, to scatter and to crush them under our great feet.

KING A stupid idea.

QUEEN Why do you make fun of it before you have discussed it?

KING It's clearly unacceptable and absurd.

QUEEN First of all, encourage him to speak and then talk things over with him.

KING (*turning to Minister; peevishly*) I have encouraged you and here I am talking things over with you. Speak. Tell me how many there will be in the army of cockroaches you want to mobilize?

MINISTER Let's say twenty. Twenty cockroaches assembled together could trample underfoot and destroy a long column of ants—nay, a whole village, a whole township.

KING Of that there is no doubt, but has it ever happened in the whole of our long history that twenty cockroaches have gathered together in one column?

MINISTER It has not, but we can try . . .

KING How can we try? We are quite different from ants. The ants know the discipline of forming themselves into columns, but we cockroaches don't know discipline.

MINISTER Perhaps by learning and training . . .

KING And who will teach and train us.

MINISTER We can look around for someone who will undertake it.

KING Marvellous! So we end up with looking around for a teacher and a trainer! Tell me, then, if we find the teacher and the trainer, after how many generations will the species of cockroaches be taught and trained to walk in columns?

MINISTER   Such information, Your Majesty, does not fall within my province. I have merely given my opinion as to the plan of action. It is for others to talk about the details.

KING   Who are those others? For example?

MINISTER   Our learned Savant for example. He is the man to be asked about such information.

QUEEN   He is right. These are things about which the learned Savant can talk.

KING   And where is the learned Savant?

MINISTER   We'll ask him to come immediately, Your Majesty.

KING   Ask for him and let him come—we are waiting.

Hardly has the Minister made a move than the learned Savant makes his appearance, panting.

MINISTER (*to the Savant*)   My dear chap, we were just about to inquire about you. His Majesty wants you on an important matter.

SAVANT   Good.

MINISTER   His Majesty will tell you . . .

KING   No, you tell him.

MINISTER   Shall I put the whole matter to him?

KING   Yes—quickly.

MINISTER   The matter in question is the problem of the ants.

SAVANT   What about the problem of the ants?

MINISTER   We want to find a decisive solution to it.

SAVANT   And what have I to do with this? This is a political problem. It is for you to solve—you in your capacity as Minister and His Majesty in his capacity as King.

MINISTER (*now baffled*)   A political problem?

SAVANT   In any case, it's an old problem. It does not fall within the province of science or scientists.

KING   But the Minister has turned it into a scientific problem, because he wants the cockroaches to be taught to walk in columns.

SAVANT   That can never happen.

MINISTER   But it must do, because we can't go on like this for ever, having the ants attacking us and not being able to drive them off.

QUEEN   The Minister is right, we must think seriously about this danger.

SAVANT   What exactly is required of me?

QUEEN   To assist with your knowledge. All hope now lies with science.

SAVANT   Define exactly what is required. What is required of me precisely? In science things must be precisely defined.

QUEEN   Define things for him, Minister.

MINISTER   You know that the ants attack us with their armies. If we also were able to mobilize an army of twenty, or even ten, cockroaches with which to attack them, we would be able to destroy their towns and villages.

SAVANT   Then mobilize ten cockroaches!

MINISTER   And who will do so?

SAVANT   You and His Majesty the King—that's your job.

KING   Our job!

SAVANT   Naturally. If the King can't order ten cockroaches to assemble together, then what authority has the King got?

KING (*haughtily*)   It seems that you're living in a daze, learned Savant!

MINISTER   The problem is how to gather these cockroaches together.

KING   Tell him! Tell him!

QUEEN   Inform us, Savant, has it ever hapened that you have seen ten cockroaches gathered together in one spot?

SAVANT   Yes, I once saw—a very long time ago, in the early days of my youth—several cockroaches gathered together at night in the kitchen round a piece of tomato.

QUEEN   Tomato?

SAVANT   Yes.

KING   An extraordinary idea—this matter of a tomato!

MINISTER   We begin from here.

QUEEN   And you say that science cannot solve the problem?

SAVANT   What has science to do with this? That was no more than a general observation.

KING   This is the modesty of a true Savant. The idea is, however, useful. If we were able to get a piece of tomato, then a number of cockroaches would gather together round it.

SAVANT   The real problem is how to get hold of a piece of tomato.

KING   How is it, therefore, that we do sometimes get hold of a piece?

SAVANT   By sheer chance.

QUEEN   And when does sheer chance occur?

SAVANT   That is something one cannot predict.

KING   You have therefore arrived at solving one problem by presenting us with another.

QUEEN   Suggest for us something other than tomatoes.

SAVANT   Any other sort of food puts us in the same position, for though we can find food we are unable to make a particular sort of food available.

QUEEN   Can't we get cockroaches together without food?

SAVANT   Neither cockroaches nor anything else.

MINISTER   That's true. The armies of the ant species themselves assemble only round food, to carry off food, or to store food.

KING   Our sole method of getting cockroaches together is food?

SAVANT   That's right—from the theoretical point of view.

QUEEN   What do you mean?

SAVANT   I mean, Your Majesty, from the practical point of view it's all neither here nor there, because the cockroaches assembling round the food won't make a bit of difference—they'll just eat and fill their stomachs, then each will take himself off.

KING   That's true. It has happened before. Remember how after I was installed as King a number of cockroaches happened to assemble round a piece of sugar we found—it was sheer good luck—and I seized the opportunity of this gathering to deliver the speech from the throne. I rose to my feet to speak, with them having eaten their fill, and hardly had I uttered two words than I found each one of them waving his whiskers and going off on his own. They left me shouting into thin air!

MINISTER   That's just our trouble!

QUEEN   Is there no cure for this, O Savant?

SAVANT   It is something ingrained.

QUEEN   There must be a reason.

SAVANT   I have thought about this a lot and have hit upon a reason. The fact is that a strong link has been observed between the assembling of cockroaches in one place and the occurrence of catastrophes of a certain sort.

MINISTER   You mean the moving mountains?

SAVANT   Exactly—and the annihilating, choking rain.

KING   That's true. I have heard news of just such calamities.

SAVANT   This has today become confirmed from a scientific point of view. If a number of cockroaches gather together in one place, and there is bright, dazzling light, mountains that have neither pinnacles nor peaks move and trample upon our troop, utterly squashing them. At other times there teems down a choking rain that destroys every one of us.

QUEEN   And what is the reason for this, O Savant?

SAVANT   Natural phenomena.

KING   And why do these natural phenomena only occur when several cockroaches are assembled?

SAVANT   Science has not yet arrived at an explanation.

KING   And what is the true nature of these moving mountains and this annihilating, choking rain?

QUEEN   These moving mountains and this choking rain, are they intended to destroy us?

SAVANT   These are all questions which cannot be answered scientifically.

QUEEN   Then why do these catastrophes only occur when we are assembled together?

SAVANT   I do not know, Your Majesty. All that science can do is to record these phenomena, to link up the connection between them and deduce a scientific law.

KING   You mean to say therefore that our fear of such calamities has made our species from time immemorial afraid of assembling together?

SAVANT   Exactly, it is from here that this characteristic has arisen—the fact that each one of us goes off on his own in a different direction: an instinctive defence mechanism.

MINISTER   But the ants do exactly the opposite to us.

SAVANT   The ants, because of their tiny size, can do what they like, but we larger creatures are in a special position.

MINISTER   But by their coming together they overcome us.

SAVANT   Yes—regretfully.

MINISTER   And the solution? We want a solution, O Savant.

KING   The Minister's son was torn to pieces by troops of ants who carried him off to their villages.

SAVANT   My sincere condolences, Minister.

MINISTER   Thank you, but this is not all we expect of you.

KING   That's right—we want of you something more useful than merely condoling with the Minister.

QUEEN   We want a definite remedy.

SAVANT   Give me time in which to examine the matter. With me everything must be done on a proper basis, with one step following another. First we must start by knowing ourselves, by discovering what is round about us in this vast cosmos. Do you know for example what is to be found behind this shiny wall underneath which we stand? (*He points at the outer wall of the bath.*)

KING   What is there behind it?

SAVANT   I have climbed to the top of it many times and have seen the strangest of things.

ALL   What did you see?

SAVANT   I saw a vast chasm—probably a large lake, though the strange thing is that it is sometimes without water, at others full of water.

ALL   And why is that?

SAVANT   I do not yet know, but after having observed this phenomenon, I was able to observe a constant factor, namely that this lake was full of water in the glare of light, but was empty of water in the darkness.

KING   And what is the relationship between light and the water?

SAVANT   There is some sort of relationship but I do not yet know the reason for it. Nevertheless we have been able to deduce a constant law in the form of a true scientific equation, namely that light equals water and darkness equals dryness.

KING   At such a moment, therefore . . .

SAVANT   At such a moment the lake is dry and it has a very beautiful appearance. Its sides are smooth and snow-white—as though strewn with jasmine flowers.

QUEEN   I wish I could see them.

SAVANT   With great pleasure. If Your Majesty would permit me, I shall lead you to the top of the wall, and then you can look down at the deep chasm—a marvellous sight.

KING   I too would like to see it.

SAVANT   I am at your disposal—let's all go.

MINISTER   Wait—the Priest is coming.

The Priest makes his appearance.

KING   Come and join us, O venerable Priest!

PRIEST   That's exactly what I'd like to do, for I have just passed by a most sad sight.

KING   A sad sight?

PRIEST   Yes, a procession of ants carrying a cockroach. The cockroach, it seems, was dead and motionless. An ant at the head was dragging him by his whiskers, while at the rear a group of them were pushing him. There was nothing I could do but to ask the gods to have mercy on him.

QUEEN   Do you not know who it was?

PRIEST   No.

QUEEN   That was the Minister's son.

PRIEST   (*turning to the Minister*)   Your son?

MINISTER   (*lowering his head in sorrow*)   Yes.

PRIEST   May the gods grant you comfort! I shall say a prayer for you.

MINISTER   Thank you!

KING   We were just now discussing what we should do about these catastrophes, for the time has come to search for a remedy. Have you any suggestion, O Priest?

PRIEST   I have only one suggestion.

KING   Don't you dare say to offer up sacrifices!

PRIEST   There is nothing else.

MINISTER   Do you see, Majesty? We have now entered into another difficulty—the search for sacrifices. We may find them and we may not. Also, who will go looking for them and bring them back? I personally am not prepared to do so—my psychological state does not permit me.

SAVANT   I certainly am not prepared to do so, because I naturally do not believe in such methods.

PRIEST   Apostasy is rife in this kingdom!

QUEEN   Do not say such a thing, O Priest! You know well that I am a firm believer.

KING   Yes, we are believers, but the question of these sacrifices has become tiresome—and a trifle old-fashioned. In the past we have offered some of the sacrifices you demanded but they gave no result.

PRIEST   The result is not in my hands—I offer the sacrifices and the gods are free to accept or refuse them.

SAVANT   Your gods always refuse the sacrifices—only the ants accept them.

MINISTER   Truly. We noticed that with the piece of sugar you demanded as a sacrifice—it was the ants who ate it.

KING   Listen, O Priest—ask the gods to help us without it costing us anything.

PRIEST   Do you want them to serve you for free?

MINISTER   And why not? Does not our King undertake his official duties for free?

QUEEN   And I myself—the Queen—no one has given me anything, not even my dear husband. I strive for my daily bread like him, without any difference at all.

SAVANT   Nor I of course—no one has laid down any salary or wage for me.

MINISTER   Nor I too. I am the Minister of the kingdom and all my official functions are performed for no wage.

KING   Then why do you demand wages for your gods?

PRIEST   I will not *demand* anything.

KING   On the contrary, you must demand of them that they help us, but on the condition that such help is free and for nothing—godsent!

PRIEST I can't put conditions on the gods.

SAVANT Do they stipulate the fee to you, or do you volunteer it?

PRIEST There is no stipulation or volunteering, but anyone who asks something of someone should aim to tempt him.

SAVANT So it's a question of tempting . . .

PRIEST Describe it how you will, but I cannot make a request of the gods while I am empty-handed.

SAVANT And do you think the gods are concerned with what you have in your hands?

PRIEST What kind of question is that?

SAVANT Have the gods ever listened to you?

PRIEST Naturally.

SAVANT When was that?

PRIEST Once, I was lying ill in a corner when I saw the armies of ants approaching. I was certain that I was done for. I called upon the gods with a prayer that came from the depths of my heart. Suddenly I saw that something looking like a large dark cloud full of water had descended from the skies and swooped down upon the armies of ants and swept them quite away, clearing them off the face of the earth.

QUEEN How extraordinary!

SAVANT The scientific composition of this cloud is well known: it consists of a network of many threads from a large piece of moistened sacking.

KING Neither the cloud's origin nor yet its scientific composition is of interest. What is important is who sent it down and wiped away the ants with it.

PRIEST Speak to him, O King, and ask him who sent it down from the sky and with it destroyed the armies of the ants. Who? Who?

SAVANT This is not a question that science can answer. However, I very much doubt the existence of any connection between this priest's prayer and the descent of this cloud.

PRIEST How is it then that the cloud descended only after my prayer?

SAVANT Pure coincidence.

PRIEST What blasphemy! What apostasy!

QUEEN I am against blasphemy and apostasy, and you, my husband who are King, must be like me in this.

KING Of course I am like you in this. Listen, O reverend Priest, I believe, must believe, that your prayer was beneficial. In any event, seeing that your prayer was efficacious and successful the once, it will clearly be so again. I would therefore ask you to pray and pray long.

MINISTER Particularly as cost-free prayer without sacrifice has been successful.

QUEEN Because, as he said, it issued forth from the depths of his heart.

PRIEST (*irritably*) Yes, all right—I shall pray.

QUEEN (*shouting*) Look! Look!

A procession of ants carrying a cockroach makes its appearance.

THE ANTS (*chanting*)
>Here is your great feast.
>We carry it together, together,
>To our towns, our villages:
>A great and splendid cockroach—
>Provision for the winter long.
>With it our storerooms we shall fill.
>None of us will hunger know,
>Because we all lend a hand,
>We're members of a single body.
>There is amongst us no one sad,
>There is amongst us none who's lonesome,
>There is amongst us none who says
>'I am not concerned with others.'

The ants move towards the wall with their heavy load, while the cockroaches continue to watch them in glum silence and stupefaction.

KING   It grieves us, O Minister, to see your son borne off in this manner.

PRIEST   May the gods have mercy upon him! May the gods have mercy upon him!

KING   It's certainly a most dignified funeral!

SAVANT   So it seems, although logic dictates that it should be otherwise, for in relation to the ants it means food, that is to say a universal blessing, and the carrying of blessings and food should be accompanied by manifestations of joy, acclamations and singing.

KING   But we hear nothing—groups walking in utter silence.

SAVANT   That is so. We hear no sound from them because they are such tiny creatures. Who knows, though—perhaps they are making thunderous sounds?

KING   Perhaps they have a language?

SAVANT   Perhaps they were singing?

KING   Naturally—for them—this was a most suitable occasion for joy and singing.

QUEEN   I implore you! I implore you! Do not stir up the grief of a sorrowing father with such talk! Let us either do something for him or keep quiet.

KING   Forgive me, Minister, this was merely general talk about the ants, but—as the Queen says—something must be done, and this has occupied us since our meeting up today.

QUEEN   This meeting which up till now has achieved nothing useful.

KING   My dear! My dear! Your Majesty! We are still at the stage of conferring and exchanging points of view.

QUEEN   What conferring and what points of view? There are the ants in front of you! They are carrying off the Minister's son to make a good, wholesome meal of him. Is it so difficult for you, being as you are four hulking males, to attack and crush them, and to rescue the Minister's son from their hands?

KING Are we four? Where's the fourth?

QUEEN You of course.

KING Ah, quite right. But I . . . leave me out of it. I am the King and the King rules and does not fight.

PRIEST Leave me also out of it. I am the Priest and the Priest prays and does not fight.

SAVANT And I too, naturally. You must leave me out of it, for I am the Savant and the Savant makes research but does not brawl.

QUEEN Then I shall go—I, the Queen—yet I shall not say I am the Queen, but merely a female. Stand, you males, and watch with folded arms while females go to war.

KING And the Minister? Is he not a male like us? Why is he standing by silently when the matter concerns him?

MINISTER I do not want to put you in such predicaments because of my son.

QUEEN As we have said, the matter is no longer merely that of your son.

MINISTER I am grateful, Your Majesty, but . . .

QUEEN The question is too important to be purely a personal one— they all know that, these most excellent leaders of the Kingdom. However, they don't want to know so they pretend not to, because they are without resolution, without willpower.

KING My dear Majesty . . .

QUEEN Shut up, you effete weakling! Leave the matter in my hands!

KING Do you want me to give up the throne in your favour?

QUEEN No, my dear sir. This throne of yours does not interest me, does not tempt me. All I want is for you to let me act.

KING Don't be so headstrong, my dear. You can do nothing. You want to attack, to make war, and to fight like the ants, but this cannot happen.

QUEEN And why not?

KING Ask the eminent Savant—he has the answer.

QUEEN Speak, O eminent Savant!

KING Speak and tell her why the ants know methods of warfare and we don't. Tell her, explain to her!

SAVANT First, the ants have a Minister of War.

QUEEN A Minister of War?

SAVANT Naturally. A minister who devotes all his attention to the business of organizing armies. Is it reasonable that all these vast troops should march with such discipline and order in serried ranks without somebody responsible behind them, somebody specialized in organizing them?

QUEEN The question's a simple one—why don't we too have a specialized Minister of War?

SAVANT That is a political matter, and I don't understand politics. Ask His Majesty about that.

QUEEN   Please be so good as to reply, Your Majesty!

KING   What's the question?

QUEEN   Why do you not appoint a specialized Minister of War?

KING   A specialized Minister of War? Is that in my hands? Where is he? Let me find him and I'll appoint him immediately. We had quite enough trouble finding one Minister, our friend here. He was good enough to accept being a general minister to look after everything without understanding anything.

MINISTER   If I do not enjoy your confidence, then I am ready to proffer my resignation.

KING   Your resignation? Do you hear? Now here's our one and only minister threatening to resign!

QUEEN   No, honourable Minister. You enjoy the confidence of everyone. Don't listen to what the King says—he sometimes lets his tongue run away with him.

MINISTER   My thanks to Your Majesty!

KING   Your most gracious Majesty!

QUEEN   Then, O venerable Savant, the whole difference is that the ants have a specialized Minister of War?

SAVANT   That is not all they have.

QUEEN   What do they have as well?

SAVANT   A brilliant Minister of Supply.

QUEEN   A Minister of Supply?

SAVANT   A brilliant one—the operation of storing food in warehouses on that enormous scale must have some remarkable economic planning behind it.

KING   We have no need for any supply or any Minister of Supply, because we don't have a food crisis and have no need to plan or store.

SAVANT   Certainly, our economy runs by sheer good luck—and we boast about it!

QUEEN   Boast about it?

KING   Certainly, my dear. Certainly we have many things to boast about which should not be sneezed at.

SAVANT   In confirmation of His Majesty's opinion I would say that we have a characteristic not found among the ants, namely birth control. The ants let their numbers increase so enormously that they are driven into a food and storage crisis, and the need for food leads to war.

KING   We are certainly in no need of food, of the storage of food, or of war.

SAVANT   And so we are superior creatures.

KING   Without doubt. We attack no living creature; we harm no one. We do not know greed or the desire to acquire and store things away.

QUEEN   Are there no creatures superior to us?

SAVANT   No, we are the most superior creatures on the face of the earth.

QUEEN That's right, and yet we suffer because of those other, inferior creatures.

SAVANT Inferiority is always a cause of trouble, but we must be patient. We cannot bring those creatures who are lower than us up to the same standard of civilization as ourselves. To each his own nature, his own environment, and his own circumstances. The ant, for instance, is concerned solely with food. As for us, we are more concerned with knowledge.

QUEEN Knowledge?

SAVANT Certainly. These long whiskers we have we do not use only to touch food. Very often we touch with them things which are not eaten, merely in order to seek out their nature, to discover their reality. Do you not, Your Majesty, often do just that?

QUEEN Certainly. Certainly. I am very interested in touching strange substances with my whiskers, not merely from my desire for food but from sheer curiosity.

SAVANT Yes, from curiosity, a love of knowledge, a desire to know.

KING And yet you say, my dear Queen, that we are weak-willed. We are the sturdiest of creatures on earth, is that not so, O venerable Savant?

SAVANT Most certainly, Majesty.

KING Are the ants stronger than us? Impossible! They do not know us; all they know is how to eat us. But they do not know who we are. Do the ants know us?

SAVANT Of course not.

KING Have they got the slightest idea of the true facts about us, about our nature? Do they realize that we are thinking creatures?

SAVANT The only knowledge they have about us is that we are food for them.

KING And so, in relation to ourselves, they are inferior creatures.

QUEEN Which doesn't prevent them eating us. We must find some way of protecting ourselves from being harmed by them.

KING The only way is for us not to fall on our backs.

QUEEN This, then, in your view is the whole solution?

KING In the view of us all.

QUEEN We have in short ended up where we began, that is to say at nought, nought, nought! Our meeting, our discussions, our investigations have all led us to nought, nought, nought!

SAVANT In research there is no such thing as nought. Every investigation is useful. When we touch things with our whiskers we derive profit even though we do not exactly understand the true nature of those things. Which reminds me, a few moments ago I was saying that I had just come from making a very important discovery but no one appeared ready to listen.

KING Ah, yes, it seems to me that I did hear you say so. And what is the discovery? Speak—I am a ready listener.

SAVANT This lake . . .

KING What lake? Ah yes, of course—we were talking about a lake and you wanted to take the Queen and me there so that we might see it.

SAVANT And we were in fact on the point of going except that the Priest came along.

KING Yes, that is true. Let us go then. Come, let's go now. That is at least more worthwhile than talking about fairy tales and fanciful projects! After you, my dear Majesty!

QUEEN I shall not go with you. I shall stay here and the Minister will stay with me. He is naturally in no psychological state for sight-seeing.

KING As you both wish. And you, O illustrious Priest, will you come with us?

PRIEST Such reconnoitrings have nothing to do with me.

KING Then let us away, O Savant!

The King and the Savant go off. The Queen, the Minister and the Priest remain.

QUEEN I am very sad about your loss. However, I am also sad and distressed about the shameful attitude of my husband.

MINISTER Do not blame your husband, Your Majesty. Your husband, the King, is capable of doing nothing.

QUEEN He is at least capable of being serious and of making up his mind; of being up to the situation.

MINISTER The situation is difficult.

QUEEN Certainly, and it needs a strong character to face up to it, but I am sorry to say that my husband is of a weak character. Have you not remarked this?

MINISTER We rely on you, Your Majesty.

QUEEN Were it not that I am at his side, what would he do? Deep down inside he feels this. I am a stronger personality than he, but he's always trying to fool himself, to make himself out as superior.

MINISTER We all have our particular natures and characteristics. He is nevertheless good-hearted.

QUEEN I don't deny that. He is a truly good person but . . .

PRIEST But going around with that atheist of a Savant and listening to his nonsense bodes no good.

MINISTER He also listens a lot to you, O venerable Priest!

PRIEST And likewise he listens to you, O high-minded Minister!

MINISTER He listens to everyone and to everything. It is only fair of us to say that he is a man with an open mind.

QUEEN You defend him despite everything because without him you'd be without a job.

MINISTER I, Your Majesty?

QUEEN Yes, you. You in particular. The Priest has things to occupy him, so does the Savant, but you the Minister would have no work to do without the King.

MINISTER And you, Your Majesty? You are the Queen and the Queen . . .

QUEEN   Understood—she too hasn't got a job without the King! I know that.

MINISTER   Sorry, I . . .

QUEEN   Don't apologize! My position is like yours. I know that. The difference, however, is that I'm female and he's always wanting to remind me that he's male—and that he's got longer whiskers than me!

> *A cockroach appears; he is singing.*

COCKROACH (*singing*)

> O night, O lovely night
> During which our eyes we close
> On things both dear and dread.
> O night, O lovely night.
> With one eye we go to sleep,
> With the other we impatiently await
> The breaking of the lucent dawn.
> O night, O lovely night.

QUEEN   Who's that singing?

MINISTER (*looking*)   He is a subject cockroach.

QUEEN   One of our subjects? Singing while we're thinking, thinking from early morning about his problem! Bring him here.

MINISTER (*calling to him*)   Hey you, come here!

COCKROACH (*approaching*)   Yes.

MINISTER   Who are you?

COCKROACH   Someone who sings and strives after his daily bread.

MINISTER   You are singing when we are thinking for you?

COCKROACH   And who asked you to think for me? I think for myself.

MINISTER   I'm the Minister.

COCKROACH (*sarcastically*)   It's an honour I'm sure.

MINISTER   We are thinking about an important problem that threatens your life—the problem of the ants. You've come along at the right time. We'd like you and others to co-operate with us. What do you think?

COCKROACH   I think you should let me be.

> *He turns his back on him and departs singing:*

> O night, O lovely night
> During which our eyes we close.

MINISTER (*to the Queen*)   It's no good!

QUEEN   It really isn't!

> *The Savant looks down from on top of the outer wall of the bath.*

SAVANT (*calling out from on top of the wall*)   Help! Help!

QUEEN   What's happened?

SAVANT   The King.

QUEEN (*anxiously*)   What's happened to the King?

SAVANT   His foot slipped—he fell into the lake!

QUEEN   Fallen into the lake? How terrible!

MINISTER   Is the King dead?

SAVANT   Not yet. The lake's dry, it's got no water in it. Its walls are slippery and he's at the foot of them trying to get out.

QUEEN   Then let's go and help him to get out. Help him! Save him! For Heaven's sake, save my husband!

SAVANT   (shouting)   Stay where you are! There is no way of saving him—you can't get down to him.

QUEEN   We must do something for him. Let's all go.

SAVANT   Do not move! The walls along the edge of the lake are slippery and your feet too may slip and you'll fall in.

QUEEN   My husband must be saved! Save my husband! I beseech you—save him!

MINISTER   Yes, the King must be saved!

SAVANT   No one can do so. He is in the very depths of the chasm. The walls are slippery. One's feet will slip on the smooth walls. Only he can save himself, only by his own efforts—or a miracle from the skies!

PRIEST   A miracle from the skies! Now *you* speak of a miracle from the skies!

MINISTER   This is your chance, O Priest!

QUEEN   Yes, I implore you, O Priest, to do something about my husband. I implore you!

PRIEST   Has not this Savant said that there is no one in the Heavens to hear us?

SAVANT   Don't seize the opportunity to be coy! Anyone who is able to do something now should do so.

QUEEN   Yes. Do something, O Priest—please!

MINISTER   It's your duty, O Priest—save the King!

PRIEST   There is nothing for me to do but pray.

MINISTER   Then we ask you to pray.

PRIEST   All of us must pray. Even this Savant must pray with us, but he will not accept to do so.

QUEEN   He will, he will accept for our sake, for the sake of my husband.

SAVANT   I shall accept to do so so that I may invalidate his argument. If there really is someone up there who hears our voices, understands our language, and pays attention to our entreaties, that's fine. If not, we have lost nothing.

MINISTER   So he has accepted.

PRIEST   A most grudging acceptance.

SAVANT   I told you he'd get coy and start making excuses.

MINISTER   Please, O Priest, be obliging.

QUEEN   Be sure that our hearts are all with you at this moment.

PRIEST   Not all of you.

MINISTER   Pay no heed to him. Pretend he's not here. Won't our three voices suffice?

SAVANT   I said I would join my voice to yours—what more do you want of me?

PRIEST   I don't want your voice to be with ours—it's enough to have one doubting voice to spoil the rest.

SAVANT   And what's my voice to you? Is it being addressed to you or to the Heavens? Leave it to the Heavens to listen or not, whether you yourself accept or not.

MINISTER   That is reasonable.

QUEEN   Truly. Leave the matter to the Heavens, oh venerable Priest, and don't bother yourself about it. Who knows? Maybe, unbeknownst to us, it will be acceptable.

PRIEST   So be it!

QUEEN   Then let us all pray.

PRIEST   Pray! Lift up your hands with me! Oh gods!

ALL (*lifting up their hands and calling out*)   Oh gods! Oh gods!

CURTAIN

Act Two—The Cockroach's Struggle

A bedroom with a bed, a wardrobe, and a small table on which rests an alarm clock. A large table stands between two chairs: on it are papers and books. The room has a small door leading to the bathroom, which contains a bath and a basin with a mirror above it, also a shelf on which are toothbrushes and tubes of toothpaste. From the bedroom another door opens onto the rest of the flat. The room is rather dark; day is beginning to dawn, light seeping through the room. As it gets lighter, Adil suddenly sits up and then gets out of bed; he performs various vigorous gymnastic movements. His wife Samia wakes up and half rises in the bed. She puts on a small bedside light.

SAMIA (*turning to her husband*)   You're up, Adil?

ADIL   Of course.

SAMIA   Has the alarm gone off?

ADIL   Of course not—as usual I got up by myself.

SAMIA   What an odd alarm! Didn't we set it for six before going to bed?

ADIL   We did—as we do every night. However, it waits till I get up by myself and then rings. (*The alarm clock goes off.*)

SAMIA   There—it's ringing.

ADIL   It does it on purpose, I assure you.

SAMIA   No harm done so long as you're . . .

ADIL   As I'm ringing in its stead?

SAMIA   And that you wake up on time.

ADIL   For you that's all that matters.

He moves towards the bathroom.

SAMIA   Where are you going?

ADIL   To the bathroom of course.

SAMIA (*jumping out of bed*)   Off with you—I'm first.

ADIL   Yes, as usual. I get up before you and it's you who get to the bathroom before me.

SAMIA   That's only right.

ADIL   How is it right? As I wake up before you I should have the bathroom first. From today onwards I'm sticking to my rights.

SAMIA   You say that every day—it's a record I've heard only too often.

ADIL   Because it's my right! It's my right, I say!

SAMIA   Off with you! Don't waste time! I'm going in before you because my work demands . . .

ADIL   Your work! I suppose I'm out of work? If you're a company employee, I happen to be also employed by the same company, and if you're in a hurry so am I. Besides, I've got to shave which you haven't.

SAMIA   I've got something more important than having to shave.

ADIL   And what might that be?

SAMIA   To do my make-up, my dear man. You don't have to make up.

ADIL   And what do you have to make up for when you're going off to work in an oils, paints, and chemicals factory?

SAMIA   What a fatuous question!

ADIL   Give me an answer.

SAMIA   Listen! Don't waste any more time. Please get away from the bathroom and let me in.

ADIL   No, you don't! Today I'll not weaken—I'll stick to my rights. I'll not give in today.

SAMIA   You're rebelling?

ADIL   Yes.

SAMIA   You say 'yes'?

ADIL   Yes.

SAMIA   And you repeat it?

ADIL   Yes.

SAMIA   I warn you. This is a warning.

ADIL   What are you going to do?

SAMIA   Get out of my way—at once!

ADIL   Only over my dead body!

SAMIA   Is that so? All right, then!

> She pushes him roughly. He almost falls, but catches hold of the bed.

ADIL   Good God! Have you gone crazy, Samia? Why are you shoving me about like this?

SAMIA   It's you who wants to use force. Everything can be settled nice and quietly. 'Bye!

> She enters the bathroom. He hurries after her. She locks the bathroom door in his face. He raps on it.

ADIL   Open it! Open it! This is no way to behave! It's not a question of force. You seize your rights by force—I mean my rights. It's my right. You seize my right by sheer force. Open up! Open up!

SAMIA (*inside the bathroom—she is doing her hair in front of the mirror and humming to herself*)   Please shut up. Don't annoy me by knocking like that!

ADIL   By what right do you go in before me?

SAMIA   I came in and there's an end to it.

ADIL   But it's a matter of principle.

SAMIA   A matter of what?

ADIL   Of principle—of principles. Don't you know what principles are?

SAMIA   I haven't yet read the morning papers.

ADIL   What *are* you talking about?

SAMIA   I'm telling you to occupy yourself usefully until I've finished having my bath.

ADIL   Occupy myself?

SAMIA   Yes, with anything, because I want quiet—quiet.

ADIL   Quiet? You tell me to be quiet?

SAMIA   Listen, Adil, turn on the radio.

ADIL   Turn on what?

SAMIA (*turning on the basin tap*)   Turn the tap on.

ADIL   The tap? You want me to turn the tap on for you as well? But the tap's where you are.

SAMIA   I told you to turn on the radio.

ADIL   The radio?

SAMIA   Yes, the radio.

ADIL   You said the tap.

SAMIA   The tap? Would I be so crazy as to say such a thing? I told you to turn on the radio! The radio! Can you hear me properly?

ADIL   I'm sorry, it's my fault. It's always my fault.

SAMIA (*moistening the toothbrush and taking up the tube of toothpaste*)   What horrible toothpaste! One of your lordship's purchases!

ADIL (*going towards the radio standing on the table*)   Why am I so weak with you? But—but is it really weakness? No, it's impossible—it's merely that I spoil you. I spoil you because you're a woman, a weak woman, the weaker sex.

He turns on the radio and the voice of the announcer bursts forth.

ANNOUNCER   And here is the summary of the news: The black nationals rose up in revolt following the occupation by the white colonialists by force of . . .

ADIL (*lowering the volume*)   They rose up in revolt!

SAMIA   I told you to turn on the radio.

ADIL   It's on.

SAMIA   But I can't hear any singing or music.

ADIL   It's the news. The news! Am I also responsible for the radio programmes?

SAMIA   Turn to another station, man.

ADIL   As you say.

He turns to another station and a song is heard:

> *'The attainment of desires is not by hoping;*
> *Things of this world are gained by striving.'*

SAMIA   (*humming the song to herself in the bathroom*)   'Things of this world are gained . . .'

ADIL   Happy?

SAMIA   Of course—it's a beautiful song.

ADIL   Things of this world are gained by striving! (*He lowers the volume.*)

ADIL   (*forcefully*)   Look here, Samia! Open up! Open up! I want to say something important to you!

SAMIA   I haven't had my bath yet.

ADIL   I want to know, I want a quick explanation: Who am I?

SAMIA   What are you saying?

ADIL   I'm asking you who I am.

SAMIA   What a question! You're Adil of course.

ADIL   Adil who?

SAMIA   Adil my husband.

ADIL   Is that all?

SAMIA   What do you mean? Do you want your surname, job, and date of birth? It's all written down for you on your identity card.

ADIL   I know. I wasn't asking about that. I was asking about my true identity. Do you know what my true identity is?

SAMIA   No, you tell me.

ADIL   I'm the world!

SAMIA   The world?

ADIL   Yes, the world that is gained by striving. You take everything I have and I take nothing of yours. You get hold of the whole of my salary and I can't touch a millieme of yours. All the payments, expenses, bills, instalments, all come out of *my* pocket: *your* dressmaker—*your* hairdresser—the instalments on *your* car—*your* petrol—*your* 'fridge—*your* washing machine—*your* Butagas . . .

SAMIA   My Butagas? Talking about the Butagas, listen, Adil—don't forget to get in touch with them to send a fresh bottle.

ADIL   And it's I who always has to get in touch!

SAMIA   I've got work to do as you know.

ADIL   And I've got no work? Your job's *work* and mine's play?

SAMIA   Won't you stop tyrannizing me with your chatter!

ADIL   And now it's I who tyrannize you!

SAMIA   Please—I've got a headache. I want to have my bath in peace—in peace, do you hear? I've told you a thousand times to occupy yourself with something, man. Read the morning paper, take a needle and thread and sew the buttons on your shirt, get the breakfast ready . . .

ADIL   Shall I get your breakfast?

SAMIA   Yes, instead of talking a lot of rubbish.

ADIL (*sitting on his bed and placing his head in the palms of his hands*) Ah . . .

SAMIA   Why are you so quiet? (*Adil remains gloomily immersed in silence.*) Adil! (*Adil does not reply. He gets up and walks about the room.*) Why are you so quiet, Adil? What are you doing out there? (*Adil does not reply but stands himself in front of her framed photo standing on the table by the bed.*) Why don't you reply, Adil? Are you in the room?

ADIL   Yes, in the room.

SAMIA   What are you doing now?

ADIL   I'm looking at your picture.

He is in fact looking at the picture—but with fury; he makes a gesture of wanting to strangle her.

SAMIA   Are you looking at my picture?

ADIL   Yes—with longing.

SAMIA   Is this the time for it? I told you to do something useful.

ADIL   Such as?

SAMIA   Go to the kitchen and put on the milk to heat until the cook comes. By the way, did you turn on the Butagas? I'll be lighting the water heater in a while—are you listening?

ADIL   I'm listening.

SAMIA   Hurry up and do it, please.

ADIL   Certainly. This is unnatural. It must be that I'm not a normal person. (*He knocks at the bathroom door.*)

SAMIA (*cleaning her teeth and rinsing her mouth*) What do you want?

ADIL (*shouting*) I'm not a normal person! Can you hear? Not normal!

SAMIA   Not normal? Who's not normal?

ADIL   I'm not—I'm not normal.

SAMIA   Are you ill?

ADIL   I shall carry out your orders: the Butagas—the heater—the bath—the heater—the bath—the Butagas—the heater—the bath —the bath—the bath—

SAMIA   Hurry up, Adil!

ADIL   Right away. (*He goes to the telephone on the table, lifts the receiver and dials a number.*) Hullo. Hullo. Raafat? Good morning, Raafat. Listen. Listen. No, no, I'm not upset. Do you think I sound upset? No, no, not at all. I . . . I'm only . . . tell me: are you awake? Ah, of course you're awake seeing that you're talking to me. No, no . . . I meant . . . have you had your bath? Oh yes . . . good. No, I haven't done anything yet. I got up early. That's the root of the problem. Tell me, talking about baths . . . yes, baths . . . has your wife . . . no, sorry . . . it's a stupid question. No, no, nothing. I only wanted to talk to you, merely to . . . merely to . . . nothing. Yes. Yes. Nothing at all. No, no . . . don't be alarmed. I'm only . . . actually, I feel that I'm . . . yes, I'm not completely all right. No, it's not all that bad. Of course I'll go out. Yes, we'll meet at the factory as usual. Samia . . . she's in the bath. In the bath, old man . . . in

the bath. I'll give her your regards. No, no, don't worry yourself. I'm
fine . . . fine, Raafat. 'Bye. 'Bye.

> *During the telephone conversation Samia has been trying in vain
> to put on the water heater. At last, as Adil puts down the receiver,
> she opens the door.*

SAMIA   Your lordship was chatting on the telephone while I thought
you'd gone to the kitchen to put on the Butagas.

ADIL   A hurried conversation.

SAMIA   With someone at the company?

ADIL   With a lady.

SAMIA   A lady?

ADIL   Yes, a lady . . . a friend.

SAMIA   Do I know her?

ADIL   No, she's a new friend—a most pleasant person.

SAMIA   Married?

ADIL   Of course not.

SAMIA   Someone who works in the company?

ADIL   No, someone far away from that atmosphere. Just a lady, a beautiful lady, a refined lady, amenable and unassuming.

SAMIA   Adil, this is no time for these glorious imaginings.

ADIL   Imaginings?

SAMIA   Of course, imaginings. After five years of marriage, don't you
think I know what you are?

ADIL   And what am I?

SAMIA   Don't go on asking me that question every moment. Will you
please note that I haven't yet had my bath, that I haven't done my
hair, in fact haven't done a thing up until now except to talk nonsense with my respected husband. I haven't even lit the heater because you've refused to be serious and have just sat around chatting
on the phone.

ADIL   God Almighty!

SAMIA   (*motioning to him to go to the kitchen*)   Do you mind?

ADIL   (*making his way meekly to the kitchen*)   Why trouble to say 'do
you mind'? You know I'll comply with the order.

SAMIA   Of course I know that. (*She examines her hair in the mirror.*)

ADIL   (*from offstage, in the kitchen*)   Of course. I'm now in the kitchen
turning on the Butagas for you.

SAMIA   Thank you. (*She goes to the heater in the bathroom and lights
it as she hums to herself.*)

ADIL   (*from offstage*)   And the bottle of milk by the door—I'm taking
it in and putting it on to heat. Any other orders?

> *Samia continues humming to herself.*

ADIL   (*entering, wiping his hands and singing*)   The attainment of desires is not by hoping.

SAMIA   (*going towards the bathroom door*)   Adil, pass me the towel, will
you?

ADIL   (*passes her the towel*)   The towel.

SAMIA   And the bathrobe too.

ADIL (*presenting her with the bathrobe*)   And the bathrobe. You've got the soap and sponge?

SAMIA   The bottle of eau-de-Cologne please.

ADIL (*passing her the bottle*)   And the eau-de-Cologne.

SAMIA   And the tin of powder.

> *Adil passes her the powder.*

SAMIA   And now get out!

ADIL   I'm out!

> *Samia closes the door of the bathroom and walks forward, humming to herself, towards the bath. She no sooner looks inside it than she lets out a scream.*

ADIL (*sitting with lowered head and then rising up in alarm at her scream*)   What's wrong?

SAMIA (*opening the door of the bathroom and screaming*)   Adil! Adil! Come quickly and look!

ADIL (*going towards the bathroom*)   What is it? What's happened?

SAMIA (*pointing to the inside of the bath*)   Look!

ADIL (*looks into the bath*)   It's a cockroach.

SAMIA   Of course it's a cockroach, but how did it get in here?

ADIL   In the same way any cockroach gets into a house.

SAMIA   I mean here, into the tub, into the bath.

ADIL   Perhaps it fell from the ceiling.

SAMIA   The bath must be cleaned at once, but first it must be killed.

ADIL   Killed?

SAMIA   At once. You've got the insecticide in the kitchen.

ADIL   It's I who's going to be entrusted with killing it?

SAMIA   Of course.

ADIL   Of course, but look! It's going to come out by itself.

SAMIA   It would be better if it came out by itself because killing it in the bath will make a mess.

ADIL   Yes, it would be preferable if it were to come out nice and quietly so that it doesn't dirty the bath for you.

SAMIA   And when it comes out you can deal with it far away.

ADIL   Yes, far away from you.

SAMIA (*looking into the bath*)   It doesn't look as if it will be able to.

ADIL (*looking closely*)   It's trying.

SAMIA   It's slipping.

ADIL   The walls of the bath are slippery.

SAMIA   Yes, no sooner does it start climbing than it slips and falls.

ADIL   But it goes on trying.

SAMIA   And goes on again and again.

ADIL   With the same procedure.

SAMIA (*continuing to look*)   Yes. Yes.

ADIL   Look, Samia. With all its strength it's climbing up the slippery wall.

SAMIA   And there it is slipping back again. There—it's fallen all the way back.

ADIL   And it's starting off to repeat the attempt.

SAMIA   Up it goes, up it goes. It's slipped! It's slipped! It's fallen!

ADIL   Don't you notice something, Samia?

SAMIA   What?

ADIL   That it's always at the same place.

SAMIA   Approximately a third of the way to the top of the bath.

ADIL   Yes, then it falls.

SAMIA   So it's unable to climb more than that.

ADIL   Because the walls of the bath are less steep near the bottom, which makes climbing easier. After that, though, it's straight up.

SAMIA   That's not the reason. Cockroaches can easily climb up a perpendicular wall, also along a ceiling. The reason is because it's slippery—no wall or ceiling is as slippery as this.

ADIL   How then can a cockroach climb up a wall of porcelain tiles, which is as slippery as this bath-tub?

SAMIA   And who told you that cockroaches can climb up a porcelain tile wall?

ADIL   Can't they?

SAMIA   Have you ever seen it?

ADIL   I rather imagined I had.

SAMIA   Imagined you had? So your lordship is imagining things!

ADIL   And you—have you seen it?

SAMIA   No, and so long as I have not seen a cockroach climbing up a wall of porcelain tiles I am unable to say that it could happen.

ADIL   Sounds logical.

SAMIA   Aren't you pleased with my logic?

ADIL   Did I say I wasn't? I was wondering, merely wondering. Is it impossible that something one hasn't seen with one's own eyes can happen?

SAMIA   Whoever said such a thing?

ADIL   I imagined you said something like that.

SAMIA   You imagined! Once again you're imagining things. Please don't imagine!

ADIL   As you say. I shall not imagine any more. As you wish me to be so positivistic, allow me to look in the dictionary.

SAMIA   Look for what?

ADIL   For the habits of cockroaches. Just a moment.

He hurries to the shelf of books by the bed and brings back a dictionary.

SAMIA   Hurry up, please.

ADIL   (*turning over the pages*)   Right away. Co . . . cock . . . cockroach, also known as black-beetle.

SAMIA   Black-beetle?

ADIL   Yes, black-beetle.

SAMIA   I prefer the word cockroach.

ADIL   I too.

SAMIA What else does the dictionary say?

ADIL The cockroach or black-beetle is a harmful insect that infests cloth, food, and paper. It is often found in lavatories and has long hairy horns or whiskers. It spoils more food than it actually requires as nourishment. It can live for about a year.

SAMIA A year? It lives for a year?

ADIL If it's not done away with and is left to enjoy its life.

SAMIA Spoiling our food and clothes!

ADIL (closing the dictionary) That's all it says in the dictionary.

SAMIA And now?

ADIL And now what?

SAMIA Are we going to go on like this looking at the cockroach?

ADIL It's an enjoyable spectacle—don't you find it so?

SAMIA What about the work we've got to do?

ADIL Quite right—work.

SAMIA We've got to put an end to it.

ADIL And how do we put an end to it? This is something which is not in our hands.

SAMIA In whose hands, then?

ADIL (pointing to the cockroach) In its hands. It's still climbing.

SAMIA And also still falling.

ADIL Yes, it climbs, then it rolls over, then it falls. Note the procedure: climbs, then slips, then rolls over, then falls to the bottom of the bath-tub.

SAMIA It climbs, then slips, then rolls over, then falls to the bottom of the bath-tub.

ADIL Exactly. Then it starts off again, without resting, without respite. It climbs . . .

SAMIA Then it slips . . .

ADIL Then it rolls over . . .

SAMIA Then it falls . . .

ADIL Then it climbs . . .

SAMIA Listen, Adil—and then what?

ADIL It hasn't had its final word.

SAMIA I think that's plenty.

ADIL Are you saying that to me?

SAMIA Please, if you've got time to waste I haven't.

ADIL Good God, and is that my fault?

SAMIA Am I going to have my bath or aren't I?

ADIL Go ahead! Have I stopped you?

SAMIA And the cockroach?

ADIL I am responsible only for myself.

SAMIA Which means that you intend to leave it like this inside the bath?

ADIL I think it's better to leave it as it is so that it can solve its problem by itself.

SAMIA Are you joking, Adil? Is this a time for joking?

ADIL On the contrary, I'm being extremely serious. Do you not see that it's still trying to save itself, so let's leave it to try.

SAMIA   Until when?

ADIL   We cannot—either you or I—decide when. That depends on
its willpower—and up until now it has shown no intention of dis-
continuing its attempts. Look! So far it is showing no sign of being
tired.

SAMIA   But I'm tired.

ADIL   Unfortunately.

SAMIA   And you? Aren't you tired?

ADIL   Of course, the same as you, but there's nothing to be done about
it.

SAMIA   In short, I'm not having my bath today, or dressing, or going
off to my job—all because of a cockroach which has fallen into the
bath-tub and my solicitous husband who stands watching it and
talking drivel.

ADIL   Thank you!

SAMIA   As one cannot depend upon you, I suppose I must act.

ADIL   What are you going to do?

SAMIA   Get the insecticide and look after things myself.

ADIL   You're going to destroy the cockroach?

SAMIA   Right away.

ADIL   Then go off and bring the insecticide.

SAMIA   I'll do just that.

> Samia hurries off to the kitchen and Adil quickly locks the bath-
> room door from the inside. Samia, noting what has happened,
> turns back and raps at the locked door. Adil, inside the bathroom,
> moves towards the bath, humming to himself.

SAMIA   What have you done, Adil? Open it!

> Adil does not reply to her: he is looking at the cockroach in the
> bath.

SAMIA   Have you done it, Adil?

ADIL   (pointing at the cockroach)   Up you go . . . up . . . up. Another
step. Go on . . . go on . . .

SAMIA   (rapping at the door)   Adil, open it!

ADIL   (to the cockroach)   Stick to it! Stick to it! Struggle for your life!

SAMIA   (knocking vigorously)   I told you to open up, Adil. Open it! Can't
you hear me?

ADIL   (to the cockroach)   They want to kill you with insecticide. Don't
be afraid—I'll not open the door. Stick to it! Stick to it!

SAMIA   (rapping at the door)   Open the door, Adil! Open up, I tell you!

ADIL   (to the cockroach)   What a shame! You slipped, you rolled over
and fell down as you do each time.

SAMIA   (rapping at the door)   Can't you hear all this knocking?

ADIL   (to the cockroach)   You want to have another go. Once again
you're starting to climb. Why don't you rest a while? Rest for a
moment, brother! Give yourself a breather? But what's the point?
(shouting) There's no point!

SAMIA   No point? You say there's no point?

ADIL Not to you!

SAMIA So you've uttered at last! Are you going to open up eventually or not?

ADIL No.

SAMIA Are you saying no?

ADIL Yes.

SAMIA Are you saying no or yes?

ADIL No and yes.

SAMIA Speak intelligibly. Are you going to open up or not?

ADIL I'll open up and I'll not open up.

SAMIA Don't annoy me—define your attitude!

ADIL You define yours!

SAMIA Mine's clear—very clear.

ADIL In relation to whom?

SAMIA To you of course.

ADIL I'm not asking about your attitude in relation to myself, I'm asking about your attitude in relation to it.

SAMIA What's it?

ADIL The cockroach.

SAMIA No, you've really gone mad! (*The telephone rings. She hurries off to it and lifts up the receiver.*) Hullo. Who is it speaking? Ah, good morning, Mr. Raafat. No, we're not dressed yet, nor had breakfast, nor done a thing all morning—neither he nor I. He spoke to you? Ah, it was he who rang you. I have, in fact, noticed something strange about him: unnatural, sick. Yes, he's in the bathroom. No, he's locked himself in. A cockroach, my dear sir. Yes, an ordinary cockroach. No. No. It's a long story. Yes, when we meet. No, I don't think he's intending to go to work. I myself am late. Quite definitely something's happened to him. No, don't you worry. The company doctor? And what can the company doctor do? I'm most grateful, Mr. Raafat. Where's Yusriyya? Good morning, Yusriyya. Your husband noticed and told you? No, don't you worry, Yusriyya. I'm very grateful to both you and Mr. Raafat. Thank you. Thank you. (*She puts down the receiver.*)

The cook enters; she is carrying the saucepan of milk.

COOK Who put the milk on the fire and left it? The milk's all boiled over on to the floor and the saucepan's quite empty.

SAMIA (*pointing to the bathroom*) It's his lordship.

COOK And what's he been interfering in the kitchen for?

SAMIA And why are *you* late today?

COOK Transport.

SAMIA Jam packed, not even a place to stand, isn't that so?

COOK Exactly.

SAMIA I know your excuse, know it in advance!

COOK Shall I prepare the breakfast?

SAMIA Breakfast? You'd better wait till we see where it's all going to end. (*She points at the bathroom.*)

COOK (*looking towards the bathroom*) It's him?

SAMIA   Yes, inside—he's locked himself in.

COOK   Why? I hope nothing's wrong.

SAMIA   The cockroach.

COOK   Cockroach?

SAMIA   Look here, Umm Attiya, did you clean the bath well yesterday?

COOK   Of course, Ma'am—with carbolic acid.

SAMIA   Impossible.

COOK   The bottle's along by the kitchen.

SAMIA   You're sure?

COOK   I swear to you.

SAMIA   Then where's this wretched cockroach come from?

COOK   From the skylight, from the stairs, from the pipes, from out of the cracks in the walls—however much you clean a house it's bound to have cockroaches and ants.

> *All this time Adil has been in the bathroom engrossed in watching the cockroach. He makes gestures to it as he follows it climbing up and falling down; by sighs and miming he expresses all his emotions and concern.*

SAMIA (*suddenly shouting*)   Oh, and where's it all going to end? My poor nerves! My poor nerves!

COOK   Shall I bring you a cup of tea?

SAMIA   No, you go about your work and let me be for the moment.

COOK   The insecticide's along by the kitchen, Ma'am. I'll bring it and . . .

SAMIA   I know the insecticide's in the kitchen but the trouble is . . . Off you go and let me alone, Umm Attiya—I know what I'm about.

COOK   As you say, Ma'am. (*She goes out.*)

SAMIA (*going towards the bathroom and rapping at the door*)   Listen, Adil, I want to have a few words with you. Are you listening?

ADIL (*without moving or interrupting his watching of the cockroach*)   I'm listening.

SAMIA   I think things have gone on quite long enough.

ADIL (*automatically echoing her words*)   Long enough.

SAMIA   And there's a limit to one's patience.

ADIL   One's patience.

SAMIA   And my nerves are in ribbons.

ADIL   In ribbons.

SAMIA   And you're behaving ridiculously.

ADIL   Ridiculously.

SAMIA (*shouting*)   This is unbearable! Won't you answer me? Answer anything! Answer! Answer! Answer!

ADIL   Answer! Answer! Answer!

SAMIA (*leaving the bathroom door in despair*)   It's hopeless! There's no longer any point in speaking to that creature. He just repeats my words like a parrot. We've now got a cockroach and a parrot in the bathroom!

COOK (*entering*)   Today you're both later than usual, Ma'am.

SAMIA   Of course.

COOK Today's a holiday?

SAMIA It's not a holiday or anything of the sort—it's a working day as usual.

COOK All right but . . .

SAMIA But what? His lordship's locked himself up in the bathroom and doesn't want to open it, nor does he want to answer me. I've given up knocking and trying to talk to him. I've come to the end of my tether with him . . . there's no way of making contact with him.

COOK Seeing that he's bolted himself in . . .

SAMIA There's only one way.

COOK Let's try it.

SAMIA Do you know what it is?

COOK No.

SAMIA Break down the door.

COOK Break down the bathroom door?

SAMIA Yes.

COOK And who's going to do that?

SAMIA Can't you?

COOK Me?

SAMIA Certainly, you'd not be able to.

COOK It's a solid door and would need a carpenter . . .

SAMIA Go and fetch a carpenter.

COOK There's no carpenter near-by in the district.

SAMIA What's to be done?

COOK Leave it in the hands of the Almighty. We'll let him be for a while until he gets fed up and opens up of his own accord.

SAMIA He won't get fed up. So long as that wretched thing's got a breath of life in it.

COOK But he'll have to come out so as to go to work.

SAMIA He'll forget work or pretend to. I know him—sometimes he forgets himself. Many times he's unable to get any control over himself or over his time.

COOK And your own work, Ma'am?

SAMIA That's the trouble. I can't go without him because they'll ask me about him. What shall I say to them? Shall I say that he hasn't turned up to work because he's engrossed in watching a cockroach in the bath?

COOK Say that he's tired, indisposed.

SAMIA They'll immediately send round the company doctor.

COOK Let him come and good luck to him!

SAMIA And if he examines him and finds he's not indisposed at all?

COOK That's true.

SAMIA He's always getting me into such embarrassing situations. If I weren't always alongside him to rescue him and guide him he'd get into any number of scrapes.

COOK May the Almighty keep you and give you strength!

SAMIA He always yields to me, he never disobeys me.

COOK That's evident.

SAMIA What's happened to him then this morning? I said to him:
Open up! Open up! but he seemed stone-deaf.

COOK All his life he's paid attention to what you have to say.

SAMIA Except for today. I don't know what's happened to him.

COOK Somebody's put the evil eye on him.

SAMIA And where will be the end of it?

COOK Be patient, Ma'am. Patience is a virtue.

SAMIA My patience has run out, it's finished, it's had it!

COOK (*looking in the direction of the bathroom*) But you mean to say
that all he's doing is just watching a cockroach?

SAMIA You don't believe it?

COOK Honestly, Ma'am, if it weren't that I believe every word you say
I'd not make head or tail of it.

SAMIA Of course—this wouldn't happen with a normal man.

COOK Shall I speak to him, Ma'am?

SAMIA You?

COOK I'll have a go.

SAMIA Go on!

*The cook knocks on the bathroom door. Adil, motionless, is still
watching what is going on in the bath-tub.*

COOK (*she knocks again, then again and again, and finally shouts
out*) I'm Umm Attiya.

ADIL (*raising his head*) Umm Attiya? What do you want?

COOK To wash the bathroom floor.

ADIL It's forbidden.

COOK Forbidden?

ADIL Today it's forbidden.

COOK I'll bring a new piece of soap for the bath.

ADIL There's soap here.

COOK A clean towel?

ADIL There is one. There's everything.

COOK Don't you need anything?

ADIL All I need is for you to take yourself off and shut up.

COOK Just as you say.

The cook returns despondently to Samia.

SAMIA I told you it was no good.

COOK You're quite right.

SAMIA So what's to be done? One's got to do something, one's simply
got to.

COOK Calm down, Ma'am, and leave things to the Almighty!

SAMIA One can't just shut up about it—one can't!

*She walks nervously about the room, while the cook watches her
and sighs. There is a ring at the door.*

COOK It's the front door!

SAMIA Who could it be?

COOK I'll go and see. (*She goes out.*)

SAMIA (*standing up and listening, then calling out*) Who is it, Umm Attiya?

COOK (*entering in a state of flurry*) It's the doctor, Ma'am!

SAMIA Doctor? What doctor?

COOK He said he was the company doctor. I put him in the lounge.

SAMIA The company doctor? Ah, no doubt Raafat sent him, thinking that the situation demanded it. And now what's to be done? This is just what I feared. (*She moves towards the bathroom door and knocks.*) Adil! Open up, Adil—there's something very important.

ADIL (*his gaze directed at the inside of the bath*) I know—very important.

SAMIA The situation's critical.

ADIL No doubt about it. (*He points to the cockroach in the bath.*) Its situation is indeed critical, and you know its situation is critical.

SAMIA Whose situation? I'm talking about your situation.

ADIL That also is only too well known.

SAMIA Open up, Adil. Open up so I can explain the situation to you.

ADIL The situation's clear and requires no explaining.

SAMIA You're wrong, something new's occurred: the doctor's come.

ADIL Doctor? You've brought a doctor?—to do away with this poor thing? An entomologist of course?

SAMIA Entomologist? What are you talking about? The doctor's come about you. Open up—the doctor's here for you.

ADIL For me? An entomologist?

SAMIA What entomologist, Adil? The company doctor; the company doctor's come to examine you.

ADIL (*jumping to his feet*) What's that you're saying?

SAMIA Open up and I'll explain to you.

ADIL (*realizing what she's up to*) Open up? Not likely! I've heard that one before!

SAMIA I'm not fooling, Adil, and I'm not playing a trick. I'm talking seriously: the company doctor has arrived and is in the lounge. It seems Raafat sent him thinking you were ill.

ADIL Me ill?

SAMIA So Raafat understood, and the doctor's actually come.

ADIL If he's actually come, why don't I hear his voice?

SAMIA He's in the lounge. I told you he was in the lounge—and please don't make him wait any longer!

ADIL In short, you want me to open up?

SAMIA Of course, in order to be able to deal with the question of the doctor.

ADIL Cut this story of the doctor out!

SAMIA Don't you believe he's here?

ADIL If he's really come for me, let him speak to me himself.

SAMIA You want him to come in here?

ADIL Isn't that the normal thing?

SAMIA   All right. (*She calls out.*) Umm Attiya—ask the doctor to come
    in here.
COOK   Certainly, Ma'am.

> *Samia hurriedly arranges her hair and clothes preparatory to
> meeting the doctor.*

COOK (*at the door*)   Please, in here, Doctor.
SAMIA (*meeting him*)   Please come in, Doctor.
DOCTOR (*enters carrying a small bag*)   Good morning.
SAMIA   Good morning. It seems we've put you out for no . . .
DOCTOR   Not at all. I was already dressed and was about to leave when
    Mr. Raafat contacted me by telephone. I came along immediately
    —my house is just near-by.
SAMIA   We are extremely grateful but . . .
DOCTOR   And how does Mr. Adil feel?
SAMIA   The fact is he's . . .
DOCTOR   In any event everything will become clear when I've exam-
    ined him. Where is he, might I ask?
SAMIA   He's . . . he's . . . he's here in the bathroom. I'll call him.
DOCTOR   Let him take his bath in peace.
SAMIA   He's not taking a bath. He's . . . just a moment. (*She knocks
    at the bathroom door.*) Adil! Open up, Adil—the doctor's waiting.
ADIL   Where is he?
SAMIA   Here in the room. Answer him, Doctor!
DOCTOR   Mr. Adil!
ADIL   Good God! It's true!
DOCTOR (*to Samia*)   What's he saying?
SAMIA (*to Adil*)   You believe me? Now open up!
ADIL (*opening the door of the bathroom and standing by it*)   Doctor?
    Truly I'm most embarrassed . . .
DOCTOR   How are you now, Mr. Adil?
ADIL   I? I'm fine.
DOCTOR   Fine?
ADIL   Naturally.
SAMIA   But he felt slightly unwell early this morning.
ADIL   I?
SAMIA   Of course you. Since early this morning you haven't been feel-
    ing right.
ADIL   And you know the reason why?
SAMIA   Whatever the reason, the doctor's come and there's an end to
    it. In any case you're late for work and there's no harm in the doctor
    giving you a day off, isn't that so, Doctor?
DOCTOR   Before prescribing anything I must make an examination.
    Please lie down on the bed, Mr. Adil.
ADIL   But I . . .
SAMIA   Listen to what the doctor has to say, Adil, and let him examine
    you.
ADIL   Examine? And say it appears . . .
SAMIA   Anyway, you're run down.

ADIL But that's not sufficient reason . . .
SAMIA It's enough for now.
ADIL I prefer him to know the real reason.
SAMIA The real reason?
ADIL Yes, come along, Doctor.
DOCTOR Where to?
ADIL (*drawing him towards the bathroom*) In here.
SAMIA You're mad, Adil! (*She draws the doctor away from the bathroom.*) Please, Doctor, come away.
ADIL Leave him alone, Samia. Let me tell him of the real reason. (*Pulls the doctor towards him.*) Come along, Doctor.
SAMIA Don't listen to him, Doctor. (*Pulls the doctor towards her.*) Come along.
DOCTOR (*at a loss, being pulled in opposite directions by the two of them*) Please! Please!
SAMIA Let the doctor go, Adil. It's not right.
ADIL You let him go!
SAMIA Allow him to examine you—that's what he's come for.
ADIL No, I'll tell him the real reason.
SAMIA But that won't . . . won't . . .
ADIL It must be done.
SAMIA You don't realize what you're doing. Come here, Doctor, please. (*She pulls him.*)
ADIL But the doctor is interested to know what it is I want to show him. I'm sure of that. Please, Doctor, listen to what I have to say. Come along! (*He pulls at the doctor.*)
DOCTOR Excuse me! Excuse me! (*He tries to release himself from the two of them.*)
SAMIA I'm sorry, Doctor, but my husband Adil doesn't appreciate . . .
ADIL Doesn't appreciate what? In what way don't I appreciate? I know exactly what I'm doing. My mind's quite made up.
SAMIA I've warned you, Adil, I've warned you.
ADIL I'll take the responsibility.
SAMIA All right, you're free to do as you please.
DOCTOR (*bewildered*) What's it all about? Please—tell me.
ADIL (*drawing him into the bathroom*) Come along with me, Doctor, and I'll explain things to you.
DOCTOR (*in astonishment*) Where to?
ADIL (*standing in front of the bath*) Here, look! What do you see inside the bath-tub?
DOCTOR (*looking*) Nothing. There's no water in it.
ADIL Of course there's no water in it, but isn't there something else?
DOCTOR No, nothing—it's empty.
ADIL Yet even so, there is something there.
DOCTOR Something? Such as?
ADIL Do you find it absolutely sparkling white?
DOCTOR Yes, absolutely.
ADIL But you can't say that it's absolutely clean.

DOCTOR   Who am I to criticize your cleanliness?

ADIL   Thank you for your kind words but the obvious truth of the matter is that there is something dirty in the bath.

SAMIA   So you've admitted it's dirty and must be done away with?

ADIL   Dirty's something and doing away with it is something else.

DOCTOR   (*looks at them both uncomprehendingly*)   If you'll allow me . . .

ADIL   Look down here into the bath, Doctor, and you'll understand.

The doctor looks down with great attention.

ADIL   Do you not see something moving?

DOCTOR   (*without interest*)   A cockroach.

ADIL   A cockroach? Well done!

DOCTOR   And so?

ADIL   This cockroach is the very core and essence.

DOCTOR   Very core and essence?

ADIL   Look at it well, Doctor. What do you notice about it?

DOCTOR   From what point of view?

ADIL   From the point of view of its behaviour.

DOCTOR   Its behaviour?

SAMIA   Keep quiet, Adil—let me explain to the doctor.

ADIL   No, please, Samia—let me do the speaking.

SAMIA   And why should I not speak? At least I won't tell it wrong.

ADIL   And I'll tell it wrong?

SAMIA   Don't complicate things for me. Let me do the talking, because I'm better than you at explaining things.

ADIL   Of course, but it's only I who . . .

SAMIA   Today you're opposing me all along the line in a quite unreasonable way.

ADIL   It's not opposition. I didn't mean . . . it's just . . .

SAMIA   Just what? Listen, Doctor . . .

ADIL   A moment, Samia, please! Let me speak first because I've got my own point of view.

SAMIA   And I too have a point of view.

ADIL   Of course. Of course—and your point of view is respected, very respected. But allow me a minute, one single minute and no more.

SAMIA   No, not even half a minute.

ADIL   Please, Samia.

SAMIA   Out of the question.

ADIL   Samia!

DOCTOR   Friends, there's no reason for all this disagreement. Explain to me first of all exactly what the problem's all about.

SAMIA   The problem, Doctor . . .

ADIL   For which of us did the Doctor come? Was it not for me? Tell me, Doctor, for whom did you come here?

DOCTOR   For you.

ADIL   For me, then it is I who shall explain to you . . .

DOCTOR   You or the lady—the important thing is for me to know what it's about.

SAMIA Do you hear, Adil: you or I, and as I'm the woman I have priority.

ADIL Heavens! Even in this, even in my own illness?

SAMIA You've now admitted you're ill.

ADIL In the doctor's view. Of course he has come because there's an ill person in the house, and the ill person is supposed to be me, but the fact, Doctor, is . . .

SAMIA The fact is that he's . . .

ADIL The fact is that I'm . . .

SAMIA (*violently*) Whatever next, Adil? Please, don't force me to . . .

ADIL It's my fault, my fault as usual, because it's always my fault.

DOCTOR The important thing, friends, is: what's it all about?

SAMIA I'm sorry, Doctor—we're taking up too much of your time.

DOCTOR No, not at all, only I'd like to understand . . .

SAMIA You'll understand, Doctor, you'll understand—if he'd just shut up for a moment I'd be able to explain to you.

ADIL Just the opposite.

SAMIA What's just the opposite?

ADIL If I keep silent he'll not understand what it's about.

SAMIA Meaning that I'm incapable of making him understand, or do you mean I'm a liar and will falsify the facts?

ADIL God forbid! Would I ever insinuate such a thing!

DOCTOR Allow me, so as to put an end to all disagreement, just let me find out what it's about by myself. Please, Mr. Adil, please lie down on the bed so that I can examine you and then I'll know the truth for myself.

ADIL No, Doctor—the truth's not to be found on the bed but in the bath.

DOCTOR In the bath?

ADIL Yes, in this bath—this cockroach.

DOCTOR Permit me, please excuse me, but I . . . I don't understand anything at all.

SAMIA It's not his fault—of course he can't understand.

ADIL I'll explain the matter in a few words—listen, Doctor, look carefully at this cockroach and tell me what it's doing now?

DOCTOR (*looking into the bath*) What's it doing? It's doing nothing.

ADIL Look carefully, Doctor.

DOCTOR What are you getting at exactly?

SAMIA What Adil is getting at is that . . .

ADIL No, no, let the doctor discover it for himself.

DOCTOR (*looking intently into the bath*) Discover?

ADIL Don't you see, for example, that the cockroach is trying to do something?

DOCTOR Of course, it's trying to get out of the bath.

ADIL Marvellous! Marvellous! We've got there.

DOCTOR (*looking at him*) Where have we got?

ADIL To the heart of the whole matter.

DOCTOR (*nodding his head*) Understood. Understood. It's all quite clear now.

ADIL   You understand what I'm driving at, Doctor? This is the point of departure and I shall explain my attitude to you.

DOCTOR   No, no, there's no need to explain—I've understood. (*He goes out of the bathroom and whispers to Samia.*) Might I have a word with you?

SAMIA (*following him*)   Of course, Doctor, go ahead.

DOCTOR (*whispering*)   He's really overdoing it. How many hours does he work at the factory?

SAMIA   The usual hours, but there's something else to it.

DOCTOR   Does he do other work?

SAMIA   He is preparing a thesis for his doctorate, but this condition of his . . .

DOCTOR   Understood. Understood. He's certainly in need of rest. I'll write down for him all that's necessary. Would you allow me, Mr. Adil?

ADIL (*coming out of the bathroom*)   What, Doctor?

DOCTOR   Nothing—it's just that having visited you at home in my capacity of company doctor, I must examine you, if only for the purpose of establishing that I've been here.

ADIL   But I'm not ill.

DOCTOR   I know that, but I am required to put in a report and the report must show that an examination has been made.

ADIL   You came in an official capacity?

DOCTOR   Of course.

ADIL   Ah, in that case I must help you. However, what are you going to write in your report seeing that I'm not ill?

DOCTOR   Leave things to me. First of all, would you just lie down here on the bed.

ADIL   I've put on weight these last years.

DOCTOR   That's obvious—you're getting flabby before your time.

SAMIA   He's grown himself a real paunch!

ADIL   From fatty food—Umm Attiya's cooking!

DOCTOR   Maybe also from lack of exercise.

ADIL   I've got no time for exercise.

DOCTOR   You overdo things at work.

ADIL   I have to.

DOCTOR (*examining his chest and back with the stethoscope*)   Take a deep breath. Enough, Enough. Do you smoke?

ADIL   A little.

DOCTOR   Drink a lot of coffee?

ADIL   A couple of cups a day.

DOCTOR   Alcohol? Drugs?

ADIL   No, no. Never, never.

DOCTOR   You naturally sometimes stay up late at night.

ADIL   Sometimes, when my work requires me to, but in any case it's never later than midnight.

DOCTOR   Do you sleep well?

ADIL   Like a log.

DOCTOR Do you have unpleasant dreams?

ADIL Neither pleasant nor unpleasant, I don't dream at all.

DOCTOR Perhaps you dream and don't remember your dreams.

ADIL Maybe.

DOCTOR You don't suffer from anything unusual?

ADIL No, not at all.

DOCTOR Thank you.

> *The doctor sets about writing out his prescription to one side of the room.*

SAMIA (*approaching the doctor*) I hope everything's all right, Doctor?

DOCTOR Fine, everything's just fine—he's in splendid health, thanks be to God. There's not a thing wrong with him. I'll write him out a prescription for some tranquillizers and give him three days' sick leave.

SAMIA Three days?

DOCTOR Too little?

SAMIA No, it's a lot, too much.

ADIL (*jumping to his feet*) What's too much?

SAMIA The doctor wants to give you three days' sick leave.

ADIL Three days?

SAMIA One day's plenty, Doctor.

ADIL Of course one day, and there wasn't even any reason to have today off if it hadn't been that you came, Doctor—so as to justify your coming here.

DOCTOR As you say—one day, my dear sir.

ADIL Thank you, Doctor.

DOCTOR On condition that you stay in bed.

ADIL Stay in bed?

DOCTOR It's necessary.

ADIL And what's the necessity?

DOCTOR For complete rest and relaxation.

ADIL And if I find complete rest and relaxation somewhere else?

DOCTOR Where?

ADIL In the bathroom, for example?

SAMIA Do you hear, Doctor? He'll be spending the day in the bathroom.

DOCTOR There's no harm in his taking a warm bath, it'll help him to relax.

SAMIA He'll not be taking a bath at all, neither warm nor cold.

DOCTOR What, then, will he do in the bathroom?

SAMIA Ask him.

ADIL I shall watch the cockroach. What's wrong with that?

SAMIA You've heard with your very own ears, haven't you, Doctor?

DOCTOR The cockroach? Again?

ADIL Come along to the bath with me and I'll explain things to you.

DOCTOR (*looking at his watch*) Another time, it's getting late and I've got some urgent work to do.

ADIL   My explanation will take no more than a minute.

DOCTOR   I promise to visit you again shortly when, God willing, your nerves will have calmed down.

ADIL   My nerves are perfectly calm. I would have liked you to stay for a while so that . . .

DOCTOR   I'll come back. I'll come back.

ADIL   When?

DOCTOR   In the afternoon. In the afternoon.

ADIL   When you return in the afternoon everything will have changed.

DOCTOR   What will have changed?

ADIL   The cockroach will—will have been destroyed. Do you think my wife will leave things as they are?

SAMIA   Of course not. You can't stop me from using the bath the whole day—it's unreasonable.

ADIL   (to the doctor)   Do you hear?

SAMIA   Judge, Doctor! Don't I have to go off to my work at the factory? Hasn't his lordship already made me late enough?

ADIL   Doctor, it's not I who've made her late. Her being late has another reason. Ask her about it!

SAMIA   What's the other reason?

ADIL   Your insistence on taking a bath today.

SAMIA   Ask him, Doctor, what the reason was for my not taking a bath today.

ADIL   I'll tell you the reason, Doctor: the reason is that she wants to destroy this cockroach.

SAMIA   There you are, Doctor!

DOCTOR   The fact is that the question . . .

ADIL   I'm certain, Doctor, you'll come down on the side of truth, for the question is clear.

SAMIA   Of course it's clear, but don't try to influence the doctor. He understands everything.

ADIL   I'm not trying to influence the doctor. It's you who from the very beginning were trying to influence him, but he understands perfectly my purpose.

SAMIA   Your purpose?

ADIL   Of course.

SAMIA   Tell us, Doctor: have you really understood anything of him?

ADIL   And have you understood anything of her, Doctor?

SAMIA   Answer, Doctor!

ADIL   Yes, answer!

DOCTOR   (at a loss between the two of them)   The truth of the matter is I . . . is I . . .

ADIL   Listen, Doctor; the essence of the matter can be put into a few words: put yourself in the same position.

DOCTOR   Your position?

ADIL   The position of the cockroach.

DOCTOR   (hurriedly taking up his bag)   No—please excuse me.

He rushes out with Samia and Adil in his wake calling out to him.

SAMIA   Wait, Doctor!

ADIL   Just a moment, Doctor!

Act Three—The Fate of the Cockroach

The same scene less than a minute later. Samia and Adil are returning to the room after the doctor's hasty departure.

ADIL   Why did the doctor leave like that?

SAMIA   Ask yourself.

ADIL   Ask myself? Why? Did I do anything wrong?

SAMIA   You? From the moment you woke up this morning you haven't stopped doing things wrong.

ADIL   Good Heavens!

SAMIA   We woke up in the morning in fine shape, got ourselves ready to go out to work, and then your lordship causes us all this unnecessary delay.

ADIL   It's I who've caused it?

SAMIA   Your cockroach!

ADIL   And was it I who placed it in the bath?

SAMIA   What it amounts to is that you've got the day off—official sick leave. As for me, I've got to go off to my work. It's true I'm late but I'll make the best of it and give as an excuse your being ill and the company doctor coming to the house.

The doctor reappears.

DOCTOR   Please excuse me! I went off in a most impolite manner.

ADIL   No, don't mention it, Doctor.

DOCTOR   I was afraid I'd be late for my other work. On thinking it over, though, I feel that my prime duty lies here. I have therefore returned quickly to ask that I might continue my examination of the case.

SAMIA   Thank you, Doctor.

DOCTOR   I'd like to have a word in private with your wife—would you allow me, Mr. Adil?

ADIL   Of course. Of course. I'll go into the bathroom.

DOCTOR   Take your time!

Adil goes into the bathroom and locks the door on himself. He goes back to watching the bath with interest. He makes signs and gestures as he follows the cockroach's movements, like someone following a game of chess.

SAMIA   Is anything wrong, Doctor?

DOCTOR   I want to ask you about certain things.

SAMIA   Go ahead!

DOCTOR   My questions will perhaps be a trifle embarrassing in that they may touch upon some personal aspects, but my duty as a practising doctor demands that I do so. May I put my questions?

SAMIA   Of course, Doctor, go ahead!

DOCTOR   What's your opinion about your husband's personality?

SAMIA   In what respect?

DOCTOR   In respect of strength and weakness.

SAMIA   In relation to whom?

DOCTOR   In relation to yourself of course.

SAMIA   I . . . I believe his personality to be weaker than mine.

DOCTOR   Does he know it?

SAMIA   Certainly.

DOCTOR   He has told you so openly?

SAMIA   No, but he believes it deep inside him.

DOCTOR   How do you know?

SAMIA   He is always stating that I boss him and make him obey my orders and tyrannize him.

DOCTOR   Tyrannize him?

SAMIA   That's what he says.

DOCTOR   Then he believes or imagines that you are tyrannizing him?

SAMIA   Yes.

DOCTOR   My diagnosis is appropriate.

SAMIA   What diagnosis?

DOCTOR   This question of the cockroach.

SAMIA   And what's the connection?

DOCTOR   You want to do away with the cockroach and he wants to save it from your hands.

SAMIA   You mean, Doctor . . .

DOCTOR   Yes, in his inner consciousness he has identified himself with the cockroach, and this is the secret of his concern and affection for it.

SAMIA   Extraordinary! D'you think so, Doctor?

DOCTOR   There can be no other reason.

SAMIA   But . . .

DOCTOR   This is a very obvious example from modern psychology. I am not a specialist in psychiatry, but I have made a private study of it as a hobby and I am indeed lucky to have come across this case today.

SAMIA   Are you certain it's a psychological state?

DOCTOR   A typical case.

SAMIA   Can it be treated?

DOCTOR   The treatment is easy, extremely easy.

SAMIA   Whatever you order me to do I shall carry out immediately.

DOCTOR   The treatment requires no more than your persuading your husband that there is no similarity between him and the cockroach.

SAMIA   And how shall I persuade him?

DOCTOR   That's the problem.

SAMIA   A way must be found.

DOCTOR First of all you must on your side show affection for the cockroach.

SAMIA Show affection for the cockroach?

DOCTOR That's essential, because any hurt done by you to the cockroach would, in your husband's view, be a hurt done to him personally.

SAMIA But this is madness.

DOCTOR Naturally—it's a pathological condition.

SAMIA But he's perfectly sane. Up until this morning he could not have been more balanced in all his behaviour, performing his company work perfectly well.

DOCTOR He is in fact extremely well balanced and will always be able to perform his company work in the best possible manner, of that I'm sure.

SAMIA Then he's a normal person.

DOCTOR Normal in all things except one—that of the cockroach.

SAMIA That's right, no sooner is the cockroach mentioned than . . .

DOCTOR Than he begins to speak and act strangely.

SAMIA That is so.

DOCTOR Yet even so there's no cause for worry. With a little wisdom and patience, kindness and adjustment, we shall quickly be able to sort things out for the best.

SAMIA You may be confident, Doctor, that I shall employ both wisdom and patience and shall be kind and compliant with him in everything he wants.

DOCTOR That is all that is now required, so let's begin trying.

SAMIA Yes, we shall try.

DOCTOR First of all, we must go along and participate in what he's doing.

SAMIA (*she goes with the doctor behind her and gently knocks on the bathroom door*) Adil!

ADIL (*getting to his feet and opening the door to them*) Have you finished your little private talk?

SAMIA Yes, the doctor was advising me . . .

DOCTOR To put you on a special diet. I'd like you to be a little slimmer.

ADIL Slimmer? Me?

DOCTOR Why not? Do you want to let your body get flabby?

ADIL Has my wife complained about my physique?

DOCTOR No, I'm talking medically—an increase in weight leads to lethargy, and you are in need of energy.

ADIL I'm exceedingly energetic, extremely energetic, which can be seen from the fact that I wake up in the morning before the alarm goes off. Ask Samia.

SAMIA Quite correct.

DOCTOR Then you admit your husband possesses this quality.

SAMIA No doubt about it—he's exceedingly energetic.

DOCTOR Do you hear that, Mr. Adil? Your wife is being very complimentary about you.

ADIL   She can't deny I'm energetic, though of course I'm not as energetic as this cockroach.

DOCTOR   The cockroach? Ah, yes, of course.

ADIL   Look, Doctor. Look, Samia. It's still struggling—with the same perseverance. I tried to catch it out slacking or giving up, but never . . . never . . . never.

SAMIA   (*looking into the bath-tub with feigned interest*)   It's certainly courageous.

ADIL   And what courage!

SAMIA   I've begun to love it.

ADIL   (*looking at her*)   Love it?

SAMIA   Yes, doesn't its courage deserve love?

ADIL   You wanted to destroy it with insecticide.

SAMIA   I was stupid.

ADIL   Thanks be to God!

SAMIA   Look at its whiskers—they're beautiful!

ADIL   Whose whiskers?

SAMIA   The cockroach's of course.

ADIL   Its whiskers are beautiful?

SAMIA   Don't you think so?

ADIL   You making fun of me?

SAMIA   Of you? No, no—I swear to you, Adil. Please don't be angry. I swear to you I'm not making fun of you. I'm being absolutely serious now. I'm sincere in what I say, and when I say that its whiskers please me, be sure that I really mean it.

ADIL   And since when did you discover its whiskers were so beautiful?

SAMIA   Since . . . since a moment ago when I looked carefully at it.

ADIL   I myself have been looking carefully at it from early morning and can't find anything beautiful about it.

SAMIA   You're being modest.

ADIL   Modest? Me? What's the connection?

SAMIA   Oh none, none at all.

DOCTOR   Certainly there's no connection whatsoever.

SAMIA   Of course, Adil, be sure there's no connection.

ADIL   (*looking at the two of them*)   What's all this confusion about?

SAMIA   Nothing at all, Adil—everything's quite in order. All that's happened is that the doctor and I have come to understand your point of view completely.

DOCTOR   Certainly. Certainly.

ADIL   (*doubting them*)   And what is my point of view?

SAMIA   It's—it's that this cockroach . . .

DOCTOR   Should not come to any harm.

SAMIA   Yes. Yes.

ADIL   Do you know why?

SAMIA   We know all right.

ADIL   No, Samia, I'm certain you don't really know. I shall explain it to you and the doctor.

SAMIA   No, there's no need, Adil, no need at all. We know and appreciate the position. God willing, everything will return to normal with a little wisdom and patience.

ADIL Yes, a little patience. All that's wanted is a little patience, because things may go on for a while. In any case, it's both interesting and exciting. I don't get bored watching, and so long as this cockroach goes on putting up such a struggle to get out of its impasse, it is not right that we should destroy it.

SAMIA Who said we were going to destroy it? On the contrary, Adil, I'll look after it with every care. I'll sacrifice myself for it.

ADIL Sacrifice yourself for it? Please, Samia—there's no need to make fun.

SAMIA Absolutely not, Adil. What can I do to convince you that I'm definitely not making fun?

ADIL When all's said and done, the struggle this cockroach is putting up stirs within me a feeling of respect.

SAMIA And who said we had less respect for it than you? We are at one with you, Adil—absolutely at one. Maybe we have even more respect and appreciation for it than you, isn't that so, Doctor?

DOCTOR Of course. Of course.

ADIL More than me? No, I don't think so.

SAMIA And why not?

ADIL Because I've been watching it since early morning, following its every movement. It amazes me the amount of strength that's stored up in it—quite remarkable strength.

SAMIA I'm in agreement with you about that, Adil, and I really do find that it has an extraordinarily strong personality.

ADIL Strong personality?

SAMIA Don't you think so?

ADIL I think it's an exaggeration to say it's got a personality.

SAMIA Honestly, Adil, it's got a strong personality—you must believe that.

ADIL Listen, Samia—don't get characteristics mixed up. The fact that a cockroach has such strength and determination is both acceptable and reasonable, but to say it's got a personality is going too far.

SAMIA I insist it has got a personality. Maybe even its personality is stronger than mine—wouldn't you agree with me there, Doctor?

DOCTOR Very likely.

ADIL What's very likely, Doctor? That this cockroach's personality is stronger than Samia's?

DOCTOR Don't, Mr. Adil, overestimate the personality of your lady wife—with all due deference to her.

ADIL I'm not overestimating but—but to compare my wife with a cockroach!

SAMIA But I'm in agreement, Adil.

ADIL It's not a question of whether you're in agreement or not in agreement—we're talking about the comparison itself.

SAMIA And why should we reject the comparison, seeing that the cockroach commands respect? It does me honour.

ADIL   Are we back again at making fun?

SAMIA   Not at all, I swear to you, Adil. I'm absolutely serious—just
ask the doctor.

ADIL   Listen, Samia, when words lose their normal dimensions, then
everything loses its seriousness. I've begun to feel that you're in
league with the doctor to ridicule my ideas.

DOCTOR   God forbid, Mr. Adil!

SAMIA   No, Adil, please don't make such an accusation against the
doctor. He is the last person to wish to harm your self-respect. He
hasn't interrupted his other work and devoted all his time to us in
order to make fun of you and your ideas.

DOCTOR   On the contrary, the . . . the fact of the matter is that I . . .

SAMIA   Don't say anything, Doctor—it's obvious what your feelings
are.

ADIL   I'm sorry—I no doubt misunderstood.

SAMIA   Be sure, Adil, that we are of the same opinion as you. There
is now no disagreement between us. The cockroach is as much an
object of affection to us as to you.

ADIL   Affection?

SAMIA   Yes, and in deference to it and to you I have decided not to
have a bath today in order to prove to you I won't attempt to harm
it.

ADIL   Thank you.

SAMIA   Doesn't that please you?

ADIL   Of course it pleases me.

SAMIA   Everything that pleases you, Adil, everything that makes you
happy, I shall at once put into effect for you.

ADIL   What's all this tenderness about?

SAMIA   I regret all my hasty actions.

ADIL   What hasty actions?

SAMIA   I haven't always been nice to you.

ADIL   That is your right as a woman and a wife, but it is my duty as
a man and a husband to endure.

SAMIA   No, from now on you shall not endure, I shall not make you
endure.

ADIL   What's happened now? What's come over the universe?

DOCTOR   Your wife is one of the best of wives, Mr. Adil, and is blindly
obedient to you.

ADIL   Since when?

SAMIA   Since today.

ADIL   And why today?

SAMIA   Because it . . . because I . . .

DOCTOR   Because she naturally doesn't want to see you being ill.

ADIL   But I'm not ill.

DOCTOR   Of course. Of course you're not ill at all.

SAMIA   What the doctor means is you're . . .

DOCTOR   Certainly. What I mean is that it's clear you're not ill. That
was established by examining you, be sure of that. However, the
whole object is to remove the *idea* of illness, not illness itself. Just

the fact of seeing a doctor in the house, a doctor who has come because of you, has made your wife feel towards you a certain . . .

SAMIA   Yes. Yes. As soon as I saw you would need sick leave . . .

ADIL   I don't need sick leave. It's the doctor who made me take it at the time he made out his report. As for me, I'm in no need of any leave.

DOCTOR   That's quite so.

SAMIA   In any case, Adil, I was unfair to you.

ADIL   Sometimes.

SAMIA   I admit it.

ADIL   Then you won't go to the bathroom before me?

SAMIA   No, never—I've turned over a new leaf, I promise.

ADIL   You won't tell me to get breakfast?

SAMIA   No, I promise. I promise.

ADIL   You won't impose your will and orders on me?

SAMIA   No, I promise. I promise.

ADIL   And what's the secret of this sudden transformation?

SAMIA   I didn't realize that this behaviour of mine towards you would have such results.

ADIL   What results?

DOCTOR   She means . . . she means your being angry.

ADIL   But I haven't been angry. I used sometimes to feel annoyance at your behaviour. I was only too often annoyed with you, but I've never been angry with you.

DOCTOR   You used to repress it.

ADIL   Repress it?

DOCTOR   Repress it deep within yourself. It's this repression that leads to . . . that leads to . . .

ADIL   Leads to what?

DOCTOR   Leads to . . . to temperamental upsets.

ADIL   Certainly I feel upset, but only for a while.

SAMIA   But maybe you keep some feeling lurking deep inside you.

ADIL   Because of you? No, not at all.

SAMIA   I almost believed this morning you hated me.

ADIL   Hated you?

SAMIA   Yes, because of the insecticide.

ADIL   Do you call that hate? A mere feeling of slight annoyance at your wish to destroy this cockroach.

SAMIA   I didn't recognize its importance.

ADIL   And do you now honestly recognize its importance?

SAMIA   Of course.

ADIL   I doubt it.

SAMIA   And why do you doubt it?

ADIL   Because you don't watch it with sufficient attention. Look! For example, it has now begun to stand for long periods on the bottom of the bath. What's the meaning of that?

SAMIA   (looking with attention)   It means that . . .

ADIL   That it's beginning to take rests.

SAMIA   Yes.

ADIL   After that continuous effort it must be in need of rest periods during which it lies prostate, as you see, quietly moving its whiskers before carrying on anew with its climbing.

DOCTOR (*looking with attention*)   It's actually begun moving slowly so as to start climbing again.

SAMIA   That's right—it's started to climb.

ADIL   Note carefully the spot at which it begins to slip.

SAMIA   Yes, yes—the same spot. There it goes—it's slipped!

DOCTOR   And fallen once more to its place at the bottom.

ADIL   Look, it's getting up from its fall and is beginning to climb again.

SAMIA   And it will slip down again. There it is—it's slipped down! The poor thing! It's been doing exactly the same thing since early morning.

ADIL   And maybe since last night, because when we got up we found it already in the bath. It must therefore have fallen into it from the ceiling during the night.

SAMIA   I have a question, Adil? May I?

ADIL   Of course, Samia—ask it.

SAMIA   Have you not thought of rescuing it from its predicament?

ADIL   Rescuing it?

SAMIA   Yes, why don't you rescue it?

ADIL   It's rescuing itself.

SAMIA   How can it rescue itself? It will never be able to. All the time its attempts are in vain because the bath is empty and slippery; there's nothing for it to climb up but the slippery sides on which it loses its foothold.

ADIL   That's up to it.

SAMIA   At least help it. Give it a little help, Adil. For example, let the end of the towel hang over inside the bath, or bring a piece of string and dangle it over the side—or anything that'll help it to get out.

ADIL   And why should we do that?

SAMIA   To get it out, to get it out alive. Don't you want it to be saved?

ADIL   Who said I wanted it to be saved?

SAMIA   How odd! You don't want it to be saved? Then you want its death?

ADIL   I don't want its death either.

SAMIA   Then what do you want for it?

ADIL   I don't want anything for it. It is no concern of mine.

SAMIA   Of course not. Of course not. It's absolutely no concern of yours. You have no connection with it, no connection at all. You are something and it is something else. We know that only too well, isn't that so, Doctor?

DOCTOR   Without doubt.

SAMIA   Be sure, Adil, that we're *completely* convinced that you have no connection with this cockroach. We wish you to know this well and to believe it.

ADIL   And don't I know this?

SAMIA   The important thing is that you should believe it deep inside you.

ADIL   Believe what?

SAMIA   Believe that there is no relationship and not the slightest similarity between you and it.

ADIL   Similarity between me and it? Whatever next, Samia? Have things come to this pass? You talk of a similarity between me and the cockroach?

SAMIA   On the contrary, it makes me happy to know there's no similarity.

ADIL   Then such a similarity does exist in your view?

SAMIA   Not in mine, Adil.

ADIL   Then in whose?

SAMIA   In your own view?

ADIL   Mine! In my view I resemble the cockroach?

SAMIA   Then you no longer think this is so?

ADIL   Think what? That I resemble the cockroach? In what way do I resemble it? Please let me know. You've really gone too far; this is too much, Samia, much too much. Me resemble a cockroach? Me? In what way? From what point of view? Whiskers? If it's from the point of view of whiskers, I am clean-shaven, as you can see. From the point of view of features? Of lineaments of face? Speak! Speak! Speak!

SAMIA   Please, Doctor, you speak!

DOCTOR   (to Samia)   Be so good as to allow us a moment in private.

SAMIA   I'll go and prepare you a cup of coffee, Doctor. (She goes out, leaving the doctor and Adil on their own.)

DOCTOR   Listen, Mr. Adil—you should, first of all, know that your wife is wholly loyal to you and does not at all intend to hurt your feelings.

ADIL   After what I've heard?

DOCTOR   Believe me, she respects you, appreciates you, and has a very high regard for you, despite your belief that your personality is weaker than hers.

ADIL   My personality weaker than hers! Who said so?

DOCTOR   No one at all—a mere supposition, a mere possibility that this was your inner belief.

ADIL   Such a supposition or possibility never occurred to me.

DOCTOR   Maybe, for example, her demands, or what might have been understood as orders, were . . .

ADIL   Certainly she is a person of many demands and orders, even arbitrary actions and a desire to be the boss.

DOCTOR   You admit this point?

ADIL   For sure.

DOCTOR   Then you find that she has a desire to be the boss?

ADIL   Of course, like most wives, and especially those who, like her, have graduated with their husbands from the same college and are employed in the same line of work.

DOCTOR   Equality, then, between the two of you is total in everything?

ADIL   In everything.

DOCTOR   And yet she wants to have the advantage, to be the boss, to dominate.

ADIL   That is exactly my wife's attitude.

DOCTOR   And you let her be the boss and dominate.

ADIL   Yes, and do you know why?

DOCTOR   Because she . . .

ADIL   No, please wait! Don't be too hasty and conclude from that that she has a stronger personality than me—those are merely her pretensions.

DOCTOR   Her pretensions?

ADIL   Tell me frankly, Doctor, was it not she who said something of that sort to you?

DOCTOR   I believe . . .

ADIL   Yes, I know this of her: deep within her she believes I have a weaker personality than her.

DOCTOR   And is that not true?

ADIL   Of course it's not at all true. She's free to believe whatever she likes about herself. If her conceit portrays things to her in that light, then let her imagine as she will.

DOCTOR   But this does not obviate the fact that you obey her and carry out all her orders.

ADIL   It's a desire on my part to please her, because she's a woman, a weak woman, taken up with her youth, her advancement, her talent. I don't like to shake her belief in her own strength and superiority. I would regard that as meanness, meanness on my part as a strong man. I hold that real manliness demands that she be made to feel her strength and her importance and to raise her morale.

DOCTOR   Raise her morale? Extraordinary! The problem's reversed.

ADIL   What problem?

DOCTOR   Another question, Mr. Adil: the problem of the cockroach?

ADIL   What about the cockroach?

DOCTOR   It's your interest in it.

ADIL   And what's the secret of your interest in my interest?

DOCTOR   None at all, it's just . . .

ADIL   Listen here, Doctor—the whole thing's becoming clear to me. I've now understood. I've understood its beauty and its whiskers and its personality and the similarity. What you were getting at, therefore, was that I . . .

DOCTOR   Frankly, Mr. Adil, sir, yes.

ADIL   Yes?

DOCTOR   Our whole object was merely to assist and to . . .

ADIL   Participate—to assist and participate with my wife in such talk.

DOCTOR   No, Mr. Adil, this is a well-known theory.

ADIL   Theory? What theory?

DOCTOR   To tell you the truth I've not specialized in psychiatry, I've only studied it purely as a hobby, and so . . .

ADIL   Quite understood. And so you came to believe that I belonged to the cockroach species.

DOCTOR   No, it's not quite like that. In any case I've now changed my opinion.

ADIL   Thank God! You now see that I'm a human being!

DOCTOR   You must excuse me, Mr. Adil, but all the surrounding circumstances drew one in that direction.

ADIL   Please, Doctor, explain to me in detail what got into your mind, according to your psychiatry.

DOCTOR   No, there's no point now. I'm sorry.

ADIL   And my wife Samia knew of this opinion of yours?

DOCTOR   Yes.

ADIL   And she it was who helped you to see me as a cockroach?

DOCTOR   No, Mr. Adil, no. It's not like that. It's not, I assure you, quite like that. I assure you.

ADIL   Listen, Doctor, I want to tell you in all frankness that any similarity between me and the cockroach is mere . . .

DOCTOR   My apologies. My apologies, Mr. Adil. Our intentions were well-meant, I swear they were.

ADIL   Allow me to complete what I had to say: if you believed that I resembled a cockroach, then you were mistaken.

DOCTOR   Of course—and how! I admit I made a wrong analysis, that I'm mistaken, a hundred per cent mistaken.

ADIL   Yes, a grave mistake, because I am unable to attain the magnificent level reached by cockroaches.

DOCTOR   What are you saying? The magnificent level?

ADIL   Yes.

DOCTOR   Are you being serious?

ADIL   Wholly serious—and I'm prepared to repeat what I said.

DOCTOR   Then you admire this cockroach?

ADIL   And I appreciate it.

DOCTOR   And you appreciate it?

ADIL   And I respect it.

DOCTOR   And you respect it?

ADIL   And I understand it well.

DOCTOR   (scrutinizing him closely) Understood. Understood. And you take after it and imagine yourself . . .

ADIL   In its place?

DOCTOR   Yes, like it.

ADIL   Yes, I imagine that.

DOCTOR   Then you, you . . .

ADIL   I what?

DOCTOR   I don't know any longer. You've bewildered me, Mr. Adil.

ADIL   Please, Doctor, that's quite enough. Once again you're applying your psychiatry to me. It's a lot simpler than all that. I shall explain it to you clearly if you'll allow me.

DOCTOR   Please go ahead.

ADIL   First of all, imagine you're a cockroach.

DOCTOR   Me?

ADIL   Or that the cockroach is you.

DOCTOR   Mr. Adil . . .

ADIL   Please don't look at me like that. I understand exactly the meaning of your glances. You are still doubting. You are really at a loss
about me, but I assure you once again that it's altogether different
from what you have in mind.

DOCTOR   Then your employment of these words is in the nature of a
pleasantry or . . .

ADIL   Take it in any meaning you like. The important thing is for you
to leave out, as far as I'm concerned, this psychiatric business and
be natural with me.

DOCTOR   Be natural?

ADIL   Yes, are you being natural now?

DOCTOR   By God, I'm . . . to tell the truth . . .

ADIL   You're not sure?

DOCTOR   I no longer know anything.

ADIL   I'll tell you what to do: just let yourself go, forget you're a doctor
and let's examine the matter with the utmost simplicity. Are you
ready to do this?

DOCTOR   Yes.

ADIL   Great! What was I asking you?

DOCTOR   You asked me about . . .

ADIL   Yes, I remember. I asked you to imagine that you . . .

DOCTOR   That I was a cockroach.

ADIL   Or that the cockroach was you.

DOCTOR   Indeed. Indeed.

ADIL   And now to the second step.

DOCTOR   But wait, in my situation I can't . . .

ADIL   Can't what?

DOCTOR   I can't be a cockroach.

ADIL   Why not.

DOCTOR   Because I've never been married.

ADIL   What's that got to do with it?

DOCTOR   It seems that I . . . that I expressed myself badly.

ADIL   No, you merely misunderstood me. I did not ask you to be a
family cockroach, in the psychological sense. No, I meant the actual
cockroach in front of you there in the bath.

DOCTOR   (pointing at the cockroach in the bath)   That?

ADIL   Yes, that hero.

DOCTOR   Hero?

ADIL   Indeed a hero. Imagine yourself in a deep well with walls of
smooth marble and that you found it impossible to get out despite
having made exhausting efforts to do so, what would you do?

DOCTOR   I'd give up of course.

ADIL   But it hasn't given up.

DOCTOR   By no means—I see it repeating its attempts dozens of times.

ADIL   Even hundreds. Since early morning I've been occupied in
counting up the number of times.

DOCTOR   Is that what you were engaged in since morning?

ADIL   Yes, I wanted to know when its struggle would come to an end.

DOCTOR (*looking into the bath with real interest*)   As of now it looks as if it won't give up yet.

ADIL   Indeed. We're tired from watching but it's not tired from trying.

DOCTOR (*continuing to watch it*)   What hope has it of escaping?

ADIL   No hope of course.

DOCTOR   Unless you were to intervene and save it.

ADIL   And I shall not intervene.

DOCTOR   Why not, seeing that you admire it?

ADIL   I must leave it to its fate.

DOCTOR   Were it able to scream, and it screamed to you for help, would you not take pity on it?

ADIL   Perhaps, but it's mute and doesn't scream.

DOCTOR   Who are you to say that?

ADIL   What are you saying?

DOCTOR   I am saying that who are we to say it is not screaming now and asking for help—just that the oscillations of its voice are not picked up by the human ear.

ADIL   Very possibly.

DOCTOR   Imagine that it is now screaming and beseeching, and you don't hear and don't understand its language.

ADIL   It also doesn't hear me and see me.

DOCTOR   Yes, every contact between the two of you is severed.

ADIL   Not completely severed, as is borne out by the fact that I am interested in it.

DOCTOR   You are interested in its struggle for life.

ADIL   This, then, is its voice, its pleading, its language which I can hear and understand.

DOCTOR   Certainly, it explains our being so interested in its struggle.

ADIL   Is that not what has kept me in front of the bath since early morning?

DOCTOR (*looking into the bath*)   It is in reality an entertaining spectacle.

ADIL (*also looking*)   Isn't it.

DOCTOR   Truly, though, I'm surprised at your refraining to help it a little, even by way of remuneration for the spectacle.

ADIL   It really deserves it.

DOCTOR   We're in this together—let's get it out of its plight!

ADIL   Get it out alive?

DOCTOR   Of course.

ADIL   And will Samia accept that?

DOCTOR   She's got a kind heart.

ADIL   I personally prefer not to introduce sentiment into a situation like this, otherwise our position is going to appear truly ridiculous.

Samia appears in the doorway carrying the coffee.

DOCTOR   Quite the contrary, the position now is no longer ridiculous at all. It's become understood and acceptable, and I myself have begun to find the subject worth following.

SAMIA (*offering him the coffee*)   Coffee, Doctor.

DOCTOR (*without raising his eyes from the bath*)   Thanks, I'll have it in a moment.

SAMIA   It seems that the cockroach is also occupying you, Doctor?

DOCTOR (*continuing his viewing*)   Certainly it's begun to interest me.

SAMIA   No doubt the disease is catching!

ADIL (*turning to her*)   What disease?

SAMIA   The doctor understands what I mean.

DOCTOR (*rousing himself*)   Come along, let's drink the coffee first.

> *They all go into the bedroom. The doctor sits down in a chair and Samia puts the tray of coffee on a small table beside him.*

SAMIA   Have you finished your examination, Doctor?

ADIL   Whose examination? My examination?

SAMIA   No, Adil, I'm just having a word with the doctor.

DOCTOR   I think it's best now to talk openly, for there's no reason or necessity for hiding anything. Mr. Adil is in perfect health and vigour, and can put on his clothes and go out as of now if he wants.

SAMIA   And the sick leave, Doctor?

DOCTOR   That's another question. However, Madam, your husband is in the right about everything and I completely endorse his behaviour, there being nothing at all untoward about it.

SAMIA   And the cockroach?

DOCTOR   What about the cockroach? I myself hope that I could become like the cockroach.

SAMIA (*winking at the doctor*)   Ah, understood. I understand, Doctor.

DOCTOR   No, honestly, I'm speaking seriously.

SAMIA   Speaking seriously?

ADIL   Of course, Samia, it's serious. The doctor has explained everything to me, has been absolutely open with me. In any case, may God be indulgent towards you!

SAMIA   Is that right, Doctor?

DOCTOR   The fact is that we had understood the situation wrongly and took up an erroneous attitude.

SAMIA   Meaning that Adil . . .

DOCTOR   Absolutely, a hundred per cent.

SAMIA   Thanks be to God. Thanks be to God. I was extremely worried about you, Adil.

ADIL   You thought there was some sort of kinship between me and the cockroach!

SAMIA   You shouldn't blame me, Adil; your great love for it . . .

DOCTOR   On the contrary, it appears it wasn't love or anything of the sort, because if he'd loved it he'd have had pity on it and saved it. Our whole hope now lies in your compassion.

SAMIA   My compassion?

DOCTOR   Yes—and I personally would ask you, I would intercede with you . . .

SAMIA   Intercede for whom, Doctor?

DOCTOR   For the cockroach.

SAMIA (*shouting*) Doctor! Doctor! Adil, what's happened to the doctor?

DOCTOR Don't be upset. Don't be upset. I'm fine and well.

SAMIA Fine and well—like my husband!

ADIL Yes, like me of course.

SAMIA What a disaster—you and the doctor! There's only Umm Attiya and I left. It'll be our turn next. No, it can't be—I'm going out at once. Umm Attiya! Umm Attiya!

ADIL What's happened, Samia? Have you gone mad?

SAMIA Is it I who've gone mad?

DOCTOR Calm down, Madam, and allow us to explain things to you.

COOK (*appearing*) You called, Ma'am?

SAMIA Yes, I'm going out. Prepare my bath.

COOK Certainly, Ma'am.

She quickly enters the bathroom and turns on the bath tap.

ADIL (*not conscious of what is happening in the bathroom, he walks towards his wife*) Calm down, Samia. Calm down a little and allow us to explain things to you.

DOCTOR Your nerves are upset, Madam, without proper reason—if you'd only allow us to say a word.

SAMIA No, there's no point, Doctor.

ADIL Don't you want to come to an understanding?

SAMIA It's enough the understanding between you and the doctor— you're both in league against me.

DOCTOR Not against you, Madam. Would it be reasonable? It's only that I've become convinced by Mr. Adil's point of view; I've understood the true meaning of his purpose and behaviour.

SAMIA And so you've become like him.

ADIL Like me? You mean like a cockroach.

DOCTOR That's an honour for me.

SAMIA You see, it really is catching!

The cook in the bathroom, having turned on the tap and filled the bath, stretches out her hand and removes the cockroach, dead, with the tip of her fingers, throwing it into a corner of the bathroom.

COOK I've run the bath, Ma'am!

ADIL (*realizing what has happened*) She's filled the bath! (*He hurries into the bathroom and gives a shout after looking into the bath.*) Come along here, Doctor—what we feared has happened.

DOCTOR (*following him*) What's happened?

ADIL The cockroach is dead.

DOCTOR Dead?

ADIL It was no doubt drowned. But where is it? Umm Attiya, where's the cockroach that was here in the bath?

COOK (*pointing to the corner of the bathroom*) I threw it down there, for the time being. (*She goes out.*)

ADIL   What a pity!

DOCTOR   Yes, it certainly is a pity.

SAMIA   Shall I get you a professional mourner? Shall we bring some music and you can walk in its funeral procession?

ADIL   That's quite enough sarcasm, thank you!

DOCTOR   Let the matter rest, Mr. Adil. What's happened has happened. In any case you wanted to leave it to its fate, and this is its fate.

ADIL   Yes, it had to end—somehow. Let us cast a last look at its corpse.

DOCTOR   Where's its corpse?

SAMIA   Its corpse? Even you, Doctor!

Adil and the doctor look round for the cockroach in the corner of the bathroom.

ADIL   Look. Look, Doctor, at these ants. Where have they come from?

DOCTOR *(looks)*   Yes, a horde of ants is carrying it off.

SAMIA   Ants?

ADIL   Yes, ants carrying off the corpse of the cockroach. Come, Samia, look! It's a really extraordinary sight—a crowd of ants carrying off the cockroach and taking it up the wall. Look, Doctor, they're taking it towards one of those cracks.

DOCTOR *(continuing to look)*   It's obviously their house, or their village, or their warehouse in which they'll store this booty.

ADIL   Take note of that ant in the front. Do you see it?

DOCTOR   Yes, it's dragging the cockroach by its whiskers.

ADIL   As though it were a ship's tow rope.

DOCTOR   And this group of ants in the rear, they're pushing it from the back. Do you see?

ADIL   The work's distributed amongst them with extraordinary discipline.

DOCTOR   And the most extraordinary thing is that they're going up at speed, despite their heavy load.

ADIL   There's only a short distance left between them and the crack or warehouse. But look, Doctor, it seems as if the opening is too small for the size of the cockroach. How can it be got in?

DOCTOR   Don't be afraid, it'll get in—nothing is too difficult for the genius of ants.

SAMIA *(looking at them from the door)*   Having finished with the heroism of cockroaches we've now started on the genius of ants!

ADIL *(continuing to watch)*   I doubt if it's possible to get the cockroach into that small crack.

DOCTOR *(also watching)*   We'll soon see.

The telephone rings.

SAMIA *(hurrying to the phone)*   Telephone, Adil! Perhaps it's for you.

ADIL *(turns and joins her)*   For me?

SAMIA *(taking up the receiver)*   Hullo. Who did you say? The doctor? Yes, he's here. Just a moment. *(She calls out.)* It's for you, Doctor.

DOCTOR (*hurrying over and taking up the receiver*)   Hullo. The company. Yes, I'm the doctor. How do you do? Where's this case? Street . . . number . . . Wait while I write it down. (*Takes out a small notebook and writes.*) What did you say the number was? Thank you. The case I'm on at present? Oh, I've finished with that now. Quite satisfactory. No, not at all serious. Merely indisposed. I'll tell him. Thanks. (*He puts down the receiver.*)

ADIL   They're asking about me at the company?

DOCTOR   Naturally.

SAMIA   They thought it was a serious case.

DOCTOR (*to Adil*)   They express their hopes for your recovery.

ADIL   Recovery?

SAMIA   And I too join my voice to theirs.

ADIL   Yes? Yes?

> *In the meantime the cook has slipped into the bathroom carrying a bucket of water and a rag and has begun cleaning it and removing the ants from off the wall. The others, occupied in their conversation, have not noticed.*

DOCTOR (*looking at his watch*)   I must leave you—there's another case waiting for me.

SAMIA   Another case?

DOCTOR   In a far-away street. I mustn't be late. Goodbye.

ADIL   Wait, Doctor. Are you going off just like that without taking a look at the ants?

SAMIA   Do you want to hold the doctor up for the ants as well?

DOCTOR   It would in fact interest me, let's go and have a look.

ADIL   Off we go, perhaps the ants will have succeeded in getting the cockroach into that crack.

SAMIA (*looking at them in wonder*)   By God, it's amazing!

> *As Adil and the doctor reach the bathroom the cook leaves it with her bucket.*

COOK (*to Samia*)   I've cleaned the bathroom, Ma'am.

> *Samia is busy taking her clothes out of the wardrobe.*

ADIL (*in the bathroom*)   What a disaster it would be if Umm Attiya's done it.

COOK (*without understanding*)   Done it?

ADIL (*shouting as he stands in front of the wall*)   What a pity! What a pity!

DOCTOR (*standing behind him and looking at the wall*)   She's done it!

ADIL   She's done it. Look—she's removed the ants, the cockroach and the lot. She's cleared the wall of everything.

DOCTOR (*coming out of the bathroom*)   Bad luck!

ADIL (*to the cook as he comes out*)   Why, Umm Attiya? Why?

COOK   What have I done?

ADIL   Nothing, nothing at all—just carry on with your work, God damn you!

The cook goes out in bewilderment. The doctor takes up his bag.

DOCTOR   I trust you'll spend your day resting and return to work to-morrow feeling a lot better, God willing.

ADIL   And what's keeping me till tomorrow? I'll get dressed now and go to work immediately.

DOCTOR   No, please, you're supposed to be on leave today.

ADIL   And what can I do now with this leave? Can't you cancel it?

DOCTOR   How can I cancel it? The company knows I'm here and that I've come to see you. What shall I say to them? Shall I say that he's . . .

SAMIA   That he's been sitting and watching a cockroach!

DOCTOR   Don't complicate things, Mr. Adil—a day's sick leave and that's that and the problem's solved.

SAMIA   (*taking up her clothes*)   I'm going into the bathroom. If you'll excuse me. I think it's no longer forbidden to go into the bathroom!

ADIL   Lucky you!

SAMIA   Advise him, Doctor, to spend his day off doing something useful.

ADIL   And what, in your view, is doing something useful?

DOCTOR   Anyway, Mr. Adil knows how to spend his time usefully and enjoyably.

SAMIA   I can bet he'll be spending the day sitting down writing mem-oirs about the fate of the cockroach!

DOCTOR   And where's the cockroach now? No sign is left of it, not even one of its whiskers.

ADIL   The important thing was its struggle for life.

DOCTOR   Yes, and that is what will remain fixed in my memory. Good-bye, everyone.

SAMIA   We're most grateful, Doctor. We're sorry for having kept you with us all this time without proper reason.

DOCTOR   Not at all. Not at all.

SAMIA   I hope that the case to which you are going is a little more serious!

DOCTOR   You may be sure that I didn't waste my time uselessly with yourselves. Goodbye. (*He leaves hurriedly.*)

SAMIA   (*as she enters the bathroom*)   Listen, Adil, you've got the day off today. You should know that I want you to spend this day usefully. D'you hear? There are my clothes and dresses all crumpled up in the wardrobe—get down to sorting them out and hang them up at your leisure one by one so that when I come back from work I'll find everything nicely sorted out and organized. Understood?

Adil remains silent, his head lowered.

SAMIA   D'you hear what I say?

ADIL   I do.

SAMIA   And let's not find a single dress creased or crumpled. Understood?

ADIL   (*shouting*)   Understoooooood!

SAMIA   I'm warning you. (*She goes into the bathroom and locks herself in.*)

ADIL (*shouting*)   Umm Attiya, bring the bucket and rag and wipe me out of existence!

CURTAIN

Humans Self Centered

56

indeed a hero

KATEB YACINE

Intelligence Powder[†]

Characters (in order of speaking)

PUFF OF SMOKE
ATTIKA
THE SULTAN
THE OFFICER
THE CHORUS LEADER
THE CHORUS
THE CADI
THE MUFTI
THE POLICEMAN
FIRST SWEEPER
SECOND SWEEPER
THE MERCHANT
ALI
THE PRINCE
FIRST YOUTH
SECOND YOUTH

Also:
COURTIERS, FELLAHS, ULEMAS, OFFICIALS, ETC.

A minimal set: two trees and a bare wall which forms a screen. Another tree upstage, a solitary palm, suggests the desert. Puff of Smoke[1] asleep on a king-sized mat. Attika, his wife, seated in a corner before a bag of dates, is illuminated by a candle.

PUFF OF SMOKE   Put out that light.

ATTIKA   I wonder what makes you so tired.

PUFF OF SMOKE   Put out the light.

ATTIKA   You're certainly not sleepy. All you do is toss and turn . . . Do you even know what day it is?

PUFF OF SMOKE   Put out that light. I haven't slept for three days and three nights . . .

† Kateb Yacine, *Intelligence Powder*, trans. from the French by Stephen J. Vogel (New York: Ubu Repertory Theater Publications, 1986). Translation copyright © 1985 by Stephen J. Vogel. Originally published in French as *La Poudre d'intelligence*, Paris. Copyright © 1959 by Editions du Seuil. Reprinted by permission of Georges Borchardt, Inc.
1. As in the title of Aristophanes' *The Clouds*, the name vaguely symbolizes a negative moral and intellectual type; in this case it implies pompousness and self-inflation.

ATTIKA What you mean is you've been asleep for three days and three nights.

PUFF OF SMOKE Well, I must have been dreaming. Put out that light.

ATTIKA You're driving me mad. We go around in circles like the hands of a clock. You're always out of work and I sit here waiting, just counting the hours.

PUFF OF SMOKE Come on, little hand, go to sleep and let me get some sleep. You're always in such a hurry. Don't you trust the revolution?

ATTIKA Some revolution! Ever since our so-called wedding, you've been soused every day. Someone's turned your head . . .

PUFF OF SMOKE Put out the light! What are you waiting for, the Last Judgment? Am I some corpse that you have to sit up all night with, burning that candle. Put out the light.

ATTIKA (*breaking open a date, then brandishing it*) Look! There are worms in this date!

PUFF OF SMOKE You see! If you'd listened to me and put out the light, you would have eaten it like the others—and we'd have peace and quiet.

Blackout. Pause. The clock strikes, six strokes of the gong. Lights. Attika opens her eyes, and wakes her husband.

ATTIKA Get up! It's six o'clock.

When he doesn't respond, she gets up, takes the water jug, and begins to sprinkle Puff of Smoke with it.

ATTIKA Get up! You told me to wake you up at six o'clock. Come on, let's get going! It's time to look for work.

PUFF OF SMOKE (*with a start*) Oh! Ah! Oh!

ATTIKA Get up! You mentioned it yourself—the house is empty. We don't even have a pinch of salt left.

PUFF OF SMOKE (*going back to sleep*) Later. Later.

ATTIKA (*sprinkling him*) Get up! It's six o'clock.

PUFF OF SMOKE (*doused, getting to his feet*) Ah! Oh! Oh! You filthy bitch! I told you to get me up, but not like that.

He dresses and leaves.

Blackout. Lights. The royal party crosses the stage. Puff of Smoke, still half asleep, runs into the horse of the Sultan, who's off to the hunt, with his Courtiers.

THE SULTAN I would have to run into this ill omen on a day like today, early in the morning, and at the opening of hunting season. (*To an Officer.*) Throw him in solitary.

The Officer takes Puff of Smoke away. Pause. The Chorus enters and, as the royal party enters, forming a magnificent hunting scene, they hide behind trees.

THE SULTAN (*half turning in the saddle*) I remember that this morning I had a man thrown in solitary confinement. Quite honestly, I didn't like the looks of him. A face like his brings bad luck. However, I must admit, I've never known such excellent hunting as today's. (*To the Officer.*) Have you thought about releasing the poor wretch of this morning?

OFFICER   I've thought about it, but he refuses.

THE SULTAN   What does he refuse?

OFFICER   He refuses to be released.

THE SULTAN   He refuses to get out of prison?

OFFICER   He says he wants to talk to you.

THE SULTAN   Well then, have him brought to me. Today I'm in the mood to rectify my injustices.

The Officer exists. Puff of Smoke enters. He bows to the Sultan.

THE SULTAN   Here, take this purse. This morning I was worried. I didn't want the hunt to start off on an unlucky note. Fortunately, thank the Lord, you didn't bring us any bad luck.

PUFF OF SMOKE   Who brought who bad luck? But bad luck always changes to good luck. It's good luck you have to be afraid of because it always turns to bad luck, and so on down the line. There are some who've built a whole philosophy on that. (*He respectfully takes leave of the Sultan and exits.*) For example, if some pickpocket stole my purse that, alas, would prove my theory.

Pause. The Sultan retires to the shadows. Puff of Smoke crosses the stage, casting suspicious glances at the Chorus. Its members divide into two groups and begin to amble about the stage, one group bowing to the other, and responding in kind to the other group's bows. The Chorus Leader, for his part, greets the entrance of Puff of Smoke with a low bow, in the oriental manner.

CHORUS LEADER   Greetings!

PUFF OF SMOKE   Greetings.

CHORUS LEADER   Greetings! Greetings! Greetings!

PUFF OF SMOKE   Greetings!

The Chorus Leader, who has slowly circled the stage, meditating, again comes face to face with Puff of Smoke, and bows mechanically, as if he hadn't met him before.

CHORUS LEADER   Greetings!

PUFF OF SMOKE (*impatiently*)   Greetings, three greetings, a thousand greetings, greetings, greetings.

THE CHORUS (*thinking the greeting is for them*)   Greetings, greetings, greetings, greetings, greetings, greetings, greetings.

A gong sounds, repeatedly. Puff of Smoke slaps the Chorus Leader.

PUFF OF SMOKE   Greetings! And greetings!

THE CHORUS (*indignantly*)   Oh scandal, scandal of scandals, scandal of scandals of scandals! To the cadi,[2] to the cadi, to the cadi.

Blackout. The gong sounds again. Lights.

THE CADI   You again. Why did you strike this man?

PUFF OF SMOKE   Greetings!

THE CADI   What did you say?

PUFF OF SMOKE (*moving away*)   Greetings!

THE CADI   Where are you going?

PUFF OF SMOKE (*moving still further away*)   Greetings!

THE CADI   Stop him!

PUFF OF SMOKE (*still moving away*)   Greetings!

THE CADI   I don't care about your greetings. Answer my question!

PUFF OF SMOKE   Answer mine first. Isn't there plenty of reason to get mad at all those never-ending greetings from all these chalky-looking townspeople, these merchants out to sell you everything and nothing, these sneaky rats who bring disaster on your head, who are just waiting, with all their skin-deep courtesy, for an innocent man, a philosopher or a traveler to fall into their greedy hands so he can lose his purse or his life . . . (*He moves further away.*) Greetings. A hundred greetings! Greetings to all the sneakthieves of the world.

The Cadi disappears into the shadow. Puff of Smoke crosses the stage again, with the same suspicious glances at the Chorus hidden behind the trees.

CHORUS LEADER   Greetings, philosopher! Where are you going in such a determined way?

PUFF OF SMOKE   Get out of my way, rabble! I'm an ex-pickpocket myself. You see this purse? The sultan himself just gave it to me along with a letter in which he names me a great philosopher, the greatest of the century, no doubt . . .

CHORUS LEADER   He's boastful.

THE CHORUS   He's boastful.

PUFF OF SMOKE (*irritated*)   Out of my way, rabble!

CHORUS LEADER (*while stealing the purse*)   At least let us know what you're going to do with all that gold.

PUFF OF SMOKE   First off, buy a donkey.

CHORUS LEADER   Good luck. Let's hope you find an animal with a better disposition than you have. (*To the Chorus.*) What arrogance! (*To Puff of Smoke.*) At least say "Inch'Allah,"[3] if God wishes, and your day will be a good one.

PUFF OF SMOKE   Whether God wishes or not, the market is right nearby, there are lots of donkeys, and I've got the sultan's purse. I

2. In Muslim communities a judge whose decisions are based on religious law.
3. Arabic: "Allah willing"; "if Allah wills it."

don't see what God has to do with it. With or without a God, I'll be
back with a donkey.

CHORUS LEADER   Oh sacrilege! Sacrilege of sacrileges!
THE CHORUS   Sacrilege of sacrileges of sacrileges!

*Puff of Smoke runs off. Pause. The Chorus moves downstage. Puff
of Smoke enters in a rage.*

CHORUS LEADER (*sarcastically*)   Greetings, philosopher!
THE CHORUS (*same tone*)   Greetings, philosopher!
CHORUS LEADER   But where's your donkey?

The Chorus dances around Puff of Smoke.

The donkey! The donkey! Where is the donkey?
PUFF OF SMOKE (*chasing the Chorus with a stick*)   Get out! Inch'Allah!
Rabble! Inch'Allah! Evil birds! Inch'Allah! At the market Inch'Allah!
I realized Inch'Allah! Someone stole my purse Inch'Allah! Thieves!
Inch'Allah! Bandits! Inch'Allah! Scum! Inch'Allah!

*With each Inch'Allah, Puff of Smoke strikes out at the Chorus
with his stick as they run away. Blackout. Lights.*

ATTIKA   What are you waiting to saw the wood for?
PUFF OF SMOKE   Bravo! Woman, you have a real gift for giving orders.
ATTIKA   Go saw the wood.

*Puff of Smoke goes off, saw in hands. He climbs a tree, sits on
the highest branch, and starts sawing, dreamily. Each time the
saw gets stuck, he changes branches and finally he begins sawing
the one he's sitting on. It breaks. A fall. Pause. Puff of Smoke
does not move.*

PUFF OF SMOKE   I'm cold, therefore I'm dead.

Pause. The Chorus enters.

CHORUS LEADER (*feeling Puff of Smoke*)   He's cold.
THE CHORUS   So he's dead.

*The gong sounds, repeatedly. The Chorus carries Puff of Smoke
away in a blanket. Suddenly the Chorus stops.*

THE CHORUS   There are several different roads to the cemetery.
CHORUS LEADER   Take the shortest one.
THE CHORUS   It's not the easiest.
PUFF OF SMOKE (*raising his head*)   Stop arguing! When I was alive we
always took the first one we came to.

*The Chorus is terror-stricken. Stampede. Blackout. Lights. Puff
of Smoke, leaning against an orange tree, holds a donkey by the
bridle. The Chorus spreads out around him.*

CHORUS LEADER   What are you doing all by yourself with this donkey?
PUFF OF SMOKE   I'm contemplating while I wait for the market to

open. I'm trying to figure out for myself who's the master and who's the slave. Is it the donkey? Is it me?

CHORUS LEADER   Do you need any help?

PUFF OF SMOKE   No. I just wish I lived in a world where people and donkeys lived apart. No disrespect intended to you,[4] of course.

CHORUS LEADER   Leave your donkey with us and go for a walk. That'll give you a new outlook on life.

> *Puff of Smoke leaves the donkey and goes off, as the Chorus murmurs.*

CHORUS LEADER (*to the Chorus*)   Take this animal, but leave me the bridle. And get out of here as quickly as you can.

> *Blackout. Lights. The Chorus and the donkey have disappeared. Puff of Smoke enters.*

PUFF OF SMOKE   Where's my donkey?

CHORUS LEADER (*the bridle around his neck*)   At your service.

PUFF OF SMOKE   I was talking about the donkey.

CHORUS LEADER   I'm your donkey. A curse from my mother has changed me to this form I have now.

PUFF OF SMOKE   It seems to me this man thinks he's a donkey. And since I think I'm a man, maybe I'm really a donkey. It must be I'm under a kind of double illusion.

> *Blackout. Lights. The Chorus is transformed into a group of Fellahs[5] selling their donkeys at the market. The Chorus Leader has Puff of Smoke's donkey.*

CHORUS LEADER   I hope our philosopher doesn't come dragging his feet around this place.

> *Puff of Smoke enters. He goes straight to the donkey.*

PUFF OF SMOKE   Greetings!

CHORUS LEADER   Greetings.

PUFF OF SMOKE   I'm not talking to you. I'm talking to the donkey.

CHORUS LEADER   That's alright. Act as though I were your donkey.

PUFF OF SMOKE (*to the donkey*)   You're a donkey, and you're going to stay a donkey.

CHORUS LEADER   Don't torment him. He's only a donkey.

PUFF OF SMOKE (*to the Chorus Leader*)   You're acting like a donkey so you can get a donkey.

CHORUS LEADER   Are you talking to the donkey? You know he can't answer you.

PUFF OF SMOKE   I used to have one donkey, now I find I've got two. Another miracle!

> *He leaps on the Chorus Leader, seizes him by the bridle which is still around his neck and attaches the bridle to the orange tree.*

4. The donkey.
5. From Arabic, "fellaheen," a peasant or laborer.

PUFF OF SMOKE   My old donkey was enough for me. As for you, if it was a curse that changed you into a donkey, you'll get your old shape back one of these days, for what it's worth. Stay where you are. Stay where you are. I'm also going back to the way I was before, and I admit that up to now, I've been acting like a donkey, myself. I let myself be taken in by the sultan's golden straw. I was really sick with it. A real poison. But I'm starting to catch on. Now I know that the sultan's gold has got to be used against him: it's the Law of the internal contradiction of Capital. Sh . . . Yes, I've decided on alchemy. I keep my hookah right by my side. The back-stabbers call me Puff of Smoke. The greedy ones call me insane. But the one who's insane is the one who believes he's insane. And I'm a great disbeliever. My knowledge is based on three scientific principles. First principle: the sultan's gold, here's what I do with it.

He searches in his pocket and gives the last remaining gold coins to his donkey, as if they were suppositories.

Second principle: we shall see what we shall see. Third principle . . .

The Sultan enters, followed and wildly cheered by the Chorus.

Bravo! I'll be able to put my discovery to the test right away. Here's the sultan now. Quiet. I'm going to demonstrate to the people our sultan's concept of political economy.

The Sultan again crosses the stage. Puff of Smoke addresses him directly.

Oh sultan, I see that you are sad and I know what it is that you need. There are three things which you lack which make a man happy, whether he be great or small: intelligence, gold and love. As far as intelligence and love are concerned, we'll see about that later. Those are only the corollaries. The essential matter is to obtain the mountain of gold which enables you to buy everything else . . . Here it is. As a result of having studied the great religions of the world, I have in my possession a very ancient manuscript which tells of a sacred donkey. Yes, a donkey, the humblest of animals, but which has the power to produce gold instead of dung . . . of which, you must be aware, a healthy animal can produce a considerable amount.

The Sultan nods his head.

Your knowledge of this subject must be extensive. In short, I have the honor to present to you this donkey: after many an invocation I finally found him, waiting for me and tied to an orange tree . . . the symbolism is obvious. Now the right thing to do, to honor him, would be to place him on a valuable carpet.

He calls to the Chorus.

Have a carpet brought to me, by order of the sultan.

The Chorus Leader brings in a carpet which Puff of Smoke puts under the donkey's hooves.

All we have to do now is wait; the animal is stuffed with hay. The best way to do this is to wait until nightfall, because magic doesn't much care for daylight . . . If I do this in the daytime it's only to prove to you that I'm no charlatan—in case you might have any doubts . . .

Pause. Then with an appropriate noise, three gold coins drop from behind the donkey.

THE SULTAN   Oh wonder! Oh benefactor of the kingdom!
CHORUS LEADER   Oh miracle! Miracle of miracles!
PUFF OF SMOKE   It's really nothing. When the divine donkey—for this is no ordinary animal, but a Friend of God, a Chosen One who is serving out his period of penitence—when the divine donkey, as I was saying, is royally fed and when, in the presence of all the civil, military and religious leaders, he can solemnly relieve himself on an even more valuable carpet—since he does like to be honored and is endowed with his own nobility—then, Oh sultan, you will have more of this miraculous gold than you know what to do with . . .

Blackout. Lights. The Ulemas, the Mufti, the Cadi are gathered around the donkey, which has been stuffed with soft grass, and which is now treading on an expensive carpet. Puff of Smoke stands facing the group, directing the magical proceedings in a newly imperious tone.)

PUFF OF SMOKE   Put out the light!

The light is extinguished.

Let the inspiration flow. When you hear the appropriate noise, then, oh great mufti, and you oh wise ulemas, extend your hands toward the carpet, all at the same time, and you shall reap the rewards of your faith.

Pause. The Ulemas and the Mufti are heard chanting.

THE SULTAN   Well . . . ?
THE MUFTI   In faith, I haven't come to anything solid yet.
PUFF OF SMOKE   Don't despair, it starts off as liquid gold.
THE MUFTI   Could it be the donkey is ill? You've been feeding it too much. We're really getting bogged down . . . And not a single coin.
THE SULTAN   Perhaps it's the darkness that's throwing you off?
PUFF OF SMOKE   Well then, let's have some light!

A light on the carpet which is overflowing with dung.

PUFF OF SMOKE   Oh evil act! The ulemas have bewitched my donkey!
THE SULTAN   I don't understand.
PUFF OF SMOKE   Sultan, I must have justice done me. I shall demonstrate publicly that these demons—never thinking that in ruining

me they were ruining you, and never thinking of all the good the magical donkey would do for the kingdom—these demons played us a nasty trick, so they could make gold in secret, their usual way, I might add. Yes, I can prove it. Just stuff these ulemas with food, and the mufti first and foremost, then put them on the carpet. You'll see with your own eyes and the people will discover it for themselves so there'll be no more doubt.

Blackout. Lights. The Chorus is arranged around the stage. In the center the Ulemas and the Mufti form a semi-circle. To the right, Puff of Smoke. The Sultan faces them. Pause. Blackout.

PUFF OF SMOKE   Courage, oh sultan. You must dig deeply into these holy remains. Have you come up with anything yet?

Pause. Blackout. Lights. Gong resounds repeatedly. Lights. Puff of Smoke alone, in front of the orange tree. He's contemplating.

PUFF OF SMOKE
Twenty years of philosophical thought!
Fifty or a hundred volumes have sprung from my head
And no one's ever had the idea, the simple idea, of their
        writing them instead of me,
Neither the people nor the sultan
Are willing to recognize that a philosopher
Needs a lot of money
And even a secretary
To have a mind that's really free.
What's more, I'm starting to lose
All my wit
Having to deal with these blockheads.
The enemies of philosophy invented the turban
To protect their arid heads
Against all forms of knowledge.
There's nothing more for me to do in this country.
Here I am, in the prime of life
Without a purse, without a pension
And I, who was called the father of the people,
Am now the least of its orphans.

A Man passes by, leading a donkey loaded down with sand. The donkey stumbles in front of Puff of Smoke and drops its load. The Man and his donkey disappear.

PUFF OF SMOKE   A nasty allegory. Now just what did that animal mean by getting rid of his holdings like that?

He remains silent for a moment. The Chorus spreads out around him.

CHORUS LEADER   Here is the madman. Here's Puff of Smoke praying before a sand heap.
THE CHORUS   The poor fool.

PUFF OF SMOKE   Let me interpret this message. Everything's symbolic for the man with nothing left to read.

Blackout. Lights. Puff of Smoke still in front of the sand heap. The Chorus is milling about.

PUFF OF SMOKE *(aside)*   My popularity is on the increase.

Pause. Puff of Smoke gets up quickly. Blackout. Lights. The sand heap is gone. The gong resounds, repeatedly.

PUFF OF SMOKE *(inciting the Chorus)*   My fellow countrymen your fortune is made! I've just made the discovery of a lifetime. Come closer! Closer! I've discovered the thing that will make sultans of you all, without the least bit of effort. Come closer!

CHORUS LEADER *(approaching)*   He's not even close to recovering his sanity.

PUFF OF SMOKE   Come closer! Come closer! I haven't been using my imagination for nothing. You can see for yourselves: what I've discovered, to put it simply, is intelligence powder! Intelligence, that's right, intelligence! Come a little closer! There's a sign-up sheet right here. I've been working all my life to come up with this magic substance. *(He shows them a small bag.)* Intelligence! Intelligence! Sign up right away.

The Crowd starts to swell. A Policeman slips through the horde.

POLICEMAN   Move along there! Move along! You know the ulemas have outlawed idolatry.

PUFF OF SMOKE   So they can have the monopoly.

POLICEMAN *(startled)*   Oh God, it's that crazy man from the desert.

He leads him off, roughly.

CHORUS LEADER   That's not fair. He said he'd discovered intelligence powder.

POLICEMAN *(astonished)*   Intelligence powder?

THE CHORUS *(excitedly)*   Take him to the sultan! To the sultan!

Blackout. Lights. The Sultan by himself. Puff of Smoke enters in the rough grip of the Policeman.

THE SULTAN   That madman again!

POLICEMAN   He was getting the people stirred up out in the square. He claims he has a powder.

THE SULTAN   A magic powder?

PUFF OF SMOKE   I've got to tell you that I didn't devise my formula with a sultan in mind. If you want to take advantage of my discovery, I'll have to revise it taking your exalted rank into account.

THE SULTAN   In other words, you haven't perfected it yet.

PUFF OF SMOKE   Oh, if I wanted to, I could do it in a flash.

THE SULTAN   Well, what are you waiting for?

PUFF OF SMOKE   I'm a little worried about not getting paid enough for my efforts.

THE SULTAN (*to the Policeman*)   Take him to solitary. And if he keeps trying to make fools of us, take away his powder by force.

PUFF OF SMOKE   We're a long way from intelligence! Why get so angry?

THE SULTAN   Alright, get your powder ready.

PUFF OF SMOKE (*intoning magic formulas*)   Wac, wac, oh sultan of sultans, your spirit shall fly into space, you shall rejoin the prophets, perhaps even the Creator . . .

THE SULTAN   Let's have no blasphemies. Is everything ready?

PUFF OF SMOKE   My fate is in your hands.

THE SULTAN (*taking the little bag*)   Let's have it. (*Considering it.*) Is there enough here?

PUFF OF SMOKE   That's enough there for four sultans, not that you aren't the only one on earth of any importance.

THE SULTAN (*indicating a silent concubine*)   This one is my favorite. I haven't quite tamed her yet, though. She'll also take some of this powder. It'll help her to understand me, no doubt . . .

PUFF OF SMOKE   You should try it on yourself first.

THE SULTAN   Let's see about this invention of yours. (*He opens the bag.*) What do you call it? Intelligence powder?

PUFF OF SMOKE   I'd advise you to inhale very fast. And very deep. Take heart, Oh sultan of sultans, and you might even take wing.

SULTAN (*sniffing the bag*)   It seems just like sand.

PUFF OF SMOKE   You see! You're beginning to understand.

> *The gong resounds repeatedly. Puff of Smoke escapes, chased by the Policeman. Pause.*

THE SULTAN   I feel very strange. Maybe the madman was right. I feel very strange. Maybe it's intelligence.

> *Blackout. Lights. Attika asleep. Puff of Smoke. The clock strikes the hour. The gong sounds.*

PUFF OF SMOKE (*staggering*)   Greetings, wife!

> *Attika grumbles, stretches and points to a plate on a low table. Then she lies down again.*

PUFF OF SMOKE   It's daybreak. Don't you hear the rooster?

ATTIKA   . . .

PUFF OF SMOKE   Get up, woman, and let out a triumphal yell.

ATTIKA   . . .

PUFF OF SMOKE   Let out a really triumphal yell.

ATTIKA (*resignedly*)   Yu, yu, yu!

PUFF OF SMOKE   Louder!

ATTIKA   Yu, yu, yu!

PUFF OF SMOKE   Put some conviction in it!

ATTIKA (*at the top of her lungs*)   Yu, yu, yu!

PUFF OF SMOKE   I have big news for you. We're rich.

ATTIKA   . . .

PUFF OF SMOKE   Listen to me. This evening I became the sultan's son-in-law.[6]
ATTIKA   . . .
PUFF OF SMOKE   Absolutely. The sultan's daughter. Good. I see you're in one of your bad moods again. Let's get some sleep.

Blackout. Lights. Attika is pensive. Puff of Smoke enters, weighed down with carpets and packages.

PUFF OF SMOKE   Whew! At last! The wedding is set for tomorrow. Here's the furniture. I got all this on credit. It's incredible. Really. Everything has changed. I'm the sultan's son-in-law. The merchants know it. It's just a matter of time. Starting tomorrow I want to get all these formalities out of the way . . . Come on, wife, cheer up! What are you worried about? A rival who's old enough to be your mother is a gift from heaven, no?

Attika, looking glum, doesn't answer.

Have it your way. Let's get some sleep. I've been on my feet all day.

He lies down next to her and covers himself with all the carpets he was carrying on his back.

Ah, it's so nice to bed down under the beneficial load of absolute power!

Pause. Puff of Smoke falls asleep. Attika slides out of bed, grabs the scissors and begins to cut up the carpets.

ATTIKA (*menacingly*)   Even if it takes all night, I'll destroy everything here right down to your moustache.
PUFF OF SMOKE   That'll teach me not to yack with women.

He gets up.

ATTIKA   Wait. I've got something to tell you. For a long time now His Majesty has been sending me his procurers . . .
PUFF OF SMOKE   We'll see about that. As a matter of fact, I'm inviting my father-in-law to dinner.

Blackout. Lights. The Sultan, welcomed by Puff of Smoke, removes his shoes, and sits in front of the low table. Attika remains off to one side.

PUFF OF SMOKE   Welcome to this humble house, oh sultan of sultans! (*aside*) How are we going to feed this glutton? (*He crosses downstage.*) Patience, my darling wife.
ATTIKA   What can I do? We haven't got a thing. Not even a pinch of salt.
PUFF OF SMOKE   Boil some water and have confidence in your man.

6. Under Islamic law, a man is permitted to have as many as four wives.

Attika disappears. Puff of Smoke grabs the Sultan's shoes and exits. Pause. The Sultan sighs deeply to remind them of his presence. Attika, having come back, plays the Sultan's game, and acts abashed.

THE SULTAN   Oh incomparable woman, ask me anything you like.

ATTIKA   I don't dare . . .

THE SULTAN   A kiss, a single kiss! Oh, you'll be the death of me.

ATTIKA   No, Majesty, I don't dare, I'm very capricious. (*aside*) I hope that man isn't at the wine merchant's!

THE SULTAN   Whatever you wish for, you shall have it. Only a kiss . . .

ATTIKA   Well then, I'd like . . . To climb up on your shoulders and ride you like a horse, to play with you . . . You see, I'm too capricious.

THE SULTAN   (*delighted*)   Not at all, you're charming. Make me suffer; I'll accept anything from you.

ATTIKA   (*leaping onto his shoulders*)   Giddyup! Get up, camel!

THE SULTAN   (*on his knees, delightedly*)   Ah! You'll be the death of me yet.

ATTIKA   Faster. Get down on all fours and I'll give you something better than a kiss!

The Sultan does as he's told, and his pleasure is so great that he whinnies.

PUFF OF SMOKE   (*entering quickly*)   Sultan you're magnificent. Come, my darling wife, let's give our great sultan some refreshment and he'll be himself again. He's accustomed to a different bill of fare!

The Sultan, breathless, doesn't know which way to turn. Attika steals away, followed by Puff of Smoke, who re-enters with a large, steaming platter. The Sultan begins to eat to show he's a good sport.

THE SULTAN   Excellent, exquisite, excellent! (*aside*) What a woman!

PUFF OF SMOKE   Whatever you do, don't force yourself.

Pause. Puff of Smoke sits next to the Sultan. They empty the platter. Then the Sultan gets up to thank him.

THE SULTAN   (*using the prescribed compliment*)   May God improve your lot.

PUFF OF SMOKE   (*cryptically*)   Don't thank me. You just ate at your own expense.

THE SULTAN   (*wandering about the stage*)   My shoes . . . Where are my shoes?

ATTIKA   (*appearing behind her husband*)   How can a camel lose its hooves?

THE SULTAN   (*menacingly, as he exits*)   I'll go see the mufti, and show him my bare feet. If he doesn't seek vengeance for this, I'll cut off his head. We'll beat this so-called philosopher at his own game, and swallow up his wife like an egg in this serpent's nest.

Blackout. Lights. The Chorus is onstage, carrying brooms.

FIRST SWEEPER (*staring at the sky*)　It's almost time to break our fast.
SECOND SWEEPER　Wait until the sun sets, at least.
FIRST SWEEPER　I tell you it's time.
SECOND SWEEPER　I tell you it isn't.
FIRST SWEEPER　Shut up!
SECOND SWEEPER　You bastard!
FIRST SWEEPER　You scum!

> *A brawl. Brooms used as clubs. Puff of Smoke. Blackout. Lights.
> The Chorus has left the stage. The Sultan on his throne. The
> Mufti enters.*

THE SULTAN　Mufti, it's a serious moment. Their thoughts are fixed on fighting. Every year, at each Ramadan,[7] it's the same turmoil.
THE MUFTI　I'm doing what I can. I pay a muezzin[8] to watch the sky and announce the exact moment when to end the fast. Every year I send messengers to Cairo and to Tunis, to consult with the greatest ulemas. The problem is, they never agree with each other!
THE SULTAN　I know that, but the people don't have to know it. It's hard enough for them to fast for an entire month. They can't accept any uncertainty from the doctors of the law. But since the religious authorities can't agree, let's ask an astrologer or a wiseman.
THE MUFTI　A brilliant idea and one I'd never thought of! I've got it: let's put our philosopher to the test. He's a pagan. He's bound to make some blunder and then we can turn the people against him . . .

> *Blackout. Lights. Attika by herself. Puff of Smoke enters in a
> rush.*

PUFF OF SMOKE (*agitated*)　It's incredible, it's amazing but it makes me suspicious.
ATTIKA　What is it this time?
PUFF OF SMOKE　The mufti, my greatest enemy . . . He's found me a job. And what a job! In short, I'm now the vice-mufti! Let's see . . . It's very simple. Hand me a container.

> *Attika, stupefied, passes him a bowl.*

PUFF OF SMOKE　Now, open your ears. Every morning you remind me to throw a pebble into this bowl. One pebble, one holy day. No harder than that. I've got it all worked out.

> *Pause. The two of them lie down on the king-sized mat. Blackout.
> The howling of a windstorm is heard. When the lights come up,
> Attika wakes her husband up, roughly.*

PUFF OF SMOKE　What's going on?
ATTIKA　A sandstorm. And you left the window open.

---

7. The ninth month of the Muslim calendar; also the daily fast that is enjoined from dawn to dusk during this month.
8. The crier who, from a minaret or other high part of a mosque, intones the call summoning the faithful to prayer.

PUFF OF SMOKE   Damn! And what about the bowl I left on the window sill?

ATTIKA   It's filled with pebbles.

PUFF OF SMOKE (*going back to bed*)   Well, that means that Ramadan is over.

> *The gong resounds repeatedly. The sounds of a brawl outside. The Chorus shouting insults, and the sound of brooms being wielded can be heard. Puff of Smoke runs downstage.*

PUFF OF SMOKE   I should have watched out for the people. Now they've got me in a tight corner. I've played into the mufti's hands.

> *The Chorus overruns the stage. The insults and brooms now threaten to be used against Puff of Smoke.*

THE CHORUS   The mufti told us to come and see you. If he picked you out, you must be a scoundrel with no respect for God, just like he is. Are we supposed to break our fast or not? And no long speeches.

PUFF OF SMOKE (*calling on all his wiles*)   Oh, true believers, do you know what I'm about to say to you?

THE CHORUS   No, no, no.

PUFF OF SMOKE   Because you're all so ignorant, I refuse to enlighten you. Come back tomorrow.

> *With those words he exits under the nose of the flabbergasted Chorus.*

THE CHORUS   He thinks we're fools.

CHORUS LEADER   No doubt about it.

THE CHORUS   Tomorrow, when we come back, he'll have to answer us.

> *The Chorus groups together. Blackout. Lights. Puff of Smoke re-enters.*

PUFF OF SMOKE (*same trick*)   Oh true believers, do you know what I'm about to tell you?

THE CHORUS   Yes, yes, yes!

PUFF OF SMOKE   Because you're all so wise, I have nothing to say to you.

THE CHORUS (*nonplussed*)   He thinks we're fools.

CHORUS LEADER   We thought we could trip you up by saying yes instead of no.

THE CHORUS   Tricky, tricky, tricky. Tomorrow, when we come back, some of us say yes, the others no! He won't know what to do then.

> *Blackout. Lights. Same trick.*

PUFF OF SMOKE   Oh true believers, do you know what I'm about to say to you?

THE CHORUS   Yes, no, yes, no, yes, no . . .

PUFF OF SMOKE   Good. Some of you know, some of you don't know. I want those of you who know to teach those of you who don't.

He escapes. Blackout. The gong resounds, repeatedly. The Chorus is heard repeating, endlessly, "He thinks we're fools. He thinks we're fools." Lights. The Sultan, the Mufti and other high Officials are conferring.

Downstage, in a thick cloud of dust, the Chorus is shaking its brooms. To one side of the two groups—the Chorus and the conferees—Puff of Smoke stands thoughtfully smoking his pipe.

PUFF OF SMOKE   Wretched, black misery, wretched miserable philosophy! Power has no need for subversive minds and the people, though they like a good speech, can't understand me, since they've been deafened by the noise of power.

A noise from the conferring Officials. The Sultan's voice is heard.

THE SULTAN   What good is philosophy? Theories won't bring in taxes. What we need is gold, and foreign trade agreements to relieve the people's woes, to say nothing of the servants of the State. God alone can help us. God protect our people. God protect our people from these ceaseless agitators. God protect us from blockheads, philosophers, poets, orators, madmen and wisemen.

OFFICIALS, LED BY THE MUFTI *(repeating)*   God protect us from these ceaseless agitators.

The Officials exit and the Chorus, one by one, fans out around Puff of Smoke, who continues to smoke in silence.

CHORUS LEADER *(pointing to Puff of Smoke)*   You see this man? He's possessed of a demon. He can read the future. He does nothing, and he smokes the hashish of slow death, like an Indian.

Pause. The Chorus begins to shake their brooms again, tightening the circle.

PUFF OF SMOKE *(gasping for breath)*   Stop, stop! Haven't you stirred up enough sand already?

CHORUS LEADER
By order of the sultan
We are condemned to sandstorms
To the sultan go gold and honors
To us, dust and flies . . .

THE CHORUS
We must work to stay alive, God has said so,
The sultan has said so, the mufti has said so,
We must work to stay alive.

PUFF OF SMOKE
Yes, yes, I understand, you stir up
The sand and I scratch my head.
Where does your work get you, what comes of my thinking?
We're losing everything, everything is lost, except for God,
Except for the sultan, except for the mufti.

THE CHORUS (*scandalized, chasing him off*) Sacrilege, sacrilege, sacrilege, sacrilege of sacrileges . . .

Fleeing, Puff of Smoke saves his pipe, but has to leave a jug on the ground behind him.

CHORUS LEADER (*raising the jug*) By God, he's a true philosopher, in full possession of his faculties: he always keeps his pipe around, but he doesn't forget his jug of cool wine, either . . .

PUFF OF SMOKE (*from the wings*) Oh Arabs, why should you die of thirst, since alcohol has been invented?[9]

Blackout. The gong strikes, repeatedly. Lights. The Chorus, visibly drunk, is dancing around the jug, shouting louder than ever: "Sacrilege of sacrileges of sacrileges of sacrileges!" The gong resounds, repeatedly. Blackout. Lights. Puff of Smoke is hard at it: stealing onions from a field.

PUFF OF SMOKE Wretched, black misery, wretched, miserable philosophy! There's no justice. Or else there's too much, because here I am, really and truly stealing onions from the mufti's garden!

The gong sounds. The Mufti enters. Caught in the act, Puff of Smoke freezes, clutching an onion, searching for an inspiration.

THE MUFTI (*sneering*) What are you up to, philosopher?

PUFF OF SMOKE . . . It was a gust of wind . . . A tremendous gust of wind. It blew me into your garden against my will . . .

THE MUFTI And what about these onions on the ground?

PUFF OF SMOKE When I said it was a gust of wind, that was an understatement. It was a real tornado! A hurricane so strong that I had to grab onto your onions, for fear of being carried away . . .

THE MUFTI (*thinking he's tripped his opponent up*) And what about these onions in your hood?

PUFF OF SMOKE You know I was trying to figure out what kind of miracle dropped them there when you showed up . . .

Blackout. The gong resounds, repeatedly. Silently, Puff of Smoke paces about. The Chorus spies him from a distance.

PUFF OF SMOKE The people are prowling around, mocking me, to say nothing of the mufti's spies . . . (*He begins to pray.*) Oh God, excuse me for beseeching you in the street like this, but I couldn't find you in the mosque.

At these words a rich Merchant leans over his balcony. Puff of Smoke, impassible, continues to pray, still more provoking in the eyes of the Merchant.

---

9. Under very strict Islamic legal precepts, drinking of alcohol is forbidden. Puff of Smoke is therefore being irreverent and sarcastic here since, in fact, tacit relaxation of the application of the law lets alcohol be imbibed widely in the Islamic world.

PUFF OF SMOKE
> Oh God, three times!
> Oh God, three times!
> Oh God, three times!

THE MERCHANT (*leaning down*)   Who is this infidel? I should have suspected it. It's that so-called philosopher again, that madman, that tramp.

PUFF OF SMOKE
> Oh God, three times!
> Hear me
> Oh God
> Three times!
> Are you listening to me?
> I need a hundred gold coins.
> You want to know what for?
> It's none of your business.
> Send me down a hundred gold coins, if you're really God,
> And leave the rest to me.

THE MERCHANT   Did you ever hear such cynicism! Ridiculing God in that fashion! And under *my* window, the builder of the mosque! I won't allow this imbecile to commit blasphemy in public.

PUFF OF SMOKE (*same trick*)
> Oh God, three times!
> Send me down a hundred gold coins, it's urgent.
> A hundred gold coins, what I need to expand my circle of
> Friends, and get through my circle of creditors.
> A hundred measly gold coins, that's less than nothing.
> Send them down to me. I want one hundred, just exactly.
> Not a hundred-and-one or ninety-nine.

THE MERCHANT (*smiling*)
> Once and for all, I'm going to shut him up.
> I'm going to catch him in the act of betraying himself.
> Yes, I've got an idea in my head, a brilliant idea that will lift my
> turban right off.

> *So saying, the Merchant removes his turban, and takes out a
> purse which he opens, adroitly.*

Yes, we merchants of Islam carry our fortune on our heads and our ideas are worth their weight in gold. Poor philosopher! I want to see you worshipping the God that you blaspheme, and I'm going to keep the whole city amused at your expense.

> *With these words, the Merchant drops ninety-nine gold coins, one
> by one, at the feet of Puff of Smoke who counts them slowly and
> carefully. With each coin he drops, the Merchant waves feverishly
> to the crowd, as if to make them witnesses.*

PUFF OF SMOKE   Ninety-nine . . . There's one missing. I knew that nothing's perfect, not even an act of God. Still, I didn't think he was such a miser. Remember, God, you owe me one. I have witnesses.

THE MERCHANT (*in a rage*) Oh, that bandit! That infidel! I knew he'd go back on his word. (*To the Chorus.*) Did you see? Did you hear?

THE CHORUS Saw nothing, heard nothing, it's none of our business.

THE MERCHANT (*coming down to the street*) Oh, thieves, bandits, wretched infidels! What, you didn't hear him? He asked God for a hundred gold coins, not a hundred-and-one, not ninety-nine. And didn't you see me, at my window, throwing him ninety-nine coins which he just put in his pocket?

THE CHORUS

Saw nothing, heard nothing.
We're not here to deliver justice.

THE MERCHANT Yes, I know that you poor wretches, you ignorant sons-of-bitches have never believed in Justice. But I believe. Without Justice, how would I have been able to defend my fortune against crooks like you? Justice. You brought it up. Let's go to the cadi. Come on, let's go! (*He shakes Puff of Smoke.*) What are you waiting for?

PUFF OF SMOKE I can't go see the cadi in these rags. You, you have a gold embroidered caftan that gives you a sense of assurance. But if I go wearing this old tunic, I'll never win my case. (*To the Crowd.*) What do you think?

THE CHORUS He's right. Justice is only just when men are equal—or at least look equal.

THE MERCHANT Of course you're on his side. But I'll defeat you all. Hola, slave! (*A Slave appears.*) Bring me down a caftan just like the one I'm wearing. (*To Puff of Smoke.*) And now are you coming with me to the Hall of Justice?

PUFF OF SMOKE Yes, but won't you be mounted on a white mare with a golden bridle? And I'll have to go on foot, under this blazing sun. So right away there's an obvious injustice.

THE MERCHANT The devil . . . I'm going to take away all of your excuses. Hola! Slave! Bring me another white mare. And now, are you coming with me to see the cadi?

PUFF OF SMOKE (*putting on the caftan*) No, not to the cadi. After all, he's only the head of the Justice Department. Now that I'm so well dressed, I want to see the person who holds absolute power—the sultan.

THE MERCHANT Very well, let's go see the sultan. Your sentence will be all the more severe.

THE CHORUS (*emphatically*) To the sultan! To the sultan!

Blackout. Lights.

THE SULTAN Time is short. Let's be brief. Now let the plaintiff complain, and the defendant defend himself, and let's get it over with.

THE MERCHANT Lord sultan, I bring you greetings. You know your humble servant well enough by now. You know that I'm an upstanding merchant who has never stinted when it comes to using my money for the good of the kingdom, and for the glory of the Moslem people.

THE SULTAN   That's a fact. You are known to us. You may reveal to us the source of your complaint, in perfect confidence.

PUFF OF SMOKE   And me, sultan? You must recognize me as well.

THE SULTAN   It's up to the plaintiff to speak. Time is short. If you two have any speeches to make, hire some lawyers.

THE MERCHANT   God forbid! I've already lost enough money. To make a long story short, this man just stole a hundred gold coins from me, right under the noses of I-don't-know-how-many-witnesses, who turned out to be his accomplices.

THE CHORUS (*murmuring*)   Saw nothing, heard nothing.

PUFF OF SMOKE   Ninety-nine.

THE SULTAN   What did you say?

PUFF OF SMOKE   Ninety-nine. Not a hundred. Ninety-nine.

THE SULTAN   What did you say? The devil . . . I don't get it at all.

PUFF OF SMOKE   Well, never mind. My worthy opponent claims I stole a hundred gold coins from him. Let's keep it at that. That's the crux of the matter.

THE SULTAN   Yes, let's keep it at that. The plaintiff has had his say. Now let the defendant speak plainly.

PUFF OF SMOKE   Sultan, you mentioned gold. My reply will be short. I tell you my opponent is plain and simply mad.

THE MERCHANT   What?

PUFF OF SMOKE   Yes, poor man, all that worrying about high finance has driven you insane. Didn't you say that I stole a hundred gold coins from you?

THE MERCHANT   Absolutely. Lord sultan, have him searched. You'll find he still has my money on him.

PUFF OF SMOKE   No need to search me. I do in fact have upon my person the sum in question, minus one coin . . . But tell me, merchant, do you think you own the whole wide world? At the rate you're going, the next thing we know you'll be saying that this caftan I'm wearing is yours . . .

THE MERCHANT   Of course it is!

PUFF OF SMOKE (*smiling*)   And the horse waiting for me outside . . .

THE MERCHANT   That's mine, too. Who else could it belong to? Didn't I just lend it to you, a little while ago?

PUFF OF SMOKE   You must admit, sultan, that the plaintiff's madness is perfectly obvious. It's even beginning to worry you. A madman, another poor old madman in our city . . .

Astonished silence from the Merchant. Consternation on the part of the Sultan. At last the Merchant, in a rage, crosses to Puff of Smoke and gives him a slap.

THE SULTAN   Come, come. Take it easy.

THE CHORUS   It's a scandal! Sultan, you're a witness to this violent deed.

THE SULTAN   Take it easy, it's nothing. Calm down. Merchant, you

made a mistake in losing your temper like that. You've put me in a
spot. I was all set to decide in your favor, and now you've made the
defendant a plaintiff. But we forgive you. Your indignation appears
justified to us. Come now, step out for a while and take a walk.
We'll take this matter up again when you've recovered your *sang-
froid*. Go now, my friend, and have no fear. We're not so easily taken
in.

THE CHORUS (*murmuring*)   It had to happen. The sultan is siding with
the merchant. That's the way things are . . .

THE SULTAN   Quiet. I have to work.

> *The Merchant steals away. The Sultan pores over an account
> book. A long silence.*

PUFF OF SMOKE   Lord sultan . . .

THE SULTAN   Quiet!

> *Pause. Puff of Smoke approaches the Sultan on tiptoe.*

PUFF OF SMOKE   Lord sultan, time is short, and you're loaded down
with work. I'll help you render a just verdict.

> *He gives the Sultan a mighty whack.*

When my opponent comes back, you can give him that slap, with
perfect justice.

> *Puff of Smoke escapes, to the great amusement of the Chorus.
> The gong sounds, more than once. Blackout. Lights. The gong
> sounds repeatedly. The Sultan on his throne. The Mufti enters.*

THE SULTAN   Tell me, mufti, are you familiar with the divine invention,
intelligence powder?

THE MUFTI (*at a loss*)   Intelligence powder? Oh yes . . .

THE SULTAN   I was sure you were. Such an invention could hardly be
unknown to our ulemas. Perhaps it's even mentioned in the Koran?

THE MUFTI   Everything is written in the Koran, in black and white.
Nothing goes unmentioned.

THE SULTAN   I knew it. Your place now is at the head of the faithful,
ready to pass along this new wealth. This discovery has come at just
the right moment to stifle all the union demands. And to think it
came our way via a progressive philosopher . . . the poor wretch!
Don't he and the others like him know that we're strong enough to
silence them, and clever enough to use their system against them?

> *Blackout. The gong resounds repeatedly. A crowd of men, wield-
> ing brooms, work amidst a whirl of dust, as hellish lights sweep
> over them in turn, for the authorities have brought in some TV
> spotlights for the occasion. Downstage, presiding over the event,
> are the Sultan, the Mufti, and Puff of Smoke.*

THE MUFTI (*hands heavenward*)   Oh creator, we glorify thee for having
lavished thy wisdom on our philosopher, Amin!

THE SULTAN   Amin.

THE CHORUS   Amin.

PUFF OF SMOKE (*to outdo the others*)   Oh creator, we thank thee. We hope that thy holy religion and the Empire of our sultan will rise ever higher . . . . And will be built on sand. Amin.

THE MUFTI (*menacingly*)   Amin.

THE SULTAN (*automatically*)   Amin.

THE CHORUS (*stifling its laughter*)   Amin, Amin, Amin.

> *Pause. The Chorus disappears into the shadow. The Sultan dismisses the Mufti with a wave of the hand and takes Puff of Smoke's arm, in a friendly gesture.*

THE SULTAN   My dear philosopher! I must admit, I had my doubts about you.

PUFF OF SMOKE   Doubt is but a grain of sand in the desert of Faith.

THE SULTAN   I'm now more inclined . . .

PUFF OF SMOKE   Your attention was somewhat taken up with your current favorite . . . A man feels rather ill-at-ease under the watchful eye of a woman, in life's most serious moments.

THE SULTAN   Oh great philosopher, you deserve a reward from me. Consider yourself officially the sole tutor to the prince, my son and heir. There is no higher service.

> *Blackout. The gong sounds, repeatedly. Near the cradle where the royal baby lies resting, Puff of Smoke is stretched out on an expensive carpet, his pipe having been traded for a magnificent hookah, the symbol of fortune.*

PUFF OF SMOKE   *Sic transit gloria:*[1] here I am, a nursemaid. From now on condemned to live day and night at the prince's bedside. I can't leave for any reason. And I'm caught in my own trap because I've got the ridiculous job of trying to discover signs of intelligence in the puny brat who's still at the thumb-sucking stage . . . Ugh! Bad luck must come in pairs . . . Now I've got to . . . How can I find it in this enormous palace . . . ?

> *Puff of Smoke circles the prince's room. His discomfort grows more and more apparent. Blackout. The gong strikes, repeatedly.*

> *Blackout. Lights. The Prince has changed positions. He now lies on the carpet.*

PUFF OF SMOKE (*in front of the empty cradle*)   Well that's too bad. I've flooded the prince's cradle. I couldn't hold it in any longer. Bah! It'll bring him good luck! Let's put him back gently, as if he were taking his bath . . .

> *He lifts the Prince and stands staring in astonishment at the carpet.*

---

1. "In glorious exaltation" or "In glorious transport." Puff of Smoke is, true to character, being pompous in using the arcane Latin phrase and being sarcastic because he is in fact "trapped" by the opulence of the scene.

I should have known it. The prince took advantage of the situation, too. The little hypocrite.

Blackout. The gong sounds, repeatedly. Lights. A spotlight at first is cast on the screen where the image of a vulture floats in wide circles, then it dims gradually and moves to the silhouette of Ali, son of Nedjma and Lakhdar, a wandering orphan. A dim light, but not yet a total blackout.

ALI

A shadow swooped down on me and I ran through the desert
Over a rocky airfield, and the shadow of the vulture was on me

The gong strikes, once.

Does anyone who hasn't spent the night in the eyes of a predatory bird
Know the speed at which the black blood flees a heart bitten by fear?
I know, and I've wept tears of fear
And the shadow of the vulture was on me, and has continued to follow me
Since the hour of the abduction and the flight, and since then, without resting,
I keep a sharp watch and I kill
To separate the bird from the shadow and the shadow from the bird
And I've wept tears of madness.

The gong resounds repeatedly. Ali lies down in the shadow of the palm tree. A pause, then the Nomads are seen arriving, very curious.

THE CHORUS

That foreigner again! So he has nowhere else to turn
And again we find him stretched out, sheltered by a tree
Having asked for nothing, said nothing, asked for nothing . . .
.

CHORUS LEADER   A vulture is gliding overhead: Could he be a condemned man? I'd like to speak to him, but it's risky to awaken any man without calling him by name.
ALI *(leaping to his feet)*   What's the matter?
CHORUS LEADER

Easy, young man, why try to defend yourself
From the people who have nothing to hold against you?
Just tell us where you're from
Allow us to offer you our hospitality, as custom requires.

Pause. Ali again settles down under the palm tree, without a word.

THE CHORUS *(angered)*   Is this scorn for us or shame, is this shame or scorn for us?

CHORUS LEADER He won't talk. He's on his guard.

THE CHORUS He's a rebel for sure, a friend of the people forced to live without friends . . . ?

CHORUS LEADER Or else a refugee who's seen too much for his age, and been brutalized by the war?

THE CHORUS There must be a reason for living like this in the desert.

CHORUS LEADER Not at all. Look at him. He sleeps without going to sleep. He's swimming in the void. His eyelids open and close as if he were on the borders of the real world.

THE CHORUS His eyes are red. The eyes of a flesh-eater.[2]

ALI (*unable to hold back*) You've guessed it. I'm from the tribe of the eagle. But the eagle is gone. A vulture has taken his place.

CHORUS LEADER A while ago he was playing dead, and now he speaks in riddles!

THE CHORUS Empty out your bag,[3] we're listening to you.

ALI Don't you believe me?

CHORUS LEADER All we want is to believe you.

ALI (*peremptorily*) The Ancestors foretold that when the last days of the tribe were at hand, the noble and mighty eagle would give way to the bird of death and defeat. But it doesn't matter. Our totem remains. He's a bird that won't give in.

THE CHORUS (*fanning out*) In every large city you can see vultures in their cages, along with their tribes.

ALI Yes, old crippled things, or else their offspring, born in captivity. A pitiful minority. Not so long ago, my mother gave me a baby vulture, captured in the wild, that they'd tied to a wineskin, after fastening a weight to his leg. So he had room enough to move around in . . . and while I was trying to tie the cord to a tree, he shrieked and struggled so hard that he would have strangled himself if I hadn't let go of the cord. But later I had to turn him loose completely, since he wouldn't touch meat or water, and his anger lasted all day. He would stop for a moment, exhausted, indignant, paralyzed as if in a bad dream, then almost at once he resumed his glorious fight for freedom. "He's going to die," my mother said, "and he won't even touch his meager rations." Of course I freed the bird, and I watched it disappear into the twilight, but not without a certain sorrow . . . I, too, would have liked my freedom. But I was bewildered the next day, and for days after that, when I saw him circling overhead. His constant presence seemed to be inviting me to make a journey. Was he waiting for my decision? It was like a game. I enjoyed following him a little further each day. One day I realized that I had left my mother behind. Besides, she lived in the open air, given over completely to magic. She already assumed I was dead. In her ghostly world I was just another spirit. So I left the valley of the wild woman and I followed the path indicated by His Highness the vulture. It was westward, always westward. At the bor-

2. Savage, cannibal.
3. Idiomatic expression for "say everything on your mind."

der, I wanted to know what country I would be going to for the first time. "This is the empire of the Maghreb," they told me. My beard wasn't a man's yet, so they let me through. "Another victim of the war," the soldiers and the government officials said . . .

CHORUS LEADER (*whispering*)   This must be due to sunstroke.

The Chorus, to one side of the stage, whispers and nods, then they point to one of the two trees, from where a thick smoke rises, and turn to Ali.

CHORUS LEADER   Do you see that tree? And do you see the smoke behind the tree?

ALI   Yes, I see.

CHORUS LEADER   Over there is a hashish smoker, a philosopher of the people. He's looking for you. He's waiting for you.

THE CHORUS (*aside*)   They're made for each other.

Blackout. Pause. The spotlight moves. Puff of Smoke is smoking his pipe in silence. Ali comes face to face with him.

PUFF OF SMOKE   It's certainly no accident if the vulture made you cross the border, and if he made the people bring you to me. It's up to me to show you why he did it, and what you have to do as the vulture's representative . . . The first thing I have to tell you is that this country is ruled by a sultan whose son will soon be called on to take command . . .

Blackout. The gong sounds once. Lights.

PUFF OF SMOKE (*his Turkish slippers in hand*)   The sultan gave me these gold-embroidered slippers as a gift. He said that a philosopher as famous as me shouldn't have to expose his toes to the pebbles. That damn monarch! Now I'm suffering twice, with these imperial slippers. Not only can't I wear them them for fear of getting them dirty, but I've also got to carry them under my arms, like a pair of illegitimate kids! That reminds me of something. It was at the mosque that I first learned how to steal. I had left my shoes at the entrance, like everyone else . . . After the prayers, I looked under all the mats . . . !⁴ Ow! Ow!

Pebbles are being hurled at Puff of Smoke. The gong sounds, repeatedly. Ali enters, followed by the Chorus which hides.

ALI   I'm here for the lesson.

PUFF OF SMOKE   We'll begin with the irregular verbs.

Pause. Puff of Smoke begins to teach. Ali takes out his slate.

CHORUS LEADER (*approaching, with a tray on his head*)   Here are some gazelle horns from the mufti.

---

4. Puff of Smoke is slyly hinting that stolen goods are (usually) hidden under prayer mats; by this he means that a great deal of stealing takes place during prayers, or more generally that piety is often a cover for brazen thievery.

PUFF OF SMOKE   Good old mufti! He knows a thing or two about horns and you can tell him to be proud of his gazelle.

The Chorus Leader sets the tray down and exits. The gong sounds, once.

CHORUS LEADER (*re-entering*)   The sultan wants to see you. It's urgent.

PUFF OF SMOKE   Obviously, I've become indispensable in this kingdom! (*To Ali.*) Be careful of that tray. There are some poisoned sweets on it intended for a conspirator. Don't touch them.

ALI   Don't worry.

Puff of Smoke exits. Ali uncovers the tray and is observed by the Chorus Leader who seems in no hurry to leave. The gong sounds, once.

ALI (*eating*)   Life is so strange. It's sweet to die from poison.

CHORUS LEADER   I'm so disgusted with life. Give me a little of your poison.

ALI (*swallowing up the last of the cakes*)   Not everyone is a follower of Socrates.

Pause. The Chorus Leader exits, crestfallen.

ALI   What bliss! I must be sailing to paradise. And yet I've got to cry . . .

He begins to whimper, getting his slate wet.

PUFF OF SMOKE (*entering, meditating on the empty slate*)   The son of a bitch!

ALI   Master, I've smeared my slate, and I've forgotten everything you taught me. Knowing how harsh your mockery can be, I wanted to die and I ate those poisoned sweets, despite your warning!

PUFF OF SMOKE   The son of a bitch! He's one of those students who just can't wait for the end of the lesson.

Blackout. Lights. The gong resounds, repeatedly. A crystal cupola representing the palace of the prince is now added to the set, near the two trees representing the forest, where we see Ali the vagabond lying down and going to sleep. Then the spotlight shines on the Chorus spread out around the cupola, through which we can make out the silhouette of the Prince sprawled across a divan.

CHORUS LEADER
    Prince, you have never passed through
    The wall of your dreams:
    Fearing to lose you, as he lost his other son
    The sultan has never wanted you to leave
    As if the whole world had to come here to bow down,
    Reduced to the image of a stain-glass window!

THE CHORUS   Prince, you have never passed through the wall of your dreams!

CHORUS LEADER

You are pining away, prince, you are suffocating in the crystal.
The earth, the forest, that's all that the bad prince wishes for . . .
But do you see the other one, the vagabond over there under that
 tree
He is stretched out like a reed.
And isn't he dreaming? Doesn't he think himself, unlike you,
In the palace of the prince, and far from all danger?
Who is the fortunate one, who is not? Even dreaming is an
 exchange . . .

THE CHORUS

Who is the fortunate one, who is not?
Even dreaming is a swindle . . .

*Silence. The Chorus hides. Pause. The gong sounds, repeatedly.
Ali, in his sleep, knocks against the crystal wall, attracting the
Prince's notice. A dream-like dialogue commences between Ali
and the Prince.*

PRINCE (*leaning against the crystal wall*)   Did someone knock?
ALI   I hear someone behind the crystal!
PRINCE (*knocking on the wall*)   Who said that? Answer!
ALI   And you, who are you? Answer! . . . You can't get out? Just a
moment.

*Ali takes a stone and shatters a good-sized portion of the cupola.
Total blackout. The gong resounds, repeatedly.*

CHORUS LEADER (*in darkness*)   They've finally broken down the wall of
 dreams.
THE CHORUS   They're free at last.
CHORUS LEADER   They're going deep into the forest.
THE CHORUS   One less prince, once more . . .
CHORUS LEADER   The vagabond has accomplished his mission.
THE CHORUS

Great events are in the offing
The people can't wait to march on the capital!

*The crystal cupola has disappeared. The Sultan, melancholy and
old-looking, is slumped on his throne. Three Youths enter and
cross to him, one of the three being Ali.*

FIRST YOUTH   We are friends . . .
SECOND YOUTH   Friends of the prince.
THE SULTAN (*rising*)   My son! Where is he?
ALI   Not far from here.

*Two male Nurses from the army of liberation[5] enter, bearing a
stretcher. Partisans are seen guarding all the exits.*

5. An allusion to peasant revolts and the Algerian anticolonial revolutionary war.

THE SULTAN (*deluded*)   It's not true. This isn't my son! Get out of here!

ALI   I'm sorry. We're sorry. You were the one who wanted war. We kidnapped the prince to shield him from your intrigues, and to make you deal with the army of liberation, which you persistently wanted to crush, even though it helped to consolidate your throne . . . The prince is dead because of your mistake.

THE SULTAN   My mistake? My mistake?

ALI   Yes, your mistake. It's true heaven had something to do with it . . . Your cavalry descended on us like locusts, though you could have counted our forces on the fingers of one hand. Being defenseless after the first assault, we were waiting to die, when a vulture suddenly appeared . . . With the second assault, we saw him settle on the prince's chest, nestle, and fold his wings as if he was going to sleep, too . . .

> *Total blackout. The gong sounds, repeatedly. Death moans from the Prince. The vulture glides across the screen.*

THE CHORUS (*in darkness*)
> The prince is dreaming his last dream,
> Vulture, fly away!

CHORUS LEADER   Vulture, fly away, he's dreaming his last dream!

CURTAIN

ATHOL FUGARD, JOHN KANI, AND WINSTON NTSHONA

Sizwe Bansi Is Dead[†]

Characters

STYLES
SIZWE BANSI
BUNTU

Styles's Photographic Studio in the African township of New Brighton, Port Elizabeth. Positioned prominently, the name-board:

> *Styles Photographic Studio. Reference Books; Passports; Weddings; Engagements; Birthday Parties and Parties.*
> *Prop.—Styles.*

Underneath this a display of photographs of various sizes. Centre stage, a table and chair. This is obviously used for photographs because a camera on a tripod stands ready a short distance away.

There is also another table, or desk, with odds and ends of photographic equipment and an assortment of 'props' for photographs.

The setting for this and subsequent scenes should be as simple as possible so that the action can be continuous.

Styles walks on with a newspaper. A dapper, alert young man wearing a white dustcoat and bowtie. He sits down at the table and starts to read the paper.

STYLES (*reading the headlines*) 'Storm buffets Natal. Damage in many areas . . . trees snapped like . . . what? . . . matchsticks . . .'

He laughs.

They're having it, boy! And I'm watching it . . . in the paper.

Turning the page, another headline.

† From Athol Fugard, John Kani, and Winston Ntshona, *Statements* (New York: Theatre Communications Group, 1986). Copyright © 1973, 1974 by Athol Fugard, John Kani, and Winston Ntshona. Reprinted by permission of William Morris Agency, Inc. on behalf of the Authors.

'China: A question-mark on South West Africa.' What's China want
there? *Yo!* They better be careful. China gets in there . . . ! (*Laugh.*)
I'll tell you what happens . . .

> *Stops abruptly. Looks around as if someone might be eavesdrop-*
> *ping on his intimacy with the audience.*

No comment.

> *Back to his paper.*

What's this? . . . *Ag!* American politics. Nixon and all his votes.
Means buggerall to us.

> *Another page, another headline.*

'Car plant expansion. 1.5 million rand plan.' *Ja*, I'll tell you what
that means . . . more machines, bigger buildings . . . never any
expansion to the pay-packet. Makes me fed-up. I know what I'm
talking about. I worked at Ford one time. We used to read in the
newspaper . . . big headlines! . . . 'So and so from America or London
made a big speech: ". . . going to see to it that the conditions of
their non-white workers in Southern Africa were substantially
improved." ' The talk ended in the bloody newspaper. Never in the
pay-packet.
Another time we read: Mr Henry Ford Junior Number two or whatever the hell he is . . . is visiting the Ford Factories in South Africa!

> *Shakes his head ruefully at the memory.*

Big news for us, man! When a big man like that visited the plant
there was usually a few cents more in the pay-packet at the end of
the week.
Ja, a Thursday morning. I walked into the plant . . . 'Hey! What's
this?' . . . Everything was quiet! Those big bloody machines that
used to make so much noise made my head go around . . . ? Silent!
Went to the notice-board and read: Mr Ford's visit today!
The one in charge of us . . . (*laugh*) hey! I remember him. General
Foreman Mr 'Baas' Bradley. Good man that one, if you knew how
to handle him . . . he called us all together:

> *Styles mimics Mr 'Baas' Bradley. A heavy Afrikaans accent.*

'Listen, boys, don't go to work on the line. There is going to be a
General Cleaning first.'
I used to like General Cleaning. Nothing specific, you know, little
bit here, little bit there. But that day! Yessus . . . in came the big
machines with hot water and brushes—sort of electric mop—and
God alone knows what else. We started on the floors. The oil and
dirt under the machines was thick, man. All the time the bosses
were walking around watching us:

> *Slapping his hands together as he urges on the 'boys'.*

'Come on, boys! It's got to be spotless! Big day for the plant!' Even
the *big* boss, the one we only used to see lunch-times, walking to
the canteen with a big cigar in his mouth and his hands in his pocket
. . . that day? Sleeves rolled up, running around us:
'Come on! Spotless, my boys! Over there, John . . .' I thought: What
the hell is happening? It was beginning to feel like hard work, man.
I'm telling you we cleaned that place—spot-checked after fifteen
minutes! . . . like you would have thought it had just been built.
First stage of General Cleaning finished. We started on the second.
Mr 'Baas' Bradley came in with paint and brushes. I watched.
W—h—i—t—e   l—i—n—e

> *Mr 'Baas' Bradley paints a long white line on the floor.*

What's this? Been here five years and I never seen a white line
before. Then:

> *Mr 'Baas' Bradley at work with the paint-brush.*

CAREFUL THIS SIDE. TOW MOTOR IN MOTION.

> *Styles laughs.*

It was nice, man. Safety-precautions after six years. Then another
gallon of paint.
Y—e—l—l—o—w   l—i—n—e—
NO SMOKING IN THIS AREA. DANGER!
Then another gallon:
G—r—e—e—n   l—i—n—e—
I noticed that that line cut off the roughcasting section, where we
worked with the rough engine blocks as we got them from Iscor.
Dangerous world that. Big machines! One mistake there and you're
in trouble. I watched them and thought: What's going to happen
here? When the green line was finished, down they went on the
floor—Mr 'Baas' Bradley, the lot!—with a big green board, a little
brush, and a tin of white paint. EYE PROTECTION AREA. Then
my big moment:
'Styles!'
'Yes, sir!'
(*Mr 'Baas' Bradley's heavy Afrikaans accent*) 'What do you say in your
language for this? Eye Protection Area.'
It was easy, man!
'Gqokra Izi Khuselo Zamehlo Kule Ndawo.'[1]
Nobody wrote it!
'Don't bloody fool me, Styles!'
'No, sir!'
'Then spell it . . . slowly.'

> *Styles has a big laugh.*

---

1. The language is Xhosa.

Hey! That was my moment, man. Kneeling there on the floor . . .
foreman, general foreman, plant supervisor, plant manager . . . and
Styles? Standing!

> *Folds his arms as he acts out his part to the imaginary figures
> crouched on the floor.*

'G—q—o—k—r—a' . . . and on I went, with Mr 'Baas' Bradley
painting and saying as he wiped away the sweat:
'You're not fooling me, hey!'
After that the green board went up. We all stood and admired it.
Plant was looking nice, man! Colourful!
Into the third phase of General Cleaning.
'Styles!'
'Yes, sir!'
'Tell all the boys they must now go to the bathroom and wash them-
selves clean.'
We needed it! Into the bathroom, under the showers . . . hot water,
soap . . . on a Thursday! Before ten? Yo! What's happening in the
plant? The other chaps asked me: What's going on, Styles? I told
them: 'Big-shot cunt from America coming to visit you.' When we
finished washing they gave us towels . . . (*laugh*).
Three hundred of us, man! We were so clean we felt shy!
Stand there like little ladies in front of the mirror. From there to
the General Store.
Handed in my dirty overall.
'Throw it on the floor.'
'Yes, sir!'
New overall comes, wrapped in plastic. Brand new, man! I normally
take a thirty-eight but this one was a forty-two. Then next door to
the tool room . . . brand new tool bag, set of spanners, shifting
spanner, torque wrench—all of them brand new—and because I
worked in the dangerous hot test section I was also given a new
asbestos apron and fire-proof gloves to replace the ones I had lost
about a year ago. I'm telling you I walked back heavy to my spot.
Armstrong on the moon! Inside the plant it was general meeting
again. General Foreman Mr 'Baas' Bradley called me.
'Styles!'
'Yes, sir.'
'Come translate.'
'Yes, sir!'

> *Styles pulls out a chair. Mr 'Baas' Bradley speaks on one side,
> Styles translates on the other.*

'Tell the boys in your language, that this is a very big day in their
lives.'
'Gentlemen, this old fool says this is a hell of a big day in our lives.'
The men laughed.
'They are very happy to hear that, sir.'

'Tell the boys that Mr Henry Ford the Second, the owner of this place, is going to visit us. Tell them Mr Ford is the big Baas. He owns the plant and everything in it.'
'Gentlemen, old Bradley says this Ford is a big bastard. He owns everything in this building, which means you as well.'
A voice came out of the crowd:
'Is he a bigger fool than Bradley?'
'They're asking, sir, is he bigger than you?'
'Certainly . . . (blustering) . . . certainly. He is a very big baas. He's a . . . (groping for words) . . . he's a Makulu Baas.'
I loved that one!
'Mr "Baas" Bradley says most certainly Mr Ford is bigger than him. In fact Mr Ford is the grandmother baas of them all . . . that's what he said to me.'
'Styles, tell the boys that when Mr Henry Ford comes into the plant I want them all to look happy. We will slow down the speed of the line so that they can sing and smile while they are working.'
'Gentlemen, he says that when the door opens and his grandmother walks in you must see to it that you are wearing a mask of smiles. Hide your true feelings, brothers. You must sing. The joyous songs of the days of old before we had fools like this one next to me to worry about.' (To Bradley.) 'Yes, sir!'
'Say to them, Styles, that they must try to impress Mr Henry Ford that they are better than those monkeys in his own country, those niggers in Harlem who know nothing but strike, strike.'
Yo! I liked that one too.
'Gentlemen, he says we must remember, when Mr Ford walks in, that we are South African monkeys, not American monkeys. South African monkeys are much better trained . . .' Before I could even finish, a voice was shouting out of the crowd:
'He's talking shit!' I had to be careful!

Servile and full of smiles as he turns back to Bradley.

'No, sir! The men say they are much too happy to behave like those American monkeys.'
Right! Line was switched on nice and slow—and we started working.

At work on the Assembly Line; singing.

'Tshotsholoza . . . Tshotsholoza . . . kulezondawo . . .'
We had all the time in the world, man! . . . torque wrench out . . . tighten the cylinder-head nut . . . wait for the next one . . . (Singing) 'Vyabaleka . . . uyabaleka . . . kulezondawo . . .'
I kept my eye on the front office. I could see them—Mr 'Baas' Bradley, the line supervisor—through the big glass window, brushing their hair, straightening the tie. There was some General Cleaning going on there too.

He laughs.

We were watching them. Nobody was watching us. Even the old Security Guard. The one who every time he saw a black man walk past with his hands in his pockets he saw another spark-plug walk out of the plant. Today? To hell and gone there on the other side polishing his black shoes.

Then, through the window, I saw three long black Galaxies zoom up. I passed the word down the line: He's come!

Let me tell you what happened. The big doors opened; next thing the General Superintendent, Line Supervisor, General Foreman, Manager, Senior Manager, Managing Director . . . the bloody lot were there . . . like a pack of puppies!

> *Mimics a lot of fawning men retreating before an important person.*

I looked and laughed! 'Yessus, Styles, they're all playing your part today!' They ran, man! In came a tall man, six foot six, hefty, full of respect and dignity . . . I marvelled at him! Let me show you what he did.

> *(Three enormous strides)* One . . . two . . . three . . . *(Cursory look around as he turns and takes the same three strides back.)*

One . . . two . . . three . . . OUT! Into the Galaxie and gone! That's all. Didn't talk to me, Mr 'Baas' Bradley, Line Supervisor, or any-body. He didn't even look at the plant! And what did I see when those three Galaxies disappeared? The white staff at the main switchboard.

'Double speed on the line! Make up for production lost!'

It ended up with us working harder that bloody day than ever before. Just because that big . . . *(shakes his head)*

Six years there. Six years a bloody fool.

> *Back to his newspaper. A few more headlines with appropriate comment, then . . .*

(Reading) 'The Mass Murderer! Doom!'

> *Smile of recognition.*

'For fleas . . . Doom. Flies . . . Doom. Bedbugs . . . Doom. For cockroaches and other household pests. The household insecticide . . . Doom.' Useful stuff. Remember, Styles? *Ja.*

(To the audience.) After all that time at Ford I sat down one day. I said to myself:

'Styles, you're a bloody monkey, boy!'

'What do you mean?'

'You're a monkey, man.'

'Go to hell!'

'Come on, Styles, you're a monkey, man, and you know it. Run up and down the whole bloody day! Your life doesn't belong to you. You've sold it. For what, Styles? Gold wrist-watch in twenty-five

years time when they sign you off because you're too old for anything
any more?'
I was right. I took a good look at my life. What did I see? A bloody
circus monkey! Selling most of his time on this earth to another
man. Out of every twenty-four hours I could only properly call mine
the six when I was sleeping. What the hell is the use of that?
Think about it, friend. Wake up in the morning, half-past six, out
of the pyjamas and into the bath-tub, put on your shirt with one
hand, socks with the other, realize you got your shoes on the wrong
bloody feet, and all the time the seconds are passing and if you don't
hurry up you'll miss the bus . . . 'Get the lunch, dear. I'm late. My
lunch, please, darling! . . . then the children come in . . . 'Daddy,
can I have this? Daddy, I want money for that.' 'Go to your mother.
I haven't got time. Look after the children, please, sweetheart!!' . . .
grab your lunch . . . 'Bye Bye!!' and then run like I-don't-know-what
for the bus stop. You call that living? I went back to myself for
another chat:
'Suppose you're right. What then?'
'Try something else.'
'Like what?'
Silly question to ask. I knew what I was going to say. Photographer!
It was my hobby in those days. I used to pick up a few cents on the
side taking cards at parties, weddings, big occasions. But when it
came to telling my wife and parents that I wanted to turn profes-
sional . . . !!
My father was the worst.
'You call that work? Click-click with a camera. Are you mad?'
I tried to explain. 'Daddy, if I could stand on my own two feet and
not be somebody else's tool, I'd have some respect for myself. I'd be
a man.'
'What do you mean? Aren't you one already? You're circumcised,
you've got a wife . . .'
Talk about the generation gap!
Anyway I thought: To hell with them. I'm trying it.
It was the Christmas shutdown, so I had lots of time to look around
for a studio. My friend Dhlamini at the Funeral Parlour told me
about a vacant room next door. He encouraged me. I remember his
words. 'Grab your chance, Styles. Grab it before somebody in my
line puts you in a box and closes the lid.' I applied for permission[2]
to use the room as a studio. After some time the first letter back:
'Your application has been received and is being considered.'
A month later: 'The matter is receiving the serious consideration of
the Board.' Another month: 'Your application is now on the director's table.' I nearly gave up, friends. But one day, a knock at the
door—the postman—I had to sign for a registered letter. 'We are
pleased to inform you . . .'

---

2. From the local apartheid administrative/municipal authorities.

Styles has a good laugh.

I ran all the way to the Administration Offices, grabbed the key, ran all the way back to Red Location, unlocked the door, and walked in!

What I found sobered me up a little bit. Window panes were all broken; big hole in the roof, cobwebs in the corners. I didn't let that put me off though. Said to myself: 'This is your chance, Styles. Grab it.' Some kids helped me clean it out. The dust! *Yo!* When the broom walked in the Sahara Desert walked out! But at the end of that day it was reasonably clean. I stood here in the middle of the floor, straight! You know what that means? To stand straight in a place of your own? To be your own . . . General Foreman, Mr 'Baas', Line Supervisor—the lot! I was tall, six foot six and doing my own in-spection of the plant.

So I'm standing there—here—feeling big and what do I see on the walls? Cockroaches. *Ja,* cockroaches . . . in *my* place. I don't mean those little things that run all over the place when you pull out the kitchen drawer. I'm talking about the big bastards, the paratroopers as we call them. I didn't like them. I'm not afraid of them but I just don't like them! All over. On the floors, the walls. I heard the one on the wall say: 'What's going on? Who opened the door?' The one on the floor answered: 'Relax. He won't last. This place is con-demned.' That's when I thought: Doom.

Out of here and into the Chinaman's shop. 'Good day, sir. I've got a problem. Cockroaches.'

The Chinaman didn't even think, man, he just said: 'Doom!' I said: 'Certainly.' He said: 'Doom, seventy-five cents a tin.' Paid him for two and went back. *Yo!* You should have seen me! Two-tin Charlie!

> *His two tins at the ready, forefingers on the press-buttons, Styles gives us a graphic re-enactment of what happened. There is a brief respite to 'reload'—shake the tins—and tie a handkerchief around his nose after which he returns to the fight. Styles even-tually backs through the imaginary door, still firing, and closes it. Spins the tins and puts them into their holsters.*

I went home to sleep. *I* went to sleep. Not them (*the cockroaches*). What do you think happened here? General meeting under the floor-boards. All the bloody survivors. The old professor addressed them: 'Brothers, we face a problem of serious pollution . . . contamination! The menace appears to be called Doom. I have recommended a general inoculation of the whole community. Everybody in line, please. (*Inoculation proceeds.*) Next . . . next . . . next . . .' While poor old Styles is smiling in his sleep! Next morning I walked in . . . (*He stops abruptly.*) . . . What's this? Cockroach walking on the floor? Another one on the ceiling? Not a damn! Doom did it yester-day. Doom does it today. (*Whips out the two tins and goes in fighting. This time, however, it is not long before they peter out.*) Pssssssss

. . . pssssss . . . pssss . . . pss (*a last desperate shake, but he barely manages to get out a squirt*).
Pss.
No bloody good! The old bastard on the floor just waved his feelers in the air as if he was enjoying air-conditioning.
I went next door to Dhlamini and told him about my problem. He laughed. 'Doom? You're wasting your time, Styles. You want to solve your problem, get a cat. What do you think a cat lives on in the township? Milk? If there's any the baby gets it. Meat? When the family sees it only once a week? Mice? The little boys got rid of them years ago. Insects, man, township cats are insect-eaters. Here . . .'
He gave me a little cat. I'm . . . I'm not too fond of cats normally. This one was called Blackie . . . I wasn't too fond of that name either. But . . . Kitsy! Kitsy! Kitsy . . . little Blackie followed me back to the studio.
The next morning when I walked in what do you think I saw? Wings. I smiled. Because one thing I do know is that no cockroach can take his wings off. He's dead!

Proud gesture taking in the whole of his studio.

So here it is!

To his name-board.

'Styles Photographic Studio. Reference Books; Passports; Weddings; Engagements; Birthday Parties and Parties. Proprietor: Styles.'
When you look at this, what do you see? Just another photographic studio? Where people come because they've lost their Reference Book[3] and need a photo for the new one? That I sit them down, set up the camera . . . 'No expression, please' . . . click-click . . . 'Come back tomorrow, please' . . . and then kick them out and wait for the next? No, friend. It's more than just that. This is a strong-room of dreams. The dreamers? My people. The simple people, who you never find mentioned in the history books, who never get statues erected to them, or monuments commemorating their great deeds. People who would be forgotten, and their dreams with them, if it wasn't for Styles. That's what I do, friends. Put down, in my way, on paper the dreams and hopes of my people so that even their children's children will remember a man . . . 'This was our Grand-father' . . . and say his name. Walk into the houses of New Brighton and on the walls you'll find hanging the story of the people the writers of the big books forget about.

To his display-board.

This one (*a photograph*) walked in here one morning. I was just passing the time. Midweek. Business is always slow then. Anyway,

---

3. The infamous "passbook" that all blacks had to carry under apartheid, especially when in the cities or "white areas."

a knock at the door. Yes! I must explain something. I get two types
of knock here. When I hear . . . (*knocks solemnly on the table*) . . .
I don't even look up, man. 'Funeral parlour is next door.' But when
I hear . . . (*energetic rap on the table . . . he laughs*) . . . that's *my*
sound, and I shout 'Come in!'
In walked a chap, full of smiles, little parcel under his arm. I can
still see him, man!

Styles acts both roles.

'Mr Styles?'
I said: 'Come in!'
'Mr Styles, I've come to take a snap, Mr Styles.'
I said: 'Sit down! Sit down, my friend!'
'No, Mr Styles. I want to take the snap standing. (*Barely containing
his suppressed excitement and happiness*) Mr Styles, take the card,
please!'
I said: 'Certainly, friend.'
Something you mustn't do is interfere with a man's dream. If he
wants to do it standing, let him stand. If he wants to sit, let him sit.
Do exactly what they want! Sometimes they come in here, all smart
in a suit, then off comes the jacket and shoes and socks . . . (*adopts
a boxer's stance*) . . . 'Take it, Mr Styles. Take it!' And I take it. No
questions! Start asking stupid questions and you destroy that dream.
Anyway, this chap I'm telling you about . . . (*laughing warmly as he
remembers*) . . . I've seen a lot of smiles in my business, friends, but
that one gets first prize. I set up my camera, and just as I was ready
to go . . . 'Wait, wait, Mr Styles! I want you to take the card with
this.' Out of his parcel came a long piece of white paper . . . looked
like some sort of document . . . he held it in front of him. (*Styles
demonstrates.*) For once I didn't have to say, 'Smile!' Just: 'Hold it!'
. . . and, click, . . . finished. I asked him what the document was.
'You see, Mr Styles, I'm forty-eight years old. I work twenty-two years
for the municipality and the foreman kept on saying to me if I want
promotion to Boss-boy I must try to better my education. I didn't
write well, Mr Styles. So I took a course with the Damelin Correspondence College. Seven years, Mr Styles! And at last I made it.
Here it is. Standard Six Certificate, School Leaving, Third Class! I
made it, Mr Styles. I made it. But I'm not finished. I'm going to take
up for the Junior Certificate, then Matric . . . and you watch, Mr
Styles. One day I walk out of my house, graduate, self-made! Bye-
bye, Mr Styles,' . . . and he walked out of here happy man, self-
made.

Back to his display-board; another photograph.

My best. Family Card. You know the Family Card? Good for business. Lot of people and they all want copies.
One Saturday morning. Suddenly a hell of a noise outside in the
street. I thought: What's going on now? Next thing that door burst
open and in they came! First the little ones, then the five- and six-

year-olds . . . I didn't know what was going on, man! Stupid children, coming to mess up my place. I was still trying to chase them out when the bigger boys and girls came through the door. Then it clicked. Family Card!

Changing his manner abruptly.

'Come in! Come in!'

Ushering a crowd of people into his studio.

. . . now the young men and women were coming in, then the mothers and fathers, uncles and aunties . . . the eldest son, a mature man, and finally . . .

Shaking his head with admiration at the memory.

the Old Man, the Grandfather! (*The 'old man' walks slowly and with dignity into the studio and sits down in the chair.*)
I looked at him. His grey hair was a sign of wisdom. His face, weather-beaten and lined with experience. Looking at it was like paging the volume of his history, written by himself. He was a living symbol of Life, of all it means and does to a man. I adored him. He sat there—half smiling, half serious—as if he had already seen the end of his road.
The eldest son said to me: 'Mr Styles, this is my father, my mother, my brothers and sisters, their wives and husbands, our children. Twenty-seven of us, Mr Styles. We have come to take a card. My father . . . ,' he pointed to the old man, '. . . my father always wanted it.'
I said: 'Certainly. Leave the rest to me.' I went to work.

Another graphic re-enactment of the scene as he describes it.

The old lady here, the eldest son there. Then the other one, with the other one. On this side I did something with the daughters, aunties, and one bachelor brother. Then in front of it all the eight-to-twelves, standing, in front of them the four-to-sevens, kneeling, and finally right on the floor everything that was left, sitting. Jesus, it was hard work, but finally I had them all sorted out and I went behind the camera.

Behind his camera.

Just starting to focus . . .

Imaginary child in front of the lens; Styles chases the child back to the family group.

'. . . Sit down! Sit down!'
Back to the camera, start to focus again . . . Not One Of Them Was Smiling! I tried the old trick. 'Say cheese, please.' At first they just looked at me. 'Come on! Cheese!' The children were the first to pick it up.
(*Child's voice.*) 'Cheese. Cheese. Cheese.' Then the ones a little bit

bigger—'Cheese'—then the next lot—'Cheese'—the uncles and aunties—'Cheese'—and finally the old man himself—'Cheese'! I thought the roof was going off, man! People outside in the street came and looked through the window. They joined in: 'Cheese." When I looked again the mourners from the funeral parlour were there wiping away their tears and saying 'Cheese'. Pressed my little button and there it was—New Brighton's smile, twenty-seven variations. Don't you believe those bloody fools who make out we don't know how to smile!

Anyway, you should have seen me then. Moved the bachelor this side, sister-in-laws that side. Put the eldest son behind the old man. Reorganized the children . . . (*Back behind his camera.*)

'Once again, please! Cheese!' Back to work . . . old man and old woman together, daughters behind them, sons on the side. Those that were kneeling now standing, those that were standing, now kneeling . . . Ten times, friends! Each one different!

An exhausted Styles collapses in a chair.

When they walked out finally I almost said Never Again! A week later the eldest son came back for the cards. I had them ready. The moment he walked through that door I could see he was in trouble. He said to me: 'Mr Styles, we almost didn't make it. My father died two days after the card. He will never see it.' 'Come on,' I said. 'You're a man. One day or the other every one of us must go home. Here . . .' I grabbed the cards. 'Here. Look at your father and thank God for the time he was given on this earth.' We went through them together. He looked at them in silence. After the third one, the tear went slowly down his cheek.

But at the same time . . . I was watching him carefully . . . something started to happen as he saw his father there with himself, his brothers and sisters, and all the little grandchildren. He began to smile. 'That's it, brother,' I said. 'Smile! Smile at your father. Smile at the world.'

When he left, I thought of him going back to his little house somewhere in New Brighton, filled that day with the little mothers in black because a man had died. I saw my cards passing from hand to hand. I saw hands wipe away tears, and then the first timid little smiles.

You must understand one thing. We own nothing except ourselves. This world and its laws, allows us nothing, except ourselves. There is nothing we can leave behind when we die, except the memory of ourselves. I know what I'm talking about, friends—I had a father, and he died.

To the display-board.

Here he is. My father. That's him. Fought in the war. Second World War. Fought at Tobruk. In Egypt. He fought in France so that this country and all the others could stay Free. When he came back they stripped him at the docks—his gun, his uniform, the dignity they'd allowed him for a few mad years because the world needed men to fight and be ready to sacrifice themselves for something called Freedom. In return they let him keep his scoff-tin and gave him a bicycle. Size twenty-eight. I remember, because it was too big for me. When he died, in a rotten old suitcase amongst some of his old rags, I found that photograph. That's all. That's all I have from him.

The display-board again.

Or this old lady. Mrs Matothlana. Used to stay in Sangocha Street. You remember! Her husband was arrested . . .

Knock at the door.

Tell you about it later. Come in!

A man walks nervously into the studio. Dressed in an ill-fitting new double-breasted suit. He is carrying a plastic bag with a hat in it. His manner is hesitant and shy. Styles takes one look at him and breaks into an enormous smile.

An aside to the audience. A Dream!
To the man. Come in, my friend.

MAN   Mr Styles?
STYLES   That's me. Come in! You have come to take a card?
MAN   Snap.
STYLES   Yes, a card. Have you got a deposit?
MAN   Yes.
STYLES   Good. Let me just take your name down. You see, you pay deposit now, and when you come for the card, you pay the rest.
MAN   Yes.
STYLES   (*to his desk and a black book for names and addresses*)   What is your name? (*The man hesitates, as if not sure of himself.*) Your name, please?

Pause.

Come on, my friend. You must surely have a name.
MAN   (*pulling himself together, but still very nervous*)   Robert Zwelinzima.
STYLES   (*writing*)   'Robert Zwelinzima.' Address?
MAN   (*swallowing*)   Fifty, Mapija Street.
STYLES   (*writes, then pauses*)   'Fifty, Mapija?'
MAN   Yes.
STYLES   You staying with Buntu?
MAN   Buntu.
STYLES   Very good somebody that one. Came here for his Wedding Card. Always helping people. If that man was white they'd call him a liberal.

Now finished writing. Back to his customer.

All right. How many cards do you want?

MAN   One card.

STYLES (*disappointed*) Only one?

MAN   One.

STYLES   How do you want to take the card?

The man is not sure of what the question means.

You can take the card standing . . .

Styles strikes a stylish pose next to the table.

sitting . . .

Another pose . . . this time in the chair.

anyhow. How do you want it?

MAN   Anyhow.

STYLES   Right. Sit down.

Robert hesitates.

Sit down!

Styles fetches a vase with plastic flowers, dusts them off, and places them on the table. Robert holds up his plastic bag.

What you got there?

Out comes the hat.

Aha! Stetson. Put it on, my friend.

Robert handles it shyly.

You can put it on, Robert.

Robert pulls it on. Styles does up one of his jacket buttons.

What a beautiful suit, my friend! Where did you buy it?

MAN   Sales House.

STYLES (*quoting a sales slogan*) 'Where the Black world buys the best. Six months to pay. Pay as you wear.'

Nudges Robert.

. . . and they never repossess!

They share a laugh.

What are you going to do with this card?

Chatting away as he goes to his camera and sets it up for the photo. Robert watches the preparations apprehensively.

MAN   Send it to my wife.

STYLES   Your wife!

MAN   Nowetu.

STYLES   Where's your wife?

MAN   King William's Town.

STYLES (*exaggerated admiration*) At last! The kind of man I like. Not one of those foolish young boys who come here to find work and then forget their families back home. A man, with responsibility! Where do you work?

MAN   Feltex.

STYLES   I hear they pay good there.

MAN   Not bad.

> *He is now very tense, staring fixedly at the camera. Styles straightens up behind it.*

STYLES   Come on, Robert! You want your wife to get a card with her husband looking like he's got all the worries in the world on his back? What will she think? 'My poor husband is in trouble!' You must smile!

> *Robert shamefacedly relaxes a little and starts to smile.*

That's it!

> *He relaxes still more. Beginning to enjoy himself. Uncertainly produces a very fancy pipe from one of his pockets.*
> *Styles now really warming to the assignment.*

Look, have you ever walked down the passage to the office with the big glass door and the board outside: 'Manager—Bestuurder'. Imagine it, man, you, Robert Zwelinzima, behind a desk in an office like that! It can happen, Robert. Quick promotion to Chief Messenger. I'll show you what we do.

> *Styles produces a Philips' class-room map of the world, which he hangs behind the table as a backdrop to the photo.*

Look at it, Robert. America, England, Africa, Russia, Asia!

> *Carried away still further by his excitement, Styles finds a cigarette, lights it, and gives it to Robert to hold. The latter is now ready for the 'card' . . . pipe in one hand and cigarette in the other. Styles stands behind his camera and admires his handiwork.*

Mr Robert Zwelinzima, Chief Messenger at Feltex, sitting in his office with the world behind him. Smile, Robert. Smile!

> *Studying his subject through the viewfinder of the camera.*

Lower your hand, Robert . . . towards the ashtray . . . more . . . now make a four with your legs . . .

> *He demonstrates behind the camera. Robert crosses his legs.*

Hold it, Robert . . . Keep on smiling . . . that's it . . . (*presses the release button—the shutter clicks*).
Beautiful! All right, Robert.

> *Robert and his smile remain frozen.*

Robert. You can relax now. It's finished!

MAN Finished?

STYLES Yes. You just want the one card?

MAN Yes.

STYLES What happens if you lose it? Hey? I've heard stories about those postmen, Robert. Yo! Sit on the side of the road and open the letters they should be delivering! 'Dear wife . . .'—one rand[4] this side, letter thrown away. 'Dear wife . . .'—another rand this side, letter thrown away. You want that to happen to you? Come on! What about a movie, man?

MAN Movie?

STYLES Don't you know the movie?

MAN No.

STYLES Simple! You just walk you see . . .

Styles demonstrates; at a certain point freezes in mid-stride.

. . . and I take the card! Then you can write to your wife: 'Dear wife, I am coming home at Christmas . . .' Put the card in your letter and post it. Your wife opens the letter and what does she see? Her Robert, walking home to her! She shows it to the children. 'Look, children, your daddy is coming!' The children jump and clap their hands: 'Daddy is coming! Daddy is coming!'

MAN (*excited by the picture Styles has conjured up*) All right!

STYLES You want a movie?

MAN I want a movie.

STYLES That's my man! Look at this, Robert.

Styles reverses the map hanging behind the table to reveal a gaudy painting of a futuristic city.

City of the Future! Look at it. Mr Robert Zwelinzima, man about town, future head of Feltex, walking through the City of the Future!

MAN (*examining the backdrop with admiration. He recognizes a landmark*) OK.

STYLES OK Bazaars . . . (*the other buildings*) . . . Mutual Building Society, Barclays Bank . . . the lot!

What you looking for, Robert?

MAN Feltex.

STYLES Yes . . . well, you see, I couldn't fit everything on, Robert. But if I had had enough space Feltex would have been here.

To his table for props.

Walking-stick . . . newspaper . . .

MAN (*diffidently*) I don't read.

STYLES That is not important, my friend. You think all those monkeys carrying newspapers can read? They look at the pictures.

---

4. The basic unit of South African currency.

After 'dressing' Robert with the props he moves back to his camera.

This is going to be beautiful, Robert. My best card. I must send one to the magazines.

All right, Robert, now move back. Remember what I showed you. Just walk towards me and right in front of the City of the Future. I'll take the picture. Ready? Now come, Robert . . .

Pipe in mouth, walking-stick in hand, newspaper under the other arm, Robert takes a jaunty step and then freezes, as Styles had shown him earlier.

Come, Robert . . .

Another step.

Just one more, Robert . . .

Another step.

Stop! Hold it, Robert. Hold it!

The camera flash goes off; simultaneously a blackout except for one light on Robert, frozen in the pose that will appear in the picture. We are in fact looking at the photograph. It 'comes to life' and dictates the letter that will accompany it to Nowetu in King William's Town.

MAN   Nowetu . . .

Correcting himself.

Dear Nowetu,

I've got wonderful news for you in this letter. My troubles are over, I think. You won't believe it, but I must tell you. Sizwe Bansi, in a manner of speaking, is dead! I'll tell you what I can.

As you know, when I left the Railway Compound I went to stay with a friend of mine called Zola. A very good friend that, Nowetu. In fact he was even trying to help me find some job. But that's not easy, Nowetu, because Port Elizabeth is a big place, a very big place with lots of factories but also lots of people looking for a job like me. There are so many men, Nowetu, who have left their places because they are dry and have come here to find work!

After a week with Zola, I was in big trouble. The headman came around, and after a lot of happenings which I will tell you when I see you, they put a stamp in my passbook which said I must leave Port Elizabeth at once in three days time. I was very much unhappy, Nowetu. I couldn't stay with Zola because if the headman found me there again my troubles would be even bigger. So Zola took me to a friend of his called Buntu, and asked him if I could stay with him until I decided what to do . . .

Buntu's house in New Brighton. Table and two chairs. Robert, in a direct continuation of the preceding scene, is already there, as Buntu, jacket slung over his shoulder, walks in. Holds out his hand to Robert.

BUNTU   Hi. Buntu.

They shake hands.

MAN   Sizwe Bansi.
BUNTU   Sit down.

They sit.

Zola told me you were coming. Didn't have time to explain anything. Just asked if you could spend a few nights here. You can perch yourself on that sofa in the corner. I'm alone at the moment. My wife is a domestic . . . sleep-in at Kabega Park . . . only comes home weekends. Hot today, hey?

In the course of this scene Buntu will busy himself first by having a wash—basin and jug of water on the table—and then by changing from his working clothes preparatory to going out. Sizwe Bansi stays in his chair.

What's your problem, friend?
MAN   I've got no permit to stay in Port Elizabeth.
BUNTU   Where do you have a permit to stay?
MAN   King William's Town.
BUNTU   How did they find out?
MAN   (*tells his story with the hesitation and uncertainty of the illiterate. When words fail him he tries to use his hands.*)
I was staying with Zola, as you know. I was very happy there. But one night . . . I was sleeping on the floor . . . I heard some noises and when I looked up I saw torches shining in through the window . . . then there was a loud knocking on the door. When I got up Zola was there in the dark . . . he was trying to whisper something. I think he was saying I must hide. So I crawled under the table. The headman came in and looked around and found me hiding under the table . . . and dragged me out.
BUNTU   Raid?
MAN   Yes, it was a raid. I was just wearing my pants. My shirt was lying on the other side. I just managed to grab it as they were pushing me out . . . I finished dressing in the van. They drove straight to the administration office . . . and then from there they drove to the Labour Bureau. I was made to stand in the passage there, with everybody looking at me and shaking their heads like they knew I was in big trouble. Later I was taken into an office and made to stand next to the door . . . The white man behind the desk had my book and he also looked at me and shook his head. Just then one other white man came in with a card . . .
BUNTU   A card?
MAN   He was carrying a card.

BUNTU   Pink card?[5]

MAN   Yes, the card was pink.

BUNTU   Record card. Your whole bloody life is written down on that. Go on.

MAN   Then the first white man started writing something on the card . . . and just then somebody came in carrying a . . .

> *Demonstrates what he means by banging a clenched fist on the table.*

BUNTU   A stamp?

MAN   Yes, a stamp. (*Repeats the action.*) He was carrying a stamp.

BUNTU   And then?

MAN   He put it on my passbook.

BUNTU   Let me see your book?

> *Sizwe produces his passbook from the back-pocket of his trousers. Buntu examines it.*

Shit! You know what this is? (*The stamp.*)

MAN   I can't read.

BUNTU   Listen . . . (*reads*). 'You are required to report to the Bantu Affairs Commissioner, King William's Town, within three days of the above-mentioned date for the . . .' You should have been home yesterday! . . . 'for the purpose of repatriation to home district.' Influx Control.

You're in trouble, Sizwe.

MAN   I don't want to leave Port Elizabeth.

BUNTU   Maybe. But if that book says go, you go.

MAN   Can't I maybe burn this book and get a new one?

BANTU   Burn that book? Stop kidding yourself, Sizwe! Anyway suppose you do. You must immediately go apply for a new one. Right? And until that new one comes, be careful the police don't stop you and ask for your book. Into the Courtroom, brother. Charge: Failing to produce Reference Book on Demand. Five rand or five days. Finally the new book comes. Down to the Labour Bureau for a stamp . . . it's got to be endorsed with permission to be in this area. White man at the Labour Bureau takes the book, looks at it—doesn't look at you!—goes to the big machine and feeds in your number . . .

> *Buntu goes through the motions of punching out a number on a computer.*

. . . card jumps out, he reads: 'Sizwe Bansi. Endorsed to King William's Town . . .' Takes your book, fetches that same stamp, and in it goes again. So you burn that book, or throw it away, and get another one. Same thing happens.

> *Buntu feeds the computer; the card jumps out.*

---

5. Labor permit or certification card.

'Sizwe Bansi. Endorsed to King William's Town . . .' Stamp goes in the third time . . . But this time it's also into a van and off to the Native Commissioner's Office; card around your neck with your number on it; escort on both sides and back to King William's Town. They make you pay for the train fare too!

MAN   I think I will try to look for some jobs in the garden.

BUNTU   You? Job as a garden-boy? Don't you read the newspapers?

MAN   I can't read.

BUNTU   I'll tell you what the little white ladies say: 'Domestic vacancies. I want a garden-boy with good manners and a wide knowledge of seasons and flowers. Book in order.' Yours in order? Anyway what the hell do you know about seasons and flowers? (*After a moment's thought.*) Do you know any white man who's prepared to give you a job?

MAN   No. I don't know any white man.

BUNTU   Pity. We might have been able to work something then. You talk to the white man, you see, and ask him to write a letter saying he's got a job for you. You take that letter from the white man and go back to King William's Town, where you show it to the Native Commissioner there. The Native Commissioner in King William's Town reads that letter from the white man in Port Elizabeth who is ready to give you the job. He then writes a letter back to the Native Commissioner in Port Elizabeth. So you come back here with the two letters. Then the Native Commissioner in Port Elizabeth reads the letter from the Native Commissioner in King William's Town together with the first letter from the white man who is prepared to give you a job, and he says when he reads the letters: Ah yes, this man Sizwe Bansi can get a job. So the Native Commissioner in Port Elizabeth then writes a letter which you take with the letters from the Native Commissioner in King William's Town and the white man in Port Elizabeth, to the Senior Officer at the Labour Bureau, who reads all the letters. Then he will put the right stamp in your book and give you another letter from himself which together with the letters from the white man and the two Native Affairs Commissioners, you take to the Administration Office here in New Brighton and make an application for Residence Permit, so that you don't fall victim of raids again. Simple.

MAN   Maybe I can start a little business selling potatoes and . . .

BUNTU   Where do you get the potatoes and . . . ?

MAN   I'll buy them.

BUNTU   With what?

MAN   Borrow some money . . .

BUNTU   Who is going to lend money to a somebody endorsed to hell and gone out in the bush? And how you going to buy your potatoes at the market without a Hawker's Licence? Same story, Sizwe. You won't get that because of the bloody stamp in your book.

There's no way out, Sizwe. You're not the first one who has tried to find it. Take my advice and catch that train back to King William's

Town. If you need work so bad go knock on the door of the Mines
Recruiting Office. Dig gold for the white man. That's the only time
they don't worry about Influx Control.

MAN   I don't want to work on the mines. There is no money there.
And it's dangerous, under the ground. Many black men get killed
when the rocks fall. You can die there.

BUNTU   (*stopped by the last remark into taking possibly his first real
look at Sizwe*) You don't want to die.

MAN   I don't want to die.

BUNTU   (*stops whatever he is doing to sit down and talk to Sizwe with
an intimacy that was not there before.*) You married, Sizwe?

MAN   Yes.

BUNTU   How many children?

MAN   I've got four children.

BUNTU   Boys? Girls?

MAN   I've got three boys and one girl.

BUNTU   Schooling?

MAN   Two are schooling. The other two stay at home with their
mother.

BUNTU   Your wife is not working.

MAN   The place where we stay is fifteen miles from town. There is
only one shop there. Baas van Wyk. He has already got a woman
working for him. King William's Town is a dry place Mr Buntu . . .
very small and too many people. That is why I don't want to go
back.

BUNTU   *Ag*, friend . . . I don't know! I'm also married. One child.

MAN   Only one?

BUNTU   *Ja*, my wife attends this Birth Control Clinic rubbish. The
child is staying with my mother.
(*Shaking his head.*) *Hai*, Sizwe! If I had to tell you the trouble I had
before I could get the right stamps in my book, even though I was
born in this area! The trouble I had before I could get a decent job
. . . born in this area! The trouble I had to get this two-roomed
house . . . born in this area!

MAN   Why is there so much trouble, Mr Buntu?

BUNTU   Two weeks back I went to a funeral with a friend of mine.
Out in the country. An old relative of his passed away. Usual thing
. . . sermons in the house, sermons in the church, sermons at the
graveside. I thought they were never going to stop talking!
At the graveside service there was one fellow, a lay preacher . . .
short man, neat little moustache, wearing one of those old-fashioned
double-breasted black suits . . . *Haai!* He was wonderful. While he
talked he had a gesture with his hands . . . like this . . . that reminded
me of our youth, when we learnt to fight with kieries. His text was
'Going Home'. He handled it well, Sizwe. Started by saying that the
first man to sign the Death Contract with God, was Adam, when he
sinned in Eden. Since that day, wherever Man is, or whatever he
does, he is never without his faithful companion, Death. So with

Outa Jacob . . . the dead man's name . . . he has at last accepted the terms of his contract with God.

But in his life, friends, he walked the roads of this land. He helped print those footpaths which lead through the bush and over the veld . . . footpaths which his children are now walking. He worked on farms from this district down to the coast and north as far as Pretoria. I knew him. He was a friend. Many people knew Outa Jacob. For a long time he worked for Baas van der Walt. But when the old man died his young son Hendrik said: 'I don't like you. Go!' Outa Jacob picked up his load and put it on his shoulders. His wife followed. He went to the next farm . . . through the fence, up to the house . . . : 'Work, please, Baas.' Baas Potgieter took him. He stayed a long time there too, until one day there was trouble between the Madam and his wife. Jacob and his wife were walking again. The load on his back was heavier, he wasn't so young any more, and there were children behind them now as well. On to the next farm. No work. The next one. No work. Then the next one. A little time there. But the drought was bad and the farmer said: 'Sorry, Jacob. The cattle are dying. I'm moving to the city.' Jacob picked up his load yet again. So it went, friends. On and on . . . until he arrived there. (*The grave at his feet.*) Now at last it's over. No matter how hard-arsed the boer on this farm wants to be, he cannot move Outa Jacob. He has reached Home.

> *Pause.*

That's it, brother. The only time we'll find peace is when they dig a hole for us and press our face into the earth.

> *Putting on his coat.*

Ag, to hell with it. If we go on like this much longer we'll do the digging for them.

> *Changing his tone.*

You know Sky's place, Sizwe?

MAN   No.

BUNTU   Come. Let me give you a treat. I'll do you there.

> *Exit Buntu.*
> *Blackout except for a light on Sizwe. He continues his letter to Nowetu.*

MAN   Sky's place? (*Shakes his head and laughs.*) Hey, Nowetu! When I mention that name again, I get a headache . . . the same headache I had when I woke up in Buntu's place the next morning. You won't believe what it was like. You cannot! It would be like you walking down Pickering Street in King William's Town and going into Koekemoer's Café to buy bread, and what do you see sitting there at the smart table and chairs? Your husband, Sizwe Bansi, being served ice-cream and cool drinks by old Mrs Koekemoer herself. Such would be your surprise if you had seen me at Sky's place. Only they weren't serving cool drinks and ice-cream. No! First-class booze, Nowetu. And it wasn't old Mrs Koekemoer serving me, but a certain lovely and beautiful lady called Miss Nkonyemi. And it wasn't just your husband Sizwe sitting there with all the most important people of New Brighton, but *Mister* Bansi.

> *He starts to laugh.*

Mister Bansi!

> *As the laugh gets bigger, Sizwe rises to his feet.*

> *The street outside Sky's Shebeen in New Brighton. Our man is amiably drunk. He addresses the audience.*

MAN   Do you know who I am, friend? Take my hand, friend. Take my hand. I am Mister Bansi, friend. Do you know where I come from? I come from Sky's place, friend. A most wonderful place. I met everybody there, good people. I've been drinking, my friends— brandy, wine, beer . . . Don't you want to go in there, good people? Let's all go to Sky's place. (*Shouting.*) Mr Buntu! Mr Buntu!

> *Buntu enters shouting goodbye to friends at the Shebeen. He joins Sizwe. Buntu, though not drunk, is also amiably talkative under the influence of a good few drinks.*

BUNTU   (*discovering the audience*)   Hey, where did you get all these wonderful people?
MAN   I just found them here, Mr Buntu.
BUNTU   Wonderful!
MAN   I'm inviting them to Sky's place, Mr Buntu.
BUNTU   You tell them about Sky's?
MAN   I told them about Sky's place, Mr Buntu.
BUNTU   (*to the audience*)   We been having a time there, man!
MAN   They know it. I told them everything.
BUNTU   (*laughing*)   Sizwe! We had our fun there.
MAN   Hey . . . hey . . .
BUNTU   Remember that Member of the Advisory Board?
MAN   Hey . . . Hey . . . Mr Buntu! You know I respect you, friend. You must call me nice.
BUNTU   What do you mean?
MAN   (*clumsy dignity*)   I'm not just Sizwe no more. He might have walked in, but Mr Bansi walked out!
BUNTU   (*playing along*)   I am terribly sorry, Mr Bansi. I apologize for my familiarity. Please don't be offended.

> *Handing over one of the two oranges he is carrying.*

Allow me . . . with the compliments of Miss Nkonyeni.
MAN   (*taking the orange with a broad but sheepish grin*)   Miss Nkonyeni!
BUNTU   Sweet dreams, Mr Bansi.

MAN (*tears the orange with his thumbs and starts eating it messily*) Lovely lady, Mr Buntu.

BUNTU (*leaves Sizwe with a laugh. To the audience*) Back there in the Shebeen a Member of the Advisory Board hears that he comes from King William's Town. He goes up to Sizwe. 'Tell me, Mr Bansi, what do you think of Ciskeian Independence?'[6]

MAN (*interrupting*) Ja, I remember that one. Bloody Mister Member of the Advisory Board. Talking about Ciskeian Independence!

To the audience.

I must tell you, friend . . . when a car passes or the wind blows up the dust, Ciskeian Independence makes you cough. I'm telling you, friend . . . put a man in a pondok[7] and call that Independence? My good friend, let me tell you . . . Ciskeian Independence is shit!

BUNTU Or that other chap! Old Jolobe. The fat tycoon man! (*To the audience*) Comes to me . . . (*pompous voice*) . . . 'Your friend, Mr Bansi, is he on an official visit to town?' 'No,' I said, 'Mr Bansi is on an official walkout!' (*Buntu thinks this is a big joke.*)

MAN (*stubbornly*) I'm here to stay.

BUNTU (*looking at his watch*) Hey, Sizwe . . .

MAN (*reproachfully*) Mr Buntu!

BUNTU (*correcting himself*) Mr Bansi, it is getting late. I've got to work tomorrow. Care to lead the way, Mr Bansi?

MAN You think I can't? You think Mr Bansi is lost?

BUNTU I didn't say that.

MAN You are thinking it, friend. I'll show you. This is Chinga Street.

BUNTU Very good! But which way do we . . . ?

MAN (*setting off*) This way.

BUNTU (*pulling him back*) Mistake. You're heading for Site and Service and a lot of trouble with the Tsotsis.

MAN (*the opposite direction*) That way.

BUNTU Lead on. I'm right behind you.

MAN Ja, you are right, Mr Buntu. There is Newell High School. Now . . .

BUNTU Think carefully!

MAN . . . when we were going to Sky's we had Newell in front. So when we leave Sky's we put Newell behind.

BUNTU Very good!

An appropriate change in direction. They continue walking, and eventually arrive at a square, with roads leading off in many directions. Sizwe is lost. He wanders around, uncertain of the direction to take.

MAN Haai, Mr Buntu . . . !

BUNTU Mbizweni Square.

---

6. An allusion to the Ciskei, one of the so-called free native states in apartheid South Africa, more properly known as "Bantustans."
7. Hut.

MAN   *Yo!* Cross-roads to hell, wait . . . (*Closer look at landmark.*) . . .
that building . . . Rio Cinema! So we must . . .

BUNTU   Rio Cinema? With a white cross on top, bell outside, and the
big show on Sundays?

MAN (*sheepishly*)   You're right, friend. I've got it, Mr Buntu. That way.

He starts off. Buntu watches him.

BUNTU   Goodbye. King William's Town a hundred and fifty miles.
Don't forget to write.

MAN (*hurried about-turn*)   Haai . . . haai . . .

BUNTU   Okay, Sizwe, I'll take over from here. But just hang on for a
second, I want to have a piss. Don't move!

Buntu disappears into the dark.

MAN   Haai, Sizwe! You are a country fool! Leading Mr Buntu and Mr
Bansi astray. You think you know this place New Brighton? You
know nothing!

Buntu comes running back.

BUNTU (*urgently*)   Let's get out of here.

MAN   Wait, Mr Buntu, I'm telling that fool Sizwe . . .

BUNTU   Come on! There's trouble there . . . (*pointing in the direction
from which he has come*) . . . let's move.

MAN   Wait, Mr Buntu, wait. Let me first tell that Sizwe . . .

BUNTU   There's a dead man lying there!

MAN   Dead man?

BUNTU   I thought I was just pissing on a pile of rubbish, but when I
looked carefully I saw it was a man. Dead. Covered in blood. Tsotsis
must have got him. Let's get the hell out of here before anybody
sees us.

MAN   Buntu . . . Buntu . . .

BUNTU   Listen to me, Sizwe! The Tsotsis might still be around.

MAN   Buntu . . .

BUNTU   Do you want to join him?

MAN   I don't want to join him.

BUNTU   Then come.

MAN   Wait, Buntu.

BUNTU   Jesus! If Zola had told me how much trouble you were going
to be!

MAN   Buntu, . . . we must report that man to the police station.

BUNTU   Police Station! Are you mad? You drunk, passbook not in order . . . 'We've come to report a dead man, Sergeant.' 'Grab them!'
Case closed. We killed him.

MAN   Mr Buntu, . . . we can't leave him . . .

BUNTU   Please, Sizwe!

MAN   Wait. Let's carry him home.

BUNTU   Just like that! Walk through New Brighton streets, at this
hour, carrying a dead man. Anyway we don't know where he stays.
Come.

MAN   Wait, Buntu, . . . listen . . .

BUNTU   Sizwe!

MAN   Buntu, we can know where he stays. That passbook of his will talk. It talks, friend, like mine. His passbook will tell you.

BUNTU   (*after a moment's desperate hesitation*)   You really want to land me in the shit, hey.

> *Disappears into the dark again.*

MAN   It will tell you in good English where he stays. My passbook talks good English too . . . big words that Sizwe can't read and doesn't understand. Sizwe wants to stay here in New Brighton and find a job; passbook says, 'No! Report back.'
Sizwe wants to feed his wife and children; passbook says, 'No. Endorsed out.'
Sizwe wants to . . .

> *Buntu reappears, a passbook in his hand. Looks around furtively and moves to the light under a lamp-post.*

They never told us it would be like that when they introduced it. They said: Book of Life! Your friend! You'll never get lost! They told us lies.

> *He joins Buntu who is examining the book.*

BUNTU   *Haai!* Look at him (*the photograph in the book, reading*). 'Robert Zwelinzima. Tribe: Xhosa. Native Identification Number . . .'

MAN   Where does he stay, Buntu?

BUNTU   (*paging through the book*)   Worked at Dorman Long seven years . . . Kilomet Engineering . . . eighteen months . . . Anderson Hardware two years . . . now unemployed. Hey, look, Sizwe! He's one up on you. He's got a work-seeker's permit.

MAN   Where does he stay, Buntu?

BUNTU   Lodger's Permit at 42 Mdala Street. From there to Sangocha Street . . . now at . . .

> *Pause. Closes the book abruptly.*

To hell with it I'm not going *there*.

MAN   Where, Buntu?

BUNTU   (*emphatically*)   I Am Not Going There!

MAN   Buntu . . .

BUNTU   You know where he is staying now? Single Men's Quarters! If you think I'm going there this time of the night you got another guess coming.

> *Sizwe doesn't understand.*

Look, Sizwe . . . I stay in a house, there's a street name and a number. Easy to find. Ask anybody . . . Mapija Street? That way. You know what Single Men's Quarters is? Big bloody concentration camp with rows of things that look like train carriages. Six doors to each! Twelve people behind each door! You want me to go there

now? Knock on the first one: 'Does Robert Zwelinzima live here?'
'No!' Next one: 'Does Robert . . . ?' 'Bugger off, we're trying to sleep!'
Next one: 'Does Robert Zwelinzima . . . ?' They'll fuck us up, man!
I'm putting this book back and we're going home.

MAN   Buntu!

BUNTU (*half-way back to the alleyway*)   What?

MAN   Would you do that to me, friend? If the Tsotsis had stabbed
Sizwe, and left him lying there, would you walk away from him as
well?

The accusation stops Buntu.

Would you leave me lying there, wet with your piss? I wish I was
dead. I wish I was dead because I don't care a damn about anything
any more.

Turning away from Buntu to the audience.

What's happening in this world, good people? Who cares for who in
this world? Who wants who?
Who wants me, friend? What's wrong with me? I'm a man. I've got
eyes to see. I've got ears to listen when people talk. I've got a head
to think good things. What's wrong with me?

Starts to tear off his clothes.

Look at me! I'm a man. I've got legs. I can run with a wheelbarrow
full of cement! I'm strong! I'm a man. Look! I've got a wife. I've got
four children. How many has he made, lady? (*The man sitting next
to her.*) Is he a man? What has he got that I haven't . . . ?

*A thoughtful Buntu rejoins them, the dead man's reference book
still in his hand.*

BUNTU   Let me see your book?

Sizwe doesn't respond.

Give me your book!

MAN   Are you a policeman now, Buntu?

BUNTU   Give me your bloody book, Sizwe!

MAN (*handing it over*)   Take it, Buntu. Take this book and read it
carefully, friend, and tell me what it says about me. Buntu, does
that book tell you I'm a man?

Buntu studies the two books. Sizwe turns back to the audience.

That bloody book . . . ! People, do you know? No! Wherever you go
. . . it's that bloody book. You go to school, it goes too. Go to work,
it goes too. Go to church and pray and sing lovely hymns, it sits
there with you. Go to hospital to die, it lies there too!

Buntu has collected Sizwe's discarded clothing.

BUNTU   Come!

Buntu's house, as earlier. Table and two chairs. Buntu pushes Sizwe down into a chair. Sizwe still muttering, starts to struggle back into his clothes. Buntu opens the two reference books and places them side by side on the table. He produces a pot of glue, then very carefully tears out the photograph in each book. A dab of glue on the back of each and then Sizwe's goes back into Robert's book, and Robert's into Sizwe's. Sizwe watches this operation, at first uninterestedly, but when he realizes what Buntu is up to, with growing alarm. When he is finished, Buntu pushes the two books in front of Sizwe.

MAN (*shaking his head emphatically*) Yo! *Haai, haai.* No, Buntu.

BUNTU It's a chance.

MAN *Haai, haai, haai . . .*

BUNTU It's your only chance!

MAN No, Buntu! What's it mean? That me, Sizwe Bansi . . .

BUNTU Is dead.

MAN I'm not dead, friend.

BUNTU We burn this book . . . (*Sizwe's original*) . . . and Sizwe Bansi disappears off the face of the earth.

MAN What about the man we left lying in the alleyway?

BUNTU Tomorrow the Flying Squad passes there and finds him. Check in his pockets . . . no passbook. Mount Road Mortuary. After three days nobody has identified him. Pauper's Burial. Case closed.

MAN And then?

BUNTU Tomorrow I contact my friend Norman at Feltex. He's a boss-boy there. I tell him about another friend, Robert Zwelinzima, book in order, who's looking for a job. You roll up later, hand over the book to the white man. Who does Robert Zwelinzima look like? You! Who gets the pay on Friday? You, man!

MAN What about all that shit at the Labour Bureau, Buntu?

BUNTU You don't have to go there. This chap had a work-seeker's permit, Sizwe. All you do is hand over the book to the white man. *He* checks at the Labour Bureau. They check with their big machine. 'Robert Zwelinzima has the right to be employed and stay in this town.'

MAN I don't want to lose my name, Buntu.

BUNTU You mean you don't want to lose your bloody passbook! You love it, hey?

MAN Buntu. I cannot lose my name.

BUNTU (*leaving the table*) All right, I was only trying to help. As Robert Zwelinzima you could have stayed and worked in this town. As Sizwe Bansi . . . ? Start walking, friend. King William's Town. Hundred and fifty miles. And don't waste any time! You've got to be there by yesterday. Hope you enjoy it.

MAN Buntu . . .

BUNTU Lots of scenery in a hundred and fifty miles.

MAN Buntu! . . .

BUNTU   Maybe a better idea is just to wait until they pick you up. Save yourself all that walking. Into the train with the escort! Smart stuff, hey. Hope it's not too crowded though. Hell of a lot of people being kicked out, I hear.

MAN   Buntu! . . .

BUNTU   But once you're back! Sit down on the side of the road next to your pondok with your family . . . the whole Bansi clan on leave . . . for life! Hey, that sounds okay. Watching all the cars passing, and as you say, friend, cough your bloody lungs out with Ciskeian Independence.

MAN (*now really desperate*)   Buntu!!!

BUNTU   What you waiting for? Go!

MAN   Buntu.

BUNTU   What?

MAN   What about my wife, Nowetu?

BUNTU   What about her?

MAN (*maudlin tears*)   Her loving husband, Sizwe Bansi, is dead!

BUNTU   So what! She's going to marry a better man.

MAN (*bridling*)   Who?

BUNTU   You . . . Robert Zwelinzima.

MAN (*thoroughly confused*)   How can I marry my wife, Buntu?

BUNTU   Get her down here and I'll introduce you.

MAN   Don't make jokes, Buntu. Robert . . . Sizwe . . . I'm all mixed up. Who am I?

BUNTU   A fool who is not taking his chance.

MAN   And my children! Their father is Sizwe Bansi. They're registered at school under Bansi . . .

BUNTU   Are you really worried about your children, friend, or are you just worried about yourself and your bloody name? Wake up, man! Use that book and with your pay on Friday you'll have a real chance to do something for them.

MAN   I'm afraid. How do I get used to Robert? How do I live as another man's ghost?

BUNTU   Wasn't Sizwe Bansi a ghost?

MAN   No!

BUNTU   No? When the white man looked at you at the Labour Bureau what did he see? A man with dignity or a bloody passbook with an N.I. number?[8] Isn't that a ghost? When the white man sees you walk down the street and calls out, 'Hey, John![9] Come here' . . . to you, *Sizwe Bansi* . . . isn't that a ghost? Or when his little child calls you 'Boy' . . . you a man, circumcised with a wife and four children . . . isn't that a ghost? Stop fooling yourself. All I'm saying is be a real ghost, if that is what they want, what they've turned us into. Spook them into hell, man!

8. Native Identification number in a person's passbook.
9. An allusion to the practice by whites in apartheid South Africa of using any name to hail a black man or woman.

Sizwe is silenced. Buntu realizes his words are beginning to reach the other man. He paces quietly, looking for his next move. He finds it.

Suppose you try my plan. Friday. Roughcasting section at Feltex. Paytime. Line of men—non-skilled labourers. White man with the big box full of pay-packets.

'John Kani!' 'Yes, sir!' Pay-packet is handed over. 'Thank you, sir.' Another one. (*Buntu reads the name on an imaginary pay-packet.*) 'Winston Ntshona!' 'Yes, sir!' Pay-packet over. 'Thank you, sir!' Another one. 'Fats Bhokolane!' '*Hier is ek, my baas!*' Pay-packet over. '*Dankie, my baas!*'

Another one. 'Robert Zwelinzima!'

No response from Sizwe.

'Robert Zwelinzima!'

MAN   Yes, sir.

BUNTU (*handing him the imaginary pay-packet*)   Open it. Go on.

Takes back the packet, tears it open, empties its contents on the table, and counts it.

Five . . . ten . . . eleven . . . twelve . . . and ninety-nine cents. In *your* pocket!

Buntu again paces quietly, leaving Sizwe to think. Eventually . . .

Saturday. Man in overalls, twelve rand ninety-nine cents in the back pocket, walking down Main Street looking for Sales House. Finds it and walks in. Salesman comes forward to meet him.

'I've come to buy a suit.' Salesman is very friendly.

'Certainly. Won't you take a seat. I'll get the forms. I'm sure you want to open an account, sir. Six months to pay. But first I'll need all your particulars.'

Buntu has turned the table, with Sizwe on the other side, into the imaginary scene at Sales House.

BUNTU (*pencil poised, ready to fill in a form*)   Your name, please, sir?

MAN (*playing along uncertainly*)   Robert Zwelinzima.

BUNTU (*writing*)   'Robert Zwelinzima.' Address?

MAN   Fifty, Mapija Street.

BUNTU   Where do you work?

MAN   Feltex.

BUNTU   And how much do you get paid?

MAN   Twelve . . . twelve rand ninety-nine cents.

BUNTU   N.I. number, please?

Sizwe hesitates.

Your Native Identity number please?

Sizwe is still uncertain. Buntu abandons the act and picks up Robert Zwelinzima's passbook. He reads out the number.

N—I—3—8—1—1—8—6—3.
Burn that into your head, friend. You hear me? It's more important than your name.
N.I. number . . . three . . .
MAN   Three.
BUNTU   Eight.
MAN   Eight.
BUNTU   One.
MAN   One.
BUNTU   One.
MAN   One.
BUNTU   Eight.
MAN   Eight.
BUNTU   Six.
MAN   Six.
BUNTU   Three.
MAN   Three.
BUNTU   Again. Three.
MAN   Three.
BUNTU   Eight.
MAN   Eight.
BUNTU   One.
MAN   One.
BUNTU   One.
MAN   One.
BUNTU   Eight.
MAN   Eight.
BUNTU   Six.
MAN   Six.
BUNTU   Three.
MAN   Three.
BUNTU   (*picking up his pencil and returning to the role of the salesman*)   N.I. number, please.
MAN   (*pausing frequently, using his hands to remember*)   Three . . . eight . . . one . . . one . . . eight . . . six . . . three . . .
BUNTU   (*abandoning the act*)   Good boy.

He paces. Sizwe sits and waits.

Sunday. Man in a Sales House suit, hat on top, going to church. Hymn book and bible under the arm. Sits down in the front pew. Priest in the pulpit.

Buntu jumps on to a chair in his new role. Sizwe kneels.

The Time has come!
MAN   Amen!
BUNTU   Pray, brothers and sisters . . . Pray . . . Now!

MAN Amen.

BUNTU The Lord wants to save you. Hand yourself over to him, while there is still time, while Jesus is still prepared to listen to you.

MAN (*carried away by what he is feeling*) Amen, Jesus!

BUNTU Be careful, my brothers and sisters . . .

MAN Hallelujah!

BUNTU Be careful lest when the big day comes and the pages of the big book are turned, it is found that your name is missing. Repent before it is too late.

MAN Hallelujah! Amen.

BUNTU Will all those who have not yet handed in their names for membership of our burial society please remain behind.

> *Buntu leaves the pulpit and walks around with a register.*

Name, please, sir? Number? Thank you.
Good afternoon, sister. Your name, please.
Address? Number? God bless you.

> *He has reached Sizwe.*

Your name, please, brother?

MAN Robert Zwelinzima.

BUNTU Address?

MAN Fifty, Mapija Street.

BUNTU N.I. number.

MAN (*again tremendous effort to remember*) Three . . . eight . . . one . . . one . . . eight . . . six . . . three . . .

> *They both relax.*

BUNTU (*after pacing for a few seconds*) Same man leaving the church . . . walking down the street.

> *Buntu acts out the role while Sizwe watches. He greets other members of the congregation.*

'God bless you, Brother Bansi. May you always stay within the Lord's mercy.'
'Greetings, Brother Bansi. We welcome you into the flock of Jesus with happy spirits.'
'God bless you, Brother Bansi. Stay with the Lord, the Devil is strong.'
Suddenly . . .

> *Buntu has moved to behind Sizwe. He grabs him roughly by the shoulder.*

Police!

> *Sizwe stands up frightened. Buntu watches him carefully.*

No, man! Clean your face.

Sizwe adopts an impassive expression. Buntu continues as the policeman.

What's your name?

MAN   Robert Zwelinzima.

BUNTU   Where do you work?

MAN   Feltex.

BUNTU   Book!

Sizwe hands over the book and waits while the policeman opens it, looks at the photograph, then Sizwe, and finally checks through its stamps and endorsements. While all this is going on Sizwe stands quietly, looking down at his feet, whistling under his breath. The book is finally handed back.

Okay.

Sizwe takes his book and sits down.

MAN   (*after a pause*)   I'll try it, Buntu.

BUNTU   Of course you must, if you want to stay alive.

MAN   Yes, but Sizwe Bansi is dead.

BUNTU   What about Robert Zwelinzima then? That poor bastard I pissed on out there in the dark. So *he's* alive again. Bloody miracle, man.

Look, if someone was to offer me the things I wanted most in my life, the things that would make me, my wife, and my child happy, in exchange for the name Buntu . . . you think I wouldn't swop?

MAN   Are you sure, Buntu?

BUNTU   (*examining the question seriously*)   If there was just me . . . I mean, if I was alone, if I didn't have anyone to worry about or look after except myself . . . maybe then I'd be prepared to pay some sort of price for a little pride. But if I had a wife and four children wasting away their one and only life in the dust and poverty of Ciskeian Independence . . . if I had four children waiting for me, their father, to do something about their lives . . . *ag*, no, Sizwe . . .

MAN   Robert, Buntu.

BUNTU   (*angry*)   All right! Robert, John, Athol, Winston . . . Shit on names, man! To hell with them if in exchange you can get a piece of bread for your stomach and a blanket in winter. Understand me, brother, I'm not saying that pride isn't a way for us. What I'm saying is shit on our pride if we only bluff ourselves that we are men.

Take your name back, Sizwe Bansi, if it's so important to you.

But next time you hear a white man say 'John' to you, don't say 'Ja, Baas?' And next time the bloody white man says to you, a man, 'Boy, come here,' don't run to him and lick his arse like we all do. Face him and tell him: 'White man. I'm a Man!' *Ag kak!* We're bluffing ourselves.

It's like my father's hat. Special hat, man! Carefully wrapped in plastic on top of the wardrobe in his room. God help the child who so much as touches it! Sunday it goes on his head, and a man, full of dignity, a man I respect, walks down the street. White man stops him: 'Come here, kaffir!' What does he do?

> *Buntu whips the imaginary hat off his head and crumples it in his hands as he adopts a fawning, servile pose in front of the white man.*

'What is it, Baas?'
If that is what you call pride, then shit on it! Take mine and give me food for my children.

> *Pause.*

Look, brother, Robert Zwelinzima, that poor bastard out there in the alleyway, if there *are* ghosts, he is smiling tonight. He is here, with us, and he's saying: 'Good luck, Sizwe! I hope it works.' He's a brother, man.

MAN For how long, Buntu?

BUNTU How long? For as long as you can stay out of trouble. Trouble will mean police station, then fingerprints off to Pretoria to check on previous convictions . . . and when they do that . . . Siswe Bansi will live again and you will have had it.

MAN Buntu, you know what you are saying? A black man stay out of trouble? Impossible, Buntu. Our skin is trouble.

BUNTU (*wearily*) You said you wanted to try.

MAN And I will.

BUNTU (*picks up his coat*) I'm tired, . . . Robert. Good luck. See you tomorrow.

> *Exit Buntu. Sizwe picks up the passbook, looks at it for a long time, then puts it in his back pocket. He finds his walking-stick, newspaper, and pipe and moves downstage into a solitary light. He finishes the letter to his wife.*

MAN So Nowetu, for the time being my troubles are over. Christmas I come home. In the meantime Buntu is working a plan to get me a Lodger's Permit. If I get it, you and the children can come here and spend some days with me in Port Elizabeth. Spend the money I am sending you carefully. If all goes well I will send some more each week. I do not forget you, my dear wife.

Your loving Husband,
Sizwe Bansi.

> *As he finishes the letter, Sizwe returns to the pose of the photo. Styles Photographic Studio. Styles is behind the camera.*

STYLES Hold it, Robert. Hold it just like that. Just one more. Now smile, Robert . . . Smile . . . Smile . . .

> *Camera flash and blackout.*

WOLE SOYINKA

Death and the King's Horseman[†]

Characters

PRAISE-SINGER
ELESIN, *Horseman of the King*
IYALOJA, *'Mother' of the market*
SIMON PILKINGS, *District Officer*
JANE PILKINGS, *his wife*
SERGEANT AMUSA
JOSEPH, *houseboy to the Pilkings*
BRIDE
H.R.H. THE PRINCE
THE RESIDENT
AIDE-DE-CAMP
OLUNDE, *eldest son of Elesin*
DRUMMERS, WOMEN, YOUNG GIRLS, DANCERS AT THE BALL

The play should run without an interval. For rapid scene changes, one adjustable outline set is very appropriate.

Scene One

A passage through a market in its closing stages. The stalls are being emptied, mats folded. A few women pass through on their way home, loaded with baskets. On a cloth-stand, bolts of cloth are taken down, display pieces folded and piled on a tray. Elesin Oba enters along a passage before the market, pursued by his drummers and praise-singers.[1] He is a man of enormous vitality, speaks, dances and sings with that infectious enjoyment of life which accompanies all his actions.

PRAISE-SINGER   Elesin o! Elesin Oba! Howu! What tryst is this the cockerel goes to keep with such haste that he must leave his tail behind?

---

† Wole Soyinka, *Death and the King's Horseman* (London: Methuen Drama, 1998). Copyright © 1975 by Wole Soyinka. Reprinted by permission of W. W. Norton and Melanie Jackson Agency, L.L.C.
1. Professional lyricists who compose and chant poems in honor of a great man or woman, for an important occasion.

ELESIN (*slows down a bit, laughing*) A tryst where the cockerel needs no adornment.

PRAISE-SINGER O-oh, you hear that my companions? That's the way the world goes. Because the man approaches a brand-new bride he forgets the long faithful mother of his children.

ELESIN When the horse sniffs the stable does he not strain at the bridle? The market is the long-suffering home of my spirit and the women are packing up to go. That Esu-harassed[2] day slipped into the stewpot while we feasted. We ate it up with the rest of the meat. I have neglected my women.

PRAISE-SINGER We know all that. Still it's no reason for shedding your tail on this day of all days. I know the women will cover you in damask and *alari*[3] but when the wind blows cold from behind, that's when the fowl knows his true friends.

ELESIN Olohun-iyo!

PRAISE-SINGER Are you sure there will be one like me on the other side?

ELESIN Olohun-iyo!

PRAISE-SINGER Far be it for me to belittle the dwellers of that place but, a man is either born to his art or he isn't. And I don't know for certain that you'll meet my father, so who is going to sing these deeds in accents that will pierce the deafness of the ancient ones. I have prepared my going—just tell me: Olohun-iyo, I need you on this journey and I shall be behind you.

ELESIN You're like a jealous wife. Stay close to me, but only on this side. My fame, my honour are legacies to the living, stay behind and let the world sip its honey from your lips.

PRAISE-SINGER Your name will be like the sweet berry a child places under his tongue to sweeten the passage of food. The world will never spit it out.

ELESIN Come then. This market is my roost. When I come among the women I am a chicken with a hundred mothers. I become a monarch whose palace is built with tenderness and beauty.

PRAISE-SINGER They love to spoil you but beware. The hands of women also weaken the unwary.

ELESIN This night I'll lay my head upon their lap and go to sleep. This night I'll touch feet with their feet in a dance that is no longer of this earth. But the smell of their flesh, their sweat, the smell of indigo on their cloth, this is the last air I wish to breathe as I go to meet my great forebears.

PRAISE-SINGER In their time the world was never tilted from its groove, it shall not be in yours.

ELESIN The gods have said No.

PRAISE-SINGER In their time the great wars came and went, the little wars came and went; the white slavers came and went, they took away the heart of our race, they bore away the mind and muscle of

---

2. Esu is the Yoruba god of chance and mischief, lord of crossroads and confuser of humans.
3. Highly valued, richly woven cloth.

our race. The city fell and was rebuilt; the city fell and our people trudged through mountain and forest to find a new home but— Elesin Oba do you hear me?

ELESIN   I hear your voice Olohun-iyo.

PRAISE-SINGER   Our world was never wrenched from its true course.

ELESIN   The gods have said No.

PRAISE-SINGER   There is only one home to the life of a river-mussel; there is only one home to the life of a tortoise; there is only one shell to the soul of man; there is only one world to the spirit of our race. If that world leaves its course and smashes on boulders of the great void, whose world will give us shelter?

ELESIN   It did not in the time of my forebears, it shall not in mine.

PRAISE-SINGER   The cockerel must not be seen without his feathers.

ELESIN   Nor will the Not-I bird be much longer without his nest.

PRAISE-SINGER (*stopped in his lyric stride*)   The Not-I bird, Elesin?

ELESIN   I said, the Not-I bird.

PRAISE-SINGER   All respect to our elders but, is there really such a bird?

ELESIN   What! Could it be that he failed to knock on your door?

PRAISE-SINGER (*smiling*)   Elesin's riddles are not merely the nut in the kernel that breaks human teeth; he also buries the kernel in hot embers and dares a man's fingers to draw it out.

ELESIN   I am sure he called on you, Olohun-iyo. Did you hide in the loft and push out the servant to tell him you were out?

> *Elesin executes a brief, half-taunting dance. The drummer moves in and draws a rhythm out of his steps. Elesin dances towards the marketplace as he chants the story of the Not-I bird, his voice changing dexterously to mimic his characters. He performs like a born raconteur, infecting his retinue with his humour and energy. More women arrive during his recital, including Iyaloja.*

ELESIN

Death came calling
Who does not know his rasp of reeds?
A twilight whisper in the leaves before
The great araba falls? Did you hear it?
Not I! swears the farmer. He snaps
His fingers round his head, abandons
A hard-worn harvest and begins
A rapid dialogue with his legs.

'Not I,' shouts the fearless hunter, 'but—
It's getting dark, and this night-lamp
Has leaked out all its oil. I think
It's best to go home and resume my hunt
Another day.' But now he pauses, suddenly
Let's out a wail: 'Oh foolish mouth, calling
Down a curse on your own head! Your lamp
Has leaked out all its oil, has it?'
Forwards or backwards now he dare not move.

To search for leaves and make *etutu*[4]
On that spot? Or race home to the safety
Of his hearth? Ten market-days have passed
My friends, and still he's rooted there
Rigid as the plinth of Orayan.

The mouth of the courtesan barely
Opened wide enough to take a ha'penny *robo*[5]
When she wailed: 'Not I.' All dressed she was
To call upon my friend the Chief Tax Officer.
But now she sends her go-between instead:
'Tell him I'm ill: my period has come suddenly
But not—I hope—my time.'

Why is the pupil crying?
His hapless head was made to taste
The knuckles of my friend the Mallam:[6]
'If you were then reciting the Koran
Would you have ears for idle noises
Darkening the trees, you child of ill omen?'
He shuts down school before its time
Runs home and rings himself with amulets.
And take my good kinsman Ifawomi.
His hands were like a carver's, strong
And true. I saw them
Tremble like wet wings of a fowl.
One day he cast his time-smoothed *opele*
Across the divination board. And all because
The suppliant looked him in the eye and asked,
'Did you hear that whisper in the leaves?'
'Not I,' was his reply; 'perhaps I'm growing deaf—
Good-day.' And Ifa spoke no more that day
The priest locked fast his doors,
Sealed up his leaking roof—but wait!
This sudden care was not for Fawomi
But for Osanyin, a courier-bird of Ifa's
Heart of wisdom. I did not know a kite
Was hovering in the sky
And Ifa now a twittering chicken in
The brood of Fawomi the Mother Hen.

Ah, but I must not forget my evening
Courier from the abundant palm, whose groan
Became Not I, as he constipated down
A wayside bush. He wonders if Elegbara[7]
Has tricked his buttocks to discharge
Against a sacred grove. Hear him
Mutter spells to ward off penalties

---

4. Ritual sacrifice placed at the crossroads to propitiate the powers that rule the universe.
5. Small, roundish fried bean cake, considered a delicacy.
6. Muslim title for one versed in the Koran; also "priest."
7. Another name for Esu.

For an abomination he did not intend.
If any here
Stumbles on a gourd of wine, fermenting
Near the road, and nearby hears a stream
Of spells issuing from a crouching form.
Brother to a *sigidi*,[8] bring home my wine,
Tell my tapper I have ejected
Fear from home and farm. Assure him,
All is well.

PRAISE-SINGER   In your time we do not doubt the peace of farmstead
and home, the peace of road and hearth, we do not doubt the peace
of the forest.

ELESIN

There was fear in the forest too.
Not-I was lately heard even in the lair
Of beasts. The hyena cackled loud. Not I,
The civet twitched his fiery tail and glared:
Not I. Not-I became the answering-name
Of the restless bird, that little one
Whom Death found nesting in the leaves
When whisper of his coming ran
Before him on the wind. Not-I
Has long abandoned home. This same dawn
I heard him twitter in the gods' abode.
Ah, companions of this living world
What a thing this is, that even those
We call immortal
Should fear to die.

IYALOJA

But you, husband of multitudes?

ELESIN

I, when that Not-I bird perched
Upon my roof, bade him seek his nest again.
Safe, without care or fear. I unrolled
My welcome mat for him to see. Not-I
Flew happily away, you'll hear his voice
No more in this lifetime—You all know
What I am.

PRAISE-SINGER

That rock which turns its open lodes
Into the path of lightning. A gay
Thoroughbred whose stride disdains
To falter though an adder reared
Suddenly in his path.

ELESIN

My rein is loosened.
I am master of my fate. When the hour comes
Watch me dance along the narrowing path

---

8. An incubus, a malevolent spirit, especially as incarnated in a carved figurine thought to be
invested with evil power.

Glazed by the soles of my great precursors.
My soul is eager. I shall not turn aside.

WOMEN

You will not delay?

ELESIN

Where the storm pleases, and when, it directs
The giants of the forest. When friendship summons
Is when the true comrade goes.

WOMEN

Nothing will hold you back?

ELESIN

Nothing. What! Has no one told you yet
I go to keep my friend and master company.
Who says the mouth does not believe in
'No, I have chewed all that before?' I say I have.
The world is not a constant honey-pot.
Where I found little I made do with little.
Where there was plenty I gorged myself.
My master's hands and mine have always
Dipped together and, home or sacred feast,
The bowl was beaten bronze, the meats
So succulent our teeth accused us of neglect.
We shared the choicest of the season's
Harvest of yams. How my friend would read
Desire in my eyes before I knew the cause—
However rare, however precious, it was mine.

WOMEN

The town, the very land was yours.

ELESIN

The world was mine. Our joint hands
Raised houseposts of trust that withstood
The siege of envy and the termites of time.
But the twilight hour brings bats and rodents—
Shall I yield them cause to foul the rafters?

PRAISE-SINGER

Elesin Oba! Are you not that man who
Looked out of doors that stormy day
The god of luck limped by, drenched
To the very lice that held
His rags together? You took pity upon
His sores and wished him fortune.
Fortune was footloose this dawn, he replied,
Till you trapped him in a heartfelt wish
That now returns to you. Elesin Oba!
I say you are that man who
Chanced upon the calabash of honour.
You thought it was palm wine and
Drained its contents to the final drop.

ELESIN

Life has an end. A life that will outlive
Fame and friendship begs another name.

What elder takes his tongue to his plate,
Licks it clean of every crumb? He will encounter
Silence when he calls on children to fulfil
The smallest errand! Life is honour.
It ends when honour ends.

WOMEN
We know you for a man of honour.

ELESIN   Stop! Enough of that!

WOMEN (*puzzled, they whisper among themselves, turning mostly to Iya-loja*) What is it? Did we say something to give offence? Have we slighted him in some way?

ELESIN   Enough of that sound I say. Let me hear no more in that vein. I've heard enough.

IYALOJA   We must have said something wrong. (*Comes forward a little.*) Elesin Oba, we ask forgiveness before you speak.

ELESIN   I am bitterly offended.

IYALOJA   Our unworthiness has betrayed us. All we can do is ask your forgiveness. Correct us like a kind father.

ELESIN   This day of all days . . .

IYALOJA   It does not bear thinking. If we offend you now we have mortified the gods. We offend heaven itself. Father of us all, tell us where we went astray. (*She kneels, the other women follow.*)

ELESIN
Are you not ashamed? Even a tear-veiled
Eye preserves its function of sight.
Because my mind was raised to horizons
Even the boldest man lowers his gaze
In thinking of, must my body here
Be taken for a vagrant's?

IYALOJA   Horseman of the King, I am more baffled than ever.

PRAISE-SINGER   The strictest father unbends his brow when the child is penitent, Elesin. When time is short, we do not spend it prolonging the riddle. Their shoulders are bowed with the weight of fear lest they have marred your day beyond repair. Speak now in plain words and let us pursue the ailment to the home of remedies.

ELESIN
Words are cheap. 'We know you for
A man of honour.' Well tell me, is this how
A man of honour should be seen?
Are these not the same clothes in which
I came among you a full half-hour ago?

He roars with laughter and the women, relieved, rise and rush into stalls to fetch rich clothes.

WOMEN   The gods are kind. A fault soon remedied is soon forgiven. Elesin Oba, even as we match our words with deed, let your heart forgive us completely.

ELESIN
>You who are breath and giver of my being
>How shall I dare refuse you forgiveness
>Even if the offence was real.

IYALOJA (*dancing round him. Sings*)
>He forgives us. He forgives us.
>What a fearful thing it is when
>The voyager sets forth
>But a curse remains behind.

WOMEN
>For a while we truly feared
>Our hands had wrenched the world adrift
>In emptiness.

IYALOJA
>Richly, richly, robe him richly
>The cloth of honour is *alari*
>*Sanyan*[9] is the band of friendship
>Boa-skin makes slippers of esteem.

WOMEN
>For a while we truly feared
>Our hands had wrenched the world adrift
>In emptiness.

PRAISE-SINGER
>He who must, must voyage forth
>The world will not roll backwards
>It is he who must, with one
>Great gesture overtake the world.

WOMEN
>For a while we truly feared
>Our hands had wrenched the world
>In emptiness.

PRAISE-SINGER
>The gourd you bear is not for shirking
>The gourd is not for setting down
>At the first crossroad or wayside grove
>Only one river may know its contents.

WOMEN
>We shall all meet at the great market
>We shall all meet at the great market
>He who goes early takes the best bargains
>But we shall meet, and resume our banter.

>*Elesin stands resplendent in rich clothes, cap, shawl, etc. His sash
>is of a bright red alari cloth. The women dance round him. Sud-
>denly, his attention is caught by an object off-stage.*

ELESIN
>The world I know is good.

WOMEN
>We know you'll leave it so.

9. Another variety of richly woven cloth.

ELESIN
>The world I know is the bounty
>Of hives after bees have swarmed.
>No goodness teems with such open hands
>Even in the dreams of deities.

WOMEN
>And we know you'll leave it so.

ELESIN
>I was born to keep it so. A hive
>Is never known to wander. An anthill
>Does not desert its roots. We cannot see
>The still great womb of the world—
>No man beholds his mother's womb—
>Yet who denies it's there? Coiled
>To the navel of the world is that
>Endless cord that links us all
>To the great origin. If I lose my way
>The trailing cord will bring me to the roots.

WOMEN
>The world is in your hands.

>*The earlier distraction, a beautiful young girl, comes along the*
>*passage through which Elesin first made his entry.*

ELESIN
>I embrace it. And let me tell you, women—
>I like this farewell that the world designed,
>Unless my eyes deceive me, unless
>We are already parted, the world and I,
>And all that breeds desire is lodged
>Among our tireless ancestors. Tell me friends,
>Am I still earthed in that beloved market
>Of my youth? Or could it be my will
>Has outleapt the conscious act and I have come
>Among the great departed?

PRAISE-SINGER   Elesin Oba why do your eyes roll like a bush-rat who
sees his fate like his father's spirit, mirrored in the eye of a snake?
And all those questions! You're standing on the same earth you've
always stood upon. This voice you hear is mine, Oluhun-iyo, not
that of an acolyte in heaven.

ELESIN
>How can that be? In all my life
>As Horseman of the King, the juiciest
>Fruit on every tree was mine. I saw,
>I touched, I wooed, rarely was the answer No.
>The honour of my place, the veneration I
>Received in the eye of man or woman
>Prospered my suit and
>Played havoc with my sleeping hours.
>And they tell me my eyes were a hawk
>In perpetual hunger. Split an iroko tree

  In two, hide a woman's beauty in its heartwood
  And seal it up again—Elesin, journeying by,
  Would make his camp beside that tree
  Of all the shades in the forest.

PRAISE-SINGER Who would deny your reputation, snake-on-the-loose
 in dark passages of the market! Bed-bug who wages war on the mat
 and receives the thanks of the vanquished! When caught with his
 bride's own sister he protested—but I was only prostrating myself
 to her as becomes a grateful in-law. Hunter who carries his powder-
 horn on the hips and fires crouching or standing! Warrior who never
 makes that excuse of the whining coward—but how can I go to
 battle without my trousers?—trouserless or shirtless it's all one to
 him. Oka-rearing-from-a-camouflage-of-leaves, before he strikes the
 victim is already prone! Once they told him, Howu,[1] a stallion does
 not feed on the grass beneath him: he replied, true, but surely he
 can roll on it!

WOMEN Ba-a-a-ba O!

PRAISE-SINGER Ah, but listen yet. You know there is the leaf-nibbling
 grub and there is the cola-chewing beetle; the leaf-nibbling grub
 lives on the leaf, the cola-chewing beetle lives in the colanut. Don't
 we know what our man feeds on when we find him cocooned in a
 woman's wrapper?

ELESIN

  Enough, enough, you all have cause
  To know me well. But, if you say this earth
  Is still the same as gave birth to those songs,
  Tell me who was that goddess through whose lips
  I saw the ivory pebbles of Oya's river-bed.
  Iyaloja, who is she? I saw her enter
  Your stall; all your daughters I know well.
  No, not even Ogun-of-the-farm toiling
  Dawn till dusk on his tuber patch
  Not even Ogun with the finest hoe he ever
  Forged at the anvil could have shaped
  That rise of buttocks, not though he had
  The richest earth between his fingers.
  Her wrapper was no disguise
  For thighs whose ripples shamed the river's
  Coils around the hills of Ilesi. Her eyes
  Were new-laid eggs glowing in the dark.
  Her skin . . .

IYALOJA Elesin Oba . . .

ELESIN What! Where do you all say I am?

IYALOJA Still among the living.

ELESIN

  And that radiance which so suddenly
  Lit up this market I could boast
  I knew so well?

---

1. Exclamation of surprise or disbelief.

IYALOJA Has one step already in her husband's home. She is betrothed.

ELESIN (*irritated*) Why do you tell me that?

Iyaloja falls silent. The women shuffle uneasily.

IYALOJA Not because we dare give you offence Elesin. Today is your
day and the whole world is yours. Still, even those who leave town
to make a new dwelling elsewhere like to be remembered by what
they leave behind.

ELESIN
Who does not seek to be remembered?
Memory is Master of Death, the chink
In his armour of conceit. I shall leave
That which makes my going the sheerest
Dream of an afternoon. Should voyagers
Not travel light? Let the considerate traveller
Shed, of his excessive load, all
That may benefit the living.

WOMEN (*relieved*) Ah Elesin Oba, we knew you for a man of honour.

ELESIN Then honour me. I deserve a bed of honour to lie upon.

IYALOJA The best is yours. We know you for a man of honour. You
are not one who eats and leaves nothing on his plate for children.
Did you not say it yourself? Not one who blights the happiness of
others for a moment's pleasure.

ELISIN
Who speaks of pleasure? O women, listen!
Pleasure palls. Our acts should have meaning.
The sap of the plantain never dries.
You have seen the young shoot swelling
Even as the parent stalk begins to wither.
Women, let my going be likened to
The twilight hour of the plantain.

WOMEN What does he mean Iyaloja? This language is the language
of our elders, we do not fully grasp it.

IYALOJA I dare not understand you yet Elesin.

ELESIN
All you who stand before the spirit that dares
The opening of the last door of passage,
Dare to rid my going of regrets! My wish
Transcends the blotting out of thought
In one mere moment's tremor of the senses.
Do me credit. And do me honour.
I am girded for the route beyond
Burdens of waste and longing.
Then let me travel light. Let
Seed that will not serve the stomach
On the way remain behind. Let it take root
In the earth of my choice, in this earth
I leave behind.

IYALOJA (*turns to women*) The voice I hear is already touched by the waiting fingers of our departed. I dare not refuse.

WOMAN But Iyaloja . . .

IYALOJA The matter is no longer in our hands.

WOMAN But she is betrothed to your own son. Tell him.

IYALOJA My son's wish is mine. I did the asking for him, the loss can be remedied. But who will remedy the blight of closed hands on the day when all should be openness and light? Tell him, you say! You wish that I burden him with knowledge that will sour his wish and lay regrets on the last moments of his mind. You pray to him who is your intercessor to the world—don't set this world adrift in your own time; would you rather it was my hand whose sacrilege wrenched it loose?

WOMAN Not many men will brave the curse of a dispossessed husband.

IYALOJA Only the curses of the departed are to be feared. The claims of one whose foot is on the threshold of their abode surpasses even the claims of blood. It is impiety even to place hindrances in their ways.

ELESIN
  What do my mothers say? Shall I step
  Burdened into the unknown?

IYALOJA Not we, but the very earth says No. The sap in the plantain does not dry. Let grain that will not feed the voyager at his passage drop here and take root as he steps beyond this earth and us. Oh you who fill the home from hearth to threshold with the voices of children, you who now bestride the hidden gulf and pause to draw the right foo. cross and into the resting-home of the great fore-bears, it is goo. at your loins be drained into the earth we know, that your last stre. h be ploughed back into the womb that gave you being.

PRAISE-SINGER Iyaloja, n. her of multitudes in the teeming market of the world, how your w. m transfigures you!

IYALOJA (*smiling broadly, comp. ly reconciled*) Elesin, even at the narrow end of the passage I kno ou will look back and sigh a last regret for the flesh that flashed pa. our spirit in flight. You always had a restless eye. Your choice has . blessing. (*To the women.*) Take the good news to our daughter a. make her ready. (*Some women go off.*)

ELESIN Your eyes were clouded at first.

IYALOJA Not for long. It is those who stand at the ะ way of the great change to whose cry we must pay heed. And then, nk of this—it makes the mind tremble. The fruit of such a union . are. It will be neither of this world nor of the next. Nor of the one hind us. As if the timelessness of the ancestor world and the unb. have joined spirits to wring an issue of the elusive being of passag . . Elesin!

ELESIN I am here. What is it?

IYALOJA Did you hear all I said just now?

ELESIN Yes.

IYALOJA The living must eat and drink. When the moment comes, don't turn the food to rodents' droppings in their mouth. Don't let them taste the ashes of the world when they step out at dawn to breathe the morning dew.

ELESIN This doubt is unworthy of you Iyaloja.

IYALOJA Eating the awusa nut is not so difficult as drinking water afterwards.[2]

ELESIN
  The waters of the bitter stream are honey to a man
  Whose tongue has savoured all.

IYALOJA No one knows when the ants desert their home; they leave the mound intact. The swallow is never seen to peck holes in its nest when it is time to move with the season. There are always throngs of humanity behind the leave-taker. The rain should not come through the roof for them, the wind must not blow through the walls at night.

ELESIN I refuse to take offence.

IYALOJA You wish to travel light. Well, the earth is yours. But be sure the seed you leave in it attracts no curse.

ELESIN You really mistake my person Iyaloja.

IYALOJA I said nothing. Now we must go prepare your bridal chamber. Then these same hands will lay your shrouds.

ELESIN (exasperated) Must you be so blunt? (Recovers.) Well, weave your shrouds, but let the fingers of my bride seal my eyelids with earth and wash my body.

IYALOJA Prepare yourself Elesin.

> She gets up to leave. At that moment the women return, leading the bride. Elesin's face glows with pleasure. He flicks the sleeves of his agbada with renewed confidence and steps forward to meet the group. As the girl kneels before Iyaloja, lights fade out on the scene.

Scene Two

> The verandah of the District Officer's bungalow. A tango is playing from an old hand-cranked gramophone and, glimpsed through the wide windows and doors which open onto the fore-stage verandah, are the shapes of Simon Pilkings and his wife, Jane, tangoing in and out of shadows in the living-room. They are wearing what is immediately apparent as some form of fancy-dress. The dance goes on for some moments and then the figure of a 'Native Administration' policeman emerges and climbs up the steps onto the verandah. He peeps through and observes the dancing couple, reacting with what is obviously a long-standing

---

2. Water typically tastes bitter after one has eaten the awusa, a West African nut.

*bewilderment. He stiffens suddenly, his expression changes to one
of disbelief and horror. In his excitement he upsets a flower-pot
and attracts the attention of the couple. They stop dancing.*

PILKINGS   Is there anyone out there?

JANE   I'll turn off the gramophone.

PILKINGS (*approaching the verandah*)   I'm sure I heard something fall
over. (*The constable retreats slowly, open-mouthed as Pilkings approaches the verandah.*) Oh it's you Amusa. Why didn't you just
knock instead of knocking things over?

AMUSA (*stammers badly and points a shaky finger at his dress*)   Mista
Pirinkin . . . Mista Pirinkin . . .

PILKINGS   What is the matter with you?

JANE (*emerging*)   Who is it dear? Oh, Amusa . . .

PILKINGS   Yes it's Amusa, and acting most strangely.

AMUSA (*his attention now transferred to Jane Pilkings*)   Mammadam
. . . you too!

PILKINGS   What the hell is the matter with you man!

JANE   Your costume darling. Our fancy-dress.

PILKINGS   Oh hell, I'd forgotten all about that. (*Lifts the face mask
over his head showing his face. His wife follows suit.*)

JANE   I think you've shocked his big pagan heart bless him.

PILKINGS   Nonsense, he's a Moslem. Come on Amusa, you don't believe in all that nonsense do you? I thought you were a good
Moslem.

AMUSA   Mista Pirinkin, I beg you sir, what you think you do with that
dress? It belong to dead cult, not for human being.

PILKINGS   Oh Amusa, what a let-down you are. I swear by you at the
club you know—thank God for Amusa, he doesn't believe in any
mumbo-jumbo. And now look at you!

AMUSA   Mista Pirinkin, I beg you, take ᵒff. Is not good for man like
you to touch that cloth.

PILKINGS   Well, I've got it on. And what's nᵉ ᵕ Jane and I have bet
on it we're taking first prize at the ball. Now, ᵒ you can just pull
yourself together and tell me what you wanted to ᵕ me about . . .

AMUSA   Sir, I cannot talk this matter to you in that drᵉ ᵕ I no fit.

PILKINGS   What's that rubbish again?

JANE   He is dead earnest too Simon. I think you'll have to haᵢ. ᵕ this
delicately.

PILKINGS   Delicately my . . . ! Look here Amusa, I think this little joᵢ.
has gone far enough hm? Let's have some sense. You seem to forget
that you are a police officer in the service of His Majesty's Government. I order you to report your business at once or face disciplinary
action.

AMUSA   Sir, it is a matter of death. How can man talk against death
to person in uniform of death? Is like talking against government to
person in uniform of police. Please sir, I go and come back.

PILKINGS (*roars*)   Now!

Amusa switches his gaze to the ceiling suddenly, remains mute.

JANE   Oh Amusa, what is there to be scared of in the costume? You
saw it confiscated last month from those *egungun*[3] men who were
creating trouble in town. You helped arrest the cult leaders yourself—if the juju[4] didn't harm you at the time how could it possibly
harm you now? And merely by looking at it?

AMUSA (*without looking down*)   Madam, I arrest the ringleaders who
make trouble but me I no touch *egungun*. That *egungun* itself, I no
touch. And I no abuse 'am. I arrest ringleader but I treat *egungun*
with respect.

PILKINGS   It's hopeless. We'll merely end up missing the best part of
the ball. When they get this way there is nothing you can do. It's
simply hammering against a brick wall. Write your report or whatever it is on that pad Amusa and take yourself out of here. Come
on Jane. We only upset his delicate sensibilities by remaining here.

> *Amusa waits for them to leave, then writes in the notebook, some-
> what laboriously. Drumming from the direction of the town wells
> up. Amusa listens, makes a movement as if he wants to recall
> Pilkings but changes his mind. Completes his note and goes. A
> few moments later Pilkings emerges, picks up the pad and reads.*

PILKINGS   Jane!

JANE   (*from the bedroom*)   Coming darling. Nearly ready.

PILKINGS   Never mind being ready, just listen to this.

JANE   What is it?

PILKINGS   Amusa's report. Listen. 'I have to report that it come to my
information that one prominent chief, namely, the Elesin Oba, is to
commit death tonight as a result of native custom. Because this is
criminal offence I await further instruction at charge office. Sergeant Amusa.'

> *Jane comes out onto the verandah while he is reading.*

JANE   Did I hear you say commit death?

PILKINGS   Obviously he means murder.

JANE   You mean a ritual murder?

PILKINGS   Must be. You think you've stamped it all out but it's always
lurking under the surface somewhere.

JANE   Oh. Does it mean we are not getting to the ball at all?

PILKINGS   No-o. I'll have the man arrested. Everyone remotely involved. In any case there may be nothing to it. Just rumours.

JANE   Really? I thought you found Amusa's rumours generally reliable.

PILKINGS   That's true enough. But who knows what may have been
giving him the scare lately. Look at his conduct tonight.

JANE   (*laughing*)   You have to admit he had his own peculiar logic.
(*Deepens her voice.*) How can man talk against death to person in

---

3. Traditionally an ancestral funerary masquerade, but generically applied to all masquerades,
   sacred or for pure entertainment.
4. A fetish with magical powers to harm one's enemies or adversaries.

uniform of death? (*Laughs.*) Anyway, you can't go into the police
station dressed like that.

PILKINGS   I'll send Joseph with instructions. Damn it, what a con-
founded nuisance!

JANE   But don't you think you should talk first to the man, Simon?

PILKINGS   Do you want to go to the ball or not?

JANE   Darling, why are you getting rattled? I was only trying to be
intelligent. It seems hardly fair just to lock up a man—and a chief
at that—simply on the er . . . what is the legal word again?—un-
corroborated word of a sergeant.

PILKINGS   Well, that's easily decided. Joseph!

JOSEPH (*from within*)   Yes master.

PILKINGS   You're quite right of course, I am getting rattled. Probably
the effect of those bloody drums. Do you hear how they go on and
on?

JANE   I wondered when you'd notice. Do you suppose it has something
to do with this affair?

PILKINGS   Who knows? They always find an excuse for making a noise
. . . (*Thoughtfully.*) Even so . . .

JANE   Yes Simon?

PILKINGS   It's different Jane. I don't think I've heard this particular—
sound—before. Something unsettling about it.

JANE   I thought all bush drumming sounded the same.

PILKINGS   Don't tease me now Jane. This may be serious.

JANE   I'm sorry. (*Gets up and throws her arms around his neck. Kisses
him. The houseboy enters, retreats and knocks.*)

PILKINGS (*wearily*)   Oh, come in Joseph! I don't know where you pick
up all these elephantine notions of tact. Come over here.

JOSEPH   Sir?

PILKINGS   Joseph, are you a Christian or not?

JOSEPH   Yessir.

PILKINGS   Does seeing me in this outfit bother you?

JOSEPH   No sir, it has no power.

PILKINGS   Thank God for some sanity at last. Now Joseph, answer me
on the honour of a Christian—what is supposed to be going on in
town tonight?

JOSEPH   Tonight sir? You mean the chief who is going to kill himself?

PILKINGS   What?

JANE   What do you mean, kill himself?

PILKINGS   You do mean he is going to kill somebody don't you?

JOSEPH   No master. He will not kill anybody and no one will kill him.
He will simply die.

JANE   But why Joseph?

JOSEPH   It is native law and custom. The King die last month. Tonight
is his burial. But before they can bury him, the Elesin must die so
as to accompany him to heaven.

PILKINGS   I seem to be fated to clash more often with that man than
with any of the other chiefs.

JOSEPH He is the King's Chief Horseman.

PILKINGS (*in a resigned way*) I know.

JANE Simon, what's the matter?

PILKINGS It would have to be him!

JANE Who is he?

PILKINGS Don't you remember? He's that chief with whom I had a scrap some three or four years ago. I helped his son get to a medical school in England, remember? He fought tooth and nail to prevent it.

JANE Oh now I remember. He was that very sensitive young man. What was his name again?

PILKINGS Olunde. Haven't replied to his last letter come to think of it. The old pagan wanted him to stay and carry on some family tradition or the other. Honestly I couldn't understand the fuss he made. I literally had to help the boy escape from close confinement and load him onto the next boat. A most intelligent boy, really bright.

JANE I rather thought he was much too sensitive you know. The kind of person you feel should be a poet munching rose petals in Bloomsbury.

PILKINGS Well, he's going to make a first-class doctor. His mind is set on that. And as long as he wants my help he is welcome to it.

JANE (*after a pause*) Simon.

PILKINGS Yes?

JANE This boy, he was the eldest son wasn't he?

PILKINGS I'm not sure. Who could tell with that old ram?

JANE Do you know, Joseph?

JOSEPH Oh yes madam. He was the eldest son. That's why Elesin cursed master good and proper. The eldest son is not supposed to travel away from the land.

JANE (*giggling*) Is that true Simon? Did he really curse you good and proper?

PILKINGS By all accounts I should be dead by now.

JOSEPH Oh no, master is white man. And good Christian. Black man juju can't touch master.

JANE If he was his eldest, it means that he would be the Elesin to the next king. It's a family thing isn't it Joseph?

JOSEPH Yes madam. And if this Elesin had died before the King, his eldest son must take his place.

JANE That would explain why the old chief was so mad you took the boy away.

PILKINGS Well it makes me all the more happy I did.

JANE I wonder if he knew.

PILKINGS Who? Oh, you mean Olunde?

JANE Yes. Was that why he was so determined to get away? I wouldn't stay if I knew I was trapped in such a horrible custom.

PILKINGS (*thoughtfully*) No, I don't think he knew. At least he gave no indication. But you couldn't really tell with him. He was rather close you know, quite unlike most of them. Didn't give much away, not even to me.

JANE   Aren't they all rather close, Simon?

PILKINGS   These natives here? Good gracious. They'll open their mouths and yap with you about their family secrets before you can stop them. Only the other day . . .

JANE   But Simon, do they really give anything away? I mean, anything that really counts. This affair for instance, we didn't know they still practised that custom did we?

PILKINGS   Ye-e-es, I suppose you're right there. Sly, devious bastards.

JOSEPH (*stiffly*)   Can I go now master? I have to clean the kitchen.

PILKINGS   What? Oh, you can go. Forgot you were still there.

Joseph goes.

JANE   Simon, you really must watch your language. Bastard isn't just a simple swear-word in these parts, you know.

PILKINGS   Look, just when did you become a social anthropologist, that's what I'd like to know.

JANE   I'm not claiming to know anything. I just happen to have over-heard quarrels among the servants. That's how I know they consider it a smear.

PILKINGS   I thought the extended family system took care of all that. Elastic family, no bastards.

JANE (*shrugs*)   Have it your own way.

Awkward silence. The drumming increases in volume. Jane gets up suddenly, restless.

That drumming Simon, do you think it might really be connected with this ritual? It's been going on all evening.

PILKINGS   Let's ask our native guide. Joseph! Just a minute Joseph. (*Joseph re-enters.*) What's the drumming about?

JOSEPH   I don't know master.

PILKINGS   What do you mean you don't know? It's only two years since your conversion. Don't tell me all that holy water nonsense also wiped out your tribal memory.

JOSEPH (*visibly shocked*)   Master!

JANE   Now you've done it.

PILKINGS   What have I done now?

JANE   Never mind. Listen Joseph, just tell me this. Is that drumming connected with dying or anything of that nature?

JOSEPH   Madam, this is what I am trying to say: I am not sure. It sounds like the death of a great chief and then, it sounds like the wedding of a great chief. It really mix me up.

PILKINGS   Oh get back to the kitchen. A fat lot of help you are.

JOSEPH   Yes master. (*Goes.*)

JANE   Simon . . .

PILKINGS   All right, all right. I'm in no mood for preaching.

JANE   It isn't my preaching you have to worry about, it's the preaching of the missionaries who preceded you here. When they make con-verts they really convert them. Calling holy water nonsense to our Joseph is really like insulting the Virgin Mary before a Roman Catholic. He's going to hand in his notice tomorrow you mark my word.

PILKINGS   Now you're being ridiculous.

JANE   Am I? What are you willing to bet that tomorrow we are going to be without a steward-boy? Did you see his face?

PILKINGS   I am more concerned about whether or not we will be one native chief short by tomorrow. Christ! Just listen to those drums. (*He strides up and down, undecided.*)

JANE (*getting up*)   I'll change and make us some supper.

PILKINGS   What's that?

JANE   Simon, it's obvious we have to miss this ball.

PILKINGS   Nonsense. It's the first bit of real fun the European club has managed to organise for over a year, I'm damned if I'm going to miss it. And it is a rather special occasion. Doesn't happen every day.

JANE   You know this business has to be stopped Simon. And you are the only man who can do it.

PILKINGS   I don't have to stop anything. If they want to throw themselves off the top of a cliff or poison themselves for the sake of some barbaric custom what is that to me? If it were ritual murder or something like that I'd be duty-bound to do something. I can't keep an eye on all the potential suicides in this province. And as for that man—believe me it's good riddance.

JANE (*laughs*)   I know you better than that Simon. You are going to have to do something to stop it—after you've finished blustering.

PILKINGS (*shouts after her*)   And suppose after all it's only a wedding? I'd look a proper fool if I interrupted a chief on his honeymoon, wouldn't I? (*Resumes his angry stride, slows down.*) Ah well, who can tell what those chiefs actually do on their honeymoon anyway? (*He takes up the pad and scribbles rapidly on it.*) Joseph! Joseph! Joseph! (*Some moments later Joseph puts in a sulky appearance.*) Did you hear me call you? Why the hell didn't you answer?

JOSEPH   I didn't hear master.

PILKINGS   You didn't hear me! How come you are here then?

JOSEPH (*stubbornly*)   I didn't hear master.

PILKINGS (*controls himself with an effort*)   We'll talk about it in the morning. I want you to take this note directly to Sergeant Amusa. You'll find him at the charge office. Get on your bicycle and race there with it. I expect you back in twenty minutes exactly. Twenty minutes, is that clear?

JOSEPH   Yes master (*Going.*)

PILKINGS   Oh er . . . Joseph.

JOSEPH   Yes master?

PILKINGS (*between gritted teeth*)   Er . . . forget what I said just now. The holy water is not nonsense. *I* was talking nonsense.

JOSEPH   Yes master. (*Goes.*)

JANE (*pokes her head round the door*)   Have you found him?

PILKINGS   Found who?

JANE   Joseph. Weren't you shouting for him?

PILKINGS   Oh yes, he turned up finally.

JANE   You sounded desperate. What was it all about?

PILKINGS   Oh nothing. I just wanted to apologise to him. Assure him that the holy water isn't really nonsense.

JANE   Oh? And how did he take it?

PILKINGS   Who the hell gives a damn! I had a sudden vision of our Very Reverend Macfarlane drafting another letter of complaint to the Resident about my unchristian language towards his parishioners.

JANE   Oh I think he's given up on you by now.

PILKINGS   Don't be too sure. And anyway, I wanted to make sure Joseph didn't 'lose' my note on the way. He looked sufficiently full of the holy crusade to do some such thing.

JANE   If you've finished exaggerating, come and have something to eat.

PILKINGS   No, put it all away. We can still get to the ball.

JANE   Simon . . .

PILKINGS   Get your costume back on. Nothing to worry about. I've instructed Amusa to arrest the man and lock him up.

JANE   But that station is hardly secure Simon. He'll soon get his friends to help him escape.

PILKINGS   A-ah, that's where I have out-thought you. I'm not having him put in the station cell. Amusa will bring him right here and lock him up in my study. And he'll stay with him till we get back. No one will dare come here to incite him to anything.

JANE   How clever of you darling. I'll get ready.

PILKINGS   Hey.

JANE   Yes darling.

PILKINGS   I have a surprise for you. I was going to keep it until we actually got to the ball.

JANE   What is it?

PILKINGS   You know the Prince is on a tour of the colonies don't you? Well, he docked in the capital only this morning but he is already at the Residency. He is going to grace the ball with his presence later tonight.

JANE   Simon! Not really.

PILKINGS   Yes he is. He's been invited to give away the prizes and he has agreed. You must admit old Engleton is the best Club Secretary we ever had. Quick off the mark that lad.

JANE   But how thrilling.

PILKINGS   The other provincials are going to be damned envious.

JANE   I wonder what he'll come as.

PILKINGS   Oh I don't know. As a coat-of-arms perhaps. Anyway it won't be anything to touch this.

JANE   Well that's lucky. If we are to be presented I won't have to start looking for a pair of gloves. It's all sewn on.

PILKINGS   (laughing) Quite right. Trust a woman to think of that. Come on, let's get going.

JANE   (rushing off) Won't be a second. (Stops.) Now I see why you've been so edgy all evening. I thought you weren't handling this affair with your usual brilliance—to begin with that is.

PILKINGS (*his mood is much improved*)   Shut up woman and get your things on.

JANE   All right boss, coming.

> *Pilkings suddenly begins to hum the tango to which they were dancing before. Starts to execute a few practice steps. Lights fade.*

Scene Three

> *A swelling, agitated hum of women's voices rises immediately in the background. The lights come on and we see the frontage of a converted cloth stall in the market. The floor leading up to the entrance is covered in rich velvets and woven cloth. The women come on stage, borne backwards by the determined progress of Sergeant Amusa and his two constables who already have their batons out and use them as a pressure against the women. At the edge of the cloth-covered floor, however, the women take a determined stand and block all further progress of the men. They begin to tease them mercilessly.*

AMUSA   I am tell you women for last time to commot[5] my road. I am here on official business.

WOMAN   Official business you white man's eunuch? Official business is taking place where you want to go and it's a business you wouldn't understand.

WOMAN (*makes a quick tug at the constable's baton*)   That doesn't fool anyone you know. It's the one you carry under your government knickers that counts. (*She bends low as if to peep under the baggy shorts. The embarrassed constable quickly puts his knees together. The women roar.*)

WOMAN   You mean there is nothing there at all?

WOMAN   Oh there was something. You know that handbell which the white man uses to summon his servants . . . ?

AMUSA (*he manages to preserve some dignity throughout*)   I hope you women know that interfering with officer in execution of his duty is criminal offence.

WOMAN   Interfere? He says we're interfering with him. You foolish man we're telling you there's nothing to interfere with.

AMUSA   I am order you now to clear the road.

WOMAN   What road? The one your father built?

WOMAN   You are a policeman not so? Then you know what they call trespassing in court. Or—(*Pointing to the cloth-lined steps.*)—do you think that kind of road is built for every kind of feet.

WOMAN   Go back and tell the white man who sent you to come himself.

AMUSA   If I go I will come back with reinforcement. And we will all return carrying weapons.

---

5. Pidgin English corruption of "come out of," meaning "scram," "get lost."

WOMAN   Oh, now I understand. Before they can put on those knickers the white man first cuts off their weapons.

WOMAN   What a cheek! You mean you come here to show power to women and you don't even have a weapon.

AMUSA (*shouting above the laughter*)   For the last time I warn you women to clear the road.

WOMAN   To where?

AMUSA   To that hut. I know he dey dere.

WOMAN   Who?

AMUSA   The chief who call himself Elesin Oba.

WOMAN   You ignorant man. It is not he who calls himself Elesin Oba, it is his blood that says it. As it called out to his father before him and will to his son after him. And that is in spite of everything your white man can do.

WOMAN   Is it not the same ocean that washes this land and the white man's land? Tell your white man he can hide our son away as long as he likes. When the time comes for him, the same ocean will bring him back.

AMUSA   The government say dat kin' ting must stop.

WOMAN   Who will stop it? You? Tonight our husband and father will prove himself greater than the laws of strangers.

AMUSA   I tell you nobody go prove anyting tonight or anytime. Is ignorant and criminal to prove dat kin' prove.

IYALOJA (*entering from the hut. She is accompanied by a group of young girls who have been attending the bride*)   What is it Amusa? Why do you come here to disturb the happiness of others.

AMUSA   Madame Iyaloja, I glad you come. You know me, I no like trouble but duty is duty. I am here to arrest Elesin for criminal intent. Tell these women to stop obstructing me in the performance of my duty.

IYALOJA   And you? What gives you the right to obstruct our leader of men in the performance of his duty?

AMUSA   What kin' duty be dat one Iyaloja.

IYALOJA   What kin' duty? What kin' duty does a man have to his new bride?

AMUSA (*bewildered, looks at the women and at the entrance to the hut*)   Iyaloja, is it wedding you call dis kin' ting?

IYALOJA   You have wives haven't you? Whatever the white man has done to you he hasn't stopped you having wives. And if he has, at least he is married. If you don't know what a marriage is, go and ask him to tell you.

AMUSA   This no to wedding.

IYALOJA   And ask him at the same time what he would have done if anyone had come to disturb him on his wedding night.

AMUSA   Iyaloja, I say dis no to wedding.

IYALOJA   You want to look inside the bridal chamber? You want to see for yourself how a man cuts the virgin knot?

AMUSA   Madam . . .

WOMAN   Perhaps his wives are still waiting for him to learn.

AMUSA   Iyaloja, make you tell dese women make den no insult me again. If I hear dat kin' insult once more . . .

GIRL   (*pushing her way through*)   You will do what?

GIRL   He's out of his mind. It's our mothers you're talking to, do you know that? Not to any illiterate villager you can bully and terrorise. How dare you intrude here anyway?

GIRL   What a cheek, what impertinence!

GIRL   You've treated them too gently. Now let them see what it is to tamper with the mothers of this market.

GIRL   Your betters dare not enter the market when the women say no!

GIRL   Haven't you learnt that yet, you jester in khaki and starch?

IYALOJA   Daughters . . .

GIRL   No no Iyaloja, leave us to deal with him. He no longer knows his mother, we'll teach him.

> *With a sudden movement they snatch the batons of the two constables. They begin to hem them in.*

GIRL   What next? We have your batons? What next? What are you going to do?

> *With equally swift movements they knock off their hats.*

GIRL   Move if you dare. We have your hats, what will you do about it? Didn't the white man teach you to take off your hats before women?

IYALOJA   It's a wedding night. It's a night of joy for us. Peace . . .

GIRL   Not for him. Who asked him here?

GIRL   Does he dare go to the Residency without an invitation?

GIRL   Not even where the servants eat the left-overs.

GIRL   (*in turn. In an 'English' accent*)   Well well it's Mister Amusa. Were you invited? (*Play-acting to one another. The older women encourage them with their titters.*)
—Your invitation card please?
—Who are you? Have we been introduced?
—And who did you say you were?
—Sorry, I didn't quite catch your name.
—May I take your hat?
—If you insist. May I take yours? (*Exchanging the policemen's hats.*)
—How very kind of you.
—Not at all. Won't you sit down?
—After you.
—Oh no.
—I insist.
—You're most gracious.
—And how do you find the place?
—The natives are all right.
—Friendly?

—Tractable.

—Not a teeny-weeny bit restless?

—Well, a teeny-weeny bit restless.

—One might even say, difficult?

—Indeed one might be tempted to say, difficult.

—But you do manage to cope?

—Yes indeed I do. I have a rather faithful ox called Amusa.

—He's loyal?

—Absolutely.

—Lay down his life for you what?

—Without a moment's thought.

—Had one like that once. Trust him with my life.

—Mostly of course they are liars.

—Never known a native to tell the truth.

—Does it get rather close around here?

—It's mild for this time of the year.

—But the rains may still come.

—They are late this year aren't they?

—They are keeping African time.

—Ha ha ha ha.

—Ha ha ha ha.

—The humidity is what gets me.

—It used to be whisky.

—Ha ha ha ha.

—Ha ha ha ha.

—What's your handicap old chap?

—Is there racing by golly?

—Splendid golf course, you'll like it.

—I'm beginning to like it already.

—And a European club, exclusive.

—You've kept the flag flying.

—We do our best for the old country.

—It's a pleasure to serve.

—Another whisky old chap?

—You are indeed too too kind.

—Not at all sir. Where is that boy? (*With a sudden bellow.*) Sergeant!

AMUSA (*snaps to attention*)   Yessir!

> *The women collapse with laughter.*

GIRL   Take your men out of here.

AMUSA (*realising the trick, he rages from loss of face*)   I'm give you warning . . .

GIRL   All right then. Off with his knickers! (*They surge slowly forward.*)

IYALOJA   Daughters, please.

AMUSA (*squaring himself for defence*)   The first woman wey touch me . . .

IYALOJA   My children, I beg of you . . .

GIRL   Then tell him to leave this market. This is the home of our
mothers. We don't want the eater of white left-overs at the feast
their hands have prepared.

IYALOJA   You heard them Amusa. You had better go.

GIRL   Now!

AMUSA (*commencing his retreat*)   We dey go now, but make you no
say we no warn you.

GIRL   Now!

GIRL   Before we read the riot act—you should know all about that.

AMUSA   Make we go. (*They depart, more precipitately.*)

The women strike their palms across in the gesture of wonder.

WOMEN   Do they teach you all that at school?

WOMAN   And to think I nearly kept Apinke away from the place.

WOMAN   Did you hear them? Did you see how they mimicked the
white man?

WOMAN   The voices exactly. Hey, there are wonders in this world!

IYALOJA   Well, our elders have said it: Dada may be weak, but he has
a younger sibling who is truly fearless.

WOMAN   The next time the white man shows his face in this market
I will set Wuraola on his tail.

*A woman bursts into song and dance of euphoria—'Tani l'awa o
l'ogbeja? Kayi! A l'ogbeja. Omo Kekere l'ogbeja.'[6] The rest of the
women join in, some placing the girls on their back like infants,
others dancing round them. The dance becomes general, mount-
ing in excitement. Elesin appears, in wrapper only. In his hands
a white velvet cloth folded loosely as if it held some delicate object. He cries out.*

ELESIN   Oh you mothers of beautiful brides! (*The dancing stops. They
turn and see him, and the object in his hands. Iyaloja approaches and
gently takes the cloth from him.*) Take it. It is no mere virgin stain,
but the union of life and the seeds of passage. My vital flow, the
last from this flesh is intermingled with the promise of future life.
All is prepared. Listen! (*A steady drumbeat from the distance.*) Yes.
It is nearly time. The King's dog has been killed. The King's favourite
horse is about to follow his master. My brother chiefs know their
task and perform it well. (*He listens again.*)

The bride emerges, stands shyly by the door. He turns to her.

ELESIN   Our marriage is not yet wholly fulfilled. When earth and passage wed, the consummation is complete only when there are grains
of earth on the eyelids of passage. Stay by me till then. My faithful
drummers, do me your last service. This is where I have chosen to
do my leave-taking, in this heart of life, this hive which contains the
swarm of the world in its small compass. This is where I have known
love and laughter away from the palace. Even the richest food cloys

---

6. "Who says we haven't a defender? Silence! We have our defenders. Little children are our
champions."

when eaten days on end; in the market, nothing ever cloys. Listen. (*They listen to the drums.*) They have begun to seek out the heart of the King's favourite horse. Soon it will ride in its bolt of raffia with the dog at its feet. Together they will ride on the shoulders of the King's grooms through the pulse centres of the town. They know it is here I shall await them. I have told them (*His eyes appear to cloud. He passes his hand over them as if to clear his sight. He gives a faint smile.*) It promises well; just then I felt my spirit's eagerness. The kite makes for wide spaces and the wind creeps up behind its tail; can the kite say less than—thank you, the quicker the better? But wait a while my spirit. Wait. Wait for the coming of the courier of the King. Do you know, friends, the horse is born to this one destiny, to bear the burden that is man upon its back. Except for this night, this night alone when the spotless stallion will ride in triumph on the back of man. In the time of my father I witnessed the strange sight. Perhaps tonight also I shall see it for the last time. If they arrive before the drums beat for me, I shall tell them to let the Alafin know I follow swiftly. If they come after the drums have sounded, why then, all is well for I have gone ahead. Our spirits shall fall in step along the great passage. (*He listens to the drums. He seems again to be falling into a state of semi-hypnosis; his eyes scan the sky but it is in a kind of daze. His voice is a little breathless.*) The moon has fed, a glow from its full stomach fills the sky and air, but I cannot tell where is that gateway through which I must pass. My faithful friends, let our feet touch together this last time, lead me into the other market with sounds that cover my skin with down yet make my limbs strike earth like a thoroughbred. Dear mothers, let me dance into the passage even as I have lived beneath your roofs.

> *He comes down progressively among them. They make way for him, the drummers playing. His dance is one of solemn, regal motions, each gesture of the body is made with a solemn finality. The women join him, their steps a somewhat more fluid version of his. Beneath the Praise-Singer's exhortations the women dirge 'Ale le le, awo mi lo.'*

PRAISE-SINGER
Elesin Alafin, can you hear my voice?
ELESIN
Faintly, my friend, faintly.
PRAISE-SINGER
Elesin Alafin, can you hear my call?
ELESIN
Faintly my King, faintly.
PRAISE-SINGER
Is your memory sound Elesin?
Shall my voice be a blade of grass and
Tickle the armpit of the past?
ELESIN
My memory needs no prodding but
What do you wish to say to me?

PRAISE-SINGER

> Only what has been spoken. Only what concerns
> The dying wish of the father of all.

ELESIN

> It is buried like seed-yam in my mind.
> This is the season of quick rains, the harvest
> Is this moment due for gathering.

PRAISE-SINGER

> If you cannot come, I said, swear
> You'll tell my favourite horse. I shall
> Ride on through the gates alone.

ELESIN

> Elesin's message will be read
> Only when his loyal heart no longer beats.

PRAISE-SINGER

> If you cannot come Elesin, tell my dog.
> I cannot stay the keeper too long
> At the gate.

ELESIN

> A dog does not outrun the hand
> That feeds it meat. A horse that throws its rider
> Slows down to a stop. Elesin Alafin
> Trusts no beasts with messages between
> A king and his companion.

PRAISE-SINGER

> If you get lost my dog will track
> The hidden path to me.

ELESIN

> The seven-way crossroads confuses
> Only the stranger. The Horseman of the King
> Was born in the recesses of the house.

PRAISE-SINGER

> I know the wickedness of men. If there is
> Weight on the loose end of your sash, such weight
> As no mere man can shift; if your sash is earthed
> By evil minds who mean to part us at the last . . .

ELESIN

> My sash is of the deep purple *alari*;
> It is no tethering-rope. The elephant
> Trails no tethering-rope; that king
> Is not yet crowned who will peg an elephant—
> Not even you my friend and King.

PRAISE-SINGER

> And yet this fear will not depart from me,
> The darkness of this new abode is deep—
> Will your human eyes suffice?

ELESIN

> In a night which falls before our eyes
> However deep, we do not miss our way.

PRAISE-SINGER
>   Shall I now not acknowledge I have stood
>   Where wonders met their end? The elephant deserves
>   Better than that we say 'I have caught
>   A glimpse of something'. If we see the tamer
>   Of the forest let us say plainly, we have seen
>   An elephant.

ELESIN (*his voice is drowsy*)
>   I have freed myself of earth and now
>   It's getting dark. Strange voices guide my feet.

PRAISE-SINGER
>   The river is never so high that the eyes
>   Of a fish are covered. The night is not so dark
>   That the albino fails to find his way. A child
>   Returning homewards craves no leading by the hand.
>   Gracefully does the mask regain his grove at the end of the day . . .
>   Gracefully. Gracefully does the mask dance
>   Homeward at the end of the day, gracefully . . .

> *Elesin's trance appears to be deepening, his steps heavier.*

IYALOJA
>   It is the death of war that kills the valiant,
>   Death of water is how the swimmer goes.
>   It is the death of markets that kills the trader
>   And death of indecision takes the idle away.
>   The trade of the cutlass blunts its edge
>   And the beautiful die the death of beauty.
>   It takes an Elesin to die the death of death . . .
>   Only Elesin . . . dies the unknowable death of death . . .
>   Gracefully, gracefully does the horseman regain
>   The stables at the end of day, gracefully . . .

PRAISE-SINGER   How shall I tell what my eyes have seen? The Horseman gallops on before the courier, how shall I tell what my eyes have seen? He says a dog may be confused by new scents of beings he never dreamt of, so he must precede the dog to heaven. He says a horse may stumble on strange boulders and be lamed, so he races on before the horse to heaven. It is best, he says, to trust no messenger who may falter at the outer gate; oh how shall I tell what my ears have heard? But do you hear me still Elesin, do you hear your faithful one?

> *Elesin in his motions appears to feel for a direction of sound, subtly, but he only sinks deeper into his trance-dance.*

PRAISE-SINGER   Elesin Alafin, I no longer sense your flesh. The drums are changing now but you have gone far ahead of the world. It is not yet noon in heaven; let those who claim it is begin their own journey home. So why must you rush like an impatient bride: why do you race to desert your Olohun-iyo?

*Elesin is now sunk fully deep in his trance, there is no longer
sign of any awareness of his surroundings.*

PRAISE-SINGER   Does the deep voice of *gbedu* cover you then, like the
passage of royal elephants? Those drums that brook no rivals, have
they blocked the passage to your ears that my voice passes into wind,
a mere leaf floating in the night? Is your flesh lightened Elesin, is
that lump of earth I slid between your slippers to keep you longer
slowly sifting from your feet? Are the drums on the other side now
tuning skin to skin with ours in *osugbo*?[7] Are there sounds there I
cannot hear, do footsteps surround you which pound the earth like
gbedu,[8] roll like thunder round the dome of the world? Is the darkness gathering in your head Elesin? Is there now a streak of light at
the end of the passage, a light I dare not look upon? Does it reveal
whose voices we often heard, whose touches we often felt, whose
wisdoms come suddenly into the mind when the wisest have shaken
their heads and murmured, It cannot be done? Elesin Alafin, don't
think I do not know why your lips are heavy, why your limbs are
drowsy as palm oil in the cold of harmattan. I would call you back
but when the elephant heads for the jungle, the tail is too small a
handhold for the hunter that would pull him back. The sun that
heads for the sea no longer heeds the prayers of the farmer. When
the river begins to taste the salt of the ocean, we no longer know
what deity to call on, the river-god or Olokun. No arrow flies back
to the string, the child does not return through the same passage
that gave it birth. Elesin Oba, can you hear me at all? Your eyelids
are glazed like a courtesan's, is it that you see the dark groom and
master of life? And will you see my father? Will you tell him that I
stayed with you to the last? Will my voice ring in your ears awhile,
will you remember Olohun-iyo even if the music on the other side
surpasses his mortal craft? But will they know you over there? Have
they eyes to gauge your worth, have they the heart to love you, will
they know what thoroughbred prances towards them in caparisons
of honour? If they do not Elesin, if any there cuts your yam with a
small knife, or pours you wine in a small calabash, turn back and
return to welcoming hands. If the world were not greater than the
wishes of Olohun-iyo, I would not let you go . . .

> *He appears to break down. Elesin dances on, completely in a
> trance. The dirge wells up louder and stronger. Elesin's dance
> does not lose its elasticity but his gestures become, if possible, even
> more weighty. Lights fade slowly on the scene.*

Scene Four

*A masque. The front side of the stage is part of a wide corridor
around the great hall of the Residency extending beyond vision*

---

7. Venerable secret order or cult of seers, diviners, and sages.
8. Large, resonant drums; also the idiom of a cultic music associated with Osugbo.

into the rear and wings. It is redolent of the tawdry decadence of
a far-flung but key imperial frontier. The couples in a variety of
fancy-dress are ranged around the walls, gazing in the same di-
rection. The guest-of-honour is about to make an appearance. A
portion of the local police brass band with its white conductor is
just visible. At last, the entrance of Royalty. The band plays 'Rule
Britannia', badly, beginning long before he is visible. The couples
bow and curtsey as he passes by them. Both he and his compan-
ions are dressed in seventeenth-century European costume. Fol-
lowing behind are the Resident and his partner similarly attired.
As they gain the end of the hall where the orchestra dais begins
the music comes to an end. The Prince bows to the guests. The
band strikes up a Viennese waltz and the Prince formally opens
the floor. Several bars later the Resident and his companion fol-
low suit. Others follow in appropriate pecking order. The or-
chestra's waltz rendition is not of the highest musical standard.

Some time later the Prince dances again into view and is settled
into a corner by the Resident who then proceeds to select couples
as they dance past for introduction, sometimes threading his way
through the dancers to tap the lucky couple on the shoulder.
Desperate efforts from many to ensure that they are recognised in
spite of, perhaps, their costume. The ritual of introductions soon
takes in Pilkings and his wife. The Prince is quite fascinated by
their costume and they demonstrate the adaptations they have
made to it, pulling down the mask to demonstrate how the egun-
gun normally appears, then showing the various press-button con-
trols they have innovated for the face flaps, the sleeves, etc. They
demonstrate the dance steps and the guttural sounds made by the
egungun, harass other dancers in the hall, Mrs Pilkings playing
the 'restrainer' to Pilkings' manic darts. Everyone is highly enter-
tained, the Royal Party especially who lead the applause.

At this point a liveried footman comes in with a note on a salver
and is intercepted almost absent-mindedly by the Resident who
takes the note and reads it. After polite coughs he succeeds in
excusing the Pilkings from the Prince and takes them aside. The
Prince considerately offers the Resident's wife his hand and danc-
ing is resumed.

On their way out the Resident gives an order to his Aide-de-
Camp. They come into the side corridor where the Resident hands
the note to Pilkings.

RESIDENT   As you see it says 'emergency' on the outside. I took the
   liberty of opening it because His Highness was obviously enjoying
   the entertainment. I didn't want to interrupt unless really necessary.
PILKINGS   Yes, yes of course, sir.
RESIDENT   Is it really as bad as it says? What's it all about?
PILKINGS   Some strange custom they have, sir. It seems because the
   King is dead some important chief has to commit suicide.

RESIDENT   The King? Isn't it the same one who died nearly a month ago?

PILKINGS   Yes, sir.

RESIDENT   Haven't they buried him yet?

PILKINGS   They take their time about these things, sir. The pre-burial ceremonies last nearly thirty days. It seems tonight is the final night.

RESIDENT   But what has it got to do with the market women? Why are they rioting? We've waived that troublesome tax haven't we?

PILKINGS   We don't quite know that they are exactly rioting yet, sir. Sergeant Amusa is sometimes prone to exaggerations.

RESIDENT   He sounds desperate enough. That comes out even in his rather quaint grammar. Where is the man anyway? I asked my aide-de-camp to bring him here.

PILKINGS   They are probably looking in the wrong verandah. I'll fetch him myself.

RESIDENT   No no you stay here. Let your wife go and look for them. Do you mind my dear . . . ?

JANE   Certainly not, your Excellency. (*Goes.*)

RESIDENT   You should have kept me informed, Pilkings. You realise how disastrous it would have been if things had erupted while His Highness was here.

PILKINGS   I wasn't aware of the whole business until tonight, sir.

RESIDENT   Nose to the ground Pilkings, nose to the ground. If we all let these little things slip past us where would the empire be eh? Tell me that. Where would we all be?

PILKINGS   (*low voice*)   Sleeping peacefully at home I bet.

RESIDENT   What did you say, Pilkings?

PILKINGS   It won't happen again, sir.

RESIDENT   It mustn't, Pilkings. It mustn't. Where is that damned sergeant? I ought to get back to His Highness as quickly as possible and offer him some plausible explanation for my rather abrupt conduct. Can you think of one, Pilkings?

PILKINGS   You could tell him the truth, sir.

RESIDENT   I could? No no no Pilkings, that would never do. What! Go and tell him there is a riot just two miles away from him? This is supposed to be a secure colony of His Majesty, Pilkings.

PILKINGS   Yes, sir.

RESIDENT   Ah, there they are. No, these are not our native police. Are these the ring-leaders of the riot?

PILKINGS   Sir, these are my police officers.

RESIDENT   Oh, I beg your pardon officers. You do look a little . . . I say, isn't there something missing in their uniform? I think they used to have some rather colourful sashes. If I remember rightly I recommended them myself in my young days in the service. A bit of colour always appeals to the natives, yes, I remember putting that in my report. Well well well, where are we? Make your report man.

PILKINGS   (*moves close to Amusa, between his teeth*)   And let's have no more superstitious nonsense from you Amusa or I'll throw you in the guardroom for a month and feed you pork![9]

RESIDENT What's that? What has pork to do with it?

PILKINGS Sir, I was just warning him to be brief. I'm sure you are most anxious to hear his report.

RESIDENT Yes yes yes of course. Come on man, speak up. Hey, didn't we give them some colourful fez hats with all those wavy things, yes, pink tassels . . .

PILKINGS Sir, I think if he was permitted to make his report we might find that he lost his hat in the riot.

RESIDENT Ah yes indeed. I'd better tell His Highness that. Lost his hat in the riot, ha ha. He'll probably say well, as long as he didn't lose his head. (*Chuckles to himself.*) Don't forget to send me a report first thing in the morning young Pilkings.

PILKINGS No, sir.

RESIDENT And whatever you do, don't let things get out of hand. Keep a cool head and—nose to the ground Pilkings. (*Wanders off in the general direction of the hall.*)

PILKINGS Yes, sir.

AIDE-DE-CAMP Would you be needing me, sir?

PILKINGS No thanks, Bob. I think His Excellency's need of you is greater than ours.

AIDE-DE-CAMP We have a detachment of soldiers from the capital, sir. They accompanied His Highness up here.

PILKINGS I doubt if it will come to that but, thanks, I'll bear it in mind. Oh, could you send an orderly with my cloak.

AIDE-DE-CAMP Very good, sir. (*Goes.*)

PILKINGS Now, sergeant.

AMUSA Sir . . . (*Makes an effort, stops dead. Eyes to the ceiling.*)

PILKINGS Oh, not again.

AMUSA I cannot against death to dead cult. This dress get power of dead.

PILKINGS All right, let's go. You are relieved of all further duty Amusa. Report to me first thing in the morning.

JANE Shall I come, Simon?

PILKINGS No, there's no need for that. If I can get back later I will. Otherwise get Bob to bring you home.

JANE Be careful Simon . . . I mean, be clever.

PILKINGS Sure I will. You two, come with me. (*As he turns to go, the clock in the Residency begins to chime. Pilkings looks at his watch then turns, horror-stricken, to stare at his wife. The same thought clearly occurs to her. He swallows hard. An orderly brings his cloak.*) It's midnight. I had no idea it was that late.

JANE But surely . . . they don't count the hours the way we do. The moon, or something . . .

PILKINGS I am . . . not so sure.

9. From his name, it is clear that Amusa is Muslim and therefore forbidden to eat pork.

He turns and breaks into a sudden run. The two constables fol-
low, also at a run. Amusa, who has kept his eyes on the ceiling
throughout, waits until the last of the footsteps has faded out of
hearing. He salutes suddenly, but without once looking in the
direction of the woman.

AMUSA Goodnight, madam.

JANE Oh. (*She hesitates.*) Amusa . . . (*He goes off without seeming to*
have heard.) Poor Simon . . .

A figure emerges from the shadows, a young black man dressed
in a sober western suit. He peeps into the hall, trying to make
out the figures of the dancers.

JANE Who is that?

OLUNDE (*emerges into the light*) I didn't mean to startle you madam.
I am looking for the District Officer.

JANE Wait a minute . . . don't I know you? Yes, you are Olunde, the
young man who . . .

OLUNDE Mrs Pilkings! How fortunate. I came here to look for your
husband.

JANE Olunde! Let's look at you. What a fine young man you've become. Grand but solemn. Good God, when did you return? Simon
never said a word. But you do look well Olunde. Really!

OLUNDE You are . . . well, you look quite well yourself Mrs Pilkings.
From what little I can see of you.

JANE Oh, this. It's caused quite a stir I assure you, and not all of it
very pleasant. You are not shocked I hope?

OLUNDE Why should I be? But don't you find it rather hot in there?
Your skin must find it difficult to breathe.

JANE Well, it is a little hot I must confess, but it's all in a good cause.

OLUNDE What cause Mrs Pilkings?

JANE All this. The ball. And His Highness being here in person and
all that.

OLUNDE (*mildly*) And that is the good cause for which you desecrate
an ancestral mask?

JANE Oh, so you are shocked after all. How disappointing.

OLUNDE No I am not shocked, Mrs Pilkings. You forget that I have
now spent four years among your people. I discovered that you have
no respect for what you do not understand.

JANE Oh. So you've returned with a chip on your shoulder. That's a
pity Olunde. I am sorry.

An uncomfortable silence follows.

I take it then that you did not find your stay in England altogether
edifying.

OLUNDE I don't say that. I found your people quite admirable in many
ways, their conduct and courage in this war for instance.

JANE Ah yes, the war. Here of course it is all rather remote. From time to time we have a black-out drill just to remind us that there is a war on. And the rare convoy passes through on its way somewhere or on manoeuvres. Mind you there is the occasional bit of excitement like that ship that was blown up in the harbour.

OLUNDE   Here? Do you mean through enemy action?

JANE   Oh no, the war hasn't come that close. The captain did it himself. I don't quite understand it really. Simon tried to explain. The ship had to be blown up because it had become dangerous to other ships, even to the city itself. Hundreds of the coastal population would have died.

OLUNDE   Maybe it was loaded with ammunition and had caught fire. Or some of those lethal gases they've been experimenting on.

JANE   Something like that. The captain blew himself up with it. Deliberately. Simon said someone had to remain on board to light the fuse.

OLUNDE   It must have been a very short fuse.

JANE   (shrugs)   I don't know much about it. Only that there was no other way to save lives. No time to devise anything else. The captain took the decision and carried it out.

OLUNDE   Yes . . . I quite believe it. I met men like that in England.

JANE   Oh just look at me! Fancy welcoming you back with such morbid news. Stale too. It was at least six months ago.

OLUNDE   I don't find it morbid at all. I find it rather inspiring. It is an affirmative commentary on life.

JANE   What is?

OLUNDE   That captain's self-sacrifice.

JANE   Nonsense. Life should never be thrown deliberately away.

OLUNDE   And the innocent people around the harbour?

JANE   Oh, how does one know? The whole thing was probably exaggerated anyway.

OLUNDE   That was a risk the captain couldn't take. But please Mrs Pilkings, do you think you could find your husband for me? I have to talk to him.

JANE   Simon? (As she recollects for the first time the full significance of Olunde's presence.) Simon is . . . there is a little problem in town. He was sent for. But . . . when did you arrive? Does Simon know you're here?

OLUNDE   (suddenly earnest)   I need your help Mrs Pilkings. I've always found you somewhat more understanding than your husband. Please find him for me and when you do, you must help me talk to him.

JANE   I'm afraid I don't quite . . . follow you. Have you seen my husband already?

OLUNDE   I went to your house. Your houseboy told me you were here. (He smiles.) He even told me how I would recognise you and Mr Pilkings.

JANE   Then you must know what my husband is trying to do for you.

OLUNDE   For me?

JANE   For you. For your people. And to think he didn't even know you

were coming back! But how do you happen to be here? Only this
evening we were talking about you. We thought you were still four
thousand miles away.

OLUNDE   I was sent a cable.

JANE   A cable? Who did? Simon? The business of your father didn't
begin till tonight.

OLUNDE   A relation sent it weeks ago, and it said nothing about my
father. All it said was, Our King is dead. But I knew I had to return
home at once so as to bury my father. I understood that.

JANE   Well, thank God you don't have to go through that agony.
Simon is going to stop it.

OLUNDE   That's why I want to see him. He's wasting his time. And
since he has been so helpful to me I don't want him to incur the
enmity of our people. Especially over nothing.

JANE   (sits down open-mouthed)   You . . . you Olunde!

OLUNDE   Mrs Pilkings, I came home to bury my father. As soon as I
heard the news I booked my passage home. In fact we were fortunate. We travelled in the same convoy as your Prince, so we had
excellent protection.

JANE   But you don't think your father is also entitled to whatever protection is available to him?

OLUNDE   How can I make you understand? He *has* protection. No one
can undertake what he does tonight without the deepest protection
the mind can conceive. What can you offer him in place of his peace
of mind, in place of the honour and veneration of his own people?
What would you think of your Prince if he refused to accept the
risk of losing his life on this voyage? This . . . showing-the-flag tour
of colonial possessions.

JANE   I see. So it isn't just medicine you studied in England.

OLUNDE   Yet another error into which your people fall. You believe
that everything which appears to make sense was learnt from you.

JANE   Not so fast Olunde. You have learnt to argue I can tell that, but
I never said you made sense. However clearly you try to put it, it is
still a barbaric custom. It is even worse—it's feudal! The King dies
and a chieftain must be buried with him. How feudalistic can you
get!

OLUNDE   (waves his hand towards the background. The Prince is dancing
past again—to a different step—and all the guests are bowing and
curtseying as he passes)   And this? Even in the midst of a devastating
war, look at that. What name would you give to that?

JANE   Therapy, British style. The preservation of sanity in the midst
of chaos.

OLUNDE   Others would call it decadence. However, it doesn't really
interest me. You white races know how to survive; I've seen proof
of that. By all logical and natural laws this war should end with all
the white races wiping out one another, wiping out their so-called
civilisation for all time and reverting to a state of primitivism the
like of which has so far only existed in your imagination when you
thought of us. I thought all that at the beginning. Then I slowly

realised that your greatest art is the art of survival. But at least have the humility to let others survive in their own way.

JANE Through ritual suicide?

OLUNDE Is that worse than mass suicide? Mrs Pilkings, what do you call what those young men are sent to do by their generals in this war? Of course you have also mastered the art of calling things by names which don't remotely describe them.

JANE You talk! You people with your long-winded, roundabout way of making conversation.

OLUNDE Mrs Pilkings, whatever we do, we never suggest that a thing is the opposite of what it really is. In your newsreels I heard defeats, thorough, murderous defeats described as strategic victories. No wait, it wasn't just on your newsreels. Don't forget I was attached to hospitals all the time. Hordes of your wounded passed through those wards. I spoke to them. I spent long evenings by their bedsides while they spoke terrible truths of the realities of that war. I know now how history is made.

JANE But surely, in a war of this nature, for the morale of the nation you must expect . . .

OLUNDE That a disaster beyond human reckoning be spoken of as a triumph? No. I mean, is there no mourning in the home of the bereaved that such blasphemy is permitted?

JANE (*after a moment's pause*) Perhaps I can understand you now. The time we picked for you was not really one for seeing us at our best.

OLUNDE Don't think it was just the war. Before that even started I had plenty of time to study your people. I saw nothing, finally, that gave you the right to pass judgement on other peoples and their ways. Nothing at all.

JANE (*hesitantly*) Was it the . . . colour thing? I know there is some discrimination.

OLUNDE Don't make it so simple, Mrs Pilkings. You make it sound as if when I left, I took nothing at all with me.

JANE Yes . . . and to tell the truth, only this evening, Simon and I agreed that we never really knew what you left with.

OLUNDE Neither did I. But I found out over there. I am grateful to your country for that. And I will never give it up.

JANE Olunde please . . . promise me something. Whatever you do, don't throw away what you have started to do. You want to be a doctor. My husband and I believe you will make an excellent one, sympathetic and competent. Don't let anything make you throw away your training.

OLUNDE (*genuinely surprised*) Of course not. What a strange idea. I intend to return and complete my training. Once the burial of my father is over.

JANE Oh, please . . . !

OLUNDE Listen! Come outside. You can't hear anything against that music.

JANE What is it?

OLUNDE The drums. Can you hear the drums? Listen.

The drums come over, still distant but more distinct. There is a change of rhythm, it rises to a crescendo and then, suddenly, it is cut off. After a silence, a new beat begins, slow and resonant.

OLUNDE   There, it's all over.

JANE   You mean he's . . .

OLUNDE   Yes, Mrs Pilkings, my father is dead. His will-power has always been enormous; I know he is dead.

JANE   (*screams*)   How can you be so callous! So unfeeling! You announce your father's own death like a surgeon looking down on some strange . . . stranger's body! You're just a savage like all the rest.

AIDE-DE-CAMP   (*rushing out*)   Mrs Pilkings. Mrs Pilkings. (*She breaks down, sobbing.*) Are you all right, Mrs Pilkings?

OLUNDE   She'll be all right. (*Turns to go.*)

AIDE-DE-CAMP   Who are you? And who the hell asked your opinion?

OLUNDE   You're quite right, nobody. (*Going.*)

AIDE-DE-CAMP   What the hell! Did you hear me ask you who you were?

OLUNDE   I have business to attend to.

AIDE-DE-CAMP   I'll give you business in a moment you impudent nigger. Answer my question!

OLUNDE   I have a funeral to arrange. Excuse me. (*Going.*)

AIDE-DE-CAMP   I said stop! Orderly!

JANE   No, no, don't do that. I'm all right. And for heaven's sake don't act so foolishly. He's a family friend.

AIDE-DE-CAMP   Well he'd better learn to answer civil questions when he's asked them. These natives put a suit on and they get high opinions of themselves.

OLUNDE   Can I go now?

JANE   No no don't go. I must talk to you. I'm sorry about what I said.

OLUNDE   It's nothing, Mrs Pilkings. And I'm really anxious to go. I couldn't see my father before, it's forbidden for me, his heir and successor, to set eyes on him from the moment of the King's death. But now . . . I would like to touch his body while it is still warm.

JANE   You will. I promise I shan't keep you long. Only, I couldn't possibly let you go like that. Bob, please excuse us.

AIDE-DE-CAMP   If you're sure . . .

JANE   Of course I'm sure. Something happened to upset me just then, but I'm all right now. Really.

The Aide-de-Camp goes, somewhat reluctantly.

OLUNDE   I mustn't stay long.

JANE   Please, I promise not to keep you. It's just that . . . oh you saw yourself what happens to one in this place. The Resident's man thought he was being helpful, that's the way we all react. But I can't go in among that crowd just now and if I stay by myself somebody will come looking for me. Please, just say something for a few moments and then you can go. Just so I can recover myself.

OLUNDE   What do you want me to say?

JANE   Your calm acceptance for instance, can you explain that? It was so unnatural. I don't understand that at all. I feel a need to understand all I can.

OLUNDE   But you explained it yourself. My medical training perhaps. I have seen death too often. And the soldiers who returned from the front, they died on our hands all the time.

JANE   No. It has to be more than that. I feel it has to do with the many things we don't really grasp about your people. At least you can explain.

OLUNDE   All these things are part of it. And anyway, my father has been dead in my mind for nearly a month. Ever since I learnt of the King's death. I've lived with my bereavement so long now that I cannot think of him alive. On that journey on the boat, I kept my mind on my duties as the one who must perform the rites over his body. I went through it all again and again in my mind as he himself had taught me. I didn't want to do anything wrong, something which might jeopardise the welfare of my people.

JANE   But he had disowned you. When you left he swore publicly you were no longer his son.

OLUNDE   I told you, he was a man of tremendous will. Sometimes that's another way of saying stubborn. But among our people, you don't disown a child just like that. Even if I had died before him I would still be buried like his eldest son. But it's time for me to go.

JANE   Thank you. I feel calmer. Don't let me keep you from your duties.

OLUNDE   Goodnight, Mrs Pilkings.

JANE   Welcome home.

She holds out her hand. As he takes it footsteps are heard approaching the drive. A short while later a woman's sobbing is also heard.

PILKINGS   (*off*)   Keep them here till I get back. (*He strides into view, reacts at the sight of Olunde but turns to his wife.*) Thank goodness you're still here.

JANE   Simon, what happened?

PILKINGS   Later Jane, please. Is Bob still here?

JANE   Yes, I think so. I'm sure he must be.

PILKINGS   Try and get him out here as quickly as you can. Tell him it's urgent.

JANE   Of course. Oh Simon, you remember . . .

PILKINGS   Yes yes. I can see who it is. Get Bob out here. (*She runs off.*) At first I thought I was seeing a ghost.

OLUNDE   Mr Pilkings, I appreciate what you tried to do. I want you to believe that. I can tell you it would have been a terrible calamity if you'd succeeded.

PILKINGS   (*opens his mouth several times, shuts it*)   You . . . said what?

OLUNDE   A calamity for us, the entire people.

PILKINGS   (*sighs*)   I see. Hm.

OLUNDE   And now I must go. I must see him before he turns cold.

PILKINGS   Oh ah . . . em . . . but this is a shock to see you. I mean
    er thinking all this while you were in England and thanking God for
    that.
OLUNDE   I came on the mail boat. We travelled in the Prince's convoy.
PILKINGS   Ah yes, a-ah, hm . . . er well . . .
OLUNDE   Goodnight. I can see you are shocked by the whole business.
    But you must know by now there are things you cannot under-
    stand—or help.
PILKINGS   Yes. Just a minute. There are armed policemen that way
    and they have instructions to let no one pass. I suggest you wait a
    little. I'll er . . . give you an escort.
OLUNDE   That's very kind of you. But do you think it could be quickly
    arranged?
PILKINGS   Of course. In fact, yes, what I'll do is send Bob over with
    some men to the er . . . place. You can go with them. Here he comes
    now. Excuse me a minute.
AIDE-DE-CAMP   Anything wrong sir?
PILKINGS (*takes him to one side*)   Listen Bob, that cellar in the disused
    annexe of the Residency, you know, where the slaves were stored
    before being taken down to the coast . . .
AIDE-DE-CAMP   Oh yes, we use it as a storeroom for broken furniture.
PILKINGS   But it's still got the bars on it?
AIDE-DE-CAMP   Oh yes, they are quite intact.
PILKINGS   Get the keys please. I'll explain later. And I want a strong
    guard over the Residency tonight.
AIDE-DE-CAMP   We have that already. The detachment from the
    coast . . .
PILKINGS   No, I don't want them at the gates of the Residency. I want
    you to deploy them at the bottom of the hill, a long way from the
    main hall so they can deal with any situation long before the sound
    carries to the house.
AIDE-DE-CAMP   Yes of course.
PILKINGS   I don't want His Highness alarmed.
AIDE-DE-CAMP   You think the riot will spread here?
PILKINGS   It's unlikely but I don't want to take a chance. I made them
    believe I was going to lock the man up in my house, which was what
    I had planned to do in the first place. They are probably assailing it
    by now. I took a roundabout route here so I don't think there is any
    danger at all. At least not before dawn. Nobody is to leave the prem-
    ises of course—the native employees I mean. They'll soon smell
    something is up and they can't keep their mouths shut.
AIDE-DE-CAMP   I'll give instructions at once.
PILKINGS   I'll take the prisoner down myself. Two policemen will stay
    with him throughout the night. Inside the cell.
AIDE-DE-CAMP   Right sir. (*Salutes and goes off at the double.*)
PILKINGS   Jane. Bob is coming back in a moment with a detachment.
    Until he gets back please stay with Olunde. (*He makes an extra
    warning gesture with his eyes.*)

OLUNDE Please, Mr Pilkings . . .

PILKINGS I hate to be stuffy old son, but we have a crisis on our hands. It has to do with your father's affair if you must know. And it happens also at a time when we have His Highness here. I am responsible for security so you'll simply have to do as I say. I hope that's understood. (*Marches off quickly, in the direction from which he made his first appearance.*)

OLUNDE What's going on? All this can't be just because he failed to stop my father killing himself.

JANE I honestly don't know. Could it have sparked off a riot?

OLUNDE No. If he'd succeeded that would be more likely to start the riot. Perhaps there were other factors involved. Was there a chieftaincy dispute?

JANE None that I know of.

ELESIN (*an animal bellow from off*) Leave me alone! Is it not enough that you have covered me in shame! White man, take your hand from my body!

> *Olunde stands frozen to the spot. Jane, understanding at last, tries to move him.*

JANE Let's go in. It's getting chilly out here.

PILKINGS (*off*) Carry him.

ELESIN Give me back the name you have taken away from me you ghost from the land of the nameless!

PILKINGS Carry him! I can't have a disturbance here. Quickly! stuff up his mouth.

JANE Oh God! Let's go in. Please Olunde.

> *Olunde does not move.*

ELESIN Take your albino's hand from me you . . .

> *Sounds of a struggle. His voice chokes as he is gagged.*

OLUNDE (*quietly*) That was my father's voice.

JANE Oh you poor orphan, what have you come home to?

> *There is a sudden explosion of rage from off-stage and powerful steps come running up the drive.*

PILKINGS You bloody fools, after him!

> *Immediately Elesin, in handcuffs, comes pounding in the direction of Jane and Olunde, followed some moments afterwards by Pilkings and the constables. Elesin, confronted by the seeming statue of his son, stops dead. Olunde stares above his head into the distance. The constables try to grab him. Jane screams at them.*

JANE Leave him alone! Simon, tell them to leave him alone.

PILKINGS All right, stand aside you. (*Shrugs.*) Maybe just as well. It might help to calm him down.

*For several moments they hold the same position. Elesin moves a
step forward, almost as if he's still in doubt.*

ELESIN   Olunde? (*He moves his head, inspecting him from side to side.*)
Olunde! (*He collapses slowly at Olunde's feet.*) Oh son, don't let the
sight of your father turn you blind!
OLUNDE (*he moves for the first time since he heard his voice, brings his
head slowly down to look on him*)   I have no father, eater of left-
overs.

*He walks slowly down the way his father had run. Light fades out
on Elesin, sobbing into the ground.*

Scene Five

*A wide iron-barred gate stretches almost the whole width of the
cell in which Elesin is imprisoned. His wrists are encased in thick
iron bracelets, chained together; he stands against the bars, looking out. Seated on the ground to one side on the outside is his
recent bride, her eyes bent perpetually to the ground. Figures of
the two guards can be seen deeper inside the cell, alert to every
movement Elesin makes. Pilkings, now in a police officer's uniform, enters noiselessly, observes him a while. Then he coughs
ostentatiously and approaches. Leans against the bars near a corner, his back to Elesin. He is obviously trying to fall in mood with
him. Some moments' silence.*

PILKINGS   You seem fascinated by the moon.
ELESIN (*after a pause*)   Yes, ghostly one. Your twin-brother up there
engages my thoughts.
PILKINGS   It is a beautiful night.
ELESIN   Is that so?
PILKINGS   The light on the leaves, the peace of the night . . .
ELESIN   The night is not at peace, District Officer.
PILKINGS   No? I would have said it was. You know, quiet . . .
ELESIN   And does quiet mean peace for you?
PILKINGS   Well, nearly the same thing. Naturally there is a subtle dif-
ference . . .
ELESIN   The night is not at peace, ghostly one. The world is not at
peace. You have shattered the peace of the world for ever. There is
no sleep in the world tonight.
PILKINGS   It is still a good bargain if the world should lose one night's
sleep as the price of saving a man's life.
ELESIN   You did not save my life, District Officer. You destroyed it.
PILKINGS   Now come on . . .
ELESIN   And not merely my life but the lives of many. The end of the
night's work is not over. Neither this year nor the next will see it. If
I wished you well, I would pray that you do not stay long enough
on our land to see the disaster you have brought upon us.

PILKINGS   Well, I did my duty as I saw it. I have no regrets.
ELESIN   No. The regrets of life always come later.

Some moments' pause.

You are waiting for dawn, white man. I hear you saying to yourself:
only so many hours until dawn and then the danger is over. All I
must do is to keep him alive tonight. You don't quite understand it
all but you know that tonight is when what ought to be must be
brought about. I shall ease your mind even more, ghostly one. It is
not an entire night but a moment of the night, and that moment is
past. The moon was my messenger and guide. When it reached a
certain gateway in the sky, it touched that moment for which my
whole life has been spent in blessings. Even I do not know the
gateway. I have stood here and scanned the sky for a glimpse of that
door but, I cannot see it. Human eyes are useless for a search of
this nature. But in the house of *osugbo*, those who keep watch
through the spirit recognised the moment, they sent word to me
through the voice of our sacred drums to prepare myself. I heard
them and I shed all thoughts of earth. I began to follow the moon
to the abode of the gods . . . servant of the white king, that was
when you entered my chosen place of departure on feet of dese-
cration.

PILKINGS   I'm sorry, but we all see our duty differently.
ELESIN   I no longer blame you. You stole from me my first-born, sent
him to your country so you could turn him into something in your
own image. Did you plan it all beforehand? There are moments
when it seems part of a larger plan. He who must follow my footsteps is taken from me, sent across the ocean. Then, in my turn, I
am stopped from fulfilling my destiny. Did you think it all out before,
this plan to push our world from its course and sever the cord that
links us to the great origin?

PILKINGS   You don't really believe that. Anyway, if that was my intention with your son, I appear to have failed.

ELESIN   You did not fail in the main, ghostly one. We know the roof
covers the rafters, the cloth covers blemishes; who would have
known that the white skin covered our future, preventing us from
seeing the death our enemies had prepared for us. The world is set
adrift and its inhabitants are lost. Around them, there is nothing but
emptiness.

PILKINGS   Your son does not take so gloomy a view.
ELESIN   Are you dreaming now, white man? Were you not present at
the reunion of shame? Did you not see when the world reversed
itself and the father fell before his son, asking forgiveness?

PILKINGS   That was in the heat of the moment. I spoke to him and
. . . if you want to know, he wishes he could cut out his tongue for
uttering the words he did.

ELESIN   No. What he said must never be unsaid. The contempt of my
own son rescued something of my shame at your hands. You have
stopped me in my duty but I know now that I did give birth to a

son. Once I mistrusted him for seeking the companionship of those
my spirit knew as enemies of our race. Now I understand. One
should seek to obtain the secrets of his enemies. He will avenge my
shame, white one. His spirit will destroy you and yours.

PILKINGS	That kind of talk is hardly called for. If you don't want my
consolation . . .

ELESIN	No white man, I do not want your consolation.

PILKINGS	As you wish. Your son, anyway, sends his consolation. He
asks your forgiveness. When I asked him not to despise you his reply
was: I cannot judge him, and if I cannot judge him, I cannot despise
him. He wants to come to you and say goodbye and to receive your
blessing.

ELESIN	Goodbye? Is he returning to your land?

PILKINGS	Don't you think that's the most sensible thing for him to
do? I advised him to leave at once, before dawn, and he agrees that
is the right course of action.

ELESIN	Yes, it is best. And even if I did not think so, I have lost the
father's place of honour. My voice is broken.

PILKINGS	Your son honours you. If he didn't he would not ask your
blessing.

ELESIN	No. Even a thoroughbred is not without pity for the turf he
strikes with his hoof. When is he coming?

PILKINGS	As soon as the town is a little quieter. I advised it.

ELESIN	Yes, white man, I am sure you advised it. You advise all our
lives although on the authority of what gods, I do not know.

PILKINGS	(opens his mouth to reply, then appears to change his mind.
Turns to go. Hesitates and stops again)	Before I leave you, may I
ask just one thing of you?

ELESIN	I am listening.

PILKINGS	I wish to ask you to search the quiet of your heart and tell
me—do you not find great contradictions in the wisdom of your
own race?

ELESIN	Make yourself clear, white one.

PILKINGS	I have lived among you long enough to learn a saying or
two. One came to my mind tonight when I stepped into the market
and saw what was going on. You were surrounded by those who
egged you on with songs and praises. I thought, are these not the
same people who say: the elder grimly approaches heaven and you
ask him to bear your greetings yonder; do you really think he makes
the journey willingly? After that, I did not hesitate.

A pause. Elesin sighs. Before he can speak a sound of running
feet is heard.

JANE	(off)	Simon! Simon!

PILKINGS	What on earth . . . ! (Runs off.)

Elesin turns to his new wife, gazes on her for some moments.

ELESIN	My young bride, did you hear the ghostly one? You sit and
sob in your silent heart but say nothing to all this. First I blamed

the white man, then I blamed my gods for deserting me. Now I feel
I want to blame you for the mystery of the sapping of my will. But
blame is a strange peace offering for a man to bring a world he has
deeply wronged, and to its innocent dwellers. Oh little mother, I
have taken countless women in my life but you were more than a
desire of the flesh. I needed you as the abyss across which my body
must be drawn, I filled it with earth and dropped my seed in it at
the moment of preparedness for my crossing. You were the final gift
of the living to their emissary to the land of the ancestors, and
perhaps your warmth and youth brought new insights of this world
to me and turned my feet leaden on this side of the abyss. For I
confess to you, daughter, my weakness came not merely from the
abomination of the white man who came violently into my fading
presence, there was also a weight of longing on my earth-held limbs.
I would have shaken it off, already my foot had begun to lift but
then, the white ghost entered and all was defiled.

> *Approaching voices of Pilkings and his wife.*

JANE   Oh Simon, you will let her in won't you?
PILKINGS   I really wish you'd stop interfering.

> *They come into view. Jane is in a dressing-gown. Pilkings is hold-
> ing a note to which he refers from time to time.*

JANE   Good gracious, I didn't initiate this. I was sleeping quietly, or
trying to anyway, when the servant brought it. It's not my fault if
one can't sleep undisturbed even in the Residency.
PILKINGS   He'd have done the same thing if we were sleeping at home
so don't sidetrack the issue. He knows he can get round you or he
wouldn't send you the petition in the first place.
JANE   Be fair Simon. After all he was thinking of your own interests.
He is grateful you know, you seem to forget that. He feels he owes
you something.
PILKINGS   I just wish they'd leave this man alone tonight, that's all.
JANE   Trust him Simon. He's pledged his word it will all go peacefully.
PILKINGS   Yes, and that's the other thing. I don't like being threatened.
JANE   Threatened? (*Takes the note.*) I didn't spot any threat.
PILKINGS   It's there. Veiled, but it's there. The only way to prevent
serious rioting tomorrow—what a cheek!
JANE   I don't think he's threatening you Simon.
PILKINGS   He's picked up the idiom all right. Wouldn't surprise me if
he's been mixing with commies or anarchists over there. The phras-
ing sounds too good to be true. Damn! If only the Prince hadn't
picked this time for his visit.
JANE   Well, even so Simon, what have you got to lose? You don't want
a riot on your hands, not with the Prince here.
PILKINGS   (*going up to Elesin*) Let's see what he has to say. Chief
Elesin, there is yet another person who wants to see you. As she is
not a next-of-kin I don't really feel obliged to let her in. But your
son sent a note with her, so it's up to you.

ELESIN I know who that must be. So she found out your hiding-place. Well, it was not difficult. My stench of shame is so strong, it requires no hunter's dog to follow it.

PILKINGS If you don't want to see her, just say so and I'll send her packing.

ELESIN Why should I not want to see her? Let her come. I have no more holes in my rag of shame. All is laid bare.

PILKINGS I'll bring her in. (*Goes off.*)

JANE (*hesitates, then goes to Elesin*) Please, try and understand. Everything my husband did was for the best.

ELESIN (*he gives her a long strange stare, as if he is trying to understand who she is*) You are the wife of the District Officer?

JANE Yes. My name, is Jane.

ELESIN That is my wife sitting down there. You notice how still and silent she sits? My business is with your husband.

> *Pilkings returns with Iyaloja.*

PILKINGS Here she is. Now first I want your word of honour that you will try nothing foolish.

ELESIN Honour? White one, did you say you wanted my word of honour?

PILKINGS I know you to be an honourable man. Give me your word of honour you will receive nothing from her.

ELESIN But I am sure you have searched her clothing as you would never dare touch your own mother. And there are these two lizards of yours who roll their eyes even when I scratch.

PILKINGS And I shall be sitting on that tree trunk watching even how you blink. Just the same I want your word that you will not let her pass anything to you.

ELESIN You have my honour already. It is locked up in that desk in which you will put away your report of this night's events. Even the honour of my people you have taken already; it is tied together with those papers of treachery which make you masters in this land.

PILKINGS All right. I am trying to make things easy but if you must bring in politics we'll have to do it the hard way. Madam, I want you to remain along this line and move no nearer to the cell door. Guards! (*They spring to attention.*) If she moves beyond this point, blow your whistle. Come on Jane. (*They go off.*)

IYALOJA How boldly the lizard struts before the pigeon when it was the eagle itself he promised us he would confront.

ELESIN I don't ask you to take pity on me Iyaloja. You have a message for me or you would not have come. Even if it is the curses of the world, I shall listen.

IYALOJA You made so bold with the servant of the white king who took your side against death. I must tell your brother chiefs when I return how bravely you waged war against him. Especially with words.

ELESIN I more than deserve your scorn.

IYALOJA (*with sudden anger*) I warned you, if you must leave a seed behind, be sure it is not tainted with the curses of the world. Who are you to open a new life when you dared not open the door to a new existence? I say who are you to make so bold? (*The bride sobs and Iyaloja notices her. Her contempt noticeably increases as she turns back to Elesin.*) Oh you self-vaunted stem of the plantain, how hollow it all proves. The pith is gone in the parent stem, so how will it prove with the new shoot? How will it go with that earth that bears it? Who are you to bring this abomination on us!

ELESIN   My powers deserted me. My charms, my spells, even my voice lacked strength when I made to summon the powers that would lead me over the last measure of earth into the land of the fleshless. You saw it, Iyaloja. You saw me struggle to retrieve my will from the power of the stranger whose shadow fell across the doorway and left me floundering and blundering in a maze I had never before encountered. My senses were numbed when the touch of cold iron came upon my wrists. I could do nothing to save myself.

IYALOJA   You have betrayed us. We fed you sweetmeats such as we hoped awaited you on the other side. But you said No, I must eat the world's left-overs. We said you were the hunter who brought the quarry down; to you belonged the vital portions of the game. No, you said, I am the hunter's dog and I shall eat the entrails of the game and the faeces of the hunter. We said you were the hunter returning home in triumph, a slain buffalo pressing down on his neck; you said Wait, I first must turn up this cricket hole with my toes. We said yours was the doorway at which we first spy the tapper when he comes down from the tree, yours was the blessing of the twilight wine, the purl that brings night spirits out of doors to steal their portion before the light of day. We said yours was the body of wine whose burden shakes the tapper like a sudden gust on his perch. You said, No, I am content to lick the dregs from each calabash when the drinkers are done. We said, the dew on earth's surface was for you to wash your feet along the slopes of honour. You said No, I shall step in the vomit of cats and the droppings of mice; I shall fight them for the left-overs of the world.

ELESIN   Enough Iyaloja, enough.

IYALOJA   We called you leader and oh, how you led us on. What we have no intention of eating should not be held to the nose.

ELESIN   Enough, enough. My shame is heavy enough.

IYALOJA   Wait. I came with a burden.

ELESIN   You have more than discharged it.

IYALOJA   I wish I could pity you.

ELESIN   I need neither your pity nor the pity of the world. I need understanding. Even I need to understand. You were present at my defeat. You were part of the beginnings. You brought about the renewal of my tie to earth, you helped in the binding of the cord.

IYALOJA   I gave you warning. The river which fills up before our eyes does not sweep us away in its flood.

ELESIN   What were warnings beside the moist contact of living earth between my fingers? What were warnings beside the renewal of fam-

ished embers lodged eternally in the heart of man? But even that,
even if it overwhelmed one with a thousandfold temptations to linger
a little while, a man could overcome it. It is when the alien hand
pollutes the source of will, when a stranger force of violence shatters
the mind's calm resolution, this is when a man is made to commit
the awful treachery of relief, commit in his thought the unspeakable
blasphemy of seeing the hand of the gods in this alien rupture of
his world. I know it was this thought that killed me, sapped my
powers and turned me into an infant in the hands of unnamable
strangers. I made to utter my spells anew but my tongue merely
rattled in my mouth. I fingered hidden charms and the contact was
damp; there was no spark left to sever the life-strings that should
stretch from every finger-tip. My will was squelched in the spittle of
an alien race, and all because I had committed this blasphemy of
thought—that there might be the hand of the gods in a stranger's
intervention.

IYALOJA   Explain it how you will, I hope it brings you peace of mind.
The bush-rat fled his rightful cause, reached the market and set up
a lamentation. 'Please save me!'—are these fitting words to hear
from an ancestral mask? 'There's a wild beast at my heels' is not
becoming language from a hunter.

ELESIN   May the world forgive me.

IYALOJA   I came with a burden I said. It approaches the gates which
are so well guarded by those jackals whose spittle will from this day
be on your food and drink. But first, tell me, you who were once
Elesin Oba, tell me, you who know so well the cycle of the plantain:
is it the parent shoot which withers to give sap to the younger or,
does your wisdom see it running the other way?

ELESIN   I don't see your meaning Iyaloja?

IYALOJA   Did I ask you for a meaning? I asked a question. Whose trunk
withers to give sap to the other? The parent shoot or the younger?

ELESIN   The parent.

IYALOJA   Ah. So you do know that. There are sights in this world which
say different Elesin. There are some who choose to reverse the cycle
of our being. Oh, you emptied bark that the world once saluted for
a pith-laden being, shall I tell you what the gods have claimed of
you?

> In her agitation she steps beyond the line indicated by Pilkings
> and the air is rent by piercing whistles. The two guards also leap
> forward and place safeguarding hands on Elesin. Iyaloja stops,
> astonished. Pilkings comes racing in, followed by Jane.

PILKINGS   What is it? Did they try something?

GUARD   She stepped beyond the line.

ELESIN (in a broken voice)   Let her alone. She meant no harm.

IYALOJA   Oh Elesin, see what you've become. Once you had no need
to open your mouth in explanation because evil-smelling goats, itchy
of hand and foot, had lost their senses. And it was a brave man

indeed who dared lay hands on you because Iyaloja stepped from one side of the earth onto another. Now look at the spectacle of your life. I grieve for you.

PILKINGS   I think you'd better leave. I doubt you have done him much good by coming here. I shall make sure you are not allowed to see him again. In any case we are moving him to a different place before dawn, so don't bother to come back.

IYALOJA   We foresaw that. Hence the burden I trudged here to lay beside your gates.

PILKINGS   What was that you said?

IYALOJA   Didn't our son explain? Ask that one. He knows what it is. At least we hope the man we once knew as Elesin remembers the lesser oaths he need not break.

PILKINGS   Do you know what she is talking about?

ELESIN   Go to the gates, ghostly one. Whatever you find there, bring it to me.

IYALOJA   Not yet. It drags behind me on the slow, weary feet of women. Slow as it is Elesin, it has long overtaken you. It rides ahead of your laggard will.

PILKINGS   What is she saying now? Christ! Must your people forever speak in riddles?

ELESIN   It will come white man, it will come. Tell your men at the gates to let it through.

PILKINGS   (*dubiously*)   I'll have to see what it is.

IYALOJA   You will. (*Passionately.*) But this is one oath he cannot shirk. White one, you have a king here, a visitor from your land. We know of his presence here. Tell me, were he to die would you leave his spirit roaming restlessly on the surface of earth? Would you bury him here among those you consider less than human? In your land have you no ceremonies of the dead?

PILKINGS   Yes. But we don't make our chiefs commit suicide to keep him company.

IYALOJA   Child, I have not come to help your understanding. (*Points to Elesin.*) This is the man whose weakened understanding holds us in bondage to you. But ask him if you wish. He knows the meaning of a king's passage; he was not born yesterday. He knows the peril to the race when our dead father, who goes as intermediary, waits and waits and knows he is betrayed. He knows when the narrow gate was opened and he knows it will not stay for laggards who drag their feet in dung and vomit, whose lips are reeking of the left-overs of lesser men. He knows he has condemned our King to wander in the void of evil with beings who are enemies of life.

PILKINGS   Yes er . . . but look here . . .

IYALOJA   What we ask is little enough. Let him release our King so he can ride on homewards alone. The messenger is on his way on the backs of women. Let him send word through the heart that is folded up within the bolt. It is the least of all his oaths, it is the easiest fulfilled.

The Aide-de-Camp runs in.

PILKINGS   Bob?

AIDE-DE-CAMP   Sir, there's a group of women chanting up the hill.

PILKINGS (*rounding on Iyaloja*)   If you people want trouble . . .

JANE   Simon, I think that's what Olunde referred to in his letter.

PILKINGS   He knows damned well I can't have a crowd here! Damn it,
    I explained the delicacy of my position to him. I think it's about time
    I got him out of town. Bob, send a car and two or three soldiers to
    bring him in. I think the sooner he takes his leave of his father and
    gets out the better.

IYALOJA   Save your labour white one. If it is the father of your prisoner
    you want, Olunde, he who until this night we knew as Elesin's son,
    he comes soon himself to take his leave. He has sent the women
    ahead, so let them in.

Pilkings remains undecided.

AIDE-DE-CAMP   What do we do about the invasion? We can still stop
    them far from here.

PILKINGS   What do they look like?

AIDE-DE-CAMP   They're not many. And they seem quite peaceful.

PILKINGS   No men?

AIDE-DE-CAMP   Mm, two or three at the most.

JANE   Honestly, Simon, I'd trust Olunde. I don't think he'll deceive
    you about their intentions.

PILKINGS   He'd better not. All right then, let them in Bob. Warn them
    to control themselves. Then hurry Olunde here. Make sure he brings
    his baggage because I'm not returning him into town.

AIDE-DE-CAMP   Very good, sir. (*Goes.*)

PILKINGS (*to Iyaloja*)   I hope you understand that if anything goes
    wrong it will be on your head. My men have orders to shoot at the
    first sign of trouble.

IYALOJA   To prevent one death you will actually make other deaths?
    Ah, great is the wisdom of the white race. But have no fear. Your
    Prince will sleep peacefully. So at long last will ours. We will disturb
    you no further, servant of the white King. Just let Elesin fulfil his
    oath and we will retire home and pay homage to our King.

JANE   I believe her Simon, don't you?

PILKINGS   Maybe.

ELESIN   Have no fear ghostly one. I have a message to send my King
    and then you have nothing more to fear.

IYALOJA   Olunde would have done it. The chiefs asked him to speak
    the words but he said no, not while you lived.

ELESIN   Even from the depths to which my spirit has sunk, I find some
    joy that this little has been left to me.

> *The women enter, intoning the dirge 'Ale le le' and swaying from
> side to side. On their shoulders is borne a longish object roughly
> like a cylindrical bolt, covered in cloth. They set it down on the
> spot where Iyaloja had stood earlier, and form a semi-circle round*

it. The Praise-Singer and drummer stand on the inside of the semi-circle but the drum is not used at all. The drummer intones under the Praise-Singer's invocations.

PILKINGS (*as they enter*) What is *that*?

IYALOJA The burden you have made white one, but we bring it in peace.

PILKINGS I said *what* is it?

ELESIN White man, you must let me out. I have a duty to perform.

PILKINGS I most certainly will not.

ELESIN There lies the courier of my King. Let me out so I can perform what is demanded of me.

PILKINGS You'll do what you need to do from inside there or not at all. I've gone as far as I intend to with this business.

ELESIN The worshipper who lights a candle in your church to bear a message to his god bows his head and speaks in a whisper to the flame. Have I not seen it ghostly one? His voice does not ring out to the world. Mine are no words for anyone's ears. They are not words even for the bearers of this load. They are words I must speak secretly, even as my father whispered them in my ears and I in the ears of my first-born. I cannot shout them to the wind and the open night-sky.

JANE Simon . . .

PILKINGS Don't interfere. Please!

IYALOJA They have slain the favourite horse of the King and slain his dog. They have borne them from pulse to pulse centre of the land receiving prayers for their King. But the rider has chosen to stay behind. Is it too much to ask that he speak his heart to heart of the waiting courier? (*Pilkings turns his back on her.*) So be it, Elesin Oba, you see how even the mere leavings are denied you. (*She gestures to the Praise-Singer.*)

PRAISE-SINGER Elesin Oba! I call you by that name only this last time. Remember when I said, if you cannot come, tell my horse. (*Pause.*) What? I cannot hear you? I said, if you cannot come, whisper in the ears of my horse. Is your tongue severed from the roots? Elesin? I can hear no response. I said, if there are boulders you cannot climb, mount my horse's back, this spotless black stallion, he'll bring you over them. (*Pauses.*) Elesin Oba, once you had a tongue that darted like a drummer's stick. I said, if you get lost my dog will track a path to me. My memory fails me but I think you replied: My feet have found the path, Alafin.

The dirge rises and falls.

I said at the last, if evil hands hold you back, just tell my horse there is weight on the hem of your smock. I dare not wait too long.

The dirge rises and falls.

There lies the swiftest ever messenger of a king, so set me free with the errand of your heart. There lie the head and heart of the favourite of the gods, whisper in his ears. Oh my companion, if you had followed when you should, we would not say that the horse preceded its rider. If you had followed when it was time, we would not say the dog has raced beyond and left his master behind. If you had raised your will to cut the thread of life at the summons of the drums, we would not say your mere shadow fell across the gateway and took its owner's place at the banquet. But the hunter, laden with slain buffalo, stayed to root in the cricket's hole with his toes. What now is left? If there is a dearth of bats, the pigeon must serve us for the offering. Speak the words over your shadow which must now serve in your place.

ELESIN I cannot approach. Take off the cloth. I shall speak my message from heart to heart of silence.

IYALOJA (*moves forward and removes the covering*) Your courier Elesin, cast your eyes on the favoured companion of the King.

> *Rolled up in the mat, his head and feet showing at either end, is the body of Olunde.*

There lies the honour of your household and of our race. Because he could not bear to let honour fly out of doors, he stopped it with his life. The son has proved the father, Elesin, and there is nothing left in your mouth to gnash but infant gums.

PRAISE-SINGER Elesin, we placed the reins of the world in your hands yet you watched it plunge over the edge of the bitter precipice. You sat with folded arms while evil strangers tilted the world from its course and crashed it beyond the edge of emptiness—you muttered, there is little that one man can do, you left us floundering in a blind future. Your heir has taken the burden on himself. What the end will be, we are not gods to tell. But this young shoot has poured its sap into the parent stalk, and we know this is not the way of life. Our world is tumbling in the void of strangers, Elesin.

> *Elesin has stood rock-still, his knuckles taut on the bars, his eyes glued to the body of his son. The stillness seizes and paralyses everyone, including Pilkings who has turned to look. Suddenly Elesin flings one arm round his neck, once, and with the loop of the chain, strangles himself in a swift, decisive pull. The guards rush forward to stop him but they are only in time to let his body down. Pilkings has leapt to the door at the same time and struggles with the lock. He rushes within, fumbles with the handcuffs and unlocks them, raises the body to a sitting position while he tries to give resuscitation. The women continue their dirge, unmoved by the sudden event.*

IYALOJA Why do you strain yourself? Why do you labour at tasks for which no one, not even the man lying there, would give you thanks? He is gone at last into the passage but oh, how late it all is. His son will feast on the meat and throw him bones. The passage is clogged with droppings from the King's stallion; he will arrive all stained in dung.

PILKINGS (*in a tired voice*)   Was this what you wanted?

IYALOJA   No child, it is what you brought to be, you who play with strangers' lives, who even usurp the vestments of our dead, yet believe that the stain of death will not cling to you. The gods demanded only the old expired plantain but you cut down the sap-laden shoot to feed your pride. There is your board, filled to overflowing. Feast on it. (*She screams at him suddenly, seeing that Pilkings is about to close Elesin's staring eyes.*) Let him alone! However sunk he was in debt he is no pauper's carrion abandoned on the road. Since when have strangers donned clothes of indigo before the bereaved cries out his loss?

She turns to the bride who has remained motionless throughout.

Child.

The girl takes up a little earth, walks calmly into the cell and closes Elesin's eyes. She then pours some earth over each eyelid and comes out again.

IYALOJA   Now forget the dead, forget even the living. Turn your mind only to the unborn.

She goes off, accompanied by the bride. The dirge rises in volume and the women continue their sway. Lights fade to a blackout.

TSEGAYE GABRE-MEDHIN

Collision of Altars[†]

A Conflict of the Ancient Red Sea Gods

A PLAY BASED ON THE FALL OF THE THIRD GREATEST POWER IN THE
WORLD: EMPEROR KALEB'S AXUMITE ETHIOPIA OF SIXTH CENTURY.

> Your god, my good brother, cannot
> set my god right; nor shall my
> dreams step down for yours to
> step up.   *Hamitic proverb.*

Characters

KING KALEB (THE HERMIT)	*The Axumite Ethiopian Emperor. Abdicated his Throne in favour of his younger son Gabre Maskel, Nezana, in AD 542 when his great expedition to Arabia failed. Instead he became a monk, but, here for the purpose of the play we make him a hermit and retain his abdication until AD 587.*
ABA PANTELEON (THIRD VOICE)	*Head Monk, Confessor, and Royal Overseer. Symbolic head of the Orthodox Christian faith in Axum. Also plays the Third Voice.*
RABBI YONA (SECOND VOICE)	*The Prince Bet Isreal, elder son of Kaleb. Symbolic head of Black Judaic faith in Axum. Also plays the Second Voice.*
NEZANA	*Kaleb's younger son, the King Gabre-Maskel, or, Servant of The Cross.*
QUEEN NOBA	*King Nezana's wife, daughter of the Chief of the Southern Lake people of 'Semri'. (Descendants of the fallen Empire of Kush.)*
ARMAH	*Nezana's son, the Crown Prince.*

† Tsegaye Gabre-Medhin, *Collision of Altars* (London: Rex Collings, 1977). Reprinted by permission of the author.

CHIEF WATTO	*Head of the elders of the Southern Lake people. Symbolic head for the old religion of the Noble Serpent in and around Axum. Also plays First Voice (priest of Atetse or Issis).*
ARAAYA	*Little Prince Araaya, the great grand-child of Kaleb, better known as Dagna Dejan.*
JAFFAR	*Jaffar Bin Abu Talib, Cousin of Mohammed, the new Prophet from Mecca. Leader of the immigrant family of Mohammed now in Axum. Also plays Fourth Voice, symbolic head of earliest Islamic faith in Axum.*
RAMIA	*Ramia Umm'Habibah, the young member of the immigrant family who is the betrothed of Mohammed, and ex-wife of Uthman Bin Huwayrith.*
ROYAL CRIER	*A blind Persian woman called Zara-dushia, serving as Royal Crier.*
MAD JULIAN	*Captain Julian, the Roman prison officer who was the Consul of Byzantium, later imprisoned and became mad.*
ABAS	*Governor of Adulis Port Town and Captain of the Palace Body Guard. Also chief Royal flogger.*
TWO GUARDS	*The two Keepers of palace gate peace, and assistant royal floggers of Axum.*
CHILDREN'S CHORUS	*A group of nine village urchins, with a range of nine to fifteen years of age, of all skin colours and sizes; all looking like thugs.*
MOTHER'S CHORUS	*A group of five lean-faced, worn, Hamitic type African mothers, in dirty and torn leather skirts. They wear beads, some are almost naked, with old Nilo-Hamite hair-dos.*
BEGGAR'S CHORUS	*A group of seven dishevelled, rather old and tattered beggars, with sticks and shrunken leather pouches.*

All characters and all chorus groups are a mixture of all colours, a result of Hamitic African, Arab, Indian, Jewish, Greek, etc. cross-breeding.

Apart from Kaleb, Nezana (Gabre-Maskel), Armah, Watto, Araaya, (Dagna Dejen), Yona (Bet Isreal), Aba Panteleon, Jaffar, Ramia and

Abas, all names are imaginary, and to a considerable extent, the mannerisms of all the characters are also imaginary.

Place

The Altars of the City of Axum: The Then Capital of Ethiopia.

Time

587 AD–629 AD

Act One
End of the Great Rise

I. CALLS OF THE INNER-VOICES

Darkness. Midnight. Axum, AD 587. Off-stage, single ritualized calls from four competitive voices, respectively. Humming in the distance more voices calling out other devotions of more primitive sects may also be echoed. Out of the darkness, the declamation of each of the four voices cause their respective symbolic signs to blaze out on a large metal frame hanging on centre back wall. The wall itself is in the shape of a huge red marble heart, the royal insignia of Axum. Each time the symbolizing voices of each of the faiths are pronounced, the large metal pieces in the heart-shaped wall blaze out, first, in the form of a writhing enormous Serpent, next, as the Star of David, third, as the Holy Cross, and finally as the Holy Crescent. Unless lighted on, the metal glows are normally less visible than the red, huge heart-wall forming the background of the stage.

VOICE ONE (*from the far dark*)
  The spirits of our dead, demand.
  The spirits of our living, obey.
    (*Serpent lights up*)
  I, Watto, speaker of their will,
  And of your dreams, command.
  Listen my children,
  Children of our life-giving lake,
  Children of our red water gate
  We have caused
  Our Noble Serpent to starve.
  From the bosom of our bright waters
  We have caused it, the Mother of Ham
  To lick at the muddy sand.
  Our eyes have strayed long
  Away from your pharoahinic roots
  Across the dirt of the salt water, and
  Towards the distant Kabah Stone of the Quaryash.
  Our ears have taken in
  The many strange gods of Sabea
  Of our Axumite brother-masters,
  The war-gods, long married
  To our land and daughters.
  We have trained our hearts to refuse
  The seasonal offerings expected of us.
  We have dared to deny our Noble Serpent Ra
  Mother of Kushite Meroe
  That which is its ancestral right.
  But listen my children,
  The spirits of our dead Ham still demand
  The spirits of our living must obey.

    Wild stifled human groans from within, then humming drums.
    Blackout on serpent. Silence.

VOICE TWO (*from the far dark*)
  Sh'maa Yisrael
    (*Star of David lights up*)
  Adonai Alohenu, Adonai Ehad.
  Hear, O Israel convert
  The Lord our God, the Lord is one.
  Sh'maa Yisrael,
  I am Rabbi Yona, servant of Jehova
  Known as the Prince Bet Israel.
  My aged, frail and tired father
  The Great Emperor Kaleb of Axumite
  Ethiopia
  Is about to abdicate his Throne
  In favour of my younger brother

The Christian Heir Apparent Prince Gabre
Maskel, Half breed of Kush Throne
Known as The Servant of The Cross.
Hear, O Israel convert
The Lord is one, and Axum is One.

> *Drums clash with horn pipes. Blackout on the Star of David.*
> *Silence.*

VOICE THREE (*from the far dark*)
Bism 'Ab, Wo-Wold,
Wo-Menfes Kidus. Amen.
Our father which art in Heaven,
　　(*Holy Cross Lights up*)
Why hast thou forsaken us!
I am the Head Monk, Aba Panteleon
Confessor of the Royal Household
Overseer for the Empire of Great Kaleb.
I speak the voice of the Savior,
I speak the will of Axum.
. . . The grace of the Lord Jesus Christ,
The love of God,
And the communion of the Holy Ghost
Be with us all.
Axumite Ethiopia stretches her hands
In supplication to God.

> *Clash of bells, drums, horn pipes and wild cries of joy. Blackout*
> *on Cross.*

VOICE FOUR (*from the far dark*)
Bism Alah Al'rahman Al'rahim,
　　(*Holy Crescent lights up*)
Praise belongs to Alah.
I, Jaffar Bin Abu Talib
Cousin of our Apostle Mohammad
—May Alah bless and preserve him—
Speak. O great Nagashi Kaleb
Kind descendent of Sabea
Protector of Mohammad's family
And of his betrothed, Ramia Umm'habibah
All here, under your good care
—May Alah bless and preserve you—.
The Prophet has bidden me to say
That Arabia is a barbarous nation
Worshipping idols, eating carrion
Fornicating, committing shameful deeds
The strong devouring the weak.
And now Alah has smitten
The enemies of the Nabi
Who seduced his faithful.
Wherefore he sends you Great Nagashi
And his people of Islam here

A message of peace and courage.
Hear, O people of the Kitab
Praise belongs to Alah
To the Lord of the worlds
To the Merciful, the Compassionate
To the Wielder of the Day of Judgement.
Him do we serve
And on Him do we call for help.

> *Horn pipes, cries of joy, crash of brass sistras and drums. Blackout on Crescent.*

II. INTRODUCTION AND THE MIME OF THE ROYAL MOCK-DEATH
PART ONE

Early morning. Dim stage light. On centre stage, a huge altar of many phases. Convertible into a massive oriental throne—Axumite Ethiopian style—into large lecterns of various denominations, and into a huge block for a tomb. A few paces towards the front of the stage, at centre left of the tomb, is a stone gate which leads to a ladder, going down to a dungeon. On both sides of the front stage, two narrow wall drops, showing the Axumite steles. There are two steps at the foot of each stele. At the foot of the steps of the left stele, a dove holding a tall batch of olive branches towards the audience. At the foot of the right one, the clutch of a hawk's claws throwing its kill of a dove at the audience. The steles have small window-sized doors opening out to the steps leading towards the front edge of the stage.

Enter mime of the Royal Mock-Death. Brass horn pipes announce the Royal entrance. The King and his entourage appear at right of Heart-shaped wall. They are, first, a uniform group under one spotlight, pausing like in a family painting. Suddenly they separate, each under different shades of different spotlights.

Emperor Kaleb, the Axumite Ethiopian monarch, at the close of his reign, (AD 587). Rather frail, aged, pale and grief-worn. His crown weighs heavily on his pointed forehead. Though old, his bearing of confidence is still there. At times, aloof, eerie, exuding an air of the unknown, of an almost unearthly bearing. Beneath his searching deep gaze, eliciting fear and a calm possessive terror, one sees he is tormented. He moves in centre forward, held supported by his grandson, Prince Armah, on his left, and the Head Monk, Aba Panteleon, on his right. Their support is merely a symbolic gesture; he finds himself leaning on his Royal cane, the long silver sceptre. He wears a life-death mask, green and red, along either side of his face. His mimed performance depicts a spiritually broken old ruler, who, just before surrendering his crown to an invisible power, fights an inner moral war with a fierce final courage of desperation. His battle looks more a mental state than real, one of being torn between two strong decisions rather than between physical forces.

*Nezana, his son, also known as Gabre-Maskel or Servant of
the Cross is about to be crowned King. He is late-middle-aged,
tall, lean, greying, sensitive and touchy. He has developed a shrill
voice, a rather slender feminine posture, smoother features, and
the demon's cunning. Rumours tell that he was emasculated, just
before the birth of his son Armah, during an expedition he led
against the neighbouring tribe of Angabe. Despite his violent fits
which possessed him at birth and thus deprived him of the full
exercise of his faculties, Nezana is regarded as active, a devout if
not a fanatic Christian. He is also a religious idealist; elegant,
subtle, and a charming death-god. Nezana has assured airs, a
cruel subtle face, but is capable at times of melancholy and bitterness to the extent of self indulgence. At present, he wears a
helmet-type mask, engraved with the cross; a determined militant appearance of an Axumite military leader set on a sense of
mission. The mime he performs depicts one who moves with
confidence, balance, and determination. His presence is also
commanding, his steps definite. The tide of a will for triumph
seems to rise in him as that of his father's is falling. His sardonic
stare elicits a vague, pitiful quiet in the father, provokes arrogance
in Prince Armah, and strikes fear in the Head Monk. While miming, he follows immediately behind his father, yet keeps an exaggerated formal distance between them.*

*Aba Panteleon, the Head Monk, is Confessor of the Royal
Household and overseer of the Empire's interests. His cross-shaped
mask is pulled down on his face from the top of his head-dress.
He is in his late seventies but very well preserved. Thickset, cor-
pulent, and heavily bearded. His intelligently imposing serene
eyes and cool manners give him the looks of one accustomed to
being listened to. He is a keen, deft diplomat, well experienced in
the petty ecclesiastical intrigues of the day. His clothing has more
pomp and ornamentation than that of the Royal family. The large
silver processional cross he holds up with both hands with reverent
awe is huge and very high above his head. His mime shows a solemn devotee, overtly compassionate, yet with an underlying will to
interpret his personal wishes into what he expects to be accepted
only as the will of Kaleb. This Panteleon is the son of a young Syrian orphan, found among the famous nine saved from a Syrian
shipwreck. His father, later on, left him in the care of the original
old bishop Panteleon. He was then re-initiated, re-baptised and
helped to make his way up to the Royal Court, by the meticulous
apprenticeship of the bishop, Abune Panteleon, who was the oldest
in the Syrian monks' group, yet the one who, until his recent death,
outlived his nine exalted friends.*[1]

1. These are the Nine White Syrian bishops who took flight to Axum during the reign of Tezana,
A.D. 463–502, and established themselves as the spiritual guides of the Empire. The party
of the Nine Holy Ones is believed to be the only group who managed to escape to Axum
from among the hundreds of the followers of Eutytyches and Dioscurus at the Council of
Chalcedon. The rest were either deposed or banished for heresy after the Fourth Ecumenical
Council of the Catholic Church, held at Chalcedone, "The City of the Blind," on 8th October, A.D. 451.

This present Panteleon is considered a near exact behavorial duplicate, raised in the true image of his long deceased finder and spiritual father, particularly where the sensitive question of contempt for the Byzantine authority is concerned. Now with a token mime support towards the spiritually agonized Monarch, he leads him ceremoniously to the Altar.

Prince Armah, Kaleb's grandson, is twenty-eight, and the only son of Gabre Maskel, Nezana. He is about to be crowned Crown Prince. Often at odds with his father Nezana, he has grown with a stronger feeling towards his grandfather. Yet his rough, crude pride checks him from exposing this attachment too obviously. His eyes gleam more hope than ambition yet his unsettled air betrays quite a relentless personal will. He too is sensitive, a little rash, at times defiant, even spoilt. His heavy limbs give him an awkward posture, but his movements are quite nimble in spite of this. Armah stands out for his amicable nature, and guileless carriage. In his lonelier moments, he plays on the church drums, no doubt an influence of 'the great hymn compiler, his friend, the Court's favourite poet, the famous old Yared, (later Saint Yared).' Armah's mask is in the shape of a gosling in fight, the edges of whose wings flicker a star-like radiance as he moves. With his left hand, he carries a golden casket which he intermittently holds up with ceremony. His mime consists of a more sincere symbolic support for his afflicted grandfather, of gesturing the highlights of his desolation, and of tempering this with an arrogance towards his father.

Each is led under his separate circle of spotlight. All movements are mute, precise, urgent and intimate. Each moves, theatrically, towards centre stage, then back to the step at the foot of the Altar. Each mimes, interprets his separate message, separately, as he stops facing the Altar. Abe Panteleon, muttering a silent prayer, stands on the right of the Altar (and stands) with his cross facing the other three. Nezana and Armah kneel, Kaleb prostrates himself with his hands stretched out to form the cross. He stays down spread-eagled with his forehead pressed against the floor. The entire mime should not last more than one minute. As the spots merge into one, they are once more framed as a group. Horn pipes, drums and the crash of instruments rise in the background. Silence. With the stage lights turning brighter, we find that the speakers of the Inner Voices are standing on either side of the heart-wall; Watto on the right, Rabbi Yona and Jaffar on the left.

ROYAL CRIER (proclaims off stage)
Now kneels great Kaleb, wrecked
Wrapped in sackcloth, fallen on ashes
Cut off from the grace of His favourite saints.
His sixty thousand strong sons of Axum
Together with the scores

Of his giant warring elephants
Are eaten up by the plague of Mecca,
Sunk into the dust of desert earth.
The winds of Arabia
Are clouded red by their young blood.
Here, Kaleb is masked
In the shade of his bated breath,
Aware of his painful days
That have come to the brink,
The great Kaleb is shorn of faith.
He has erased his memory of Sobok
Of Ethiopis, of Endebis, and of Tezana
His triumphant forefathers,
Of mighty Ezana
Who reduced the Nations of Tiawa, Agame,
And the distant Arabetics
Beyond the Khybar water's gate
To his iron will.
Here, kneels great Kaleb, tired.
He will not allow himself
To come forward any more
And have the dead homes
Of his people in his sight.
Here, his noble spirit torn into shreds,
His mettle brow hit into the dust of earth
He will not allow his face of grief
To pry upon the wounds
Of his left-over people.
A people now melted down
To a nation without sons.

MOTHERS' CHORUS (*A group of wailing, lean mothers, not less than five,
of all sizes and ages, of all skin colours, and of Axum's and her neigh-
bouring hair styles, with beads and clay masks, in leather rags, some
almost naked, humming a litany in the half-dim, like shadows sway
and crawl across the stage beneath the Heart-wall.*)
Our wombs cry for our sons,
Whose tender bloods
The plague of Arabia claimed.
Our eyes ache for their sight
But the desert vultures
That slit out their beautiful eyes
Have perched back on our castrated homes.
They scratch for the worms in our roofs.
Where are the flowers of our lives, Kaleb?
Why have you pinned down our love
To rust in a scavenging day?
Where are our men, Kaleb?
Why have you hung our wombs to dry
Beyond the darkness of time?
Our breasts hurt, demanding

What visitation ravaged our essence.
The sleepless spirits
Accuse our thoughts, Kaleb.
The season of mothers
Question our dreamless nights.
Our wombs cry for our sons,
Our feet fret for their sight.
Where are the flowers of our lives, Kaleb?

> *They go out crawling. Kaleb rises. Tears his gown off his shoul-*
> *ders. Makes an effort to keep his head high. Lights half-dim. The*
> *altar turns immediately into his throne. Lights brighten. On ei-*
> *ther side of the throne are two golden statues of unicorns. Aba*
> *Panteleon steps back and raises the cross. As Kaleb staggers and*
> *sits himself on the throne, Nezana and Armah stand on either*
> *side of it. Except for Kaleb, the others remove their masks by*
> *pulling them down to the back of their necks. We find that Ne-*
> *zana has a dusky light-brownish Arab complexion with a slight*
> *African bone structure. Aba Panteleon has a whitish Syrian skin,*
> *and Armah, a dark-brown complexion with a heavier African*
> *bone structure. Kaleb gestures an elaborate hand-clap and horn*
> *pipes bleat in the background.*

ABA PANTELEON
Call the Southern Princess, Noba
Daughter of the Chief Watto of Semri
Wife of the Servant of The Cross
Mother of the Prince Armah.
Also call the child Prince Araaya
Great-grandson of Great Kaleb,
Born of a Yemenite slave girl
To the young Prince Armah.

> *Noba enters. In her late forties still a black elegance. Shy, ma-*
> *ternal, impervious, and with unaffected high-breed bearing. She*
> *is the mother of Armah, through marriage to Nezana, being the*
> *daughter of the Berber Chief Watto, of the Southern Lake Re-*
> *gion. She bows low ceremoniously, Ethiopian style, to the throne,*
> *then stands on the left of Nezana, keeping Prince Araaya beside*
> *her.*
>
> *Araaya is a nine-year-old, timid child with intelligent eyes. Has*
> *a dark brown complexion, long old Ethiopian hair style, and large*
> *earrings. He carries a David's toy-harp slung across his shoulders.*
>
> *Aba Panteleon formally opens the golden casket which Armah*
> *is holding. Draws out a rolled goat-skin parchment, a feather pen*
> *with a bamboo handle and a horn ink pot. Leaning the large*
> *cross at the foot of the throne, he prepares to write. Kaleb gestures*
> *the writing of his final will. Seated, regal, he gestures his instruc-*
> *tions. Royal Crier commences interpreting his mute mime into*
> *words. (Stage lights slightly dim.)*

ROYAL CRIER (*Spot light on Royal Crier coming out of the left side stele
on to the front step. She is blind, a bell on her left arm, a stick with
the other hand. She is Persian, about thirty but dishevelled, tattered
and looking over fifty.*)
In the absence, by sudden disappearance
Of Cosmos, the royal scribe,
Our Greek slave-scholar from Egypt
We commend our Head Monk
Confessor and Royal Overseer Aba Panteleon
To write our final will to our people.
ROYAL CRIER (*proclaims*)
Write.
(*Panteleon writes*)
Our fathers were the chosen sons
Of the god Mahrem
The god Astar and the god Beher
Since the memory of time.
Driven by the Hymerites
And led by their Sabean gods
They floated to this promised land
Where the water is milk
And the soil, bread.
Our fathers humiliated boastful Egypt,
Brought Nubia to her knees,
Drove Mahas and Faras into slavery.
Seven generations of Kings lived
Initiated into the house of Abraham
Before it was revealed to them
That they should take the new ways of Christianity.
Since the great King Ezana
Cousin of our father's great grandfather
Seated himself, by will of God, on Meroe and
On this throne of his Axumite Fathers,
The sovereign vow
That only Christian Orthodox Kings
Born of the same royal blood should rule
Has been successfully carried out
To this day of our reign.
Many are the altars on this land of Kush
But Christ chose the faith of her Kings.
And when Justinian of Byzantium
Called on us
In the name of the Cross,
To raise our arms
Against those Judaic persecutors
Of the lonely Nagran Christians,
We accepted, and rose
In the name of the Mother of Jesus,
In the name of our forefather King of Kings
And the Christians elect of God.

Seven years we toiled
At our port of Aduliss.
We built boats,
Trained charging elephant bulls
Bought and made arms.
We raised our young and strong
In the cunning art of war.
We punished our fanatic Jewish brethren
Who were the murderers of the helpless Christians.
We carved and erected there
The monumental church of Nagran in Arabia.
Yet it became the will
Of our Elector-Father-God
That at the doors of Mecca
A single moon of pestilence
Should smother our entire army,
And flatten it against the heathen soil of Kabah.

BEGGARS' CHORUS (*Lights half-dim. A disheveled, tattered very old men's chorus group, not less than seven, of all colours, of old-type African facial and hair makes, cross the stage, chanting, stampeding and swaying under the heart-wall.*)
We are your dung-sweating peasant horde, Kaleb.
We are the humbled bones
Bent in the thick of your silence.
Ask of your father God who elected you
Why he has foresaken us.
Why the earth is flattened tight
On the guts of our sons.
Why fate has grabbed our hopes
Out of our mouths.
Our laughter racks in nakedness, Kaleb
Our folk-tales taste of blood.
Dry tears tear at our throats
And our fingers have failed
To scratch a living out of the poisoned Soil.
Our huts are dank, rat-ridden,
Our dreams mired in destitution,
Our pride churned and blown to the winds.
Ask of your God, Kaleb
Ask why.

> *They go out. Kaleb struggles to a half-kneeling posture, shrunk and crouching on his throne. He lifts his crown which appears to weigh heavily on his hands. He places it between his knees. With a hand-clap from him, horn pipes blare out off stage.*

PANTELEON (*rising*)
Call the young woman, Ramia Umm'Habibah
Divorcee of the baptized Meccan
Uthman Bin Huwayrith,

Daughter of the Nation of Islam
And the betrothed of the Nabi Mohammad.

*Habibah enters and stops near Jaffar. She is a modest, middle-
sized young Yemenite, in pink and silver armlets. Large black
eyes, bushy eyebrow, and rich hair as dark as night. Her hair is
a bit delicate for a peasant. An olive-skinned and rather shy oriental beauty. Her slender arms and long neck seem to elongate
themselves in a deliberate contrast to her full, round chest and
sound hips. Kaleb gestures Aba Panteleon to continue the writing
of the will. Royal Crier commences to interpret.*

ROYAL CRIER (*proclaims*)
Write.
    (*Panteleon squats to write*)
We, sole elect of God
Of the chosen house of Abraham
Master of Axum, the Angabe, the Barbara
Patron of the Tziamo and the Zoa
Conqueror of the Aua and the Kaloa
Protector of the Thiamoe, the Agame
The Himyar and the Raydon,
Have on this seventh day
Of our Lord's Sabath
In the year of his birth
Five hundred and eighty seven
Decided, of our own discretion
To abstain ourselves
From all matters of throne.
To curtail our wishes
Entirely within our person.
And thus to die here and now
A total death from all authority.
    (*Horn pipes moan, drums tremble*)
Also by the will of God
We hereby bequeath our throne and crown
Of this Christian kingdom
To our son and heir apparent Nezana
Servant Of The Holy Cross,
The reign of queenship, to his wife Noba,
The Crown Princeship, to our grandson, Armah,
All of them being elects of Jehova.
The king Nezana and the Crown Prince Armah
As true royal members
Of the chosen house of Abraham,
And the Queen Noba
By right of holy matrimony. Amen.

*Crash of instruments. Simultaneously with the last words, Kaleb
lifts his crown with both hands, passes it to Aba Panteleon, who
holding it high and muttering the prayer 'Bism Ab, Wo-Wold,
Wo-menfes Kidus . . .' etc., places it ceremoniously on Nezana's*

head. Out of the casket carried by Armah he draws a large crown for Noba which he places on her head. He also divests Kaleb of his imperial robe, draws out an ordinary monk's head-dress, a tattered gown and a small wooden cross. Spreads these separately at the foot of the throne. At the same time he takes the crown of the Crown prince from Nezana's head and holding it up places it on Armah's head. Crash of Instruments.

ROYAL CRIER (*proclaims, interpreting Kaleb's mime.*)
By force of custom
The old rule.
  (*Panteleon writes*)
By urge of the gods of seasons
The young question to defy.
By command of time
Life crawls on.
And now, I, says Kaleb the Hermit,
I, a naked creature born of the sweat of dust
I, common mud among the herd
A drift of shadow in no man's abode,
Do, here and now
Of my own free will, choose
To deny my person
The pleasures of worldly vanities.
I choose to hide and creep
In the clouds of my last seasons
To snuggle my tired breath
Into the isolated shade
Of mute silent hermitage.
There, my son and King Nezana,
Upon your shoulders rest the burden of Axum.
Send the great Crown of our fathers
To the Holy City, Jerusalem
To lie beside the grave of Jesus.
Consider with great caution
The rising of the Zarathustran pagan hordes
That shade the skies of Persia.
Look with kindness
Upon the people of your wife,
The tribe of the house of Watto
Along with all the other tribes
Who, before the memory of history
Peopled this promised land.

   Watto, the thin, graceful, old, stooping, masked chief, steps forward armed with a ceremonial spear, shield and arrows. The metal Serpent lights and dims out on him as he bows.

Protect, care and defend
The family of the young Mohammad
Also called Rasul and Prophet
Who are here in our shelter

From the angry swords
Of the Umm'Ayalid Amirs.
He has sent us his word of supplication
From the caves of Hira
Where he meditates in hiding.
He has informed us in secret
That the terrible Califs
Asked for the return of his family
Only in order to put them to the sword.
Send back the gifts
Of these Califs, my son.
You should not
Give up Mohammad's families
Who have taken refuge with our Cross
Even if they were to offer you
A mountain of gold.

> *Ramia Umm'Habibah with Jaffar Bin Abu Talib, leader of the*
> *first escape to Axum, step forward and bow. Crescent lights and*
> *dims out on them. Jaffar is on the young side of his middle age,*
> *dressed in white gown, a blue turban with simple ornament, and*
> *is lightly bearded. A pair of dull, unimpressive eyes seem to hold*
> *back a storm of anxiety in his head. His smooth face clearly shows*
> *the hard lines of time and exhaustion. The wet, hanging lips give*
> *him a foolish look. His sense of mission seems to dominate his*
> *will even in spite of himself. He is quite eager to impress, but*
> *much quicker to defend himself. He is quite eager to impress, but*
> *much quicker to defend his new faith.*

Grant my elder son
Your half-brother Rabbi Yona
The right to worship in his Synagogue,
Since, because of his Talmudic Faith,
He has now lost to you
The throne of his fathers.

> *Rabbi Yona, the short Ethiopian black Jew of indeterminate age*
> *and impressive figure, steps forward and bows. The Star of David*
> *lights and dims out on him.*

Permit the release of the Roman Officer Julian
The messenger of Constantinople
Whose letter was the ill cause
Of our sending the sons of Axum
On that expedition to calamity.
He is now unable to feel
The slow pains of our vengeance
Since his nineteen years in the dungeon
Have watered his wits into ruin.

ABA PANTELEON (*rising*)
Command our Captain of the guards, Aba,

To summon out
The Roman prisoner-officer
From the royal dungeon.

> *With a characteristic theatrical elaboration, Nezana makes a
> hand-clap, and horn pipes sound out. Chained and under two
> guards, a middle-aged, broken Byzantine officer with a blank face
> and lost wits is pushed up from the opening in the floor. He falls
> between Captain Abas and the two guards who bring him out.
> Abas, Governor of Adulis Port-town, is Chief of Royal Bodyguard.
> A step-son of the former Adulis Governor also called Abas, (one
> of Kaleb's able commanders during the expedition on Dhu Nu-
> was). It was on the death of the former that the present inherited
> the post. He is often reported for secretly conducting a private
> slave trade with his mother's relatives, the Bedouin nomads hiding
> in the islands of the Khaybar. His brute mind is what attracts
> Nezana, since he needs him to curb the unrest now affecting
> Axum. Abas is impulsive, rough, doctrinaire, ruthless and even
> lustful. Often looked down upon at the Court, because of his
> unaccepted Bedouin blood, he uses the excuse of Nezana's law
> and his own brutal scourge, to punish the society that has denied
> him identity. Armed with his sharp hippo-skin lash, he stands over
> the head of Mad Julian, the Roman prisoner.*

ROYAL CRIER
There my son and King, Nezana,
Says the Great Kaleb, now Hermit,
Grant . . .

> *(Mad Julian cuts in with a wild shout.)*

MAD JULIAN (*Stammers with a private but bewildered melancholy, and
retarded wit. He recites his often repeated words as if from a blank
memory.*)
Justinian the Emperor, bid me say, O King
Constantinople is the daughter of Rome,
Sister of Christian Axum,
Great heart-beat
Of the greater Roman past.
He bid me say, O King
That the poor Christians of Arabian Nageran
Are chased, slain, burnt
By the fanatic Jew king Dhu Nuwas.
Stand by the poor, he bid me say,
Byzantium shall stand with Axum.

> *(Suddenly lost in memory, and then with excitement)*

Consequently O King,
Your army of sixty thousand
And your elephant bulls
Brought Dhu Nuwas to his death.
You did to him
As he did to the Nageran Christians.

In the name of the Cross
Your army rode down Arabia,
Slaughtered a third of Yemen
Laid waste a third of the land
Brought a third of the people
As slaves in your bondage.
      (*Now melancholic, sobbing*)
But O your valiant army
Was suddenly hit
And fed to the plague
That felled it at the gates of Mecca.
      (*Frightened, crawling*)
And Byzantium failed
To stir in your aid
But Justinian, with his mistress Theodoras
Is long dead and buried O King,
And I am still in your dungeon
Buried alive, Kaleb.
      (*Contemplative*)
His heirs Maurice and Phocas,
Themselves locked at each other's throats,
Dared to ask you
To stay as their exarch
On your own land and throne
Representing their altar
Against the altar of your fathers.
They dared you, O Kaleb.
But their fight of greed
Is weakening our Constantinople
To stand against the gods of Zoroaster
For none escape their anger.
Not even Axum, nor king.
      (*Now up and raging*)
Nineteen years, old Kaleb
You held me captive,
Merged my daylight in darkness,
Denied me the warmth of Sun.
Nineteen years, old man
Bats pissed in my eyes,
Rats nibbled at my flesh.
I worshipped the darkness
Of your eternal dungeon, you.
      (*Grows wilder. Points at Royal Crier, and sobs.*)
You tore out the eyes
Of my Persian woman, Zaradushia, there
Hung the blind bell round her neck
And made a royal crier out of her
O, you bloodless ogre,
You made my young blood cold
Like the blood of reptiles in holes.
      (*Lashes from Abas cut down and shrivel him into silence.*)

Suddenly, a rioting, kicking, stampeding wild noise from a group of Children's Chorus, not less than nine. Drums, horn pipes and clash of instruments. They hurl themselves on stage on the narrow strip of level at the foot of the Heart-wall. They jump about, rolling in a cult-dance game. Their skin colour is even more mixed, their hair make-up more impressive, some are in masks, beads, ivory and ebony necklaces for the girls, animal claws and teeth tied around the arms of the thug-like boys. The smallest is nine and the oldest among them only fifteen years old. The game is an interpretation of the Angabe funeral dance. Their song sounds like a militant nursery-rhyme. All are armed with bow, toy arrow, toy dagger, axe and spear, except the two girls.

CHILDREN'S CHORUS
    We are the bearers
    Of the fallen shields of our fathers.
    The eagle's eggs
    Deliver no dove chicks.
    We are the children of vengeance.
    We are the bearers
    Of the broken lance of Axum.
    The womb of the panther
    Delivers no lambs, Kaleb,
    And we ask for vengeance.
    (They exit across the stage, out rioting.)
ROYAL CRIER
    Write.
    (Aba Panteleon kneels and writes.)
    There, my son and king
    Royal Servant Of the Holy Cross
    Upon your shoulders
    Stay the burden of Axum.
    And now please grant,
    My good Confessor,
    The Head Monk Aba Panteleon
    To pronounce me, Kaleb
    An ordinary hermit of no consequence.

    A long eerie moan from horn pipes. Smoke swells from the dungeon and fills the stage.

ABA PANTELEON *(Rises. Takes up the ordinary wooden cross, the long ordinary tattered gown and head-dress, from the foot of the throne. Muttering his usual prayer in a sing-song low tone, he takes deliberate religious steps towards Kaleb. He ceremoniously dresses him, gown first, head-dress second, then hands him the wooden cross, proclaiming.)*
And so be it. Amen
    (Drums tremble)
The stigma of your historical storm
Has cut deep into your soul.

The instinct for quiet
Is long starved in you.

ROYAL CRIER
Let it not be inscribed
On the royal tombs of Axum
Begs the poor hermit Kaleb,
That I forsook my wounded people
At the hours of their plight.
That my reign of much crying
At the altars of the good saints
And much throwing up
At the mortals of the land
Brought about the visitation
That sunk our sons
In the deserts of Arabia.
Let it not be inscribed
   (*Panteleon writes*)
That the saints opposed
Their mightier strength
Against that of our vanquished sons.
That their angry truth
Closed down on my royal house.
Let it be only said, he begs
   (*Panteleon stops writing and rises*)
That I died, only
The common death of my human lot.

ABA PANTELEON (*helping Kaleb lie slowly across the throne, proclaims
appeasingly*)
Amen.
   (*Drums tremble*)
In you who was long sleepless
Peace shall temper the day
For her crushed crusader.
Peace shall appease the sun
Of her cutting shafts.
In you who is long burdened
Under the weight of a broken-down faith
In you, peace shall cleanse the air
Of its slanderous whispers.

> *Stepping back he stands holding a large silver cross with both
> hands, and religiously lowers it on the throne. Horn pipes moan,
> drums tremble. All chorus groups incant and wail their repeated
> ululation off stage. The throne slowly turns into a large tomb,
> with Kaleb taken inside with it. Lights cold, half-dim. Panteleon
> resumes his pronouncement with a ritualized sing-song moan,
> Ethiopian church style.*

Like the homeless hermit he is
Like the wilted leaf left adrift
He shall stray among crowds, unfelt.

Like the piece of rag
Held against a frosty sky.
Like the lone figure in a crowd
Flapping to keep his feet a-ground,
He shall linger among his own, unknown.
Amen.

> *Drums and horn pipes. Clash of instruments and church bells.
> Smoke rises thicker. Incantation intense. Spotlights on Royal
> Crier brighter.*

ROYAL CRIER   Hear all, hear all
   (Drums)
May the gods open the ears
They gave you to hear with.
Hear all
   (Horn pipes)
The King Kaleb is dead.
   (Clash of instruments)
Hear all
Long live the King Gabre-Maskel
Servant Of The Holy Cross.

> *Clash of instruments. Church bells peal from a nearby church of
> Our Lady of Tsion. Spotlights die out on The Royal Crier.*

PART TWO

> *Long silence. Stage lights remain cold and half-dim. Panteleon
> reaches out with the Cross towards Nezana, with Kaleb's Royal
> robe still on it. The Queen Noba dresses Nezana. He moves cer-
> emoniously to the tomb, then throws a handful of earth into the
> opening of the block. The rest follow suit in turn, with Nezana's
> permission, and perform the 'earth to earth' ritual. As Nezana
> points at her, Noba performs, proclaiming:*

NOBA
My fathers built
A heritage of songs and laughters.
Your fathers built
Monuments of wars
An historic mass of ruins.
Your sinners came
Crossed out red water fortress
To make our innocent repent.
They came to accuse our Serpent
Of causing their women to sin.
They condemned it
To be beaten on the head
By all who walked the earth.
They insulted our Ra god
And the memories of Meroe.
Chains of feud rose between our peoples

Till we smoked the incense of peace
Conducted the rites of marriage
And you let our Noble Serpent be.
Though, instead of sweet grass
You made us burn
The dung of bullocks for it,
You still did let our Noble Serpent be.
In your wisdom, Kaleb
You did away with the strange gods
Zeus, Ares and Poseidon,
Their lustful Apollo, married
To his own sister,
Who hunted little pigs and vipers,
You did away with their Zekhuera
The fornicator, their evil Zukhal
The eater of young sons.
You let the Serpent
And its bright irit-Ra be.
You destroyed their dream interpreters
And medicine mixers
And let our original gods of Semri and Kush
Triumph over them,
The god of our Noble Serpent
To ever stay with us in Atete
And fertilize our nile abode,
And for us to bleed rams for it.
You have taken us for your people
Respected that which is ours
And considered us as one of yourselves,
Therefore your death, Kaleb
Is the death of my people too.
Your victory was mine
And now your pain is my pain Kaleb.

CHIEF WATTO
And now great Kaleb
Without you our heavens are rent.
In your wisdom great King
You did away with the slave trade
That drove my people to Arabia
To the market on the Burnt island.
Instead, you made of them
The army of your cross
Who vanquished Arabia
And sent us a multitude of slaves.
But now, without you
Our proud mountains bend
Into the dust below their feet.
We await your spirit
To ride the mountains
And proclaim to our sad fate

Which you left down with us, moaning.
We await your spirit
To ride out of our red water
To immerse into your son
Into our new King Nezana,
And into the abode
Of your broken people, Kaleb.

ARAAYA (*timidly, and with awkward embarrassment performs the earth-to-earth ritual accompanying his broken words on the tune of his toy harp*)

Farewell, I hope angels receive you.
I do not know where you go.
But I know we are being separated.
Farewell, I hope angels receive you.

RABBI YONA

But my father Kaleb
Is lost to the God of Moses
To the pride of his own past
And to the roots of his true heritage.
Like the kings since Ezana
He deserted the true God
Of his father Abraham,
Vowed with the power of Byzantium
And abused the Covenant.
He sent our arms
Upon King Dhu Nuwas of Arabia
And upon his innocent Judaic followers.
He crushed them
And the terror of the Talmud rose
To smother our misled sons.
Your pride received a wound, grandfather
That perhaps only death can heal,
An inherent wound of the spirit
That I fear has lived
To inflict its cult
On the generation of my age
With the strength of our men
All sold out by the wars
Our dead city is now thrown
Between the clutches of scavengers.
And without you, grandfather
We are now left
With mere drums
Names, emblems and shame.

With a sweep of his arm Nezana silences Armah. He points down at him and Armah kneels. Nezana then makes an elaborate commanding gesture at the rest who immediately make way for him. Drums and horn pipes, clash of instruments and Church bells. Spotlight on Royal Crier.

ROYAL CRIER
  The King Kaleb is dead.
  Long live the King Nezana.
  People of Axumite Ethiopia,
  Your King Nezana, Servant of The Holy Cross
  Sole elect of God
  And of the Chosen house of Abraham,
  Speaks.

> Lights up below where the Chorus Groups have entered under
> separate spots beneath the Heart-wall. On the right the Mothers'
> Chorus, in the middle the Children's Chorus, and on the left the
> Beggar's Chorus.

NEZANA (As he speaks, he grows gradually violent and enraged.)
  Beloved Axumites, hear.
  Hear people of our region
  Of the great Southern Lake.
  Peoples of Koloa, Nubia, Barbara, Gambala
  Yeha, Agau, Adulis, Angabe
  Of Himyar, Raydon, Cyeneum and Kasu, hear.
  We children of the cross
  Take heed
  Not to will ourselves to bitterness.
  Not to lose
  Our concept of struggle
  And the confidence in our arms
  Which had failed us only just once.
  Beloved Axumites,
  The revenge of the Cross
  Shall yet give meaning
  To your present life
  Of barren wastage.
     (Children's Chorus scream approval.)
  In these vast godless lands
  All closed in around us
  We are still
  The lone Christian players of history.
  The only hope left to us
  Is to scratch day by day
  Into our only path of light.
  To try and once more will
  The completeness of our manhood.
  Our Christian manhood
  In the service of the Cross.
     (The Beggar's Chorus whisper, sigh and spit)
  Have we then forsaken our manhood
  And delivered it in pawn?
  Did Axum produce
  A people unequal to the task that faces it?
  Have we given up the memory

Of why our fathers were men
And of why they died men?
(*The Mothers' Chorus shiver, sway and groan with pain.*)
But I shall not allow
Our great Axumite spirit
To opt out of life in castration.
I shall not be the sovereign
Of a toothless Axum.
I shall not, during my reign
Allow her history
To be ripped out of her
And thrown
Between the waters and desert sand.
The breath of her new youths
Shall refuse, now
To slumber with the past.
It shall shake itself
And waken, now
Into the bright temper
Of its own future.
  (*The Children's Chorus scream, kick and riot with gusto, and Ne-
  zana's rage grows more incited.*)
Beloved Axumites
By our natural authority
Endowed on us by the will of God
And the rightful heritage
Of this throne of our fathers
We warn that you rid yourselves
Of your resigned attitudes.
For, ware you beloved
To lead is to rule
And to be king is to kill.
But to any who dreams
To go against this will
We warn, now,
That he sneak out with the evening dusk
Before the last sun sets on him.

> Nezana, though exhausted, elaborately lifts the crown off his head
> then holds it up with the sceptre in both hands. Panteleon leans
> and rests the large Cross against the crown. Abas turns his scourge
> at the Chorus with vehement threat. Violent drums ensue. Horn
> pipes bleat. All kneel except Nezana. Holy Cross shines on him.
> Suddenly from left of Heart-wall the hermit enters, without mask,
> slightly stooping but stiff as a statue. Though his hands are in
> chains, he holds a hammer and chisel. His dark brown complex-
> ion and strong African bone structure resemble those of Armah.
> He kneels by mad Julian, enchains himself to him and slowly
> takes him down into the dungeon.
>   Only Nezana sees him, for all the rest are kneeling with their
> heads bent. As soon as the hermit and Mad Julian have disap-

*peared into the dungeon, the metal cross from the Heart-wall
shines brighter on Nezana. Blackout.*

Act Two
Reign Without Tears

I. RITES OF THE FLOGGING OF THE PRINCE

*A few years later. Darkness. The silence is broken with scourges
whizzing in the background. Whisper, hiss, incantations, Coptic
Church chant, wailing and occasional scream mingle. The whizz
of scourges grows tedious in long drawn-out frictions. Lights up
in half-dim. To indicate Nezana's rigid ecclesiastical reign, and
the degenerate period of a people humiliated with defeat, poverty
and fear, we note in the dim light that both the Mothers' and the
Beggars' chorus groups now have their chins pressed to the ground
at the spots where they were last seen kneeling. The stage atmosphere equipment and costume is dusty, the props dusty, spider-
webbed and worn out. The eternal whistle of the whips in the
background is interpreted by the scourge of Abas intermittently
lashing at the Chorus groups. A gradual change of lights into a
colder distant dim with echoes of the tedious lashes underscore
fatigue and a crawling rigid period. As the whips and the ecclesiastical incantations grow more violent off stage, the two chorus
groups mime violent shivers and grind their faces into the ground.
At the same time the metal cross becomes animated into a writhing eery figure. The limbs of both chorus groups are now unruly
and sprawl about making the mark of age obvious on them. As
spotlight slowly reveals the Royal Crier on the steps of the left
stele, the sound of scourges gradually dies out in the background.
At the same time as that of the Royal Crier, a dimmer spotlight
also reveals Prince Araaya sitting on the steps of the right side
stele playing with his toy David's harp. As Royal Crier speaks,
Araaya accentuates the words with a low key on his harp.*

*The whole effect of both background sound and chorus mime
should not last more than fifteen seconds. As soon as the sound
stops, both Chorus groups crawl out in opposite directions under
the heart-wall with Abas following the Beggars' one. Blackout on
stage. Spotlight on Royal Crier, slightly brighter.*

ROYAL CRIER (*assumes a more personal intimacy and a less official man-
ner of tone*)
For several long pitiless years
Fear crawled in each night
To hug this dying city of altars.
Tempers rose in the ranks
And grew horny each day.
With each stab of pain
Each ferment of deception
The wooden hearts of the god-makers

Throbbed with contempt for each other.
There is no measuring the walls
That rose between
Each interpreter of dreams.
Each preached, ranted and collided
In the minds of the strong
And in the hearts
Of the weakest of worshippers.
In this lone city
Where they never cease praying for man
Men die most.

ARAAYA (*Spotlight dimmer on Royal Crier, brighter on Araaya.*)
   (*Sings*) Ayee! Ayhaey! honey-fly.
   Who tore your womb
   Who killed your song?
   Ayee! honey-fly
   Who slit your breast
   Who made your hive
   A grave-alive?
   Ayhaey! honey-queen
   Who made you rave
   Who killed your song
   Your song of birth?
   Ayee! Mother-fly
   Ayhaey! honey-queen
   Who cut your breath
   Who killed your song
   Who slit your breast
   And made your womb
   A living tomb?
   Ayhaey! Ayee! honey-queen.

   *Spotlight dimmer on Araaya, brighter on Royal Crier. Araaya slips
   out of sight through the door of the right stele. Off stage, a sudden
   crash of instruments. Then the pealing of Church bells out-
   sounds the instruments.*

ROYAL CRIER (*proclaims with rigid solemnity*)
   Hear all, hear all
   May the gods open the ears
   They gave you to hear with.
      (*Church bells gradually die out in the back-ground. Drums and
      incantations echo. Royal Crier, with an even more official tone and
      manner announces.*)
   Our King Nezana, Gabre-Maskel
   The Great Servant Of the Holy Cross,
   Hear all, hear all
   Has pronounced his royal judgement
   Upon the Young Crown Prince Armah
   Who, in presence
   Of the Closed Throne Council,

Declined to lead the expedition of the Cross
Against the South lake dragon
Called the Noble Serpent,
And against its obstinate worshippers
The people of the Chief Watto,
Now officially declared godless.

> *Drums, hornpipes and church bells. Clash of instruments. Lights up. The entire cast is on stage, in the same spot and position as on the end of the last scene before the blackout. Only Armah is prostrated face down across the tomb, with the two guards holding him tight down from either end. Abas is on the tomb, with his scourge raised, pausing in a position to begin the flogging. The Chorus groups lightly whisper, mumble and sigh. Nezana, with the crown and sceptre still held high, aggressively takes several deliberate steps centre forword, abruptly stops, then turns his back on the audience to face the Chorus groups. Their slight commotion and noise is suddenly swallowed by angry drums and horn pipes. Except for Julian and the Hermit, the rest, who are still on stage and on their knees, hold their heads up to face Armah who is prostrated on the tomb.*

ROYAL CRIER
Seventeen fierce lashes,
The rites of blood-letting
By the royal scourge,
—Hear, people of Axumite Ethiopia,—
Shall flay the bare skin
Of your Crown Prince Armah,
The only son
Of your beloved King Nezana,
To make of him
An example for you,
For his tongue has questioned
The unquestionable will
Of this royal throne of Axum.

NEZANA (*proclaims*)
We drip the blood of our son
Into this Royal Tomb of Axum
Bearing the dust of our forebears.
A symbolic offering
Of our own embodiment
To our heritage and our past,
A living example
To you, my beloved.
That you look more to the Holy Cross
And less to your private impulses.
We have for long
Tolerated, with much pain
Your playing the clients
Of strange gods and demons

Within our holy Empire.
You have also stayed long
Inside your mist of idolatry
In which you enclose our reign.
You haunt our throne
And wallow in idle demonism.
We shall not tolerate it any longer, beloved.
Behold the thrust of the scourge
Ripping the tender flesh
Of our only son
And let the thick crust of your ill sloth
Vanish with his pains.
Rid yourselves, beloved
Of the dark cry in your brains.

> *Nezana replaces the crown on his head. Drops a decisive left
> hand. The blows Abas deals Armah are elaborate and stylized, yet
> deliberate.*

ROYAL CRIER   One, Two, Three, Four, Five, Six, Seven,

> *The Queen Noba and Chief Watto hide their heads between their
> legs. Araaya silently sobs on Noba's shoulders. The Mothers' and
> Beggars' Chorus spread out their hands in supplication to Ne-
> zana. Aba Panteleon triumphantly holds the cross against Armah's
> head. Habibah stares into Armah's eyes as if obsessed. Only Mad
> Julian, and Rabbi Yona seem to enjoy this with calm.*

NEZANA (*raving*)
You shall lift your arm
For our Cross, Armah
Against the people of Watto,
Against the demon of the South Lake.
Go Armah,
Before the deadly teeth
Of our judaic past
Consume them alive
As it did our region of Agau.
Go Armah, Go.

> *Serpent writhes vehemently making an unearthly satanic shriek.*

ROYAL CRIER   Eight, Nine, Ten, Eleven, Twelve,
NEZANA (*outraged*)
Go Armah, Go
Before the eastern Zoroaster horde
Overwhelms our light,
Before the rising of the Kitab
Puts Axum to its Jihad sword.
You shall take the light of the Cross
Against the darkness
Of your mother's people in plight.
ROYAL CRIER   Thirteen, Fourteen, Fifteen, Sixteen,

NEZANA (*vehement, almost obsessed and breathless*)
  You shall lead, Armah
  Our Axumite army of the Cross
  Against . . .
    (*Breaks down in a fit. All freeze. Black-out.*)
ROYAL CRIER (*in the dark*)
  Hear all, hear all.
  With the sudden attack
  Of the noble shiver
  That broke down our King
  The remaining one lash
  To be dealt by the royal scourge
  Shall stay, until the God of Holy Axum
  Brings back the full health
  Of our beloved Sovereign.

> *Slight whisper and commotion in the background is immediately crushed by sudden drums and the ferocious peal of church bells.*

II. NIGHTS WITHOUT LOVE

> *Immediately after. Late evening. Beyond the heart-wall, a sky in deep red cloud dominates the horizon. Lights up only in the area of the tomb. Armah is still left prostrated on it. In the distance, the two guards are standing on watch, with their backs to the audience. Though there seems to be a feeling of them being spied on, the stage is empty except for Habibah and Araaya who are still with Armah. Araaya is seated crouching under the tomb. As Habibah rises with her eyes still on Armah, and comes closer to the tomb, Araaya rises to leave.*

HABIBAH
  Please don't leave.
  I have some medicine
  For your father.
    (*She draws out two bird eggs from her lap. Leaves one with Armah.*)
  Help me give it to him.
    (*Gently she breaks the one egg between her palms. Then begins to rub the flow smoothly over Armah's flayed back.*)
  Where I come from, Prince
  The egg of the crane bird
  Is administered
  On a torn skin like yours.
ARMAH
  And what, Ramia Habibah,
  Do you administer
  On torn memories of men?
  I understand
  You are to leave us tonight
  With the first Hejira to Mecca.
  The influence of your new prophet

Is now strong enough
For the security of his family,
And I hear that on your arrival
Your marriage ceremony to Mohammad
As his ninth chosen wife
Will immediately take place.
Your eleven years of exile here
Must have been a waste
Of the best years of your youth.
For your wedding present
The royal house of Axum is sending
Four hundred golden dinars,
Silk, ivory, frankincense and incense.
It is not much
But you know Axum is no more
What she used to be.
I am also sending with you
My son Araaya
To meet and sing for a while
With Mohammad's son, Ali.
Our people say, Ramia
That out of childhood games
Grow the sizes of whole men.
I know you will care for him
Together with the good Prophet
Whose kingdom of the Kitab
And the strength of the Jihad
Is securing many more today.

HABIBAH

Not the kingdom of the Jihad sword, Prince,
But peace in the kingdom of the Kitab.

ARMAH

There can be no kingdom, Ramia
Without the grip on the sword.
Neither the worldly one
This realm of human-gods,
Nor the heavenly one
That realm of the spirit-gods.
Only, the terror grows more immediate
Where humans often claim
To transport heavenly spirits
At the beck of their noses.
Yes. It is the rise of a new day
That always announces
The birth of a new night.
See, the evening sun there
Yielding to the bite
Of the mightier darkness,
Shooting out her blood at us
Through the thin desert clouds,
Bearing witness to the same sword truth?

HABIBAH
>   Have you not heard. Prince?
>   —Swear not by the evening glow
>   By the sun that gathers darkness
>   On her trail,
>   By the moon that shifts her mane
>   With little shine:
>   I should beware Prince
>   Lest your words of conceit
>   Blind the sight of my faith.

ARMAH
>   But that, Ramia
>   I am not able to do to you, anymore.
>   Only a while ago, remember
>   You were faith to me
>   When my bare flesh
>   Was being ripped off my bones.
>   Perhaps, I might not have pulled through
>   Had I not drawn some courage for life
>   Form the source of your eyes
>   Which suffered with me all along.
>   There Ramia. Do you not see
>   The dying sun, now
>   Sending her last plaint to nature
>   Through the glare
>   Of her blood-stained skies?
>   Like the free wind
>   Her suffering reaches us
>   In spite of ourselves.
>   Like a mutilated lowest field
>   She keeps back nothing of her shame.
>   Not us, but only the gods
>   Can afford to watch her stark stiff
>   Or even mock her without pain.
>   Yet only a whole love from us
>   Can hold her in
>   From the painful fears
>   Of her inevitable end.

HABIBAH
>   Please Prince. I must go.
>   Those who look on us
>   And do not hear us
>   May interpret our whispers.

ARMAH
>   Those who know you by your whispers
>   Never interpret your real dreams, Ramia.

HABIBAH
>   Yes, I have not been able
>   To remain faithful in my dreams
>   Even to the saints I trust, Prince.
>   Is it not that, what you meant?
>   Yet you know, I must leave.

ARMAH

Go then, strange woman.
May the Saints of your choice
Stay with you
For the man who begrudges them
Turns only against himself.
Only, help me up a little
Before darkness is complete.
  (*Holding his arms, Habibah and Ayaaya try to help him sit up on the tomb. Footsteps approach in the distance.*)
Please, always remember,
As a token of farewell, strange woman
That, only the living nip in us,
Which addicts us to painful habits
Which condemns us to ruthless needs,
Remains the only truth of value
Our guts should cope with.
Here, I leave my son
In your good care now,
Teach him how to make friends
With the son of your Nabi.

Habibah and Araaya, helping Armah between them, exit. The shadow of Jaffar closes on the tomb behind them.

III. EXODUS AND RANT OF THE TEACHERS
PART ONE

As darkness gradually blots out the evening dusk beyond, the shadow of Jaffar is enlarged to shade and fall across the area of the tomb. Crescent light slightly comes up on him. With his left hand his double-bladed Jihad sword points to the east. He makes three blaring calls on his trumpet. With the change of light, the tomb suddenly turns into the Holy Kabah Stone, the Altar at Mecca.

JAFFAR (*calling out to the audience from behind the Altar*)

Bism Alah, Al Rahman, Al Rahim
  (*Crescent brighter on him*)
Praise belongs to Allah.
Rise people of the house of Islam.
You, who have long striven
In the cause of Allah,
For we start tonight
On our home-coming Hijra.
The Apostle whom God gave us
From among ourselves,
He, with whose lineage and purity
We are happily acquainted
Now calls us all, back to Mecca.

Rise people of the nation of Islam,
You who have established the prayer
And paid the Zakat,
For the Sacred Mosque of Qibla
Is now appointed
As your holy place of worship.
O ye who, have Judaised
Ye the infidel, who assert
That you are friends of Allah
To the exclusion of his people,
Ye who hide the Covenant
From the people of God,
Desire death.
For Allah shall curse
And make stones of your hearts.
Rise people of the Kitab,
Do not choose Jews, nor Christians
For your friends,
For they befriend only each other.
And any who make friends of them
Is one of them,
Since he shall learn from them
To accuse God
Of taking to himself an offspring.
To accuse Allah
Of being brought forth
And of having brought forth.
Rise. And twist not our tongues
To make a botch of faith.
Rise. Turn thy face in heaven
And face the Sacred Mosque of Mecca,
Lest you are cast into Al-Hutama
The fire of Gjehanna set alight
Which shall mount over your hearts
And close you into
its long-drawn tongues of flame.
Rise people of the Kitab.

> *Commotion and mass movement in the background. Lights grad-*
> *ually dim down on Kabah Altar. Jaffar exits blaring his trumpet.*
> *Crescent light blacks out.*
>
> *Spotlight on Watto who emerges out on to the step of the right*
> *stele. In the distance, a faint Serpent shine. Watto is addressing*
> *the Hermit, who, rigid as a statue, and with his back to the au-*
> *dience is kneeling in silent prayer below the steps of the stele.*
> *Mad Julian is still chained to him.*

WATTO
What is to become of my people?
Tell me then
You who are now the estranged hermit,

You who are for ever
Mute, in silent call to your silent God,
You who are speechless
In the tongue of the living, tell me.
The revenge of a wounded spirit
In the body of our Noble Serpent
Attacked the person of Nezana,
Locked his jaw upon his tongue
Made him squirt red foam
And rendered him
To a life of living silence.
You, the Stranger who is detached
From earthly causes,
What is to become of my people?
Of my people who
Have no one to face,
No other spirit
To call them of its own?
We were not of the Cross
Though we died in its cause,
We are not of the Crescent
Nor are we of the Star,
But only of the Serpent
But only of the Serpent Mother
Nurse of Biahank and Sobok
Our pharaonic ancestors
Now being killed of wounded spirit.
Nezana is determined to end
What little is left
Of that dying spirit
In the body of his son, Armah,
By commencement of the royal scourge
On the tender scars of his flesh.
The revenge of our Serpent
Of our limitless all-powerful
Before the world arose,
Has now taken on eternal vow
To share Nezana's own body
With the Cross that possesses it,
Or even die
Only locked up in it.
In vain, old Yared
The King's learned friend
Spent many nights
Of wisdom and water
Singing purifying words
Over his charmed head.
Unlike his great father
In whose cause, the strength
Of my peoples was sapped
And with whom their pride suffered

Nezana rose to kill, now
Our initial spirit-essence.
Our possessor of immortal breath,
Who, with its thong of flame
Split the frown of the skies
He rose to kill our Serpent Mother
The womb of Kush and Nubia
In defence of that
Which is still foreign in us,
Of that which was brought in to us
Only in borrowing,
Nezana rose to dry up in us
The roots of our spiritual heritage
The waters of Biahank and Ra
Which fertilized the wombs of our being
Ever since the birth
And rise of our red water
Ever since the memory of man.
He aborted our spirit-originator
Out of the body of my people
And instead forced upon us
His adopted stranger spirit-child
Which shall ever deny
The pride of its roots
Against the pride of my heritage.
Against the Serpent Mother
In the abode of the great red water.
Now that ours is dying in us
My people are open, naked
To the choice of foreign gods
Who, in neglect and enslavement
Of their spirit-pride
Haunt their emptiness.
What is to become of my people
Estranged Hermit of the unknown?
What is to become of my people?

> *Spotlight blacks out on them. The faint shine of the Serpent dies out in the distance. With a change of light the area of the Holy Kabah Altar has turned into a Holy Synagogue Altar with a Jewish candelabra, revealing Rabbi Yona with his Staff of Moses pointed at the audience. The Star of David shines on him.*

YONA
Adonai Alohenu, Adonai Ehad.
And the Lord of Hosts
Shall lend you his might.
Like Samson, with a jaw bone of an ass
You shall smite a thousand men.
As an eagle
That stretches up her chest
Hovers over her young

Spreads aboard her nest
Takes them
Bears them on her wings,
The Lord of Moses
Shall bear you with his care.
But you have sinned, Axum,
The wrath of God
Has come upon you
And upon your misguided children.
It is now the will
Of the true God of Abraham
That those among you
Who have not yet succumbed
To the guilt of Axum,
Who have not gone astray
With the corrupt uncircumcized
Into the dark ways of the gentiles,
Shall leave this city of death
For the northern Region of Agau
Where more of your kind await you.
Slay the ram
For your peace offering,
The calf and the anointing oil
For your sin offering.
Sprinkle the altar
As thy Lord commandeth.
Make an atonement
For the sins of your fathers.
Slay the bullock
For your burnt offering.
Burn it with its hide
Its flesh and its dung
And put incense thereon.
Soak your garments with the blood
Lest a fire cometh from the Lord
To devour you.

> *A commotion of exodus in the background rises to die with a
> sudden blackout. As the shine on the Star of David darkens and
> an immediate spotlight comes up on the area of the dungeon
> entrance, it is the Queen Noba, disguised as a maiden, who car-
> ries food to Julian. Yona, also disguised in an ordinary outfit,
> suddenly emerges from the darkness to join her.*

NOBA

You too, my Rabbi
Have finally turned a deserter?
YONA

I never deserted you, my queen.
But Axum, yes.
She deserted me first, remember.

NOBA
It was your will
Against the will of Axum's throne.
You chose your own.

YONA
My little, feeble, toothless will
Against that of a throne?

NOBA
Not entirely feeble, my Rabbi.
You were well gritting
Even that toothless will of yours
While that of the throne
Was left to decay of neglect.

YONA
You begrudge me then
The last wish left of me?

NOBA
You mean your sense of cause
For deserting Axum?

YONA
Not just that, my queen
Nor even the rights
Of a rightful regent heir
Derooted, dispossessed of his own.
But you, your person . . .

NOBA
Me? I was never one
Of your corrupt imperial pawns.

YONA
Please, You know very well
I am not implying that.
You also know
That is it not altogether impossible
For one to have faith
In the person of another
Without having to share his altar.
What is more, you certainly know
That if it were not
For what you call my choice,
You could have almost been my betrothed.

NOBA
What you call 'could-have-been'
Is long, long dead
And can no longer be.

YONA
No?

NOBA
How dare you insinuate . . .

YONA
Why then are you disguised

In this servant's outfit
In the dead of night, my queen?
To make your humble royal turn
At feeding that Roman imbecile
Or the mad Hermit
Who, of his own will
Carves mad words on the caves
Of your dingy royal dungeon, my queen?

NOBA

Go on ask
You, who must ask everything
And win at your every little cause,
Go on ask. And stop
Hissing, 'my-queen' at me
Between your little rats' teeth,
But go on ask, my Rabbi.

YONA

It is hard enough as it is, God knows
And you make it harder for me, why Noba?
You know that I know
That in that naked inert throne
There is more than Axum's will
Decaying of utter silent neglect.
You yourself, your person, yes Noba.
And you know how I care,
How the very presence of your scent
Blinds the light of my wit,
Burns my burnt blood to shame
Even in spite of myself.
No, it is not easy for me, God knows.

NOBA

Nor any easier for me.
For me, a nominal queen
Unable to appease the wound
Of my humiliated people
Even at the cost of my own humiliation.
Me, abandoned by the ancestors
Whose scorn I bear
In my shamed breath,
Yet commanded to remain faithful
To the one that dirties my pride,
Insults my human body
For feeling life and want,
And still chokes my nights
In his sterile outrage.
Spirits are the absolute, Prince
And I have none to turn to
Where their silence judges me
In my absolute loneliness.
Yes, you have known, Bet-Israel
This bread for the enchained

Is only an excuse I took
To share my pains of neglect
With someone like you
Who says he has also known
The silent flaming chains
Of that same loneliness.
The ancestors give us flesh
Maybe, only to judge others by
Those like you and I
Who finally have no strength
But bend in human homage
Before the rites of their fire.

As she speaks, they carry the prison bread between themselves and descend into the dungeon. Slow blackout on them while the carver's hammer and chisel begins to sound from within the dungeon.

PART TWO

A few months later, but scene commences immediately after. Spotlight on Royal Crier seated at the foot of the left-side stele.

ROYAL CRIER
That's it. In this mute city
Of love-forsaken screaming whores
Who scratch in the nightmares
For men who long ceased to exist,
Such gross fornication is a rarity
Reserved for the privileged.
(*The sound of hammer and chisel die out.*)
But for many seasons, now
The lost news of that little angel
The young Prince Araaya
Has the news or is little angel left Armah?
With a still heavier heart.
Since the great expedition
And the regional wars of the Cross,
The feud of greed, the poverty
The rant of the god-makers
And then the exodus of dissenters
Has left his city of lost prides
Haunted only by senile old men
Shrunken old mothers
And depraved little urchins.
Islam has grown mightier,
Kaleb's church in Southern Najran
Is burnt down to ashes
By the men of Ibrahim the Thaquafite,
The regions of Tziamoe, Zoa, Gambala
And Kaloa ceased paying tribute,
Slave market on the Burnt Island

Has grown fast and ruthless,
Watto's humiliated people await
With mad revenge in their eyes,
Throne rumours now tell
That Rabi Yona, the Prince Bet Israel
For whom the Queen Noba is pregnant
Is up to crown himself King
In the northern Agau Region.
The tyrannical reign of Phocas
Who snatched the throne of Constantinople
by killing Maurice
The heir of Emperor Justinian
Is also being overrun
By the great Khosrau II of Persia,
Son of the Fire of Zarathushtra,
Born in the lands of Aryan Vaj,
Teacher of the genius of obedience.
    (*On centre stage, a faint tongue of flame rises out of a simple chalice*
    on the plain altar, as symbol of Zarathushtra.)
Teacher of Ashura Mazda
The Supreme Lord of Creation,
Conferer of the epithet of 'the wise',
Follower of the Sexless Oramoazdes
Who founded the wisdom of the Magi,
Winner of the blessed 'God'
The holy title of the Wild Ass,
Caretaker of the inexhaustible Cow,
Judge of the general ordeal,
Singer of the chariot of Zeus
In the Fire Temple of Ormoazd.
And whatever is left
Of this ghost-ridden altar-city
Now trembles in its last terror.
Yes. I am happy
To be the bearer of the news
For I was a Zarathushtran too
Till the sex in my flesh
Brought me here with that mad Roman
Where I was reduced
To a blinded Royal Crier
By the elegant satan
Of this infirm Habashite's realm.
But the pig-headed zeal of Panteleon
Deaf to all, save the Cross
Is sworn to re-baptize
The last wretched loafer in Axum
'So that he died, at least
The death of a Christian dog.'
His ranting words of plague
Turned the urchin lot god-crazed.
Turned them into no ordinary lot.

Quick blackout on Royal Crier and on the altar flame. At centre front area of the stage, lights reveal three young urchins from the Children's chorus group: A big boy, a small boy and a girl, loitering about. Big boy whispers in little boy's ear.

SMALL BOY (*with a start*)
No, no. That was not what he said.
Our newly baptized Meccan Arab
—Uthman Bin Huwayrith—
Has his own art
For saying all things his own way.
    (*Imitating an old new believer who has just seen the light.*)
'We the poor, my son,
Have an eternal future to think of,
To arrange and prepare for,
An endless heavenly happiness, you see,
While our unfortunate poor-rich
Our wretched poor masters
Have nothing but our tepid sweats,
Our frail splintered bones
To leak at and look forward to.'

BIG BOY
So that's the kind of faith
That caused our old-new convert
The famous divorcee of Ramia
To sneak out of Jaffar's Hijra herd.
It leaves one with a feeling
That there is something missing, though.

GIRL (*pompous*)
Of course, they also say
He remained behind
For some political reasons.

BIG BOY (*lost*)
Political what!
What is this 'political reasons'?

SMALL BOY (*bored*)
May be another new religion?

GIRL (*all-knowing*)
No, It's only a new name
For a respectable, religious
Holy Byzantium type of knife
In the old Arab's cloak.

BIG BOY (*amused, but indulgent*)
What a bastard lot we all are!
What an accursed, deluded
Mixed up lot we Habashites are.

SMALL BOY
But of that too
Our new convert confided in me,
'My son, do not lose faith in faith,
The future is all
In you, the brighter mixtures.'

GIRL

   The bastard.
      (*Suddenly sulking*)
   But I do not understand
   Both of you looking ready, even eager
   For this re-baptismal zeal of Panteleon.

SMALL BOY

   Here comes the woman
   Who, when Adam looked about
   For his second sweet rib
   Climbed up the tree, and spoke
   With the tongue of the snake.
   It isn't just the re-baptismal
   Our little lady hog,
   It also means a free
   Handful of oiled malt as well
   Special, from the royal kitchen itself
   So, go eat your clever words.

GIRL

   Not just the free oiled malt, either
   You snake-eating Zoan bastard,
   Your big monk-Royal-Confessor
   Had ordered stinking slat water
   Down from the Khaybar
   To drown your clever head in
   And for you to suck it up
   Through your fat nostrils.
   So, his re-baptismal feat
   Includes burning filthy water
   To be rubbed into your eyes, as well.

SMALL BOY

   What is so bad in a fast
   Salt water bath, lady glutton
   As long as it meant
   A large handful of oiled malt
   For your noisy belly.

GIRL

   Sorry, I forgot that's supposed to be a
   Luxury, one risked his neck for
   In the parts you come from.

BIG BOY

   Particularly in these hungry times
   You mean, don't you,
   When the chief of the city beggars
   Has shut out his father,
   Expelled him from the group
   And abandoned him
   To the valley of the damned.
      (*Girl expresses surprise*)
   Yes. Haven't you heard?

Suddenly, his father's miserable skin
Started releasing white pus,
His eyes watered little silver balls,
Then his poor nose and fingers
Were being eaten into flat bones
So, that was that.

SMALL BOY

That is a stinking lie
And you know it.
The truth is, he refused to share
His frugal bit of alms
With your greedy chief-of-beggars uncle
Who then created this big lie
To have him thrown out.

GIRL

Don't fume, I understand now
My damned Zoan bastard
Why you are so bent
On earning your oiled malt
Even at the cost of Panteleon's
Salt water re-baptismal feat.

SMALL BOY (*bowing in mock courtesy*)

Please do dry up our dear lady-hog.
  (*Then his sudden leap at her is stopped short by Big Boy.*)

BIG BOY

Speaking of feats, though,
The exarch of North Egypt
Has asked for twenty more
Virgin slaves: breast buttocks
And all, in return for a word of news
His messenger hissed at Panteleon,
And our poor King, they say
Is having another of his attacks.

SMALL BOY

That is not true, again.

BIG BOY

O, No? How would you know
Since your type stays inside
Scratching at his father's itching skin
When all your betters
Go out for better things?
In fact it has been agreed upon
That the tender slave girls
Get picked up from your Zoan Region.
You people are the slowest on tax
So, it might as well turn up
That the flowers of merchandise
Be your own blooming sisters, son.

SMALL BOY

In the first place
My big, dear, Kasu bull

I am a Zoan, but
Only on my mother's side.
And unlike you Kasu female servitors
Mother's sides are not so considered
According to my father's people.
Besides, what you say is still untrue,
And even if it were
They should slit your tongue
For saying so, aloud.

GIRL (*surprised*)

But who would tell them
That he said so, aloud?

BIG BOY

Who else but he?
He'll go hiss out
In the father Confessor's wet ears.
    (*To girl*)
Didn't you hear yet
Of what he confessed to
    (*With the cross, sprinkles holy water on their heads and on their
    toy-arms.*)
I re-baptize you, Children-Of-The-Cross.
I baptize you with water
But may Christ of the Cross
Baptize you with fire.
In the name of God the Father
God the Son, and
God the Holy Ghost
I re-name you, Children-Of-The-Cross.
God gave His Son
To die for you,
And He expects you
To die for His Cross.
He has chosen His might
To act through your arms,
And may he Baptize you with fire.
    (*Puts the cross aside and drowns each urchin's head and toy-arm
    into the pit of water with obsessive seriousness which looks almost
    mad.*)
Cast your nests now,
Catch His lost souls back.
Bring the light of life
To their pit of darkness.
Beware of seductive spirits
Of the double tongued
Of those sewing diverse lusts
Lest the warmth of sin
Eat into your flesh,
And the day of the Lord
Spring on you
Like a cutthroat

In the dead of night.
God laid down
His own life for you
And He expects you
To lay down your lives
In his sleepless dreams?
Last night, he wetted his own thighs
Right on his fire-side rug,
Then suddenly shot up
In his usual sleep walk
Screaming out aloud,
'I have sinned. Sinned again
O, great father confessor.'
And his poor Zoan mother
Had to slap him out of dream.
   (*To boy*)
That's you, my rock-worshiping
Little godless Zoan mule.

> *They jump on each other and fight. Black out. Rioting, stamped-*
> *ing, then drums, rise in the dark background. Stage lights reveal*
> *that the area of the altar is now a baptismal pit of the Orthodox*
> *Ethiopian order. Rising above the pit, is Panteleon. Immediately,*
> *Children's Chorus hurl themselves on stage beneath the heart-*
> *wall rolling with their cult dance. They are armed with toy spears,*
> *daggers and axes.*

CHILDREN'S CHORUS (*singing what sounds like a militant nursery rhyme,*
and swinging their arms in rhythm)
Amen. We are the new men of Axum.
We are the will of the Cross.
The womb of the panther
Delivers no lambs.
We are the will of the Cross.
We are the will of its vengeance. Amen.

PANTELEON (*Vehemently, raises the large silver cross with both hands*
and all is silent. Metal Cross blazes on him. He dips the large silver
cross religiously in the baptismal pit. Immediately, they all kneel sub-
missively with their rear to the audience and their heads lined on the
edge of the pit.)
Take heed. The day of the Lord
Shall spring on you
Like the pains of labour
Upon a woman with child.
For the will of his Cross.
I baptize you with water
But may He baptize you
With his eternal fire.
   (*Critically, he looks down at the sprawling Children's Chorus. Dis-*
   gusted, he leaves abruptly.)
CHILDREN'S CHORUS (*exhausted, choked with water and sprawling about*)

Amen. We are the new men of Axum.
We are the will of the Cross
We are the will of its vengeance. Amen.

Panting and defeated, all stay down. Armah enters right of Heart-wall. Slowly lifts the large silver cross which he finds very heavy. Drags it centre stage with effort. Spot light encircles and follows him while all lights on metal Cross, Children's Chorus and baptismal area blacks out. Breathless and spent he kneels down with cross resting across his shoulders. He has now dragged it, Golgotha-style, far forward across centre stage between the two steles. The hammer and chisel sound from within the dungeon and stop only when Armah kneels tired out.

ARMAH
Suddenly, I hoped,
A tiny forlorn hope
And even felt unlike myself.
A scrap of dignity
I dared throw at my failure,
Then I was accused of sin
For letting your past
Walk in my blind dreams, Axum.
And no sooner have I felt this
Than I screamed it all aloud
And it tasted moth-eaten.
O, why have you so narrowed
Your fertile womb my Axum,
Why have you refused
The birth of whole men?
Must the cottage your past built
Dwarf the size of your present?
Must your past glory linger
Where your weakest still hide?
Ah my Axum, how you must die!
Not my mother, not the Queen Noba
For she is made the embodiment of shame,
Nor my father, the King Nezana
For he sees only his brand of a cross,
A cross of self-hate, secret death
And misdirected revenge.
But you Axum, my song of birth
Whom I can't accuse on their account,
You, on whose fragile hands
My fairy dreams bent mountains,
Whose sweet eyes of care
Like opals in a clear spring
Spread open in my innocent face,
You, whose vital guide of my footsteps
Against the scar of goring nights
Protected my moments of innocence,

O, how you must die, my twilight.
(*With extra effort, he manages to get back on his feet, stopping
under the weight of the cross. Hammer and chisel sound from
within the dungeon gradually growing louder.*)
But now my Axum
My soul is wedded to hating
Everything that surrounds you,
And I strain to crawl
From one dark day to another long night
On the soothing pains of your memory, alone.
I have long forgotten how to laugh,
I only search for your night cloak
Where you last left it hung
For it is my only cradle, Axum,
I listen to your silence
For it is my only music.
The vital life you once gave me free
Is lost somewhere along the way
In the service of your mordant custom.
I have long forgotten how to laugh
And, it is now my habit
To worship your grave, my Axum.

> *Gradually the sound of hammer and chisel rises to grow louder,
> insistent, piercing and fills the stage. At the same time, smoke
> swells from the dungeon and clouds the stage. Armah covers his
> ears, breaks under the weight, and hides his head between his
> legs. The cross now falling across his neck seems to crash down
> on him. Spotlight on the area of the dungeon entrance reveals
> Hermit and Julian kneeling respectively right and left, on the far
> end of the foot side of the cross. They are both in chains and
> enchained to each other, with the Hermit holding the hammer
> and chisel. At the same time as the slow spotlight reveals the two,
> sound of hammer and chisel stop. As the Hermit, now kneeling
> as stiff as a statue, mimes the words of his speech, an eerie, un-
> earthly echo rises from the dungeon to pronounce the words
> which, with a ghostly underscored echo overwhelm the audito-
> rium. On the other hand, the echo of Julian's words is not as
> loud, hardly eerie and almost natural. Also the manner of his
> kneeling is far from stiff, with his head drooping and his body
> half resting on his limp calf.*

HERMIT (*mimes*)
How can you who are unable
To save yourself
Justify her lust to me?
Your Axum, Armah
Bent the backs of my people
In vain, to stiffen
her dust-eaten bones.
She sank her claws

In my weak and destitute
To vent her anger at the God
Who shamed her pride.
Her laughter now raking with madness
Grew fat on the tears of my weak.
Her greed rose on their corpses
And she made holes in their dreams.
And how can you who are unable
To save yourself
Justify her lust to me?

MAD JULIAN (*interrupts with his mime*)
Take me to your side, O Prince.
Your germ-pissing bats
Your death-spurting rats
Are clotting my blood
Into that of a mad dog.
Take me to your side, O Prince.

HERMIT (*out-shouting Julian to silence*)
Your Axum has tired of love, Armah
Of the dialogue of life
Of the eternal ale of songs.
She has dispelled the charm of hope
Out of my people
Only to play at fear,
To turn their healthy laughter
Into short scornful grins.
And now that my weak ones
Out of the terrible fear she created
Are made to teach themselves
How to band together
Like a family of animals,
She makes them bend anew, only
To fresh layers of her evil habits
Grown over her old skeleton.
Confront your fate, Prince
You are the bearer
Of my people's fate,
Speak for their muted words.
See for their blinded lot.
Think for their raked dreams.
Not with your veins on fire
But with your heart open to them
As it is to your Axum, Armah.
For you who are unable
To save yourself from her grip
Cannot justify her lust to me.

   Silence. Blackout.

Act Three
"Have You Forgotten the Year of the Elephant?"

I. DEATH-WATCH BEETLES CHANT
PART ONE

A few months later. Darkness. Echoes of whizzing lashes crack across the stage. Rear lights up at the foot of Heart-wall. The Beggars' Chorus enters from right of Heart-wall flanked by the First Guard who is lashing at them. The area of the baptismal pit is dim and only faintly visible. Abas enters left of Heart-wall armed with spear and shield. He stands on the narrow strip of a level at the foot of the heart-wall attending to the lashing. Second Guard lashes to drive out the Children's Chorus from the dim baptismal area to the light at the left side of heart-wall. As Guards work themselves into a frenzy of whipping, both chorus groups remain huddled into each other, snarling like cornered animals. From the dim area of center stage, Mothers' Chorus violently sing out what sounds like a protest dirge. Each time the Beggars' or the Children's Chorus make a move to join in with the Mothers' Chorus, they are severely lashed back to their respective corners.

MOTHERS' CHORUS (*dirge*)
    Awake, leftovers of Axum.
    The cunning master god-makers
    Who sow the plague of words
    Have made cowering dogs
    Out of your noble nature.
    You have fallen a sacrifice
    To their bestial outlet.
    Awake, out, wretched of Axum, Awake.
ABAS (*hisses threateningly at both chorus groups who trying to rise are being whipped back.*)
    You watered down guts.
    You screeching jangled nerves.
    Enemies of your fathers' cross.
    Where is the manhood in you?
FIRST GUARD (*lashing the Beggars' Chorus to silence.*)
    You exist by instinct.
    You vegetate by habit.
    What are you men for
    You broken guts of Axum?
MOTHERS' CHORUS (*dirge, marching closer*)
    Awake, our lost of Axum.
    Death has caught on your sleep.
    You have allowed its clutch
    To perch upon your dreams,
    You have allowed the vultures of Axum
    To fight over your lean souls.
    They have long instilled
    Your littleness in your spirit,

Your belly is left to sulk,
The morsel you peck at
Gets lost in your throats.
Awake now and demand,
Our wombs are ashamed of you. Awake.

SECOND GUARD (*lashing the Children's Chorus down to silence*)
Do not listen to their humming bum,
You whimpering wet-pants of Axum.
How dare you sit about moping
When the King's will awaits,
You broken siblings?

MOTHERS' CHORUS (*dirge, marching closer still*)
Where the eagles have fallen
Timid bats are creeping,
Where fire blazed
Ahses are blowing.
Awake, little men of Axum.
Must we sift
Our living from among your dead?
Must you leave us
Only with the undertaker's task?
You have grown weak and senile
Without growing up and alive.
You grind hungry lice
Between your dead claws
When stiff-necked boors
Turn you into villains
In the land of your loves.
Awake, our miserable of Axum, Awake.

> *Under a storm of lashes both the Beggars' Chorus and the Chil-*
> *dren's Chorus rush to join the Mothers' Chorus who have now*
> *moved very close to them. They make a cry of joy but the Two*
> *Guards, enraged, rush in on them to brutally beat and separate*
> *them. Each is made to crawl back to his corner, except a mother*
> *and child, who in each other's arms fall beneath the level, at the*
> *feet of Abas, Suddenly Abas makes a sharp war cry, 'Zaraf!', and*
> *menacingly draws his sword on them. Quick black out.*

PART TWO

> *Though she begins speaking her first few lines in the dark, a slow*
> *spotlight reveals Royal Crier at the steps of the left stele.*

ROYAL CRIER
Her own jackals have out-circled
her strangled dreams,
The dreams of a deadly wounded tigress.
Turbulence straps at her gates
Yet within her walls
The way of her ogres
Still stayed and held sway.

Now, even her young
Who were then caught
By the cult-tales of her glory
Have joined in with her wrecks
Against the stale vomit of her sins
No sooner have they grown up
Than they grew wise and crafty
Yet, there was no spark of reason left
To defend these bonded skeletons
From the beast among themselves.
The strong were let loose on them
With crude naked claws
To break and re-make out of them all
A defence for Nezana's splintered Cross
If only to give the depraved Axum
A mock-honourable funeral
News of the approach
Of a special caravan from Mohammad
Led by Jaffar Bin-Abu Talib
And accompanied by little Prince Araaya
Has been in the air for some time,
But is kept secret here.
As the long pregnant terror
Begins to explode all around us,
What cannot be kept secret
Is this moral wreckage of Axum,
Where, in the mysterious interest
Of the altars and the Throne
The strong still devour the weak,
The weak still compelled to self-hate.
Sons turned against mothers,
Mothers, against their little ones.

> *Slow lights up on the area of the baptismal pit, which is now turned to the Throne. As Armah looks on, Nezana, with an effort, slowly rises out of the Throne and is helped by Noba to stand on his feet. Very carefully, but with determined effort he stretches his legs. He has managed to move. Regal, swelled up, detached, and growing more confident, he silently walks out. Armah's stare is fixed on Noba.*

ROYAL CRIER
Yes, Nezana has somehow managed
To get back on his feet.
Somewhat risen, pale and haunted
But with his old rugged soul
Still his own lethal-cross brand.
At the same time
Right under his limp nose
The little nipple in his wife's womb
Has blossomed fast and set forth.

*(As spotlight slowly blacks out on her and stage lights grow brighter
on the throne area, her last words are heard in the dark.)*
And this mystery was loudly whispered
Both in the rat-ridden danks
And within the sin infested
Royal beds of Axum.

ARMAH

Now that he has pulled through
I say that even he has a right to know
That which all Axum whispers aside

NOBA

He knows all right Armah
But tell him what he knows
And he will murder you for it.
He has also ears for Axum's whispers
But only in the shade of rigid quiet
For he has well drilled
His art of dead silence in her.
And you yourself my son
Are not above that rule.

ARMAH

Not I. You.
You must tell him mother
You owe it to him, to yourself
To your people, to Axum.

NOBA

And to you as well, Armah?

ARMAH

Yes, to me as well mother
If you still abide
By that truth of motherhood.
Me to whom you gave life
Then smeared it with corruption.
To your husband as well
Even though he is a spectre
That kills everything he touches.
And to your people
Whose stink of death
Spout under your wooden feet.
To them and to the honour of Axum
Which the gods entrusted in your hands
But you discharged for the smell of sin.

NOBA

Honour? Do you imply to my face
That there is more honour
In the kind of death
You still dream will absolve Axum?
Why don't the gods
Who, as you say, entrusted
Such honour in my hands,
Ride over on their anger

To clamp down on me, then?
Why not, my all-noble
Little sneaking Prince of Axum?
Yes, I should know best
My own make of a slink
Hiding in his molten stream of sweat
Unable to face the truth of life?
I am a kush, and of this land of Ra
On whose roots the first sun rose,
My body living
As my head is true.
Mine is unlike your hybrid
Devious, little Sabaean mind
Where the quibbles of your Geez tongue
Outlive the living body by far.
With us, the body has a language
The mind cannot speak.
Both live. Without the one
The other is dead: and
The one cannot live
The other's complete life.
First, try and win yourself back
Then go win for Axum, my son.

ARMAH
You talk of the flesh
As if it were the holiest of gifts
Even with that evil fruit of copulation
Your phantom husband's evil brother
Planted there, now threatening
To overwhelm not only yours
—If you have any left—
But the honour of all Axum as well.

NOBA
Your gods, Armah, not I.
Defiled your Axum's honour.
Or is it your honour,
The loss of a crippled coward's glory
That you mean to blame on me?
In that case, it is not I
But the substance you are made of
That should answer the mystery
Of why you go on living in self-deceit,
Why you indulge
In your blind accusations
To replace your lost pride,
Why you indulge
In your sensuous desperation
To substitute for hope.
As for my 'people's pride'
It is your sick father-king
Who publicly murdered it in you,

Or are you grudging me my survival
For which I still pay
Through pain, shame and peril?
I never struggled
For things beyond my reach, son
But that piece of the life
I stooped my honour for
I paid. Yes, I paid
Through insult, toil and unmerited injury.
And as for what you call
A fruit of evil planted in my womb
You are no less a fruit of evil
My timid little mongrel.
You are not a child of love, either
But of that ugly name for love
The foetus in my womb
You said, is a fruit of.
I was pawned to your father, Armah
And you came as a result
Of a cheap affair, in the days
When he was not yet a disabled demon,
But he could release his frustrations on me.
And yet, unlike you, little Sabean bastard
He will not be indulged with
Not pitied, even though
He needed pity the most.

ARMAH (*enraged*)
Now you stop there
My loving, funny, mother queen
You stop there.
I am not your little Sabaean bastard
Nor just your little Semri
Of your great South Lake
Nor just a little anything
Of this or that begot denomination,
I am an ordinary human man first
Please Mother, an ordinary human man, first.

NOBA
An ordinary human man
Up to the mark of man, Armah?
A man coming to his own?
A man who owns his own
And is able to win himself back?
I ask no forgiveness, Armah
For I don't confess
To such a sinner as you are,
Who is too weak to win himself back,
For there is no noble spirit
Left in you to offer forgiveness.
But, I should warn you, little man
That if you tried to tell Nezana

The shame he very well knows
He will either cut you for it
Or make your skin speak
With the fire of that thong
Only to mete you out
With fresher wounds
To remind you of your mixed littleness.
And what you call
The honour of the people, Armah
Will always find in plenty
That same royal blood it seeks
For it spouts like a wild plant
In the shade of any mother's womb.

Nezana enters with restrained effort, but regal and imposing. His superior air dwarfs the others. Armah remains stunned like a cornered animal. Noba makes for the exit. Long awkward silence ensues. Black out.

II. END OF NOBLE SHIVER

Spotlight on a frustrated, enervated Aba Panteleon seated at the foot of the right side stele.

ABA PANTELEON
We await at the sordid edge
Driven to the margin of our corner,
Torn with the gasp
That scratches in our anxious heads.
We await. We look down at the hell
The Jihad pit for the Cross,
The Cross for the Serpent.
We await. We are the hunters turned hunted
With our feebled backs to the wall
Unable to find our escape holes.
There is no compromise
With the new angles of the sword
Whose glory is in the ultimate fall
Of those who stood with their past.
The rule is, first make your kill
Then come to terms with your God.
And now, we of the Cross
Have lost the terms
To come to our God with.
The Zarathushtran gods of Persia
Who yesterday shook Constantinople
Now shiver under the blows of Mohammad.
Our Indian trade ships
Are now warned away
By the Bedouin bandits of Khaybar.
Here, Chief Watto's people are turned Islam

By the sword of the Jihad.
Our regions of Barbara, Nubia, Meroe
Yeha, Endebis and Cyeneum
Are made to embrace it as well.
Rabbi Yona, now the self-made king
Of our region of Agaw
Brandishes his Jewish Talmud
Against the weakened Cross.
Our port town of Adulis
Is burnt, and buried
By the sands of the sea.
Out protectorate peoples of Zoa,
Kaloa, Gambala and Faditcha
Riot, impatient of our law.
The air is pregnant and ennerved
Since the news of the caravan
Approaching with Araaya and Jaffar
Might only mean the end for us.
All around are the angels of the sword.
Everywhere the Jihad. Everywhere the fire.
And we only await
With death bites in our jangled nerves.
   (*Suddenly rising*)
Still, except for the Mad hermit
Who goes on carving the word
Into the dingy walls of the Dungeon,
Only the great diehard Nezana
The True Servant Of The Cross
Holds his lance of faith
Rather than sit and bewail his lot,
Like his foul-tongued son Armah.

     Blackout. Horn pipes and drums. From rear stage, Royal Crier
     approaches in the dark, proclaiming. She appears under spot
     light on the steps of left side stele only after the end of the first
     part of her announcement.

ROYAL CRIER (*from rear stage*)
  Hear all, hear all.
  May the gods open the ears
  They gave you to hear with.
    (*Horn pipes*)
  Our King Nezana, Gabre Maskel
  Upon full recovery of his health
  He has found the Crown Prince Armah
  Guilty, of spreading ill rumours,
  Of ostracizing the blameless names
  Of the great King, his own father
  And the good queen, his own mother.
  Guilty, also, of ever declining

To lead the expedition of the Cross
Against the dragon of the South Lake.
Guilty of exciting, through negligent stealth,
The rebellion of the godless people
Of Zoa, Kaloa, Agau and Kasu.
    (*Appearing under spotlight*)
The rites of blood-letting
By the royal scourge,
Shall now commence.

> *Full lights on stage reveal Armah being lifted by the two guards, prostrated and trussed down on the tomb which is now just replacing the baptismal pit. Abas climbs the tomb with his scourge. All Chorus groups are interspersed, sprawling at the foot of the heart-wall where they were last seen being flogged.*

One of the fierce lashes
Remaining from the last seventeen,
Three more, for his abusive false rumours
Against his august, loving royal parents.

> *Abas and the Guards stand ready. Drums, horn pipes and clash of instruments announce the Royal entourage: Nezana, Noba, Watto and Panteleon enter right of heart-wall. Except Watto, who has lost his dignity, they are in full ceremonial pomp, with Panteleon holding the large silver cross above their heads.*

And the other one
For his unsympathetic silence
On the revolt of the protectorate lands,
Bringing the total number
To twenty one terrible lashes.

> *Nezana makes a pompous hand sign. Chorus groups make a deep agonized sigh. Noba and Watto kneel: Panteleon holds the large cross against Armah's head. Abas begins whipping. Camel and horse hoofs overwhelm background. Drums grumble. Horn pipes blare. Clash of instruments. Abas stops whipping. A tremendous commotion, then a riot in the background develops, then is taken up by the Chorus groups who have suddenly sprung up to life. Clash of instruments is mingled with the riot, but Nezana holds up his sceptre, and with an angry sweep brings all to silence. The Chorus groups fall down sprawling about. He makes a desperate effort to speak but manages only to mime 'Beloved Axumites', which he releases only as a shrill impotent dumb noise. Royal Crier takes over from him and announces.*

Jaffar Bin Abu Talib
Of the Holy army of Jihad
Demands immediate royal audience,
For he brings an urgent message
From His Sainthood the Nabi Mohammad.

Also the young Prince Araaya
Asks permission to enter with Jaffar.

Drums and horn pipes. Both Jaffar and Araaya enter unceremo-
niously and stand opposite each other. Araaya kisses Noba's fore-
head. As Jaffar approaches Nezana, who scornfully turns his face
away from him, he in turn defiantly throws his message, a parch-
ment scroll, at the foot of Nezana, Then commences to recite its
content with a threatening tone. The Holy Crescent blazes on
him.

JAFFAR
'Glory be to Allah,
The Only One, The Holy One,
The Peaceful and Faithful Protector,'
Wrote to you, King,
Our great Nabi Mohammad
—May He bless and preserve him.
'I, testify,' says our great prophet
To you, King, Nagashi of the Habashites
'That Jesu, the son of Mary
Is the Spirit and Word of Allah
And that he sent them both
Down into Mary
The blessed and immaculate Virgin
And she conceived,
He created Jesu of His own Spirit
And made him to live
By His own breath
Even as He did Adam.
I now summon you',
Says the Nabi, to you king
'To worship the One Allah
Who is without counterpart
And rules heaven and earth.
Accept my mission. Follow me.
Become one of my disciples
For I am the Apostle of Allah.'
He sends me
Along with his other believers
For you to care and supply our request.
'Set aside thy pride of sovereignty.
The Nabi calls upon you,
And upon your people
To accept the worship
Of the Only Supreme Being.
Finally he says to you, King
'My mission is over.
I have preached and done my share.
May heaven grant
That my councils be of benefit

To you, and to those who hear.
Peace shall be only with he
Who walks in the life
Of the Only True Belief.'
I have said my message, Negashi,
And I await your reply.

> *Nezana, with his face still turned against Jaffar, makes a furious gesture at Abas who commences the whipping.*

ROYAL CRIER   Twenty, Twenty One.

JAFFAR
The great Nabi Mohammad
Expects prompt reply, Nagashi.

> *Nezana turns on Jaffar. Makes a tremendous effort to say something but is choked, and his rage overwhelms him. With one hand holding on to his sceptre, he staggers and falls. Shakes violently in a long fit, then expires. Abas and the two Guards draw back from the tomb. Armah rises slowly, torn and beaten. He kneels by the body of Nezana and with effort releases his clutch on the sceptre. After a long meditating pause and a formal kiss on his forehead, he rises on his feet, moves centre stage, and raises the sceptre high. Horn pipes, drums and instruments clash timidly.*

ROYAL CRIER
Hear all, hear all.
The King Nezana, Gabre Maskel
Great Servant Of The Holy Cross, is dead.

> *Horn pipes blare disheartened.*

JAFFAR
The great Prophet's Nation of Islam
Demands immediate reply, Nagashi.

ARMAH
What do you say
Of the new Prophet's Message
Our Confessor Father Panteleon?

> *Panteleon fixes his eyes on the body of Nezana, but does not reply.*

Isn't this revelation
And that of the ancient Moses
And that of the man Christ
From the same source?

> *Panteleon does not reply.*

JAFFAR
Is there no reply, then
To our Apostle's message. Nagashi?

ARAAYA (*timidly, and with restraint he kneels*)
I ask permission to speak
O king, for the Great Nabi Mohammad

Has also sent his message of peace.
My friend, his young son Ali
Has also joined him
In this message of peace.
Mohammad has declared, O King
To his entire Jihad Army
And the Holy Islam war
'To leave the just land
Of our Ethiopians, in peace.'
JAFFAR (*enraged, frothing*)
Have you forgotten, then
The year of the Elephant
When the wrath of Allah
Smote your cross and your guileful plans?
Repulsed your proud army
With his fire of Al'Hutama
At Mughamas, the raped gate of Mecca?
   (*Holy Crecent grows larger, sinister looking and blood red.*)
Do not cling to your sin, Nagashi
For Allah is the Prince of Forgiveness.
Submit to his will, now
Or the Jinn created of the Blaze
Shall pound your earth, small, small,
ARAAYA (*rushes closer and hanging on to the staggering legs of his father*)
But the good Nabi Mohammad
Has certainly declared, O father
'To leave the just land
Of Axumites in peace.'
JAFFAR (*shouting what sounds like a war cry.*)
Glory belongs to Allah!
And to Mohammad Rasul Allah!

> *Draws his sword. Echo of riot rises in the background. Jaffar points his sword at the holy crescent, now enlarged in dark red to dominate the Heart-wall. The Star, the Serpent and the Cross tremble. Heart-wall cracks. The stage shakes. Flames leap up between the cracks of the Heart-wall. All shiver. Jaffar turns round to disappear behind the Heart-wall. Heart-wall breaks, falls, revealing a naked desert sky in the distance. The royal tomb caves in. Silence. Blackout.*

III. WAY OUT TO VOMITURITION

Darkness. Night. A cold, red spotlight, on the steps of a now torn, tattered right side stele, where a shocked Royal Crier just begins to gain consciousness. Silence. Distant wind howls, then silence.

ROYAL CRIER
Everything is still. Mute.
Everything silent. Extinct.
Though, on Mohammad's special wish

Axum herself escaped direct destruction,
Everything around her, is dead.
Hers became the bleak fate
Of the surrounded-vanquished,
Cut off from all warmth
Locked out by a plague of hostility.
From the mouth of Memphis
Across the red water Khaybar
To the gates of lower Barbara
The race of Ham is humiliated
By the hordes of Arabia.
The cow of Athor and Isis
The Serpent Mother of Kush
Are raked by the hoofs of Jihad.
True Egypt is no more.
Nubia and Meroe are no more.
Azum licks her death blow.
Around her stood only naked rifts,
Hills shaven down to dust
And riven with pestilent leak.
Far, far around her walls
And close, close to the skin of her teeth
Fell bodies eroded by flames
Faces eaten into rat holes
Limbs reduced to black ashes.
Even my trusted gods of Zarathushtra
Crawled in my dreams
Like a depraved family of degenerates,
And the stink of death around
Made all hope impossible.
Axum is reduced to a den for rats
A reek for fat flies,
A lone spot lapped in heat
Where only cracking pillars gaped.
And roofs threatened to cave in.
Life is rendered silent. Still.
The sun, by sheer force of habit, rose
Shone on a deserted emptiness.
The wind came. Howled,
The Kush man is dead
And lone lean ghosts in toppled walls
Ached. Echoed and moaned.
Everything living was rendered mute,
Silent, Still. Dead.

> *Spotlight slowly dims out on her. Darkness. Full red moon in*
> *naked sky. Silence is broken by a faint hammer and chisel sound.*
> *It builds up gradually then fills the stage. A faint church bell*
> *peals in mass call, but is submerged by the insistent re-echoes.*
>   *As lights come up, the Hermit, now with a staff, rigid, frail but*
> *commanding, with Mad Julian, both still in chains, ascend from*

the dungeon. Except for Jaffar, all are where they were seen last. Hermit and Julian approach Armah, who has remained stunned on his last spot. The Hermit casually points towards the silver cross which Panteleon had left lying by Nezana's body. Armah drags himself and kneels by the cross trying to carry it Golgotha style. He manages to shoulder the head part. The sprawling Chorus groups collect their broken bodies together and pull themselves up, at the same time separating into their three sections. The two Guards lift the body of Nezana high above their heads on a simple stretcher with elephant skin covering.

Led by the Hermit and Mad Julian the mute-mime procession begins to descend into the dungeon, the sound of hammer and chisel increases, echoed by a church-type chant from the dungeon. Stage light turns bluish cold, with shafts of red showering on the audience.

As the procession circles its way down into the dungeon, the two Guards with Nezana's body follow immediately on the heels of the Hermit and Mad Julian. Behind them, Panteleon and Noba. Then Armah bent under the cross, crushed but resilient, with Abas behind him ready with his scourge. Then Chief Watto, alone. Mothers' Chorus behind him followed by Children's Chorus, then Beggars' Chorus. After the Chorus groups. Royal Crier, alone. The whole movement mime is like a dream withdrawn, pulled towards the dungeon sound as if something stronger than themselves is reaching out for them.

Finally, Araaya follows striking on his toy-harp the tune of hammer and chisel. Only the crack of Abas' scourge breaks the beat now and then. All descend except for Araaya, who now looks back at the audience with half of his body already in the dungeon. Lights slowly fade out except for the spotlight that encircles him. Long silence. As he speaks, his voice seems distant, changed and aged. Even his harp looks larger, and his face wiser.

ARAAYA

Let me stay a while
For a few words of farewell
Before the storm
Prevents me the sooner.
I asked my father, sometime back,
What 'she' was like.
I meant my mother,
The slave girl
Who died at my birth.
He thought for a long while
His contemplation gone adrift,
Then replied with sorrow
—She was like a rising honey-fly, son
Whom twilight embraced
Welcomed into the rays of life
Then abruptly buried in its lethal caress—

I knew he meant Axum. His Axum,
And not my mother
Not even Ramia Umm'Habibah
That woman of his painful memories,
But Axum, his eternal Axum.
Yet, that catch, in a way
Often ran in the family trait,
Taking out of your memory of the land
On that of your woman
On whose behalf you suffered shame
Pain and hard toil
Has always been the Sabean's lapse.
    (Wind howls)
And so, not everything of Axum
Got lost to time, as fast.
Yes, things broke apart,
But they lingered on too.
Things tided over in time,
And the sound of the hammer and chisel
Whiled away through thick and thin.
The word they cut on wood and stone,
Carved in and around the caves of Axum,
In her now remote island lakes
In the rocks of her gorges
In the up-turned depth
Of her insurmountable mountains
Survived, lingered, and still linger on.
Some Axumites took to Islam
Of their own will,
Some stayed in their own right
With the old star of David
And with what they believed, and hoped
Would always be theirs.
But there were many, many more of those
Who held tight on to their earliest ways
And with what they knew with confidence
To be for ever theirs: Hamite.
Others still, ran far, far out of Axum
Towards the woodlands of sunset
And far, far to the south
To discover new peoples.
To live among other's ways,
And for others to discover theirs.
My father, Armah spent his life-time
Breaking down his uncle, Bet Israel
To come down to harsh, revengeful terms.
Like my slave mother
The Queen Noba died of labour too,
And not without the child
Which also died inside her.
Some say I poisoned her,

And there's the chink
In the human love story.
Particularly in our Axum's evasive
Eternal, folk-tale of passion heritage
That ever tasted painfully bittersweet,
That notch born of power
Flowing wider as you stretch out
In reach for its fangs.
After me, my sons ruled
And after my sons
Other kings of the Cross stayed on.
Usinas, Ebana, Alal Mez, Gersem
And others, and others, had their turn,
Until much, much later
Another self-made Jewess queen
The terrible Yodit of Agau half-breed
Ransacked her remains to the ground.
Yes: It took longer for Axum to die.
She lingered, but never the same.
With the Serpent Mother womb
The true Ham man is dead in her.
Our beggars' folk-song says
That once the huge oak tree is felled
It is the termites alone
That creep in its roots.

He descends. Distant winds howls. Full stage light up. Curtain.

AMA ATA AIDOO

The Dilemma of a Ghost†

Characters

THE BIRD OF THE WAYSIDE
ATO YAWSON, [Ebow] *A young Ghanian graduate*
EULALIE YAWSON (*née* RUSH), *Afro-American graduate*
ESI KOM, [Maami] *Ato's mother*
MONKA, *His sister*
NANA, *His grandmother*
AKYERE, *His elder aunt*
MANSA, *His younger aunt*
PETU, *His elder uncle*
AKROMA, *His younger uncle*
1ST WOMAN ⎫ *Neighbours*
2ND WOMAN ⎭
BOY ⎫ *Two children in a dream. The boy being the*
GIRL ⎭ *ghost of Ato's fonner self*

*The action takes place in the courtyard of the newest wing of the
Odumna Clan house. It is enclosed on the right by a wall of the
old building and both at the centre and on the left by the walls
of the new wing. At the right-hand corner a door links the courtyard with a passage that leads into the much bigger courtyard of
the old house. In the middle of the left wall there is a door leading
into the new rooms. A terrace runs round the two sides of the
new sector.*

*In the foreground is the path which links the roads leading to
the river, the farm and the market.*

Prelude

I am the Bird of the Wayside—
The sudden scampering in the undergrowth,
Or the trunkless head
Of the shadow in the corner.
I am an asthmatic old hag

† Ama Ata Aidoo, *The Dilemma of a Ghost* (New York: Collier Books, 1965). Reprinted by
permission of the author.

Eternally breaking the nuts
Whose soup, alas,
Nourished a bundle of whitened bones—
Or a pair of women, your neighbours
Chattering their lives away.
I can furnish you with reasons why
This and that and other things
Happened. But stranger,
What would you have me say
About the Odumna Clan? . . .
Look around you,
For the mouth must not tell everything.
Sometimes the eye can see
And the ear should hear.
Yonder house is larger than
Any in the town—
Old as the names
Oburumankuma, Odapadjan, Osun.
They multiply faster than fowls
And they acquire gold
As if it were corn grains—
But if in the making of
One Scholar
Much is gone
You stranger do not know.
Just you listen to their horn-blower:
   "We came from left
   We came from right
   We came from left
   We came from right
   The twig shall not pierce our eyes
   Nor the rivers prevail o'er us.
   We are of the vanguard
   We are running forward, forward, forward. . . ."

Thus, it is only to be expected that they should reserve the new addition to the house for the exclusive use of the One Scholar. Not that they expect him to make his home there. No . . . he will certainly have to live and work in the city when he arrives from the white man's land.

But they all expect him to come down, now and then, at the week-end and on festive occasions like Christmas. And certainly, he must come home for blessings when the new yam has been harvested and the Stools are sprinkled. The ghosts of the dead ancestors are invoked and there is no discord, only harmony and a restoration of that which needs to be restored. But the Day of Planning is different from the Day of Battle. And when the One Scholar came . . . I cannot tell you what happened. You shall see that anon. But it all began on a University Campus; never mind where. The evening was cool as evenings are. Darkness was approaching when I heard the voices of a man and woman speaking. . . .

EU   Graduation! Ah well, that too isn't bad. But who's a graduate? What sort of creature is it? Why should I have supposed that mere graduation is a passport to happiness?

ATO (*harshly*) If you must know, woman, I think you do get on my nerves. Since you do not think much of a degree, why for heaven's sake did you go in for it?

EU   Don't shout at me, if you please.

ATO Do keep your mouth shut, if you please.

EU   I suppose African women don't talk?

ATO How often do you want to drag in about African women? Leave them alone, will you. . . . Ah yes they talk. But Christ, they don't run on in this way. This running-tap drawl gets on my nerves.

EU   What do you mean?

ATO I mean exactly what I said.

EU   Look here, I don't think that I'll stand by and have you say I am not as good as your folks.

ATO But what have I said, for goodness sake?

EU   Well, what did you mean by running-tap drawl? I only speak like I was born to speak—like an American!

ATO (*contrite*) Nonsense, darling. . . . But Sweetie Pie, can't we ever talk, but we must drag in the differences between your people and mine? Darling, we'll be happy, won't we?

EU   (*relaxing*) I'm optimistic, Native Boy. To belong to somewhere again . . . . Sure, this must be bliss.

ATO Poor Sweetie Pie.

EU   But I will not be poor again, will I? I'll just be "Sweetie Pie." Waw! The palm trees, the azure sea, the sun and golden beaches . . . .

ATO Steady, woman. Where did you get hold of a tourist brochure? There are no palms where we will live. There are coconut trees . . . coconut palms, though. Unless of course if I take you to see my folks at home. There are real palm trees there.

EU   Ah well, I don't know the difference, and I don't care neither. Coconut palms, palm-palms, aren't they all the same? And anyway, why should I not go and see your folks?

ATO You may not be impressed.

EU   Silly darling. Who wants to be impressed? Fine folks Eulalie Rush has herself, eh? Could I even point to you a beggar in the streets as my father or mother? Ato, can't your Ma be sort of my Ma too?

ATO (*slowly and uncertainly*) Sure she can.

EU   And your Pa mine?

ATO Sure.

Following lines solemn, like a prayer

And all my people your people. . . .

EU   And your gods my gods?

ATO Yes.

EU   Shall I die where you will die?

ATO Yes . . . And if you want to, you shall be buried there also.

Pause

EU (*anxiously*)   But darling, I really hope it won't matter at all?

ATO   What?

EU   You know what, Native Boy.

ATO   'Lalie, don't you believe me when I tell you it's O.K.? I love you,
Eulalie, and that's what matters. Your own sweet self should be O.K.
for any guy. And how can a first-born child be difficult to please?
Children, who wants them? In fact, they will make me jealous. I
couldn't bear seeing you love someone else better than you do me.
Not yet, darling, and not even my own children.

EU   You really sure?

ATO   Aren't you the sweetest and loveliest things in Africa and America rolled together? My darling, we are going to create a paradise,
with or without children.

EU   Darling, some men do mind a lot.

ATO (*vehemently*)   Look at me, we shall postpone having children for
as long you would want.

EU   But still, I understand in Africa . . .

ATO   . . . Eulalie Rush and Ato Yawson shall be free to love each
other, eh? This is all that you understand or should understand
about Africa.

EU (*delighted*)   Silly, I wasn't going to say that.

ATO   Then forget about what you were going to say.

EU (*persistently*)   I only hope it's O.K.

ATO   It shall be O.K.

EU   Ato!

Act One

*Evening. The two village women are returning from the river with
their water pots on their heads.*

1ST W   Ah! And yet I thought I was alone in this . . .
The lonely woman who must toil
From morn till eve,
Before a morsel hits her teeth
Or a drop of water cools her throat,

2ND W   My sister, you are not alone.
But who would have thought that I,
Whose house is teeming with children,
My own, my husband's, my sister's . . .
But this is my curse.
"Shall I do this when
This and that have nothing to do?"
No. And they all sit
With their hands between their knees.
If the courtyard must be swept,
It is Aba's job.
If the *ampesi* must be cooked,

It is Aba's job.
And since the common slave[1] was away all day
There was no drop in the pot
To cool the parched throat,
I am telling you, my sister,
Sometimes we feel you are luckier
Who are childless.
1ST W   But at the very last
You are luckiest who have them.
Take Esi Kom, I say.

> *Esi Kom enters from the door on the right with two stools which
> she puts on the centre of the stage. For the rest of the scene, she
> moves stealthily but swiftly in and out of the stage arranging six
> stools in preparation for the next scene.*

2ND W   What has happened?
1ST W   You know her son
That was away beyond the seas
Is now come back?
2ND W   So, that explains the new paint. When?
1ST W   Yesternight.
2ND W   Is he here?
1ST W   I do not know.
2ND W   I heard her younger children
Crying for eggs.
1ST W   Which means that those of us
Who are in this neighbourhood
Are going to have our mouths watering
With the aroma of the fryings and stewings.
2ND W   Of course, that is what she always does.
And meanwhile the debts pile up.
1ST W   Yes, but the arrival of the son
May mean the paying of all the debts at last.
Her soul is a good one.
2ND W   Hmm. For my part, I would be ashamed
To live in a Clan house for
As long as she has done.
But let us hurry, my sister
For my food is getting cold.

> *They go out. After a minute or so, Esi Kom goes out too, having
> finished arranging the stools.*

> *Later. It is quite dark now. The old woman totters in supported
> by her stick. In her youth, she had been a short, dark petite
> femme with a will like iron. Now, though she is weak, her tongue
> is as sharp if not sharper for her eighty plus. She sits on one of*

---

1. Herself; i.e., the wife is the "common slave" of the household.

the stools in the centre of the stage. She props her chin on her stick. Presently Ato enters from the door on the left. For a few seconds the old woman continues sitting motionless as if she has not seen him, then suddenly she speaks.

NANA   I am glad you came and found me alive.

ATO   I am glad too.

NANA   And what is on your mind, my grandson.

ATO   There is nothing else on my mind, Nana.

NANA   Were you not thinking, nay hoping, you will come and find me dead?

ATO   Oh!

NANA   Do not be pained my grand-child. I just wanted to trouble you a little. But go and tell your mother that if she and the others do not come early, I will be angry. (*Ato leaves by the door on the right.*) Already, naughty slumber is stealing over my senses. (*A clanging noise from within.*) Yes, someone has tripped in the doorway, eh. One day the people in this house will commit murder. Do they not know that if the heavens withdraw their light, man must light his own way? But no. They will let us all lie in darkness. How will he find his way around this dark place should the ghost of one of our forebears pay us a visit? But this is something one should not speak about. They say they buy *kresin*[2] and pay for it with money . . . ah, as if the penny will shine and light our way when it is tied in a cloth. . . . But of course, they will say I talk too much. . . . Are they not coming? They are now removing their pans, tchia! Are these women? I shit upon such women. When we were young, a woman cleared her eating place after the last morsel had hardly touched her tongue. But now, they will allow their noise-making pans to lie around for people to trip over. But it is not their fault. If they had to use earthenware pots which broke more easily than eggs, they would have learnt their lessons long ago.

ATO   (*from within*)   Maami, why do not you and my Uncles hurry? Nana is getting impatient. (*He reenters.*)

NANA   Have your Uncles Petu and Akroma come?

ATO   Yes, Nana. (*Voices from within.*)

MANSA   (*from within*)   Oh, the old woman again!

NANA   Are those speaking your aunts?

ATO   Yes, Nana.

NANA   But what are they doing there?

Several voices, Petu and Akroma come in. The two men sit down.

PETU   Old woman, we greet you.

NANA   I respond, my Royal Ones. And how are you?

PETU   We are all well, Old One.

Ato slips into his room, left.

---

2. "Kerosene"; Aidoo uses the pidgin form for "local flavor."

NANA   Akroma, how is your wife's stomach?

AKROMA   It is a bit better.

NANA   I notice you do not feel clear in your own inside. You people always say I talk too much. So I try not to put my tongue in your affairs. But I hope you would think of what I always say. Have we not had enough of the white man's medicines? Since they do not seem to do anything for your wife, why do you not take her to Kofikrom? The herbalist there is famous. . . .

AKROMA   I have heard you, Old One. I would put it to her people and hear what they have got to say too.

NANA   (*with her eyes turned towards the entrance*)   I say, what are you doing there? Why are you doing this thing to me?

FEMALE VOICES   Ah, here we are. (*Esi Kom, Akyere and Mansa enter. The stage is well-lit now. The women sit around on the terrace.*)

NANA   Ah, your characters are not pleasing. What were you really doing by the hearth. I thought you know that I must not sit here until the dew falls on me.

MANSA   Old One, it is all right. We won't do this again.

AKROMA   But where is our master, the white man himself?

ATO   (*from within*)   I am coming, Uncle. (*He comes out.*)

PETU   But where are you sitting? . . .

ESI   (*overlapping Petu and directing her voice to the old sector*)   Monka, are you not bringing your brother a chair?

MONKA   (*from within*)   *Hei* Ebow!

ALL   What is it?

MONKA   (*coming back with a chair*)   The way some people become scholars is fearful.

ATO   What is the matter?

MONKA   The master scholar was sitting on the chair studying, so he could not move off! (*Ato laughs.*) After all, what is he learning? Is it the knowledge of the leopard skin? (*Sucks her teeth.*)

ESI   If it had been in any other home, he, Ebow, would have seen to it that we were all seated.

AKROMA   But I do not know what he has done for all of you to pick on him in this way.

ESI   Let us say what we cannot keep in us any longer, for the day Ebow becomes like you, he will kick us all around as if we were his footballs.

NANA   Esi Kom, leave that child alone, for no one knows what the man of fame and honour was like when he was a child.

AKROMA   But Old One, we can soon know the bird which will not do well, for his nest hangs by the wayside.

ATO   Let us give him, too, some time.

MONKA   I always say that one can always know the man who is civilised.

NANA   I think you should all know that Ato was always a humble one.

PETU   Of course, he is a first born. Our eldest hold that first borns are always humble. Our white master, we welcome you.

ATO   I thank you, Uncle.

PETU   Ah, we have been here at home but you . . .

AKYERE   I say . . .

PETU   What is it?

AKYERE   I say, Esi. For a long time I have not been seeing that sheep which you were rearing in Ato's name.

AKROMA   As for you women.

ESI   Ho, I have sold it.

MANSA AND AKYERE   Sold it!

ESI   But yes.

AKYERE   What did you do with the money?

ESI (*indirectly addressing Ato*)   I have not done anything with it. It had a good market and I thought I would find some more money and add to it to give to Ato's father to pay for the bride price for its owner.

AKYERE   That is very good.

PETU   But women, can you not wait for us to finish what we came here to say? The child has just come from a journey. You have not welcomed him but already you want to marry for him.

ATO (*as if just awake from sleep*)   Ei, Uncle, are you talking of marriage?

ESI   It is nothing. I was only telling your aunt that I have sold your sheep to pay the bride price for you when you make up your mind to marry . . .

ATO (*casually*)   But I am already married, Maami.

ALL   You are married? Married? Married!

ESI (*overlapping*)   Who is your wife?

AKYERE (*overlapping*)   When did you marry?

MANSA   Who is your wife?

MONKA (*overlapping*)   What is her name?

ESI   Where does she come from?

Everyone repeats her words to create confusion.

PETU   You must all be quiet. One must take time to dissect an ant in order to discover its entrails.

MONKA (*laughing wickedly*)   Ei, so I have a sister-in-law whom I do not know?

AKROMA   Ei, Monka, keep quiet.

NANA (*who has been sleeping since she last spoke*)   What is all this noise about? Have you asked the child news from his journey?

Silence while everyone stares at Ato.

PETU   Ato, when did you marry?

ATO   That is what I was going to tell you. One week ago.

NANA (*spitting*)   My grand-child, so you have married? Why did you never write to tell us?

ESI   Ato my son, who is your wife?

ATO (*quite embarrassed*)   Eulalie.

ALL   Eh!

ATO   I said "Eulalie." (*By now all the women are standing.*)

MONKA   Hurere!

ESI   Petu! Akyere! What does he say?

THE W   Hurere!

MONKA   Oh, let us say, let us say that some of the names that are coming into the world are fearful.

ESI   Ato, you know that some of us did not hear the school bell when it rang. Therefore we will not be able to say this name. This Uhu-hu . . . I want her real name, my son.

ATO   But Maami, this is her only name.

MANSA   Our master, isn't your wife . . . eh . . . Fanti?

ATO   No, aunt.

AKYERE   (*Contemptuously*)   If so, what is her tribe?

ATO   She has no tribe. She does not come from . . .

NANA   (*Looking up at him*)   She has no tribe? The story you are telling us is too sweet, my grand-child. Since I was born, I have not heard of a human being born out from the womb of a woman who has no tribe. Are there trees which never have any roots?

PETU   Ato, where does your wife come from? (*A short silence. All look at Ato.*)

ATO   But no one is prepared to listen to me. My wife comes from . . . America.

ESI   (*Putting her hands on her head*)   Oh Esi! You have an unkind soul. We always hear of other women's sons going to the white man's country. Why should my own go and marry a white woman?

MONKA   Amrika! My brother, you have arrived indeed.

AKYERE   But we thought that we too have found a treasure at last for our house. What have you done to us, my son? We do not know the ways of the white people. Will not people laugh at us?

ATO   (*Very nervously*)   But who says I have married a white woman? Is everyone in America white? In that country there are white men and black men.

AKROMA   Nephew, you must tell us properly. We do not know.

ATO   But you will not listen to me. (*All quiet. Eyes are focused on Ato.*) I say my wife is as black as we all are. (*Sighs of relaxation.*)

ESI   But how is it, my child, that she comes from Amrika and she has this strange name? (*The old woman spits significantly.*)

NANA   Is that what people call their children in the white man's country?

ATO   (*irritably*)   It is not the white man's country.

ALL   O . . . O . . . Oh!

ATO   Please, I beg you all, listen. Eulalie's ancestors were of our ancestors. But (*warming up*) as you all know, the white people came and took some away in ships to be slaves . . .

NANA   (*calmly*)   And so, my grand-child, all you want to tell us is that your wife is a slave? (*At this point even the men get up with shock from their seats. All the women break into violent weeping. Esi Kom is beside herself with grief. She walks round in all attitudes of mourning.*)

ATO (*wildly*)   But she is not a slave. It was her grandfathers and her grandmothers who were slaves.

NANA   Ato, do not talk with the foolishness of your generation.

The two village women come into the path.

1ST W   My sister, what can be the meaning of this?

2ND W   That is what I cannot see.

1ST W   Probably the old woman is dead.

2ND W   She has not been very well lately.

1ST W   This is life.
Some are going
While others are coming.
That is the road to the life hereafter.

2ND W   Then let us start weeping, my sister.

They begin to weep and walk up stage, then they notice Nana.

1ST W   Ah, but look, she is sitting there.

NANA (*hobbles towards the women*)   Yes, I am sitting here. So you thought I was dead? No, I am not. Go home good neighbors and save your tears for my funeral. It cannot be long now. . . . Go.

The women turn back.

No, do not go yet. I still need your tears.
(*All eyes turn on the women.*) My grand-child has gone and brought home the offspring of slaves. (*Women's faces indicate horror.*) A slave, I say.

Esi Kom enacts horror and great distress.

Hear what has befallen our house.

ATO (*moving to the front of the stage*)   Heavens! Is there any reason why you should make so much fuss? All because I have married an American Negro? If you only know how sweet Eulalie is! (*He looks at the women and whistles.*) Now all this racket you are putting on will bring the whole town here. (*He turns back abruptly, goes to his door, enters and closes it on the scene. All eyes are turned to the closed door now.*)

NANA   My spirit Mother ought to have come for me earlier.
Now what shall I tell them who are gone? The daughter of slaves who come from the white man's land. Someone should advise me on how to tell my story.
My children, I am dreading my arrival there
Where they will ask me news of home.
Shall I tell them or shall I not?
Someone should lend me a tongue
Light enough with which to tell
My Royal Dead
That one of their stock

Has gone away and brought to their sacred precincts
The wayfarer!

   Everyone except Nana starts leaving the stage.

They will ask me where I was
When such things were happening.
O mighty God!
Even when the Unmentionable
Came and carried off the children of the house
In shoals like fish,
Nana Kum kept his feet steadfast on the ground
And refused to let any of his nephews
Take a wife from a doubtful stock.

   She turns to leave, and walks towards the door on the right.

If it is true that the last gets the best of everything
Then what is this
Which my soul has drawn out for me?

   Lights go out.

Act Two

   *A fortnight later. Afternoon. The two village women are returning
from the woods where they have gathered some faggots.*

2ND W *Ei,* Esi Kom.
  Some child bearing is profitable.
1ST W What has happened now?
2ND W Nothing. It is only that I remember
  Her and her affairs when we pass their house.
1ST W Child bearing is always profitable
  For were not our fathers wise
  Who looked upon the motion of our lives
  And said,
  They ask for the people of the house
  And not the money in it?
  There is nothing that can compare with
  Being a parent, my sister.
2ND W Not always, my sister
  If you perchance hear on a silent afternoon
  The sound of a pestle hitting a mortar,
  Go get out your mortar too
  For they are only pounding cassava.
1ST W Perchance they are pounding yam.
2ND W Have you forgotten the daughter of this same
  Esi Kom? Have you not heard it whispered?
  Have you not heard it sung
  From the end of the East road
  To the beginning of the West
  That Monka never marries well?

1ST W   But if Esi Kom bears a daughter
   And the daughter finds no good man
   Shall we say
   It is Esi Kom's fate in childbirth,
   Or shall we say it is her daughter's trouble?
   Is not Monka the sauciest girl
   Born here for many years?
   Has she not the hardest mouth in this town?

2ND W   That is as it may
   But Esi Kom suffers for it.

1ST W   My sister, even from bad marriages
   Are born good sons and daughters.

2ND W   Who shall look after them?

1ST W   Do you ask that of me
   When everybody knows
   A son is back from the land beyond the seas?
   Shall he not help to look after his nephews
   And nieces when it was somebody else who
   Looked after him in the days of his childhood?
   You talk, my sister,
   As if the days are gone
   When the left hand washed the right
   And the right hand washed the left.

2ND W   Perhaps they are not, my sister.
   But those days are over
   When it was expedient for two deer
   To walk together,
   Since anyone can see and remove
   The beam in his eye with a mirror.

1ST W   These are sad sayings, my sister.
   But where is his wife?

2ND W   I do not know, my sister.
   But I heard them say that his mother
   Had gone to knock the door of Yaw Mensa
   To ask for the hand of his daughter for him.

1ST W   Oh, he would have had a good woman.
   I saw that girl when she came home last Christmas.
   School has not spoilt her, I think.

2ND W   And that is the sad part of it, my sister.
   He has not taken this girl
   Whom we all know and like,
   But has gone for this
   Black-white woman.
   A stranger and a slave—
   But that is his and Esi Kom's affair.
   I hear in the distance the cry of a child
   That cry is meant for my ear.
   Let us hurry home, my sister.

    She takes the lead.

1ST W   Oh, Eternal Mother Nature,
  Queen Mother of childbirth,
How was it you went past my house
    Without a pause
    Without a rest?
Mighty God, when shall the cry of an infant
Come into my ear;
For the sun has journeyed far
In my sky.

  Lights out.

---

  *Late afternoon of the next day. Everywhere is quiet. Ato is asleep
  in the inner room. Eulalie comes in with a packet of cigarettes,
  a lighter, an ash tray and a bottle of Coca-Cola. She sits on the
  terrace facing the audience. She begins sipping the Coca-Cola
  and soon the voice of her mind comes across the courtyard. Later
  her mother's voice is also heard. As the voices speak on, her body
  relaxes except for her mouth which breaks into a light smile or
  draws up tightly; and her eyes, which stare in front of her or dart
  left and right generally expressing the emotions that her thoughts
  arouse in her. (On the other hand the passage could be spoken
  as a soliloquy with the mother's voice interrupting from back
  stage.)*

VOICE   So at last here am I in Africa. . . . Joseph and Mary! I hope
  I've done the right thing. What good fun I'm going to have here!
  (*Smiles.*) Just reckon. I hear the cottons are exactly the thing! You
  hold on until I go to the shops . . . (*She starts as she hears a rumble
  of drums.*) . . . And anyway, supposing this is just an ugly mess I've
  let myself into, what am I going to do? You got a heart, Eulalie Rush?
  No. Now it's over to you Eulalie Yawson . . . Yawson. That surely is
  a name. (*Smiles.*) Life can be funny at times, that's what Fiona used
  to say. Now, I must sort of confess that I am finding all this rather
  cute. Ato says there will be two boys in the house. Fiona, if you
  could only see me now. (*Mouth grim.*) Or is it rather if I could only
  see you now? Sometimes a girl would just like to have someone she
  loves and knows to tell things to and laugh with. But there is no
  one for me here who would have understood like you would, Fiona.
  There is no one even back in the States . . . Christ, Fiona, Pa and
  Ma! There was no one left, was there? (*Bends her head.*) And how
  can one make a family out of Harlem? Ma . . . with her hands
  chapped with washing to keep me in College . . . I say (*smiles*), I
  never knew there is Coke in these parts. (*Holding the Coca-Cola
  bottle affectionately.*) Fiona would have been shocked to hear it. How
  we used to talk of the jungle and the wild life . . . And I haven't
  seen a lion yet! As for his folks, they are cute. I adore the old one
  . . . His mother gives me a feeling, though. (*She starts and stares as
  she hears the drums again.*) Ma, I've come to the very source. I've
  come to Africa and I hope that where'er you are, you sort of know

and approve. " 'Lalie, you shall not stop. Chicken, you must have it
all." And I had it all, Ma, even graduation. "You'll be swank enough
to look a white trash in the eye and tell him to go to hell." Ma, ain't
I telling the whole of the States to go swing! Congress, Jew and
white trash, from Manhattan to Harlem . . . "Sugar, don't sort of
curse me and your Pa every morning you look at your face in the
mirror and see yourself black. Kill the sort of dreams silly girls dream
that they are going to wake up one morning and find their skins
milk white and their hairs soft blonde like them Hollywood tarts.
Sugar, the dear God made you just that black and you canna do
nothing about it." Ma, it was hard not to dream but I tried . . . only
I wish you were not dead . . . I wish you were right here, not even
in the States, but here in this country where there will be no washing for you no more and where . . . where . . . Oh Ma! But I know
you would pat me on the back and say, "Sugar, you sure done fine."
Native Boy is the blackest you ever saw . . .

> Suddenly the drums just roll and roll. Eulalie throws away her
> cigarette, her eyes pop out. She is really scared. She mutters
> "Christ, Christ" like a caged animal. She rushes towards the room
> and crashes into Ato's arms.

ATO   Hullo, my sweet. (*Then he notices her frightened look.*) What is
the matter?

EU   Can't you hear?

ATO   Ah, what is it?

EU   Can't you hear the drums?

ATO   (*cocks his ears*)   Oh, those!

EU   Aren't you afraid? I am.

ATO   Don't be absurd, darling. (*Holds her close.*) But I thought that
one thing which attracted you about Africa was that there is a lot
of drumming here.

EU   (*relaxes and thinks*)   Y-e-s. But, you know, I didn't guess they'll
be sort of like this.

ATO   You thought they would sound like jazz?

EU   Sure. Or rather like, you know, sort of Spanish mambo.

ATO   I see. (*Chuckles.*)   But there is nothing specially frightening
about this, is there?

EU   I don't know. I only thought it was witch-hunting.

ATO   What?

EU   Witch-hunting.

ATO   Witch . . . (*He bursts out laughing till he is quite breathless.*)
Witch-hunting? O mine, who put that idea into your head?

EU   But I understand there is always witch-hunting out here in Africa.

ATO   But still, why were you so scared? You aren't a witch yourself,
are you?

EU   Don't tease.

ATO   I'm not teasing. For after all, only a witch should be afraid of
witch-hunting. For the rest of the community, it is a delightful sport.

EU   (*curious*)   How quaint. Tell me more.

ATO   I will, but first, you tell me: how were Hiawatha and Minnehaha
    when last you met them?

EU   Now you are really teasing, Native Boy. But I thought I would
    learn about all these things.

ATO   (*chuckles*)   Especially witch-hunting? (*He takes her arm.*) Sorry,
    I don't know much about them myself. Those were only funeral
    drums. But I think you must have a siesta. If you don't, you'll have
    a nervous breakdown before you've learnt enough to graduate in
    primitive cultures . . .

EU   (*looking up accusingly*)   Native Boy.

    Ato turns to look at her and sees the Coca-Cola bottle.

ATO   Have you been drinking Coke?

EU   Mm . . . yes.

ATO   Excellent of you. I can't bear it warm.

EU   And of course you carried a refrigerator down here.

ATO   I am sorry.

EU   Christ, what are you apologising for? After all, I was only feeling
    a little homesick and I drank it for sentimental reasons. I could have
    had a much cooler, sweeter and more nourishing substitute in co-
    conuts, couldn't I?

ATO   (*confused and unable to say anything for some time*)   I am thirsty
    too but I'll have a gin and water.

    *Eulalie's eyes follow him as he goes back to the room and she is
    still looking in his direction when he returns some minutes later
    with the bottle of gin, water and a glass. He catches the look in
    her eyes and sits on the terrace facing her.*

ATO   (*mixing the drink*)   Darling, what is it?

EU   What is what?

ATO   Well, there was such a look on your face. Were you going to say
    something?

EU   (*gets up and moves closer to him*)   Yes.

ATO   (*lightly*)   Box on then.

EU   Ato . . .

ATO   (*interrupting*)   By the way, are you interested? (*Indicating the gin
    and water.*)

EU   Yes.

ATO   Oh, I beg your pardon then. (*He gives her the mixture, and forgets
    about one for himself.*)

ATO   Aha-a.

EU   Ato, isn't it time we started a family?

ATO   (*surprised*)   Why? I thought . . .

EU   Ya, I remember I bought the idea, but I got the feeling . . .

ATO   Heavens, women! They are always getting feelings. First you got
    the feeling you needed a couple of years to settle down and now you
    are obviously getting a contradictory feeling.

EU   (*her turn to look confused*)   I hope you aren't taking it so . . . badly?

ATO (*boldly*) Not at all. It's only that I think we better stick to our original plans.

EU (*tiredly*) Okay! (*Long pause.*) I'd better go and rest now.

She turns towards the door and the drink is entirely forgotten. Ato follows her into the room.

Act Three

Six months later. Saturday afternoon. Ato and Eulalie have come to spend a week-end. Her sunhat is lying on a chair in the court-yard. Two village children run in.

BOY What shall we do now?

GIRL *Kwaakwaa.*

BOY All right. I will hide, you find me.

GIRL No, I will not find you, I will hide.

BOY I say, I will hide.

GIRL No, I will.

BOY I will not allow you.

GIRL Then I will not play.

BOY If you do not, I will beat you. (*Hits her.*)

GIRL (*crying*) Beast!

BOY Oh, I did not mean to hurt you. But you too! I have told you I want to hide . . . Let us play another game then. What shall we do?

GIRL Let us sing "The Ghost."

BOY Ghost . . . Ghost . . . ah, yes! (*They hold hands and skip about in circles as they sing.*)
"One early morning,
When the moon was up
Shining as the sun,
I went to Elmina Junction
And there and there,
I saw a wretched ghost
Going up and down
Singing to himself
'Shall I go
To Cape Coast,
Or to Elmina
I don't know,
I can't tell.
I don't know,
I can't tell.' "

They repeat, but halfway through the lights go out. When the lights come up a few seconds later, the children have vanished. Ato bursts in immediately. His hair is dishevelled, his trousers creased and his face is looking sleepy-eyed and haggard.

ATO (*looking right and left and searching with great agitation*) Where are they? Where are those two urchins? Heavens! Those scruffy urchins and the racket of noise they were making. Why should they come here? But . . . where are they? Or was it a dream? (*Panting.*) Ugh! That's why I hate siesta. Afternoon sleep always brings me afternoon dreams, horrid, disgusting, enigmatic dreams. Damn this ghost at the junction. I loved to sing that song. Oh yes, I did. But it is all so long ago. I used to wonder what the ghost was doing there at the junction. And I used to wonder too what it did finally . . . Did it go to Elmina or to Cape Coast? And I used to wonder, oh, I used to wonder about so many things then. But why should I dream about all these things now?

Petu enters. He is in an old pair of trousers and a smock which make up his farm clothes.

Probably I am going mad?

PETU   Oh-o!

ATO   *Ei*, Uncle.

PETU   I heard you are come and that is why I am coming to greet you.

ATO   You went to the farm?

PETU   My master, where else have I to go? (*He sits on the terrace while Ato still stands.*) Since the morning has found us, we must eat. And as you know, some of us are not lucky enough to be paid only to sit in an office doing nothing. And that is why I have to relieve the wayside herbs of their dew every morning.

ATO   But my Uncle, we too work hard.

PETU   (*sarcastic*) You believe that . . . But nephew, why were you talking so hard to yourself when I came in?

ATO   (*uneasily*) I had had a queer dream.

PETU   Is that long ago?

ATO   No. It was only this afternoon when I lay down to rest.

PETU   An afternoon dream? (*His face shows he is not terribly pleased even about the idea of it.*) What was the dream?

ATO   I dreamt that there were two children in this courtyard singing that song about the ghost who did not know whether to go to Elmina or to Cape Coast.

PETU   Ah. (*He laughs.*) How funny!

ATO   But Uncle, the boy looked like me when I was a child.

PETU   (*serious*) Ei, this needs thinking about. Do not be disturbed, although I do not like afternoon dreams myself. I will tell your grandmother and hear what she has to say about it. (*He rises to go and sees Eulalie's hat.*) Did you bring your wife?

ATO   Yes. She too is resting.

PETU   (*turns towards the door on the right*) Yo-o. I am going now. When your wife wakes up, tell her I give her welcome. I have brought some cocoyams from the farm and I will be sending her some by and by. Do not think too much about the dream.

ATO   Thank you, my Uncle. When you go, tell my mothers that we will be coming to see them this evening. (*Petu goes away. Ato stands confused. Eulalie comes in.*)

ATO   Hullo, 'Lalie.

EU   Hullo. (*They kiss each other on the cheeks.*) I heard talking here, didn't I?

ATO   My Uncle came to give us welcome.

EU (*anxious*)   Oh, this means the whole lot of them will be coming to see us.

ATO   Would you rather we went to see the new Methodist School?

EU   Lovely. (*She kisses him on the cheek again, and takes her lovely sunhat. She puts it on and cocks her head for admiration. Ato says "Exquisite" and hand in hand they come down the courtyard following the path leading to the left.*

   Lights go off.

────────────

   Two hours later. Esi Kom enters from the door on the right carrying two bundles wrapped in sack cloth. She opens the door to Ato's apartment. She puts the bundles in the outer room, comes out and is closing the door when Ato and Eulalie enter the courtyard from the path.

EU (*sees the woman*)   I say! (*She glares at Esi Kom for a second or two and then turns on Ato.*) Ato, would you care to ask your mother what she wants in our room?

ATO   Eh . . . Maami, were you looking for us?

ESI   Hmm . . . They told us when we arrived from the farm that you and your wife have come to spend today and tomorrow with us. So I thought I would bring you one or two things for I hear food is almost unbuyable in the city these days. And your nephews are so naughty that I knew if I did not bring them here they would steal the snails and roast them all in an hour's time.

EU   What is she saying?

ATO   Oh, she only brought us food to take back with us.

EU   What kind of food?

ATO   Maami, what did you bring?

ESI   Can not your wife herself go and see? After all, these are all women's affairs. Or do our masters, the Scholars, know what goes on in their wives' kitchen?

ATO (*persuasively*)   Darling, will you go and check up, please?

   Eulalie walks rather puzzled into the room. As she enters, she exclaims "Sweet Jesus" and rushes out closing the door behind her.

ATO   Darling, what is it?

EU   Eh . . . some crawling things! (*Composing herself.*) Anyway, tell your mother we are very grateful.

ATO   Maami, my wife says she thanks you a lot for the things.

ESI   Tell her I am glad she likes them . . . Now, I think I will go and prepare the evening meal. Monka will cook you and your wife some rice and stew. If you need anything, you come and tell us or just shout for any of the children.

She turns off. Then turns back.

(*To Eulalie*) "My lady," I am saying goodbye.

> *Accompanied by a wave of hand, Eulalie waves back. The moment she is through the door on the right, Eulalie rushes to close it. Then she rushes into their room and brings out the sack bundle. She is crossing towards the path when Ato stops her.*

ATO   What's all this?

EU   Those horrid creatures of course!

ATO   Where are you taking them?

EU   Throwing them away, of course.

ATO   What rubbish.

EU   What do you mean? What rubbish? If you think I am going to sleep with those creatures, then you are kidding yourself.

ATO   But how can you throw them away just like that? Haven't you seen snails before?

EU   My dear, did you see a single snail crawling on the streets of New York all the time you were in the States? And anyway, seeing snails and eating them are entirely different things!

> *She turns off as if to go on. Ato reaches her in two strides. He grabs a part of the sack.*

ATO   But at least, I could give them to my mother to cook for me alone.

EU   And give them the opportunity to accuse me of unadaptability. No, thank you. (*She wrenches the bundle from Ato and as she turns off, Monka opens the door on the right door. Her eyes take in the scene. Eulalie hurries down and dumps the sack near the path. At the same time, Monka disappears closing the door on the right behind her. Eulalie and Ato just stare at each other.*)

MONKA (*from within*)   Maami, Maami, Ato's Morning Sunshine has thrown away the snails you gave them.

> *Ato and Eulalie are still staring at each other when Esi Kom enters.*

ESI (*addressing Ato*)   Is it true that your wife has thrown away the snails I brought?

ATO   Who informed you?

ESI   That is not important, but is it true?

ATO (*defensively*)   She does not know how to eat them . . . and . . .

ESI   And what, my son? Do you not know how to eat them now? What kind of man are you growing into? Are your wife's taboos yours? Rather your taboos should be hers.

> *Monka re-enters and stands watching. Ato turns on her.*

ATO   Yes, you went and told Maami, eh?

MONKA   Ei, take your troubles off me. Have you seen me here this afternoon?

ESI These days, the rains are scarce and so are snails.
But the one or two I get for you, you throw away.

Eulalie goes into their room.

ATO But Eulalie . . .
MONKA (*derisively*) That's the golden name . . .
ESI Yes, Hureri, Hureri. . . . What does my lady say today? . . .

*Eulalie comes back, sits on the terrace and starts puffing her
cigarette.*

MONKA She reminds me of the words in the song:
"She is strange,
She is unusual.
She would have done murder
Had she been a man.
But to prevent
Such an outrage
They made her a woman!"
Look at a female!

*Eulalie ignores Monka although her face shows she guesses at
what is going on.*

ESI Hureri. Hmm. All the time I have been quiet as if I were a tortoise. But I have been watching, hoping that things would be different, at least, in this house.
ATO (*moving towards his mother*) Maami, this is only a small affair,
what are you trying to say now?
ESI What am I trying to say now?
MONKA If nothing scratched at the palm fibre, it certainly would not
have creaked.
ESI If you listen, you will hear what I want to say. This is not the
first time I have fallen into disgrace for bringing you things. Only it
is my own fault. I should have learnt my lesson. The same thing
happened the day I came to visit you at Accra . . .
ATO Ah, are you still harbouring this grievance?
ESI Do not annoy me, please. How can I forget it? I had travelled
miles to come and visit you and your wife. And if you threw my gifts
into my face and drove me out of your house, how can I forget it?
ATO (*in desperation*) Maami, you make me too unhappy.
ESI Listen to what he is saying.
ATO We asked you and Monka to stay but you insisted on coming
back.
MONKA There are two kinds of offers. One which comes right from
the bowels and the other which falls from the lips only. My brother,
yours fell from your lips.
ESI I had thought I would do as other women do—spend one or two
days with my daughter-in-law, teach her how to cook your favourite
meals. But as if I was not noticing it, neither you nor your wife

bothered to give us seats to sit on or what to cool our parched throats . . .

ATO   I remember that Monka drank water.

MONKA   I begged for it!

ESI   . . . How can I then sleep in a house where I am not welcome? . . . Where did you throw the snails?

> *Ato looks left and right, uncertain of what to do. Monka rushes to where Eulalie dumped the bundle and retrieves it.*

MONKA (*coming back*)   Here they are . . .

ESI   Bring them; at least we shall find a beggar to give them to. (*Eulalie makes as if to stand and speak but sits down again and continues puffing at her cigarette.*)
Oh, Esi, of the luckless soul. It is true,
Living a life of failure is like taking snuff
At the Beach. Just consider the troubles I
Have had—the school fees, the uniforms . . .

MONKA   As for the balls of *kenkey*,[3] they are uncountable.

ESI   The tears I have shed . . .

ATO   Must you go on in that way, Maami?

ESI   Keep quiet, my son and let me speak now, for something has pricked my wound. My knees are callous with bending before the rich . . . How my friends must be laughing behind me now. "After all the fuss, she is poorer than ever before."

MONKA   Even I should not be such a pitiable creature now, after all, my brother is now a great man.

ESI (*overlapping*)   Apart from the lonely journeys I made to the unsympathetic rich, how often did I weep before your Uncles and great Uncles while everyone complained that my one son's education was ruining our home.

MONKA (*to herself*)   I remember the time he was preparing to go to the white man's land where he went to take up (*indicating Eulalie*) this "Wonder"! The money . . . the money . . . This is something which no one should hear anything about. A great part of the land was sold and even that was sufficient for nothing . . . Finally, the oldest and most valuable of the family heirlooms, *kentes* and golden ornaments, which none of us younger generation had ever seen before, were all pawned. They never brought them into daylight . . . not even to celebrate the puberty or marriage of a single girl in this house. But since our master must buy coats and trousers, they brought them out on this occasion. They were pawned, I say. And have they been redeemed? When, and with what? Ask that again.

ESI   For what do I still trouble myself, giving unacceptable gifts? . . . I cannot get a penny to pay the smallest debt I owe. Hureri must have eh . . . what do they call it?

ATO   Maami, is it not enough now? Give me time to work.

---

3. A Ghanaian food item that is a staple of the local diet; made by a long process of fermenting corn flower in water and steam-cooking the soaked flour in the fermented water.

ESI   No, my son, I shall speak. You have been back a long time yet. The vulture, right from the beginning wallows in the soup he will eat. Have your Hureri got all her machines now? Hureri must have a *sutof*.[4] Hureri must have something in which to put her water to cool. Hureri, Hureri. Oh, the name keeps buzzing in my head like the sting of a witch-bee! (*And with that she turns quickly off. Monka turns to follow up, taking the sack with her.*)

MONKA   We are going. Ato, we wish you and your "Morning Sun" a prosperous marriage. (*She too goes away, banging the door behind her. The couple are silent, Ato with a bowed head and Eulalie still puffing at a cigarette. Presently Ato speaks.*)

ATO   (*quietly*)   Now you have succeeded in making trouble for me. Won't you congratulate yourself?

> *Eulalie continues to puff her cigarette. After what seems to be a long time, she puts the cigarette down, stamps on it, cries "Blast" and gets up to go into the room. Ato comes out of the courtyard, and following the path on the left, walks ever so slowly into the night.*

Act Four

Another six months later. The door to Ato's room is open. A great deal of noise comes over from the old sector of the house. The two women are on their way from the market where they have bought fish, pig's feet, seasoned beef, etc., for their evening fufu.

2ND W   My sister, do not say it loudly,
  Even fish is too dear to eat these days.
1ST W   If I think I have spent
  So much on fish . . .
2ND W   And what shall I say?
1ST W   Why is there so much noise from that house today?
2ND W   Do you not know
  Tomorrow is their "Sprinkling of the Stools"?
  The son has come from the city.
1ST W   This reminds me of something
  I had wanted to ask these many days.
  If her son gets a goodly bag by the month
  Why has Esi Kom still not . . .
2ND W   I crave pardon
  For snatching the word from your mouth.
  But my sister, roll your tobacco and stuff your pipe.
  It has not been good going,
  The roof leaks more than ever before.
1ST W   But how can it be?
2ND W   If Nakedness promises you clothes,
  Ask his name.

---

4. Corruption of "suit of clothes"; i.e., a rich wardrobe.

1ST W　But I ask, how can it be?
2ND W　You ask me?
1ST W　But you know, my sister,
That my name is Lonesome.
I have no one to go and listen
To come back and tell me.
2ND W　Then scoop your ears of all their wax
And bring them here.
Esi Kom is not better than she was.
1ST W　Why?
2ND W　They never ask "Why?"
Is it not the young man's wife?
1ST W　What has she done now?
2ND W　Listen, I hear she swallows money
As a hen does corn.
1ST W　Oh, Esi Kom!
2ND W　One must sit down
If one wants to talk of her affairs.
They say that the young man gets
No penny to buy himself a shirt . . .
But the strangest thing is that
She too works.
1ST W　Then how does she spend all that money?
2ND W　By buying cigarettes, drinks, clothes and machines.
1ST W　Machines?
2ND W　Yes, machines.
Her water must be colder than hailstone.[5]
I heard it said in the market place
Monka's teeth were set on edge
For drinking water in her house.
And her food never knows wood fire.
1ST W　Does she tear at it uncooked?
2ND W　As for you, my sister!
She uses machines.
This woman uses machines for doing everything.
1ST W　Is that why their money
Never stays in their palms?
2ND W　But yes.
1ST W　This is very hard to understand.
Before God-up-there
My breasts have never given suck to a child,
But if what I hear mothers say are true,
Then the young people of the coming days
Are strange . . . very strange.
2ND W　Fear them, my sister.
If you meet them, jump to the wayside.
Have I not born eleven from the womb here?
I know what I am talking about.

5. Referring to a refrigerator.

1ST W   But this is too large for my head
   Or is the wife pregnant with a machine child?
2ND W   Pregnant, with a machine child?
   How can she be?
   Does she know what it is to be pregnant
   Even with a child of flesh and blood?
1ST W   Has she not given birth to a child since they married?
2ND W   No, my sister,
   It seems as if the stranger-woman is barren.
1ST W   Barren?
2ND W   As an orange which has been scooped of all fruit.
   But it is enough, my sister.
1ST W   Barren?
2ND W   One should not tell too much of a tale
   And we must eat tonight.
1ST W   Barren! . . .
2ND W   I must leave you then.
   You know Esi Kom's troubles are many . . .
1ST W   Barren! . . .
2ND W   The mouth will twist that says too much of them.
   And as for her son's marriage,
   The ear will break that hears too much of it.
1ST W   Barren!
2ND W   I say let us go. (*She takes the lead.*)
1ST W   Barren! . . .
   If it is real barrenness,
   Then, oh stranger-girl,
   Whom I do not know,
   I weep for you.
   For I know what it is
   To start a marriage with barrenness.
   You ought to have kept quiet
   And crouched by your mother's hearth
   Wherever that is—
   Yes. With your machines that cook
   And your machines that sweep.
   They want people.
   My people have a lusty desire
   To see the tender skin
   On top of a child's scalp
   Rise and fall with human life.
   Your machines, my stranger-girl,
   Cannot go on an errand
   They have no hands to dress you when you are dead . . .
   But you have one machine to buy now
   That which will weep for you, stranger-girl
   You need that most.
   For my world
   Which you have run to enter
   Is most unkind to the barren.

And for you—
Who shall talk for the stranger?
My daughter or my sister,
Whom I have never set eyes upon,
You will cry until your throat is dry
And your eyes are blind with tears.
Yes, my young woman, I shall remember you.
I shall remember you in the hours of the night—
In my sleep,
In my sleepless sleep.

> *Lights go out.*

> *Next morning. Petu enters with a wooden bowl full of white and oiled* Oto *(mashed yam), Arroma comes behind him carrying a brass tray containing a herbal concoction and a kind of sprinkling broom. They go round the courtyard sprinkling the walls and the floor first with* Oto, *then with the potion. The gong man beats the gong behind them. They circle thrice round the courtyard and are just leaving when Petu calls to Ato.*

PETU Nephew!
ATO (*comes from the room and for the first time in cloth*)
Here I am, my Uncle.
PETU We have killed the goats and chickens. The women will send you and your wife some of the *Oto* and then you can eat a proper breakfast. But do you not think you and your wife should come near the Stool Rooms?
ATO *Yoo*, Uncle. We are coming.
PETU But you are a man. So you must come and drink with the men first.
ATO Then I am coming with you now.

> *He goes into the room and returns in a minute.*
> *They all leave the courtyard by the door on the right.*

> *Lights go out.*

_____

> *Several hours later,* Eulalie *enters from the door on the right. She surveys the courtyard with disgust.*

EU What a blasted mess! Well. (*She shrugs her shoulders.*) I suppose folks must have their customs. Though if you ask me, I think there has been enough messing round for one day. (*She goes into the room and returns with a glass of whisky and, as usual, a packet of cigarettes and a lighter. She lights her cigarette and moving to the door on the right, peeps out into the old apartment. She makes a face. Ato enters from that direction.*)
EU (*moving to him*) Native Boy, I have missed you dreadfully.
ATO But you left us barely five minutes ago.
EU That shows you that after a year of marriage I am still in love with my husband which, incidentally, is a wonderful achievement.

ATO By what standards? Because I am still in love with my wife. (*They burst out laughing. Ato looks down at the glass in her hand.*) Sweetie Pie, don't drink too much.

EU But I have not been drinking at all.

ATO This looks too strong.

EU I needed it so badly. I was getting rather nervy when I came back.

ATO Well, now that I am back I don't think you need it, do you, Sweetie Pie?

EU Just let me finish this. (*Voices behind the door to the right.*)

ATO I think some of my people are coming. (*Anxiously*) Let me put your drink in the room for you.

EU Why?

ATO I don't think they'll approve.

EU (*taking a sip*) Nonsense. (*Voices draw nearer.*)

ATO (*trying to take the glass from her*) But 'Lalie, don't let them find you in the very act.

EU (*sarcastically*) Is this a taboo? (*She laughs and goes into the room. Just then, Petu and Akroma enter followed by Monka carrying the brass bowl containing the herbal concoction. Close behind her enter Esi Kom, Mansa, Akyere and Nana.*)

ATO Ei!

> He gives the two chairs in front of the door to the two men who sit down. Everyone cries cheerfully to him 'Afenhyiapa'. Monka puts her bowl down between the two men. The women sit round on the terrace.

ATO (*addressing Petu*) How is it I found you here, my elders.

NANA (*from her corner*) Young man, one does not stand in ant-trail to pick off ants. You find somewhere to sit and then ask us for the purpose of the visit.

> Ato hurries off into the room, returning with a chair on which he sits.

ATO What brings you here this afternoon?

AKROMA Aha, now you are moving in the right path, young man. If I am not putting my mouth into an affair which does not concern me, may I ask you where your wife is?

NANA Who says it is not your affair? It's his affair, isn't it? (*Addressing this to Petu.*)

MANSA If this isn't your affair, whose affair is it? It's everybody's affair isn't it? (*Addressing Akyere.*)

ESI Ei, these days, one's son's marriage affair cannot always be one's affair. (*Ato enters the room.*)

NANA It may be so in many homes. Things have not changed here. (*Knocking the ground with her stick. Ato returns with Eulalie who shows great surprise at seeing so many people around.*)

EU But why so many people? (*Ato does not say anything. Everyone just stares at her. She looks round for somewhere to sit. Ato notices that and jumps up to give her his chair.*)

PETU   And where shall you sit?

ATO   Oh, there. (*Indicating a place on the terrace. Cries of 'Ei, Odo from the gathering.*)

PETU   Our master, we are going to talk to you and you must be near enough to hear without our having to shout. (*Ato looks with consternation at Eulalie. Their eyes meet and they withdraw to a side where they have a tête-à-tête which is inaudible to the audience. At the end, Eulalie walks away into their room.*)

AKROMA   What has happened now?

ATO   Nothing, Uncle.

PETU   Ah, is she going away?

ATO   Eh . . . eh . . . eh . . .

AKROMA   But what we are going to say concerns her.

ATO   Eh . . . since she will not understand it, you tell me and I will tell her everything.

NANA   I have not heard the like of this before. Is the woman for whom stalwart men have assembled herself leaving the place of assembly?

ESI   Yet, this is something which must not be mentioned.

PETU   And if she leaves now, whose stomach shall we wash with this medicine?

MONKA   Let us say! (*Followed by meaningful looks from the women folk.*)

ATO   Uncle, did you say you are going to use the medicine to wash my wife's stomach?

PETU   Yes.

ATO   Why?

AKROMA   Have patience, our master.

PETU   (*looking round*)   I hope I can deliver my message now.

ALL   Go on.

PETU   It was a couple of days ago that we met. What came out of the meeting is that we must come and ask you and your wife what is preventing you from giving your grandmother a great-grandchild before she leaves us. (*Everybody nods his/her head. Nana more violently than the others.*)

ATO   Oh!

PETU   We were to choose this day because, as you know, on this day we try to drive away all evil spirits, ill luck and unkind feelings which might have invaded our house during the past year. You know also, that we invoke our sacred dead to bring us blessings. Therefore, we are asking you to tell us what is wrong with you and your wife so that first we will wash her stomach with this, then pour the libation to ask the dead to come and remove the spirit of the evil around you and pray them to bring you a child.

ATO   (*gripping his chair*)   Good Heavens!

PETU   So my nephew, this is what we bring you. (*All eyes on Ato.*)

ATO   Oh!

AKROMA   Ato, they sent us to bring you a message and they asked us to take words from your own mouth to them. And I do not hope that you think we can go and tell them you only said "Oh!" What has been the cause?

ATO   Nothing . . . oh!

PETU   Haven't you got anything more to say? When two people marry, everyone expects them to have children. For men and women marry because they want children. Or I am lying, Akroma?

AKROMA   How can you be lying? It is very true.

PETU   Therefore, my nephew, if they do not have children then there is something wrong. You cannot tell us it is nothing. There is no disease in this world but it has a cure. It may cost a great deal, but money is worthless if it is not used to seek for people. If it is your wife . . .

ATO   (*aggressively*)   Why do you say it is my wife's fault?

PETU   Oh, my witness is your Uncle Akroma here. (To *Akroma*.) Akroma, you heard me. Did I say it is his wife? All the words which came out of my mouth were. "If it is your wife . . ." How can I say it is your wife?

AKROMA   Petu could not have said that. Does he know what is in your marriage?

AKYERE   What sin would you have committed even if you said that?

ESI   I am very quiet.

AKYERE   Who does not know that she smokes cigarettes? And who has not heard that she can cut a drink as well as any man?

Cries of assent from all.

ATO   Heavens!

PETU   Nephew, we are still waiting.

AKROMA   He will say it is nothing.

PETU   What is wrong?

ATO   Nothing.

AKROMA   I told you so.

PETU   (*angrily*)   Monka, come carry the medicine. (*The women are too shocked. They stare vacantly. Monka carries the brass bowl. They all stand up.*) Nephew, we will go our own way. I cannot be angry with you. I was only a messenger. Now, I remember your dream. I was going to ask the dead to come and take away the evil spirit which is haunting you. Now I know it is not a foreign evil spirit, my nephew. (*He strides out, followed by Akroma, Monka and the other women. Esi Kom turns back and standing akimbo, stares at Ato for a long time. She only moves when the old woman turns back too and urges her to move, with her stick. But then she herself spits, before hobbling away. Eulalie peeps out and discovering that the people are gone, comes out. She paces round for some time and then walks up to Ato. He does not stir.*)

EU   Native Boy, what did they say? (*Silence.*)
Ato, what's the matter?

ATO   They came to ask why we haven't started a family.

EU   And what did you tell them?

ATO   Nothing.

EU   What do you mean by "nothing"? I should have thought the answer to that question is very simple.

ATO   They would say we are displeasing the spirits of our dead ancestors and the Almighty God for controlling birth . . .

EU   (*bitterly*)   You knew all this, didn't you, my gallant black knight?
Now you dare not confess it before them, can you? (*She yawns*) Oh
God! What an awful mess!

> *The lights go out.*

Act Five

> *The next morning. Church bells are ringing in the distance. It is
> Sunday. Ato comes in wearing a mourning cloth. He is attending
> the Thanksgiving Service[6] of a cousin, fourth removed, who had
> died the previous year. He walks up and down, obviously irritated.*

ATO   (*going to the door that leads to their room*)   Eulalie, how long does
it take you to put on a dress? (*There is no reply. He paces up and
down.*) I say Eulalie am I to wait here for ever?

> *Eulalie comes in wearing a house coat. She looks very excited.*

EU   If you must know, darling Moses, I am not coming along.

ATO   What do you mean?

EU   You know what I mean, or don't you understand English neither?

ATO   (*turning his back to her*)   I am waiting for you. If we aren't there
by nine, the place will be full up and I wouldn't care to stand
through a whole Thanksgiving Service.

EU   Of course, you'd only have to come back here to sleep. (*She gig-
gles.*) I would, only I repeat "I ain't coming" eh. Or you are too
British you canna hear me Yankee lingo?

ATO   (*miserably*)   Eulalie, you've been drinking!

EU   Sure, Moses.

ATO   Again? (*In a horrified voice*) And on a Sunday morning?

EU   Poor darling Moses. Sure, I have been drinking and on a Sunday
morning: How dreadful? But surely Moses, it ain't matters on which
God's day a girl gets soaked, eh?

ATO   (*anguished*)   Eulalie!

EU   Yeah . . . That jus whar yar beautiful wife as com teh, soaking on
God's holy day . . . My lord, whar a morning!

> *Hums "My Lord what a Morning"*

ATO   (*looking tenderly at her*)   Sweetie Pie.

EU   (*laughing again*)   Ain't you going teh say Poor Sweetie Pie? Ain't
I poorer here as I would ave been in New York City? (*In pathetic*

---

6. An institutionalized practice of West African Christianity in which a special commemorative
worship honors the memory of a departed relative and "gives thanks" for his or her life.

imitation of Ato) "Eulalie, my people say it is not good for a woman to take alcohol. Eulalie, my people say they are not pleased to see you smoke . . . Eulalie, my people say . . . My people . . . My people . . ." Damned rotten coward of a Moses. (*Ato winces.*) I have been drinking in spite of what your people say. (*She sits on the terrace facing the audience.*) Who married me, you or your goddam people?

> *She stands and moves closer to Ato.*

Why don't you tell them you promised me we would start having kids when I wanted them?

ATO They won't understand.

EU Ha! And so you make them think I am incapable of having kids to save your own face?

ATO It isn't that.

EU Then what is it?

ATO They simply won't understand that one should begin having children only when one is prepared for them.

EU Sure not. What else would they understand but their own savage customs and standards?

ATO Eulalie!

EU And of course, you should have known that. Have they appreciation for anything but their own prehistoric existence? More savage than dinosaurs. With their snails and their potions! You afterwards told me, didn't you, that they wanted me to strip before them and have my belly washed? Washed in that filth! (*She laughs mirthlessly.*) What did you tell them I was before you picked me, a strip-tease? . . . (*She sits down again.*) Go and weep at the funeral of a guy you never knew. These are the things they know and think are worthwhile. (*At this point, she is certainly very sober.*)

ATO Look here. I won't have you insult . . .

EU . . . "My people." Add it, Moses. I shall say anything I like. I am right tired. I must always do things to please you and your folks. . . . What about the sort of things I like? Aren't they gotten any meaning on this rotten land?

ATO (*with false forcefulness*) When in Rome, do as the Romans do.

EU (*contemptuously*) I thought you could do better than cliches. Since you can preach so well, can't you preach to your people to try and have just a little bit of understanding for the things they don't know anything about yet?

ATO Shut up! How much does the American Negro know?

EU Do you compare these bastards, these stupid, narrow-minded savages with us? Do you dare? . . . (*Like the action of lightning, Ato smacks her on the cheek and goes out of the house going by the path on the left. Eulalie, stunned, holds her cheeks in her hands for several seconds. She tries to speak but the words do not come. She crumples, her body shaking violently with silent tears, into the nearest chair. This goes on for a while and then the lights go out.*)

*It is midnight of the same day. Ato stumbles from the path into
the courtyard. He can barely see his way because it is very dark.
As he comes along, he cries, "Maami, Maami," and goes to stand
behind the door on the right. The two village women, each
wrapped only in a bed cloth run into the path. They are carrying
little tin lamps.*

1ST W   My sister, what is it?
2ND W   Oh, are you awake too?
1ST W   Is this noise not enough to wake the dead?
    Why so much noise at midnight?
2ND W   It is very dark.
    I cannot make out the figure at the door,
    It looks like a . . . ghost.

    Tired, Ato crumples on the terrace.

1ST W   I think it is the son.
2ND W   Ah, you are right.
1ST W   But what does he want at this hour?
2ND W   I do not know, my sister.
    But it seems as if
    Between him and the wife
    All is not well.
1ST W   How do you know?
2ND W   Oh, I could tell you
    The Bird of the Wayside
    Never tires of chirping.
    But this is no secret.
    My sons tell me this:
    On their way home
    From laying their snares
    They saw the lady wife
    Sitting on the grass in the school
    With her head bowed.
1ST W   Oh . . . And when was this, my sister?
2ND W   Just this evening.
    Darkness was approaching.
1ST W   Unlucky prophecies coming true,
    I could excel one
    Who has swallowed the dog's eye.
    . . . But what was she doing there?
2ND W   I do not know.
    And it is not part of my worries.
    Besides, marriage is like *Oware*
    Someone is bound to lose
    And another gain.
1ST W   But if both players are good,
    The game may end equally.
2ND W   And how do you know
    The players in this set are not equal?

1ST W   One has backers
        Another has not!
2ND W   People have been known to win
        Who even continue on other people's losses.
1ST W   You are right.
        And this is only the beginning.
2ND W   If we know this
        Then, my sister,
        Let us go back to mend our broken
        Sleep.

> *They leave. Ato gets up and starts pounding on the door again and at the same time keeps calling his mother. Esi Kom opens the door and comes out. Ato stares at her as she starts speaking.*

ESI   *Hei*, what has happened that you wake folks from their beds? Is it very serious? Shall I go and call your uncles? Why did you and your wife not attend the Thanksgiving this morning? Where did you go? All the food we reserved for you is cold. Is it the custom of educated people not to bid goodbye when they are leaving people?

ATO   It is not that. Eulalie is gone.

ESI   (*moving towards the front of the courtyard followed by Ato*)   Where is she gone to?

ATO   I do not know.

ESI   (*sighing*)   Or is she gone to your house in the city?

ATO   I am coming from there.

ESI   Then where can she be? We thought the two of you went away together.

ATO   No.

ESI   But why should she behave in such a strange way?

ATO   I slapped her.

ESI   You slapped her? What did she do?

ATO   She said that my people have no understanding, that they are uncivilised.

ESI   (*exclaims coolly and nods her head*)   Is that it?   (*She paces round then turns to Ato.*)   My child, and why should your wife say this about us?

ATO   I do not know.

ESI   But do you never know anything? I thought those who go to school know everything . . . So your wife says we have no understanding and we are uncivilised . . . We thank her, we thank you too . . . But it would have been well if you knew why she said this.

ATO   (*miserably*)   I only asked her to come to the Thanksgiving with me. But she refused and . . .

ESI   And will she not refuse? I would have refused too if I were her. I would have known that I can always refuse to do things. (*A pause.*) Her womb has receded, has it not? But did you make her know how important it is for her to . . .

ATO   But her womb has not receded!

ESI   (*unbelieving*)   What are you telling me?

ATO   If we wanted children, she would have given birth to some.

ESI   *Ei*, everyone should come and listen to this. (*She walks round in all attitudes indicating surprise.*) I have not heard anything like this before . . . Human beings deciding when they must have children? (*To Ato*) Meanwhile, where is God? (*Ato is confused since he does not know how to reply to this*) . . . yet only a woman who is barren will tell her neighbours such a tale.

ATO   But it can be done.

ESI   *Yoo*, if it can be done, do it. But I am sure any woman who does it will die by the anger of the ghosts of her fathers—or at least, she will never get the children when she wants them.

ATO   But, Maami, in these days of civilisation . . .

ESI   In these days of civilisation what? Now I know you have been teaching your wife to insult us . . .

ATO   Oh, Maami!

ESI   Is this not the truth? Why did you not tell us that you and your wife are gods and you can create your own children when you want them? (*Ato is shame-faced and in spite of wide speculations and several attempts to speak, no words come out. There is a long pause.*) You do not even tell us about anything and we assemble our medicines together. While all the time your wife laughs at us because we do not understand such things . . . yes, and she laughs at us because we do not understand such things . . . (*Here, mother and son face each other for a long time and it is Ato who is forced to look down at last.*) . . . and we are angry because we think you are both not doing what is good for yourselves. (*She is almost addressing herself now.*) . . . and yet who can blame her? No stranger ever breaks the law . . . (*Another long pause.*) Hmm . . . my son. You have not dealt with us well. And you have not dealt with your wife well in this. (*Ato makes more futile attempts to speak.*) Tomorrow, I will tell your grandmother, and your uncles and your aunts about all this, and I know they will tell you that . . . (*At this point Eulalie enters from the path on the right. She is weak and looks very unhappy. She nearly crumples in front of the courtyard while Ato stares dazedly at her. It is Esi Kom who, following Ato's gaze and seeing her, rushes forward to support her on. After a few paces into the courtyard, Eulalie turns as if to speak to Ato. But Esi Kom makes a sign to her not to say anything while she herself continues to address Ato . . .*)
. . . Yes, and I know
They will tell you that
Before the stranger should dip his finger
Into the thick palm nut soup,
It is a townsman
Must have told him to.
And we must be careful with your wife
    You tell us her mother is dead.
If she had any tenderness,
Her ghost must be keeping watch over
All which happen to her . . .

There is a short silence, then clearly to Eulalie.

Come, my child.

And with that, Esi Kom supports Eulalie through the door that leads into the old house. Ato merely stares after them. When they finally disappear, he crosses to his own door, pauses for a second, then runs back towards the door leading to the family house, stands there for some time and finally moves to the middle of the courtyard. He looks bewildered and lost. Then suddenly, like an echo from his own mind the voices of the children break out.

Shall I go to Cape Coast
Shall I go to Elmina?
I can't tell
Shall I?
I can't tell
I can't tell
I can't tell
I can't tell . . .

The voices fade gradually out and the lights dim on him, gradually, too.

NGUGI WA THIONG'O and NGUGI WA MIRII

I Will Marry When I Want[†]

To all those who have been at the forefront in the development of literature in Gĩkũyũ language through songs and books: Mũthĩrĩgũ and Mau Mau composers; contemporary composers like Kamaarũ, D. K. Kĩraatũ, Wahoome, Rũguĩti, Gathaithi Choir, Mwĩkũ Mwĩkũ Orchestra; and to all the other Kenyans who have been developing literature in all the other Kenya national languages through songs and books.

In particular, we can never forget the contribution of Gakaara wa Wanjaũ who long before the Mau Mau armed anti-imperialist struggle used to write books in Gĩkũyũ language. And even after Gakaara was detained by the British for his patriotic anti-imperialist literature, he never gave up his struggle to create a patriotic literature in Gĩkũyũ language. On being released from political detention, he continued to write and publish books and magazines in Gĩkũyũ:

All patriotic Kenyan writers, accept this, our offering!

Characters

KĨGŨŨNDA, *Farm labourer*
WANGECI, *Kĩgũũnda's wife*
GATHONI, *Their daughter*
GĨCAAMBA, *Kĩgũũnda's neighbour, a factory worker*
NJOOKI, *Gĩcaamba's wife*
AHAB KĨOI WA KANORU, *Wealthy farmer and businessman*
JEZEBEL, *Kĩoi's wife*
SAMUEL NGUGIRE, *Nouveau riche farmer and shopkeeper*
HELEN, *Ndugĩre's wife*
IKUUA WA NDITIKA, *Kĩoi's business partner*
DRUNK
WAITER
SECURICOR WATCHMAN

---

† Ngugi wa Thiong'o and Ngugi wa Mirii, *I Will Marry When I Want* (London: Heinemann, 1986). Copyright © Ngugi wa Thiong'o and Ngugi wa Mirii 1982. Reprinted by permission of East African Educational Publishers Ltd.

SINGERS, DANCERS, MUSICIANS, CHILDREN, WORKERS, MAU-
MAU GUERRILLAS, BRITISH SOLDIERS, AFRICAN HOMEGUARDS

Act One

*Kīgūūnda's home. A square, mud-walled, white-ochred, one-
roomed house. The white ochre is fading. In one corner can be
seen Kīgūūnda and Wangeci's bed. In another can be seen a pile
of rags on the floor. The floor is Gathoni's bed and the rags, her
bedding. Although poorly dressed,* GATHONI *is very beautiful. In
the same room can be seen a pot on three stones. On one of the
walls there hangs a framed title-deed for one and a half acres of
land. Near the head of the bed, on the wall, there hangs a
sheathed sword. On one side of the wall there hangs Kīgūūnda's
coat, and on the opposite side, on the same wall, Wangeci's coat.
The coats are torn and patched. A pair of tyre sandals and a basin
can be seen on the floor.*

As the play opens, WANGECI *is just about to finish peeling potatoes. She then starts to sort out the rice on a tray and engages
in many other actions to do with cooking.*

*KĪGŪŪNDA is mending the broken leg of a folding chair. Gath-
oni is busy doing her hair. The atmosphere shows that they are
waiting for some guests. As Kīgūūnda mends the chair, he acci-
dentally causes the title-deed to fall on the floor. He picks it up
and gazes at it as if he is spelling out the letters.*

WANGECI
What do you want to do with the title-deed?
Why do you always gaze at it
As if it was a title for a thousand acres?
KĪGŪŪNDA
These one and a half acres?
These are worth more to me
Than all the thousands that belong to Ahab Kīoi wa Kanoru.
These are mine own,
Not borrowed robes
Said to tire the wearer.
A man brags about his own penis,
However tiny.
WANGECI
And will you be able to mend the chair in time
Or are our guests to squat on the floor?
KĪGMŪŪNDA *(laughing a little)*
Ahab Kīoi son of Kanoru!
And his wife Jezebel!
To squat on the floor!
WANGECI
Go on then and

Waste all the time in the world
Gazing at the title-deed!

> *Wangeci continues with her cooking chores. Kĩgũũnda puts the*
> *title-deed back on the wall and resumes mending the chair. Sud-*
> *denly a drunk passes through the yard singing.*

DRUNK (*singing*)
I shall marry when I want,
Since all padres are still alive.
I shall get married when I want,
Since all nuns are still alive.
   (*Near the door he stops and calls out*)
Kĩgũũnda wa Gathoni!
Son of Mũrĩma!
Why didn't you come out for a drink?
Or are you tied to your wife's petticoats?
Do you suckle her?
Come, let's go!

WANGECI (*runs to the door and shouts angrily*)
Go away and drink that poisonous stuff at the bar!
You wretch!
Has alcohol become milk?
Auuu-u!
Have you no shame urinating there?
   (*She looks for a stone or any other missile. But when she again*
   looks out, she finds the drunk disappearing in the distance. She goes
   back to her seat by the fireplace.)
He has gone away, legs astride the road,
Doing I don't know what with his arms.
Has drinking become work?
Or have beer-halls become churches?

KĨGŨŨNDA
Was that not Kamande wa Mũnyui?
Leave him alone,
And don't look down upon him.
He was a good man;
He became the way he now is only after he lost his job.
He worked with the Securicor company.
He was Kĩoi's nightwatchman.
But one day Kĩoi finds him dead asleep in the middle of the night.
From that moment Kamande lost his job.
Before the Securicor company he was an administrative
      policeman.
That's why when he takes one too many,
He swings his arms about as if he is carrying a gun.

WANGECI
Alcohol will now employ him!

KĨGŨŨNDA
Poverty has no heroes,
He who judges knows not how he will be judged!

Suddenly a hymn breaks out in the yard. Kĩgũũnda stops work and listens. Wangeci listens for a little while, then she continues with her activities. Gathoni goes out into the yard where the singers are.

SOLOIST
The Satan of poverty
Must be crushed!

CHORUS
Hallelujah he must be crushed,
For the second coming is near.

SOLOIST
He destroys our homes,
Let's crush him.

CHORUS
Hallelujah let's crush him and grind him
For the second coming is near.

SOLOIST
The Satan of theft
Must be crushed!

CHORUS
Hallelujah he must be crushed,
For the second coming is near.

SOLOIST
Crush and cement him to the ground,
Crush him!

CHORUS
Hallelujah crush and cement him to the ground,
For the second coming is near.

SOLOIST
He oppresses the whole nation,
Let's crush him!

CHORUS
Hallelujah let's crush and grind him,
For the second coming is near.

SOLOIST
The Satan of robbery
Must be crushed!

CHORUS
Hallelujah he must be crushed,
For the second coming is near.

SOLOIST
Bury him and plant thorn trees on the grave.

CHORUS
Bury him and plant thorn trees on the grave,
For the second coming is near.

SOLOIST
He brings famine to our children,
Let's crush him!

CHORUS
Hallelujah let's crush and grind him,
For the second coming is near.

SOLOIST
The Satan of oppression
Must be crushed!

CHORUS
Hallelujah he must be crushed,
For the second coming is near.

SOLOIST
Crush and cement him to the ground,
Crush him!

CHORUS
Hallelujah crush and cement him to the ground,
Crush him!

SOLOIST
He holds back our rising awareness
Let's crush him.

CHORUS
Hallelujah let's crush and grind him,
For the second coming is near.

SOLOIST
Our people let's sing in unity,
And crush him!

CHORUS
Hallelujah let's crush and grind him,
For the second coming is near.

SOLOIST
I can't hear your voices
Let's crush him!

CHORUS
Hallelujah let's crush and grind him,
For the second coming is near . . .

> *The group Leader now enters Kīgūūnda's house and stands by the*
> *door holding a container for subscriptions. Gathoni also enters*
> *and stands where she had previously sat.*

LEADER
Praise the Lord!

KĪGŪŪNDA ⎫
WANGECI ⎭ (*Looking at one another as if unable to know what to say*)
We are well,
And you too we hope.

LEADER
We belong to the sect of the poor.
Those without land,
Those without plots,
Those without clothes.
We want to put up our own church.
We have a haraamble.[1]

---

1. Public fund-raising.

Give generously to the God of the poor
Whatever you have put aside
To ward off the fate of Anania and his wife.[2]

KĪGŪŪNDA (*Making a threatening step or two towards the Leader*)
We can hardly afford to feed our bellies.
You think we can afford any for haraambe?

The Leader goes out quickly. The group resumes their song.

SOLOIST
The devil of stinginess
Must be crushed!

CHORUS
Hallelujah let's crush him
And press him to the ground,
For the second coming is near.

SOLOIST
He is making it difficult for us to build churches,
Let's crush him!

CHORUS
Hallelujah let's crush him and press him down,
For the second coming is near.

SOLOIST
The devil of darkness
Must be crushed . . .

KĪGŪŪNDA (*rushing to the door*)
Take away your hymn from my premises
Take it away to the bush!

They go away, their voices fading in the distance. Gathoni sits down and resumes doing her hair.

KĪGŪŪNDA
That we build a church in honour of poverty!
Poverty!
Even if poverty was to sell at five cents,
I would never buy it!
Religions in this village will drive us all crazy!
Night and day!
You are invited to a haraambe fund-raising for the church.
Which church?
Of the White Padre and Virgin Mary.
You are invited to a haraambe for the church.
Which church?
Of the P.C.E.A.[3] The Scottish one.
Haraambe for the church.
Which church?
Of the Anglicans.

---

2. A reference to the biblical story of Anania and his wife, Sapphira, who lost their lives as punishment for keeping some of their possessions from the collective property of the early, communal church.
3. Presbyterian Church of East Africa.

Of the Greek Orthodox.
Of Kikuyu Independent.
Of Salvation Army.
Of the Sect of Deep Waters.
Are we the rubbish heap of religions?
So that wherever the religions are collected,
They are thrown in our courtyard?
And now the sect of the poor?
Religion, religion, religion!
Haraambe, haraambe, haraambe!
And those church buildings are only used once a week!
Or is this another profitable business?

WANGECI
You know they were here the other day
Trying to convert me!

KĨGŨŨNDA
Who? The same lot?

WANGECI
What do they call themselves?
The ones that came from America very recently,
Those ones: their haraambe is not local
They say you take them a tenth
Of all you earn or harvest.
Even if it's a tenth of the maize or beans
You have grown in your small shamba[4] . . .

KĨGŨŨNDA
All that haraambe,
To America.

WANGECI
What are they called now?

KĨGŨŨNDA (*pretending anger at her*)
And why don't you follow them
To Rome, Greece or that America
Singing (*sings in mimicry*)
The devil must be crushed,
Crush him!
For darkness is falling . . .

        Wangeci and Gathoni laugh

WANGECI
That voice of yours attempting foreign songs
Could frighten a baby into tears.

KĨGŨŨNDA (*suddenly seized by a lighthearted mood*)
This voice that belongs to Kĩgũũnda wa Gathoni?
Don't you remember before the Emergency[5]
How I used to sing and dance the Mũcũng 'wa dance?
Was it not then that you fell in love with these shapely legs?

---

4. Farm.
5. Kenya was under a British-imposed State of Emergency from 1952 to 1962.

WANGECI
  You, able to dance the Mũcũng'wa?
KĨGŨŨNDA
  Gathoni,
  Bring me that sword on the wall.

  Gathoni goes for the sword

I want to show this woman
How I then used to do it!

> *Gathoni hands the sword to Kĩgũũnda. Kĩgũũnda ties the sword round his waist. He starts the Mũcũng'wa. In his head he begins to see the vision of how they used to dance the Mũcũng 'wa. Actual dancers now appear on the stage led by Kĩgũũnda and his wife.*

KĨGŨŨNDA (*soloist*)
  I am he on whom it rained
  As I went up and down
  The Mũitĩrĩri mountain.
DANCERS
  I am he on whom it rained
  As I went up and down
  The Mũitĩrĩri mountain.
KĨGŨŨNDA
  I was late and far away from home
  I spent the night in a maiden's bed
  My mother said they should go back for me
  My father said they should not go back for me.
DANCERS
  I was late and far away from home
  I spent the night in a maiden's bed
  My mother said they should go back for me
  My father said they should not go back for me.
KĨGŨŨNDA
  Maiden lend me your precious treasures
  And I will lend you my precious treasures
  Maiden, the treasures I'll lend you
  Will make you lose your head
  And when you lose your head you'll never find it again.
DANCERS
  Maiden lend me your precious treasures
  And I will lend you my precious treasures
  Maiden, the treasures I'll lend you
  Will make you lose your head
  And when you lose your head you'll never find it again.
KĨGŨŨNDA
  Whose homestead is this
  Where my voice is now raised in song,
  Where once my mother refused a marriage offer
  And I wetted the bed?

DANCERS

> Whose homestead is this
> Where my voice is now raised in song,
> Where once my mother refused a marriage offer
> And I wetted the bed?

KĪGŪŪNDA

> My mother's bridewealth was a calf taken in battle,
> The calf was tended by young warriors.
> Many hands make work light.

DANCERS

> My mother's bridewealth was a calf taken in battle,
> The calf was tended by young warriors.
> Many hands make work light.

KĪGŪŪNDA

> Mother ululate for me,
> For if I don't die young I'll one day sing songs of victory.
> Oh, yes, come what come may
> If I don't die young I'll one day sing songs of victory.

DANCERS

> Mother ululate for me,
> For if I don't die young I'll one day sing songs of victory.
> Oh, yes, come what come may
> If I don't die young I'll one day sing songs of victory.

KĪGŪŪNDA

> The crown of victory should be taken away from traitors
> And be handed back to patriots
> Like Kīmaathi's[6] patriotic heroes.

DANCERS

> The crown of victory should be taken away from traitors
> And be handed back to patriots
> Like Kīmaathi's patriotic heroes.

> All the dancers leave the arena. Kīgũũnda goes on alone and
> repeats the last verse.

KĪGŪŪNDA

> The crown of victory should be taken away from traitors
> And be handed back to patriots
> Like Kīgũũnda wa Gathoni . . .

WANGECI (cutting him short)

Sit down!
An aging hero has no admirers!
  (Kīgũũnda unties the sword and hangs it back on the wall)
Who prevented you from selling out?
Today we would be seeing you
In different models of Mercedez Benzes,
With stolen herds of cows and sheep,
With huge plantations,
With servants to look after your massive properties.
Yes, like all the other men around!

---

6. Dedan Kīmaathi, Mau Mau guerrilla leader.

They are now the ones employing you,
Jobs without wages!
Hurry up and mend that chair,
Kīoi and his family are about to arrive.
Hasn't that chair been in that condition all this time,
Without you doing anything about it?
If they arrive this very minute,
Where will they sit?

KĪGŪŪNDA (*hurrying up with the work. When he finishes repairing it, he sits on it, trying to see if it's firm*)
What can they do to me even if they enter this minute?
Let them come with their own chairs
Those spring and sponge ones that seem to fart
As you sink into them.
 (*He sings as if he is asking Wangeci a question*)
Whose homestead is this?
Whose homestead is this?
Whose homestead is this?
So that I can roll on the dust
Like the calf of a buffalo!

> Kīgūūnda waits for an answer. Wangeci merely glances at him for about a second and then continues with her work. Kīgūūnda now sings as if he is answering himself. Still singing, he stands up and walks to the title-deed, pulls it off the wall and looks at it.

This is mine own homestead
This is mine own homestead
This is mine own homestead
If I want to roll on the dust
I am free to do so.

WANGECI
I wonder what Mr Kīoi
And Jezebel, his madam,
Want in a poor man's home?
Why did they take all that trouble to let us know beforehand
That they would be coming here today?

KĪGŪŪNDA
You, you woman,
Even if you see me in these tatters
I am not poor.
 (*He shows her the title-deed by pointing at it. Then he hangs it back on the wall*)
You should know
That a man without debts is not poor at all.
Aren't we the ones who make them rich?
Were it not for my blood and sweat
And the blood and sweat of all the other workers,
Where would the likes of Kīoi and his wife now be?
Tell me!
Where would they be today?

WANGECI
Leave me alone,
You'll keep on singing the same song
Till the day you people wake up.
A fool's walking stick supports the clever.
But why do you sit idle
While this bedframe
Also needs a nail or two?

> *Kĩgũũnda takes the hammer and goes to repair the bed. Wangeci
> turns her face and sees Gathoni's bedding on the floor.*

Gathoni, Gathoni!
GATHONI
Yes!
WANGECI
Gathoni!
GATHONI
Yeees!
WANGECI
Can't you help me
In peeling potatoes,
In sorting out the rice,
Or in looking after the fire?
Instead of sitting there,
Legs stretched,
Plaiting your hair?
GATHONI
Mother you love complaining
Haven't I just swept the floor?
WANGECI
And what is that bedding doing over there?
Can't you put it somewhere in a corner,
Or else take it outside to the sun
So the fleas can fly away?
GATHONI
These tatters!
Are these what you call bedding?
And this floor,
Is this what you call a bed?
WANGECI
Why don't you get yourself a husband
Who'll buy you spring beds?
GATHONI
Mother, why are you insulting me?
Is that why you refused to send me to school,
So that I may remain your slave,
And for ever toil for you?
Picking tea and coffee only for you to pocket the wages?
And all that so that you can get money
To pay fees for your son!

Do you want me to remain buried under these ashes?
And on top of all that injury
You have to abuse me night and day?
Do you think I cannot get a husband?
I'll be happy the day I leave this home!

WANGECI (*with sarcasm*)
Take to the road!
There's no girl worth the name
Who is contented with being an old maid
In her mother's homestead.

GATHONI
Sorry!
I shall marry when I want.
Nobody will force me into it!

WANGECI
What? What did you say?

GATHONI
I shall marry when I want.

WANGECI
You dare talk back to me like that?
Oh, my clansmen, come!
You have started to insult me at your age?
Why don't you wait until you have grown some teeth!
   (*with sarcasm*)
You! Let me warn you.
If I was not expecting some guests
I would teach you never to abuse your mother.
Take these potato peelings and throw them out in the yard.

> Gathoni takes the peelings. As she is about to go out, her father
> shouts at her

KĨGŨŨNDA
Gathoni!
   (*Gathoni looks at her father fearfully*)
Come here.
   (*Gathoni makes only one step forward still in fear*)
If ever I see or hear that again . . . !
Utaona cha mtema kuni.
Do you think that we mine gold,
To enable us to educate boys and girls?
Go away!
Na uchunge mdomo wako.

> Gathoni takes the peelings out.

WANGECI
What's wrong with the child?
She used not to be like this!

KĨGŨŨNDA
It's all the modern children.
They have no manners at all.

In my time
We could not even sneeze in front of our parents.
What they need is a whip
To make them straighten up!

WANGECI

No!
When children get to that age,
We can only watch them and hope for the best.
When axes are kept in one basket they must necessarily knock
     against each other.
She'll soon marry and be out of sight.
There's no maiden who makes a home in her father's backyard.
And there's no maiden worth the name who wants to get grey
     hairs at her parents' home.

KĪGŪŪNDA

Do modern girls marry,
Or do they only go to the bars
Accompanied by men old enough to be their fathers,
And the girls cooing up to them, sugardaddy, sugardaddy!
Even for those who have gone to school up to secondary
Or up to the Makerere grade of Cambridge
The song is still the same!
Sugardaddy, sugardaddy!

> *Gathoni enters and goes back to where she was before and con-*
> *tinues with doing her hair as if she is getting ready to go out.*

WANGECI

Have you gone back to your hair?
What's wrong with this child!
Bring me the salt.
     (*Gathoni brings soda ash instead*)
Oh, clansmen, did I ask you for soda ash?

GATHONI

I did not find any salt.

WANGECI

So you suggest we put soda ash in the stew?
Look for the salt.

GATHONI

There is no salt.
Wasn't it finished last night?

WANGECI

Where shall I now turn?
Give me some money so Gathoni can run for salt!

KĪGŪŪNDA (*searches his pockets*)

I have no money. I gave it all to you.
Didn't you buy cooking oil, rice and salt?

WANGECI

Thirty cents' worth of cooking oil
And half a kilo of sugar!
Was that all that exhausted your pockets?

KĨGŨŨNDA
  The given does not know when the granary is empty.
  Do you think that taking out is the same thing as banking?
WANGECI
  He who puts on dancing finery knows how he is going to dance in
      the arena!
  You were the one who said that we should cook food for the
      visitors, not so?
KĨGŨŨNDA (*not happy with the subject, trying to change it*)
  Do you know that in the past,
  The amount of money I gave you
  Would have bought more than three kilos of sugar?
  Today, am I expected to cut myself to pieces
  Or to increase my salary by force
  To enable me to keep abreast with the daily increase in prices?
  Didn't they increase the price of flour only yesterday?
WANGECI (*sarcastically*)
  The difference between then and now is this!
  We now have our independence!
KĨGŨŨNDA
  I ran away from coldland only to find myself in frostland!
WANGECI
  But even if prices rise
  Without the wages rising,
  Or even if there are no jobs,
  Are we expected to eat saltless food?
  Or do they want us to use ashes?
  Gathoni!
GATHONI
  Yees.
WANGECI
  Can you run over to Gĩcaamba's place
  And ask them for some salt!
  Those are never without anything
  Because of their fortnightly pay.
      (*Gathoni begins to move*)
  And Gathoni!
GATHONI
  Yees.
WANGECI
  And . . . eem . . . and . . . eem,
  Don't tell them that we have guests.
  This food cannot feed guests
  And feed the whole village.

      Gathoni goes out.

KĨGŨŨNDA (*as if his thoughts are still on wages and price increases*)
  You talk about prices,
  But tell me a single item whose price has not gone up?
  In the past a mere thirty shillings,

Could buy me clothes and shoes,
And enough flour for my belly.
Today I get two hundred shillings a month,
And it can't even buy insecticide enough to kill a single bedbug.
African employers are no different
From Indian employers
Or from the Boer white landlords.
They don't know the saying
That the hand of a worker should not be weakened.
They don't know the phrase, 'increased wages'!

WANGECI
Are we the pot that cooks without eating?

> *Gathoni enters panting. It looks as if she has something on her mind.*

GATHONI
We have been given a lot of salt!

> *Before Gathoni sits down a car hoots from the road. Gathoni does not know if she should sit down or run out; she shuffles about doubtfully.*

WANGECI
What kind of a person is this?
He never enters the house to greet people!

> *The car hoots again, now with more force and impatience.*

WANGECI
Go, you are the one being called out by John Mūhūūni.
Why don't you get out before he makes us deaf with the hooting?
    (*Gathoni goes out.*)
Do you know that Gathoni began to be difficult
Only after this son of Kīoi started this business of hooting for her?
    (*Kīgūūnda goes on with his work as if he has not heard anything.*)
The son of Kīoi!
What does he want with Gathoni?
Gathoni being a child,
Does she realize that men have prickly needles!

KĪGŪŪNDA
You should have said that it is the modern men
Who have got prickly needles.
Give me water to wash my feet.

> *Wangeci brings him water in a basin. Kīgūūnda goes and gets his tyre sandals from the floor. He now imitates the gait of young men as he walks towards the basin talking all the time.*

Modern young men?
You can never tell!
Ask them to put on bell bottoms
And to put on platform shoes,
And then to whistle whistles of hypocrisy,

That's all they are able to do.
But it has well been said that
The father and mother of the beautiful one have no ears.

WANGECI (*starts as if an idea has suddenly occurred to her*)
Could it be the reason why . . . ?

KĨGŨŨNDA
Why what?

WANGECI
Mũhũũni's father and mother, Kĩoi and Jezebel, are visiting us?
They have never before wanted to visit us!

KĨGŨŨNDA
To visit, yes—to say what?

WANGECI
It could be that . . .

KĨGŨŨNDA
You women!
You are always thinking of weddings!

WANGECI
Why not?
These are different times from ours.
These days they sing that love knows no fear.
In any case, can't you see
Your daughter is very beautiful?
She looks exactly the way I used to look—a perfect beauty!

KĨGŨŨNDA (*stopping dusting up the tyre sandals*)
You? A perfect beauty?

WANGECI
Yes. Me.

KĨGŨŨNDA
Don't you know that it was only that
I felt pity for you?

WANGECI
You, who used to waylay me everywhere all the time?
In the morning,
In the evening,
As I came home from the river,
As I came home from the market,
Or as I came back home from work in the settlers' farms?
Can't you remember how you used to plead with me,
Saying you had never in your life seen a beauty like me?

KĨGŨŨNDA (*going back in time*)
That was long before the state of Emergency.
Your heels used to shine bright,
Your face shone like the clear moon at night,
Your eyes like the stars in heaven.
Your teeth, it seemed, were always washed with milk.
Your voice sounded like a precious instrument.
Your breasts were full and pointed like the tip of the sharpest
    thorn.
As you walked it seemed as if they were whistling beautiful tunes.

WANGECI (*also mesmerized by memories of their past youth*)
  In those days
  We used to dance in Kĩneenĩ forest.
KĨGŨŨNDA
  A dance would cost only twenty-five cents.
WANGECI
  In those days there was not a single girl from Ndeiya up to
      Gĩthĩĩga
  Who did not die to dance with you.
KĨGŨŨNDA
  You too would swing your skirt
  Till the guitar player was moved to breaking the strings.
  And the guitars used to sound tunes
  That silenced the entire forest,
  Making even the trees listen . . .

> *The sound of guitars and other instruments as if Kĩgũũnda and
> Wangeci can hear them in the memory. Kĩgũũnda and Wangeci
> start dancing. Then they are joined by the guitar players and
> players of other instruments and dancers. They dance, Kĩgũũnda
> and Wangeci among them.*

Nyaangwĩcũ let's shake the skirt
Nyaangwĩcũ let's shake the skirt
Sister shake it and make it yield its precious yields.
Sister shake it and make it yield its precious yields.

Nyaangwĩcũ is danced on one leg
Nyaangwĩcũ is danced on one leg
The other is merely for pleasing the body.
The other is merely for pleasing the body.

Wangeci the beautiful one
Wangeci the beautiful one
With a body slim and straight like the eucalyptus.
With a body slim and straight like the eucalyptus.

Wangeci the little maiden
Wangeci the little maiden
When I see her I am unable to walk.
When I see her I am unable to walk.

Wangeci let's cultivate the fruit garden
Wangeci let's cultivate the fruit garden
This garden that belongs to Kĩgũũnda wa Gathoni.
This garden that belongs to Kĩgũũnda wa Gathoni.

Wangeci, our mother, we now refuse
Wangeci, our mother, we now refuse
To be slaves in our home,
To be slaves in our home.

> *When this is over, Wangeci says, 'Oh my favourite was Mwom-
> boko.' And Kĩgũũnda replies: 'Oh in those days we used to tear*

the right or left side of trouser legs from the knee downwards.
Those were our bell bottoms with which we danced Mwomboko.'
Now the guitar players and the accordion players start. The
Mwomboko dancers enter. Kĩgũũnda and Wangeci lead them in
the Mwomboko dance. Guitars, iron rings and the accordions are
played with vigour and the dancers' feet add embellishments.

The Mwomboko dance is not difficult,
It's just two steps and a turn.
I'll swing you so beautifully that,
Your mother being in the fields,
Your father in a beer feast,
You'll tell me where your father's purse is hidden.
    Take care of me
    I take care of you
    Problems can be settled in jokes.
Limuru is my home
Here I have come to loaf about
Wangeci, my young lady
Be the way you are
And don't add frills
To your present gait.
    Take care of me
    I take care of you
    Problems can be settled in jokes.
This is your place
Famed for ripe bananas
I'll sing to you till you cry
Or failing to cry
You'll be so overcome with feelings
That you'll take your life.
    Take care of me
    I take care of you
    Problems can be settled in jokes.
I brewed liquor for you
And now you've turned against me!
A cripple often turns against his benefactors
Our son of Gathoni
Good fortune, unexpected, found Wacũ in the Field
And she sat down to feast on it.
    Take care of me
    I take care of you
    Problems can be settled in jokes.
Have you taken one too many
Or are you simply drunk
I'll not say anything,
Oh, Wangeci my little fruit,
Until seven years are over . . .

The voices of men and the sound of guitars, accordions and other
instruments end abruptly. The dancers leave the stage. Kĩgũũnda

and Wangeci remain frozen in the act of dancing. Kĩgũũnda
shakes his head as if he is still engrossed in memories of the past.
They disengage slowly!

KĨGŨŨNDA
Oh, the seven years were not even over
When we began
To sing new songs with new voices,
Songs and voices demanding
Freedom for Kenya, our motherland.

A procession enters the stage singing freedom songs.

Freedom
Freedom
Freedom for Kenya our motherland
A land of limitless joy
A land rich in green fields and forests
Kenya is an African people's country.

We do not mind being jailed
We do not mind being exiled
For we shall never never stop
Agitating for and demanding back our lands
For Kenya is an African people's country . . .

As the singers leave the stage Wangeci takes over the remem-
brance of things past.

WANGECI
I myself have always remembered
The Olengurueni women,
The ones driven from their lands around Nakuru
To be exiled to Yatta, the land of black rocks.
They passed through Limuru
Caged with barbed wire in the backs of several lorries.
But still they sang songs
With words that pierced one's heart like a spear.
The songs were sad, true,
But the women were completely fearless
For they had faith and were sure that,
One day, this soil will be returned to us.

A procession of women singers enter the stage singing.

Pray in Truth
Beseech Him with Truth
For he is the same Ngai[7] within us.
One woman died
After being tortured
Because she refused to sell out.
Pray in Truth

7. God.

Beseech Him with Truth
For he is the same Ngai within us.
Great love I found there
Among women and children
A bean fell to the ground
And it was shared among them.
    Pray in Truth
    Beseech Him with Truth
    For he is the same Ngai within us.

    The singers leave the stage.

KĪGŪŪNDA
It was then
That the state of Emergency was declared over Kenya.
Our patriots,
Men and women of
Limuru and the whole country,
Were arrested!
The Emergency laws became very oppressive.
Our homes were burnt down.
We were jailed,
We were taken to detention camps,
Some of us were crippled through beatings.
Others were castrated.
Our women were raped with bottles.
Our wives and daughters raped before our eyes!
    (*Moved by the bitter memories, Kīgūūnda pauses for few seconds*)
But through Mau Mau
Led by Kīmaathi and Matheenge,[8]
And through the organized unity of the masses
We beat the whites
And freedom came . . .
We raised high our national flag.

    A jubilant procession of men, women and children enters the
    stage singing songs and dances in praise of freedom.

It is a flag of three colours
Raise the flag high
Green is for our earth
Raise the flag high
Red is for our blood
Raise the flag high
Black is for Africa
Raise the flag high.

    They change to a new song and dance.

SOLOIST
Greet our patriots for me . . .

---

8. Stanley Matheenge, lieutenant of Dedan Kīmaathi in the Mau Mau anticolonial guerrilla war.

Where did the whites come from?

CHORUS
Where did the whites come from?
Where did the whites come from?
They came through Mūrang'a,
And they spent a night at Waiyaki's home,
If you want to know that these foreigners were no good,
Ask yourself:
Where is Waiyaki's grave today?
We must protect our patriots .
So they don't meet Waiyaki's fate.

SOLOIST
Kĩmaathi's patriots are brave
Where did the whites come from?

They continue singing as they walk off the stage.

KĨGŨŨNDA
How the times run!
How many years have gone
Since we got independence?
Ten and over,
Quite a good number of years!
And now look at me!
    (*Kĩgũũnda looks at himself, points to the title-deed and goes near it*)
One and a half acres of land in dry plains.
Our family land was given to homeguards.
Today I am just a labourer
On farms owned by Ahab Kĩoi wa Kanoru.
My trousers are pure tatters.
Look at you.
See what the years of freedom in poverty
Have done to you!
Poverty has hauled down your former splendour.
Poverty has dug trenches on your face,
Your heels are now so many cracks,
Your breasts have fallen,
They have nowhere to hold.
Now you look like an old basket
That has lost all shape.

WANGECI
Away with you,
Haven't you heard it said that
A flower is robbed of the colours by the fruit it bears!
    (*Changing the tone of voice*)
Stop this habit of thinking too much about the past
Often losing your sleep over things that had better be forgotten.
Think about today and tomorrow.
Think about our home.
Poverty has no permanent roots!

Poverty is a sword for sharpening the digging sticks . . .
  (*Pauses, as if caught by a new thought*)
Tell me:
What does Kĩoi and his family
Want with us today?

KĨGŨŨNDA

Well, they want to see how their slave lives!
To see his bed for instance!

WANGECI

Of all the years you have worked there,
Is it only now that they have realized you have a home?

KĨGŨŨNDA (*lightheartedly*)

They want . . . to come . . . to tell you . . . that . . .
You must tell . . . your daughter . . . to stop . . .
Going places with their son!

WANGECI

Yes, for I myself did not feel birth pangs for Gathoni?
Should they dare to say such a thing,
I'll make them tell me whether it's Gathoni
Who goes to hoot a car outside their home day and night.

KĨGŨŨNDA (*suddenly remembering something*)

Wait a minute!

WANGECI

What is it?

> Kĩgũũnda puts his hands in his pockets, obviously searching for
> something. He takes out a letter. He reads it silently. Then he
> goes to where the title-deed is and pulls it off.

WANGECI (*repeating the question*)   What is it?

KĨGŨŨNDA

You know the rich fellow
They call Ikuua wa Nditika?

WANGECI

The great friend of Kĩoi?

KĨGŨŨNDA

Yes. That's the one.
It's really true that a rich man
Can even dig up forbidden sacred shrines!
He wrote me this letter
And told me that there is a company
Belonging to some foreigners from America, Germany
And from that other country, yes, Japan,
Which wants to build a factory
For manufacturing insecticide
For killing bedbugs!
They want to buy my one and half acres
For they say the plot is well situated in a dry flat plain
And yet very near a railway line!
Ikuua wa Nditika and Kĩoi wa Kanoru
Are the local directors of the company.

It's therefore possible that Kīoi is coming
To talk over the matter with me.

WANGECI
Stop. Stop it there.
Aren't they the real bedbugs,
Local watchmen for foreign robbers?
When they see a poor man's property their mouths water,
When they get their own, their mouths dry up!
Don't they have any lands
They can share with these foreigners
Whom they have invited back into the country
To desecrate the land?

> A knock at the door. Kīgũũnda quickly hangs back the title-deed
> and puts the letter back into his pocket. Wangeci runs about
> putting things straight here and there for she thinks that Kioi and
> his family have arrived. She exclaims: 'They have come and the
> food is not yet ready!' Another knock. Gīcaamba and Njooki en-
> ter. They are a worker and his peasant wife and they look mature
> in mind and body. Gīcaamba is dressed in overalls. Kīgũũnda
> and Wangeci are obviously disappointed.

KĪGŨŨNDA }
WANGECI } So it's you?

GĪCAAMBA }
NJOOKI   } Yes . . . How are you?

WANGECI }
KĪGŨŨNDA } We are well.

NJOOKI
Give us what you have cooked.

WANGECI
The food is still cooking.

KĪGŨŨNDA
Karibu,[9] karibu.

WANGECI
Aren't you sitting down?

> Gīcaamba takes a chair. Kīgũũnda also takes a chair near
> Gīcaamba. They sit in such a way that the men are able to talk
> to one another, and the two women the same.

NJOOKI (to Wangeci)
Gathoni told us that you had visitors.
And so I asked myself,
Who are these secret guests?
Could they be whites from abroad?
And you know very well a white has no favourite?

WANGECI
Gathoni is too quick with her tongue.
It's Kīoi and his family

9. Welcome.

Who said they would like to pass by
On their way from the church.

NJOOKI

Just passing by? I wonder.
Since when have rich men been known to visit their servants?

WANGECI

We don't know what they really want.
In fact you found us asking ourselves the same question.
They sent a word the day before yesterday.
Even their son, John Mūhūūni,
Has just come for Gathoni this very minute.
He is a real particle of Godhead.
But he hardly ever talks with people.
He, for instance, never enters the house.
He just hoots and whistles from the road.

NJOOKI

Let me caution you for even a wise man can be taught wisdom.
Ask Gathoni to cut off that relationship.
Rich families marry from rich families,
The poor from the poor!
Can't you see that the children of the big men,
And of these others who brag that they are mature men
All go to big houses!
Or have you become Jesus-is-my-saviour converts
And I have never heard you shouting 'Praise the Lord!'
And giving testimony . . .

KĪGŪŪNDA

. . . but you are slightly better off,
For you are paid every fortnight.

GĪCAAMBA

Even though we are paid fortnightly
Wages can never equal the work done.
Wages can never really compensate for your labour.
Gīkūyū[1] said:
If you want to rob a monkey of a baby it is holding
You must first throw it a handful of peanuts.
We the workers are like that monkey
When they want to steal our labour
They bribe us with a handful of peanuts.
We are the people who cultivate and plant
But we are not the people who harvest!
The owners of these companies are real scorpions.
They know three things only:
To oppress workers,
To take away their rights,
And to suck their blood.

> *The two women stop their own chatter to listen to Gīcaamba.*
> *Gicaamba speaks with a conviction that shows that he has*

---

1. Name of the founder of the Gīkūyū nationality, but in this context refers to the whole community.

thought deeply about these matters. He uses a lot of movement, gestures, mimicry, miming, imitation, impersonation, any and every dramatic device to convey his message.

GĪCAAMBA

Look at me.
It's Sunday.
I'm on my way to the factory.
This company has become my God.
That's how we live.
You wake up before dawn.
You rub your face with a bit of water
Just to remove dirt from the eyes!
Before you have drunk a cup of milkless tea,
The Sirena cries out.
You dash out.
Another siren.
You jump to the machine.
You sweat and sweat and sweat.
Another siren.
It's lunch break.
You find a corner with your plain grains of maize.
But before you have had two mouthfuls,
Another siren,
The lunch break is over.
Go back to the machine.
You sweat and sweat and sweat.
Siren.
It's six o'clock, time to go home.
Day in, day out,
Week after week!
A fortnight is over.
During that period
You have made shoes worth millions.
You are given a mere two hundred shillings,
The rest is sent to Europe.
Another fortnight.
You are on night shift.
You leave your wife's sweat.
Now you are back at the machine.
You sweat and sweat and sweat,
You sweat the whole night.
In the morning you go home.
You are drunk with sleep.
Your wife has already gone to the fields.
You look for the food.
Before you have swallowed two mouthfuls,
You are dead asleep.
You snore and snore.
Evening is here!
You meet your wife returning from the fields.

Bye, bye,
You tell her as you run to the machine.
Sweat.
Another fortnight.
Here, take this
Two hundred shillings.
The rest to Europe.
By that time you have sold away
Your body,
Your blood,
Your wife,
Even your children!
Why, because you hardly ever see them!
There are some who sell away their blood,
And they end up dying in there.
But many more end up as cripples.
Remember the son of . . . eeeh . . . you know who I mean . . .
The chemical dust
Accumulated in his body
Until the head cracked!
Did they take him to hospital?
Oh, no.
Was he given any compensation?
He was summarily dismissed, instead.
What about the son of . . . eeh . . .
You know the K.C.A.[2] elder? The one
Who, with others, started the freedom struggle? . . .
His son used to work in the cementing section
Where they keep retex and other dangerous chemicals.
The chemicals and the dust accumulated in his body,
He was forced to go to the Aga Khan Hospital for an operation.
What did they find inside him? A stone.
But was it a stone or a mountain!
It was a mountain made of those chemicals!
He was summarily retired with twenty-five cents as compensation.
What has life now got to offer him?
Is he not already in his grave though still breathing?
Since I was employed in that factory,
Twenty-one people in that section have died.
Yes, twenty-one people!

KĨGŨŨNDA

Oooh, this is a very serious matter!
If I were to be told to work in that retex section
I, son of Gathoni,
Would then and there part ways with that company.

GĨCAAMBA

I wouldn't mind, son of Gathoni,
If after selling away our labour,
Our village had benefited.

---

2. Kikuyu Central Association, a militant political movement.

But look now at this village!
When was this company established?
Before the Second World War.
What did it bring into the country?
A few machines,
And money for erecting buildings to house the machines.
Where did they get the land on which to build?
Here!
Where did they get the charcoal for use by the machine?
Here!
Was it not this factory together with the railways
Which swallowed up all the forests around?
Is that not why today we cannot get firewood
And we can't get rain?
Where do they get the animal skins?
Here!
Where do they get the workers to work those machines?
Here!
Where do they get the buyers for those shoes?
Here!
The little amount of money they give us,
We give back to them;
The profit on our work,
On our blood,
They take to Europe,
To develop their own countries.
The money they have already sent to Europe
Paid for those machines and buildings a long time ago.
Son of Gathoni, what did I tell you?
A handful of peanuts is thrown to a monkey
When the baby it is holding is about to be stolen!
If all the wealth we create with our hands
Remained in the country,
What would we not have in our village?
Good public schools,
Good houses for the workers,
Good houses for the peasants,
And several other industries
In which the unemployed could be absorbed.
Do you, son of Gathoni, call this a house?
Would you mind living in a more spacious house?
And remember the majority are those
Who are like me and you!
We are without clothes.
We are without shelter.
The power of our hands goes to feed three people:
Imperialists from Europe,
Imperialists from America,
Imperialists from Japan,
And of course their local watchmen.
But son of Gathoni think hard

So that you may see the truth of the saying
That a fool's walking stick supports the clever:
Without workers,
There is no property, there is no wealth.
The labour of our hands is the real wealth of the country.
The blood of the worker
Led by his skill and experience and knowledge
Is the true creator of the wealth of nations.
What does that power, that blood, that skill
Get fortnight after fortnight?
Something for the belly!
Wa Gathoni, just for the belly!
But it's not even enough for the belly!
It's just to bribe the belly into temporary silence!
What about the three whom I mentioned?
Today all the good schools belong
To the children of the rich.
All the big jobs are reserved
For the children of the rich.
Big shops,
Big farms,
Coffee plantations,
Tea plantations,
Wheat fields and ranches,
All belong to the rich.
All the good tarmac roads lead to the homes of the rich.
Good hospitals belong to them,
So that when they get heart attacks and belly ulcers
Their wives can rush them to the hospitals
In Mercedes Benzes.
The rich! The rich!
And we the poor
Have only dispensaries at Tigoni or Kĩambu.
Sometimes, these dispensaries have no drugs,
Sometimes people die on the way,
Or in the queues that last from dawn to dusk . . .

WANGECI
   Oh, well, independence did come!

NJOOKI (*sings Gĩtiiro*[3])
   Let me tell you
   For nobody is born wise
   So although it has been said that
   The antelope hates less he who sees it
   Than he who shouts its presence,
   I'll sing this once,
   For even a loved one can be discussed.
   I'll sing this once:
   When we fought for freedom
   I'd thought that we the poor would milk grade cows.

3. A dance song, a form of opera.

In the past I used to eat wild spinach.
Today I am eating the same.

GĨCAAMBA (*continuing as if he does not want his thought to wander away from the subject of foreign-owned companies and industries*)
Yes,
What did this factory bring to our village?
Twenty-five cents a fortnight.
And the profits, to Europe!
What else?
An open drainage that pollutes the air in the whole country!
An open drainage that brings diseases unknown before!
We end up with the foul smell and the diseases
While the foreigners and the local bosses of the company
Live in palaces on green hills, with wide tree-lined avenues,
Where they'll never get a whiff of the smell
Or contract any of the diseases!

KĨGŨŨNDA (*sighs and shakes his head in disbelief*)
Oooh!
I have never worked in a factory.
I didn't know that conditions in industries are that bad.

GĨCAAMBA
To have factories and even big industries
Is good, very good!
It's a means of developing the country.
The question is this: Who owns the industries?
Who benefits from the industries?
Whose children gain from the industries?
Remember also that it's not only the industrial tycoons
Who are like that!
Have you ever seen any tycoon sweating?
Except because of overweight?
All the rich wherever they are . . .
Tajiri wote duniani . . .
Are the same,
One clan!
Their mission in life is exploitation!
Look at yourself.
Look at the women farm labourers,
Or those that pick tea-leaves in the plantations:
How much do they get?
Five or seven shillings a day.
What is the price of a kilo of sugar?
Five shillings!
So with their five shillings:
Are they to buy sugar,
Or vegetables,
Or what?
Or have these women got no mouths and bellies?
Take again the five shillings:
Are they for school fees,
Or what?

Or don't those women have children
Who would like to go to school?
Well, independence did indeed come!

NJOOKI

You'll have to shut those mouths of yours!
It hates less he who sights it
Than he who shouts its presence.
Was it not only the other day
That the police beat you
When you went on strike
Demanding an increase in wages?
Did you get anything
Apart from broken limbs?
Your rumour-mongering
Will cost you lives.

WANGECI

Was it not the same language
You people used to talk during the rule of the wealthy whites?
When will you ever be satisfied? You people!
Dwellers in the land of silence were saved by silence!

KĪGŪŪNDA

Discussions breed ideas.
And ideas cannot be hauled about like missiles.
Discussions breed love, Gĩkũyũ has stated.

> *Gĩcaamba lifts up Kĩgũũnda's arm. They sing. Gĩcaamba sings solo and then they both join in the chorus. They dance around the stage, the two women looking on.*

GĨCAAMBA

Here at wa Gathoni's place
I will spend night and day
Till I am sent for by post.

CHORUS

Here at wa Gathoni's place
I will spend night and day
Till I am sent for by post.

GĨCAAMBA

I'll talk about workers
And also about peasants
For in unity lies our strength.

CHORUS

I'll talk about workers
And also about peasants
For in unity lies our strength.

GĨCAAMBA

Foreigners in Kenya
Pack your bags and go
The owners of the homestead have come.

CHORUS

Foreigners in Kenya

Pack your bags and go
The owners of the homestead have come.

ALL
I'll defend my fatherland
With the sword of revolution
As we go to the war of liberation.

ALL
I'll defend my fatherland
With the sword of revolution
As we go to the war of liberation.

GĨCAAMBA
Poverty! Poverty!
Nobody can govern over poverty
For poverty is like poison in a body.
Exploitation and oppression
Have poisoned our land.

> A knock at the door: all turn their eyes to the door. Ahab Kĩoi
> wa Kanoru, Jezebel, Samuel Ndugĩre and Helen enter and stand
> near the door, so that for a time there are two opposing groups
> in the house. Ahab Kĩoi and Jezebel are dressed in a way that
> indicates wealth and wellbeing. But the Ndugĩre family is dressed
> in a manner which shows that they have only recently begun to
> acquire property. Kĩoi for instance is dressed in a very expensive
> suit with a hat and a folded umbrella for a walking stick. Jezebel
> too has a very expensive suit with expensive jewellery. But Ndu-
> gĩre and Helen have clean, tidy but simpler clothes. They all take
> out handkerchiefs with which they keep wiping their eyes and
> faces because of the smoke in the house. They also cough and
> sneeze rather ostentatiously. Kĩgũũnda and Wangeci are worried
> because there are not enough seats in the house. Gĩcaamba and
> Njooki look at the visitors with completely fearless eyes. As Kĩoi
> and his group enter moving close to one wall of the house to avoid
> contact with the Gĩcaambas, one of them causes the title-deed to
> fall to the ground. They don't pick it up. And because of their
> worry about seats and the excitement at the arrival of the Kĩois,
> Kĩgũũnda and his wife do not seem to have their minds on the
> fallen title-deed. Gĩcaamba walks to the title-deed and picks it
> up. All eyes are now on Gĩcaamba and they give way to him.
> Gĩcaamba looks at the title-deed, then at the Kĩoi group then at
> the Kĩgũũnda family. He hangs the title-deed back on the wall.
> Gĩcaamba and Njooki go out.

KĨGŨŨNDA (relieved)
Come in, come in
Why are you standing?

> As he says that, he is giving them seats. Kĩoi sits on the chair
> which Kĩgũũnda had been repairing. Ndugĩre and his wife sit
> on the bed, and Kĩoi's wife sits on an empty water tin or small
> water drum. They sit in such a way that the Kĩoi group is on

one side and the Kĩgũũnda family on the other side, at least they should be seen to be apart, or to be in two opposing camps. Wangeci now cleans her hand with a rug or with her upper garment or with her dress, and shakes hands all round. She then removes the pot from the fire and busies herself with plates and engages in other chores connected with the reception of the visitors.

KĨOI

We are not staying . . .
You were at our place this morning,
I take it?

KĨGŨŨNDA

Yes, I am the one who milked the cows
And I even helped the tractor driver to load it.
But it was very early,
You had not yet woken up.
The only other person whom I saw was the Securicor guard
As the company car came to fetch him away.

NDUGĨRE

Who is the tractor driver?

KĨOI

He is an old hand at the farm.
Even when the farm belonged to the white man
We had nicknamed him Kanoru . . .
We gave him the same name as my father . . .
The tractor driver worked there.

KĨGŨŨNDA

Kanoru's?
I too used to work there
Before I was sent to detention at Manyani.

JEZEBEL (*to Ndugĩre but loud enough for everybody to hear*)

That tractor driver is very mature.
He does not argue back.
He does not demand higher wages.
He just believes in hard work,
Praising our Lord all the time.
He is a true brother-in-Christ.

NDUGĨRE

You have spoken nothing but the truth.
If all people were to be saved,
And accepted Jesus as their personal saviour,
The conflicts you find in the land would all end.
For everybody,
Whether he does or does not have property,
Whether an employee or an employer,
Would be contented
To remain in his place.

Wangeci scoops out rice on plates and hands a plateful to everyone.

JEZEBEL (*looks at the food as if she is finding fault with the cooking*)
    You know, with me, when lunch time is over,
    However hungry I might have been,
    I am not able to swallow anything!
KĨOI
    I am also the same,
    But I could do with a cup of tea.
WANGECI
    I'll make tea for you.
    But you can't come into my house
    And fail to bite something.

> Kĩgũũnda starts to eat heartily. Wangeci is busy putting water for
> tea on the firestones.

KĨOI
    Let's say grace.
    Sister-in-Christ!
    Say grace before we eat.
HELEN (*eyeing the Kĩgũũndas with ferocious disapproval*)
    Let's all pray . . .
    God, Creator of Heaven and Earth,
    You the owner of all things on earth and in heaven,
    We pray you bring to an end
    The current wickedness in the land:
    Breaking into banks and other people's shops,
    Stealing other people's coffee,
    Placing obstructions on highways,
    All this being Satan's work to bring ruin to your true servants.
    Oh, God our Father
    Tame the souls of the wicked
    With thy sword of peace,
    For we your servants are unable to sleep
    Because of the terror inflicted on us by the wicked.
    You to whom all the things on earth do belong
    Show the wicked that everybody's share comes from Heaven,
    Be it poverty or riches.
    Let us all be contented with our lot.
    We ask you to bless this food,
    And add unto us that of the Holy Spirit;
    We ask you in the name of your only Son,
    Jesus Christ, our Lord.
ALL
    Amen.

> After the grace, Kĩoi and Jezebel take a spoonful each and then
> they are satisfied. But Ndugĩre and Helen eat without any inhi-
> bitions.

KĨOI
    You might perhaps be wondering
    Why we have come here today.

Do you know him?
He is our brother-in-Christ.

NDUGĪRE (*standing up to give testimony*)
My name is Samuel Ndugīre
I am a man who has received the tender mercy of the Lord,
Since the year 1963.
Before then I used to be a very bad homeguard.
I used to kill people,
And to do many other terrible deeds
As was the habit among the homeguards of those days.
In our village they had baptized me Kīmeendeeri
Because of the way I used to crush people's heads.
But the Lord called unto me in 1963,
It was the midnight of December twelve,
And he told me:
Ndugīre . . . the only good freedom is that of the soul.
Leave your fishing net behind
Follow me now,
And I shall make you a fisher of men.

> *The Kīoi group sings*

I shall make you fishers of men
Fishers of men, fishers of men,
I shall make you fishers of men,
If you follow me
> *If you follow me*
> *If you follow me*
I shall make you fishers of men
If you follow me.

Since then my affairs started improving.
I and my sister-in-Christ
Were given a few shops by God.
It's from those shops,
That we now and then get a shilling or two
For clothes for our children,
For school fees,
And for petrol.
And quite recently,
God showed us a tiny garden in the settled area.
It is a tiny garden of about a hundred acres.
But it has a good crop of tea.
The same Lord then took us by the hand,
To inside a bank
Where he enabled us to get a loan with which to buy it.
Now you see I did not take out
Even a cent from my pocket.
And yet I am milking cows,
And I am harvesting tea.
That's why I always praise the Lord
Without any fear.

*Kĩoi, Jezebel, Helen and Ndugĩre sing while Kĩgũũnda and Wan-
geci sit completely amazed.*

We praise you
Jesus lamb of God
Jesus your blood cleanses me
I praise you Lord.

> *As they come to the end of the verse they are seized by the spirit.
> Ndugĩre starts another hymn. He claps and the other three join
> in, dancing about with joy.*

I step gently on the road
On my way to heaven.
I am sure that I'll get there
To rest for ever with the other saints.

Thank you Lord my guide
With Jesus Christ as my bread of life
And the Holy Spirit as my water of life
I'll never go hungry or thirsty.

Wild animals and diseases
And even poverty can't get at me
For they are frightened by the bright flames around me
For I am completely dressed up in the splendour of God.

KĨGŨŨNDA (*shouting at them*)
    What do you want?

> *Jezebel is startled by the sudden unexpected shout and she falls
> down. Ndugĩre and Helen rush to where she has fallen on the
> floor. They fuss around her, lift her to her feet and dust off her
> clothes, all the time casting murderous glances at Kĩgũũnda.
> Wangeci is worried and she tries to make the tea. She looks about
> for the tea-leaves. Then she shouts:*

WANGECI
    Oh, dear, we have no tea-leaves.
    They were finished last night
    And I forgot to buy more.
        (*Showing them the sugar*)
    I only remembered to buy sugar.
KĨOI
    It does not matter . . .
    Even without having given witness,
    I would like to say this:
    The other day the Lord our Master
    Came to me and to my sister-in-Christ
    And he told us:
    How can you light a lamp,
    And then cover it with a tin?
    After praying hard and humbling ourselves before him,
    The Lord our Master told us
    That we should show people the way

To enter the church of God
So that we can all praise the Lord together!
KĨGŨŨNDA (*slowly, without shouting*)
  What do you want?
KĨOI
  We want you to enter the Church!
JEZEBEL
  You and your wi-wi-wi-
  And Wangeci.
HELEN
  Come out of the muddy trough of sins!
NDUGĨRE
  Praise the Lord.
KĨOI
  To enter the Church is easy.
  But you must first stop living in sin.
JEZEBEL
  You must be baptized.
NDUGĨRE
  You do a church wedding.
HELEN (*showing her wedding ring*)
  Give Wangeci a wedding ring.
KĨGŨŨNDA
  Sin, did you say?
JEZEBEL
  Yes, you and Wangeci have been living in sin.
WANGECI
  But God has blessed us and given us children.
HELEN
  Children of sin.
KĨGŨŨNDA
  Sins . . . Sins!
KĨOI
  We have brought you the tidings
  So that when our Lord comes back
  To separate goats from cows
  You'll not claim
  That you had not been warned.
  Repent. Come out of the darkness.
KĨOI
JEZEBEL
HELEN   } (*singing*)
NDUGĨRE

When Jesus comes back
To take home his amazing ones,
The amazing ones being the people
Saved by the Lord.
They will shine bright as the star
The great northern star
And the beauty of his amazing ones

Will shine like the stars
And you children, and you children . . .

> *Kīgūūnda shouts at them, moving threateningly towards them,*
> *mimicking them at the same time. In fright, Jezebel drops her*
> *bag on the floor. She does not pick it up as she and Helen flee*
> *to near the door. Near the door, Jezebel remembers her handbag*
> *on the floor and she tries to gesture to Helen to go back for the*
> *handbag. But Helen refuses. Jezebel moves stealthily towards the*
> *bag, picks it up and runs back to where Helen is standing. All*
> *this time Kīgūūnda is giving Kīoi and Ndugīre a piece of his*
> *mind. As he moves towards them, they move backwards (eyes to*
> *the door) at the same time gesturing to Kīgūūnda to be cool and*
> *patient.*

KĪGŪŪNDA
And you the children!
The amazing ones!
Sins! sins!
Wapi!
This is mine own wife,
Gathoni's mother,
I have properly married her
Having paid all the bridewealth
According to our national ways.
And you dare call her a whore!
That we should now be blessed by a human like me!
Has he shaken hands with God?
Let me tell you one thing Mr Kīoi.
Every home has its own head
And no outsider should interfere in other people's homes!
Go away, you devils!

> *As he says the last words, he rushes for the sword. Seeing him*
> *take the sword, the Kīois and the Ndugīres flee followed by Kī-*
> *gūūnda holding the sword. Kīgūūnda comes back, laughing and*
> *swinging the sword in a kind of victory dance, mimicking them.*

KĪGŪŪNDA
Jesus should hurry up
And come back for his amazing ones . . .
WANGECI (*upset*)
See what you have now done,
Chasing away our guests.
You did not let them say what had really brought them here.
Tomorrow you'll be without a job!

> *Before Kīgūūnda answers, a car hoots. After a second* GATHONI
> *comes, running. She is dressed in new clothes, new platform shoes*
> *and has a new handbag. She has also got new earrings. She now*
> *stands as if she is in a fashion parade.*

WANGECI
Gathoni, from where did you get these clothes?

*Gathoni removes her handbag from one shoulder to the other,
then she walks across the stage haughtily, and she cannot take
her eyes from her new self. She walks about as if she is still in a
beauty contest or fashion parade.*

GATHONI
Oh, this dress?
John Mūhūūni bought it for me.

WANGECI
What about these shoes?

GATHONI
Platform shoes! He bought them too.

KĪGŪŪNDA
Mūhūūni, son of Kĩoi?
Son of Ahab Kĩoi wa Kanoru?

GATHONI
Yes!

*Another hooting. Gathoni takes out a lipstick and begins to paint
her lips red.*

KĪGŪŪNDA
Listen.
When did Kĩoi's son marry you?
I want you to take back this dress to him!
And all these other fineries of a whore.

WANGECI
Even these shoes worn by rebels!

GATHONI
And I go back to my rags?

KĪGŪŪNDA
A man brags about his penis however small.
A poor house, but mine!
Don't overstep the boundaries, else you get lost.

GATHONI (*for a second stopping applying lipstick*)
Who is the girl who does not like being well dressed?
Who does not like to feel that she is human at times?
So that when now and then she steps on the road
People's eyes turn to her,
And gasp, there goes Miss Gathoni.
It's poverty and not riches
That forces a woman to go without perfume.

WANGECI
Do you see how you answer your father?
Don't you know a maiden once drowned in a sea of sweetness!
And where are you going?

GATHONI
John Mūhūūni wants me to accompany him to the coast.
Mombasa, for a week.

WANGECI
    Mombasa! Swahililand?
    Do you think to be smiled at is to be loved?
    You'll now get lost.
KĨGŨŨNDA
    If you go to Mombasa,
    Then find another home!

> *Now the hooting continues. Gathoni puts things back in her handbag. For a time it looks as if she is torn between her loyalty to her parents and her loyalty to John Mũhũũni. When she hears another hooting sound, she walks to the door, turns once to her parents and says 'Goodbye'. She goes out. Kĩgũũnda sits down on a chair and supports his head in his cupped hands, dejected. Wangeci slowly walks to the door and peers outside. Then she comes back and she too slumps into a seat. There is silence between them, there is complete silence in the house. After some time, Wangeci begins to nod her head as if a new idea has occurred to her. She stands up and walks slowly to her husband's side, and puts a hand on his shoulder.*

WANGECI
    Don't be so dejected.
    A parent is never nauseated
    By the mucus from his child's nose.
    A she-goat suckles its young
    However deformed.
    I have just thought of something,
        (*smiling*)
    Couldn't that be the reason?
KĨGŨŨNDA
    The reason what?
WANGECI
    Why the Kĩois want you and me
    To first have a church wedding?
KĨGŨŨNDA
    Why?
WANGECI
    You have eyes and can't see?
    Or has the language of the eyes
    Become as hard as the language of the ear?
        (*Wangeci walks to the title-deed and takes it off the wall*)
    You yourself had earlier thought
    That they were visiting us
    To talk to you about this, your one acre,
    Because of the insecticide factory
    They and their foreign friends want to build.
    Didn't you even show me the letter from Ikuua wa Nditika?
    Kĩoi did not say a thing about it.
    And if they had come here
    On account of your piece of land,

Kīoi would have brought Ikuua along.
Our title-deed is now out of danger!
   (*Wangeci returns the title-deed to its original place on the wall*)
So what else would make them want
To see us two in a church wedding?
Think!

KĪGŪŪNDA
So what?

WANGECI
Gathoni! Gathoni and John Mūhūūni!
Didn't you also think that they were coming
To tell us that
Our daughter should not keep the company of their son?
Did they mention anything of the sort?
Did they say they don't want Gathoni and John Mūhūūni
   together?

   *Kīgūūnda raises his head. He and Wangeci look at each other.
   Then Kīgūūnda nods his head several times as if he too has suddenly seen the light.*

END OF ACT ONE

Act Two

SCENE ONE

*Inside Kīgūūnda's house. Another day. Kīgūūnda, Wangeci, Gī-
caamba and Njooki are all seated as if in an intense discussion.
They are eating porridge. Wangeci and Njooki are also shelling
maize grains from maize cobs. They are all wearing working
clothes. It's evening. The sun is setting. In the course of this scene,
it progressively gets dark and Wangeci has to light a hurricane
lamp.*

GĪCAAMBA
   . . . Leave these people alone.
They are just playing about with you,
In the same way a cat plays about with a mouse,
Knowing that the mouse will end up in the cat's belly!

KĪGŪŪNDA
We are looking at it this way!
It's obvious that Kīoi does not want his son
To marry from mere pagans!

GĪCAAMBA (*doubtingly*)
Ahab Kīoi wa Kanoru.
Is that what he told you?

KĪGŪŪNDA
Eh . . . Eh . . . What?

GĪCAAMBA
That he wants his son
To marry Gathoni, your daughter?

WANGECI
  Not in so many words
  They only hinted at it . . .
GĨCAAMBA
  Promises do not mean delivery.
  Clouds may be in the sky
  But it does not mean it'll rain!
NJOOKI
  You people! You people!
  A tooth smiles at a spear.
  The rich never marry from the poor.
  The rich only want to find ways
  Of continuing to drink people's blood.
GĨCAAMBA
  And how does religion come into it?
  Religion is not the same thing as God.
  All the religions that now sit on us
  Were brought here by the whites.
  Even today the Catholic religion
  Is still called the Roman Catholic Church.
  P.C.E.A. belongs to Scottish protestants.
  The Anglican church belongs to the English.
  The Orthodox belongs to the Greeks.
  The Baptist belongs to the Americans.
  There are many more religions
  Which have been brought here by imperialists from America,
  And which tell us we should give them a tenth of all that we
      produce.
  Where does the ten per cent go?
  To America.
  Then they send back to us ten shillings
  Taken from the tenth portion we sent them,
  And they tell us:
  This is American aid to your local churches.
  And we give them a standing ovation.
  When the British imperialists came here in 1895,
  All the missionaries of all the churches
  Held the Bible in the left hand,
  And the gun in the right hand.
  The white man wanted us
  To be drunk with religion
  While he,
  In the meantime,
  Was mapping and grabbing our land,
  And starting factories and businesses
  On our sweat.
  He drove us from our best lands,
  Forcing us to eke a living from plots on road sides
  Like beggars in our own land,
  Some of us dying in his tea and coffee plantations

Others dying in his factories.
Had we not woken up
And sworn a readiness to die
Fighting against the British imperialists,
Where would Kenya be today?
The white man had arranged it all
To completely soften our hearts
To completely cripple our minds with religion!
And they had the audacity to tell us
That earthly things were useless!
　(*Singing*)
Goats and cows and money
Are not important.
What is important
Is the splendid face of Jesus.

I glance here
I glance there
And I see a huge bonfire
In Devil's Hell
And I ask myself:
What can I do
To avoid the Hell's fire?

But they, on this earth, this very earth,
They are busy carousing on earthly things, our wealth,
And you the poor are told:
Hold fast unto the rosary,
Enter the church,
Lift up your eyes unto the heavens.

NJOOKI　　　 ⎫
GĨCAAMBA ⎭ (*singing*)

Believe in God
And He'll take care of all your problems,
He will show you all the good things
And remove all the evils from you
Through Jesus you'll get your share in heaven.
　Believe in God
　Believe in God
　Believe in God
　And trust in Him.

GĨCAAMBA
Can't you remember
The days of our freedom struggle?
Was it not the religious leaders
Who used to be sent to us in detention camps
At Manyani
Mageta
Hola
Mackinon Road
Wamũũmũ

To tell us:
Surrender, surrender, confess the oath,
That's what Jesus tells you today!
    (Sadly)
I remember one man,
Whom we had nicknamed Patriot Son of Njeeri,
Because of his patriotic courage.
He was a brave fighter,
So feared by the enemy
That the enemy soldiers would not go near any place
Rumoured to be wa Njeeri's area of operations.
When he was finally caught,
His gun having jammed,
Wa Njeeri was sentenced to hang.
I remember one priest,
Even today he is still around preaching,
Who used to trail wa Njeeri in the cell:
Repent, repent.
Confess the oath,
Reveal where the others are hiding.
All this as if we were not fighting
For the liberation of our country,
The liberation of our lands and our wealth!
Patriot Son of Njeeri
Just shot saliva into the fellow's priestly mouth
And told him that
He, a patriot, would never betray the other patriots to foreigners
Because of his belly!
He told him with great courage:
I Patriot Son of Njeeri
Will never sell the masses
Or sell my country for money!
I would rather die.

      Njooki starts a song and they all join in:

I'll never betray this land,
I'll never allow the greed for money to guide me
Like Warũhiũ and Luka wa Kahangara.

GĨCAAMBA
    The same colonial church
    Survives even today.
    Did the leopard ever change its spots?
    A kid steals like its mother.
    The chameleon family
    Has never changed its backridge.
    Wa Gathoni, the war was hard fought!
WANGECI
    The church has changed a lot.
    They now beat drums and play guitars in church!
    They sometimes use traditional tunes
    To fit in religious words!

NJOOKI
  Yes!
  But the song is the same song . . .
  The word the same word . . .
  The aim the same!
  And the intentions are still the same!
  You!
  You don't need to have words rammed down your throat!
  You!
  The earthly water is bitter!
GĨCAAMBA (*singing*)
  And even today the earthly water is still bitter
  From homesteads to workplaces,
  From the children to grown-ups
  The earthly water is bitter, what shall we drink?
ALL (*joining in*)
  If you go to any office to seek help,
  You find the occupant is glum,
  If you try to enter inside,
  He growls at you, 'I'm busy'
  All because the earthly water is bitter.
NJOOKI (*continues singing alone to prove that the aim of all these relig-
  ious hymns is to point the way to heaven*)
  Even now, the earthly water is bitter
  From homesteads to workplaces,
  Drink Jesus and he'll quench your thirst
  For the earthly water is bitter.
    (*Stops singing but changes to preaching*)
  Rest not your souls on this earth.
    (*Goes to the wall, takes the title-deed and raises it high*)
  Lay not your treasures on this earth.
ALL (*singing*)
  This world is not my home
  I am just a passer-by.
  All my joys await me in heaven
  Where all the saved have gone.
  I'll never worry over earthly homes.
GĨCAAMBA
  What about their homes of twenty storeys and more?
  Have they burnt them down?
  It's simply that they don't want us
  To think too much about our shanties,
  And ask ourselves, why!
NJOOKI (*to Kĩgũũnda, as if preaching to him but still holding high the
  title-deed*)
  Blessed are they that go thirsty and hungry
  And endure tribulations in their hearts
  For they shall inherit the Kingdom of God!
GĨCAAMBA (*now really worked up*)
  The Kĩois of this earth
  Where do they rest their souls?

Njooki points at the title-deed as if she is answering Gĩcaamba's question. She then hangs back the title-deed on the wall, walking as if she has a rich man's big belly. She then walks back to her seat still imitating the walk of a rich man with a big protruding belly.

GĨCAAMBA

Why didn't Kĩoi come
To tell you that he has increased your wages?
Or to give you a piece of his own lands?
Yes, for the earthly treasures are not that important!
Or is it a sin to increase a worker's wages?
Religion . . . religion . . . !
Religion is the alcohol of the soul!
Religion is the poison of the mind!
It's not God who has brought about our poverty!
All of us were born equally naked.
Wa Gathoni,
It's not that we don't work hard:
I drive a machine all the day,
You pick tea-leaves all the day,
Our wives cultivate the fields all the day,
And someone says you don't work hard?
The fact is
That the wealth of our land
Has been grabbed by a tiny group
Of the Kĩois and the Ndugĩres
In partnership with foreigners!
Accompany them to church, if you like!
No one regrets the going as the returning.
Take care you don't lose four
While running after eight.

KĨGŨŨNDA

Listen.
I am not much after the church.
I don't even go to these haraambes
For stone church buildings
Daily being erected
As if in competition.
But,
And there you have not answered me,
Shall I punish my own daughter and ruin her future
By refusing to have our marriage blessed?

GĨCAAMBA

There is no marriage which is not blessed.
How else would God have given you Gathoni?
Didn't you pay the bridewealth,
Seeking our people's communal blessings?
Isn't the Ngurario ceremony the true blessings
Of all your family and the nation?
The voice of the people is the voice of God.

NJOOKI
  Marriage is between a man and a woman.
  Marriage is a covenant between two people,
  Their flesh and soul becoming one
  Without money coming into it,
  Love pulled by love:
  Love the price of love.
  Today it's not one human that marries another
  But property marrying property,
  Money marrying money,
  This House marrying that House,
  Hearts being taken to the market
  And the customers asked:
  How many kilos of love do you want?
  That's why you find that
  Even if modern couples go to church
  Or to the District Commissioner,
  With the rings and flowers,
  They don't spend more than two nights together!
  Darling, I'm sorry, but it was not you I loved.
  Sugarmummies and sugardaddies
  Are now all over the land:
  Boys with their mothers,
  Girls with their fathers!
  What happens to the herd
  When the leader has broken legs?

GĨCAAMBA
  They go to church as a fashion.
  Some go back to the church only on the day
  They are being buried.

WANGECI
  You!
  They can't say prayers over your body
  Unless you have been baptized
  And you have been a churchgoer.

GĨCAAMBA
  Yes, if you are poor.
  But if you are a man of property
  Or if you have been a leader of this or that
  They will pray for you
  And sing aloud
  How hardworking you used to be.
  Haven't you heard it said that
  A rich man's fart does not stink?
  How many bishops came to the funeral
  Of the rich old man who died recently,
  And you know very well that
  He never even knew the door to any church?
  Do you want to say that
  If Ikuua wa Nditika died today
  His body would not be taken to the altar

By his friends the Kīois?
Don't tell me this and that.
A blessed marriage is when
A human quality is attracted by another human quality.
A blessed marriage is when
Two people accept to be two patriots
Defending their home and nation.

WANGECI
What's wrong in having a marriage blessed?

NJOOKI
Were you not told just now?
There's no marriage which is not blessed
Except the one founded on measured love
Or on bank savings!
My wedding for instance was very blessed
Though I didn't take it to their churches.
The Ngurario ceremony[4] was attended by the whole land.

GĪCAAMBA
Men, women and children,
The whole community rejoiced together.

KĪGŪŪNDA
I too was there
And I saw it all!
The women's ululations
Were like trumpets of purest joy . . .

> The national Ngurario wedding ceremony of Gīcaamba and
> Njooki. Women from the side of the bridegroom enter from one
> side carrying liquor and other gifts trilling the five ululations for
> a boy. Women from the bride's side enter from the other side
> answering back with the four ululations for a girl. They meet in
> the middle and form a circle and the two sides exchange com-
> pliments and gifts through the Gītiiro opera dance and song.

AAGACIKŪ (the bride's clan)
Let me give away the hand of Njooki,
I swore I would never exchange her
For anybody's property.
But I'll exchange her for a gourd of honey.
Give me now the honey
For which I once took an oath.
I'll now keep the honey beside the bed
So every time I wake up I taste a little.
I, woman of the Njikū clan,
Have cultivated hills and slopes
Making sure that Njooki has enough to eat.
That's why I swore I would never exchange her for property
That I would only exchange her for honey.

---

4. The final ceremony in a marriage. Once a couple go through this ritual, they are legally married.

Huuu! I said I would take her to the home of Gĩcaamba Son of
     Kĩhooto
Where rich honey is kept in skin drums.
Yes, this is Njooki whom I now take
Where honey is kept in skin drums,
Delicacy of many seasons
A feast in valleys far away.

AAMBŨI (*women from the bridegroom's clan*)
Woman with a beautiful gap in the teeth
I'm still on my way to the Njikũ clan
Looking for Njooki, my bride.
For I keep on asking myself
Where will I get the woman
Who will fill my granary with millet grains?
I'll come to you, stealthily walking against the walls,
The same walls against which
The black goats of the Mbũi clan
Warm themselves and scratch their skins.
Woman of the Njikũ clan
I have everything you may now demand of me,
Except that which was stolen from me by the whites.
I have got your honey.
But I'm also hungry though I'll not beg.
Hand me now my Njooki
Through the main entrance into my homestead
And even then, woman of the Njikũ clan,
You'll give me my yam with which
To fill the broken gap in my mouth,
For I long ago tightened a belt around my waist
And I swore I would only unite the belt
At Njooki's mother's homestead.

AAGACIKŨ
Here is the millet gruel, woman of the Mbũi clan,
You who know how to welcome guests!
Now hand me my honey
And my earrings and tobacco
For the beautiful one from the Njikũ clan.
As for you the beautiful one from the Mbũi clan,
I have got your yam,
And a crop of ripened bananas.

> *The Aagacikũ clan trill the four ululations for a girl. The Aambũi*
> *trill the five ululations for a boy.*

AAGACIKŨ
Now you have seen
We have given away the hand of Njooki
To the Mbũi clan
So famous in war and peace.
Let's now go back to cultivate our fields
While seeking ways of getting back

Lands stolen from us by the whites.
AAMBŪI
  Yes, we join our two hands
  To see if we can defeat the enemy
  Of this, our land,
  Our beautiful land of Mount Kenya.

  When they finish the Gĩtiiro opera sequence they sing and dance
  yet another sequence, expressing joy and triumph.

  Give way
  Give way
  Else you'll be trodden
  By the herds belonging to the Mbūi clan
  Herds with bells around their necks.

  As soon as they finish and exit, children rush onto the stage pull-
  ing the bride, encircling her, singing and dancing.

  Hail our herds
  Hail our bride
  She'll fetch water for us from the valley
  And should she refuse.
  We back-a-bite her

  And as soon as the children exit, men now enter the stage singing
  and dancing. They form a big circle.

In whose homestead do you raise the dust of vigour?
In whose homestead do you raise the dust of happiness?
  I holding a gun in the mountains
For I see the soot here hangs long and loose from the roof
  I holding a gun in the mountains.
Whose homestead is this?
Whose homestead is this?
  I holding a gun in the mountains
So I can roll down like the young of a rhino
  I holding a gun in the mountains.
Mother ululate for me
Mother ululate for me
  I holding a gun in the mountains
For a white woman once raised hue and cry against me
  I holding a gun in the mountains.

  Women ululate. The dancers get off the stage still singing and
  dancing. Gĩcaamba takes over.

GĨCAAMBA
  It was soon after this
  That the colonial government
  Forbade people to sing or dance,
  It forbade a gathering of more than five.
  But we went on meeting clandestinely.
  We the workers in factories and plantations said in one voice:

We reject slave wages!
Do you remember the 1948 general strike?

> *A procession of workers with placards bearing political slogans enter. They shout different slogans: 'We want higher wages; Down with prices; Up with Uhuru, Down with Imperialism; Down with traitors, Up with patriots; the factories and the country belong to us.' They then form a line sitting in twos, ready to take the oath of unity in struggle. The leader utters a particular resolution and the mass repeats after him. After each resolution, two people go through the arch of banana leaves to the other side, where two patriots, a woman and a man, are standing giving out guns. As soon as they get the guns, they stand in a line marking time ready for the war of liberation.*

LEADER
  I speak the truth and swear before God
  And before the people present
  And before the ancestors
  I swear by the oath of the masses
  And by the blood of the Kenyan people.
ALL (*repeat*)
LEADER
  I'll never let this soil go with foreigners
  Leaving the people of Kenya wretched!
  If I ever let it go,
  May this, the people's oath, destroy me
  And the blood of the masses turn against me.
ALL (*repeat*)
LEADER
  I'll never aid the missionaries in their preaching
  Or follow them
  Betraying our culture and national traditions.
  If I do so,
  May this, the people's oath, destroy me
  And the blood of the masses turn against me.
ALL (*repeat*)
LEADER
  If I am asked to hide weapons
  I shall obey without questions.
  If I am called upon to serve this organization
  By day or night,
  I'll do so!
  If I fail to do so
  May this, the people's oath, destroy me
  And the blood of the poor turn against me.
ALL (*repeat*)
LEADER
  I'll never make a girl pregnant
  And then leave her without a husband
  If I do so,

May this, the people's oath, destroy me
And the blood of the masses turn against me.
ALL (*repeat*)
LEADER
  I'll never never divorce
  If I do so,
  May this, the people's oath, destroy me
  And the blood of the masses turn against me.
ALL (*repeat*)
LEADER
  I'll always help this organization,
  With all my strength and property,
  I'll help members of this organization,
  So that if a bean falls to the ground
  We split it amongst ourselves.
ALL (*repeat*)
LEADER
  Therefore I'll never eat alone
  Forgetting fellow comrades and patriots,
  If I do so,
  May this, the people's oath, destroy me
  And the blood of the masses turn against me.
ALL (*repeat*)

> *When all are in line with weapons, the Leader makes them go*
> *through military drills, he then inspects a guard of honour (or*
> *the other way round), and then they march out singing joyfully*
> *and defiantly.*

We were happy as we went to battle
We were happy as we returned victorious
Our spirits were high
As we went and returned.

When we got to Rũirũ River
We found it in floods
Warũingĩ ordered us to make a bridge
Death in struggle is welcome.

A little further on
We came across a traitor,
Who threatened to shout our presence,
Waruingĩ said, let him shout
And a bullet will shout him down.
GĨCAAMBA
  It was soon after this that
  I too fled into the mountains
  To join the people's guerrilla army
  Here in Limuru
  We were led by Warũingĩ and other patriots.

A battle between Mau Mau guerrillas and British soldiers with their African homeguards breaks out. The Mau Mau guerrillas are victorious, killing a few enemy soldiers, capturing some of their weapons and clothes, capturing one or two enemy soldiers, and making the others run away. The Mau Mau patriots now march on the stage singing victory songs.

When our Kĩmaathi ascended the mountains
He asked for strength and courage
To defeat the imperialist enemy.

After marching, they go out, still singing.

GĨCAAMBA
We were not given freedom
We bought it with our blood,
We the peasants, workers and children.
Wa Gathoni,
Do you want to say that
That blood was not blessed?
If we had agreed with those
Who used to tell us,
Get saved, surrender,
Think of your life only and
You'll go to heaven,
Kenya would still be under colonial rule.
Blessings! Blessings!
Blessings are born of patriotic unity!
Blessings come to a people,
When they love their country
And they unite to produce wealth,
Uniting in toil
And in sharing out without greed,
And without discrimination between sexes!
Blessings come to a people
When they reach a stage where
If a bean falls to the ground
They split it among themselves.
Blessings will come to us
When we struggle and fight for our rights
And defend Kenya against internal and foreign exploitation.
WANGECI (*standing up and speaking bitterly*)
I don't much care
If Gathoni marries into the Kĩoi family or not.
All I care is for Gathoni to marry a man
Who will look after her.
Whether she marries into a rich man's home
Like that of Kĩoi's business partner,
Ikuuwa wa Nditika,
Even though he never goes to church,
Or she marries one of your sons, Gĩcaamba,

All I want is for her
To live well.

*Wangeci starts collecting things together and lighting up the lamp
in a way that shows that the Gīcaambas are no longer welcome.*

NJOOKI (*getting the hint and turning to Gīcaamba*)
You have talked too much
A priest without a collar!

GĪCAAMBA
I am a priest of peace
And patriotic unity.

NJOOKI
Why then don't you go to a seminary!
Let's go home now
For tomorrow is back to work.

GĪCAAMBA
Give us leave to go.
But think about what I've said.
For although Gīkūyū once said
That nobody ever repents another man's sins
Yet a leader who never listens
Is not a leader at all.

*Njooki and Gīcaamba leave. Kīgūūnda remains seated but deep
in thought. But Wangeci goes on with her activities still angry.*

KĪGŪŪNDA
The spear of Gīcaamba's words
Has truly pierced my heart.

WANGECI (*angrily*)
Go ahead and let your daughter suffer
All because of the words of a political agitator.
Since when did a person
Try to build his hut
Exactly like that of his neighbour?

KĪGŪŪNDA
Gīcaamba is an honest man.
He has never turned his back against the people.
He has never betrayed the Mau Mau oaths.

WANGECI
It's all alright.
You join Gīcaamba in his drunkenness.
You listen to him and get lost.
You!
The burdens of the masses
Are tied with a cord easy to cut
Or carried in a basket full of holes.
Remember when we received Uhuru!
Some people roamed the whole land
Telling us that we should not buy land
For which we had all shed blood!
Wasn't Ikuua wa Nditika one of those agitators

And he had been in detention at Mageta?
Those who had the money
And those who joined hands with homeguards
Or those that got loans
And did not listen to foolish words,
Weren't they the ones
Who bought all the best lands?
We who listened to foolish words,
Where are we now?
Just this verandah for a house.
    (*She goes to the wall and pulls off the title-deed*)
And this piece of waste land,
One and a half acres only.
And even then Ikuua wa Nditika
Is still after it!
Let me tell you.
The coward went home safely to tell the tale
And left the brave lying for ever safe on the battlefield!
Gathoni's father,
Let us go to Kīoi's place early tomorrow morning.
Let's go and tell him that we agree with his plans.
His words are good.
His ways are straight.
His style of life is proper.
His church is holy.
His church shows us the only way to life and happiness.
Gīcaamba's words arise out of envy.
Do you hear,
Or am I talking to the deaf?

KĪGŪŪNDA (*He is still deep in thought. He stands and in confusion and agitation walks about the stage. Then he goes and stands near Wangeci*)

We shall not wait for tomorrow morning.
Let's go there this very minute.
Hand me my sword
For a man does not go in the dark with empty hands.

> *Wangeci puts the title-deed on the seat. She goes to get the sword. Kīgūūnda puts on his coat. Then he takes the sword from Wangeci and hides it under the coat. Wangeci also puts on her coat. Then Kīgūūnda sees the title-deed on the seat. He picks it up. He looks at it. Then he slowly walks to the wall and hangs it back, Wangeci looking on. Kīgūūnda then turns to Wangeci:*

KĪGŪŪNDA

Let's not go there now, in the dark, for it is very late.
Let's go there tomorrow early in the evening!
Come to think of it,
We do not even have the money
For the wedding ceremony.

END OF SCENE ONE

SCENE TWO

*Kĩoi's home, in the evening. A big well-furnished house. Sofa
seats, TV, radiogram, plastic flowers on the table, and so on. Electric lights. On the walls are several photographs. On one wall can
be seen a board with the words:* 'CHRIST IS THE HEAD OF THIS
HOUSE, THE UNSEEN GUEST AT EVERY MEAL, THE SILENT LISTENER
TO EVERY CONVERSATION'. *There is also a picture of a hairy Nebuchadnezzar turned into an animal. Jezebel, Ndugĩre and Helen
are at table. The table has all sorts of dishes. There is also water
on the table in a huge glass container. A waiter stands by. Ikuuwa
wa Nditika, a man with a belly as huge as that of a woman about
to deliver, is seated away from the dining table and is busy collecting his things, bits of paper and so on into a small suitcase.
Kĩoi is standing near him waiting for Ikuua to go so he can join
the others at table. As soon as Ikuua finishes collecting his things,
he stands up and makes as if to move.*

JEZEBEL
   Are you sure you won't take a bite?
   A cup of tea even,
   And it is easy to get it ready.
IKUUA
   I prefer a beer
   Or a glass of wine,
   But I know that you are all saved, Jesus-is-my-Saviour.
      (They all laugh)
   Anyway you know very well that
   When I am not in a hurry
   I do take your meals.
   I left my Range Rover way down at the gate
   And the driver might fall asleep.
   Besides, his home is very far from my place
   And on driving me home he has to walk back all that way.
   Let me go.

      *He makes as if to move and then he turns to Kĩoi. They walk a
      step or two and talk as if in a private conference but loud enough
      for the others to hear.*

Listen Mr Kĩoi.
Don't forget that business about the insecticide factory.
Our foreign friends want to start as soon as possible.
As you know,
The main problem with such a factory
Is that it's bound to produce a lot of smelly gases
And therefore it cannot be built in an area
Where important people live.
What we need is a place like Kĩgũũnda's

Or any other place similarly situated.
The poor are many in Kenya.
(*They laugh*)
Their laziness is what is driving them
To sell their strips of land.
But if you don't want your name as one of the local directors to
    appear,
We can use your wife's name
Or that of John Mūhūūni, your son.
That's what most people are doing these days,
Because of income tax,
And also to cover up a little,
For poverty has no governor.
It's better to sometimes cover up our eating habits
Rather than show the poor our mastications!
Being a local director of foreign firms
Is not a very taxing job;
What they want is just an African's name.
All we are required to do
Is to be their watchmen.
Yes, we could be called their watchdogs!
    (*They laugh*)
Yes, watchdogs for foreign interests!

JEZEBEL
Your words Mr Ikuua are very unbecoming,
They might send you into the everlasting fire.
You have even refused to renew your marriage in church!
All you would have been required to do
Is to throw away one wife.
It does not matter if the knife falls on the eldest
And you are left with the youngest
Provided you go through a proper church ceremony!

IKUUA (*laughing*)
I am contemplating marrying a third!
Mr Kīoi think about the matter,
But anyway I am coming back soon
So we can go over the accounts again.

Goes out. Kīoi joins the others at table.

HELEN
That man has become really wealthy.

JEZEBEL
Oh, he is wealth itself!

NDUGĪRE (*trying to change the subject*)
So your son John Mūhūūni
Has not yet returned?

KĪOI
From Mombasa? No.
I had also sent him to Malindi,
To check on a plot I bought near Watamu Bay!

HELEN

What for, so far away?

KĨOI

I just want to erect a small hotel!
About three storeys or so.
That's why in fact I'm dragging my feet
Over this business of an insecticide factory.
At Mombasa and Malindi
Hotels are very profitable.
Profits from hotels are more than
You can get from factories
Or even from smuggling in coffee or gold or ivory,
All because of our visitors from abroad!
What do you call them? Watalii.
Yes, tourists from America, England, France and Germany.

HELEN

Are those the ones I normally see in buses
Passing by Kĩneenĩĩ on the way to the Rift Valley,
Sometimes stopping by the roadside
To buy fruit and sheepskins?

NDUGĨRE

Tourists?
I have heard on the radio,
That there is not a single government ministry
Which brings as much money into the country
As the Ministry of Tourism.
I have heard it said
That a man blessed by the Lord
With the ability to provide tourists with all sorts of earthly
    pleasures
Can get lots of money.
Although I believe in self-reliance,
I am also convinced that
Partnership with foreigners can bring quick wealth.

KĨOI

True,
But these workers cannot let you accumulate!
Every day: I want an increment.
Workers are like the ogres said to have two insatiable mouths.
When they are not demanding a rise in wages
They are asking you for an advance.
My mother is in hospital!
My child has been expelled from school,
Because I have not yet paid his school fees!
My wife has just delivered!

JEZEBEL

And you know
They won't hear of going to family planning clinics!

KĨOI

And when a worker decides to go
He does not even give you any notice!

NDUGĨRE

Do you know what I do with them?
I give them this month's salary
In the middle of the next month.
If you do that,
A worker will never leave you
Unless you sack him.
Of course there are one or two who complain!

JEZEBEL

This business of not being satisfied,
And of not being contented with one's station in life
As clearly ordained by God,
Comes from not being a good Christian.

HELEN

These are earthly trials.
We should pray for these people,
Knowing at the same time that
There are many sects
Now misleading the masses.

NDUGĨRE

Like the sect that calls itself
The church of the poor?
They make us all lose sleep
By their endless night drumming
Shouting: 'Crush Satan!'
Don't they know that Satan is not visible?

JEZEBEL

I don't blame them.
Many of them cannot read or write,
They don't know A or B or C.

KĨOI

And even some of these Kikuyu independent churches which are
    being revived
Are rather dangerous.
    (*Whispering*)
Don't you remember that
Mau Mau oaths used to be taken
Under the cover of those churches?

NDUGĨRE (*fearfully*)

Is Kĩgũũnda one of those people?
Is he a Mau Mau type?
I have never liked that man's eyes.
Do you recall the night he took out his sword against us?

KĨOI

No, no, Kĩgũũnda is not that type at all.
The other workers fear and respect him.
That's why I think that should he be saved
He would lead the other workers into the church.
Some of those workers who waste their energy in beer-halls
Would give up the habit altogether.

Besides, Kĩgũũnda is a hard worker
And that's why although he raised a sword against us
I did not dismiss him.

JEZEBEL
You?
Don't you remember those Mau Mau days?
Wasn't it the servant, supposed to be faithful,
Who used to spy on and betray his European employer?

Dogs bark fiercely. There is a knock at the door. They all look to the door with terrified faces. No one wants to open the door. Kĩoi turns to the waiter.

KĨOI
Go . . . and . . . and . . . open the door.

The servant/waiter is also a little scared. He gingerly walks to the door and opens it. A Securicor watchman enters and speaks in Kiswahili.[5]

WATCHMAN
Sir!
Madam!
There is a man and woman here
And they say they want to see you.
Shall I let them enter?

KĨOI
Tell them to enter.

Enter Kĩgũũnda and Wangeci. Kĩoi and his friends are relieved. They literally sigh with relief.

ALL
So it was you?

KĨGŨŨNDA ⎫
WANGECI   ⎭ Good evening?

The Watchman goes out.

THE OTHERS
Good evening.

KĨOI
We are at table.
Take seats over there.

KĨGŨŨNDA
We have come because . . .

KĨOI
Let's first eat,
We are going to talk after.

The waiter brings tea and passes near where Kĩgũũnda and Wangeci are sitting. As the waiter passes by, Wangeci, thinking that

5. The watchman speaks in Kiswahili, not in Gikuyu, because the authors wish to establish some distance between him and the working-class protagonists.

the tea is meant for them, stretches her hand out to pick up one cup. The waiter quickly moves the tray away leaving Wangeci's hand hanging in the air empty. Wangeci is very humiliated.

JEZEBEL

Please excuse us!
I am afraid we had cooked just enough
For invited guests.

WANGECI *(trying to cover up her humiliation)*

It does not matter.
We have just eaten,
A supper of a mixture of beans and maize.

> *Helen turns up her nose as if she can smell the foul smell of bean and maize.*

KĪGŪŪNDA

Our only problem is water.
The water around has dried up.
Now our women have to walk for miles.
Wangeci has today been roaming all over
Looking for water,
And even then she could not get any.
Give me a little water
To push down the meal of maize and beans.

JEZEBEL *(to the waiter)*

Go and fetch water from the drum outside,
You know the one near the pig-sty.

> *Waiter hurries out.*

NDUGĪRE

Oh, without water life is such misery!
  (He deliberately takes a glass and fills it with water from the huge jar on the table and empties the glass.)
Before I eat an egg in the morning
I have first to drink a full glass of water.
Some people don't realize that
Water is very vital to the body.
Water is better than tea or even milk.

HELEN

A well-cared-for body is only possible with water.

> *The waiter brings water, in a cup, and gives it to Kĩgũũnda who drinks it.*

JEZEBEL

Yes, because without water,
You cannot clean the body.

KĨOI

That's why Jesus told the woman from Syria,
I am the water of . . .

NDUGĪRE
  Life!

> *The others sing: the Kīgũũndas watch*

> *Thirst and hunger for earthly things*
> *Is the sleep and death of life.*
> *Cry unto God your Lord*
> *And he will save you.*
>   *Life, life,*
>   *The everlasting life*
>   *And you'll never get thirsty.*

JEZEBEL
  Let's now say a prayer
  To thank God for the food
  We have just eaten.
    (*She looks at the Kīgũũndas*)
  We thank you Lord our God
  For the food you have given us.
  Now we humbly lower our eyes
  Before your holy presence, Oh Jehovah,
  You who are the head of this house
  You the unseen guest at every meal
  You the silent listener
  To every conversation.
  We do not want to be like Nebuchadnezzar
  Who was turned into a beast
  For forgetting to thank you.
  That's why we now humbly beg you
  To give us spiritual food
  And to give us the water of life
  So that we shall never never get thirsty.

ALL
  Amen.

> *The Kīois and the Ndugīres now leave the table and take more*
> *comfortable seats facing the Kīgũũndas. The servant/waiter begins*
> *to clear the table.*

KĪOI
  What do you want?
KĪGŨŨNDA (*clearing his throat*)
  We have come because of that matter.
WANGECI
  We have thought a great deal about the matter,
  And we came to the conclusion that
  We should not put obstacles
  To your larger purposes.
KĪOI
  If you have agreed to our plans
  We shall now become true friends,
  Your house and mine becoming one
  In the name of the Lord.

ALL (*They sing clapping joyfully. Kīgũũnda and Wangeci join in the singing but they obviously don't know the tune and they often clap out of step.*)
Good news
About our Saviour
Has come to us
This is good news.

Yes good news has come
Telling us all
How He forgives
And how he loves us.

Great love is this
Of Christ the helper;
He came down from heaven
Because he felt pity over us.

His name will be sung
From place to place
And all the nations
Will give up their wickedness.

KĪGŨŨNDA
But there's a small problem!
A modern church wedding
Requires a lot of things.
We cannot enter the holy church
The way we are
With muddy feet
And these rags ever on our shoulders.

JEZEBEL
You don't need a great deal.
You only need the following:
First is the fee for the officiating priest.
And then robes for the bride.

NDUGĪRE
And a suit for the bridegroom.

HELEN
And clothes for bridesmaids and best man.

JEZEBEL
And for the children,
Who will hold the train!
Then you'll have to set aside a little sum of money
For bread, milk, butter, jam,
And of course for the wedding cake.

HELEN
Oh, yes, the cake!
The cake is central to a Christian wedding!

NDUGĪRE
The Christian Ngurario.
    (*Laughs at the comparison*)

JEZEBEL
    You!
    Ikuua seems to have taught you unbecoming language!
HELEN
    What about rings and flowers?
JEZEBEL
    Oh, yes, I was forgetting those.
KĪOI
    And you can buy all those
    From my supermarket at Wabera Street.
WANGECI
    Where shall we get the money for all that?
KĪOI
    Kĩgũũnda earns a lot of money.
    Don't you deposit some of it
    In a Post Office savings account?
NDUGĪRE
    You know that we black people
    Have never really mastered the word, savings.
    Yes, setting aside something
    For a rainy day.
KĪGŨŨNDA
    What do I get a month?
    Two hundred shillings,
    And you call that a lot of money?
    Two hundred shillings a month
    With which to buy clothes, food, water,
    And you know very well
    That prices are daily climbing up!
    A person earning two hundred shillings,
    Can he really cope with the rising prices?
NDUGĪRE (cutting him short)
    But do you think it possible to have two price categories,
    For those with property
    And those without?
    Does God's rain fall on a rich man's fields
    Bypassing a poor man's field?
KĪOI
    Not only that my brother-in-Christ.
    I give all the workers a hundred or a hundred and fifty!
    You, Kĩgũũnda and the tractor driver
    Are the only workers who get two hundred shillings.
JEZEBEL (as if cracking a joke)
    The tractor driver is very well behaved
    And not like you, father of Gathoni.
    He never complains about anything.
    He never complains about his wages!
KĪGŨŨNDA
    I didn't come here to ask for an increment
    Although I won't mind a rise in wages
    It's only that the wedding ceremony will cost a lot of money.

KĨOI

    Kĩgũũnda, you are a very wealthy man,
    Only that you don't care to know:
    You have a lot of land, one and a half acres.
    You have a full-time job.
    How many thousands who in Kenya today
    Cannot boast about a space large enough for a grave even?

NDUGĨRE

    A grave is not even the best comparison
    Since there are many state-owned graveyards.
    But how many hundreds of Kenyans
    Are now roaming all over the country
    Looking for any type of job whatever the pay
    And they can't get any?

KĨGŨŨNDA

    I wanted to find out
    If you could lend us money
    To meet the cost of the wedding ceremony.

     *Ndugĩre, Kĩoi, Helen and Jezebel stare at one another in obvious
     dismay. Kĩoi is rapt in thought.*

KĨOI

    That's an easy matter.
    I like you.
    The other day I even visited you in your home.
    But remember what God told Adam and Eve:
    There are no free things!
    Hakuna cha bure!
    No more manna from heaven.
      (*Turning to Ndugĩre*)
    If anyone wants free things
    He should go to Tanzania
    Or to China.

NDUGĨRE

    I have heard it said that
    In China there's no private property,
    That everything, including women, is shared out.

JEZEBEL
            } What! Women shared out!
HELEN

NDUGĨRE

    Yes, they say that in China there's no rich or poor.
    But how can a country progress
    Unless led by the rich?

KĨOI

    In China, they don't even believe in God.

JEZEBEL

    Didn't the missionaries get there?
    Does it mean that all the Chinese,
    The whole country, will burn in hell?

KĨOI
Yes, eight hundred million souls.
To burn for ever!

NDUGĨRE
Nebuchadnezzar's clansmen.
Let them burn.

HELEN
Flames jumping in the sky.

NDUGĨRE
Like flames from a pile of dry firewood.

JEZEBEL
Their bones breaking: crack! crack!

KĨOI
And all because of
Getting rid of the rich.

KĨGŨŨNDA
Does it mean that in China
People do not now have food, clothes and shelter?

NDUGĨRE
Who knows!

KĨOI
Just imagine!
All the people . . .
If all the people are to become equal like these teeth
Who would do the work?
Anyway we in Kenya are very lucky,
Because we are a Christian nation.
We worship at the feet of the Lord,
The same Lord who commanded us all
To forever sweat over whatever we eat or drink.
Mr Kĩgũũnda your words are good
And I am willing to help you.

KĨGŨŨNDA
Thank you! Thank you!

KĨOI
There are two alternatives.
You have got one and a half acres of land.
There is an American-, German- and Japanese-owned company
Which wants to build an insecticide factory.
I think Mr Ikuua has already written to you about it!
If you sell that piece of land,
You'll get a lot of money.
With some of that money,
You can buy land in the Rift Valley
Or in Maasailand
And the rest you can bank.

KĨGŨŨNDA
I will never sell the piece of land.
I just wanted . . .

KĨOI

I have not finished. I told you there were two alternatives.
You have rejected the first.
The other alternative is to borrow money from a bank
With your one and half acres as security.

KĨGŨŨNDA }
WANGECI } What! Our title-deed to go to a bank!

KĨOI

Yes, because no bank will lend you money
Without some security.
In fact borrowing from a bank is better
Than borrowing from an individual like me,
Because the bank only requires you
To pay back a little each month.
Now this is how I'm going to help you:
First I'll myself take you to the bank
Of which I am a director
And I will vouch for your integrity.
I'll pledge to withhold from your wages
Whatever the monthly amount
You and the bank will agree.

HELEN

You, our brother-in-Christ, are very kind-hearted.
Praise the Lord.
   (*Turning to Kĩgũũnda*)
Do you know that not many people today
Would agree to become a surety
In order that a mere worker might get a bank loan?

NDUGĨRE

Yes, because a propertied man like Kĩoi
Naturally fears that such a worker
Might fall ill or even die suddenly.

WANGECI

Anybody can die.
Even millionaires do die.

NDUGĨRE

Yes, but you will agree that the
Death rate is worse among the poor!

KĨOI

Mr Kĩgũũnda, what do you have to say?

KĨGŨŨNDA

Whether I borrow from you or from a bank
It is all the same to us.
I didn't come here to beg.
But you people are the bankers
Of what we the poor produce!
Tomorrow I shall bring the title-deed;
You and I will take it to the bank.

END OF ACT TWO

Act Three

Kĩgũũnda's home. The interior is very different from what it was in previous scenes. A new dining table with chairs. On the table is a big suitcase, also new. New plates, cups, basins and so on. A suit hangs on the wall where Kĩgũũnda's old coat used to hang. On one wall hangs the picture of Nebuchadnezzar exactly like the one in Kĩoi's home. On another wall, exactly on the spot where the title-deed used to be, now hangs a board with the inscription: 'Christ is the head . . . etc', again like the one in Kĩoi's house. The title-deed is not now anywhere in the house.

The scene opens with Kĩgũũnda and Wangeci busy bringing in new things into the house, such as sofa seats, a big standing mirror, a radio and so on. Wangeci and Kĩgũũnda are full of joy at the sight of each item. They are very happy, particularly because their house now looks like the Kĩois'. Kĩgũũnda goes to the board with the inscription 'Christ is the head', takes it off and studies it before putting it back on the wall. Wangeci in turn goes to it, dusts it, and then looks at it as if she is studying each letter. Kĩgũũnda goes to the radio and turns the knobs until he gets a song. He tries to dance to the tune. He then goes to the mirror where he tries on his wedding suit, in the process discarding his old rags and tyre sandals. Wangeci goes to the radio, tries the knobs this way and that way, occasionally standing back to admire it or walking about with it or swinging it. She turns to Kĩgũũnda.

WANGECI
    Why did you buy this?
KĩGŨŨNDA (*turning round*)
    Didn't I tell you to try on your clothes?
WANGECI
    I was admiring you.

> *Wangeci goes to the suitcase. She opens it. She starts undressing, getting rid of her old rags. She seems fascinated with the different items of clothing, lifting each in turn, as if she cannot make up her mind where to start. She takes out a huge brassière.*

WANGECI
    How does one put on this?
KĩGŨŨNDA
    Why don't you simply wear it as pants?
WANGECI
    I'll try it on, on the wedding day.

> *Wangeci puts on her wedding robes.*

KĩGŨŨNDA (*dusting himself up and admiring himself in his new suit*)
    On that day

I'll wake very early,
And put on this suit!
(*Turning round, he is completely mesmerized by Wangeci in her white wedding dress.*)
You have turned into a teenager!
Do you know what this white wedding dress means?
Its whiteness means that
You have never known any man.
(*Laughs*)
On that day
I shall ask Jishinde Ushinde Studio
To take a colour picture of you.
We shall send one picture to the papers
Taifa Leo. The wedding column.
I hear that the paper belongs to the Aga Khan
And they send him a copy of the paper in Europe!
Imagine!
Your picture and mine going to the Aga Khan in Europe!
On that day you and I will walk down the holy aisle
Holding hands.

> *He tries to hold Wangeci's hand.*

WANGECI
No, it's the bridegroom who enters first.
The bride follows, led by her father.
KĪGŪŪNDA
O.K. O.K.!
(*He goes to the radio and stops the music.*)
I'll then walk ahead with the best man.
(*He walks ahead and then turns his head to see if Wangeci is following.*)
Aren't you following behind me?
WANGECI
I'm coming.

> *They start walking as if they are really in a church on the wedding day. A church choir accompanies their mimed enactment of the wedding ceremony.*

The good news of life
Is all about Christ the Lord.
He is our strength.
He will guide us.
And should any evil
Come near us
Christ is able
To defend us from evil.
And when our days on earth are over
We shall dwell with Jesus
For ever and ever.

Now Wangeci and Kīgūūnda are standing before an invisible priest. They then kneel down before 'him'. The voice of the invisible priest is heard raised in prayer:

VOICE

Oh, God, our Lord
We lower our eyes before you today
Asking you to bless this bride
And this bridegroom.
For you were the one who wrote in the holy book.
Thus shall a man leave his father and mother
And be joined to his wife
And the two shall become one.
That's why, oh Jehovah, we humbly ask you
To bless this ceremony.
For you also said:
Two people are better than one
For they can see the fruits
Of their labour.
And should one person fall
The other can raise him.
But cursed is the man who falls
And he has no one to raise him.
And if two people should sleep together,
They can warm one another,
But if one sleeps alone,
How can he warm himself?
That's why you Christ the Lord
Went to the holy wedding at Galilee
And you turned water into wine,
The wine which was your blood.
Bless this house of
Winston Smith Kīgūūnda and Rosemary Magdalene Wangeci.
Double the fruits of the labour of their hands.
We ask you all this
In the name of Jesus Christ
Our Lord, Amen.

The prayer is followed by a hymn sung by an invisible church choir:

God blessed
The very first wedding
Of Adam and Eve.
Even today he still blesses
Holy matrimony
When Christians
Are marrying.
And afterwards
When Jesus comes back,
They'll ascend with him to heaven
The bride and bridegroom of the Lord.

As the hymn is being sung Kĩgũũnda takes out an invisible ring and puts it on Wangeci's finger. Wangeci does the same. Kĩgũũnda now lifts the veil from Wangeci's face and kisses her. They kneel down, holding hands. The invisible choir now takes up another hymn.

Jesus I have now put on my cross
To marry my Lord
Even though
Others may leave him.
And you my friend hurry up
And put on robes of faith
So that you'll ascend to heaven
To dwell in God's eternal happiness.

While the hymn is going on Kĩgũũnda and Wangeci rise and slowly walk to the reception. They sit, waiting for speeches and gifts.

KĨGŨŨNDA
Speeches bore me.
WANGECI
Me, too.
The man who is now talking
Never misses a single wedding.
KĨGŨŨNDA
And he makes the same speech
In all the wedding receptions.
WANGECI
Look at that one
Who has just stood to speak.
He advises couples to do
What he himself never practises.
KĨGŨŨNDA
Yes, he is always beating his wife.
WANGECI
Oh, dear,
That one again!
She never says anything
Apart from how beautiful her own wedding was.
And she ends up crying.
See.
There she goes.
She has started.
She is weeping . . .
KĨGŨŨNDA
When will they start bringing us gifts?
Today I want to know
Who our true friends are!
I wonder what the Kĩois and the Ndugĩres
Will bring us?
Some people can play nasty tricks;

They'll hand you a closed envelope,
But on opening it
You will find they have enclosed only five shillings!
Wait a minute.
That one has stood up.
He will now read the whole Bible
From cover to cover,
And then he will preach
Until tomorrow . . .

WANGECI
Oh, dear, before we have cut the cake?
Cutting a wedding cake
Which is as white as snow
Or as white as this wedding dress
Is a most wonderful thing.
A wedding without a cake
Is not a Christian wedding at all!

KĪGŪŪNDA
The speeches are now over.
Let's stand up to cut the cake.
It's a cake, five storeys high!

They stand up holding an invisible knife. They start cutting the cake. The choir sings another hymn. They give each other a piece of cake. They continue cutting it. Suddenly the hymn stops. A car hoots rudely. But Kĩgũũnda and Wangeci do not hear it. They are totally absorbed in the ceremony of cutting the cake. Another rude hooting and a car moves away. Gathoni comes in. She is at first taken aback by the changes in the house and by the strange behaviour of her parents. She then slumps into a seat and starts weeping. Without realizing that they are still holding each other's hands, her parents stare at Gathoni.

KĪGŪŪNDA ⎫ What's the matter?
WANGECI ⎭ Where's John Mũhũũni?

Gathoni goes on weeping. Wangeci lets go Kĩgũũnda's hand and goes to where Gathoni is sitting.

WANGECI
What's the matter, my daughter?

GATHONI
He . . . he . . . he has jilted me.

WANGECI
Who?

GATHONI
Jo . . . John . . . Mũhũũni . . .

KĪGŪŪNDA
To be jilted is nothing.
There are many more eligible men in the world.

WANGECI
Stop weeping.

GATHONI

It . . . is . . . not . . . just . . . that . . .

WANGECI

What else?

Speak. Quickly.

GATHONI

We went to Mombasa.

When we came back to Nairobi

I told him that

I was pregnant.

KĪGŪŪNDA ⎱
⎰ Pregnant?
WANGECI

GATHONI

He used to tell me that

He wanted us to have a baby

That he would never marry a girl

Who had not conceived

In case he married someone barren.

At Nairobi, he did not say anything.

But when we reached the village

He suddenly shouted at me

And ordered me to get out of his car,

That he was not responsible for the pregnancy

And that he would never marry a prostitute.

KĪGŪŪNDA

Do you now see the fruits of your obstinacy?

Did I not forbid you

To go to Mombasa?

WANGECI

Leave her alone.

Let's go to Kīoi's place now.

He is a good old man,

A Christian,

A man of the church,

A man of integrity,

A man who likes to help others.

He is not the sort who would endure

To see a child like this suffer.

Didn't he tell you that

He wanted your house and his to become one?

let's go there now,

Even though it is dark,

And tell him.

Let the children marry first.

> *Kīgūūnda collects his old rags, about to change. Then he takes
> the sword. He shouts at Wangeci, 'Change into your old clothes!'*

END OF SCENE ONE

*Kĩoi's home. Kĩoi and Ikuua are alone in the sitting room. They
are busy counting money and cheques. Their words can be heard:
'This million and a half comes from the sale of tusks and of lion
and leopard skins to Japan. And these two million come from the
maize and salt we sent to Uganda. . . . And these eight millions
come from Chepkumbe coffee . . .' etc. Ikuua is doing most of
the talking, while Kĩoi is merely grunting assent, and receiving
some of the heaps of notes and cheques, and writing down the
figures. As soon as they have finished counting, Ikuua tells Kĩoi:
'It's now your turn to take all this to the bank tomorrow. And
beware of robbers.' Ikuua stands up:*

IKUUA

Let me leave now
For I have to rush to the airport.
Our friends from America and Germany,
You know, the ones involved in this factory,
Arrive at midnight.
By the way don't worry about the site,
The peasant whose land adjoins Kĩgũũnda's
Has agreed to sell us three acres,
So that he can buy some shares
In a land-buying scheme in the Rift Valley
Of which I am the leader.
But should Kĩgũũnda agree to sell his,
It's alright,
For the factory will need space for expansion.
And what did you decide
About you becoming one of the local directors?
It's not much work.
It's just a matter of one or two board meetings.
You become overseer
Just as you oversee their banks.
You and I will be like watchdogs!
Holding fleshy bones!
   (*He laughs.*)

KĨOI

It's alright.
But I think we'd better forward the name of John Mũhũũni.
Let him become a director,
So that our sons can begin to exercise responsibility!
Charity begins at home.

IKUUA

So he has come back from Mombasa?

KĨOI

Yes, and he reported that
All my properties on the coast
Are in good condition.

IKUUA
Bye, bye.

Ikuua goes out. Kīoi goes on calculating a bit and jotting a few things down. Suddenly there is an urgent knocking at the door. He hides the money. Before he has hidden everything away, Kīgūūnda and Wangeci, in their old working clothes, enter.

KĪGŪŪNDA
We have come
Because something unexpected has happened.
Instead of Wangeci and I marrying in church
The children had better marry first.

KĪOI
Children?
Which children?

WANGECI
Mūhūūni and Gathoni.

KĪOI
John Mūhūūni!
Which Mūhūūni are you talking about?

KĪGŪŪNDA
Has he not told you?

KĪOI
What?
Tell me.

KĪGŪŪNDA }
WANGECI   } That he has made Gathoni pregnant.

KĪOI (*very angry*)
My son can't do a thing like that.
We have brought him up in Christian ways . . .
Go away from here.
I don't want to hear any nonsense from you.
Why are you unable to look after your children?

WANGECI
Aaa—uuu—u!
We shall go to court.
We are all equal before the law.

KĪOI (*smiling*)
Did you say 'court'? Law?
Run. Hurry up.
We shall see on whose side the law is!
Your side or our side!
There are no laws to protect parents
Who are unable to discipline their children,
Who let their children become prostitutes.
I am a mature person,
I've been made mature by Christ.
And I can let my son marry
Only from the home of a mature person.

KĪGŪŪNDA (*pulling out the sword*)
> So I'm not a human being?
> So I have no feelings?
> Is that why you dare call my daughter a whore
> In my very presence?
> Don't you know how it pains
> When I truly know that
> It's your son who lured her away from home?
> Now I'll prove to you that
> I am a human being!
> This sword is my law and my court.
> Poor people's lawcourt.
>> (*Kĩoi is trembling with hands raised.*)
> You'll die now.
> Kneel down.
> Kneel!
>> (*Kĩoi kneels down.*)
> Look at yourself, you Nebuchadnezzar.
> You are the one turned into a beast.
> Walk on all fours.
> Walk on your feet and hands.
>> (*Kĩoi walks on all fours.*)
> Eat grass,
> Christ, the Head, is watching you,
> Walk!
>> (*Wangeci is beseeching Kĩgũũnda not to kill him.*)

WANGECI
> Don't kill him.
> Let him sign an agreement.

KĪGŪŪNDA
> This one?
> To sign an agreement?

KĪOI
> Yes, I'll sign.
> I'll sign anything you want me to sign.
> Even if you want them to go to church tonight
> They'll go!

KĪGŪŪNDA (*with pride*)
> Church, your churches?
> Let me tell you a thing or two Mr Ahab Kĩoi.
> Even if you were now to give me all the wealth
> Which you and your clansmen have stolen from the poor,
> Yes, the wealth which you and your Asian and European clansmen
> And all the rich from Kenya share among yourselves,
> I would not take it.
> Just now,
> No amount of gold or ivory or gemstones
> Would make me let Gathoni marry your son.
> But as for signing something,
> You will!
> Earthly debts must be paid here on earth.

It is said the fart of the rich never smells
But yours Kīoi stinks all over the earth.

*Jezebel peeps in and quickly rushes back to the inner rooms. The
Securicor watchman and Ndugīre and Helen enter. Kīgūūnda is
not afraid. But Ndugīre and Helen are trembling with fear, and
they don't seem to know what to do. The watchman takes out his
whistle and starts blowing it and threatening Kīgūūnda from a
safe distance. But whenever Kīgūūnda moves a step towards them
they all run to an even safer distance.*

KĪGŪŪNDA
Wangeci bring a piece of paper from that table.
I want all these to witness
Ahab Kīoi wa Kanoru's signature.

*The watchman goes on blowing his whistle and threatening
Kīgūūnda, but with his eyes very much on the door. Before
Kīgūūnda gets the piece of paper, Jezebel enters with a gun, a
pistol. The Watchman and the Ndugīres give way and follow behind her, now all acting brave. With her eyes on Kīgūūnda's
sword and pointing the gun at him she walks to where her husband is and helps him to his feet with a hand. Wangeci goes to
where Kīgūūnda is and tries to get the sword from him. But Kīgūūnda pushes her away. Now it is the confrontation between the
gun and the sword.*

JEZEBEL
Put that sword down.

*Kīgūūnda at first refuses, then he reluctantly lets the sword fall
to the ground. Jezebel bends down and pushes away the sword,
while still pointing the gun at Kīgūūnda.*

JEZEBEL
Get out. Get out of here.

*Kīgūūnda and Wangeci start to leave. But at the door, Kīgūūnda
quickly turns round as if finally determined to regain his sword
and fight it out. Jezebel fires the gun. Kīgūūnda falls.*

END OF SCENE TWO

SCENE THREE

*Kīgūūnda's home. About two weeks after. Kīgūūnda is not in.
Most of the new things are no longer there. The house is very
much like the way it was at the beginning of the play, except for
the picture of Nebuchadnezzar and the board with the inscription
'Christ is the Head' which still hang from the walls as if in mockery. Note that the board with the inscription 'Christ is the Head'
hangs on the spot where the title-deed used to hang. Wangeci is
sitting on a chair, dejected. Njooki is standing near her, trying to*

comfort her. Gĩcaamba is standing near the board with the inscription, as if he is reading the letters, shaking his head from side to side in disbelief.

WANGECI
What shall I now do?
Where shall I now turn?
Oh, oh, my child!

GĨCAAMBA
Where is Gathoni?

WANGECI
My friends: don't ask me.

NJOOKI
But why? Where is Gathoni?

WANGECI
Her father threw her out of the house.
I stayed for a week without knowing
Where she had gone.
Now I hear that she is a barmaid.
My daughter!
A barmaid!
Gathoni my child!
To become a whore?

GĨCAAMBA (*moving away from the board*)
Let's not call our children prostitutes.
A hyena is very greedy
But she does not eat her young.
Our children are not to blame.
Gathoni is not to blame.
When a bird in flight gets very tired
It lands on the nearest tree.
We the parents have not put much effort
In the education of our girls.
Even before colonialism,
We oppressed women
Giving ourselves numerous justifications:
    (*Sings*)
    Women and property are not friends,
    Two women are two pots of poison,
    Women and the heavens are unpredictable,
    Women cannot keep secrets,
    A woman's word is believed only after the event.

And through many other similar sayings,
Forgetting that a home belongs to man and woman,
That the country belongs to boys and girls.
Do you think it was only the men
Who fought for Kenya's independence?
How many women died in the forests?
Today when we face problems
We take it out on our wives,

Instead of holding a dialogue
To find ways and means of removing darkness from the land.
(*Sings*)
Come my friend
Come my friend
Let's reason together.
Our hearts are heavy
Over the future of our children.
Let's find ways of driving darkness
From the land.

NJOOKI
Gathoni now has no job.
She has no other means of earning a living
And she would like to dress up
Like all her age-mates.

WANGECI
Would she were a housemaid!

NJOOKI
A housemaid?
To be collecting all the shit in somebody else's house?
And when the memsahib is out of sight,
The husband wants the maid to act the wife!
Thus the maid doing all the work for memsahib!

GĪCAAMBA ⎫ (*Sing as if continuing the song*
NJOOKI ⎬ *Gīcaamba has just sung*)
Yes we find out why
It's the children of the poor
Who look after rich people's homes,
Who serve them beer in beer-halls,
Who sell them their flesh.
　Come my friend
　Come my friend
　We reason together.
　Our hearts are heavy
　Over the future of our children.
　Let's find ways of driving away darkness
　From the land.

WANGECI
Oh, my child!

NJOOKI
She will come back!
Our children will one day come back!

GĪCAAMBA
And where now is Kīgūūnda?

WANGECI
I don't know!
He might be in a beer-hall.
Ever since he lost his job,
He had become married to Chibuku liquor!
And now he has lost his piece of land.

GĨCAAMBA
NJOOKI } What?

WANGECI

Didn't you hear about it over the radio?
You too have forgotten us.

NJOOKI

No!
We have not forgotten you,
Gĩcaamba has been on night shifts.
And again we noticed
That since you started friendship with the Kĩois,
You did not really want our company.

WANGECI

Nobody repents the sins of another.
Nobody regrets the going as the returning.

GĨCAAMBA

What about the piece of land?

WANGECI

We went to Kĩoi's place
To tell him about Gathoni and Mũhũũni.
Kĩoi and Kĩgũũnda exchanged heated words.
Kĩgũũnda took out his sword.
Kĩoi's wife took out a gun.

GĨCAAMBA
NJOOKI } What? A gun?

WANGECI

What can I say?
We are now breathing
Only because the bullets missed us
Death was not ready to receive us.
Kĩoi said he would not pursue the matter further,
But he dismissed Kĩgũũnda from his job.

NJOOKI

If only I could catch that Kĩoi.
With these hands that know toil
I would teach him a thing or two!

WANGECI

After a week
Kĩgũũnda got a letter from the bank's lawyers.
The letter said: pay back the loan
Or we shall sell your piece of land.
Kĩgũũnda has no job.
He has tried to sell the goods
We foolishly bought with the loan money
And they are not fetching much.
So the radio announced that
The piece of land would be auctioned.

NJOOKI

We never heard the announcement.
When will it be auctioned?

WANGECI
> Today.
> It was being auctioned today.

NJOOKI
> Today?

WANGECI
> Today! This day!
> Today was the day
> The Kīois buried us alive.

> KĪGŪŪNDA's *drunken voice can be heard. He is singing.*

> *I shall marry when I want*
> *While all padres are still alive*
> *And I shall get married when I want*
> *While all nuns are still alive.*

> *Kīgūūnda enters, very drunk.*

KĪGŪŪNDA
> How are you?
> Son of Kīhooto,
> Why didn't you join me for a drink?
> Chibuku for power.
> Kill me quick: Chibuku.
> You Gīcaamba have become tied
> To your wife's apron strings.
> Do you suckle her?
> Women are useless.
> A woman is a pot full of poison.

WANGECI
> And so Chibuku has married you?
> Everyday. In the morning. In the evening.
> Whenever you sell anything
> To get money to pay back the loan,
> You go to a beer-hall where Chibuku is sold.
> Chibuku!
> Chang'aa liquor!
> Poison poured into our country!

GĪCAAMBA
> Yes, yes, by the whites
> And their local followers.
> Servants to foreigners!

KĪGŪŪNDA (*sings and dances*)
> *Greet Chibuku for me*
> *Chibuku chased away my bitterness*
> *Chibuku chased away pain, sorrow and thoughts.*

WANGECI
> Go away,
> Go back to the beer-halls
> Where your daughter is selling beer
> And dance and sing in there.

KĨGŨŨNDA
Shut up, woman!
Gĩcaamba, never trust a woman.

WANGECI
Was I the one who told you
To go for loans from other people's banks?

KĨGŨŨNDA
Who wanted a church wedding?
You an old woman
Wanting to go through a humiliating ceremony!
And all because of looking down upon our culture!
You saw fools going for foreign customs
And you followed in their footsteps.
Do you think that it's only foreign things
Which are blessed?

WANGECI
You are not the one talking.
It's liquor speaking through you.

KĨGŨŨNDA (*worked up*)
You now insult me!
You dare insult me!
Have church weddings entered your brains?

> *He takes the picture of Nebuchadnezzar and breaks it to pieces.
> He does the same for the board with the inscription, 'Christ is
> the Head'.*

WANGECI
Do you think that breaking those
Will bring back the piece of land?

> *Wangeci and Kĩgũũnda fight. Gĩcaamba and Njooki separate
> them. Wangeci is crying and shouting all sorts of insults.*

WANGECI
Kill me!
Let him murder me!
Murder me before the whole population!
Kĩoi has proved too much for you.
Chibuku has proved too much for you.
Your daughter has proved too much for you.
O.K., kill me! Kill me now!
Leave him alone, the poor wretch.
Let him now kill me
So he can have meat for supper.

> *Kĩgũũnda suddenly changes as if a mortal blow had been struck at
> his own identity. He slumps into a seat, completely dejected, but
> rapt in thought. Wangeci is also dejected as she too takes a seat.*

GĨCAAMBA
Whatever the weight of our problems,
Let's not fight amongst ourselves.

Let's not turn violence within us against us,
Destroying our homes
While our enemies snore in peace.

KĨGŨŨNDA

You have spoken the truth.
For from today Kĩoi has become my enemy.
Either I die, or he dies.
Why, they have buried me alive!

NJOOKI

The piece of land . . . was it sold?

KĨGŨŨNDA (pause)

Yes. (Shows them his hand.)
Now we have only our hands.

GĨCAAMBA

Who . . . Who bought it?

KĨGŨŨNDA (pause)

Ahab Kĩoi wa Kanoru.

NJOOKI

A-uuu-u!
That man should now be baptized
The Oppressor, Son of Grab-and-Take.

ALL

The Oppressor, Son of Grab-and-Take.

KĨGŨŨNDA

When I left the auction place
I thought I should revisit the piece of land
For a last glance,
A kind of goodbye.
Who did I find there?
Kĩoi wa Kanoru, Ikuua wa Nditika
Plus a group of whites.
I fled.
But their open laughter followed me . . .

GĨCAAMBA

The laughter from the clansmen of . . .

KĨGŨŨNDA ⎫
NJOOKI   ⎬ The Oppressor, Son of Grab-and-Take.
WANGECI   ⎭

> *The same group of people who had sung in Act One now come
> back and break into the same song.*

The devil of robbery
Must be crushed
Hallelujah let's crush him
For the second coming is near.
He has brought famine to this land
Let's crush him.
Hallelujah let's crush him
For the second coming is near.

The devil of oppression
Must be crushed.

  The Leader of the group enters with a container.

LEADER
It's a haraambe to build a church
For those troubled at heart
For those carrying pain in their hearts!

  *Wangeci unties a handkerchief and takes out a shilling which
  she puts into the container. She stands at the door and watches
  the group as they now sing a hymn of harvest:*

We bring you this offering, oh Lord,
It is the fruit of our toil on the land.
Take it Lord and bless it.
Take it Lord and bless it.
  If you give in a tiny calabash,
  In heaven you'll be paid in a similar container.
  If you give in a big wide basin,
  In heaven you'll be paid in a similar container.
  And if you don't give anything,
  You too will never receive blessings.
  Lord take it and bless it.
We bring you this offering, Oh Lord,
It's the fruit of our toil on the land.
Take it Lord and bless it.
Take it Lord and bless it.

  *The singers go away singing. Wangeci returns to her seat.
  Gĩcaamba is shaking his head from side to side.*

GĨCAAMBA
This has become too much for us.
The Kĩois and the Ikuuas,
For how long will they continue oppressing us?
The European Kĩoi, the Asian Kĩoi,
The African Kĩoi,
What's the difference?
They are clansmen.
They know only how to take from the poor.
When we took the Mau Mau oath,
We used to make this vow:
I'll always help this organization
With all my strength and property
I'll always aid members of this organization.
If a bean falls to the ground
We shall split it equally among us.
If I fail to do so,
May this, the people's oath, destroy me
And the blood of the masses turn against me.

ALL (*They repeat as if renewing a political vow.*)

GĪCAAMBA

Our nation took the wrong turn
When some of us forgot these vows.
They forgot all about the people's movement
And they took over the programme of the homeguards,
They said that a vulture eats alone
That no bird of prey preys for another.
They turned into sucking, grabbing and taking away.
That group is now ready to sell the whole country to foreigners.
Go to any business premise;
Go to any industry;
Go to any company;
Even if you find an African behind the counter,
Smoking a pipe over a protruding belly,
Know that he is only an overseer, a well-fed watchdog,
Ensuring the smooth passage of people's wealth
To Europe and other foreign countries.
Grabbers
Exploiters
Oppressors
Eaters of that which has been produced by others:
Their religion,
Their hymn,
Their prayer
Are all one:
Oh, God in heaven,
Shut the eyes of the poor,
The workers and the peasants
The masses as a whole
Ensure that they never wake up and open their eyes
To see what we are really doing to them!
Wa Gathoni,
We too should think hard,
Let's wake up and reason together, now.

ALL (*They sing. Wangeci stands up and sings facing and looking at Kĩgũũnda. Kĩgũũnda also stands up and walks towards her. They meet and hold hands as they continue singing*)

> Come my friend
> Come my friend
> Let's reason together.
> Our hearts are heavy with worry
> Because of the future of our children.
> Let's drive away the darkness
> From all our land.

GĪCAAMBA

The question is this:
Who are our friends? And where are they?
Who are our enemies? And where are they?
Let us unite against our enemies.

I don't need to elaborate!
He who has ears, let him hear,
He who has eyes, let him see.
I know only this:
We cannot end poverty by erecting a hundred churches in the
    village:
We cannot end poverty by erecting a hundred beer-halls in the
    village;
Ending up with two alcoholics.
The alcoholic of hard liquor.
The alcoholic of the rosary.
Let's rather unite in patriotic love:
Gĩkũyũ once said:
    (*Sings*)
    Two hands can carry a beehive,
    One man's ability is not enough,
    One finger cannot kill a louse,
    Many hands make work light.
Why did Gĩkũyũ say those things?
Development will come from our unity.
Unity is our strength and wealth.
A day will surely come when
If a bean falls to the ground
It'll be split equally among us,
For—

    They sing

SOLOIST
    The trumpet—
ALL
    Of the workers has been blown
    To wake all the slaves
    To wake all the peasants
    To wake all the poor.
    To wake the masses
SOLOIST
    The trumpet—
ALL
    Of the poor has been blown.
SOLOIST
    The trumpet!
ALL
    The trumpet of the masses has been blown.
    Let's preach to all our friends.
    The trumpet of the masses has been blown.
    We change to new songs
    For the revolution is near.
SOLOIST
    The trumpet!

ALL

The trumpet of the masses has been blown.

SOLOIST

The trumpet!

ALL

The trumpet of the masses has been blown.
We are tired of being robbed
We are tired of exploitation
We are tired of land grabbing
We are tired of slavery
We are tired of charity and abuses.

SOLOIST

The trumpet!

ALL

The trumpet of the poor has been blown.
Let's unite and organize
Organization is our club
Organization is our sword
Organization is our gun
Organization is our shield
Organization is the way
Organization is our strength
Organization is our light
Organization is our wealth.

SOLOIST

The trumpet!

ALL

The trumpet of the masses has been blown.

SOLOIST

The trumpet—

ALL

Of the workers has been blown
There are two sides in the struggle,
The side of the exploiters and that of the exploited.
On which side will you be when

SOLOIST

The trumpet—

ALL

Of the workers is finally blown?

CURTAIN

FEMI OSOFISAN
Esu and the Vagabond Minstrels[†]

A Fertility Rite for the Modern Stage

Characters
(In Order of Appearance)

CHIEF
ADE
YOUTH CORPERS
MINSTRELS
OMELE
EPO OYINBO
JIGI
SINSIN
REDIO

Worshipers:
PRIEST IN LOINCLOTH
WOMEN WITH BASKETS
MAN

Spirits:
ESU
ESU'S FOLLOWERS
PREGNANT WOMAN
MALE LEPER/ORUNMILA
FEMALE LEPER/YEYE OSUN
OBALUAYE

One: Orchestra

Lights come up on a festive scene. A community in obvious celebration. The community in the author's mind is a National

Youth Service Corps[1] *camp, but note that, in production, this could be substituted for—an end-of-year school's gathering, a village assembly at the close of harvest, a tourists' holiday camp, a workers' commune, a military barracks, a gathering of beggars and/or criminals in their usual havens after a heavy haul, or prison inmates or seminarists on an "open" day—any community will do, and the appropriate vocabulary adjustments should then be made. Community leaders sit on a slightly raised platform, while the rest are on mats, stools, etc. Each holds a calabash cup, while younger men and women, bearing large gourds, go around serving. Noise of conversation, chanting, quarreling, bantering, etc. Some musicians can be picked up here and there among the crowd, although they are not all necessarily playing. Soon the community leader—whom we shall name Chief for convenience—calls for silence.*

CHIEF   Thank you, everybody, thank you! I believe you're all well served? Good! May we continue to have days like this, when happiness and prosperity sit so solidly in our midst! (*responses*) Before we close, however, I think this an appropriate moment to ask our players what they have ready for the competition next week. (*noises of assent*) Okay, Ade, where are you? Ade! Has anyone seen our lead singer?

(*Voices rise, calling Ade, till he answers, offstage.*)

A VOICE   But, chief . . . the competition, is it still on? I mean, with the coup d'état and the change of government in the capital . . . ?

(*He is interrupted by some voices, some laughing, some hissing.*)

CHIEF   The competition is still very much on, my friend! What do they say? "The government changes, the people remain!" Let them go on with their fighting over there in the capital! It doesn't concern us, does it? (*A thundering response of "Noooo!" Then someone starts the "Song of Khaki and Agbada," which everybody picks up.*)

THE SONG OF KHAKI AND AGBADA

Chorus: *Jo mi jo!*   Chorus: *Jo mi jo!*

Olufe, wa gb'akara	*Darling, chop akara!*
Ma d'olosi lohun	*Make you no mind de rumors*
Wole, ko ti'lekun!	*Shut de door and window*
Khaki toun t'agbada	*Khaki and Agbada*
Awon lo jo nrin	*De two dey waka together*
Ti khaki ba gba power	*Khaki come to power*
A fese bi agbada!	*Imitate Agbada!*
T'Agbada ba gb'agbara	*Agbada come to power*
A tunse bi soja	*And go dey do like Khaki*
Agbara dun tabi kodun!	*Power de sweet man pickin!*

---

1. A government-run institution that coordinates the compulsory one-year national service of college graduates in Nigeria.

"With immediate effect."	*"With immediate effect."*
Non fi nkowo ilu mi	*He don chop de treasury*
"With immediate dispatch!"	*"With immediate dispatch!"*
Won nwo jet lo Mecca	*He buy jet for Mecca*
Won a lo Rome fun "shopping"	*Fly to Rome for shopping*
Ko ni sonje loja	*Food go dear for market*
Aiye o ni le gbadun	*Man go suffer—suffer*
Won ma so'lu d'ahoro	*Farm go dry like desert*
Awon Oje lu pansaga!	*Still Agbada no go care*
But, Khaki o gba'ru e	*Then Khaki go thunder*
Ani, Soja o gba se!	*Soldier don vex finish*
Adie ba l'okun tan	*Na fowl tanda for rope*
Kiniun gb'o de l'ehin	*Hunter dey for lion back . . .*
Aroye ni mo wa ro!	*But, I too dey talk—talk*
Emi ele nuso biri	*With my mouth like shovel*
Bi mba dake ma ro'ran!	*And I go henter for trouble*
Olufe, tilekun!	*Darling, make you shut de door!*

(*They end the song in great laughter.*)

CHIEF   Thank you, thank you! I wonder why many of you here are not in the acting troupe! (*Ade enters.*) Ah, Ade, there you are! Your players, are they here?

ADE (*looking around*)   Yes, I should think so. Except for Leke.

CHIEF   Well, what play are you people taking to the competition? Or is it not ready?

ADE   Not quite, but have no fear at all! I promise everyone here that we shall not fail you (*cheers*) We have an excellent play that we are working on seriously. It's going to beat anything our rivals may bring up! (*cheers*)

CHIEF   That is the kind of thing I love to see in the community! A winning spirit! But . . . is it possible . . . I mean, can we see some bit of it before we disperse today? Just to give us a foretaste?

ADE   Oh yes, why not? I'm sure the Players will love it. It will give us a chance to test it out before a live audience. That is, if you don't mind our doing it without costumes and the necessary props.

CHIEF   Come on, what are costumes? What are props? Are they not just embellishment? It's the story we want, not so? (*responses*)

ADE   Okay, we have some costumes and props anyway. If you give us your go-ahead, we'll get started. Players, where are you? (*They assemble round him.*) Taju, run and fetch Leke. Tell him it's a rehearsal, and he's needed. Now let's see . . . ah, yes, clear the center here, please; that will be our stage. Right here, at the center. We are putting a crossroads there. A crossroads, which as you all know is Esu's homing ground! Where's Esu! Come on, take position here with your followers. Er, Chief, you won't mind, will you, if we borrow the signpost over there? Dele, go and fetch it and put it up in the center here. Yes! This will be the spot for Esu's homing ground. (*looking out*) What! (*laughs*) Okay, Chuks, run quickly and give Dele a hand with the signpost. Meanwhile, Esu, where are you again?

Let's have you and your followers to this side. (*Dele and Chuks appear with a large signpost that has crossed arms.*) Here! Good. Esu, come on, take position now, with your men. (*Esu and the followers sit or squat around the road sign. Then one of the players whispers in Ade's ears.*) All right, all right. I think I'll ask the women present to help us. Can you please lend us your shawls? Thank you. Thank you. These people, or what shall we call them? Gods? Esu and his followers need them. When they wrap themselves, as they are doing now, they turn to stones. Yes, just like that. See? Ah, there's Leke! I knew you'd fly here, once you hear the word *rehearsal*! (*to the crowd*) He doesn't want to lose his part to another player! Even though he's going to be a mere vagabond! Well, ladies and gentlemen, here are your lead players, these five. They are what I said before, vagabonds! Vagabond musicians. They've been jobless for months—since the change of government actually, and the proscription of entertainers like them. And they've been forced therefore to trek from town to town, village to village, searching for work, all in vain, till they arrived here, at this crossroads. That's where our story will start. Please watch well, and let us have your comments after the show. Ah, what changes, what unexpected changes, a new government can bring to people's lives! (*The crowd starts the "Song of Khaki and Agbada" again, as they disperse into the orchestra. The sitting arrangements now must be such that, except for the open space at the center, there is no real separation between the players and the assembled audience. Players not directly needed onstage, or in the orchestra, should mix with the audience. Lights dim gradually, till the next scene is ready.*)

Two: Overture

The lights come up on a crossroads. Dawn. Later clearing into morning. Sounds of cockcrow. Five bedraggled minstrels—three men and two women—come wearily onto the stage.

OMELE   This is the place.

EPO OYINBO   Where?

OMELE   Here.

JIGI   This crossroads?

OMELE   Yes. Where the roads meet. You can put down your things. We've arrived.

SINSIN   At last! My poor feet!

EPO OYINBO   But . . . where's the food?

OMELE   Put down your things.

EPO OYINBO   I said, where's the food?

OMELE   I don't know Epo Oyinbo! Are you the only one hungry here?

EPO OYINBO   Well show us then!

OMELE   You mean you can't wait?

EPO OYINBO   Wait for what?

OMELE   Look, I'm tired . . .

EPO OYINBO You hear that!

REDIO Now, what's the game, Omele?

EPO OYINBO He's tired!

OMELE All I'm saying is that . . .

EPO OYINBO Nonsense! What are you saying? A feasting house, that's what you promised us! Food in abundance! That's why we dragged ourselves through the dust and followed you all this distance! And now, see, you are "tired," and the place is as barren as a graveyard!

OMELE And so what! Are you better than a corpse anyway?

EPO OYINBO (*furious*) You hear him, Oga Redio? You hear his filthy mouth!

JIGI But he's right, isn't he? Corpses, Epo Oyinbo! Is that not what we've become! We crawl from one hole to another, scrounging. And the smell of the grave follows our every step.

EPO OYINBO You too, Jigi? You too?

JIGI Hunger, my friend. Hunger makes a life meaningless!

EPO OYINBO And all those words of rubbish that you keep mouthing, is that what will feed us?

JIGI Corpses, my friend!

SINSIN Yes, but living corpses! The dead don't have a stomach howling for food.

REDIO Stomach! You must be damn lucky! What I have here (*pointing at his stomach*) is a furnace of rioting embers! I don't know where you fellows find the strength to quarrel like this.

EPO OYINBO But that's just it, Oga Redio! Eggs! Yams! Palm oil! Bananas! What else did he promise us? And now this—a forlorn crossroads!

SINSIN I can't even curse him! My voice is swallowed in my aching belly.

OMELE If only you'll be patient . . .

EPO OYINBO I should have known! After the prank you played last week! Only last week! But here I am, an imbecile, following you again! Don't I deserve it!

OMELE (*angry now*) It wasn't a prank, and you know it! Or would I play a prank on myself too?

JIGI You're going too far, Epo Oyinbo. Raking up such memories.

EPO OYINBO I'm starving!

JIGI And him? Has he eaten more in the last three days than the groundnuts we scavenged from that poor woman?

OMELE (*bitterly*) A prank! I wanted to help! It was my hometown, wasn't it? Where I was born and raised! How could I have known that the place had changed so much? How? That was my mistake . . .

EPO OYINBO Which almost killed us! A mistake!

OMELE Charity! That was the creed we were all raised on, and the whole village practiced it! Not even a stranger passed by without finding a roof, or a warm bed. They taught us to always give, freely, like Mother Nature. They said God owned everything, and that every man was a creature of God. Created in his image! So, how was I to know that in just five years, five years since I left, all that would have changed? How could I have foreseen it, that a day would come when these same people, my own people, would see men in torment, and drive them back into the wind?

JIGI   And how they drove us! Omele ran like a squirrel, when the hunters suddenly emerged behind us!

SINSIN   And you! You didn't run?

JIGI   I was the first to turn, I admit it! And then I saw Epo Oyinbo zooming past, with his scattered legs . . .

EPO OYINBO   Who? Whose legs are scattered? (*Jigi flees, laughing.*)

JIGI   (*to Omele*)   Don't blame your people, my dear. In those days you talk of, there was a different God in this land. The locusts had not come to power. The priests of austerity, drought, and perennial shortages. The greedy men with their gleaming teeth, calling themselves politicians . . .

EPO OYINBO   But is this the time for sermons! What's wrong with all of you? I'm starving!

OMELE   If only you'll be patient! I told you . . .

REDIO   Tell us, Omele! Tell us again! If there's no food, why have you brought us here?

OMELE   There'll be food. But Oga Redio, you all agreed to follow me, remember, because no one else had a better idea?

EPO OYINBO   What! I suggested the bridge! We would have found shelter at least under it, instead of having to roam around like this, like beggars!

JIGI   That would have been all right for you! No doubt. You would have been quite comfortable. They're your type, the scum who live under the bridge. You would have been comfortable with them!

EPO OYINBO   You'd better watch your tongue, Jigi!

SINSIN   I suggested the market. The stalls are warm and empty in the night.

OMELE   Empty? Where do all the roaming lunatics go to roost at sundown?

JIGI   And the soldiers on patrol! Who wants to wake up with a gun pointing down her throat?

SINSIN   Oga Redio suggested the beach! We could have stayed there with the aladuras.[2]

OMELE   And feed on what, Sinsin? On sand and salt water?

SINSIN   On fish!

JIGI   But we went through all these arguments before! We all agreed Omele's idea was the best.

EPO OYINBO   Yes! But did he say it would be a barren crossroads?

OMELE   It isn't a barren crossroads, Epo Oyinbo! Has any of you never heard of Sepeteri?

SINSIN   Sepeteri?

2. Members of a Christian evangelical sect.

REDIO   What is Sepeteri?

EPO OYINBO   It rings a bell, let me see . . . (*shouts in alarm*) Yeeh-pa! Sepeteri! Is that where we are?

OMELE   Yes. This is the crossroads of Sepeteri.

EPO OYINBO   Sepeteri! My friends, let's go quickly! Let's go!

SINSIN   Why?

EPO OYINBO   You're strangers here, to the legends of the land. You don't know where he's brought you, this crazy man. But just follow me quickly out of . . .

REDIO   Wait. Let him explain to us.

EPO OYINBO   No, not here! Later! Please heed my advice!

REDIO   (*laughing*)   This is getting intriguing. To see you trembling, Epo Oyinbo! You, who used to laugh at death as you turned somersaults on the dashboard of lorries, before I brought you into the band! So something can turn you into a woman!

EPO OYINBO   You don't understand! You don't understand at all, Oga Redio! This place . . . Sepeteri! This is the home of Esu himself! Esu, the dreaded god of mischief, this is his homing ground! We are standing on his head! (*Jigi and Sinsin scream in alarm.*)

REDIO   Indeed! Calm yourself . . .

EPO OYINBO   I swear it to you! Tales are told of . . . of people going mad here! Suddenly losing their senses and beginning to bark! Like dogs dying of rabies! Of men suddenly transfixed and having to be carried stiff to the home of herbalists! And of course they never recover to recount their experience! Or of women turning into screaming monsters! Of . . .

OMELE   Calm yourself, Epo Oyinbo. I know these stories too.

EPO OYINBO   So why did you bring us here? And at this time of night?

OMELE   It's already morning as you can see. You heard the cocks crow.

EPO OYINBO   What does that matter? Is there any time of day or night when it is safe to share Esu's bed?

OMELE   We're not sharing his bed. We're only going to share his food.

EPO OYINBO   Soponna[3] O! What did you say?

JIGI   Can you explain to us, Omele? Now, I'm getting frightened.

SINSIN   And I! What's this about Esu and his food?

OMELE   Those stories, my friends, they are for children. Or those with the brains of kids. But it's all going to be a boon for us, as you'll see.

REDIO   I'm not afraid of Esu. I know he can be kind too to those he favors. But what precisely is this story about sharing his food?

OMELE   I'll explain. This place . . . this crossroads, I used to live here. After I left the village, they brought me here, to train as a mechanic. My master's workshop was over there, by that tree. So I saw a lot of things, here. People used to bring a lot of food and leave it at this crossroads.

SINSIN   Why? What for?

OMELE   As offering to Esu. From those looking for children, or for

---

3. In Yoruba mythology and religion, the "god" of smallpox.

riches, or for a long life. You see, Sepeteri is the last point between the town behind us and the sacred grove of Orunmila, over there. So Esu, the lord of Sepeteri, is regarded as a kind of intermediary, between men and their wishes, between destiny and fulfillment. If you wait, in a short while you will see. They will soon begin to arrive with their baskets and pots, to placate Esu. The whole place will be laden with food!

SINSIN   And then what happens?

OMELE   What else? The feasting will begin!

EPO OYINBO   Have I gone mad, or am I hearing you correctly, Omele? Are you telling us to steal food from a god?

OMELE   Steal! Is it stealing to eat food that will only go to rot, or at best will be devoured by stray dogs and goats?

EPO OYINBO   But . . . Omele, that's an abomination! Have you thought of the god himself, how he will take it? Or are you going to risk the wrath of Esu?

OMELE   With a full belly, yes! Go and sit down my friend. If your god does not object to vermin eating his food, why should he be angry that human beings, driven by hunger, feed themselves?

EPO OYINBO   You're mad! Completely insane! Your hunger has turned your head!

OMELE   Well, that is my plan anyway. And I am going to wait here for those baskets!

EPO OYINBO   Oga Redio, you've heard him. Let's go away and leave him alone to dare the anger of Esu if he wants to.

REDIO   Wait, Epo Oyinbo. Let's think about this.

EPO OYINBO   Wait? Think? You mean it's not obvious enough this crazy plan? Oga Redio! Sinsin! Jigi!

SINSIN   How do I know? How can I think on an empty stomach?

JIGI   I think I'll stay and eat. Yes, I'll eat first, and then repent afterward. The god will understand.

SINSIN   He definitely will. I'm sure he knows that we have no other choice. It's not our fault after all that we're jobless.

REDIO   I think I agree with you. At worst, we'll repay it all when we find work again.

EPO OYINBO   When, Oga Redio? Speak now, as our leader. The band has been proscribed. They said we played too much for the politicians. We were banned, and all our assets seized! So when do you think the new government will change its mind about us?

REDIO   Governments are not eternal. Someday there'll be another one, with its own ideas. But first, we must survive, which means we must eat. Who knows in fact, there may come a government tomorrow, headed by a fellow musician!

SINSIN   I like that! His Excellency, Commander of the Charmed Voices!

JIGI   Ah, to have a governor who will dance *bata* with me! On television!

OMELE   (*laughing too*)   Dreams, my friends! That will be the day! What do you think a government is? A musical jamboree?

SINSIN Hear him! Haven't we seen worse?

JIGI Better to have a musical jamboree than a dance of corpses!

SINSIN Yes! Better to have singers than slayers.

JIGI Better storytellers than treasury looters!

SINSIN Better leaders than murderers!

OMELE I'm sure you understand me. The leaders the people need must provide, not music, but food. Food!

JIGI Wrong, Omele. They need music too!

OMELE They do? So why are you complaining of hunger? You're the best singer in the band. You've got music. Eat it!

REDIO (*chuckling*) I like that! And it's her song too, you know!

JIGI What?

REDIO Your song! The one Omele wrote for you: "The Maiden and the Music Man"!

OMELE (*laughing*) Oh yes! How appropriate! (*He begins to sing the "Song of the Maiden and the Music Man." They all join, except for Epo Oyinbo, who turns his back in disgust.*)

THE SONG OF THE MAIDEN AND THE MUSIC MAN (I)

1. *And the Music Man, he said
"I've brought my band:
See, my songs are mellow!
I've cooked them well,
Put in your names like sugar-ah-ah
Oh, like sugar!"*

2. *But the broken girl, on her bed
Was crying, and
The tears poured down on her pillow:
"You sing so well,
But you don't see the hunger around,
Oh, the hunger!*

3. *"You've helped me, to shred
The magic wand
Of blind love, so adieu!
Lock the door well
As you go, Mister Singer-ah-ah
Oh, Mister Singer! . . ."*

> *Epo Oyinbo, unable to contain his anger, finally shouts them down.*

EPO OYINBO Just look at you! Look at you! Singing, at a time like this! (*But none of them seems affected by his anger.*)

REDIO (*merrily*) Ah Omele, that's a cruel song! No one told me anything like that in my youth! And now! I mean, how can an old man like me suddenly begin to change profession now?

OMELE We learned the trade our fathers taught us. And we learned it well. Pity, that the season turned bitter, and the leaders grew corrupt. We had to eat! And how those politicians sprayed when we sang for them!

JIGI They loved the sound of their names! My voice wrapped them in lovely fantasy!

SINSIN No one! No one could have known that times would change like this! That the feasting would end, the dancers would go to prison. And we, the singers, so many times decorated, would turn to vagabonds.

REDIO "Go back to the land!" "Go and farm!" Crows the government radio. But with hands like these, made for drumming? The hands that have felt the trembling skin of a drum, how can they condescend to hold a hoe? Is there no limit at all then to the vulgarity of the age?

JIGI (*laughing*) Ah, soldiers! You remember that one, that night at the police station . . . ? He came up to me . . . They'd just picked us up at the hotel . . . yes, I had just finished one of my numbers, and the audience was clapping, when . . . suddenly, soldiers everywhere . . . the stampede, ah! . . . so, at the station, where they took us, the man said to me—"Why don't you go and farm? Why waste your life away in the corruption of the city?"—That's what he called it, corruption! (*hisses*) Well, I told him. I said, "Soldier, what do you mean? How can I go and farm, when I myself, I am a farm already?" He was puzzled by that. You should see his face. "I beg your pardon?" he asked. "You don't understand? No? Well, it's like this . . . the man brings his shovel where I am lying. He digs. Yes, he digs! And I respond, like this! (*makes a suggestive movement with her buttocks*) Soldier, don't turn away. Let me tell you . . . how the seeds pour in!" (*They all laugh, except for Epo Oyinbo, who has been looking around furtively.*)

EPO OYINBO God! God! To see all of you laughing like this, with all the problems on our hands! I'm going! I won't . . .

> At that moment, from offstage, comes the sound of a bell, followed by incantations. The actors freeze.

SINSIN What . . . is that?

OMELE (*in whispers*) A bell . . . shhh, listen! (*The bell and the voice of incantations become more audible, approaching.*)

EPO OYINBO You see! It's beginning!

OMELE (*taking command*) Okay, quick! Let's hide! I think they're beginning to come! (*They scramble for cover behind the stones. Enter a priest, in a white loincloth, ringing a bell, holding a pot in his other hand. He puts down the pot at the center of the crossroads, kneels briefly, chanting. Then he rises and exits. As soon as he goes, the musicians rush out to the pot—then recoil, in disgust.*)

REDIO Omele . . . what's this?

OMELE (*baffled*) I . . . I don't know . . .

EPO OYINBO You see? You see now?

REDIO   You goat! You accursed animal! This is what you call food!

SINSIN   Cow dung! What an insult! (*Omele carries the pot and throws it away.*)

JIGI   Leave him. Let's not be so hasty. That was only the first man to come after all . . . let's wait . . .

OMELE   I don't understand . . . I just don't understand . . . (*Esu and his followers laugh out suddenly, briefly.*)

SINSIN (*cowering*)   What's that?

REDIO   I'm beginning to hate it all, you know. The whole bloody setup! Let's listen again. (*They listen. But now it is the voice of women, chanting, from offstage. Omele signals again, hurriedly, and the musicians scramble for cover as before. Now some women enter, with baskets. They put the baskets down at the center of the crossroads and go out again, chanting. The musicians come out to look, cautiously now, and apprehensive, and are again disappointed.*)

REDIO (*angry*)   I can't believe it! This is obviously a rubbish dump! Rubbish, Omele! You've been playing tricks with us!

SINSIN   Oh, my stomach! My stomach!

OMELE   But I don't understand! They'll not dare . . . Things could not have got as bad as that! They can't bring rubbish to Esu!

REDIO   No, it's food! Food! Eat it! Eat! (*He plunges Omele's face into the basket. When Omele stands up, he is covered in sawdust. Jigi comes to help him brush it off.*)

SINSIN   Let's go, *jare!* I've had enough of this!

EPO OYINBO   If only you'd listened to me! (*He kicks the basket away savagely into the bush.*)

JIGI (*quick to defend Omele*)   Quiet! Are you any better? Were you not expecting food too? All you said was that we should not eat it, not that it would be sawdust!

REDIO   Let's go! Let's leave this place at once! (*They try, but find they cannot move.*)

SINSIN   What . . . what's happening?

EPO OYINBO   I . . . I can't move! My legs are stuck!

JIGI   And me too! As if there's a clamp on my feet!

REDIO   We're stuck! Stuck!

OMELE   What's happening? It's not possible!

REDIO   Go on, move then!

OMELE   I can't! My legs, they're . . .

EPO OYINBO   I warned you, didn't I? I warned you, but no one would listen to me!

REDIO   Omele, do something! You brought us here!

OMELE   I don't know what to do!

SINSIN   We're lost! We're going to die here!

JIGI   Omele, you must remember! What the men used to do when they came here. You must have seen them from your workshop.

OMELE   I can't remember . . .

JIGI   Think! There must be something!

OMELE   Maybe . . . ? A song! Yes, a song! There's a song that every one of them sings when he come here.

REDIO   A song!

JIGI   How does it go? Maybe we can sing it?

OMELE   It's Esu's song of supplication. You know it. One of those we sang before. Maybe if we try it?

> *They begin to sing "Esu's Theme Song." Slowly, as they sing, hooded figures begin around the signboard to come alive and the static figure of the signboard begins to shake, till a man gradually emerges from it in a cloud of smoke and fire. It is an old man, and the now animated figures gather round him, singing too. There is a brief dance round the Old Man, although the musicians, stunned, have stopped singing, to watch in fascination.*

ESU'S THEME SONG

Esu O, Esu O!	*Esu O, Esu O!*
Esu O, Laaroye	*Esu O, Laaroye*
Se oun gbo'gbe, baba?	*Father, please hear our prayers,*
Araiye de'ri wa mo konga	*We've been pushed down the well of despair;*
A o ti se ka yo o?	*We long to surface again;*
Awa ti de gboin gboin	*We have our backs pinned to the wall;*
Dede'eni kongun, baba o!	*Completely lost and undone!*
Eranko o inu iboji	*The mighty beasts, who rule the jungles,*
Won ra ma ko s'omi lo o?	*How can they drown at sea?*
Akere e—ema ik'osa	*Will the crab leave his home in rivers*
Ko poun k'ori b'oko?	*And then take to the bush?*
Gbawa o, we de sim'edo,	*We call you, and crave your pity*
Ko gbo t'eni o!	*Please do not shun our prayers!*

The Old Man stops the song abruptly.

OLD MAN (*stern*)
> The Owner of the World
> Has created balance between the forces of Good
> And those of Evil. He appointed Esu
> To watch over them, and I am his priest.
> But everywhere, Evil is in the ascendant!
> My ears fill daily
> With the woes of the afflicted.
> Speak! Tell me your wishes, you who would eat
> The Offerings of Esu!

Epo Oyinbo runs forward and prostrates.

EPO OYINBO   I warned them, sir! They would not listen! I told them it was sacrilege!

JIGI   We were hungry. Please, forgive us. We do not normally live by stealing.

OMELE   The times are desperate. We've not eaten for days. It was I who brought them here. If there's to be any punishment, let it be mine alone.

OLD MAN
    Those are fine words, such as
    I seldom hear from human beings.
    But I know you:
    You used to eat in abundance, yes!
    At the feasts of the wealthy, once,
    You sang the praise-songs,
    While their victims perished at the door.

SINSIN   We were earning a living, like everyone else! Sir, we did not make the laws, we only tried to live by them.

OLD MAN
    You learned to live
    Like pests. Feeding on other pests.

OMELE   We did, but we have paid dearly for it. Look at the condition we are now in! Pity us!

REDIO   Old Man, we've come to the end of the road. And it looks like you can help us, as a priest of the gods.

OLD MAN
    Esu loves to help men, but only
    When they show that they can live
    Happily among other human beings.
    For human beings are greedy . . .

JIGI   Help us, servant of the King of the Crossroads! We've learned our lesson!

OLD MAN
    Esu does not see into the hearts of men,
    Only their actions.
    Are you ready
    To help those among you, who are in distress?
    To bring redress to the wronged?
    And justice to the exploited?

ALL   Yes! Yes! We're ready!

OLD MAN   If you are, I can change your lives! I can make you really prosperous again!

ALL   We are! Priest of the Crossroads! Help us!

Again, they begin Esu's theme song, the "Song of Supplication."

OLD MAN
    That is enough. Songs alone
    Do not prove a man's sincerity.
    But I am going to give you a chance
    To help yourselves. Come forward.

The retinue begin a soft chant and dance.

I am going to give you a power
That can raise you from dust
Onto a throne of gold! But, careful!
If you misuse it, you'll be punished
Heavily! It's a power, and it's also a test.
Take these seeds, one for each of you.
Eat it. Swallow it. Done?
Now, let each one find a suffering man,
Someone unhappy, and sing to him.
Sing to him your favorite song,
And make him dance with you. That's all.

He sees their puzzled looks and smiles.

As you sing and dance, whatever his pain,
Whatever his suffering, it will end!
If he is thirsty, he will be satisfied.
If crippled, he will walk. Whatever
His agony, your song will relieve it,
Your dance will bear it all away.
Are you listening to me? Sing and dance,
Let the suffering man heal, and
Afterward, ask for anything.
Anything you wish! His gratitude
Will make you rich, or make you poor.
It depends on what you ask. Find a man
This morning, and by evening
You become a millionaire,
Or return to the gutter!
So, now it depends on you. Choose your targets
Carefully, according to your personal wishes
Choose those truly capable of gratitude.
And you will be well repaid!
As for me, I'll be back here tomorrow
To see the result. And whatever you have
Won, Esu will double it for you!
You hear? Esu will multiply by two,
Whatever you have used the power to acquire!
But if you have gained nothing,
If you have misused the power,
Chosen the wrong targets, I promise,
You will be severely punished.
So I leave now. You have all eaten
The seed of wishes. Good luck to you.

The Old Man leaves, with his retinue chanting and dancing.

SINSIN (*after a while*) A song and a dance! Do you think it will work?
OMELE We'll soon find out, won't we?
EPO OYINBO Hm, Esu, god of mischief! I don't trust him! Or his priest!
JIGI But he's also a god of justice, remember? And a friend to Orun-

mila.[4] On the tray of divination, he takes a forward place. I don't think he'll deceive us more than we deceive ourselves.

OMELE   You're right. Esu is not destiny, only the way to it. He is like a loom in the market of fate. But we each hold the shuttle, free to swing it the way we like.

SINSIN   Anyway I've eaten the charm, and I am ready to sing! Strange how my belly no longer feels the pang of hunger!

REDIO   And mine too! I feel heavy with hope. I know I shall choose the right person.

EPO OYINBO   Well, how do we begin? Shall we go and look for them?

OMELE   No. I think this is a good place to wait.

SINSIN   You think so?

OMELE   Look at it. A crossroads! One way to the market, there. This one to town. And that to the stream, and beyond, to the sacred grove. Think of it. Anyone in trouble must pass by here.

JIGI   Yes! Besides, this is the shrine of Esu, isn't it? This is where you say all those invalids come with their offerings?

REDIO   You're right. We'll wait wait here.

SINSIN   Ah, let them come quickly! I'm dying to be rich!

JIGI   Fortune, please smile on us today! (*They spread out, relaxing, and sing the rest of the "Song of the Maiden and Music Man."*)

THE SONG OF THE MAIDEN AND THE MUSIC MAN (II)

4. *As the man turned, she shouted*
   with command:
   "Listen, Singer, to the willow:
   The trees can tell
   How winds wake to anger-ah-ah
   Oh, to anger!

5. *"And the waters have repeated*
   On the sea-sand,
   On the ocean breeze and the billow:
   They all can tell
   That wars breed on hunger-ah-ah
   Oh, on hunger!

6. *"And the voices of the wretched*
   Of the land,
   While your songs are so mellow,
   They speak of hell,
   And they scream of danger ahead,
   Oh, of danger!"

   The lights fade slowly here, to indicate the passage of time. End of Overture.

---

4. In the Yoruba orisa religion, the god of wisdom and divination, patron of healers and diviners.

Three: Opium

*Same situation. A few moments after the last scene. The musi-
cians are apparently sleeping, as a man, middle-aged, enters carrying a basket of fruits. The man looks around carefully, does not
see the musicians apparently, and then goes to put down his load
at the center of the crossroads. He kneels to pray. The musicians
stir and stand up at the sound of his voice. Mistaking them for
armed robbers, however, the praying man leaps up, his hands in
the air.*

MAN   Please! Please, spare me! I'll give you anything you want! Anything!

SINSIN   What's the matter with him?

MAN   (*falling on his knees piteously*)   Sir . . . Madam . . . I beg you!
In the name of Orunmila! Spare my life!

REDIO   Stand up my friend! We've not come to harm you.

JIGI   You see, Epo Oyinbo? You see how your evil face scares honest
people!

EPO OYINBO   Nonsense! Oga, don't be afraid. We've come to help you.

MAN   (*uncertain*)   To . . . help me?

REDIO   Yes. We're musicians, as you can see. We're not robbers.

MAN   (*still unconvinced*)   Yes, yes . . .

JIGI   Put your hands down. And tell us your problems. Maybe we can
help.

MAN   (*putting his arms down, but scornful*)   You! You can help?

SINSIN   Yes. Why not try us?

MAN   Thanks. I thank you all. But . . . my problems, you see . . . No
one can help. Except the gods! No one on earth can help! Especially
not musicians, if you don't mind my saying so . . .

OMELE   You may be right, but I'll advise you to try us first. We may
not look like much, but we do have the power to help those in need.
There's no harm in trying.

MAN   I have been to . . . how many herbalists! I've been to doctors all
over the world. All of them made me try one thing or the other.
Even prayer houses, how many! But all in vain, my friends! My
manhood won't come back!

SINSIN   (*laughing*)   So that's it!

MAN   Yes, laugh, dear lady! That's how they've been laughing at me
for five years! My manhood! I've lost it and become a husk, an empty
husk! (*sobbing*) Ah, the shame of it! I can't even get it up anymore!
I'm only an empty, walking shell!

OMELE   Calm yourself, mister. We can help you, I'm sure.

MAN   You can't imagine how bad it is! To have so much wealth but
not to . . .

EPO OYINBO   Eh, repeat that. You are wealthy?

MAN   Yes, alas! Perhaps more than wealthy. Houses! Cars! A private
jet! What don't I have? I've bought them all. But all for what, I ask

you? (*sobbing again*) For whom? I cannot father children to inherit them. My life's a waste!

EPO OYINBO   I will help you! Now! Come with me!

SINSIN (*with others*)   What! Why you? Who says I myself, I don't . . .

EPO OYINBO (*turning on them*)   Now, no interference from any of you! This one is my own. I saw him first!

JIGI   But we all saw him together!

EPO OYINBO   Well, I am the first to volunteer to help! And he's mine!

SINSIN   Nonsense! You have no right to claim him!

EPO OYINBO   Are you going to fight me then? Come on! We can decide it that way, if that's what you want. (*Takes out a knife. The women flee, screaming, toward Redio, who also backs away.*)

REDIO (*finally*)   Shut up! Shut up all of you! And put that knife away. I'll decide.

SINSIN   Yes, good! Let the band leader decide.

REDIO   There's no need for us to begin to quarrel like this. The day is still young, and this is only the first man to come along. Who knows, the day may still bring richer prizes! Let each wait his turn then! Okay? (*sees the knife again*) Right, Epo Oyinbo, since you want this one, go ahead. He's all yours.

MAN   Wait a minute! What do you mean, I'm all his? Am I some meat to be shared . . . ?

EPO OYINBO   My dear man, all it means is that your troubles are over! I can cure you of your impotence!

MAN   Look, look, swear you're not joking! You really can?

EPO OYINBO   Yes, I can. But what are you ready to offer?

MAN   Everything! I'll give anything to be cured of this disgrace! Anything!

EPO OYINBO   Talk, man! "Anything" is not definite enough!

MAN   What do you want? Houses? Lands? Take them all! You'll be one of the wealthiest men in the land!

EPO OYINBO (*exultant*)   You hear, all of you? All his property! (*hesitates*) But how do I know I can trust you?

MAN   Take, here's my ring! Gold, all of it! Just rid me of this shame, and I'll show you who I am! Please!

EPO OYINBO   You are cured! You'll be fit and prancing again, like a festive drumstick! Just sing with me!

MAN (*disappointed*)   Sing! At a moment like this!

EPO OYINBO   Sing! And dance!

MAN   Can't we do all that afterward? I mean, I don't see why I should begin to celebrate before I can . . .

EPO OYINBO   You're wasting your own time, my friend. This is no celebration. It is the cure itself. Join me! (*He begins to sing. The others first refuse to join him. He begs them.*)

REDIO   Let your knife sing with you!

> But finally they yield to his entreaties and sing "Let the Snake Rise."

LET THE SNAKE RISE *(led by Epo Oyinbo)*

1. Eyin ero, mo fe korin
   —Yes, a ngbo, Epo Oyinbo!

1. Listen to me, I have a song
   —Yes, sing your song, Epo
   Oyinbo!

2. Mo fe korin, mo fe sure
   —A ngbo, Epo Oyinbo,
   Sise sise o ni talakose

2. I have a song, I have a prayer
   —Sing your song, Epo Oyinbo,
   May your prayers, may they
   come true

3. E ba mi gbe, eyin ore mi

3. I need your help, sing along
   with me

—A mo e, Epo Oyinbo
   Orin aladun ni tire

—Start your song, Epo Oyinbo,
   We are willing to sing along.

4. Eni iowo iowo
   ti o bimo o
   O ti gbe s'aiye.
   Ka sise sise
   Ka si romo fun logun
   B'ogede ba ku,
   soun fomo ropo ni,
   Ile o to,
   Aso o p'eniyan
   L'ojo ale,
   Omo nikan lo le sin ni!

4. Any man of wealth
   Who has no children
   Wastes his life on earth,
   May we have a son
   To inherit everything,
   Like the banana
   Whose tree dies to be reborn;
   When the clothing
   And the money have gone
   With our dust,
   Children will prolong our
   name!

5. E ma pe ko se—Ase!
   Igi wa a ruwe—Ase!
   Igi wa a ruwe—"
   Konga wa a ponmi—"
   ojola a dide—"
   A dide a s'ogbe—"
   Ekun iya aburo—"
   Ekun omo a so—"
   Layo n'igbehin orin—"

5. Say after me: Amen!—Amen!
   Say after me: Amen!—Amen!
   Our trees will be green—"
   Our wells fill to brim—"
   And the snake will rise—"
   Snake will rise and strike—"
   Then a mother's cries—"
   Welcome, new baby!—"
   May sweetness end our song—"

> As they sing, the Old Man's retinue, apparently unseen by the minstrels and the Impotent Man, return to dance along. They gradually involve the Impotent Man in a kind of ritual and then dance away. As soon as they disappear, the man, as if awakening from a trance, shouts out in surprise.

MAN   Soponna O! By God, it's working! I'm coming alive!
SINSIN *(laughing)*   Look! It's working!
MAN *(We now see a bulge under his cloth. The man runs after Sinsin, who flees, then after Jigi. Finally he grasps Epo Oyinbo.)*   My friend! Your name is Epo Oyinbo, isn't it? Your fortune is made, you hear

me! I have to hurry away now, you understand? It's five years, and I just have to be sure! Excuse me, I'll be back! (*He rushes out. Epo Oyinbo, recovering from his laughter, makes as if to follow him.*)

OMELE   No, let him go. He'll be back.

EPO OYINBO   You think so?

SINSIN   You have his ring.

EPO OYINBO   Yes, a golden ring! Am I not lucky!

SINSIN   It's going to be my turn next, Oga Redio! I insist!

REDIO   All right, you can have the next person. Meanwhile, as for me . . . (*He moves to the basket abandoned by the Impotent Man, takes out fruits, and begins to eat. The others join him. They eat, humming their theme song. Soon, a new sound is heard. A woman, wailing. They hastily drag the basket to one side and hide. A woman, heavily pregnant, but half-nude, her hair disheveled, enters. She looks truly wretched, and carries a small earthen pot, crying. She kneels with great difficulty and begins to pray.*)

WOMAN   (*through her sobs*)   Onile Orita! Esu, god of the crossroads! I have been bearing this burden now for nine years! Nine years with this stone inside me! It won't let me stand, it won't let me sit! I can't even lie down, it's all pain, pain, pain! What have I done? Which god have I offended? Priests, herbalists, doctors, I've seen them all! I've undergone, oh, how many operations! Various men have opened me up! All kinds of fingers have probed inside me! Why? Why don't you let me die and forget it all! Orisa, why not kill me! . . . (*As she prays, the musicians are discussing at the other side of the stage.*)

OMELE   A truly pathetic case!

REDIO   Well, here you are, Sinsin. Here's your chance.

SINSIN   No, I don't want it!

REDIO   What? I beg your pardon?

SINSIN   It's a trick, and I won't have it!

JIGI   But you yourself insisted, just now!

SINSIN   So what? Why don't you take her yourself? Just look at the woman. Look at her condition! What kind of reward do you think this one will be able to offer?

OMELE   Sinsin!

EPO OYINBO   She's right! Can't you see? The woman looks really wretched. She can't have anything. Let her go.

OMELE   I'll help her then!

SINSIN   Don't be a fool, Omele!

OMELE   We can't let her go like this! Look at her! She's in torment.

JIGI   Listen to me, Omele. I know how you feel about the woman. I am a woman myself, and I should be the first to step forward. But remember, it's the only chance we have, this song, to make something of our lives at last, to cease our wandering in the slums of the world, give reality at last—Oh God—to our dreams . . .

OMELE   I know, Jigi. Thank you for caring. But money is not the only road to happiness. I cannot let her go like this.

REDIO   Omele, maybe I should stop you. After all, I trained you, made you into the accomplished musician that you are. I am also responsible for your future. I won't be happy to be rich, while you take the wrong turning at this crucial crossroads, and walk back to wretchedness . . .

OMELE   Thank you, sir. Now step back. (*Redio is offended.*) I'll carry my own future in my hands. (*calls*) Woman! Wipe your tears, I'll help you!

WOMAN (*startled, seeing them*)   Sir? . . . I beg your pardon, sir?

OMELE   Orisa has listened to your prayers. I'll help you out of your pain.

WOMAN   Sir . . . whoever you are, let me beg you, sir, not to make a jest of me. I'm a poor woman, you can see. Since I've been carrying this curse around, I've lost everything! Everybody has run away from me! My friends, my relations, and my husband! My relatives were the first to stop calling. And then my husband went across the threshold one day and has never returned! Sir . . . you say you can help me?

OMELE   Yes, I can. Trust me.

WOMAN   This baby, my first pregnancy . . . but it has stayed inside me for nine years! Nine years! And you mean, sir . . . you mean you can . . . can . . .

OMELE   Yes, I mean it, poor woman. Stand up.

WOMAN   Oh God, I dare not! I'm afraid! No, I must not dare to hope . . . Sir . . . Sir, perhaps you do not understand. I have nothing. I won't be able to pay you!

OMELE (*helping her up*)   Will you be able, at least, to say "thank you"?

WOMAN   I'll crawl at your feet! I'll be your slave forever!

OMELE   A small "thank you," that's all I'll need. Now are you ready?

WOMAN   Oh God! Oh God! I don't know how to answer! Will it hurt very much?

OMELE   It may be hard a little. You have to dance.

WOMAN   Dance?

OMELE   Yes, I'm afraid. I'll be singing, with my friends.

WOMAN   Is that all I have to do?

OMELE   Yes. Will you try?

WOMAN   Try, sir? Ask me to jump! To run over to the stream and back! What's all that compared to the relief that's coming! To be able to bring this baby to the world at last, and rest . . .

OMELE   All right then, let us begin.

> *He begins to sing, his friends accompanying him, at first reluctantly, then enthusiastically. The chorus of Esu followers appear, as usual, as Omele leads the woman in a slow dance.*

THE CHILD INSIDE IS CALLING (*led by Omele*)

1. *Ba mi se o, Yeye Osun*
 Jowo gbo temi, Yeye Osun
 —*Jowo ba mi se o, Yeye Osun*
 Dakun gbo temi, Yeye Osun.

2. *Ebe la be e o, Yeye Osun*
   Dakun gbo temi, Yeye Osun.
   —Jowo ba mi se o, Yeye Osun
   Dakun gbo temi, Yeye Osun.

3. *Oh please hear my cry, Yeye Osun*
   Don't abandon me, Yeye Osun
   —Will you hear my cry, Yeye Osun
   Don't abandon me, Yeye Osun.

4. *Fill me with your love, Yeye Osun*
   Fold me in your arms, Yeye Osun
   —Will you hear my cry, Yeye Osun
   Don't abandon me, Yeye Osun.

5. *Iwo lo l'oyun, to tun l'omo*
   Iwo lo l'ekun abiyamo
   Iwo lo l'erin yeye omo
   —Fill me with your love, Yeye Osun
   Fold me in your arms, Yeye Osun.

6. *Iwo lo ni wa, ki la le se?*
   Yeye ma ni t'atare
   Pupo pupoo l'omi okun
   Dakun ba mi se o, Yeye Osun
   —Fill me with your love, Yeye Osun
   Fold me in your arms, Yeye Osun.

7. *Eni gb'omo pon lo le so'tan*
   Iwo to l'oyun, iwo la pe
   Dakun wa gb'ohun abiyamo o
   K'oloyun s'amodun o tomotomo
   —Fill me with your love, Yeye Osun
   Fold me in your arms, Yeye.

   The woman collapses suddenly.

WOMAN   He-e-elp! (*The chorus of Esu followers dance hastily off.*)
OMELE (*anxious*)   What? What is it?
WOMAN   The baby! I can feel it! It's moving!
JIGI   It's working again! The power works!
OMELE   Come on, let's sing harder! (*They sing. The woman rises, painfully.*)
WOMAN   My dear sir, I must be going now . . . I think I have to find a midwife quickly—it's my first time, you see, and I don't want to make a mess before you . . . I shall return, you'll see, with the baby! We'll come to thank you . . . But, just in case it takes a while—for it's my first time, you see, and I don't know how long I'll be down —just in case I don't come back by tomorrow, sir, please come around, if you can do us the honor. My house is not hard to find. It's the only one opposite the market, with a half-fallen roof. And everybody knows the house of Mama Oloyun, the Ever-pregnant

Woman . . . I'm talking too much, I'm so excited. I'm going to be the first mother of the season! (*pausing as she goes*) Can I beg you sir, for a token? Something to hang on the child when he comes? . . .

OMELE   Oh yes, of course! Here's my chain, take it!

WOMAN (*going*)   Thank you sir. Thank you all! Until tomorrow!

OMELE (*watching her go*)   What a woman! What a woman!

SINSIN   Omele! Even your chain into the bargain!

OMELE   She was so happy! I wish I could be there, when the baby comes!

SINSIN   You're just a fool, that's all! Who's stopping you from following her?

EPO OYINBO   Since you've so stubbornly gone ahead and blown your chance, I hope you're not depending on me to help you in the future! You won't get anything! I will not share a kobo[5] of the fortune coming to me! Everyone must reap his own harvest.

REDIO   Of course, he knows that. He pushed me back! Me! Nobody here is going to bail him out when the time comes!

OMELE   I accept. I won't complain.

JIGI   Poor Omele.

REDIO   Well, two gone, three more to go! Who'll be next now?

SINSIN   What do you mean, Oga Redio? You know of course that I'm next!

REDIO   No, I think I'll go next, or ask Jigi. You lost your chance.

SINSIN   No! No! It's me, I insist. (*beginning to wail*) It's me next!

REDIO   Come on, don't be childish . . .

JIGI   Let her go next, Oga Redio. I can wait; I'm not in a hurry.

REDIO   Well, if you say so. But only because of you.

JIGI   Take the next man, Sinsin.

SINSIN   Of course, provided he's not a wretch like the last one!

JIGI (*smiling*)   Ah, Sinsin! Anyway, you're lucky! Look! The man coming looks like he owns the Central Bank! Take him, he's all yours!

> Enter a tall, richly dressed man, limping. He is also coughing badly at intervals. But his looks are fierce and arrogant.

MAN (*with difficulty*)   Good . . . day to you all!

SINSIN   Good day to you, sir.

MAN   Tell me . . . young lady . . . is this the way to Ife?

> Baffled, Sinsin turns to Omele, who nods.

SINSIN   Yes, sir. You're right.

MAN   And the hospital? Can you direct me to the hospital?

OMELE   He means the Specialist Hospital in the town. (*to the man*) Sorry sir, the hospital is closed.

MAN (*in alarm*)   Closed! Since when?

OMELE   For some months now. There was a riot there. Some policeman died, under treatment, and his colleagues came and stormed

---

5. Penny; idiomatic for "a cent's worth" of anything.

the place. So the doctors withdrew their services, pending an apology from the police. The place has been closed down since then, because the doctors won't work.

MAN   Oh, God! Oh, God!

OMELE   The government has ordered an inquiry, which is still going on. The hospital won't reopen till they submit their findings.

MAN (*hoarsely*)   And when will that be?

OMELE   Who knows? Maybe another couple of months . . .

MAN   Months! I'll be dead by then!

SINSIN   Dead!

MAN   Yes, alas! Look . . . (*He unbuttons his shirt. It is all splattered with blood. The musicians scream.*) It was fierce! Fierce! They must have pumped a hundred bullets inside me, the hounds! . . . But I still managed to escape, you see . . . thinking that if I got to the hospital here . . . They have a good reputation don't they, the doctors at the . . . ah, at the hospital . . . ? But now . . . (*He falls gradually, groaning.*)

JIGI   He's going to die! (*running to him*)

SINSIN (*pushing her back*)   No! He's mine, remember? I'll save him!

REDIO   That's all right, Sinsin, but first, who's he? Let's find that out first! This talk about fighting and bullets . . .

SINSIN   It doesn't matter. I'll save his life if he's rich.

MAN (*on his knees, battling bravely*)   Rich! What a joke! So . . . none of you . . . none of you knows me!

SINSIN   Talk quickly. Are you a rich man?

MAN (*laughing weakly*)   It . . . must be a joke! Fate is . . . is . . . playing pranks on me, in my dying moments! To think that . . . that there's a place in this land where I am unknown, and imbeciles . . . imbeciles ask whether I am rich!

The angry minstrels are held back by Sinsin.

SINSIN   So speak! Are you rich or not? Your life hangs on it!

MAN   Well . . . what does it matter anymore? Let me go like this then, unknown, among ignorant fools from some unknown planet. I have lived a life of fantasy, chasing adventures, daring death itself! I anchored my name to the winds, so that everywhere, whenever I touched down, I arrived like fear itself! Yes, when I found that men had made money their god, I conquered it! . . . You know how? With the blood of virgin children, the sperm of virile men, a pair of succulent breasts, such as yours . . . (*reaches toward Jigi, who slaps his hand*)

JIGI   Keep your hands off! I thought you were dying!

SINSIN   Sh! Let's hear him. Gently now . . .

MAN   . . . Yes, bye bye! (*regretfully, to Jigi*) Breasts like yours, they could have fetched a fortune! But no more! (*laughs weakly*) I've reaped more than my share of the commerce in human seeds! Ah, yes, I made gold my servant, built a palace of gems . . . so well, now . . . (*His voice is now very feeble.*) . . . no matter. Adieu, fools! My candle has burned out . . .

SINSIN   Wait! You say you built a palace of gems! I'll save you!

MAN   No, dear lady. It's too late.

OMELE   Sinsin, didn't you hear him? How he made money? (*She is not listening to him.*)

SINSIN   Try! All you have to do is sing, and you'll recover! Don't laugh!

MAN (*laughing*)   A miracle, eh? If anyone can save me now he can have all my wealth!

SINSIN   I won't forget that! Now, let's see you try. (*She goes to help him.*) Rise a little. Yes, hang on to me. That's it! Hang on! I'm going to sing now. And dance. No, don't shut your eyes yet! All you have to do is just sway along. No, Omele, don't help me, I'll manage. Don't give me your bad luck. Hang on, man, for God's sake! (*She begins to sing.*)

I SING TO END YOUR PAIN (*led by Sinsin*)

1. Sekere yeni ola
   Sekere yeni owo
   Oloomi o ba dide o jo sekere o

   Sekere yeni ola o

1. Sekere beats for the rich,
   Sekere sounds just for kings;
   My sweetheart, it's for you
        gourds are rattling,
   Celebrating your wealth!

2. Ikoko omo aiye le o
   Erupe ponmi oro—

   Olojo oni ma ma je Ka mu
        nibe o
   Ikoko omi oro o!

2. The pots of men can deceive;
   You drink from them at your
        risk;
   May bad luck not descend
        upon us
   When we drink with our
        friends!

3. Oro l'eiye ngbo
   Oro ase iye
   Eiyekeiye gberu l'orule o

   Oro l'eiye ngbo o

3. Bird of death in our sky;
   We dance to drive you away;
   You will not alight on our
        rooftop;
   Bird of death, fly away!

4. Arun l'orin nle lo o
   Aisan l'orin nle
   Ore mi tete jijo ajomole o

   Aisan l'orin nle lo!

4. I sing to end all your pain,
   My song commands your relief
   My friend, dance along with
        abandon,
   And that will cure your
        disease.

For a more dramatic effect, as discovered in the Ife production, Sinsin and her friends sing the English version first. At the end of it, the chorus of Esu followers do not disappear, but stand trembling like leaves, shaken by a silent laughter. The Wounded Man, who seems revived, rushes forward in joy toward Sinsin, only to collapse and die. There is general consternation. Wailing, Sinsin begins the Yoruba version of the song, like a dirge now, and the others gradually join in. The Esu chorus then dance *away, as the Wounded Man finally recovers, carries Sinsin up, and dances with her.*

MAN (*setting her down finally*)   Lady, what's your name?

SINSIN   They call me Sinsin.

MAN   Sinsin! You saved my life! You actually did!

SINSIN   Yes, and you remember your promise?

MAN   Of course, how could I forget! But we can settle all that to-morrow. Let me go and deal with those rascals first, or you may find you have nothing to receive! If I know them well, they'll be busy sharing my inheritance now among themselves! Let me go quickly! Tomorrow, let us meet here again!

SINSIN   Right, sir, but give me a token. Something to assure me you'll be back.

MAN   I'll be back! I never break my word! (*He sees that his path has been blocked by Epo Oyinbo with his knife out.*) All right, take this anyway. It's my necklace, and it's got my insignia on it in diamond. I'll see you tomorrow! (*He runs out.*)

SINSIN (*dancing*)   I made it! Dance with me! I made it! I'm going to be rich!

They crowd around her, hugging her happily. Then she starts the "Song of Rejoicing," which they pick up.

THE SONG OF REJOICING (*led by Sinsin*)

1. *E wa ba mi jo*
   Ke gberin
   E wa ba miyo
   Ke korin

2. *E wa ba mi jo*
   Ke korin
   E wa ba mi yo
   Ke gberin

3. *Mo royin nita*
   Mo riyo nita
   Keregbe mo fi bu lo le

   Solo: *Keregbe mo fi bu lo o-ee*

   Chorus: *Keregbe mo fi bu lo le!*

1. *Come and dance my friends*
   Sing my song
   Let your voices ring
   Like a bell

2. *Stand and dance, I say,*
   Sing my song
   Come rejoice with me,
   Ring my bell

3. *Where I found honey,*
   And discovered salt,
   I carried calabashes home.

   Solo: *I carried calabashes of them*

   Chorus: *I carried calabashes home*

Dancing lustily, they do not notice the three businessmen who enter, apparently in a hurry, until one of them coughs. Three different accents of local speech—e.g., Hausa, Yoruba, Igbo—are suggested for these strangers.

FIRST STRANGER   We're sorry to interrupt your celebration. But we need help urgently.

REDIO You need help! All three of you?

FIRST STRANGER Yes, all of us. We're searching for a man. And if we don't find him by sundown, we hope to find death.

JIGI Death! This is such a beautiful day!

SECOND STRANGER Not for us. A man has swindled us. And because of him, the new government has tied a noose around our throat.

THIRD STRANGER Don't bother them with our problem! Just go to the essentials.

FIRST STRANGER Has any of you seen a short, yellow man, with side whiskers and mustache? He has greyed a bit at the temples . . .

The Second Stranger takes a photograph around.

EPO OYINBO No, no man with such a description passed by. And we've been here all morning.

SECOND STRANGER Then all is lost, my friends! Lost!

THIRD STRANGER Let's not waste more time. Better death than public disgrace!

FIRST STRANGER Please, can you show us the way to the house of death?

OMELE Tell us first, what is the problem? We may be able to help.

SECOND STRANGER Thank you, but there's nothing you can do. The man we are searching for was our Manager.

THIRD STRANGER We own the Lagbaja Trading Company, you see!

EPO OYINBO (*whistling*) So you're the owners of LTC!

REDIO I'm sorry, Jigi, you'll have to wait. This is definitely going to be my case! (*Jigi tries to protest.*) Quiet! (*pushes her back*) Please go on.

FIRST STRANGER Six months ago, we were able to win the bid for an import license. To bring in two million bags of rice.

SINSIN Two million bags!

FIRST STRANGER A paltry number, my dear, considering what we paid out for the contract. And then our Manager vanished with the license! Can you believe that! No one has seen him since! Not even his family!

THIRD STRANGER Six months now! Six months since he disappeared! But we're probably boring them with our . . .

REDIO No, please, go on! I am interested!

SECOND STRANGER Well, the Manager disappeared. At that time, with the old government, it didn't seem to matter at all. They had all got their kickbacks and didn't care a hoot for rice. Even the Minister told us not to bother ourselves, to simply put in for another license. For fertilizers.

JIGI Indeed! Just like that!

FIRST STRANGER Yes, just like that. We did, and it was approved, through the same process.

THIRD STRANGER And then, the coup came, and with it, a new government! Go on with the story, make it brisk!

FIRST STRANGER And the soldiers have said—Produce the fertilizers, and the rice, or return the money!

SECOND STRANGER   Three hundred and fifty million!

FIRST STRANGER   Within seven days!

SECOND STRANGER   Or pay the price!

THIRD STRANGER   Friends, today is the seventh day!

FIRST STRANGER   And we haven't got the rice! Or the fertilizer!

SECOND STRANGER   Or the license!

THIRD STRANGER   And the Manager is still missing!

REDIO   Well, is that all?

FIRST STRANGER   Yes, except that our wives and children, they've been taken away, to detention . . .

SECOND STRANGER   Our passports have been seized . . .

THIRD STRANGER   Our property confiscated . . .

SECOND STRANGER   Our accounts frozen . . .

FIRST STRANGER   All our friends have fled . . .

SECOND STRANGER   All our mistresses . . .

THIRD STRANGER   And today is the seventh day!

REDIO   I can help you!

FIRST STRANGER   I beg your pardon?

REDIO   I can help you, I said.

SECOND STRANGER   You know where he is, the Manager?

FIRST STRANGER   You know about the license!

THIRD STRANGER   You have friends in the new government?

REDIO   No, no. I don't know where the Manager or the license is. And I know no one in the cabinet. But still, I can help. You can recover your license!

FIRST STRANGER   When?

THIRD STRANGER   How?

REDIO   You can have it back right now!

SECOND STRANGER   Impossible!

REDIO   And you won't believe it, merely by dancing!

THIRD STRANGER   Let's go. The man is mad.

SECOND STRANGER   He's mocking us, the devil!

THIRD STRANGER   Let's go. Quickly!

REDIO   I am the last chance you have. Today, as you said, is your final day. You can try me, or go on to find your death.

SINSIN   He's offering you life! Your whole life back! Will you refuse?

THIRD STRANGER   Can you imagine such frivolity, at a moment like this! To begin to . . . (*demonstrating a dance*)

FIRST STRANGER   Maybe, if he explains . . . ?

REDIO   And I must have your solid promise first. You'll have to offer me some reward if I succeed.

FIRST STRANGER   Oh that's no problem. Ask for anything you want.

SECOND STRANGER   Well, I suppose there's no harm in trying?

REDIO   What will you give me, if I save your honor and your life?

SECOND STRANGER   I have a newly built estate in Lagos. It has thirty-five flats. You can have it all.

FIRST STRANGER   I own the majority shares in the Magna Profit Bank. What does it yield now? Some few millions a year, after tax. I'll give it to you.

REDIO   An estate and a bank! What lovely prizes! Omele, you see what it means, not to be in haste, to use one's head (*to the Third Stranger*) And you, sir, I'm waiting! What are you going to give me?

THIRD STRANGER   Well, what do you want? I own the Imole Shipping Line. The biggest in the country, but I'm ready to forfeit it. Will you want that?

REDIO   It's not bad—for a start. From anybody else, that would be quite substantial, I confess. But from you, sir, come, that's rather miserly!

THIRD STRANGER   Okay, add the Wilson Associates. We sell furniture worth—er, how much now? Some millions a year. Take it, and tell us quickly how to recover the license!

REDIO   Don't worry, it will come straight into your pockets. I am going to sing now with my friends. As we sing, you will dance along with us. As best as you can. Okay? It's as simple as that. Now come on! (*He sings and dances, with the three strangers copying his footsteps rather badly, their looks showing great scepticism. The Esu chorus appear and join the dance.*)

NA MONEY RULE DE WORLD (*led by Redio*)

1. Awon eniyan lo wa saye
   Taye dun mo won lara
   Sebi eniyan lo ngbaye
   Taye ro fun won jare
   Oba Naira, Iwo la nsin o

   Ma kehin si'gba wa o
   Wa pese s'oja ta wa

2. Awon miran wa saye
   Won tosi lo ma ni
   Awon yen o je kogbon
   P'Owo, Oba osi ni

3. Iwo Esu lo wa saye
   Pelu ogun orin kiko
   O si ti seleri
   Lori esun ibi kibi
   Awon meta wonyi, daakun o

   Ma kehin si'gba won o
   Wa f'ere soja ta won

4. Awon ijoye lo nfole
   Laye oni, se mo yen!
   Tori eniyan o nilari
   Bi ko le jale o.

1. Some men we know today
   Belle dey sweet for dem
   Dem chop better so-tay
   Dem mouth na honey oh!
   God of Naira, we your
      worshipers
   Beg for your favors now
   Come to our stalls today!

2. Some others waste away
   Dem die in misery!
   Dem never learn at all
   Na money rule de world!

3. Esu, na you talk am
   Say song be medicine,
   You tell us make we dance
   And play for all disease;
   Dis three people, we dey beg
      you oh,
   Ask for your helping hand,
   Carry their problems away!

4. The chiefs na dem be thiefs
   Nowadays no be lie!
   For man wey be somebody
   He find money first to steal.

Tani o mo p'Owo lo laye
  Aje ni iranse re,
  Ofin ni!
  A si gbodo sa
  Ka bowo fun!

  Finally, touching his pockets, one of the three strangers exclaims.

FIRST STRANGER   I feel something! There's something in my pocket!
SECOND STRANGER   And me too!
THIRD STRANGER   And me!

  They reach frantically inside their pockets and bring out documents.

THIRD STRANGER   By God, it's . . .
STRANGERS   The LICENSE!!
FIRST STRANGER (*embracing them childishly*)   It's true! It's the license! The license! We're saved!
THIRD STRANGER   Yes! Hurry! We must beat the deadline! (*Redio runs to stop them.*)
REDIO   And what of me? How do we settle our bargain?
THIRD STRANGER (*in a hurry*)   Here, take my card. Call tomorrow in the office.
REDIO   A card, after all I did! Do you think . . .
FIRST STRANGER   Have my wristwatch, as a token for now.
REDIO   Now that's something!
SECOND STRANGER (*irritated*)   Have my lighter and cigarette case. Gold, both of them, and inscribed. Just show them at the gate!
THIRD STRANGER   He won't need to show anything. We ourselves will be back here, tomorrow. Then he'll see how we keep our promises! Meanwhile have this too, as a token. (*He gives him one of his coral beads.*) You say your name is . . . ?
REDIO   Redio! That's what they call me, sir.
FIRST STRANGER   Right, Radio, or Television. It doesn't matter. We'll see you tomorrow! (*They hurry off.*)
REDIO (*dancing*)   You see? You see! My friends, rejoice with me also! My fortune is made!
EPO OYINBO   Congratulations! The ball we shall have after this, you and me!
REDIO   You and who? Insult! With what's coming to me I can employ you as a houseboy!
EPO OYINBO   Me, houseboy! What of Sinsin then?
SINSIN   Sinsin's going to be a billionairess, you just watch! And if I hear any nonsense from you then . . . (*They laugh.*)
JIGI   Poor Omele. How bad you must feel!
OMELE   I won't be rich, I know. But perhaps . . . perhaps . . .
JIGI   Perhaps what?
OMELE   Perhaps I can be happy . . . ? I know I will be happy!
REDIO   Happy! What can be happy in: "Come here, boy! Have you swept the carpet this morning? The cars, you've washed them? And

madam's dirty clothes? Yes? You've bathed the kids? What of the
dog, have you taken it for a walk? And, God, all this dust on the
furniture! Why do you think I'm paying you all that money? As soon
as you take your pay tomorrow, you leave! You hear? You are sacked!
Pack your load and leave the boys' quarters! Don't ask me where
you're going, idiot! Go to hell if you wish! . . ." And so on! For you
know, don't you, that that is the only future waiting for you?

OMELE   Yes, but even amid it all, even as I pack my load, I'll remember
and say: "One woman came to me in great pain, and she left
smiling."

EPO OYINBO   I don't know why you even bother yourself with him, Oga
Redio. There's obviously a curse of poverty on his head!

SINSIN   Ah, tomorrow, when I collect! When I collect!

REDIO   Hey, wait! I'm going after them!

SINSIN   I beg your pardon? After who, Oga Redio?

REDIO   Those three businessmen.

SINSIN   Why? What's the need?

EPO OYINBO   They'll be here tomorrow and . . .

REDIO   Tomorrow! That's just it! I don't trust the words of the rich!

SINSIN   Well, there's nothing you can do about it now. You have to
wait at least till Jigi gets her own chance.

REDIO   Who says so? Does she need my mouth to sing her song?

OMELE   Ah, Oga Redio! Are you the one saying this!

REDIO   I've just thought of it. All this premature rejoicing! Suppose
the men fail to turn up?

EPO OYINBO   We have their tokens, don't we?

REDIO   I see! You have their tokens! Wait for me! (*He goes out.*)

SINSIN   What! After him, Epo Oyinbo! We can't abandon Jigi like this!

EPO OYINBO   Come with me, Omele! We'll force him back!

OMELE   You wait here, Jigi. Something's gone wrong with the old man.
But we'll not abandon you!

> *They run out after Redio, leaving Jigi alone on stage. She goes to
> wait for them, withdrawing to one side of the stage, so that her
> back is turned when the next man enters. The man looks around
> furtively, then tiptoes to the road sign. He stops when he finds a
> rope, which he picks up and tests. This could be his trouser belt.
> He makes a noose quickly, to string it on one arm of the road
> sign. Putting the noose round his neck, however, he finds the rope
> short, even when he jumps. He searches around desperately for
> something to stand on. At that moment Jigi turns, and sees him.*

JIGI   What are you doing!

MAN   Please . . . don't make a noise! Come and help me!

JIGI   Help you do what?

MAN   Please, it'll take maybe a few seconds of your time. But you must
help me! Just a brief ride . . . on your shoulder . . .

JIGI   Indeed. You think I don't know what you're trying to do!

MAN   Please! It's a matter of honor.

JIGI   I won't be an accomplice, sir!

MAN   Just a little ride, and then you can run from here!

JIGI   Hear him! My friend, I am a dancer, not a donkey!

MAN   I'll make it worth your while.

JIGI   Besides, how am I sure I can hold your weight?

MAN   You can, I assure you. I know about such things.

JIGI   You do!

MAN   Yes, . . . I was born into it, you see! I've ridden on shoulders more fragile and more gaunt than yours. I am . . . er . . . I was a prince, you see . . .

JIGI   (*laughing*)   Ah, Kabiyesi! Greetings, Your Majesty! But you'll have to find someone else to give you her shoulder!

MAN   (*stern*)   It's no laughing matter, young woman! I must kill myself before they get here!

JIGI   Who? Before who gets here? And why must you kill yourself?

MAN   Will you . . . promise? Promise me! Say you will help me, if I explain to you.

JIGI   But of course! That's what I've been trying to make you see! I can help you. But not to hang yourself! I can help save your life.

MAN   No! No! I don't want it! You'll have to promise to help me die. I cannot live in dishonor. The women will strip me naked, put hot ashes in my . . . hair . . .

JIGI   They adore you that much?

MAN   Listen. They will burn my hair with ashes. Then they will lead me in a disgraceful procession back to the town. Through the open streets, while they beat me with their pestles and cooking spoons, and mock my dangling manhood! I will be the butt of every filthy urchin on the street! After which they will chain me and sell me off at the border! Do you hear? Slavery! That's the fate pursuing me hotly down here! Do you want me to face it, or will you help me simply to die?

JIGI   But why? Why would your people want to treat a prince like this?

MAN   Barbaric, isn't it? A pagan custom. But no one in the town will listen to me! Not even the Christians and Muslims among us! When it comes to brutality, we are all united! We call it keeping our traditional customs! (*laughs bitterly*) But one day I said, no, no more! The past must end, so we can clear the way for the future! Why, other men elsewhere are sending astronauts to the moon! We too must march into the future! . . . So I seized the royal python, symbol of the whole decadence! I poured petrol on it! I set it on fire! And was I sorry for the poor thing, as it writhed to death! But, well, it died! Yes! The immortal serpent, whom they said could never die, I turned it into ashes.

JIGI   You mean you . . . you dared to . . .

MAN   I wanted to free my people, liberate them from superstition. Just think of it! A mere snake! How can it be the harbinger of harvest? Why should adults, balls in their pants, consent to dance for it year after year, in the stupid belief that the ritual will bring rain? That a python can exercise power on the spirits of the soil, make them nurture seeds into exuberant crops? I turned it to ashes! . . .

JIGI   And . . . what happened?

MAN   At the news . . . my father, at the news, died from shock! Yes!
Just fell back and died! Only the priest, the old priest, was strong.
He alone was stronger than me. He told the people: "He is Evil! He
is the scourge foretold in our prophecies! You must kill him!" And
you should see the people swaying to his words as he ranted!

JIGI   So what did you do? You ran?

MAN   Not then. I tried to buy time. I had to say something, fast. I
said—oh, I am ashamed to confess it. It was the only thing that
came to my mind. I promised them a miracle! Another superstition.
I told them the snake would resurrect, today!

JIGI   And they believed you?

MAN   All, except the old priest. He was not fooled. His bread was at
stake! But, well, my father was dead now, and I was already heir
apparent. There was little he could do. He had to wait, like others.
But he told them: "We'll see! If the day comes, and there is no
miracle, you know what to do! The Prince must be treated as a
carrier,[6] as is the custom!" So that's the story, young woman. The
day has come, with no miracle. I must die!

JIGI   Suppose I save you? Suppose the serpent resurrects?

MAN   It can't! That was only a ruse I thought up.

JIGI   But suppose it does? You become the king, don't you?

MAN   Yes, of course.

JIGI   And you'll have lands?

MAN   I'll give them up! Back to the people, to whom they originally
belonged!

JIGI   And jewels?

MAN   Thousands of them in the palace collection! We were once a
mining people, you see . . .

JIGI   What else will you inherit?

MAN   Lots of other things. But I am not interested. They were all
accumulated through exploitation.

JIGI   Will you give some of it to me?

MAN   Why? What for?

JIGI   Because I am poor, and I want to be rich. I want to change from
these rags into the best finery available! I want princes like you to
see me, and be filled with lust! I want you to smell my scented
breath, and swoon in the perfume of my mouth! I want to sing, and
dance, and I wish to see powerful monarchs grovel as they watch!
All the dreams that have followed me all my life, laughing at me,
because I was poor, and they could not be fulfilled! Prince, will you
give me your wealth, in exchange for your life?

MAN   Wealth, that is immaterial. You can have all you want. But how
will you give me back my life?

> *The other musicians return, holding on to an obviously displeased
> Redio.*

6. In rituals of cleansing or appeasement of divine powers, the person who "carries" the sacrificial objects to a sacred grove, the sea, or any other designated place.

JIGI I'll resurrect the serpent for you. Look at my friends here. We're all musicians, and we've got some magic from some passing old man, a priest. Believe me, it works! All I have to do is sing and dance, and your serpent will come back to life!

MAN No, I don't want the serpent back. It will mean that those superstitions have won!

JIGI Well, what then?

MAN Well . . . let me think . . . The priest, yes! The priest is leading the women down here! Without him, the rest are nothing. Kill him! Let him tumble and fall dead!

JIGI That's easily done then. As you wish! Just come forward and dance with me as I sing! Come, my friends, this is Jigi's chance to rise from the gutter! Sing with me!

They begin to sing and dance, accompanied by the unseen chorus of Esu's followers, as before.

MY BEADS ARE JINGLING *(led by Jigi)*

Ise aje o	Road of business
Ona toro f'erin	Opens wide for lions,
Ise owo	Road of money
Ona fere f'ejo	Narrows down for rabbits;
Bi o se o	If you walk it
Owuro re a ro	Pain will fill your morning,
Bi we se o	And if you don't
Ale ojo a le	Hardship for your evening;
Owo baba Orisa	Business, prime Orisa
Aje, oko okunrin	Money, husband of men!
E maa pe Jigi—Jigi Aro!	Announce my name—Jigi Aro!
E maa mi jigi—jigi ileke	And bend and ripple—to my rhythm
Ileke sa so—sa so Oyinto	My beads are jingling—like Oyinto
Oyinto dara—o di wura	Oyinto the maiden—a song of gold
Wura a mi jigi—jigi ileke	The gold of beauty—like singing beads
Ileke Jigi—Jigi Aro!	The beads of Jigi—Jigi Aro!
Aro nro gboun—gboun bata	A name like music, a call of drums,
Bata olota—ota kongo	When drums are throbbing, who can sleep?
Kongo a dun keke—keke bula	You dance in the blood, like fire,
Bula a ke roro—bi ti soja	The fire of battle, you pretty soldier,
A ke roro titi—ebi gbode	You eat our insides, like a hunger,
Ode Eleko—ilu Owo!	The hunger of Lagos, town of riches!

Suddenly there is a scream, from offstage, followed by the noise of wailing. The singing and dancing stop abruptly, and the chorus of dancers disappears.

MAN   What's that?

SINSIN   A scream! I heard it!

JIGI (*smiling*)   I think someone here has just lost an important enemy and is going to become king!

The noise of keening women approaches. Then the townsmen arrive—this may be a large or small number, as is convenient for the Director. They fall on their faces before the Prince. Their spokesman speaks.

SPOKESMAN   Ka-a-a-bi-ye-siii! King-to-be! We've been sent as emissaries from the homeland. The people have asked us to tender their apologies and bring you back. We now know who the forces of evil were, and they're dead! You must come back to sit on the throne of your fathers!

SECOND SPOKESMAN   We are sent with these—sandals, so your feet will always go forward henceforth on steps of ease.

Each of these gestures is henceforth punctuated with a shout of "Ka-a-biyesi!"

ANOTHER   And this wrapper for your waist, as only splendor can robe you!

ANOTHER   This shawl, for your shoulders! Grace becomes them.

ANOTHER   Finally, this sparkling cap, for your royal head. Only the crown can henceforth displace it!

ALL   Ka-a-a-a-bi-ye-siiiii!!!

SPOKESMAN   Come, your majesty! Now to lead you home!

MAN (*to the musicians*)   Goodbye, my friends. At least for a while. You have helped me so much!

JIGI   And my reward, Prince?

MAN   Sh!! Tomorrow, at the palace! Come and see me! Everything will be settled!

JIGI   And how shall I enter? Who'll show me in?

MAN   Take this, my royal bangle. It's heavy, but you can carry it. When they see you wearing it, they'll open the gate!

JIGI   Goodbye then. Until tomorrow!

The townspeople, singing the royal praise-songs, follow the Prince out. Jigi dances.

JIGI   My friends, my friends, rejoice with me!

SINSIN   Jigi! So you too, you made it!

EPO OYINBO   You've joined the league of the big spenders!

REDIO   We'll all see tomorrow! Tomorrow, when we will say goodbye to poverty forever!

OMELE (*pointing out suddenly*)   Hey, look!

They look and shrink back immediately.

EPO OYINBO By God, they're not coming here!

SINSIN Drive them away! Don't let them get near!

JIGI How? How!

> *They run to one side, except for Omele, as two lepers enter. Male and female, they are badly deformed and look hideous. They stop, however, at a good distance, making no attempt to go near the musicians.*

MALE LEPER Good day to you all.

> *There is a brief silence, when no one answers. Then Omele steps forward.*

OMELE Good day, children of the earth.

MALE LEPER We know how you must feel, just to look at us. We've seen ourselves in the mirror, and we see each other every minute. But that's why we need help, my wife and I. We've walked here from a far country, and hopefully, this will be our last stopping point. And if we don't get help here, we'll have to give up, for it will be too late anyhow. Can you help us?

OMELE You need help! Oh God, it's too late! We've used all our powers! Why didn't you come five minutes before?

FEMALE LEPER We walked as fast as we could. But hunger, and the blisters on our feet, slowed our progress.

MALE LEPER The help we need will be useless only after midday. So it can still be done, if you wish.

OMELE What do you mean?

MALE LEPER Last season, the drought came, bringing a terrible wind. That was when the epidemic swept our land. At the height of the ravaging disease, one day, a priest came by. He said—"There's a way you all can be cured. If you can find a man bold and selfless enough."

OMELE Yes? What will the man do?

MALE LEPER That's what I asked him exactly. And he replied; a simple but rather difficult thing. He will come forward and take you in his arms!

SINSIN What! You hear that!

MALE LEPER Those were his very words. "The man will embrace you, and thereby confirm to the gods that you're still one with the living, that your humanity is intact! That's all you need to be cured!"

EPO OYINBO You mean . . . you want someone to embrace you!

REDIO Not on your life, sir! Not for all the riches in the world.

OMELE How I wish you had come earlier!

MALE LEPER It's a gamble I know. Is none of you brave enough, to step forward, in the name of humanity?

SINSIN A gamble he calls it! It's a summons to suicide!

EPO OYINBO I'd rather drink a bucket of poison!

MALE LEPER (*to his wife*) It's just as I feared, Lewa! Just as I feared!

FEMALE LEPER Well, we must keep walking.

MALE LEPER But to where?

FEMALE LEPER Today is the last day he gave us, remember?

MALE LEPER Well then, let's go quickly. We may still find someone, who knows?

FEMALE LEPER (*desperately*) Friends . . . look at us! We were beautiful too, once, like you! We had ambitions, dreams . . .

MALE LEPER Let's go, Lewa. They are healthy, young. They have their future before them! They cannot listen to such arguments . . .

OMELE Wait! (*He is visibly disturbed.*)

JIGI (*apprehensive*) Let them go Omele! Why are you calling them back? You're not going to do something rash again?

OMELE I'm thinking—the Old Man, he gave us each this tremendous power. He said nothing about using it twice . . .

SINSIN He did! He warned us not to even try!

OMELE Why not? Why not, if it's to help people like these?

REDIO Well go ahead. I'm tired of trying to talk sense into your brain. Go ahead, it's your own funeral!

JIGI Omele, you're crazy!

EPO OYINBO I can even understand, if it's to try and repair the chance you bungled the first time. But, look, they haven't even told you that they have anything to offer.

OMELE It doesn't matter. I don't want anything. Come here, my dear people. I'll do it! I'll take the risk!

JIGI I'm going! I don't want to witness this! (*She's nearly in tears.*)

SINSIN And me too! I don't want to see it! I know what will happen.

EPO OYINBO We don't have to be back here anyway, till tomorrow.

REDIO That's right. Let's go.

OMELE You won't stay, to help me with the song?

REDIO Help yourself! Idiot! (*They go, Jigi sobbing.*)

FEMALE LEPER Young man, maybe after all . . . maybe you shouldn't try. I'm afraid suddenly, afraid for you! Look at you. You're so young! We're older at least. We've known life, given birth to children, made something of our lives! Even if death comes now, it cannot come with too much regret. But you . . .

MALE LEPER Yes, Lewa! You're right, he shouldn't do it!

OMELE It's my choice!

MALE LEPER Yes, but it's our disease! Look, your friends have all fled. You're alone, and you're young. Leave us to our plight.

OMELE It's no use now. If I let you go, I'll never grow old. For I'll never know happiness again! I'll be thinking only of this single moment of cowardice, when I turned away some human beings in need. So come on. I'll do it, even though I'm trembling! I've used my chance up, Old Man, but I'm going to try again a second time! If your power was good, it should work always, wherever suffering is found! But we shall not know that, shall we, unless we take the risk! So you, sir, you first! Like this! (*He embraces the male leper.*) And you, dear lady, like this! I'll hold both of you together now while I sing and dance with you. See if you can sing with me! (*He holds them and begins to sing, slowly, till they join him in the singing. The Esu dancers do not appear for this song.*)

WHEN OTHERS RUN *(led by Omele)*

Bo ba ya o ya	*If the time comes*
Bo ba je ewo	*When sympathy's wrong*
Iranlowo le pa ni	*And to help a friend can kill,*
Ka s'okunrin	*Cowards will run:*
Bo ba ya se	*If courage fails*
Bo ba je ese	*And tears are treason,*
Igba kan l'okunrin nlo	*Pity helps a man to stand*
Ka s'okunrin	*When others run:*
Omele ti rubo	*Omele takes the risk,*
Mo rubo nile Orin	*Dares to fight leprosy,*
Eru oje k'eniyan sere	*Fear never lets some men*
Fun eni to nwa're	*Feel compassion when they can.*
Onile Orita!	*Onile Orita!*
Ajantala Orun!	*Ajantala Orun!*
Esu ma tan mi o:	*Esu, weave your spell*
Adete o ye'ni	*Leprosy disappear!*
Se'wo lo fun wa l'agbara	*Invoke a magic remedy,*
Orin kiko:	*My melody,*
Eru o je k'eniyan se're	*Fear never lets some men*
Fun eni to nwa're	*Feel compassion when they can.*

> *Soon, the changes begin. The limbs of the lepers begin to stretch out again, the spots disappear from their faces and skin; they begin, literally, to glow. They shout out joyously.*

MALE LEPER   Lewa! Lewa! Look at you!

FEMALE LEPER *(incredulous)*   Love, it's you! Your old self again! You're cured! *(Omele collapses in great pain.)*

MALE LEPER   We're cured! We're cured!

FEMALE LEPER   My dear young man—*(She runs forward, only to see Omele writhing on the ground. A transformation has also taken place in him: his limbs have retracted, and there are spots all over him. The woman screams, while her husband stands, trembling.)*

MALE LEPER   Lewa! What have we done?

FEMALE LEPER *(sobbing)*   He's got it, love! We've given him the disease!

OMELE *(in panic, his voice changed)*   My God, I've got it! I've been marked! Help me!

FEMALE LEPER *(shaken)*   What have we done? There's no help we can give!

MALE LEPER   We've passed it to him! The priest tricked us!

FEMALE LEPER   We've ruined his life! We've ruined another man's life. Oh God, what shall we do?

> *Omele stand up, hideously deformed. But he is calm now.*

OMELE It doesn't matter. I accept. Don't blame yourselves, it was my decision. What was I before now anyway? A corpse! So what does it matter? I remain a corpse. I accept . . .

Blackout

Four: Hangover

Same situation. Next morning. On one side, the four lucky singers, eating and drinking merrily, all finely dressed. On the other side, alone, the leprosy-infested Omele, driving flies off his body.

EPO OYINBO Yes, my friends! That's how I got the food. I walked up to her in the stall and said: Give me, on credit! And she looked up at me and said, yes sir! Without any argument, just like that!

REDIO Yes, incredible, isn't it, Epo Oyinbo? Money, even just the promise of it, gives you power! Walk, and everybody catches the smell of it! Dance, and the world tumbles down at your feet.

SINSIN It was the same story at the clothes' store. (*She throws a bone across to Omele.*) Take that. (*Omele turns disdainfully away from it.*) Yes, at the stores. They let us pick the clothes and dresses we wanted! All on credit!

JIGI When my Prince comes this morning—ah, when the Prince arrives, I don't want him to find me still unkempt! So I went to the hairdresser's. I said, Go on, the Prince will be paying! And see, they turned me into a fairy queen!

EPO OYINBO I hope you're listening, Omele? We warned you, but you would not listen! You see now!

OMELE I'm not complaining.

EPO OYINBO No? You can have the leftovers. (*laughs*) Here, have this . . .

JIGI No! Don't give him anything!

EPO OYINBO Why, Jigi? It's only a bone!

JIGI He doesn't deserve anything! He made his choice. He wanted to stand alone. He didn't care for any of us. So don't give him anything! Let him also eat his own reward!

SINSIN She's right! He doesn't deserve any pity! Always that holier-than-thou attitude! Let him pay for it!

JIGI He doesn't even deserve to remain here! His presence alone infuriates me! He contaminates the air!

REDIO That's true, you know! Staying by him, any of us could get infected!

SINSIN Good God, you're right! This vermin could ruin the rest of our lives, just as he's wrecked his own! We must drive him away!

OMELE But Sinsin! My friends . . .

JIGI Shut up and go away! You have no friend here!

OMELE Jigi!

EPO OYINBO You heard her! What are you waiting for?

OMELE You can't drive me away. This is a public place. I have a right
  just like any of you, to . . .

JIGI A right! Look at the leper talking of rights! Are you going to go,
  or do you want us to treat you the way lepers are treated?

SINSIN Torches! Let's burn him out! (*They rush to find matches and
  dry sticks.*)

EPO OYINBO No, that will only bring the government down on our
  back. But stones! Use stones to drive him away! (*picks up a stone
  and throws it at Omele*) Go!

OMELE (*hit*) Epo Oyinbo! It's me!

EPO OYINBO Go away, leper!

> The others also pick up stones and begin to throw them at Omele,
> shouting for him to go away. He calls them one by one, in pain
> as he is hit, but the rain of stones only increases. He falls down
> and begins the "Song of Tomorrow," to which the other musicians
> reply in antiphony.

THE SONG OF TOMORROW (*led by Omele*)

OMELE
> 1. Remember tomorrow,
>   For evil will sprout,
>   And like seedlings grow,
>   Your deeds will come out.
>
> 2. You'll pay back with pain
>   When you cause people sorrow
>   But you'll reap the gain
>   From the good you sow.

OTHERS
>   In vain we talked to you,
>   You shunned all our warnings,
>   Whoever calls Sango,
>   Sango, Oba Koso o,
>   Sango, voice of thunder,
>   Brings him home for lunch.
>   If lightning wrecks your house,
>   You cannot complain.

OMELE
> 3. You hassle for glamour,
>   For material gains,
>   But money does not endure,
>   Friendship remains,
>
> 4. To others be kind,
>   And think of tomorrow,

The actions of humankind
Bear fruits to show.

OTHERS

In vain we talked to you,
You shunned all our warnings,
Whoever calls Sango,
Sango, King of Koso,
Wears rainstorms for clothing,
Brings him to your farm,
And floods destroy your crops,
You cannot complain!

> *Omele falls down, the stones rain on him again. Finally he turns and runs. The other minstrels return laughing to their feasting.*

JIGI Good riddance to bad rubbish!

REDIO Yes! His sight would have driven back my business tycoons! Just imagine that!

JIGI Now, my Prince can come! Ah, even if he doesn't pay any more! If he merely twists his finger, and says, Come along! What happiness! What a promise of luxury!

REDIO It's the only song people like us live our lives for, the song of wealth! Otherwise, when we reach the crossroads at last, at a place like this—we may choose the wrong direction. But, Edumare, you created this jungle we live in, and you made some animals with teeth. Don't forget us, listen to our song!

> *They begin the "Song of the Jungle."*

SONG OF THE JUNGLE *(led by Redio)*

1. *Obangiji o, oba to laje,*

   Feti sebe mi:
   Kiniun l'oba, gbogbo aginju

   Nitori ehin
   Iwo lo ma fun, Edumare O!

2. *Aje wu'niyan, ise aje pe*

   Nitori owo
   Nitori afe, aiye to l'ero,

   Nitori aje,
   Iwo le se o, Edumare O!

1. *Obangiji o, the owner of wealth,*
   Listen to my plea:
   The lion it is, who rules the jungle
   Because he can kill:
   You gave him his teeth, Edumare O!

2. *We cheat and scramble, because business pays,*
   Money in the bank,
   Money in the hand, and a life of ease,
   Lots of luxury
   Make me rich today-o, Edumare o!

3. *Ko fun mi l'ehin, to mu sasa*

   Feti sebe mi
   Se mi n'kiniun, I'oja araye

   Nitori aje
   Iwo le se o, Edumare o!

4. *Tantara!*
   Oro aje ni!—Tantara!

   O wu ni'yan—Tantara!
   Ise aje dun o Tantara!

   Aiye afe ni—Tantara!

   O wu ni'yan—Tantara!
   Aiye afe dun o Tantara!

3. *Give me teeth, I pray, sharper*
      than the blade,
   For this is my plea:
   Make me the lion, in the busi-
      ness world,
   With the power to kill,
   Make me rich today-o, Edu-
      mare o!

4. *Tantara!*
   Money will be mine!—
      Tantara!
   World of luxury—Tantara!
   O what a golden dream—
      Tantara!
   Comforts will be mine—
      Tantara!
   World of fantasy—Tantara!
   O what a lovely dream—
      Tantara!

But suddenly, in counter-chorus, Esu's theme song rises, as the Old Man and his followers, hooded, arrive. The musicians give them a rousing welcome.

OLD MAN (*smiling*) Good day, my children, I am glad to see you all gay and happy like this. That means you made good for yourselves!

REDIO Indeed we have, Old Man! The charm you gave us, it worked wonderfully! In a few hours, if you wait long enough, all the people we helped will be arriving here to repay their debts!

OLD MAN I am glad to hear that! How you must all have helped to reduce suffering in the world!

EPO OYINBO The important thing is—because I hate beating about the bush—the important thing is that we have reduced suffering for ourselves! No more hunger and no more wandering for us! Finished, the vagabond life. We've planted our feet down firmly in fortune!

OLD MAN Good! Where's your other comrade?

SINSIN Gone, Old Man.

OLD MAN To where?

JIGI He alone, he wasted your power! He's always been foolish and pig-headed. As if an eternal curse followed him, never to let him make good! You see, with your power, he did not pick up prosperity, like us! He picked up leprosy!

OLD MAN Leprosy! How? . . .

EPO OYINBO First, he wasted his power on a pauper. A woman with no money or means. And then, he tried again, a second time. Yes, despite your warning, he tried to use your power a second time!

OLD MAN So where is he?

REDIO We drove him away, to avoid contamination. Because . . .

Enter Omele.

OMELE   Because of your greed! But I'm here. Here also to give account!

JIGI   Is that what brought you back, you shameless man?

OMELE   Everywhere I went, they drove me away. So I returned here. Old Man, punish me. I have not grown wealthy like the others.

OLD MAN   All is set then! The hour has come for your reward, all of you. (*to his followers*) Reveal yourselves, my children. (*The hoods fall off, one by one, to reveal the same characters who had been helped by the musicians, all except the pregnant woman and the lepers. The musicians jump with shock.*)

OLD MAN   Look at them well. Don't say you don't recognize them?

REDIO   But . . . but . . . (*Jigi runs forward in ecstasy.*)

JIGI   Prince! I know you're an adventurer! Still, what a spectacular manner this is of making a reappearance! (*The Prince laughs.*) Well, the Old Man is a magician, although you probably know that already, since I see you're friends. He was the one who gave me the power I used for you, to save you from that priest. Thank you for coming back to settle acc . . .

PRINCE   Woman! What are you talking about? Saved me! From what priest?

JIGI   Prince! Yesterday! Here, in this very place, when you . . .

PRINCE   Quiet woman! And move back! How you smell! Old Man, this is extraordinary! Is this why you asked me here, to talk with commoners like this?

JIGI   (*bursting into tears*)   It's not possible! Prince, my beloved! This, this is your bangle . . .

PRINCE   Where did you steal it from?

JIGI   Oh God! Why are you . . . ?

OLD MAN   Stand back! Give way to the next person!

REDIO   I come next, and I make my claim with these items. A wristwatch, a lighter, and a cigarette case. They belong to him, and him, and him. They gave me these yesterday, when I helped them retrieve a license. I know they are rich and generous and will reward me well, as they promised. So go ahead, Old Man, ask them. (*The strangers laugh.*)

FIRST STRANGER   Really! Where did these people get their fanciful dreams?

SECOND STRANGER   Who did you help retrieve a license, my dear fellow?

REDIO   You, of course! Yesterday!

THIRD STRANGER   Was that when you woke up from your nightmare?

REDIO   Please . . . please! You can't do this to me! These are your tokens!

SECOND STRANGER   (*laughing*)   Ours, those tinsels!

FIRST STRANGER   Old Man, this is past a joke! Why force us to come here to listen to riff-raff?

REDIO   No! Old Man, I swear . . .

OLD MAN   Enough! Stand back! I warned you! I told you to choose well, and you all made your choice. So what about you, my dear? (*to Sinsin*) Are you ready to make your claim?

SINSIN   I don't know . . . I don't know any more . . . It all happened here, before our eyes. But now they're all lying, denying! So, I don't know. But he was here, all covered in blood. He was dying. Yes, you! You were wounded, and I saved you! You promised me half of your wealth!

MAN   Indeed! Why would I do such a reckless thing?

SINSIN   But see! This is your necklace! The one you gave me for—

MAN   Keep it, if indeed it's mine. Whatever next!

OLD MAN   Stand back then, woman! You—why are you drawing a knife?

PRINCE   Bandits! Old Man, you've brought us among bandits!

EPO OYINBO   I'm not a bandit, but no one's going to trifle with me and get away with it! I've lived in prison before, and I'm willing to be hanged. But sir . . . yes, you! (*to the former Impotent Man*) You sir, say a word amiss! Say I didn't help you, one wrong word, and we'll both go to hell!

MAN   Old Man, do something! The man is dangerous!

OLD MAN   This is childish! Put the knife away!

EPO OYINBO   I want him to talk! He came here! He didn't have children. He couldn't even get it up! And I cured him! Yes, with your power, Old Man! I cured him!

MAN   What vulgarity! But if you wish to know, I have forty-something wives in my harem! Children by the dozens! Grandchildren too numerous to count! They couldn't all have been born yesterday? So what are you saying, my dear fellow?

EPO OYINBO   (*thundering*)   . . . I've been cheated! He's lying! And by Sango, I'll . . . (*He lunges forward, but the Old Man stops him, with a gesture. Transfixed, he replies henceforth like a robot.*)

OLD MAN   Naughty boy. Go and throw that toy away! (*He does so mechanically.*) And don't let me see you repeat that foolishness again, or you'll be punished! Move back. Now, for the last man . . .

OMELE   That's me, Old Man, but it's no use. I know I helped a woman, who is not here now. But even if she was, it would not change a thing, for she has nothing, and I asked for nothing. I was glad merely to see that she was happy. So I make no claim for myself. I too, I wasted your power. Instead of getting rich, I caught a disease. Punish me along with the rest.

OLD MAN   They tell me you were greedy. That you tried to use the power twice.

OMELE   Yes, I confess. I tried a second time, but not out of greed. The people who came were really desperate, and I made them happy. I have no regrets.

OLD MAN   Where are they now? Will they be ready to give witness?

OMELE   Who knows? Leave them alone. Let them enjoy their happiness.

OLD MAN   Well, I'll summon the woman at least . . .

OMELE   No! (*But it's too late. The Old Man has already gestured toward the wings. Sound of a woman answering as if to a call. She enters, with her baby strapped to her back.*)

WOMAN (*entering*)   I heard my name and . . . (*sees Omele*) Oh God! Whatever happened to you!

OMELE (*evasive*)   Congratulations! You've had your baby!

WOMAN (*near tears*)   Come with me! We'll find a doctor!

OLD MAN   You know him, woman?

WOMAN (*angry*)   No, I don't know him! (*hisses*) One of you, one of you here probably did this to him. And I swear the person is going to pay for it!

OLD MAN   But who are you? And where do you come from? You're not one of my followers . . .

WOMAN   And who would want to follow such an evil-looking man like you? Please . . .

OLD MAN (*shouting*)   You were not sent by Orunmila?

WOMAN   If you don't mind, you old man, I have no time for idle questions. (*to Omele*) Come, *jare* . . .

OLD MAN   All right, please don't be angry, woman. It's just that I don't know where or how you entered the game. And I should know, since I laid the rules.

WOMAN   But which game are you talking about? Listen if . . .

OLD MAN   All right, forget it. Just the suspicions of an old man, perhaps. But tell me now . . . why? Why are you sticking up for this man like this?

WOMAN   Because he saved me! Nine years, the child was inside me! And then he . . .

EPO OYINBO (*quickly stepping in*)   It's a lie!

WOMAN   No! You, you were even singing and . . .

EPO OYINBO   It's a lie! A conspiracy between you two! Isn't it, you fellows?

JIGI   It is! You're lying!

WOMAN   But . . .

SINSIN   Yes! It's a lie! A filthy lie!

EPO OYINBO   Go away!

REDIO   Get out of here, at once! Liar!

WOMAN (*overwhelmed*)   But . . . but . . .

MINSTRELS   Get out!! Go away!! Get lost!! Bitch!! (*They scream at her, frightening her, till she runs out sobbing.*)

EPO OYINBO   Forget all about her, Old Man! They hatched the clever plot together, but it won't work. You've got to punish all of us together!

JIGI   Yes, let's all be punished!

OLD MAN   That was your witness, Omele. She's fled!

OMELE   Yes, I know. They chased her away.

OLD MAN   So, what are you going to do?

OMELE   Nothing. What shall I do against them? They were once my comrades. They taught me all I know. How to sing, and lie, and fight. Shall I turn all that against them? I am part of them.

OLD MAN Do something at least. Put up a fight for yourself . . .

OMELE No. Not against them. (*enter the former lepers, now looking very healthy, although worried*)

FEMALE LEPER Ah, there he is!

MALE LEPER Young man, where have you been?

OMELE I . . . I didn't expect to see you back here!

FEMALE LEPER We've been searching for you all over the place!

OLD MAN Who are you?

FEMALE LEPER (*sharply*) Please keep out of this, whoever you are! We are in a hurry.

MALE LEPER We went and met the priest again. And he said we can take our disease back. Provided we embrace you again before noon. So, come . . .

OMELE No! Stand back!

FEMALE LEPER (*surprised*) But what's wrong with him?

OMELE You've been cured. Stay cured!

MALE LEPER Nonsense! Isn't it our disease?

FEMALE LEPER We want it back!

OMELE Stay away from me! (*a short play, while they advance and he retreats*)

MALE LEPER But be reasonable! Old Man, are you a friend of his?

OLD MAN In a way, yes.

MALE LEPER Well, judge for us. This man, to help us, did an extraordinary thing. He didn't know us; we had never even met before. But he saw us in our anguish, covered all over in leprous spots, and he had the courage to embrace us! Yes, he embraced us, and we were cured at once! Just as our priest had foretold, his embrace cured us of the dreadful disease! But alas, we could not rejoice for long. No! For he himself had become infected in the process!

FEMALE LEPER So we ran back to seek the priest again. And we told him: No, Baba! We don't like the bargain! We'd rather take our disease back and let the young man go free! So that's why we have returned here. All we need, said the priest, is to embrace him again and he will return to what he was, in his sparkling health!

OMELE No! Let things stay as they are! (*another short chase*)

OLD MAN I don't understand! How can you keep someone else's disease, if the owner wants it back?

OMELE Because it doesn't matter to me. I have only one life, and it's not worth much. I've always lived in want, as a vagabond. Oh yes, my life itself has been like a leprosy. So I am used to it, I can live like this for the rest of my wretched life. But look at them, aren't they handsome as they are? They have a name, a career; they have kids. They have money in the bank, an insurance policy no doubt. Their life is a hymn to the future. Society needs them, not dregs like me. I'll keep the disease!

MALE AND FEMALE LEPERS We refuse!!!

MALE LEPER   Every life is as precious as the other. Including yours.
It's not for you to give a value to any human life!

OLD MAN   I know what to do, but I think I need some advice first
before I act. Who'll advise me? (*The minstrels eagerly volunteer.*)
You, I don't trust. You've been caught in the mischief of my followers, and I can see you're hungry for vengeance! No. You'll wait there
till I decide your punishment. So who will advise me?

MALE LEPER   (*exasperated, steps forward*)   Look here, Esu! This is
enough! You know what you have to do! Or why else do you think
we came here?

OLD MAN   You? Who are you?

MALE LEPER   (*smiles, to the Female Leper*)   My dear, how terrible you
can be, even to a god! See, you've wrapped his mind so completely
in your cobweb!

FEMALE LEPER   (*smiling*)   Well, you know that when you play with the
master trickster himself, you have to be ruthless. I put his mind in
a season of drought, and Edumare obliged. But he can go now.
(*gestures*) Winds, unfreeze! Roots, resume your growing!

OLD MAN   That voice! Those words! I've heard them before!

MALE LEPER   Close your eyes, Esu. Look deeply, where the gods look.
Look below the surface.

OLD MAN   (*does so, recoils*)   No, not you! Not you again, Orunmila!
And . . . (*turns to Lewa*)

FEMALE LEPER   (*smiling*)   Yes, its me, Esu. You forgot, didn't you, that
even the cleverest fox can still be fooled.

OLD MAN   (*angry*)   I see. I see now, Yeye Osun![7] Both of you, you sent
that woman with the baby here.

FEMALE LEPER   You hatched your clever plot, Esu, as usual. And as
usual, I am using it to retrieve my children.

OLD MAN   And to frustrate me, of course! All right, both of you! You
think you've won, but I still have a last card. I'm going to throw the
question to the audience and let their fellow human beings decide!
(*to the audience*) You! Don't just sit there and let an injustice be
done. Say something! Should Omele return the disease, or should
he keep it? Speak up, we need your answers to decide! Yes, you sir?
And you, madam! . . .

> *A debate is now encouraged among members of the audience,*
> *while the actors freeze on stage. The lights come half down. The*
> *Old Man finally calls for a vote between the Aye's and the No's.*

OLD MAN   Again, please? Let's here the aye's, those who want the
disease returned! Okay now, the no's! Well, I'm sorry—maybe my
ears are failing—but no side has won! (*The Male Leper tries to intervene.*) No need, Orunmila, I know what you want. As well as the
goddess Osun, by your side. These tricks you play on behalf of humanity! It's called cheating!

---

7. An appelation for Osun, goddess of rivers in the Yoruba orisa religion.

MALE LEPER Decide quickly, now. It's not just what we want, but
what you must do. You know you have no choice.

OLD MAN (*sighs*) Yes. Let's end the play then, old spoilsport. And yet
so much fun still to be had! Well, as you like it! Let the disease go
to those who have won it, those who seek to be rich without labor.
Who have put their selfish greed first before everything, including
their humanity! I mean you, my dear fellows! Take your reward! (*The
minstrels cringe in terror.*) Obaluaye, it's your turn now! They're
yours!

> *Obaluaye, the god of smallpox, detaches himself with a terrifying
> laughter from the retinue, and comes forward as his praise-song
> rises. The transformations begin: with Omele being cured, and
> his comrades writhing in agony as they are caught by the dreadful
> god, and are gradually covered in spots. Obaluaye finally leads
> them out in a dance.*

OLD MAN Come, Orunmila, and you, mother of fertility. You know I
am not unkind. We've all played the game. And now, it is time to
reward the only man we have found truly worthy to be called a
human being! Salute!

> *Omele is led in, again, now decorated with cowrie beads. The
> once-pregnant woman holds him by the hand.*

MALE LEPER (*as Orunmila, steps forward*)
My son, this is no time for speeches,
And I shall spare you one.
Esu Laaroye, lord of the crossroads,
Trickster, he set you a test, to see
Whether between compassion and greed,
You would know the road to take;
Between hollow material wealth,
So ephemeral,
And the unseen riches of tenderness,
You alone passed the test, you alone
Pitied the woman we sent along
Even in spite of her wretchedness
So we said, let's test him again,
Just to be sure, and we came down ourselves.
Me and Yeye Osun, disguised in
The frightful skin of Obaluaye, as lepers.
But again you did not let us down!
Again, you let your humanity
Yield to unusual compassion. Salute,
My friend! So, let's bring the play
To an end here. Let the parable
Come to a close. Let the gods disappear,
As we must, to where we came from,
In a fairy tale. The rest is for our audience
To learn from your example
For every man . . .

The other minstrels, half undressed, burst in, and join, raucously, in completing the sentence.

. . . has a lamp in his hand,
Waiting to be lit!

The other actors onstage watch, in astonishment.

REDIO (*in great laughter*)
   "Every man carries the key . . ."
JIGI (*same game*)
   ". . . To a door of happiness!"
EPO OYINBO (*to Orunmila*)   Go on! Complete your speech!
MALE LEPER   But . . . what happened? I thought we just got rid of you?
REDIO   Not tonight, my friend. Not again. Today the play's going to end differently.
OLD MAN   Indeed! And have you told the author about it!
SINSIN   Let him watch, like everybody else. But we're tired of taking part in deceit.
FEMALE LEPER   What do you mean? Where's Obaluaye?
OBALUAYE (*appearing*)   Here. I am on their side. Let the audience know the truth.
OLD MAN   Which truth? Where has it ever happened before, that the characters in a play rewrite the script?
MALE LEPER (*appealing*)   Please, go back into the wings, and die as you've been doing before. Let's end the play.
REDIO   That's the easiest way out, we know. But it's a lie. There's just no miraculous answer to life's disasters. Even a play must face the truth.
FEMALE LEPER   For whom are you speaking?
JIGI   For ourselves, both as actors and as citizens.
EPO OYINBO   There's no magic to the riddle of evil.
SINSIN   Kindness cannot be willed by the waving of a wand.
REDIO   No incantations can cure the anguish caused by the greed of politicians.
JIGI   And prayers are not sufficient to counter the violence in the street.

Some of the actors begin to gather from the wings.

EPO OYINBO   Neither prayers nor good wishes.
REDIO   But only the actions of struggling men . . .
EPO OYINBO   Only many fists, waving together . . .
REDIO   For only the muscles behind a wheel can turn it.
JIGI   Only many voices rising together, to shout "NO!" this moment . . .
SINSIN   "YES!" another moment . . .
EPO OYINBO   And "LET US MARCH!" all the moments . . .
REDIO   And "LET US BUILD, FOR WE CAN BUILD!"
MINSTRELS   "FOR WE CAN BUILD!"

JIGI   Only such determined voices can change the course of history . . .

SINSIN   And bring the true compassion that people need.

JIGI   And bring the compassion that really endures.

OBALUAYE   So, tell the audience, that I, Obaluaye, I do not exist . . .
   (*as he removes his costumes*)

SINSIN (*doing the same*)   The story you heard does not exist . . .

JIGI   And I, I do not . . .

MALE LEPER   Enough! Thank you! (*claps*) Fools!

EPO OYINBO   What . . . !

MALE LEPER

   If only you'd waited for our last song!
   Now the joke's on you. For, clearly,
   You've missed the difference between reality
   And its many mirrors. All of us,
   What else are we, but metaphors in a
   Fading tale? Just the props of a parable,
   The drums on which the message is beaten.
   But it is time to go. Call the others in the wings.
   Let us end the play with our final song
   As the author wants it. And remember,
   Sing only as farmers plant seeds:
   Sing well, And—please remove your costumes
   And masks. Bring back the house lights!
   Let us restore the audience back to reality.
   Okay—are we set! After three!
   One! Two! Three!

   *The actors, who have gathered round him in their own clothes,
   as he requested, begin to sing the song "Esu Does Not Exist."*

ESU DOES NOT EXIST (*led by Orunmila*)

1. *HERE HE STANDS our dear friends*
   And as our story ends
   The man we call the hero
   He will now take a bow:
   All we have tried to say
   Through this gay storytelling
   Is that compassion pays
   Kindness has its own reward;
   Life's not all buying, selling,
   Cheating, amassing wealth;
   And greed is the way to death:
   God is one loving word!

2. *AND SO WE END our show*
   And we are about to go
   But don't take our story light
   Like some tale on moonlit night:
   All this magic we've shown

All this miracle of healing
They're devices that you've known,
Spices to our narration—
But though it's fascinating
Till your mind can't resist,
Esu does not exist
Save in your imagination!

3. *ESU DOES NOT exist*
And if evil does persist
We must each search our soul
What we've set ourselves as goal:
If wealth is all we seek
And don't care what means we're using,
If our ways seem so sleek
When we keep strange rendez-vous,
One day we'll come to reason
At some Sepeteri
Where Esu—or History—
Waits in ambush with his noose!

The actors join the audience. The theatre empties. Life resumes.

BACKGROUNDS AND CRITICISM

African Drama and Theatre

FRANTZ FANON

On National Culture†

To take part in the African revolution it is not enough to write a revolutionary song; you must fashion the revolution with the people. And if you fashion it with the people, the songs will come by themselves, and of themselves.

In order to achieve real action, you must yourself be a living part of Africa and of her thought; you must be an element of that popular energy which is entirely called forth for the freeing, the progress, and the happiness of Africa. There is no place outside that fight for the artist or for the intellectual who is not himself concerned with and completely at one with the people in the great battle of Africa and of suffering humanity
—Sékou Touré.[1]

Each generation must out of relative obscurity discover its mission, fulfill it, or betray it. In underdeveloped countries the preceding generations have both resisted the work or erosion carried by colonialism and also helped on the maturing of the struggles of today. We must rid ourselves of the habit, now that we are in the thick of the fight, of minimizing the action of our fathers or of feigning incomprehension when considering their silence and passivity. They fought as well as they could, with the arms that they possessed then; and if the echoes of their struggle have not resounded in the international arena, we must realize that the reason for this silence lies less in their lack of heroism than in the fundamentally different international situation of our time. It needed more than one native to say "We've had enough"; more than one peasant rising crushed, more than one demonstration put down before we could today hold our own, certain in our victory. As for we who have decided to break the back of colonialism, our historic mission is to sanction all revolts, all desperate actions, all those abortive attempts drowned in rivers of blood.

* * *

---

† From *The Wretched of the Earth,* trans. Constance Farrington (New York: Grove Press, 1963) 206–07, 214–23. Copyright © 1963 by Presence Africaine. Reprinted by permission of Grove/Atlantic, Inc.

1. "The political leader as the representative of a culture." Address to the second Congress of Black Writers and Artists, Rome, 1959.

This historical necessity in which the men of African culture find
themselves to racialize their claims and to speak more of African culture than of national culture will tend to lead them up a blind alley.
Let us take for example the case of the African Cultural Society. This
society had been created by African intellectuals who wished to get to
know each other and to compare their experiences and the results of
their respective research work. The aim of this society was therefore
to affirm the existence of an African culture, to evaluate this culture
on the plane of distinct nations, and to reveal the internal motive
forces of each of their national cultures. But at the same time this
society fulfilled another need: the need to exist side by side with the
European Cultural Society, which threatened to transform itself into
a Universal Cultural Society. There was therefore at the bottom of this
decision the anxiety to be present at the universal trysting place fully
armed, with a culture springing from the very heart of the African
continent. Now, this Society will very quickly show its inability to
shoulder these different tasks, and will limit itself to exhibitionist demonstrations, while the habitual behavior of the members of this Society
will be confined to showing Europeans that such a thing as African
culture exists, and opposing their ideas to those of ostentatious and
narcissistic Europeans. We have shown that such an attitude is normal
and draws its legitimacy from the lies propagated by men of Western
culture, but the degradation of the aims of this Society will become
more marked with the elaboration of the concept of negritude. The
African Society will become the cultural society of the black world and
will come to include the Negro dispersion, that is to say the tens of
thousands of black people spread over the American continents.

The Negroes who live in the United States and in Central or Latin
America in fact experience the need to attach themselves to a cultural
matrix. Their problem is not fundamentally different from that of the
Africans. The whites of America did not mete out to them any different
treatment from that of the whites who ruled over the Africans. We
have seen that the whites were used to putting all Negroes in the same
bag. During the first congress of the African Cultural Society which
was held in Paris in 1956, the American Negroes of their own accord
considered their problems from the same standpoint as those of their
African brothers. Cultured Africans, speaking of African civilizations,
decreed that there should be a reasonable status within the state for
those who had formerly been slaves. But little by little the American
Negroes realized that the essential problems confronting them were
not the same as those that confronted the African Negroes. The Negroes of Chicago only resemble the Nigerians or the Tanganyikans in
so far as they were all defined in relation to the whites. But once the
first comparisons had been made and subjective feelings were as-
suaged, the American Negroes realized that the objective problems
were fundamentally heterogeneous. The test cases of civil liberty
whereby both whites and blacks in America try to drive back racial
discrimination have very little in common in their principles and objectives with the heroic fight of the Angolan people against the de-

testable Portuguese colonialism. Thus, during the second congress of the African Cultural Society the American Negroes decided to create an American society for people of black cultures.

Negritude therefore finds its first limitation in the phenomena which take account of the formation of the historical character of men. Negro and African-Negro culture broke up into different entities because the men who wished to incarnate these cultures realized that every culture is first and foremost national, and that the problems which kept Richard Wright or Langston Hughes on the alert were fundamentally different from those which might confront Leopold Senghor or Jomo Kenyatta. In the same way certain Arab states, though they had chanted the marvelous hymn of Arab renaissance, had nevertheless to realize that their geographical position and the economic ties of their region were stronger even than the past that they wished to revive. Thus we find today the Arab states organically linked once more with societies which are Mediterranean in their culture. The fact is that these states are submitted to modern pressure and to new channels of trade while the network of trade relations which was dominant during the great period of Arab history had disappeared. But above all there is the fact that the political regimes of certain Arab states are so different, and so far away from each other in their conceptions, that even a cultural meeting between these states is meaningless.

Thus we see that the cultural problem as it sometimes exists in colonized countries runs the risk of giving rise to serious ambiguities. The lack of culture of the Negroes, as proclaimed by colonialism, and the inherent barbarity of the Arabs ought logically to lead to the exaltation of cultural manifestations which are not simply national but continental, and extremely racial. In Africa, the movement of men of culture is a movement toward the Negro-African culture or the Arab-Moslem culture. It is not specifically toward a national culture. Culture is becoming more and more cut off from the events of today. It finds its refuge beside a hearth that glows with passionate emotion, and from there makes its way by realistic paths which are the only means by which it may be made fruitful, homogeneous, and consistent.

If the action of the native intellectual is limited historically, there remains nevertheless the fact that it contributes greatly to upholding and justifying the action of politicians. It is true that the attitude of the native intellectual sometimes takes on the aspect of a cult or of a religion. But if we really wish to analyze this attitude correctly we will come to see that it is symptomatic of the intellectual's realization of the danger that he is running in cutting his last moorings and of breaking adrift from his people. This stated belief in a national culture is in fact an ardent, despairing turning toward anything that will afford him secure anchorage. In order to ensure his salvation and to escape from the supremacy of the white man's culture the native feels the need to turn backward toward his unknown roots and to lose himself at whatever cost in his own barbarous people. Because he feels he is becoming estranged, that is to say because he feels that he is the living haunt of contradictions which run the risk of becoming insurmountable, the native tears himself away from the swamp that may suck him down and accepts everything, decides to take all for granted and confirms everything even though he may lose body and soul. The native finds that he is expected to answer for everything, and to all comers. He not only turns himself into the defender of his people's past; he is willing to be counted as one of them, and henceforward he is even capable of laughing at his past cowardice.

This tearing away, painful and difficult though it may be, is however necessary. If it is not accomplished there will be serious psychoaffective injuries and the result will be individuals without an anchor, without a horizon, colorless, stateless, rootless—a race of angels. It will be also quite normal to hear certain natives declare, "I speak as a Senegalese and as a Frenchman . . ." "I speak as an Algerian and as a Frenchman . . ." The intellectual who is Arab and French, or Nigerian and English, when he comes up against the need to take on two nationalities, chooses, if he wants to remain true to himself, the negation of one of these determinations. But most often, since they cannot or will not make a choice, such intellectuals gather together all the historical determining factors which have conditioned them and take up a fundamentally "universal standpoint."

This is because the native intellectual has thrown himself greedily upon Western culture. Like adopted children who only stop investigating the new family framework at the moment when a minimum nucleus of security crystallizes in their psyche, the native intellectual will try to make European culture his own. He will not be content to get to know Rabelais and Diderot, Shakespeare and Edgar Allan Poe; he will bind them to his intelligence as closely as possible:

> La dame n'était pas seule
> Elle avait un mari
> Un mari très comme il faut
> Qui citait Racine et Corneille
> Et Voltaire et Rousseau
> Et le Père Hugo et le jeune Musset
> Et Gide et Valéry
> Et tant d'autres encore.[2]

But at the moment when the nationalist parties are mobilizing the people in the name of national independence, the native intellectual sometimes spurns these acquisitions which he suddenly feels make him a stranger in his own land. It is always easier to proclaim rejection than actually to reject. The intellectual who through the medium of culture has filtered into Western civilization, who has managed to become part of the body of European culture—in other words who has exchanged his own culture for another—will come to realize that the cultural matrix, which now he wishes to assume since he is anxious to appear original, can hardly supply any figureheads which will bear

---

2. The lady was not alone; she had a most respectable husband, who knew how to quote Racine and Corneille, Voltaire and Rousseau, Victor Hugo and Musset, Gide, Valéry and as many more again (René Depestre: "Face à la Nuit").

comparison with those, so many in number and so great in prestige, of the occupying power's civilization. History, of course, though nevertheless written by the Westerners and to serve their purposes, will be able to evaluate from time to time certain periods of the African past. But, standing face to face with his country at the present time, and observing clearly and objectively the events of today throughout the continent which he wants to make his own, the intellectual is terrified by the void, the degradation, and the savagery he sees there. Now he feels that he must get away from the white culture. He must seek his culture elsewhere, anywhere at all; and if he fails to find the substance of culture of the same grandeur and scope as displayed by the ruling power, the native intellectual will very often fall back upon emotional attitudes and will develop a psychology which is dominated by exceptional sensitivity and susceptibility. This withdrawal, which is due in the first instance to a begging of the question in his internal behavior mechanism and his own character, brings out, above all, a reflex and contradiction which is muscular.

This is sufficient explanation of the style of those native intellectuals who decide to give expression to this phase of consciousness which is in the process of being liberated. It is a harsh style, full of images, for the image is the drawbridge which allows unconscious energies to be scattered on the surrounding meadows. It is a vigorous style, alive with rhythms, struck through and through with bursting life; it is full of color, too, bronzed, sunbaked, and violent. This style, which in its time astonished the peoples of the West, has nothing racial about it, in spite of frequent statements to the contrary; it expresses above all a hand-to-hand struggle and it reveals the need that man has to liberate himself from a part of his being which already contained the seeds of decay. Whether the fight is painful, quick, or inevitable, muscular action must substitute itself for concepts.

If in the world of poetry this movement reaches unaccustomed heights, the fact remains that in the real world the intellectual often follows up a blind alley. When at the height of his intercourse with his people, whatever they were or whatever they are, the intellectual decides to come down into the common paths of real life, he only brings back from his adventuring formulas which are sterile in the extreme. He sets a high value on the customs, traditions, and the appearances of his people; but his inevitable, painful experience only seems to be a banal search for exoticism. The sari becomes sacred, and shoes that come from Paris or Italy are left off in favor of pampooties, while suddenly the language of the ruling power is felt to burn your lips. Finding your fellow countrymen sometimes means in this phase to will to be a nigger, not a nigger like all other niggers but a real nigger, a Negro cur, just the sort of nigger that the white man wants you to be. Going back to your own people means to become a dirty wog, to go native as much as you can, to become unrecognizable, and to cut off those wings that before you had allowed to grow.

The native intellectual decides to make an inventory of the bad habits drawn from the colonial world, and hastens to remind everyone of the good old customs of the people, that people which he has decided contains all truth and goodness. The scandalized attitude with which the settlers who live in the colonial territory greet this new departure only serves to strengthen the native's decision. When the colonialists, who had tasted the sweets of their victory over these assimilated people, realize that these men whom they considered as saved souls are beginning to fall back into the ways of niggers, the whole system totters. Every native won over, every native who had taken the pledge not only marks a failure for the colonial structure when he decides to lose himself and to go back to his own side, but also stands as a symbol for the uselessness and the shallowness of all the work that has been accomplished. Each native who goes back over the line is a radical condemnation of the methods and of the regime; and the native intellectual finds in the scandal he gives rise to a justification and an encouragement to persevere in the path he has chosen.

If we wanted to trace in the works of native writers the different phases which characterize this evolution we would find spread out before us a panorama on three levels. In the first phase, the native intellectual gives proof that he has assimilated the culture of the occupying power. His writings correspond point by point with those of his opposite numbers in the mother country. His inspiration is European and we can easily link up these works with definite trends in the literature of the mother country. This is the period of unqualified assimilation. We find in this literature coming from the colonies the Parnassians, the Symbolists, and the Surrealists.

In the second phase we find the native is disturbed; he decides to remember what he is. This period of creative work approximately corresponds to that immersion which we have just described. But since the native is not a part of his people, since he only has exterior relations with his people, he is content to recall their life only. Past happenings of the byegone days of his childhood will be brought up out of the depths of his memory; old legends will be reinterpreted in the light of a borrowed estheticism and of a conception of the world which was discovered under other skies.

Sometimes this literature of just-before-the-battle is dominated by humor and by allegory; but often too it is symptomatic of a period of distress and difficulty, where death is experienced, and disgust too. We spew ourselves up; but already underneath laughter can be heard.

Finally in the third phase, which is called the fighting phase, the native, after having tried to lose himself in the people and with the people, will on the contrary shake the people. Instead of according the people's lethargy an honored place in his esteem, he turns himself into an awakener of the people; hence comes a fighting literature, a revolutionary literature, and a national literature. During this phase a great many men and women who up till then would never have thought of producing a literary work, now that they find themselves in exceptional circumstances—in prison, with the Maquis, or on the eve of their execution—feel the need to speak to their nation, to compose the sentence which expresses the heart of the people, and to become the mouthpiece of a new reality in action.

*   *   *

WOLE SOYINKA

Theatre in African Traditional Cultures: Survival Patterns†

Even where other resources of pre-colonial society are unevenly shared, culture tends to suggest a comparatively even-handed distribution or—perhaps more simply—mass appropriation. This may help to explain why it is always a primary target of assault by an invading force. As an instrument of self-definition, its destruction or successful attrition reaches into the reserves of racial/national will on a comprehensive scale. Conversely, the commencement of resistance and self-liberation by the suppressed people is not infrequently linked with the survival strategies of key cultural patterns, manifested through various art forms. The experience of West Africa has been no different. The history of West African theatre in the colonial period reveals itself therefore as largely a history of cultural resistance and survival. Confronted by the hostility of both Islamic and Christian values, in addition to the destructive imperatives of colonialism, it has continued until today to vitalize contemporary theatrical forms both in the tradition of 'folk opera' and in the works of those playwrights and directors commonly regarded as 'Westernized'.

We must not lose sight of the fact that drama, like any other art form, is created and executed within a specific physical environment. It naturally interacts with that environment, is influenced by it, influences that environment in turn and acts together with the environment in the larger and far more complex history of society. The history of a dramatic pattern or its evolution is therefore very much the history of other art forms of society. And when we consider art forms from the point of view of survival strategies, the dynamics of cultural interaction with society become even more aesthetically challenging and fulfilling. We discover, for instance, that under certain conditions some art forms are transformed into others—simply to ensure the survival of the threatened forms. Drama may give way to poetry and song in order to disseminate dangerous sentiments under the watchful eye of the oppressor, the latter forms being more easily communicable. On the other hand, drama may become more manifestly invigorated in order to counteract the effect of an alienating environment.

Nigeria offers a valuable example of the dual process of cultural

† From *Art, Dialogue and Outrage: Essays on Literature and Culture* (Ibadan: New Horn Press, 1988) 134–46. Copyright © 1962, 1988, 1993 by Wole Soyinka. Used by permission of Pantheon Books, a division of Random House, Inc., and Melanie Jackson Agency, L.L.C.

attenuation and resurgence. For example, theatrical professionalism was synonymous, by the middle nineteenth century, with the artistic proficiency and organisation of a particular theatrical form which had emerged from the burial rituals associated with the Oyo monarchy, the *egungun*. The question of when a performed event became theatre as opposed to ritualism is of course a vexed one that we need not bother about in this context. It is, however, commonly agreed that what started out—probably—as a ritualistic ruse to effect the funeral obsequies of an Oyo king had, by the mid-century, evolved into a theatrical form in substance and practice. From an annual celebration rite of the smuggling-in of the corpse of that king and its burial, the *egungun* ancestral play became, firstly, a court re-enactment, then a secular form of performance which was next appropriated by the artists themselves. Its techniques were perfected by family guilds and township cults. About this time, however, Islam had begun its push southwards. The Oyo empire, already in disintegration from internal rivalries and other stresses, found itself under increasing military pressure from the Hausa-Fulani in the north, a situation which came on the heels of a rebellion of tributary states to the south. The fall of Oyo took down with it the security which the theatrical art had enjoyed under its patronage. The Muslims, victorious in northern Yorubaland, banned most forms of theatrical performance as contrary to the spirit of Islam. The *Agbegijo, Alarinjo* and allied genres, with their dramatic use of the paraphernalia of carved masks and other representations of ancestral spirits, came most readily under religious disapproval. It did not matter that, by now, they had lost most of their pretence to the mysterious or numinous.

Southern Nigeria and its neighbouring territories were, however, only temporary beneficiaries from this disruption of political life in the old Oyo empire. The Christian missionaries had also begun their northward drive, usually only a few steps ahead of the colonial forces. The philistinic task begun by the Moslems was rounded out by the Christians' ban on the activities of suspect cults. The Christians went further. They did not content themselves with banning just the dramatic performance; they placed their veto also on indigenous musical instruments—*bata, gangan, dundun* and so on—the very backbone of traditional theatre. It was into this vacuum that the returned slaves stepped with their Western (and therefore Christian) instruments, their definitely Christian dramatic themes and their Western forms.

Another historical factor aided the temporary eclipse of indigenous theatre forms: the slave trade and its supply which involved inter-state wars, raids and casual kidnappings. The missionary compounds often offered the securest havens from these perennial hazards, just as did (in West Africa) submission to the protective spheres of the Muslim overlords. It is difficult to imagine a group of refugees from the old Oyo empire encouraged by their Muslim or Christian protectors to revert to the ways of their 'pagan art'. The records do not reveal any such acts of disinterested artistic patronage. Artistic forms might be appropriated, but only in the cause of religious promotion; thus, for example, the appropriation of musical forms by the nineteenth-century Christian missionaries in Buganda for hymns. This, however, was only a later refinement, a sensible strategy for rendering the patently alien words and sentiments less abrasive to the indigenes by coating them in traditional harmonies.

It is difficult to trace, at present, the effect of the Oyo *egungun* dispersal on the development of theatrical forms in neighbouring areas. This is always the case with any situation of artistic hiatus—a period, that is, when a particular form of art goes underground or disappears temporarily, especially under the pressures of a dominant political and artistic ethos. The records simply ignore them, or treat them merely as isolated nuisances. The substitution of new forms belonging to the dominant culture takes pride of place in records, and this is the situation we encounter in the development of Western 'concerts' and variety shows in the colonized territories of West Africa.

At this point, therefore, let us clarify in our minds what theatre is. That this is more than a merely academic exercise is easily grasped if we refer to a sister art, sculpture, an achievement which the missionary-colonizer pioneers found convenient to deny to the African. The redressing assessment was made by other Europeans—the artists themselves, notably the Expressionists; they had no overriding reasons to deny the obvious, to ignore what was even a potential source of inspiration to their own creative endeavours. The vexed question of what constitutes drama and what is merely ritual, ceremony, festival and so on, while it continues to be legitimately argued, must always be posed against an awareness of early prejudiced reading of the manifestations encountered by culture denigrators, definitions which today still form the language of orthodox theatre criticism. To assist our own definition we need look only at any one cultural event within which diversified forms are found, forms which—through their visual impact—tend towards the creation of differing categories for a comparative description. In other words if, within one performance or cluster of performances (say, a festival or a celebration) in any given community, we discover consciously differing qualitative enactments, we are obliged to rummage around in our artistic vocabulary for categories that reflect such differences. Thus we find that, sooner or later, we arrive at the moment when only the expression 'drama' or 'theatre' seems apposite, and then the search is over. We will take an example from the Afikpo masquerades of south-east Nigeria.

A contrast between the *okumkpa* event and the *oje ogwu*, both being components of this Afikpo festival, actually furnishes us with the basic definition we need. This masquerade, which is the professional handiwork of a male initiation society, varies, we discover, from basically balletic sequences as contained in the *oje ogwu* to the *mimetic* as contained in the *okumkpa*. The latter is indeed performed as a climax to what appears to be the prominent *oje ogwu* turn by the masquerades. Both are basically audience-oriented—in other words, we are not really concerned here with the complication of a *ritual* definition but one of performance and reception. The audience plays a prominent appreciative role in this outdoor performance, judging, booing or approving on purely aesthetic grounds. Whatever symbolism may be contained in the actual movements of the *oje ogwu* is of no significance in the actual judgement. What the audience looks for and judges are the finer points of leaps, turns, control and general spatial domination. The poorer performers are soon banished to the groups sessions— which demonstrates the importance given to individual technical mastery.

The *okumkpa* event, by contrast, consists of satirical mimesis. Masks are also used but the *action* forms the basis of performance. This action consists of a satirical rendition of actual events both in neighbouring settlements and in the village itself. Personalities are ridiculed, the events in which they were involved are re-enacted. In short, events are transformed artistically both for audience delectation and for the imparting of moral principles. Additionally, however, one standard repertoire consists of the taking of female roles by the young male initiates, this role being of a rather derogatory character. The satirized female is invariably what we might call 'the reluctant bride'. As the young actor minces and prances around, sung dialogues accompany him, built around the same theme: 'How much longer are you going to reject all suitors on the grounds that they are not sufficiently handsome/strong/industrious etc., etc.?' Competition is keen among the initiates for the honour of playing this central female impersonator. The various sketches in this vein are rounded off in the end by a massed parade of the various actors in the *njenji* where the less accomplished actors have their own hour of glory and the entire female world is satirically lectured on the unkindness of keeping the male rooster waiting too long.

We will not examine the sociological motivation of this kind of drama except to point out that this example is actually more rewarding, in our search for an explanation of man's motives in *dramatizing*, than, for instance, the theory of the origin in the Oyo masquerade. Clearly, in the Afikpo masquerade we encounter a male-prejudiced device. It ensures man's claim to social superiority and creates guilt in the woman for not fulfilling on demand man's need for female companionship. It is of no more mystifying an order of things than, for instance, the disparagement by male undergraduates in their press of female undergraduates who have not submitted to their own desires —except, of course, that traditional society imposed heavy penalties on libellous fabrication (which is, by the way, a reliable indication of artistic barrenness). What we obtain from one, therefore, is genuine art; from their modern progeny, alas, only dirty pictures and fevered fantasies. The *okumkpa* provides us with drama—variety, satire. We are left with no other definition when we contrast it with its consciously differentiated companion piece—the *oje ogwu*.

Similarly, festivals such as the Ogun or Osun (River) festivals in Yorubaland provide us with multi-media and multi-formal experiences within which it is not at all difficult to find unambiguous examples of dramatic enactments. The high point of the festival of the Yoruba hero-deity Obatala is, for instance, undoubted drama, consisting of all the elements that act on the emotions, the excitations of conflict and resolution and the human appreciation of spectacle. We begin to understand now why dating the origin of African drama, locating it in a specific event, time and place is an impossible task—indeed, a meaningless one. In the study of art forms, it is clearly more appealing to look into extant material for what may be deduced as primitive or early forms of the particular art, noting along the way what factors have contributed to their survival in the specific forms. Festivals, comprising as they do such a variety of forms, from the most spectacular to the most secretive and emotionally charged, offer the most familiar hunting-ground. What is more, they constitute in themselves *pure theatre* at its most prodigal and resourceful. In short, the persistent habit of dismissing festivals as belonging to a 'spontaneous' inartistic expression of communities demands re-examination. The level of organization involved, the integration of the sublime with the mundane, the endowment of the familiar with properties of the unique (and this, spread over days) all indicate that it is into the heart of many African festivals that we should look for the most stirring expressions of man's instinct and need for drama at its most comprehensive and community-involving. Herbert M. Cole renders this point of view in penetrating terms:

> A festival is a relatively rare climatic event in the life of any community. It is bounded by a definite beginning and end, and is unified thereby, as well as being set apart from the above daily life. Its structure is built on a core or armature of ritual. The festival brings about a suspension of ordinary time, a transformation of ordinary space, a formaliser of ordinary behaviour. It is as if a community becomes a stage set and its people actors with a battery of seldom-seen props and costumes. Meals become feasts, and greetings, normally simple, become ceremonies. Although dependent upon life-sustaining rituals, the festival is an elaborated and stylised phenomenon which far surpasses ritual necessity. It often becomes the social, ritual and political apotheosis of community life in a year. At festival time one level of reality—the common and everyday—gives way to another, a more intense, symbolic and expressive level of reality.[1]

What this implies is that instead of considering festivals from one point of view only—that of providing, in a primitive form, the ingredients of drama—we may even begin examining the opposite point of view: that contemporary drama, as we experience it today, is a contraction of drama, necessitated by the productive order of society in other directions. That is, drama undergoes parallel changes with other structuring mechanisms of society. As communities outgrow certain patterns of producing what they require to sustain themselves or of transforming what exists around them, the structures which sustain the arts are affected in parallel ways, affecting in turn the very forms of the arts. That the earlier forms are not necessarily more 'primitive'

1. Herbert M. Cole in *African Arts*, VIII (3).

or 'crude' is borne out by the fact that more and more of the highly developed societies are turning to the so-called 'primitive' forms of drama as representing the significant dramatic forms for contemporary society. These societies, which vary from such ideologically disparate countries as the United States and East European countries, are reintroducing on stage, in both formal theatre structures and improvised spaces, dramatic forms such as we have described, from the macro-conceptual (as represented in festivals) to the micro-conceptual, as ritual may be held to epitomize.

In this vein, what are we to make of the famous Return-to-the-Village Festival of the Koumina canton in Bobo-Dioulasso, Upper Volta?[2] Here we encounter a people who, like many others in West Africa, have experienced the culturally disrupting influences of Muslim and Christian cultures. The traders came first, the Mande traders, in the early sixteenth century. In their next significant migration, the mid-eighteenth century, they were accompanied by Muslim clerics, with the cultural results with which we are by now familiar. By 1775 proselytization had become so successful that an Imamate had been established by the famous Saghnughu family of scholars. The late nineteenth century saw the take-over by colonial administrators and Christian missionaries. Yet under this double assault, Bobo traditional arts have survived until today, and nowhere are they given more vital expression than in the 'Tagaho' season festival which marks the return of the Bobo to their village after their seasonal migrations to their farmsteads. The festival, which has for its core the funeral ceremonies for those who died during the period of farmland migration, has a far more important function for the living: the re-installation of the co-hering, communal spirit and existential reality. Costumes are elaborately prepared, formal patterns both of 'ritual' and 'pageant' worked out and rehearsed, individual events enacted by masked figures for a delayed participation by the community as one entity. It is all of course a conscious performance, informed and controlled by aesthetic ideas, by the competitive desire also of 'showing off' dramatic skills. Simultaneously it is an affirmation of social solidarity. Can this form of theatre, considered in its most fundamental purpose and orientation, be viewed much differently from the theatre of 'happenings' which began in America and Europe in the sixties and is still encountered in parts of those societies today? To be sure, the former is more disciplined, formal and community-inspired, which are all attributes that we experience from unalienating forms of theatre.

At this point, it may be useful to consider instances where an art form evolves into another art form in one geographical/cultural area but fails to do so in another. The heroic tradition is one that is common to most parts of Africa (and, indeed, to most societies). Within this tradition may be grouped, at any level of its development, the epic, saga, praise-chants, ballads and so on, but here we are concerned with the performance aspect from which dramatization most naturally

2. Now renamed Burkina Faso.

evolves. East, Central and South Africa are particularly rich in the tradition of the heroic recitative. Among the Luo of Kenya and Uganda, for instance, we may note the form known as the *pakrouk*, a kind of virtue-boasting which takes place at ceremonial gatherings, usually to the accompaniment of a harp. The individual performer emerges from the group, utters praises of his own person and his achievements, and is replaced or contended with by another. Similar manifestations are found among the Ankole tribes, while further south, among the Sotho and the Zulu, sustained lyrical recitations on important historical events have become highly developed.

Among the Ijaw people of south-eastern Nigeria, however, the same tradition has actually developed dramatic variants, has moved beyond the merely recited to the enacted, a *tour de force* sustained by a principal actor for over three days. The saga of *Ozidi*, the principal source for J. P. Clark's play of the same name, is an example. By contrast, the history of the performance arts in Central and Southern Africa reveals a tendency towards virtual stasis of the putative dramatic elements. Even the dramatic potential of such rituals as the *Nyasi-iye*, the boat-building and launching ceremonies of the Luo, with its symbolic cutting of the 'umbilical cord' as the boat is freed from its moorings, even the abundant parallelisms with nuptial rites, have somehow failed to move towards a truly dramatic rendering of the significance and life-intertwining role of the boats in the daily pre-occupations of the Luo. One need only contrast this with the various rites and festivals of the coastal and riverine peoples of West Africa, where both religious observances and economic practicalities of the same activity have taken on, over the centuries, a distinctly dramatic ordering. One may speculate at length on the reasons for this contrast; the reality remains, however, that drama as an integral phenomenon in the lives of the peoples of Central and Southern Africa has followed a comparatively meagre development.

Well then, let us, using one of our early examples, follow how traditional theatre forms adjusted or re-surfaced from the preliminary repressions of alien cultures. We find that the 'pagan' theatre ultimately withstood the onslaught, not only preserving its forms but turning itself consciously into a base of resistance against both dominating systems. We are able to witness the closing of a cycle of cultural substitution in a curious irony of this slavery-colonial experience. Having first broken up the cultural life of the people, the slave era, now in its dying phase in the first half of the nineteenth century, brought back the sons of the land with a new culture in place of the old. The returnees constituted a new elite: they possessed after all the cultural tools of the colonial masters. But—and now we emphasize the place of theatre among these cultural tools—even where they were fully assimilated into the cultural values of their erstwhile masters (or saviours), they found on their return company servants, civil servants, missionary converts who belonged in the same social class as themselves, but were culturally unalienated. These stay-at-homes had had what was more or less an equivalent colonial education, yet had also acquired a nationalist awareness which manifested itself in cultural attitudes. As the nineteenth century entered its last quarter, the stay-at-homes were able to provide a balancing development pattern to cultural life on the West Coast which came predominantly under the creative influence of the returnee Christians, despite the latter's confidence in the superiority of their acquired arts and their eagerness to prove to the white population that the black man was capable not only of receiving but also of practising the refined arts of the European.

The cultural difference between the settlers of Liberia and Sierra Leone on the one hand, and the coastal societies of Ghana and Nigeria on the other can be translated in terms of the degree of cultural identification with, and adaptation of the authentic resources of the hinterland. To the former—mostly returnee slaves—the indigenous people remained savage, crude and barbaric, to be regarded only as material for missionary conversion and possible education. The converts who had remained at home, however, set off a process of schisms within social and religious institutions whose value-system was Eurocentric, delving again and again into the living resources of indigenous society. Naturally there were exceptions on both sides, but this dichotomy did hold in general. The direction of *new* forms of theatrical entertainment therefore followed an eastward pattern from the new returnee settlements; inevitably it received increasing native blood-transfusion as it moved further east away from the bastardized vaudeville of the 'Nova Scotians', so that by the time it arrived in Ghana, Dahomey (now Benin) and Nigeria, both in form and content, a distinct West African theatrical idiom had evolved.

'Academies', to begin with, were formed for the performance of concerts which were modelled on the Victorian music hall or the American vaudeville. The Christian churches organized their own concerts, schools were drawn into the concert rage—prize-giving days, visits of the District Officer, Queen Victoria's birthday and so on. The black missionaries refused to be outdone; Rev. Ajayi Crowther was a famous example, a black prelate who patronized and encouraged this form of the arts, while the Rev. James Johnson turned the famous Breadfruit church in Lagos into a springboard for theatrical performances. The Brazilian returnees added an exotic yet familiar flavour, their music finding a ready echo in the traditional melodies of the West Coast and the Congo whose urban suppression had not occurred long enough for such melodies to be totally forgotten. At the turn of the century and in the first decades of the twentieth century, Christmas and New Year saw the streets of the capital cities of Freetown and Lagos transformed by mini-pageants reminiscent of Latin fiestas, of which the 'caretta', a kind of satyr masquerade, appears to have been the most durable.

Cultural nationalism was, however, constantly at work against a total usurpation by imported forms. Once again religion and its institutions provided the base. Unable to accept the excesses of the Christian cultural imperialism, such as the embargo on African instruments and tunes in a 'universal' church, and the prohibition of drumming on tranquil Anglican Sundays, the breakaway movements began. The period 1888 to the early 1930s witnessed a proliferation of secessionist movements, mostly inspired by a need to worship God in the cultural mode of the forefathers. And now began also a unique 'operatic' tradition in West Africa, but especially Lagos, beginning with church cantatas which developed into dramatizations of biblical stories until it asserted its independence in secular stories and the development of professional touring troupes. The process, reminiscent of the evolution of the 'miracle' or 'mystery' plays of medieval Europe, is identical with the evolution of the Agbegijo theatre (then temporarily effaced) from the sacred funeral rites of the Alafin of Oyo to court entertainment and, thereafter, independent existence and geographical dispersion. From the genteel concerts of classical music and English folk songs by the 'Academy' of the 1880s to the historical play *King Elejigbo* of the Egbe Ife Church Dramatic Society in 1902, a transformation of thought and sensibility had recognizably taken place even among the Westernized elite of southern Nigeria. The churches did not take kindly to it. They closed their churchyards and schools to the evolving art. Alas, they only succeeded in accelerating the defiant erection of theatre halls, specifically designed for the performing arts. It was in reality a tussle between groups of colonial elites, fairly balanced in the matter of resources. By 1912 the secularization of theatrical entertainment in southern Nigeria was sufficiently advanced for the colonial government to gazette a 'Theatre and Public Performance Regulations Ordinance', which required that performing groups obtain a licence before going before the public. In the climate of cultural nationalism which obtained in Lagos at that time, it is doubtful whether this disguised attempt at political censorship would have worked; it is significant that the ordinance was never made into law.

Ironically, yet another breakaway church, the Cherubim and Seraphim movement, swung the pendulum back towards a rejection of traditional forms and was followed shortly by other emulators in the Christian re-consecration of theatrical forms. The furthest these churches would go in the use of musical instruments was the tambourine; local instruments which had created a new tonality in the operettas now touring the West Coast—sekere, dundun, gangan, and so on—were damned as instruments of the Devil. Secular stories, even of historic personages and events, were banned and the new theatre halls, church halls and schoolrooms echoed once more to the Passion of Christ, the anguish of Nebuchadnezzar, the trials of Job, and other dramatic passages from the Bible. The Aladura, Cherubim and Seraphim, and their adherents did not however stop there. These 'prophetist' cults spread rapidly along the West Coast waging a crusade against all 'pagan' worship and their sacred objects. Descending on the provinces of the established churches, they ignited bonfires with their hot-gospelling in which perished thousands of works of art, especially in Nigeria, Cameroons, Ghana and the Ivory Coast. The vision of a fifteen-year-old girl, Abiodun Akinsowon, about 1921, was to prove a costly dream for the cultural heritage of West Africa, the heaviest

brunt of which was borne by Yoruba sculpture. This period may also
be justly said to constitute the lowest ebb in the fortunes of traditional
theatre, participation in the cultural life even of the villages being
subjected to lightning descents from the fanatical hordes of the pro-
phetic sects. In the physical confrontations that often took place, the
position of authority was predictable. Embarrassed as they sometimes
were by the excesses of the sectarians, the European missionaries and
their black priests had no hesitation about their alliances—and their
voice was weighty in the processes of imposing the colonial peace.

But the 'vaudeville' troupes prospered. Names of groups such as we
encounter in 'Two Bobs and their Carolina Girl' tell us something of
the inspiration of much of these. Master Yalley, a schoolteacher, is
credited with having begun the tradition of the vaudeville variety act
in Ghana. His pupil Bob Johnson and his 'Axim Trio' soon surpassed
the master and became a familiar figure on Ghana's cultural landscape, also later in Nigeria. More important still, Bob Johnson's innovations must be credited with having given birth to the tradition of
the 'concert party' of Ghana, groups which specialize in variety routine:
songs, jokes, dances, impersonations, comic scenes. However, the
most notable achievement in the sense of cultural continuity was their
thrusting on to the fore-stage of contemporary repertoire a stock character from traditional lore, the wily trickster Anansi. This quickly developed into a vehicle for social and political commentary, apart from
its popularity in comic situations.

The Jaguar Jokers, for example, transformed Anansi into the more
urban character of Opia, while Efua Sutherland's more recent *The
Marriage of Anansewa* takes this tradition into an even more tightly-
knit and disciplined play format—the term 'disciplined' being employed here merely in the sense of reducing the areas of spontaneous
improvization, without however eliminating them. Those who saw this
piece during Festac 77 will have observed how attractively the element
of formal discipline and free improvisation blended together to encourage a controlled audience interaction. By the middle 1930s, Bob
Johnson had become sufficiently established to take his brand of
vaudeville to other West African cities. West Africa in this decade
could boast of a repertoire of shows displaying the most bizarre products of electric art in the history of theatre. Even cinema, an infant
art, had by then left its mark on West African theatre: some of Bob
Johnson's acts were adaptations of Charlie Chaplin's escapades,
not omitting his costume and celebrated shuffle. And the thought
of Empire Day celebration concerts at which songs like 'Mini the
Moocher' formed part of the evening musical recitals, side by side with
'God's Gospel is our Heritage' and vignettes from the life of a Liberian
stevedore, stretches the contemporary imagination, distanced from the
historical realities of colonial West Africa.

Again, another irony of colonial intentions: while Bob Johnson was
preparing his first West African tour and Hubert Ogunde, later to
become Nigeria's foremost 'concert party' leader, was undergoing his
aesthetic formation from the vying forces of a clergyman father and a

grandmother who was a priestess of the *Osugbo* cult, a European ed-
ucationist, Charles Beart in Senegal, was beginning to reverse the policy of European acculturation in a leading secondary school in
Senegal. The extent of this development—including also an appreciation of the slow pace of such an evolution—will be better grasped by
recalling the educational charter of assimilationism, spelt in diverse
ways by the publications of such dedicated African Francophiles as the
Abbe Boillat, Paul Holle and so on. Boillat, in spite of extensive sociological research (*Esquisses senegalaises*),[3] the result of his examination of the culture and philosophy of the Bambara, Sarakole, Wolof,
Serer, the Tukulor and Moorish groups in Senegal, found no lessons
to be drawn from African society for modern cultural development, no
future but to witness the fall of all those 'gross, if not dishonourable,
ways known as the *custom of the country'*. If his addresses to the metropolitan centre of the French world did not become the cornerstone
of French assimilationist policies, they undoubtedly played a key role
in their formulation. Against this background, and ensuring decades
of such conservatism, the Ecole William Ponty was founded. A famous
teachers' college, it served Francophone Africa in the same way as did
Achimota College in the Anglophone West and Makerere College in
East Africa. They were all designed to provide a basic European education for would-be teachers and low-echelon civil servants. Such hu-
manistic education as came into the curriculum of the Ecole William
Ponty was of necessity French—French plays, poetry, music, art, history. Charles Beart, during his principal-ship, embarked however on a
new orientation of the students' cultural instructions. From 1930 onwards the students were encouraged to return to their own societies
for cultural directions. Assignments were given which resulted in the
students' exploration of both the form and the substance of indigenous
art. Groups from every colonial territory represented at William Ponty
were then expected to return from vacation armed with a theatrical
presentation based on their researches, the entire direction being left
in the hands of the students themselves. Since the new theatrical sociology did not confine itself to the usual audiences of European officials and 'educated' Africans, nor to Senegal alone, its influence
spread widely through different social strata of French-speaking Africa.
Was it, however, a satisfying development of the culture from which
it derived?

The answer must be in the negative, though the experiment was not
without its instructive values. It would be too much to expect that, at
that period, the classic model of French theatre could yield completely
to the expression of traditional forms. The community represented by
William Ponty was an artificial one. It was distanced from the society
whose cultural board it rifled both in qualitative thought and material
product. The situation was of course not peculiar to William Ponty
since it also obtained in the other schools and institutions set up by
the colonizer for the fulfilment of his own mission in Africa. Thus the

3. Abbe Boilatt, Esquisses Sénégalaises, 1858; new edition, Paris, 1984, Editions Karthala.

theatre of William Ponty served the needs of exotic satisfaction for the community of French colonials. Even when it 'went to the people', and with their own material, it remained a curiosity that left the social life and authentic cultural awareness of the people untouched.

We will conclude with the 'new' theatre form which has proved the most durable; hybrid in its beginnings, the 'folk opera' has become the most expressive language of theatre in West Africa. What were the themes that mostly engaged the various groups spread along the Coast? The Nigerian Hubert Ogunde provides a convenient compendium, since he does appear to be more consistently varied in his dramatic fare than any comparable group to date in West Africa. His repertoire ranges from outright fantasy through biblical dramatizations to social commentary and political protest, both in the colonial and post-colonial era. A comparative study of the repertoire of the Jaguar Jokers, the Axim Trio, or the current Anansekrom groups of Ghana for example would reveal that these concentrate almost exclusively on social commentary, mostly with a moralistic touch—the evils of witchcraft, maladjustment in the social status of the cash-crop *nouveaux riches*, generational problems, changing status of women in society, sexual mores and so on, all of which also preoccupy the pamphlet drama of the Onitsha market literateurs. Hubert Ogunde explored these themes in his plays and more. His biblical adaptations became in effect a vehicle for direct commentaries on contemporary society. Reference is hardly necessary to those plays which have earned him the ire of colonial and post-colonial governments: *Bread and Bullets,* a play not merely on the famous Iva Valley strike by miners in eastern Nigeria but on the general inequity of labour exploitation; and *Yoruba Ronu,* an indictment of the corruption and repression of the government of the then Western Region. Both plays were proscribed by the affected governments. They have entered the lore of theatrical commitment in Nigeria.

And additionally, Hubert Ogunde exemplifies what we have referred to up until now as the survival patterns of traditional theatrical art. From the outset of his theatrical career, Ogunde's theatre belonged only partially to what we have described as the 'Nova Scotian' tradition. His musical instrumentation was all borrowed from the West, movement on stage was pure Western chorus-line night-club variety. Nevertheless, the attachment to traditional musical forms (albeit with Western impurities) gradually became more assertive. Encouraged no doubt by the appearance of more tradition-grounded groups such as Kola Ogunmola and Duro Ladipo, Hubert Ogunde in the early sixties began to employ traditional instruments in his performance, his music delved deeper into home melodies, and even his costumes began to eschew the purely fabricated, theatrically glossy, for recognizable local gear. Rituals appeared with greater frequency and masquerades became a frequent feature—often, it must be added, as gratuitous insertions. Ogunde's greatest contribution to West African drama—quite apart from his innovative energy and his commitment to a particular political line—lies in his as yet little appreciated musical 'recitative' style, one which he has made unique to himself. It has few imitators, but the success of his records in this genre of 'dramatic monologue' testifies to the responsive chord it elicits from his audience. Based in principle on the Yoruba *rara* style of chanting, but in stricter rhythm, it is melodically a modernistic departure, flexibly manipulated to suit a variety of themes. Once again, we find that drama draws on other art forms for its own survival and extension. It is no exaggeration to claim that Hubert Ogunde's highest development of the chanted dramatic monologue can be fixed at the period of the political ban on his *Yoruba Ronu*. Evidently all art forms flow into one another, confirming, as earlier claimed, that the temporary historic obstacles to the flowering of a particular form sometimes lead to its transformation into other media of expression, or even the birth of totally different groups.

This survey stops at the emergence of the latest forms of traditional drama. The finest representatives of this to date have been the late Kola Ogunmola (comedy and satire) and Duro Ladipo (history and tragedy). Their contribution to contemporary drama and their innovations from indigenous forms require a far more detailed study, just as Moses Olaiya (Baba Sala) demands a chapter of his own iconoclastic brand of theatrical wit. The foregoing attempts to highlight ways in which artistic forms return to life again and again after their seeming demise, ways by which this process emphasizes the fundamental unity of various art forms and the social environment that gives expression to them; how certain creative ideas are the very offspring of historic convulsions. Finally, while for purposes of demarcation we may speak of Nigerian, Ghanaian or perhaps Togolese drama, it must constantly be borne in mind that, like the economic intercourse of the people themselves, the various developments we have touched upon here in drama and the arts do not obey the laws of political boundaries though they might respond to the events within them. The various artistes we have mentioned had, and still enjoy, instant *rapport* with audiences far from their national and linguistic boundaries. Their art finds a ready response in most audiences since their themes are rooted in everyday experience, fleshed out in shared idioms of cultural adjustment.

NGUGI WA THIONG'O

Enactments of Power: The Politics of Performance Space†

I

The struggle between the arts and the state can best be seen in performance in general and in the battle over performance space in particular. Performance is representation of being, the coming to be, and the ceasing to be of processes in nature, human society, and thought. If before the emergence of the state the domain of culture embodied the desirable and the undesirable in the realm of values, this was expressed through performance. The community learnt and passed on its moral codes and aesthetic judgements through narratives, dances, theatre, rituals, music, games, and sports. With the emergence of the state, the artist and the state became not only rivals in articulating the laws, moral or formal, that regulate life in society, but also rivals in determining the manner and circumstances of their delivery.

This is best expressed in Plato's dialogue the *Laws*. The Athenian describes how, as the representatives of the state, they must respond should the tragic poets come to their city and ask for permission to perform:

> We will say to them, we also according to our ability are tragic poets, and our tragedy is the best and noblest; for our whole state is an imitation of the best and noblest life; which we affirm to be indeed the very truth of tragedy. You are poets and we are poets, both makers of the same strain, rivals and antagonists in the noblest of dramas, which true law can alone perfect, as our hope is. Do not then suppose that we shall all in a moment allow you to erect your stage in the agora, or introduce the fair voices of your actors, speaking above our own, and permit you to harangue our women and children, and the common people, about our own institutions, in language other than our own, and very often the opposite of our own.[1]

The war between art and the state is really a struggle between the power of performance in the arts and the performance of power by the state—in short, enactments of power. The conflict in the enactments of power is sharper where the state is externally imposed, a situation of the conqueror and the conquered for instance, as in colonialism.

Jomo Kenyatta dramatizes this confrontation in *Facing Mount Kenya*. The story goes that there was a brief period of kingship in

---

† From *Penpoints, Gunpoints, and Dreams: Towards a Critical Theory of the Arts and the State in Africa* (Oxford: Clarendon, 1998) 37–69. Copyright © Ngugi wa Thiong'o 1998. Reprinted by permission of Oxford University Press.
1. Plato, *Laws*, book 7, in Hofstadter and Kuhns (eds.), *Philosophies of Beauty* (Chicago: University of Chicago Press, 1976), 52.

Agikuyu society. This was replaced by a new, more egalitarian system rooted in the family as the basic unit. The replacement was effected through a revolution, *ituĩka*, which literally means a break, a complete break with what has gone before. The new revolutionary councils, all the way up to the highest coordinating body of elders, derived their authority from below. The coming-to-be of this new system was celebrated through a ceremony called Ituĩka every twenty-five years or so. The ceremony also marked the passing of power from one generation to another. The festival was spread over a period of six months and involved the entire land inhabited by the Agikuyu. Thirty years after the British colonial state was established in about 1895 the Agikuyu community was involved in a flurry of activities to celebrate the Ituĩka ceremony, but this was stopped by the colonial state. The performance of Ituĩka was taken as a challenge to its power. The annual parade of British military might at the opening of the new sessions of the legislative assembly replace *ituĩka*-type performances.

The main ingredients of performance are space, content, audience, and the goal, whose end, so to speak, could be instruction or pleasure, or a combination of both—in short, some sort of reformative effects on the audience. The state has its areas of performance; so has the artist. While the state performs power, the power of the artist is solely in the performance. The state and the artist may have different conceptions of space, content, goals of performance, either of their own or of the other, but they have the audience as their common target. Again the struggle may take the form of the state's intervention in the content of the artist's work, which goes by the name of censorship, but the main arena of struggle is the performance space—its definition, delimitation, and regulation.

II

'I can take any empty space and call it a bare stage,' says Peter Brook in the opening line of his book *The Empty Space*. A man walks across the empty space while someone else is watching him, and this is all that is needed for an act of theatre. I want to pose the question: is a performance site ever empty as in the title of Peter Brook's book?

There are many ways of looking at performance space. One is to see it as a self-contained field of internal relations: the interplay between actors and props and light and shadows—the *mise-en-scène*—and between the *mise-en-scène* as a whole and the audience. The outer boundaries of this space are defined by a wall, material or immaterial. The material could be stone or wood or natural hedges. The immaterial is the outline formed by the audience in what is otherwise an open space. The director utilizes the entire playing-field, *ithaakĩro*, to maximum effect on both the actors and the audience. He will look for various levels, heights, centres, and directions of force in the acting area. But these levels and centres acquire their real power only in relationship to the audience. The entire space becomes a magnetic field of tensions and conflicts. It is eventually transformed into a

sphere of power revolving around its own axis like a planet in outer
space. This is the real magic and power of performance. It incorporates
the architectural space of material or immaterial walls into itself and
becomes a magic sphere made still by its own motion, but it is potentially explosive, or rather, it is poised to explode. That is why the state,
a repressive machine, often targets its nervous eyes on this aspect of
the performance space. For even if it does not explode, might it not,
by its sheer energy, through its laser-beams of power, ignite other
fields? For the magic sphere is not suspended in total isolation. There
are other social centres and fields of human actions: farms, factories,
residences, schools. Life goes on there, births, marriages, deaths, and
their representations in celebratory festivals of welcome or in dirges
of farewell.

Which brings us to another way, the second way, of looking at performance space. The performance space is also constituted by the totality of its external relations to these other centres and fields. Where
are they all located relative to each other? Who accesses these centres
and how frequently? It matters, in other words, whether, say, the
artist's space is located in a working-class district, in a bourgeois res-
idential neighbourhood, in the ghettos, or in the glossy sections of our
cities. The real politics of the performance space may well lie in the
field of its external relations; in its actual or potential conflictual engagement with all the other shrines of power, and in particular, with
the forces which hold the key to those shrines. The shrines could be
the synagogue, the church, the mosque, the temple, parliament, law-
courts, television and radio stations, the electronic and print media,
the classroom, playing-fields of all sorts and guises. In other words, it
is often not so much a question of what happens or could happen on
the stage at any one time, but rather the control of continuous access
and contact.

These questions of access and contact become very pertinent in a
colonial and post-colonial state, where the dominant social stratum is
often not sure of its hegemonic control, and particularly where the
population is divided not only on the traditional lines of the urban and
the rural but also on racial and ethnic fissures. And within those run
class divisions. The gap between the poor and the rich is so glaring,
so immediate, and so visible, that the state may want to get rid of the
performance spaces which keep on chafing this area of friction. In
such a situation, the question whether the space should be inside a
building or not may acquire a deep symbolic value and become the
site of intense power struggles.

And thirdly, the performance space, in its entirety of internal and
external factors, may be seen in its relationship to time, in terms, that
is, of what has gone before—history—and what could follow—the
future. What memories does the space carry and what longings might
it generate?

It is clear from this that the performance space is never empty. Bare,
yes; open, yes; but never empty. It is always the site of physical, social,
and psychic forces in society. It is the instinctive awareness of this

which prompts the Athenian in Plato's *Laws* never to want to permit the serious performing artist to harangue women, children, common people about 'our institutions'. And hence the battles over performance space.

Drawing concretely on my own experiences in theatre in Kenya, and on specific productions, I want to look at the performance space of the artist. Then I shall briefly look at the state's own areas of performance, and finally at their interactions and consequences on the body and mind of the artist and the population as a whole. We shall see that the politics of post-colonial performance space is a complex interplay of the entire field of internal and external relations of these forces in the context of geography, time, and history.

III

First the space of the artist. That this space, however bare it looks, is not empty came home to me when in 1976 I became involved in the production of the play *The Trial of Dedan Kīmathi*, whose national and world première was in Nairobi on 20 October that year. The script was a joint effort by Mĩcere Mũgo and me. We were then colleagues in the Literature Department of the University of Nairobi. Although she and I had for a long time discussed the possibility of collaborating on a play, it is ironic that what actually triggered intensified efforts on our part was a call by the state. The venue for the Second World Black and African Festival of Arts and Culture originally scheduled for Zaïre had been changed to Lagos, Nigeria, for February 1977. Kenya would be represented in all the events from displays of material culture to performing arts, including theatre.

With the representation of Kenya in Lagos in mind, the Ministry of Social Services, under which culture and cultural institutions were administered, had set up a national committee to oversee all the preparations. This in turn set up subcommittees for the various events. The Drama Subcommittee was given the task of coming up with two plays. I was initially the chairman of this subcommittee, but later, when the play in which I had collaborated with Mĩcere Mũgo was submitted for consideration, I gave up the chair, and Seth Adagala took up the position. Seth Adagala then worked with the Ministry, having resigned, a few years before, as the first and then the only African director of the Kenya National Theatre. The Drama Subcommittee eventually selected two plays, *The Trial of Dedan Kīmathi* and *Betrayal in the City* by Francis Imbuga. The two plays were to be run under the name Kenya Festac 77 Drama Group. Tirus Gathwe was to direct *Betrayed in the City* and Seth Adagala, *The Trial of Dedan Kīmathi*. As chairman of the Ministry's subcommittee, Seth Adagala was to be in overall charge.

In June 1976 the Festac 77 Drama Group came up with a brilliant but really common-sense proposal: since the two plays were supposedly going to represent Kenya in Lagos, it was important that they were performed first to audiences in Kenya, as a matter not of privilege but of right and necessity. There was an added reason: Kenya was going to host a Unesco general conference; there would be many delegates from all over the world, and it would do Kenya's image a world of good were the delegates to see effective African theatre. The question now was simply one of the best 'symbolic' time and venue.

The month of October was finally selected for two reasons. The Unesco meeting was to be held that month. But October was also the month in which Kenyans celebrated the heroes of anti-colonial struggles. We were also unanimous on the question of the venue: the Kenya National Theatre. After all it was called National; and it was under the Ministry of Social Services; and surely, apart from anything else, it would be the focal point for the Unesco delegates. Guardians of international education and culture, they would surely be interested in what the Kenya National Theatre would offer during their stay in the country. Thinking that everybody would applaud this, the leadership of the Festac 77 Drama Group presented the proposals to the management of the National Theatre. We were sure that there would be no problems: logic and good sense pointed to the selected time and place.

The first wake-up call took us all by surprise. The management, which was almost entirely composed of Europeans linked to the major European amateur and semi-professional groups, told us that there was no room in the inn! But this was in 1976, thirteen years after formal independence under the presidency of Jomo Kenyatta. We drew their attention to the symbolism of the event; the dignity of Kenya before the world; the fact that Kenyans needed to see the play before Lagos; and surely apart from anything else Kenyans needed to remind themselves that their independence was won through sweat and blood and the deaths of many. No room in the inn. The management was already committed to Bossman's *Jeune Ballet de France* and the City Players' *A Funny Thing Happened on the Way to the Forum*. At this crucial moment and in a national venue, Kenya would be seen through the eyes of a French ballet and a British farce.

In the course of the struggle over dates and venues there now arose basic questions of principle. Shouldn't the Kenya National Theatre and the Kenya Cultural Centre be catering primarily for national interests? In planning for cultural activities over the year, did the management not take into account the Kenyan image inside and outside the country? What shows should be performed on national days? And for the eyes of the world like the forthcoming Unesco conference? So many questions, so few answers, except that, for us, there was simply no room.

The management argued that the dates had been booked months before; that African plays never attracted theatre-lovers anyway. Statistics were even quoted as evidence. They had never stopped to ask why, even assuming their allegations to be true, there had always been a low turn-out of Africans at the theatre. Were the reasons not very evident in what they were proposing to offer as Kenyan culture before the eyes of the world in October? Could it not be that over the years the National Theatre had created the image of a service station for Western shows like *Godspell, The Boyfriend, The King and I, Jesus Christ Superstar?* Or more truthfully a service centre for the kind of theatre described as deadly in Peter Brook's book?

Actually behind the conflicting positions and arguments were deeper questions of the performance of history. The story of the space defined as national theatre was intertwined with that of the subject-matter of *The Trial of Dedan Kĩmathi,* and that of the entire country. Three stories locked together in the unfolding drama of times and venues.

The National Theatre complex was actually constructed by the colonial state. According to Richard Frost, former head of the Empire Information Services and the British Council's first representative in East Africa, the theatre had been put up under direct instructions from the Colonial Office to meet the urgent needs of good race relations in the colony through cultural practices. The National Theatre and the Cultural Centre complex were to be a place where 'people of culture and position' could meet. In the book *Race Against Time,* Frost elaborates on this thus:

> At that time no Africans were able to live anywhere near the site which was selected, but the site was selected because it was hoped that in due time the residential apartheid would be brought to an end and Muthaiga, Westlands, the Hill and other areas, which were then open only for Europeans, would become districts where leading people of all races would live. As it was not to be a 'working-class' theatre, it was built in the middle of the 'well-to-do' Nairobi.[2]

The National Theatre space was also going to be the host site of the Kenya Schools Drama Festival. The British Council, which had hatched the scheme in 1951, had hoped to 'win the goodwill of Europeans and to help them keep at a high standard the cultural heritage of Britain'. Theatre was the perfect instrument:

> Drama was a cultural activity enjoyed by both actors and audiences and it was also an activity in which Africans and Asians engaged. It was hoped that through the theatre the goodwill of the European community could be gained, and, later on, members of the different races could be brought together by participation in a common pursuit which they all enjoyed.[3]

So, right from the start, the place had been seen as an empty space on which a predominantly British theatre was going to help in the construction of a new chapter of good race relations in the country.

But the site was not a space empty of history and in which, now, a narrative of new race relations could be written through the mediating eyes of the Colonial Office in alliance with a colonized people of goodwill. Next to the National Theatre site was, and still is, the Norfolk Hotel, built by Lord Delamere, one of the early British settlers, at the

---

2. Richard Frost, *Race Against Time* (London: Rex Collings, 1975), 73.
3. Ibid. 196.

turn of the century. It was in fact known more popularly among the settlers as the House of Lords because that was where the colonial white nobility, or pretenders to nobility, used to meet for drinks and gossip and politics. The Norfolk Hotel overlooks the site where in 1922 African workers were massacred by the British police. The workers were marching to the central police station to demand the release of their leader, Harry Thuku, who had been arrested and later imprisoned for eight years because of his involvement in the nascent workers' movement. Their march was interrupted by gunfire from the police. The police were also joined in the massacre by the white lords on the terraces of the Norfolk Hotel. The figures of the dead are in dispute. The British admit to twenty-two only; but there were at least 150 dead. The bodies of the dead and wounded lay sprawled on the ground on the site which years later was to house the National Theatre complex and the University of Nairobi. Harry Thuku became a nationalist hero, the subject of many songs and dances. But opposed to Harry Thuku and his workers' politics were the colonial-appointed chiefs who had even founded the first ever loyalist movement in the country. The colonial state and the loyalist chiefs were on the same side in blaming the massacre on the victims.

The massacre had also attracted international protest. Marcus Garvey, on behalf of the Universal Negro Improvement Association, dispatched a telegram of protest to the British prime minister Lloyd George, in which, *inter alia,* he said: 'You have shot down a defenceless people in their own native land exercising their rights as men. Such a policy will aggravate the many historic injustices heaped upon a race that will one day be placed in a position to truly defend itself not with mere sticks, clubs and stones, but with modern implements of science.'[4] Garvey's prophecy came true in 1952 when a 22-year-old former primary school teacher and accountant escaped the tight security net and slipped into the mountains to become the most formidable leader of the Mau Mau armed guerrilla forces. His name was Dedan Kĩmathi.

Under his leadership the Mau Mau guerrillas put up one of the most heroic struggles against imperialism in the twentieth century. It is often forgotten that while liberation movements in places such as Guinea-Bissau, Mozambique, Angola, and Algeria had free neighbouring territories which served as rear bases, Mau Mau guerrillas were completely surrounded by the enemy administration. They had to depend almost entirely on what arms they could steal from the enemy forces and what they could make in the underground arms factories in the country's cities and forests. Before Kĩmathi's capture in 1956 and execution in 1957, even the British government and the colonial state had to admit that, despite thousands of soldiers brought from the British bases all over the world, and despite bombings on a scale reminiscent of the Second World War, there were virtually two gov-

---

4. Quoted in Ngũgĩ, *Detained: A Writer's Prison Diary* (London: Heinemann, 1987), 40.

erning authorities in Kenya: the colonial authority led by the Governor and Mau Mau, led by Dedan Kĩmathi.

The period saw the most incredible upsurge of Kenyan culture. It was a general grass-root-based performance of hope. There were several newspapers in Kenyan languages. Songs and dances celebrating the African past, condemning colonial practices, and calling for freedom had erupted. In the educational field, people had developed their own schools under the Kikuyu Independence Schools Movement and Kikuyu Karĩng's Schools Association. This educational movement culminated in the building by the people themselves of the first ever institute of higher learning in the country under the name Gĩthũngũri African Teachers' College, led by Mbiyũ wa Koinange, a Columbia University graduate. The symbolic importance of this can be seen in the fact that not until 1960, three years before Independence, was the second institute of higher learning, the University College of Nairobi, built, ironically on a site next to both the Norfolk Hotel and the National Theatre.

The colonial state retaliated. In October 1952 a state of emergency was declared. African-run schools were closed down because they were seen as performance sites for the nationalist forces. Gĩthũngũri Teachers' College was closed as an educational institution and the building turned into a prison where captured Mau Mau guerrillas and sympathizers were hanged. All cultural performances were stopped. And on 20 October 1952 Kenyatta and hundreds of leaders of KAU, the Kenya African Union, and of Mau Mau, were arrested. Kenyatta and seven others were later tried in what became one of the most celebrated trials in colonial history, now immortalized in the book by Montague Slater *The Trial of Jomo Kenyatta*. The defendants were found guilty of leading Mau Mau and were imprisoned for eight years with hard labour. The colonial state did not bother with the trials of hundreds of others; they were summarily sent to concentration camps all over the country.

The play *The Trial of Dedan Kĩmathi* tries to capture that heroism and the determination of the people in that most glorious chapter of their history, not only a moment that helped to break the back of the British Empire and its entire colonial policy, but also, for Kenyans, a moment that was the culmination of all the previous struggles waged by the other resistance heroes of our history such as Waiyaki, Me Katilili, and Koitalel. Kĩmathi saw himself in the tradition of that struggle, but also in that of the Peasants' Revolt in Britain, an event he referred to in a letter addressed to the British from his hide-out in the mountains. The play tries to capture the fears and the hopes, the promises and the betrayals, with hints that history could repeat itself.

It is now evident that both the venue and the time—the days and the month of October—carried different memories. For the management, 1952 was the year the National Theatre was constructed and opened. And between 1952—the year that saw the declaration of a state of emergency, the banning of independent African performances, and the outbreak of the Mau Mau armed struggle—and 1963—the year of formal independence—the National Theatre space had remained a site for basically British theatre into which Africans could be admitted as they matured into people of culture and position.

It was these men and women of culture and position who after Independence were indeed able to integrate into those special areas that Frost talks about: Muthaiga, Westlands, and the Hill. Independence removed racial apartheid but retained economic barriers. Some of these African Kenyans defined by the British as men of culture and position were also to assume very important seats in the new post-colonial government. One of these was Charles Njonjo, the son of one of the early colonial chiefs who were part of the loyalist movement opposed to the nationalist politics of Harry Thuku. He became Attorney-General and, as a patron of one of the European performing groups and with his social linkage to most of the members of the management of the Kenya National Theatre and Cultural Centre, he was to play a crucial role in ensuring the uninterrupted control of the space by men and women who could maintain standards already set by the colonial state. And for him, although he himself was a black African, the only people who could ensure that continuity were British white. In other words, colonial practices were to be the yardstick for performative culture at the space. It was not surprising, therefore, that the management of the Centre could sincerely feel they were doing their duty to Kenya by staging a French ballet during the historically significant month of October and during a Unesco conference hosted by Kenya. For them the symbols of French ballet and a British farce stood for the authentic tradition of an Anglican Kenya.

The Trial of Dedan Kīmathi stood for a different tradition. It was celebrating the Mau Mau heroism and its centrality in bringing about independence for Kenya. But even more importantly, it was linking itself to the culture and aesthetic of resistance developed by the Mau Mau activists as they fought in the mountains, as they resisted in prison and concentration camps and villages, and as they called for a new Kenya and a new Africa. A good number of these songs and dances, now available in a collection of Mau Mau patriotic songs edited by Maina Wa Kīnyattī under the title *Thunder from the Mountains,* were incorporated in both the text and the performance of the play.

So the conflict over the performance space was also a struggle over what cultural symbols and activities represented the new Kenya. The country had emerged from an anti-colonial struggle: could a colonial culture and heritage effectively form the basis of its nationhood and identity? Even small acts could carry conflicting visions of the new Kenya. At a time when the Festac 77 Drama Group was trying to carry out a performance that reflected national history and to devise emblems that symbolized this, the management of the Kenyan National Theatre were selling Christmas cards of the National Theatre building as it was in 1952. It was then of course flying the Union Jack, the British flag, and this was quite prominent on the cards.

IV

The Ministry, probably embarrassed by press notices that a Kenyan play had been handcuffed on Kenyatta Day, intervened, and the Festac 77 Drama Group was given eight days between 20 and 30 October to use the space. So in effect the two plays, *The Trial of Dedan Kĩmathi* and *Betrayal in the City*, were crammed into four nights each between Bossman's *Jeune Ballet de France* (10 to 18 October) and the City Players' *A Funny Thing Happened on the Way to the Forum* (1 to 21 November). That in effect meant that the two European shows would take up a total of thirty-one days to our eight.

Despite this, the success of the two productions was astounding, especially in terms of the reception by African audiences. Every single one of the eight nights was sold out. The opening night of *The Trial* was particularly memorable because Kĩmathi's wife and children were prominent guests, and they later stayed with the cast almost the night long telling stories of the war and singing many of the songs over and over again. As one newspaper put it, 'never before has the story of Kenya's freedom struggle been told with such force and conviction'. Nor, if I might add, had any previous production at the National Theatre been received with so much enthusiasm by a Kenyan audience. For those eight nights, the space had been truly nationalized by the feet of so many from all walks of life who came on foot, in private cars, and in hired vehicles to sing and dance with the actors.

But the dramatic highlight still belongs to the opening night. As the actors sang their last song and dance, through the middle aisle of the auditorium, they were joined by the audience. They went outside the theatre building still dancing. What had been confined to the stage had now spilled out into the open air and there was no longer any distinction between actors and the audience. It became a procession, and they weaved their way towards the historic Norfolk Hotel, towards the terraces from where in 1922 the settlers had helped the police in their massacre. Even in 1976 it was still largely patronized by whites, mostly tourists. As the procession was about to cross the road, they were met by a contingent of police, who now told them, politely but firmly, to turn back. There was no antagonistic physical confrontation. The actors danced back to the National Theatre, formed a circle outside, and continued with their dances and songs, which talked about all the heroes of Kenyan resistance. The scene outside the theatre building continued every night of the four days allocated to *The Trial,* but the attempt to dance onto the premises of the Norfolk Hotel was not repeated. Nevertheless, it was as if the cast and the audience were trying to create an open space all around the Kenya National Theatre building, a space which would allow them to communicate better with the spirits of those who had died in 1922. A name which kept on cropping up in the singing was that of Mary Mũthoni Nyanjirũ, the woman who led the workers' procession and the first to fall under the hail of colonial bullets.

After the eight days allocated to the two plays, we all vacated the space, peacefully. The Europeans came with their productions. One day Seth Adagala and I were summoned to the Nairobi Headquarters of the Criminal Investigation Department for a few questions about performances at the theatre—actually, one question: why were we interfering with European performances at the National Theatre? The only possible 'interference' we could think of was the very success of our venture. No charges were filed against us, but there was an implied threat in the fact of the police summons and questions.

V

For some of us it was clear from that experience that, if Kenyan theatre was ever to thrive, it would have to find and define its own space in terms of both physical location and language. *The Trial of Dedan Kīmathi* had been staged in English in a controversial location. The real national theatre surely lay where the majority of the people resided: in the villages in the countryside and in the poor urban areas. It would have to be the site of a combination of what Peter Brook describes as holy theatre, rough theatre, and immediate theatre. It would have to be a theatre that went to the root of the historical space of the people's experience in order to speak to their immediate presence as they faced their tomorrow. To achieve any of that, it was important, we felt, to have a performance space directly under the control of the people. Those are some of the concerns that led to the foundation of the Kamīrīīthū Community Education and Cultural Centre.

I have told bits and pieces of Kamīrīīthū's story in three of my books, *Detained: A Writer's Prison Diary, Decolonizing the Mind,* and *Barrel of a Pen,* so I shall not go into too many details here. The project which was started in 1976—a literacy and cultural programme with theatre at the centre—became a truly community affair involving peasants and factory and plantation workers then resident in the village of the same name. In 1977, together with the community of this village about thirty kilometres from the capital, Nairobi, we developed a play, *Ngaahika Ndeenda,* 'I Will Marry When I Want', in which people sang songs about their own history. Here were peasants and workers who only the year before were illiterate, who were used to singing songs of praise about the leadership and what it had done for the people, but who now could not only read and write but were actually singing with pride about their own abilities, what they had done in history, and now their hopes of what they could do tomorrow. What is more, they had built an open-air theatre in the centre of the village by their own efforts, and with no hand-outs from the state. They had reclaimed their historical space.

They tried to do the same when in 1982 they attempted another play, *Mother Sing for Me.* Again it was pride in their own history and faith in their own abilities, and hence their hope for the future, which was important. Professor Ingrid Bjorkman, who did research on Kamīrīīthū, has written a book that really testifies to this aspect. She came to Kenya in 1982 in the aftermath of the government repression and interviewed the actors and members of the audience who had come to see the play in the public rehearsals before the ban. She closes her main text with the words of one of those who had attended the show:

> The remarkable thing is that in our kind of system it is believed that we have people who have to think for us. As workers and peasants, people who actually toil, we are not supposed to use our heads. And you are not supposed to be mentally productive. You are not supposed to associate things and see a picture. You are always supposed to see things in isolation and you always know that you are being led into anything. Now here Ngũgĩ showed in *Mother Sing for Me* that peasants can think and they can communicate those thoughts—the understanding of their environment to other people. They can understand what makes them that which they are. It beats somebody, who has always known that he is a thinker, to think that a peasant could act and could also form songs that could express himself. . . . So this feeling that the peasants can understand a situation and actually communicate what they are thinking is what became the biggest threat. Because to be led you have to be 'sheep'. And when you show that you are not 'sheep', the leader becomes disturbed.[5]

The attempt to locate theatre among the people would raise new questions and answers about the content, form, and language of African theatre. But in November 1976 I did not realize that the attempt to locate culture where it belonged would raise even more problems and questions, not only about the performance space of the artist but about that of the state as well to the consideration of which we now turn.

VI

'All the world's a stage', said Shakespeare in *As You Like It,* 'And all the men and women merely players; They have their exits and their entrances.' The nation state sees the entire territory as its performance area; it organizes the space as a huge enclosure, with definite places of entrances and exits. These exits and entrances are manned by companies of workers they call immigration officials. The borders are manned by armed guards to keep away invaders; but it is also to confine the population within a certain territory. The nation state performs its own being hourly, through its daily exercise of power over the exits and entrances, by means of passports and visas and flags.

Within that territorial enclosure, it creates others, the most prominent being prison, with its entrances and exits guarded by armed might. How did prison, a much narrower stage, come to be such an important site for the state's performance of punishment? The state would prefer to act out its power, watched by an audience over the entire territory. In the television age, this is possible, though there are restraints. Historically, punishments were not always enacted in a hid-

5. Ingrid Bjorkman, *'Mother Sing for Me': People's Theatre in Kenya* (London: Zed, 1989), 97.

den enclosure. In *Discipline and Punish,* Foucault has described in minute detail scenes of punishment in eighteenth-century Europe very much in terms of spectacle—what he calls the theatrical representation of pain by the state. 'There were even some cases of an almost theatrical reproduction of the crime in the execution of the guilty man—with the same instruments, the same gestures.'[6] These used to happen in the open. 'In the ceremonies', writes Foucault, 'the main character was the people, whose real and immediate presence was required for the performance. An execution that was known to be taking place, but which did so in secret, would scarcely have had any meaning. The aim was to make an example, not only by making people aware that the slightest offence was likely to be punished, but by arousing feelings of terror by the spectacle of power letting its anger fall upon the guilty person.'[7]

In his article 'Theater for an Angry God', Mark Fearnow has described a similar phenomenon in eighteenth-century America. He talks of the public burnings and hangings in colonial New York in 1741 in terms of performance—what he describes as the most revolting ends to which theatrical techniques can be applied: 'public execution as popular entertainment, the display of rotting and exploding corpses as triumphant spectacle'.[8] But this spectacle did not always produce the desired ends, particularly on the audience. The condemned, by his reaction to the pain, could sometimes win the sympathy and even the admiration of those watching, and there was always the danger of the crowd intervening. The people drawn to a spectacle that was meant to terrorize them could express their rejection of this punitive power and sometimes revolt. 'Preventing an execution that was regarded as unjust, snatching a condemned man from the hands of the executioner, obtaining his pardon by force, possibly pursuing and assaulting the executioners, in any case abusing the judges and causing an uproar against the sentence—all this formed part of popular practices that invested, traversed and often overturned the ritual of public execution.'[9] And even after his death the so-called criminal could turn into a saint and come back to haunt the state. The condemned found himself transformed into a hero by the sheer weight of the drama and publicity surrounding his case. 'Against the law, against the rich, the powerful, the magistrates, the constabulary, or the watch, against taxes and their collectors, he appeared to have waged a struggle with which one all too easily identified.'[1]

There were precedents before the eighteenth century. The most famous case in biblical antiquity is that of Jesus Christ, whose public execution was later to haunt the Roman state and empire. So in time this open-air theatrical representation of pain was withdrawn from the open space into an enclosure. But, wryly comments Foucault, 'What-

6. Michel Foucault, *Discipline and Punish* (New York: Vintage, 1979), 45.
7. Ibid. 57–8.
8. *TDR* (*Theater Drama Review*), T150 (Summer 1996), 16.
9. Foucault, *Discipline and Punish,* 59–60.
1. Ibid. 67.

ever the part played by feelings of humanity for the condemned in the abandonment of the liturgy of the public executions, there was, in any case, on the part of the state power, a political fear of the effects of these ambiguous rituals.'[2]

Fearnow describes the same fear—the threat to public order in the fairs that developed spontaneously around such executions—as being what lay behind the banning of the gibbet in England in 1845. The truth of these observations is attested by real historical cases as described by Foucault, but also in literature. The Dickensian condemned man could always win sympathy, even if only that of a small boy like Pip for the Magwitches of the world. In Kenya the colonial state tried public executions and displays of bodies of the Mau Mau condemned, but this always aroused more anger against the state, as I have dramatized in my novel *A Grain of Wheat*. And when in 1984 the post-colonial state ordered processions to watch my effigy being burned and the ashes thrown into rivers, lakes, and the ocean, the spectacle only aroused more sympathy for me and the cause I was espousing: the release of all political prisoners in Kenya. Although the practice of public punishment still continues in some countries, and certainly in other more indirect ways throughout the world, removing the spectacle of punishment from the larger territorial space into an enclosure becomes a logical development. No state wants its designated criminals transformed into heroes and saints, with the possibility of their graves becoming some kind of revolutionary shrine.

But though the punishment was removed from the open into an enclosure, the element of performance remained particularly so for political and intellectual prisoners—artists, mostly. The prison yard is like a stage where everything, including movement, is directed and choreographed by the state. The *mise-en-scène*, the play of light and shadows, the timing and regulation of actions—even of eating and sleeping and defecating—are directed by armed stage-hands they call prison warders. It is a proscenium stage with the fourth wall added and securely locked so that there is no question of a privileged spectator peeping through it and seeing the action. Nevertheless, both the state and the condemned artist are aware that there is an interested audience outside the walls of the enclosure. The state tries to interpret, for the audience outside, what is happening inside the closed walls: the prisoner has confessed, the prisoner is healthy, or whatever fabrications it wants to feed the world.

The prisoner tries to counter the government propaganda by whatever means are at his disposal. Escape is impossible, suicidal even. So he resorts to pen and paper when he can find them. Hence the struggle for the literary means of production that I alluded to in my last lecture. Prison narratives by artist-prisoners are essentially a documentation of the battle of texts and of the continuing contest over the performance space of the state. This contest, while aimed at the groups of interested watchers outside the gates—Amnesty International, International Pen,

---

2. Ibid. 65.

and other human rights groups—is ultimately aimed at the real audience: the people waiting in the territorial space. The state is trying
to direct the drama of the prisoner's self-condemnation—a confession
of crimes of thought, his own guilt so to speak—and this has parallels
with the gallows speeches of medieval and feudal Europe: 'The rite of
execution was so arranged that the condemned man would himself
proclaim his guilt by the *amende honorable* that he spoke, by the placard he displayed and also by the statements that he was no doubt
forced to make. Furthermore, at the moment of execution, it seems
that he was given another opportunity to speak, not to proclaim his
innocence but to acknowledge his crime and the justice of his conviction.'[3] The artist-prisoner resists in every fibre of his being displaying
'the placard of self-condemnation', and even if he is forced, through
torture, to display it, he will try to dispatch to the world, through some
of the more sympathetic stage-hands, another placard denying the content of the first. This contest over the prison performance space of the
state is also a means of resistance, a means of staying alive in this
torture-chamber of the spirit. It is, in other words, one of the ways of
denying the state a triumphant epilogue to its performance.

VII

There is no performance without a goal. The prison is the enclosure
in which the state organizes the use of space and time in such a way
as to achieve what Foucault calls 'docile bodies' and hence docile
minds. The struggle for subjugation of the mind of the artist-prisoner
is paramount. That is why once again books and reading materials
become such vital objects of struggle. Prison narratives are full of in-
cidents about books that one is not allowed to read and those one can
read. The authorized and banned list, a kind of index of the prison
inquisition, can be an insight into the mind of the state. In his book
Kenya: A Prison Notebook, historian Maina wa Kĩnyattĩ records many
episodes in which he is not allowed to read any of my works. Ngũgĩ's
novels are political, they are dangerous, he is told over and over again
during his six and a half years in various maximum-security prisons.
But he has to find ways of reading these books, or similar ones, and
Maina wa Kĩnyattĩ is amused by the fact that he can read Richard
Wright and Maxim Gorky without problems. A political prisoner in
fact is acting out an aesthetic of resistance through bodily or mental
gestures. He is fighting against the intended docility of the mind. Even
within the prison walls he will try to create a physical, social, and
mental space for himself. He will try to use his allotted time and space
and his limited social interactions in a manner that gives him maximum psychic space.

We have a humorous illustration of this in Hama Tuma's *The Case
of the Socialist Witchdoctor.* In the story The Case of the Prison-

3. Foucault, *Discipline and Punish.*

Monger', Hama Tuma tells of an Ethiopian intellectual who describes himself as a prison maniac. He claims that he really loves prison. Every time he comes out of prison, he commits a crime, however petty, so that he can be sent back to gaol. The prosecuting team asks him, 'Doesn't it bother you to spend ten years of the prime of your life behind prison walls?' 'No', he replies. He argues that people are really in prison only when they believe themselves to be so. A house can be a prison. Even a palace can be a gilded prison for a king. On the other hand, the monk who shuts himself up in total isolation in a cave is not in prison. 'In prison, I met very many really free people', he asserts to the utter astonishment of the judge-prosecutor, who cannot understand this logic. Then follows this exchange:

> What sentence do you now expect for your crime?
> I should be sent to prison for five years as article 689 of the penal code states.
> What if you are set free?
> That will be a crime, the accused says, really shocked at the possibility of freedom.
> But if you are set free, would you commit a crime again?
> I couldn't avoid it. For the public good and mine.
> If you commit three more crimes, you will be killed.
> Then death will be a relief indeed. Not punishment but real salvation.[4]

And now comes the judgement:

> You, the accused, you are a no-good, fast-talking, lazy, strange, crazy person. You are a parasite. You are also dangerous. Whoever finds joy in prison, whoever feels free in our jails goes against the order of things, goes against the expected. A cow can't give birth to a puppy. Prison is a punishment, not a source of calm and freedom. If such feelings as yours spread, our security will be in chaos. I agree with the prosecutor. You are hereby sentenced to immediate freedom.[5]

The accused almost faints with shock at his sentence. When he recovers, he is shouting and screaming at the judge, 'You can't do this! You must send me back to prison!' The point is now made. For him the actual prison, the enclosure, is less evil than the wider territorial space under the military regime. The entire country is one vast prison where people's movements are tightly controlled, where they can be dislocated from familiar spaces into those easily patrolled. In any case, dislocation and dispersal can be one way of removing any basis of a collective performance of identity and resistance. The method had been tried during plantation slavery in America and the Caribbean islands.

4. Hama Tuma, *The Case of the Socialist Witchdoctor* (London: Heinemann, 1993), 120–I.
5. Ibid. 121.

VIII

In *Song of Ocol,* by Okot p'Bitek, the leading character, a member of the post-colonial ruling élite, actually wants to ban all performance so that they may not reflect his blackness. He wails, 'Mother, mother, why was I born black?' But the easiest way is to obliterate the rural space altogether, because this is the site of those performances that most remind him of his African being. His vision for post-colonial Africa is in terms of a huge city that swallows the rural completely:

> I see the great gate
> Of the city flung open
> I see men and women walking in.[6]

The rural person has only two alternatives:

> Either you come in
> Through the city gate
> Or take the rope
> And hang yourself.[7]

Do we hear in this echoes of English economic history with its enclosures in the eighteenth century? The goal is to take away the land which is the basis of the peasantry and turn the tillers into wage-slaves in the urban enclosures called factories and ghettos. It is another way of restricting the performance space of the tiller.

Prison then is a metaphor for the post-colonial space, for even in a country where there are no military regimes, the vast majority can be described as being condemned to conditions of perpetual physical, social, and psychic confinement. The state performs its rituals of power not only by being able to control exits and entrances into the territorial space, its entire performance space, but also by being able to move people between the various enclosures within the national territorial space. But the aesthetic of resistance that applies in both the smaller prison and the territorial one may force the state to try other measures. So sometimes it acts out those rituals of absolute control by forcing people, citizens, out of the territorial space of the nation state to become anchorless wanderers on the global space. There are the special cases of penal colonies, the most striking being Australia, where a whole people deemed undesirable are removed from one territorial space into another, equally big or bigger. In Africa, there is the example of Angola, which was used as a penal settlement. In a historical note to her translation of Pepetela's novel *Yaka,* Marga Holmes says that in addition to Portuguese colonial officials and troops, 'the white community in the nineteenth century included ex-convicts, political exiles,—Republicans, anarchists,—and some who had fled from the newly Republican Brazil.' Forcing writers and artists into exile is a variant form of penal settlement at the level of the individual. The only difference is that, unlike a penal settlement, the global space where

6. Okot p'Bitek, *Song of Ocol* (Nairobi: Heinemann, 1988), 149.
7. Ibid.

such writers may find themselves is not controlled by the same state. But the spiritual effects might be the same.

IX

A writer floating in space without anchorage in his country is like a condemned person. Nawal el Sa'adawi feels as if she is in jail whenever she is away from her Egypt. For her, exile becomes like another prison. So exile is a way of moving the writer from the territorial confinement where his acts of resistance might ignite other fields into a global 'exclosure'. The hope is that his actions from this exclosure, whatever they are, will not directly affect those confined within the vast territorial enclosure. But here, as inside a prison, there are many contradictions for both the state and the artist. The artist in exile knows that he has been removed from the space which nourishes his imagination. He will nevertheless try to break out of the exclosure and reach into the territorial space. From exile he will still try to challenge the state's absolute hold on the territorial space. And because of this, the state is also in a dilemma. To let an artist go into global space means a continuation of the contest for the attention of a global audience. Besides, the word of the exile may very well travel back to the territory to go on haunting the state. Which is what happened in 1984. Dan Barron-Cohen, an Oxford graduate, and I directed a London production of *The Trial of Dedan Kīmathi* at the Africa Centre using techniques developed at Kamīrīīthū. The Kenya state sought to have the performances, both at the Africa Centre and at the Commonwealth Institute, stopped. They wanted the British government to do it for them, but this time they did not get co-operation. Similarly, in Zimbabwe Ngũgĩ wa Mīriī has utilized and extended the Kamīrīīthū experience to create one of the most continuous community theatre movements in Africa. The Kenyan state tried in vain here too to make the Zimbabwean state act against Ngũgĩ's activities. In other words, the Kenyan state under Moi wanted us all back under its watchful eye in the territory under its control.

That is why banning performances or confining artists in prison or killing them are the actions to which the state frequently resorts. But to avoid the contradictions of prison, exile, and physical elimination, like possible condemnation by the national or international audience, the state may find it much easier to deny the artist space altogether. It is the path that invites least resistance and condemnation, and it is the method highly recommended by Plato: 'And therefore when any of these pantomime gentlemen who are so clever that they can imitate anything makes a proposal to exhibit himself and his poetry, we shall send him away to another city.'[8]

The next city could very well turn out to be a replica of the first, so that the performers could end up being homeless wanderers in search of space.

8. Plato, *Republic*, book 3, in Hofstadter and Kuhns (eds.), *Philosophies of Beauty*, 23.

X

We can now make some tentative observations: that the more open the performance space, the more it seems to terrify those in possession of repressive power. This can be seen through a quick comparison of the actions of the colonial and the post-colonial state to performances in the open space.

The pre-colonial African performance area was often the open space in a courtyard or in an arena surrounded by wood and natural hedge. It could also be inside buildings, as when stories are told in the evening around the fireside. But the open space was more dominant, and even in the intimate circle around the fireside, it is the openness of the performance area that is marked: the story-teller and the interactive listeners are in the same area. Visitors could come into the scene, at any time, for the main door was not barred to would-be guests. Equally well, any of the listeners could go in and out. Any space could be turned into a performance area as long as there were people around. Thus the performance space was defined by the presence or absence of people.

To a certain extent the open space of the pre-colonial African performance has parallels with the social space of the carnival spirit of pre-capitalist Europe of the Middle Ages as described by Mikhail Bakhtin, particularly where he argues that the carnival spirit does not know footlights—that is, it does not acknowledge any distinction between actors and spectators.

> Carnival is not a spectacle seen by the people; they live in it and everyone participates, because its very idea embraces all the people. While carnival lasts there is no other life outside it. During carnival time life is subject only to its laws, that is, the laws of its own freedom. It has a universal spirit; it is a special condition of the entire world, of the world's revival and renewal, in which all take part.[9]

Colonial conquests resulted in clear-cut boundaries that defined the dominated space with controlled points of exit and entrance and the formation of a colonial state to run the occupied territory. And right from the beginning the colonial state was very wary of the open air. It was not sure of what was being done, out there, in the open spaces, in the plains, in the forested valleys and mountains. It was even less sure of people dancing in the streets, in market squares, in church-yards and burial places. And what did those drumbeats in the dark of the night really mean? What did they portend?

The post-colonial state has the same fear of the uncontrolled space, a fear which long ago Euripides dramatized in a confrontation between maenads and the state in the play *The Bacchae*. Pentheus, king of the Theban state, cannot stand it that women are out there in the woods and mountains, beyond the control of the city, even though all they are doing is celebrating Dionysus, the god of wine, whose gifts are joy

9. Mikhail Bakhtin, *Rabelais and His World* (Bloomington: Indiana University Press, 1984), 7.

and the union of the soul with dancing. Darkness in open space is dangerous to women, Pentheus claims, and he vows to use force to bring them back to controllable space within the city. He orders the arrest of Dionysus, and imprisonment in a dark stable, where he will have all the darkness that he wants. You can dance in there! As for these women whom you've brought to aid and abet you, I shall either send them into the slave market, or retain them in my household to work at the looms; that will keep their hands from drumming on the tambourines.[1] The parallels with the authoritarian colonial and post-colonial state are very striking, and that is one of the reasons which may have prompted Wole Soyinka to write an adaptation of it, with a post-colonial African setting, under the title *The Bacchae of Euripides*. Both the colonial and the post-colonial state acted as if they were taking a leaf out of Pentheus's book. The open space had to be limited.

Thus under colonialism there followed attempted suppression or strong limitation of all open-air performances within the territorial space. A few examples from Kenya. I have already mentioned the stoppage of the Ituĩka ceremony. This was one of many such stoppages. After the 1922 Harry Thuku massacre, women devised a song and dance sequence called Kanyegenyũri. It needed no permanently defined ground on which it could be performed. The song-poem-dance was banned by the colonial regime: it could not be sung or danced or recited anywhere on Kenyan soil. The colonial state treated another dance sequence, Mũthĩrĩgũ, developed after the Second World War, in the same manner. And in 1952 the colonial regime once again acted against the nation-wide upsurge of anti-colonial dances and songs, banning all open-air performances in any part of the country, whatever the performance at a particular moment. Every performance, even a simple gathering for prayers, had to be authorized. Communication between one space and the next had to be authorized. The entire territory was one vast performance space full of threatening motions of innumerable magic spheres. Similarly, in the era of apartheid in South Africa, an elaborate pass system regulated the entire territory as a space for daily performance.

The post-colonial state exhibits similar sensitivities. Collective expressions of joy or even grief outside the watchful eyes of the state, may, in some instances, constitute a crime. So the post-colonial state tries to enact limitations similar to those of the colonial state. In Kenya, under the Chief's Act, a gathering of more than five people, no matter where and on whatever occasion, needs a police licence. The performance space for prayers, funeral dirges, marriage ceremonies, naming tea-parties, family gatherings, sports, are dependent on the issuance of a permit. Thus when the police break into any gathering and break up story-telling sessions in people's homes, they are absolutely within the law. Performances have to be contained in controllable enclosures, in licensed theatre buildings, in schools, especially, but not in open spaces where the people reside.

1. Euripides, *The Bacchae and Other Plays* (Harmondsworth: Penguin, 1961), 197.

In other words, says Guillermo Gomez-Peña in his article 'The Artist as Criminal', describing similar scenes of suppression of street performances in Mexico in 1994, 'it is one thing to carry out iconoclastic actions in a theater or museum before a public that is predisposed to tolerating radical behavior, and quite another to bring the work into the street and introduce it into the mined terrain of unpredictable social and political forces'. For as opposed to the official feast of the dominant social forces represented by the state in containable places, the carnivalistic spirit, embodied in the performance of the open space, people's social space, celebrates and marks 'temporary liberation from the prevailing truth and from the established order' and 'suspension of all hierarchical rank, privileges, norms, and prohibitions'. Bakhtin, mindful of twentieth-century state dogmatisms, talked of carnival as 'the feast of time, the feast of becoming, change and renewal' opposed to all that which had been sanctified by the state and declared complete.[2]

A comparison between the first performance of *The Trial of Dedan Kĩmathi* on 20 October 1976 within an enclosure of stone and concrete called the Kenya National Theatre and of *I Will Marry When I Want* at Kamĩrĩĩthũ village in 2 October 1977 at an open-air theatre, a construction without roof and stone walls, is instructive. The production of *The Trial of Dedan Kĩmathi* was by university students in English; that of *I Will Marry When I Want* by a cast of peasants and workers in the Gĩkũyũ language. Thus in 1976, despite the tensions and the publicity surrounding the productions of *The Trial of Dedan Kĩmathi*, and despite the police questions, no action was taken by the state against the performance. But on 16 November 1977 the state banned further performances of *I Will Marry When I Want*. And in 1982 they barred the same Kamĩrĩĩthũ group from performing anywhere, even the National Theatre. The government also ensured that the Kamĩrĩĩthũ performers would not take advantage of an invitation to perform in the then newly independent state of Zimbabwe by outlawing the group. Moving to the next 'city' was therefore not even an option because to do so they would still have needed passports, and governments do not give passports to groups who do not legally exist.

But the state's reaction to the two spaces is even more instructive. In 1976 and 1982 the post-colonial state could bar people from the National Theatre but the building was never destroyed. In 1982, after the same cast of village actors tried to perform another play, *Mother Sing for Me*, the state reacted, not only by refusing to license the performances but by sending armed policemen to raze the Kamĩrĩĩthũ open theatre to the ground. Again this is so reminiscent of the actions of Pentheus in Euripides' *Bacchae*, written and performed more than 2,000 years ago. Pentheus has just proclaimed his intention to use force against the Bacchantes, for, in his contempt of women, he believes that 'when the sparkle of sweet wine appears in their faces no

2. *TDR* T149 (Spring 1966), 112; Bakhtin, *Rabelais and His World*, 12.

good can be expected from their ceremonies'.[3] Tiresias, the blind seer, opposes his move against the women's performance in the space of their choice and his reliance on force, warning him that it is not force that rules human affairs. Pentheus is incensed at the seer's resistance, but, unable to inflict bodily harm directly, he orders his men to go to Tiresias' religious performance place, and 'smash it with crowbars, knock down the walls, turn everything upside down, fling out his holy fripperies to the wind. That will sting him more than anything else.[4] In the same way dictator Moi singled out the women of Kamīrīīthū for special censure, and then thought to 'sting' all of us where it hurt most by the physical destruction of the Kamīrīīthū performance space. Performances, not only at the Kamīrīīthū centre, but throughout Limuru county, were banned. The state attached so much value to the destruction of the open-air space that the whole performance of the ban on the Kamīrīīthū players on 12 March 1982 was televised for all the country to see. There was the provincial commissioner, with all the regional bureaucrats under him and guarded by armed troops, summoning the village to a meeting where the ceremony denying space to the Kamīrīīthū players was preceded by prayers from leaders of the various established religious denominations. But it was also noticed that most of the prayers took the form of asking God to endow the human heart with the spirit of tolerance.

In 1976 Seth Adagala and I could get away with police questioning, but in 1977 I was arrested and taken to a maximum-security prison for a year, released only after the death of the first head of state, Jomo Kenyatta; and in 1982 I found myself in exile from Kenya. The open space among the people is the most dangerous area because the most vital. Thus the Kenyan state performance of its ritual of power over the territorial space took the form of removing me from the people, first by confining me to prison, and then by forcing me out of the territorial space altogether. They could have done worse and removed me from the global space, as happened to Ken Saro Wiwa,[5] and also to thousands of Kenyans.

XI

The performance space of the artist stands for openness; that of the state, for confinement. Art breaks down barriers between peoples; the state erects them. Art arose out of human struggle to break free of confinement. These confinements could be natural. But they are also economic, political, social, and spiritual. Art yearns for maximum physical, social, and spiritual space for human action. The state tries demarcation, limitation, and control. Two spatial and temporal borders with the inevitable border clashes between two hostile territories, to

3. *The Bacchae and Other Plays*, 189.
4. Ibid. 192.
5. Nigerian playwright, novelist, and environmental activist, executed by the Abacha military dictatorship in November 1995 [*Editor*].

paraphrase Michael Holquist's comment on Bakhtin's characterization of the state and the carnival in the Middle Ages.[6] Bakhtin's words are equally applicable to the colonial and post-colonial performance space of both the artist and the state. Carnival laughter, Bakhtin has written, 'builds its own world versus the official world, its own church versus the official church, its own state versus the official state. Laughter celebrates its masses, professes its faith, celebrates marriage and funerals, writes its epitaphs, elects kings and bishops',[7] which brings us back to the issue of rivalry between art and the state in a class society.

That is why the question of the politics of the performance space is basic to any theorizing about the post-colonial condition. For the politics of the performance space is much more than a question of the physical site for a theatrical show. It touches on nearly all aspects of power and being in a colonial and post-colonial society. It is germane to issues of what constitutes the national and the mainstream. In a post-colonial state this takes the form of a struggle between those who defend the continuity of colonial traditions and those who want to see reflections of a new nation and a new people in the performance space as a unified field of internal and external relations.

But ultimately the politics of the performance space and its location is a class question. For human labour is the real artist in the world. All other forms of artistic expression imitate that of the human hand and mind. And the human hand and mind have the entire limitless space and time for their performance of the struggle for human freedom and self-realization. But the class society which has come into being has created all sorts of borders, enclosures, to confine that freedom. The enclosures could be the nation state, religions, race, gender, ideology, languages—any social variations on those themes. Questions of the performance space are tied to those of democracy, of civil society, of which class controls the state.

One of the most effective ways of ensuring minority social control of labour and the products of labour is the exclusion of whole classes of people from effective participation in the national life. Whole classes of people can be put into psychic enclosure—slaves and serfs in feudal societies, the working people in most advanced capitalist countries today, and women in most societies. In such societies this is done through what Gramsci described as hegemonic rather than formal exclusionary laws. But in Africa, the exclusion of the majority and their enclosure in narrowed psychic space is achieved through the dominance of European languages. * * *

6. Michael Holquist, 'Prologue', in Bakhtin, *Rabelais and His World,* p. xxi.
7. Bakhtin, ibid. 88.

BIODUN JEYIFO

The Reinvention of Theatrical Tradition†

> "We could start all over again, perhaps."
> "That should be easy."
> "It's the start that's difficult."
> "*You can start from anything.*"
> "Yes, but you have to decide."
> "True."
> —Samuel Beckett, *Waiting for Godot*

> One of the most perverse myths invented by ethnology . . . is the myth of primitive unanimity, the myth that non-Western societies are "simple" and homogenous at every level, including the level of ideology and belief. What we must recognize today is that pluralism does not come to any society from outside but is inherent in every society . . . The decisive encounter is not between Africa as a whole and Europe as a whole. Pluralism in the true sense did not stem from the intrusion of Western civilization into our continent . . . it is an internal pluralism, born of perpetual confrontations and occasional conflicts between Africans themselves.   —Paulin Hountondji

> A break in historical continuity is a tribulation, but it is also an opportunity.   —Arnold Toynbee

Introduction: An African Shingeki?

Peter Brook's famous journey to Africa in 1973 remains one of the most controversial experiments in interculturalism in the contemporary international theatre movement. At the heart of the experimental project of this journey was a search for a truly intercultural "grammar" of theatrical communication, a simple, powerful, universal "language" of theatre which beyond the divisions of nationality, culture and class, would communicate directly to all audiences in all places, at all times. John Heilpern, a member of Brook's entourage and the quasi-official diarist of the journey, has described the purpose of the journey in the following words:

> A way must be found to create a direct response. The event had to justify itself totally, living or dying on human terms alone. And so one is forced to create a new language, more powerful ways of communicating than anything these actors had known. But how? What is simplicity? Perhaps Africa would tell us.[1]

Now, it is important to note that Brook in this journey did not set out, like Conrad's fictional Marlowe, and like so many other famous Western cultural and intellectual pundits before him, by presuming to be

---

† From *The Intercultural Performance Reader,* ed. Patrice Pavis (New York: Routledge, 1996), 149–61. Reprinted by permission of Taylor & Francis Books Ltd.
1. John Heilpern, *The Conference of Birds,* London, 1977, p. 91.

journeying into an African "heart of darkness": Brook apparently did
not set out conceiving of the theatrical landscape in Africa as a void,
a *tabula rasa* on to which he could inscribe the discoveries of his neo-
Romantic search for a universal theatre "language". According to Heilpern, Brook had some knowledge of the contemporary African theatre
situation, he had some definite notions about the larger cultural and
historical contexts of the contemporary theatre scene in Africa. More
precisely, Brook went to Africa with a *textualized* construction of what
was happening "over there," a textualization which contained representations of the African theatrical landscape which pose serious questions for our attempts to create an appropriate, adequate *discursive
practice* for contemporary international theatrical interculturalism.
Before we state what some of these questions and issues are, it is instructive and pertinent to explore important aspects of Brook's representations of the African theatrical "Other" as the backdrop of his
search for the universal grammar of theatrical communication. These
aspects are particularly notable in Brook's admonitions to his actors
before their first performance in Nigeria:

> They'll be expecting a *show*. And we must give them some *real*
> skill. We must do things for the pleasure of doing them. It's par-
> ticularly exciting because what's happening here is comparable to
> Greek drama . . . because in Nigeria there's a fascinating mixture
> of buzzing popular theatre sometimes based on everyday life and
> sometimes on epic and mythic local material. And the unique
> fascination of this theatre is that it spontaneously recreated the
> conditions of Elizabethan drama on the one hand, and ancient
> Greek drama on the other. It's the beginning of a whole new
> culture, not commercialized or set, but in its first roots. So we
> must try to give them the best that we possibly can.[2]

Brook's excitement about the African theatre scene as a backdrop for
his experiment is only too evident in these observations. It is also apparent that for Brook, contemporary African theatre seemed to be offering something akin to his own project: exciting new beginnings,
fresh initiatives, and correspondingly, a uniquely auspicious environment for his actors to give the best of their skills. But if we carefully
read the subtexts of these otherwise open-minded and positive representations of the African theatrical Other, if we deconstruct its surface
praise and high regard for the Nigerian theatre and its audience(s),
Brook's "text" turns out to be very ambiguous, it turns out to be solidly
inscribed in an established tradition of critical discourse(s) of the Nigerian and African theatre whose apprehension of the phenomenon of
interculturalism is the subject of this essay, especially as this apprehension pertains to the interactions and oppositions between, on the
one hand, the "Western", the "foreign", and on the other hand, the
"African", the "indigenous". In this regard, it is particularly instructive
to draw attention to Brook's notion of a "spontaneous" recreation of

2. Ibid., pp. 173–74.

the conditions of classical Greek drama and Elizabethan theatre: does "spontaneous" here not signify de-historicized, non-determinate, purely serendipitous? Equally ambiguous is the bald assertion that this "new", "exciting" Nigerian theatre is in its very "first roots". In effect then, two problematic representations of the contemporary Nigerian theatre are encountered here: a "spontaneously" new recreation of theatrical expressions which are strangely familiar and easily assimilated to received Western theatre traditions and paradigms; an absolute first age of origination. Extrapolated from their "positive" verbal context, these two representations return us rather insidiously to aspects of the established critical discourse on African theatre in which we read of an absent or suspended African provenance for the contemporary theatre expressions of the continent. It is necessary to repeat: this problematic construction features positively in Brook's perspectives by analogy with the first epigram to this essay, the ruminations of Estragon and Vladimir in *Waiting for Godot* concerning the need "to start all over again". Brook after all is neither the first nor the last major theorist and practitioner of the Western theatre to call for a break, a new beginning from the presumed Spenglerian exhaustion and enervation of the Western theatre. But with regard to its pertinence to the critical discourse on interculturalism in the contemporary African theatre, what this problematic formulation involves can best be represented heuristically as a sort of African mutation of the tradition of the Japanese Shingeki: a "new" theatre suspended in time and place, bracketed from discernible roots in powerfully sedimented and historically perpetuated indigenous theatre traditions like the Noh and the Kabuki. This essay is a brief attempt to review the critical discourses on contemporary African theatre which have either subsumed or challenged the perspectives inherent in this notion of an African Shingeki without its subtending Noh, Kabuki, or Bunraku. As I hope to demonstrate, nothing less than the possibility and necessity of the "decolonization" of the discourse on interculturalism in the modern theatre is implicated in this review.

One writes deliberately of *discourses*, and not of one discourse with different strands or currents, in order to frame and reveal a coherent pattern of tensions, refutations and contestations which attend the appraisal of the "indigenous" and the "foreign", the "African" and the "Western" in the African theatre. Three separate, distinct discourses are identified. The first discursive formation turns, explicitly or implicitly, on the notion of the mutant African Shingeki that we have briefly elaborated above. In *this* discourse, which we may describe as "dominant", Eurocentric or colonialist, perspectives from a powerful, imperializing scholastic Western critical orthodoxy are deployed in debates on the existence or non-existence of indigenous African theatre traditions, or in formalistic and facile debates over the degrees of Western influence on the African theatre. It is a measure of the decisive impact of this dominant discourse on the African theatre that it foists an "originary" obsession, a fervent search for lost origins and historical continuity on the discourse which it engenders and which seeks to displace it. Thus, in the second composite discourse, what we have is a *counter-discourse,* a putatively "Afrocentric", "anti-colonialist" riposte to the "dominant" discourse: the positions and judgements of the latter are contested, and in some cases refuted, but almost always within the same scholastic, formalist premises. In the third composite discourse, the parameters of apprehending interculturalism in the African theatre are broadened beyond the polarized "Western" and "African" binarism, and often in a resolutely anti-scholastic, non-formalist spirit. The underlying premise here may be expressed in the words of the Beninoise philosopher, Paulin Hountondji: "the decisive encounter is not between Africa as a whole and Europe as a whole".

It should be added that it will not be the task of this short essay to provide either a comprehensive profile of these discourses or an exhaustive bibliographic location of their main proponents and followers. Rather, the more modest intention is to give, in each respective case, a short but sharply defined sketch of the essential positions and the rhetorical, discursive strategies with which they are advanced. A brief concluding section then makes more explicit, more openly polemical, the ideological and philosophical premises which undergird the whole essay.

Three distinct but interlocking theses or composite views make up the orthodoxy of the dominant critical discourse on interculturalism in the African theatre. It is useful for our purposes in this essay to extrapolate and restate them from their inscription in innumerable books, essays and articles.

First, there is the thesis of the non-existence of indigenous "native" traditions of drama or theatre in Africa, a view which we may ascribe to the not-so-distant prehistory of this dominant critical discourse. This thesis was later revised or modified to "concede" that if Africa does indeed have indigenous theatrical traditions, they are nonetheless properly "quasi-theatrical" or "proto-dramatic". The second thesis holds that compared with Europe and Asia, Africa does not possess well-developed theatrical traditions, especially in terms of the formalization of technique, style and aesthetic principles, and their historical transmission through successive ages and periods. These two theses are best summed up by the famous, controversial opening paragraph of Ruth Finnegan's chapter on "Drama" in her influential book, *Oral Literature in Africa:*

> How far one can speak of indigenous drama in Africa is not an easy question . . . Though some writers have very positively affirmed the existence of native African drama, it would perhaps be truer to say that in Africa, in contrast to Western Europe and Asia, drama is not typically a widespread or a developed form.[3]

3. Ruth Finnegan, *Oral Literature in Africa*, Nairobi, 1970, p. 501.

The third thesis, building both on a subsumation of the two previous theses and a one-sided empirical apprehension of the massive cultural impact of Western colonization on Africa, asserts that what there are today of theatrical expressions on the continent are wholly, or pervasively derivative of Western sources, forms and traditions. Having given a broad outline of the main theses of this critical discourse, we may more usefully examine its more intricate nuances and inflections.

If the assertion that Africa possesses no "native" theatrical traditions belongs to the "prehistory" of the Eurocentric critical orthodoxy on interculturalism in the African theatre, and if virtually no critic or scholar makes this assertion any more, we should note that this view belongs to a not-so-distant past. And what is more important is that subtle variations of the theme persist in the scholarship on the African theatre, and they are promoted as much by African scholars as they are by Western critics. Sometimes indeed—so ambiguous is the operation of this critical formation—a scholar starts with the intention to refute its positions, only to be entrapped by the coils of the unexamined foundations and premises on which the critical orthodoxy rests. This is particularly evident in Anthony Graham-White's important book, *The Drama of Black Africa*, especially in the book's best researched section, the Appendix titled "A Chronology of African Drama". Here, in one entry for 1932 in the subsection dealing with the entire continent, we are given a piece of information whose cryptic brevity carries much critical force: "British Drama League sponsors a conference on Native African Drama and formally decides that there is no indigenous drama".[4] But then, another entry under the country-by-country listings gives the date around 1600 for the emergence of the Yoruba *Alarinjo* or *Apidan* Masquerade Theatre.[5] The effect of juxtaposing these two separate entries is unmistakable: the arrogant but ignorant 1932 pronouncement of the British Drama League is effectively demolished. But then Graham-White himself soon ends up in a quandary which places him in the colonialist critical orthodoxy he so evidently wishes to refute, for the next significant date after the 1600 entry is 1882 and this is *not* for an indigenous African theatrical tradition which has been historically consolidated or perpetuated, but for amateur European-style dramatic performances in Lagos by a "Brazilian Dramatic Company" formed by freed ex-slaves returned from the Americas. We are thus left with a wide lacuna between 1600 and 1882; moreover, after the latter date there is a total disappearance from Graham-White's "Chronology" of *any* theatrical expression not derived wholly or in part from Western sources and forms. The colonialist, Eurocentric foundational premise is thus subtly restored: theatre expressions in Africa have a history, an objective intelligibility as an object of scholarly research and critical study only to the extent that they derive from Western forms and traditions.

---

4. Anthony Graham-White, *The Drama of Black Africa*, New York, 1974, p. 168.
5. Ibid., p. 172.

If this premise accords only too well with the underlying premises in a discipline like the colonial historiography which was established under the aegis of European intellectual triumphalism, if we sense here a congruence with the vast project outlined by Eric Wolf in his monumental book, *Europe and the People Without History,* we must emphasize that in the domain of African theatre scholarship, this orthodoxy was produced, *could only have been produced,* by the confident, unexamined and triumphalist application of a positivist *scholasticism,* a sort of neo-Aristotelian formalism to African theatre traditions. In concrete terms, only on the basis of applying previously established and institutionally textualized criteria of determining what is, and is not drama, only on the basis of the operation of a rhetoric of scholarly discourse largely blind to its own constructedness, could the supposed definitional "elements", or combinations thereof which make drama, be applied to Africa in order to pronounce the traditions of the continent as either non-existent or not well-developed. Here, quoted at some length, is Ruth Finnegan's classic, if rather awkward expression of this scholasticism in application to African drama:

> It is clearly necessary to reach at least some rough agreement about what is to count as "drama" . . . Most important is the idea of enactment, of representation through actors who imitate persons and events. This is also usually associated with other elements, appearing to a greater or lesser degree at different times or places: linguistic content; plot; the represented interaction of several characters; specialized scenery, etc.; often music; and—of particular importance in most African performances—dance.
>
> Now it is very seldom in Africa that all these elements of drama come together in a single performance . . . What is clear is that while dramatic elements enter into several different categories of artistic activity in Africa and are thus worth consideration here, there are few or no performances which obviously and immediately include all these dramatic elements.[6]

A clarification, a gloss on the genealogy of the discourse of scholasticism on African theatre is perhaps necessary here. Before the pedantry of the scholar, the authoritative voices of commentary on African theatre were those of the *missionary* and the *anthropologist.* Graham-White has given a good short account of the prejudices and predilections which coloured the commentaries of these precursors of the *scholar,* this in a context which personally for Graham-White amounts to an annunciation of the arrival of the "objective scholar" to replace and displace the inexpert, jaundiced gaze of the missionary and the anthropologist.[7] It then becomes paradoxical for the scholar to be in turn unconscious of the freight of methodological principles she or he brings to bear on the body of African theatrical traditions by assuming, with a tenacious logocentrism, that "reality" lies at the other side of scholastic discourse. This premise achieves its massive

6. Finnegan, op. cit., p. 501.
7. Graham-White, op. cit., p. 13.

occlusion if the "real" in fact refuses to appear at the other side of the discourse of scholasticism. The twists and turns of this occlusion are best perceived in the endless debates over the identification of *genres* in the African theatre, and the consequent debates over criteria of classification and taxonomy.[8] Only this peculiar brand of scholastic self-mystification could produce Graham-White's absurd suggestion that in African theatre (and traditional culture in general) "Tragedy does not seem to exist",[9] as if *any* culture could exist, romantic Rousseauian anthropologists notwithstanding, which did not develop a "tragic" or "sorrowful" sense of life and the ritualized, formalized means of representing it. The absurdity however dissolves once we part company with the self-misrecognition of Western positivist scholasticism, once we recognize that "Tragedy" exists only in its own hermetic definitional universe. As we shall see presently, the need to combat this particular Western scholastic query on the existence of tragic expression in African drama empowered what is perhaps Soyinka's most important theoretical essay on drama, "The Fourth Stage".

Nothing expresses the fact that the "Afrocentric" counter-discourse on interculturalism in the African theatre is basically *reactive* to the orthodoxy of the dominant discourse as the former's subsumation of the binary Africa–Europe polarity initially constructed by the Eurocentric orthodoxy. Given the fact of this binarism, it was inevitable for this reactive counter-discourse to take much of its methodological and thematic cues from the very discourse it sought to displace. Especially notable is the formalism, the academicism with which this counter-discourse took up the ruling academic *telos* of official Western theatre historiography—theatre develops from ritual to drama—both to prove the existence of African drama, and to assimilate it to the supposed "universal" pattern.[1]

Although the "Afrocentric" counter-discourse cannot be said to have transcended its basic *reactive* constitution, its maturation can be deemed to have come when it sundered its methodological filiation to those "constitutive elements", those given, defining criteria of apprehending and describing the *theatrical* set up by the assumed universalism of Western scholasticism. By ceasing to speak in the Name of the (European) Scholastic Father, a separate nomenclature, a different set of criteria and "elements" were constructed with which to apprehend and describe the theatre traditions of the continent, even if many of these seemed makeshift and awkward.[2] The informing new premise

8. Yemi Ogunbiyi (ed.), *Drama and Theatre in Nigeria*, Lagos, 1981, pp. 3–53, 57–74.
9. Graham-White, op. cit., p. 43.
1. H. I. E. Dhlomo, "Nature and Variety of Tribal Drama", in *Bantu Studies* XIII, 1939; M. J. C. Echeruo, *Research in African Literatures*, vol. 4, no. 1, 1973; Andrew Horn, "Ritual, Drama and the Theatrical: The Case of Bori Spirit Mediumship", in Yemi Ogunbiyi (ed.), *Drama and Theatre in Nigeria*, Lagos, 1981.
2. Joel Adedeji, "Traditional Yoruba Theatre", in *African Arts/Arts d'Afrique*, III, Lagos, 1969; Osmond Enekwe, "Myth, Ritual and Drama in Igboland", in Yemi Ogunbiyi (ed.), *Drama and Theatre in Nigeria*, 1981.

here was that one culture's set of criteria may very well be another culture's non-criteria, a view powerfully advanced by Obiechina's distinctions between "evolutionists" (Eurocentric) and "relativists" (Afrocentric) in African theatre scholarship.[3] Thus African theatrical expressions and traditions which the critical orthodoxy of Western academicism had declared "quasi-theatrical" and "protodramatic" were reappraised in the light of different criteria and affirmed as valid indigenous traditions of theatrical performance.

It is incontestable that this move was particularly liberating, for in place of the apologetic, halting accents of the initial phase of this counter-discourse[4] at the portals of abstract universalism we now find a voice, admittedly *monologic*, but insistent in its declaration of Africa as a continent endowed with rich, varied, expressive and performance arts of the theatre. The liberation was doubly consummated, for also in place of the apologia for not having adequate *written* records, we now find the privileging of *orality* as an equally valid, equally empowering medium of historical transmission of accumulated skills and cultural patterns.[5] Moreover, the all-important, overarching question of a historical break, a historical lacuna, was engaged by some scholars who sought to establish an unbroken chronological line of development and perpetuation of some indigenous African forms and traditions whose origins lie in precolonial times, and which were neither snuffed out by colonial rupture, nor greatly impacted upon by Western forms.[6] This liberating notion of vital contact with an archaic cultural energy, of contact with autochthonous expressive paradigms which have survived the colonial sundering of so much of Africa's cultural capital from its sources, this is perhaps what fuels the work of many of Africa's most influential theatre companies and individual dramatists like Soyinka, Rotimi, Clark, Aidoo, Sutherland, Osofisan, Rugyendo and the late Duro Ladipo. It is this spirit which also imbues Soyinka's most important theoretical reflection on the theatre, the essay "The Fourth Stage" with its considerable interest.[7] This essay indeed marks what is quintessentially paradoxical about the "Afrocentric" counter-discourse on interculturalism in the African theatre: the Nietzschean echoes, the exploration of parallels between Greek and Yoruba classical tragic paradigms both mark the deeply conditioned, *reactive* nature of the essay; at the same time however, its confident self-assurance about the scope and range of indigenous sources available to the modern artist marks a crucial tactical move to reappropriate an indigenous, precolonial performance idiom; in other words, to *reinvent* theatrical tradition.

---

3. Emmanuel Obiechina, "Literature—Traditional and Modern—in the Nsukka Environment", in G. E. K. Ofomata (ed.), *The Nsukka Environment* (Fourth Dimension Publishers), 1978.
4. H. I. E. Dhlomo, op. cit., for example.
5. J. P. Clark, *The Ozidi Saga*, Ibadan, 1980.
6. Joel Adedeji, "The Alarinjo Theatre: A Study of Yoruba Theatrical Art from the Earliest Beginnings to the Present Times", unpublished dissertation, University of Ibadan, 1969; Ziky O. Kofoworola and Yusuf Lateef, *Hausa Performing Arts and Music*, Lagos, 1987.
7. Wole Soyinka, "The Fourth Stage", in *Myth, Literature and the African World*, Cambridge, 1976.

As already indicated in this essay, in our third discourse on intercul-turalism in the African theatre we encounter critics, scholars and prac-titioners who push analysis of the issue beyond the Africa–Europe binarism of both the dominant discourse and the counter-discourse that it engendered. Only in this respect may we describe this "third" discourse as a post-Negritude, post-manichean apprehension of inter-culturalism in the African theatre. In *this* discourse the issue is now problematized beyond the parameters of the two previous sets of dis-courses since analysis characteristically now turns on questions like: *Which* African or European sources and influences do we find oper-ative and combined in any given African theatrical expression? What motivates the interaction and combination of the "foreign" and the "indigenous", for instance, an escapist, nostalgic retreat into neotra-ditionalism, or a liberating and genuine artistic exploration of the range and diversity of styles, techniques, paradigms and traditions available within both the "foreign" and the "indigenous"? What social and ide-ological uses and functions mediate, legitimize or problematize the intercultural fusion of the "foreign" and the "indigenous"? And what aspects, within the reinvented "indigenous" forms, appear "foreign" to an indigenous audience and conversely, what absorbed "foreign" ele-ments seem "familiar"? Among many other critics and scholars I would identify Kavanagh's *Theatre and Cultural Struggle in South Africa* (1985), Etherton's *The Development of African Drama* (1982) and, rather self-consciously, my own *The Yoruba Travelling Theatre of Ni-geria* (1984) and *The Truthful Lie* (1985), as important book-length texts of this "third" discourse.

It is of course important to emphasize that this "third" discourse builds on some of the strengths and insights of the "first" and "second" discourses, while trying to avoid some of their inherent weaknesses, especially the tendency to make facile, over-hasty generalizations about singularity or normative unproblematic identity in theatrical expres-sion. The debt to the "second" discourse, the "Afrocentric", nationalist discourse, is perhaps incalculable, especially with regard to the fact that it brought to light the ignored orally transmitted forms of per-formance indigenous to Africa, in their communalistic, professional or amateur expressions, and with the stock of cultural energy which, over the centuries, have perpetuated them among the people. Equally note-worthy is the debt owed to the "Afrocentric" discourse in the unbur-dening of a new generation of African critics, scholars and theatre practitioners from the complexes of earlier generations, complexes de-rived from the suppositions of "people without history". If the debt owed to the "first" discourse is not so remarkable, if, indeed, a per-manent ambivalence, not to say antipathy, surrounds the conse-quences of the orthodoxy of this "first" discourse, one debt must nevertheless be acknowledged: the scholars' passion and dedication to reconstructing the "facts" with a scrupulous, meticulous eye for the details while clearly keeping the total picture in mind. It is important to recollect that even with the heavy baggage of a scholasticism blind to its methodological foibles, it was the *scholar* who effectively terminated the regime of the missionary and the anthropologist as the intellectual pundits of African theatre.

To acknowledge these debts of our "third" discourse to its precedent discourses however is not to become complacent. Nothing would be more naive, more unrealistic than to suppose that their respective premises and perspectives have either been routed from the field of African theatre scholarship, or indeed no longer continue to hold sway over the field. A cursory glance at any of the latest bibliographic surveys of doctoral theses or master's dissertations, or an encounter with recent, up-to-the-minute scholarly disputations in review articles in learned journals will only too readily confirm that the "third" discourse has not effectively moved us into a fully liberated, truly de-colonized space of discourse on interculturalism in the African theatre.

By way of concluding the reflections in this essay on discourses on interculturalism in African theatre scholarship, I would like to draw these reflections into a wider frame of reference which embraces basic issues and problems of interculturalism in the international theatre movement. What I wish to do here is make even more explicit, more polemical some ideological and philosophical premises which inform my own views on the subject. However, I wish to do this by pushing these ideological and philosophical premises through some central views of three contemporary thinkers on the relations of dominance, control and resistance which always operate between knowledge, power and discourse, namely Eric Hobsbawm, Michel Foucault and Frantz Fanon.

The discourse on interculturalism in world theatre is a cultural and intellectual novelty in theatre research and exchange of ideas between scholars and theatre practitioners perhaps comparable to the ecumenical movement among the clergy and laity of the world religions. However, according to Hobsbawm, though historical novelty implies innovation, it is almost always a "reinvention of tradition", a means of achieving intelligibility and legitimacy through establishing continuity with the past, even when the claim of absolute novelty is aggressively touted. Obviously this applies to our explanations of interculturalism, especially with regard to the second of Hobsbawm's three types of "invented traditions": "those establishing or legitimizing institutions or relations of authority."[8] The question which arises here in the context of our reflections in this essay is whether "interculturalism" would be a kind of "fourth" discourse, conscious or unconscious as the case may be, of those discourses which, in Africa and Asia in particular, have preceded it, discourses which have either perpetuated or challenged dangerous forms and modes of paternalistic "knowledge" about the world's theatre traditions. And here Foucault's ideas become particularly relevant, especially the notion of the "archives" or ground rules which establish the very possibility of a discourse and, often irrespec-

---

8. Eric Hobsbawm and Terence Ranger, *The Invention of Tradition*, Cambridge, 1983, p. 9.

tive of the views and intentions of a "discussant", subsume established relations between knowledge and power. Pointedly, one may push this notion to a query on whether those of us who now seek to explore contemporary theatrical interculturalism in a world-wide context are sufficiently aware and "free" of the structure of the global "information order", the global relations of knowledge which make our exchanges possible, but which also undergird the complex relations of unequal exchange between the nations and regions of the earth.

Finally, Frantz Fanon. His relevance here pertains to the outline he once gave of the shifts and transformations in the ideological contexts and the intellectual climates which determine modern views of culture and cultural exchange, and more particularly, his elaboration of three decisive phases.[9] In the first phase, according to Fanon, it is asserted that there are human groups with culture, and human groups without culture, the assertion of this theory being coincident with the inception of European colonization of non-European peoples of the earth and its attendant justificatory crudely biologically determined cultural racism. This, Fanon observes, is later refined to a more "accommodating" phase in which it is asserted that all human groups possess culture, that it is absurd to assert that any human group could be without a culture; it is only the case that there is a hierarchy to the complement of human cultures. Finally, Fanon observes that the liberalization of colonialism, and its formal termination, lead to the espousal of *cultural relativism* and the abandonment of the notion of a hierarchy of cultures. This then produces the view that the "validity", the worth, of each culture is established by its own internal reference points.

Obviously, this last stage coincides somewhat with our present milieu. In which case we might wish to consider Fanon's cautionary observations on the pitfalls of the liberal facade of cultural relativism: abstract, formal acceptance of difference and diversity, while being undoubtedly an advance on the blatant prejudices and paternalism of the past, can co-exist perfectly with actual, material relations of dominance and exploitation.

I began this essay with the controversial, problematic nature of Peter Brook's journey to Africa in 1973 as a practical expression of interculturalism in contemporary world theatre. Brook's company on this trip was drawn from all the continents of the world, and the object of the trip was a search for a common, universal "language" of theatre performance. With this lofty purpose, and this preparation, Brook went to Africa. We have seen that Brook and "Africa" met in this encounter with received codes, signs, parameters of discourse, and agenda of tasks and priorities which overdetermined that encounter. It seems to me that those of us engaged in the current exchanges on interculturalism in the international context ought, whether our explorations take

9. Frantz Fanon, "Racism and Culture", in *Presence Africaine*, nos. 8/9/10, 1956.

us to Africa, the Americas, Asia or Europe, to take the message of that
encounter to heart.

REFERENCES

Michael Etherton, *The Development of African Drama*, New York, 1982.
Biodun Jeyifo, *The Popular Yoruba Travelling Theatre*, Nigeria, 1984.
Biodun Jeyifo, *The Truthful Lie: Essays in a Sociology of African Drama*, London, 1985.
Robert Kavanagh, *Theatre and Cultural Struggle in South Africa*, London, 1985.
Eric R. Wolf, *Europe and the People Without History*, California, 1982.

DON RUBIN

African Theatre in a Global Context†

The American expatriate poet Gertrude Stein once said that the problem in dealing with Los Angeles as a geographical entity was that
'there's no there there'. For many brought up on the professionalized
Euro-American spoken theatre or even on many formalized Asian sung
and/or danced drama forms, the problem in dealing with Africa's dynamic performative traditions, most of which involve music and dance,
is—to paraphrase Stein—the theatre there seems to be without theatre there. Which is to say that it is easy not to see the continent's
sophisticated and often ancient theatrical traditions if one is looking
only for theatre buildings, raised stages, complicated infrastructures,
advanced technology, expensive sets and published scripts.

Sub-Saharan Africa—Black Africa, if you will—has a multitude of
its own traditions and has evolved its own contemporary forms based
on those traditions. In francophone Africa much of it is based on the
griotic tradition rooted in each community's oral history. A number of
francophone Africa's most theatrically advanced groups—particularly
in Côte d'Ivoire—are, in fact, now re-examining the role of the *griot*
through crossover forms that connect past to present, storytelling to
collective creation.

In parts of anglophone Africa the Concert Party with its many well-
known travelling companies brings together elements of burlesque
comedy and communal improvisation, folk song and social satire. Particularly strong in east Africa are the still vital storytelling traditions
and a powerful and extraordinarily advanced Theatre-for-Development
movement, a movement rooted in both urban and rural communities,
a movement involving health, educational and social issues in the belief that it is possible to find communal solutions to communal
problems.

Those who wish to connect to Euro-American theatrical styles—
French cuisine when visiting, say, the ancient African cultural and
educational centre of Timbuktu (in modern Mali)—there is no better
connection to be found in sub-Saharan Africa than the plays of the

† From *The World Encyclopedia of Contemporary Theatre*, vol. 3, ed. Don Rubin (London and
New York: Routledge, 1997) 14–16. Reprinted by permission of Taylor & Francis Books Ltd.

Nobel Prize-winning Nigerian dramatist Wole Soyinka, whose unique voice brings the most dynamic of African performative traditions and mythology together with the socially rooted traditions of western spoken drama. His work has already taken its deserved place in contemporary theatrical discourse.

Purely spoken drama in Africa, however, is still very much of a minority art form, a late development that emerged as part of colonial impositions and missionary training within the indigenous communities, impositions that failed to respect or even recognize in many cases either ethnic differences (there are more than a thousand different ethnic groups in sub-Saharan Africa alone) or differing religious traditions. In many countries, the spoken drama was used to try to replace traditional forms but in only a few countries did it succeed. Nevertheless, important dramatists did emerge—Bernard Dadié and Bernard Zadi Zaourou in Côte d'Ivoire, Soyinka and Ola Rotimi in Nigeria, Sony Labou Tansi in Congo, Sénouvo Agbota Zinsou in Togo, and Athol Fugard in South Africa—to name just a few of the many original and profound talents. Interestingly, since the mid-1960s, attempts have been made right across the continent by these and other dramatists to return traditional African performing arts to a more central place within the continent's theatrical experience, even in works that are essentially spoken.

To look at these issues in a slightly different way, it would seem that an argument could be made that western classical art divided—probably by the end of the fourth century BC—into a populist art aimed primarily at entertainment and escape, and a more elitist and often state-controlled or state-supported art primarily aimed at discussion and/or at the moral education of the community. The Roman poet and satirist Horace certainly recognized this when he argued in his *Ars Poetica* for the value of bringing both approaches together, to reunite *delicare* with *docere*, delight with teaching, entertainment with learning. Too rarely, however, have the two come together in the west. Shakespeare was perhaps the most successful at achieving such union in English drama; Brecht the closest in the Euro-American tradition during the twentieth century.

But the dichotomy that took place in western art did not, for the most part, occur in traditional African art. Even today, elements of that earlier cultural wholeness can still be seen across the continent. Art within these traditional societies is not perceived of as *either* educational *or* escapist but rather both simultaneously. Even in crossover forms, it is this union that is most apparent, this sense of the totality of theatrical form. It is this, then, that non-Africans seem to have the most trouble with in trying to 'read' African theatre whose dances, songs, plays and even grammatical constructions are layered with recognizable significance to those properly attuned. It is also this that is at the root of the difficulties many Africans have in trying to read 'meaning' into disengaged western popular art.

Yet these differences must be articulated and recognized if one is to begin to grasp the nature of theatre in African culture. To do so, one must be open to larger definitions of the word than are normally found in western tradition, alternative definitions or perhaps just more accurate definitions. This is part of what our two African volume editors are suggesting when they make distinctions between traditional and modern theatre in their introduction to this volume. And this is what east African scholar Penina Mlama of the University of Dar es Salaam means when she speaks of the connections between artist and community in her survey of theatre in Tanzania. This is what Joseph Tomoonh-Garlodeyh Gbaba means when he speaks of the importance of traditional aesthetics in his examination of theatre in Liberia today.

Obviously, if one is *only* interested in spoken drama one will not be able to understand the essence of contemporary African theatre, the rich fusions that are being made now even by traditional artists or those who, trained in western dramatic form, are beginning to reintroduce indigenous traditions into their work. It is this that is at the root of *didiga* in Côte d'Ivoire, the modern *koteba*[1] in Mali, much of Soyinka's work, and the work of many experimental Theatre-for-Development groups in east Africa. It is, in fact, among the most exciting of evolutions in the performing arts to be found anywhere in the world today. Living traditional forms in vital discourse with alternative dramatic visions.

It is also at the root of the new interdisciplinary science of theatre anthropology, an extraordinary late-twentieth-century investigation into the nature of the performative being created by groundbreaking theorists and practitioners in this growing field such as Victor Turner, Richard Schechner, Eugenio Barba, Jerzy Grotowski, Augusto Boal and, in his own way, Peter Brook. All are seeking to recognize and understand the role of the performative in daily life, to enlarge the notion of the theatrical to make all of us realize that theatre is not necessarily limited to a few hours in a closed, darkened building with a carefully prepared text being spoken to a group that has somehow been allowed entrance. It is an attempt to make us aware that theatre, the theatrical and the performative are quintessentially connected to universal human experiences: birth, death, rites of passage, marriage, namings and even funerals. The theatrical—as Africa well knows—is to be found in sporting events and in circuses, in storytelling and in public scenes, in dances and other mating events, in clothing and hairstyles. And, yes, the theatrical is even to be found in theatre buildings and scripts from Johannesburg's Market Theatre to Addis Ababa's National.

All of these are part of a continuum of the performative that we can and do participate in daily, a theatre that requires active rather than passive involvement, to be lived as well as watched. Not theatre *or* ritual but theatre *and* ritual. * * *

---

1. *Didiga* and *koteba* are neotraditional theatre forms [*Editor*].

JOACHIM FIEBACH

Dimensions of Theatricality in Africa†

Human behavior (presentation of the self) and social interrelationships (acting out roles) have been quite often understood in Western
cultures, at least since the sixteenth century, as theatrically structured.
Given the prevalent assumption that there was a rigid line of demarcation between society as the objective reality, and theater as a subjective, constructed, fictional representation (mimesis), the two realms
were mostly compared and interrelated on a metaphorical level. This
has changed in the twentieth century. Scholars and artists themselves
have come to conceive of social realities as more or less made up by
the very components, structural relations, and "techniques" that com-
prise the phenomenon of theater art. In the 1920s the German anthropologist Helmuth Plessner took an actor's activity on stage as the
paradigm for human attitudes and interaction with others in real life
and in the sociopolitical world. Humans, Plessner argued, act and interact in "real life" the same way as a performer does in theater arts
(109-29, 399-418). In the 1930s–early 1940s, Brecht described the
acting out of social roles and, implicitly, the display of the self in "real
life" as "natural theater" and "everyday theater."[1] In 1959 Erving Goffman summed up this line of thinking: theatrical techniques, he wrote,
were constituents of the individuals' interaction in real life.[2] Since the
1960s larger groups have been re-thinking societal realities as "theatrical" or forms of performance. This, for instance, has resulted in the
establishment of special academic institutions for performance studies
in North America and in a joint research project "Theatralität/Theat-
ricality" conducted by several universities in Germany. Different
strands of postmodernist theorists focus in particular on developments
in highly industrialized societies. They claim that the exponentially
accelerating production and circulation of commodities and audiovisually mediated images have created an entirely new historic situation.
Some hold that it has been only since the 1950s that performance and
theatricality have become decisive agencies (constituents) of reality.
Most tend to assume the distinction between "reality" and "image circulation" is being blurred to such an extent that reality (realities) appear to be lost or dissolve altogether.[3]

This essay's general interest is to provide an outline demonstrating
that African cultures do bear out what Western anthropologists, sociologists, and artists like Brecht have advanced about theatricality and

† From *Research in African Literatures* 30.4 (Winter 1999): 186–201. Reprinted by permission
  of Indiana University Press.

1. Bertolt Brecht, "Die Staßenszene," *Schriften Zum Theater*, vol. 5 (Berlin: Aufbau-Verlag,
   1964), 74–106; *Arbeitsjournal* (Berlin: Aufbau-Verlag, 1977), 131–32, 300.
2. Erving Goffman, *The Presentation of Everyday Life* (New York: Doubleday, 1959), 254–55.
3. Walter T. Anderson, *Reality Isn't What It Used to Be: Theatrical Politics, Ready-to-Wear
   Religion, Global Myths, Primitive Chic and Other Wonders of the Postmodern World* (San
   Francisco: Harper, 1990), 3–6.

performance beginning in the 1920s. Its special goals are twofold. First, it attempts to contribute to further research into the vast range of African "theatrical phenomena" that may exist beside the already widely discussed performance formats. It seeks to indicate that theatricality has been a major dimension for upholding and contesting power structures and social (general) difference. Second, elaborating on pre-industrial African cultures, the essay argues that performance as symbolic action was a decisive agency in constituting societal realities well before the advent of the "age of television," as Martin Esslin calls it.

I will start by considering four examples of acts of performance described by foreign visitors to Africa from the Middle Ages to the nineteenth century. I will then proceed to comment on each of those performances. The first is by Ibn Battuta. Looking back at his travels in the Mali empire of the fourteenth century, Ibn Battuta described the audiences the sultan (king) held in the palace courtyard on certain days. There was a platform under a tree, with three steps, silk carpeting, and cushions placed on it, and with a huge umbrella protecting it from the sun. The king made his appearances from a door in a corner of the palace, with a bow in his hand and a quiver on his back. He was preceded by musicians who carried two-stringed guitars; behind him came hundreds of armed slaves. He walked in a leisurely fashion, affecting a very slow movement, and even stopped from time to time. On reaching the platform he halted and looked round the assembly, then ascended it "in the sedate manner of a preacher ascending a mosque-pulpit." As he took his seat, drums, trumpets, and bugles were sounded. Three slaves went running out to summon the king's deputy and military commanders, who then came and sat down. When the king summoned any of his subjects, the person called would take off his clothes and put on worn garments, remove his turban, and don a dirty skullcap, then approach the king with his garments and trousers raised knee-high. He went forward in an "attitude of humility and dejection," according to Ibn Battuta, and knocked the ground hard with his elbows. Then that person would stand with bowed head and bent back listening to what the king said. If anyone addressed the king and received a reply from him, he uncovered his back and threw dust over his head and back, "like a bather splashing himself with water." When the sultan delivered remarks, all those present at his audience would take off their turbans and set them down, listening in silence to what he said. Sometimes one of them stood up and recalled his deeds in the sultan's service, saying, "I did such-and-such on such a day" or "I killed so-and-so on such a day." Others who knew of his deeds would confirm his words by plucking the cord of their bow and releasing it with a twang, just as an archer did when shooting an arrow. If the sultan said "truly spoken," the man would remove his clothes and "dust."[4]

4. Ibn Battuta, "Travels in Mali," in *The African Past: Chronicles from Antiquity to Modern Times*, ed. Basil Davidson (Harmondsworth: Penguin, 1964), 89–90.

The second example is drawn from eighteenth-century Benin, where chiefs were described as presenting their selves/social roles in the following manner: When they went to the king's palace or other places, they dressed themselves like the women of Spain. From the waist down they wore clothes resembling sheets and farthingales. Two men who remained beside them served as attendants so that they could rest their arms on the attendants' shoulders. Thus they moved about with great solemnity. When on horseback, they struck similar poses that conveyed solemnity, especially when they were going to the king's palace for festivals or sacrifices. Each chief had a large following and his own band, some playing ivory flutes, others small guitars, others calabashes with small stones inside, and still others drums. An observer remarked that those who cut the most fearsome figure were accounted the finest.[5]

In the nineteenth century, a French general received a grand reception by a paramount chief who apparently had authority over quite a few West African villages. The chief descended from his horse and, according to the general's description, prostrated himself and then sat down beside the high-ranking, powerful European. The chief's relations, friends, and virtually all villagers formed a circle around him. Three griots were playing on their music instruments. All of a sudden, a warrior stormed into the circle, with a sword in his hand. He moved to the general, stretched his arm toward the earth, and then started to jump and yell, as the general put it, moving his sword about as if he were attacking and then defending himself. Other warriors stood up and followed suit. Their movements (presentations) developed into a wild dance accompanied by music and illuminated by a big fire. The griots came and challenged the chief who then took his rifle and began to dance. The relatives, who had stood up together with the chief, joined in, keeping their distance respectfully. When the chief ended his dance, everyone saluted and praised him profusely. He resumed dancing, then after some time stopped, apparently exhausted, according to the general's observation.[6]

The fourth and last example is about story-telling in South Africa. After characterizing, in the beginning of his study undertaken in the 1950s, the *ntsomi* of the South African Xhosa as a traditional form of oral literature, Harold Scheub ended up considering the accompanying oral performance of those stories as an essentially theatrical phenomenon, a type of theater. The narrative, that is to say, the performance of Xhosa story-telling, often moves with breathtaking speed from image to image, from one signifying action and signified event to the other. The performances depend heavily on gesture:

> The body is actively involved in creating the actions expressed in the *ntsomi*. Thought and stream of consciousness may be indi-

5. A. F. C. Ryder, *Benin and the Europeans 1485–1897* (Ibadan History Series, Ibadan: Longmans, 1969), 314.
6. R. Cornevin, *Le théâtre en Afrique noire et à Madagascar* (Paris: Le livre africain, 1970), 16–17.

cated by a lowering of the voice, a sinking of the head. To indicate dialogue, the performer often tilts her head to the left, then to the right, to differentiate between the two characters who are speaking; this may be coupled with vocal dramatics, to distinguish them further. [. . .] At times, gesture is utilized purely for rhythmic purposes, the hands and body in harmony with the movement of the words rather than their content, the body thus becoming an echo of the sound of language rather than its meaning. [. . .] The audience provides [. . .] accompaniment and commentary, or total involvement as actors. In accompanying and commenting, it simply reflects the rhythmic movement and action of the narrative as it is being developed by the artist.[7]

The first three cases could be considered highly demonstrative symbolic actions, or "cultural performances" of different significance that were at the same time the actual communicative practices of the respective societal entities. They were activities to conduct public life, to mediate characteristic attitudes of individuals (self-presentation), and to act out the actual positions and interrelationships of different social strata and groups in the given society or, so to speak, to construct its "real fabric." The performance of sociocultural power and the ostentatious display of pertinent individual (social) attitudes constituted the very realities of court life and of interrelationships between ruling strata in ancient African states. This comes out even more graphically in the third example of a paramount chieftainship that was receiving the mighty representative of the new colonial power. The presentations of *ntsomi*-stories (narratives) are clearly separated out from normal, everyday life, let alone from political activities. They could be categorized as aesthetically dominated communicative events, as a distinct artistic/aesthetic production called theater. In the West, the concept derives from a specific cultural phenomenon that originated in ancient Greece. Since then the term *theater* has mostly been used to describe events that resemble or are almost identical to those separated-out (compartmentalized) cultural productions that developed in Europe, corresponding to similar types in Asia. However, components (techniques) of that specific phenomenon called "theater" made up the symbolic actions at the court in Mali, the public appearance of the Benin chiefs, and the encounter between the Senegalese chief and his followers as well. Those techniques consisted of ostended gestures and facial expressions, the positioning and grouping of persons and objects in ways that define social space, rank, and interrelationships. Rhythmical or ostended physical movements, ranging from

7. Harold Scheub, *The Xhosa Ntsomi* (Oxford: Clarendon, 1975), 71–73. Isidore Okpewho emphasized "The Mimetic Principle" governing "oral performance" (*The Epic in Africa: Toward a Poetics of the Oral Performance* [New York: Columbia UP, 1979], 14–19). Paul Zumthor devoted a whole chapter to "The Performance" and a paragraph to "Théâtralité"/Theatricality in his book on oral poetry (*Introduction à la poésie orale* [Paris: Seuil, 1983], 147–208). In 1986, still taking oral epic and poetry as "oral literature" ("littérature orale"), Jacques Chevrier nevertheless pointed to the interrelationship between the narrator and the recitation on the one hand and the audiences on the other as an essential element of oral performances. The theatrical ability of the narrator would be essential (*L'arbre à palabres: Essai sur les contes et récits traditionnels d' Afrique Noire* [Paris: Hatier, 1986], 17).

gesturing to dancing, constituted the very reality of the given societal entities, and at the same time signified social allegiances, disparities, and antagonistic cleavages. "Real" social attitudes and political relations unfolded in a theatrical way, or for that matter as the expressive presentation of (social) selves and/or the acting out of (social) roles. Thus, theatricality not only appears as a defining characteristic of artistic (aesthetically dominated) productions markedly set apart from other practices, but as an essential dimension of sociocultural and political praxis, at least to a large extent. In any case, it is a defining characteristic of the wide range of cultural performances that are often constituents of sociopolitical processes. Tracing ways in which India was modernizing in the 1940s–1950s, Milton Singer called cultural events such as weddings, temple rituals, festivals, recitations, plays, dramas, and musical concerts "cultural performance."[8] Extending the notion of performance to audio-visual productions in 1972, he claimed that performances were "the elementary constituents of the culture."[9] They elucidate processes of social and cultural change to a large extent.[1]

My understanding of theatricality in this all-encompassing, expansive sense[2] is similar to views and notions that have been advanced mainly by Western theater people, social and cultural historians, anthropologists, sociologists. A few examples of these notions will illustrate the point. Analyzing the power struggle between the gentry and plebeian strata in England in the eighteenth century, E. P. Thompson elaborated on the theatricality of their respective stances and interaction, and generalized that many forms of public political activities were theater.[3] In his studies on "performance," Richard Schechner describes activities and events that are not specifically framed as "theater art" as theater and drama[4]—activities such as "social dramas, personal experience, public displays, political and economic interaction."[5] Discussing reality as a "highly contestable notion," David Parkin claimed that a false distinction is made by asking the "usual question" of the extent to which reality is an "objective condition that can be represented." If power, for instance, is "immanent in all social inter-

---

8. Milton Singer, *Preface to Traditional India: Structure and Change,* ed. Milton Singer (Philadelphia: American Folklore Society, 1959), xii–xiii.
9. Milton Singer, *When a Great Tradition Modernizes* (London: Pall Mall, 1972), 71.
1. Ibid., 77. Publishing conference papers on "cultural performance" in 1984, John J. MacAloon claimed that the conferees were in agreement that "performance is constitutive of social experience and not something merely added or instrumental" ("Introduction: Cultural Performance, Cultural Theory," in *Rite, Drama, Festival, Spectacle,* ed. John J. MacAloon [Philadelphia: Institute for the Study of Human Issues, 1984], 2).
2. Joachim Fiebach, "Theatralitätsstudien unter kulturhistorisch-komparatistichen Aspekten," in *Spektakel der Moderne: Bausteine zu einer Kulturgeschichte der Medien und des darstellenden Verhaltens,* ed. Joachim Fiebach and Wolfgang Mühl-Benninghaus (Berlin: Vista, 1996), 9–54; *Keine Hoffnung Keine Verzweiflung: Versuche um Theaterkunst und Theatralität* (Berlin: Henschelverlag, 1998), 35–53.
3. Edward P. Thompson, *Plebejische Kultur und moralische Ökonomie. Aufsätze zur englischen Sozialgeschichte des 18. und 19. Jahrhunderts* (Frankfurt/Main: Ullstein, 1980), 176–202, 299–301.
4. Richard Schechner, *Performance Theory 1970–1976* (New York: Drama Book Specialists, 1977), 86–87, 124, 145–46.
5. Richard Schechner, *Between Theater and Anthropology* (Philadelphia: U of Pennsylvania P, 1985), 150.

action," then we need to ask what is special about power "emanating from cultural events." Thus Parkin pointed to the "transformative qualities" of the symbolic or of the cultural becoming "the political and vice versa."[6] He believed, according to Edward L. Schieffelin in his 1998 study problematizing "performance," that there was something fundamentally performative "about human being-in-the-world." He posited cautiously there would be no culture and no society without "living human body expressivity."[7]

Victor Turner and Georges Balandier should be mentioned in particular. Their respective ideas derived primarily from encounters with African realities; rites of passages of various types; African attitudes toward death and practices dealing with the dead; healing processes; and complex cultural performances inextricably intertwined with possession or mediumship. Claiming that the self was "presented through the performance of roles,"[8] Turner referred to Goffman's question of the "critical ways" in which the world would not be theater (72).

Balandier delineated historical trajectories along which the theatrical construction of social and political structures (realities) moved in different and changing historical processes. On the one hand, he outlined how and why social interrelationships, specific mechanisms for upholding power structures, and hierarchical (class, caste, gender) disparities between the ruling and the ruled have been structured and thus bolstered and cemented by theatrical activities. On the other hand, he sketched the extent to and manner in which groups have always tried to subvert, resist, or even change those realities through what I would like to call symbolic actions. His book, *Le pouvoir sur scènes*, traces relevant phenomena from stateless and oral societies to what he calls the "thélé" societies of today, also touching on African sociopolitical and cultural performances such as those described by the above-cited Arab and French observers. In the 1960s, Balandier had already pointed to the decisive role that symbolic actions played in the construction of everyday life in the old Congo kingdom.[9] In *Le pouvoir sur scènes*, he begins by dealing with the role of symbolic actions or, for that matter, theatrically constructed practices in the consolidation or contestation of various types of power structures and social hierarchies in oral and stateless societies. This does not mean, according to his emphasis, that such activities, as performances, are reduced to "mere appearances" and "illusory play." A society is not "held together" as an entity (only) by means of coercion and relations of legitimate forces but also by the whole set of transfigurations. They

6. David Parkin, "The Power of the Bizarre," in *The Politics of Cultural Performance*, ed. David Parkin, Lionel Caplan, and Humphrey Fisher (Oxford: Berghahn Books Providence, 1996), xx, xvi.
7. Edward L. Schieffelin, "Problematizing Performance," in *Performance, Media, Ritual*, ed. Felicia Hughes-Freeland (London: Routledge, 1998), 195. For a classic example of the study of politics as theater in a pre-industrial state, see Clifford Geertz, *Negara: The Theatre State in Nineteenth-Century Bali* (Princeton: Princeton UP, 1980).
8. Victor Turner, *The Anthropology of Performance* (New York: PAJ, 1986), 81–82.
9. Georges Balandier, *La vie quotidienne au Royaume de Kongo du XVIᵉ au XVIIIᵉ siècle* (Paris: Hachette, 1965), 174, 201; Georges Balandier, *Le Pouvoir sur scènes* (Paris: Balland, 1980).

function as agency(ies) to constitute a society and to make it work. That ensemble has a rather vulnerable structure. It is even a factor in threatening existing structures, and can generate forms of dramatization that show power as a negative phenomenon. (*Le pouvoir* 50–51).

I cautiously take the view that symbolic action and the theatrical performance of social and political realities are essential characteristics of oral societies or predominantly oral societies before the communications (and thus cultural) revolution ushered in by the invention and spread of the printing press. They unfold(ed) in essential ways as symbolically fraught praxis, as a "signifying practice,"[1] or for that matter signifying performances, or vice versa.[2]

There is a rich body of material (e.g., descriptions of travelers, analyses of anthropologists) to support my contention that large portions of public communication (sociopolitical interaction) in many African societies, before and during the period of full-scale colonization that began in the nineteenth century, have been structured in similar theatrical ways.[3] Francois N'Sougan Agblemanon thus considered the "theatrical approach" (*strategème théâtral*) a fundamental feature of African oral societies. With regard to story-telling performances as a "school for education" (*école d'éducation*), he claimed that the "theatrical approach" not only played a role in reducing the tensions between the individual and society but created an environment conducive to the cohesion of a given group and enhanced the individual's receptiveness of community values. Music and dance as essential components of performance were essential factors in molding almost all domains of society. Public life was a "permanent scene" (*scène ininterrompue*) in which "attitudes and stances became roles in a theatrical sense" (*les comportements deviennent des rôles, au sens théâtral*).[4]

Agbelamnon emphasized the power of the "theatrical approach" to enable individuals to open up more easily to collective values, and thus to become integrated into cohesive social units. He highlighted the role it could play in forming and stabilizing social structures and communal solidarity. It appears, however, that this was not the main or only trajectory or set of functions of theatricality in conducting essential parts of public life in many African oral societies. The first three cases presented above are examples of what could be called "representative theatricality," or performances that demonstrate the distinct social status of different ruling groups and their most powerful individuals. The public behavior of the latter signified and thus under-

---

1. Raymond Williams, *Culture* (Glasgow: Fontana, 1981), 208–09.
2. As to the European Middle Ages and their mainly orally communicating societies, I refer to LeGoff, who, explaining why an autonomous, clearly separated-out theater art seemed to have fully developed only since the seventeenth century, claimed that the "whole mediaeval society stages itself" (qtd. in Michel de Certeau, *The Writing of History* [New York: Columbia UP, 1988], 202).
3. Joachim Fiebach, *Die Toten also die Macht der Lebenden: Zur Theorie und Geschichte von Theater in Afrika* (Berlin: Henschelverlag, 1986), 7–159.
4. François N'Sougan Agblemanon, *Sociologie des sociétés orales d' Afrique Noire: Les Ewe du Sud-Togo* (Paris: Mouton, 1969), 149, 114.

scored social cleavage and difference, rather than fostering communal cohesion and solidarity, which Agbelamnon seems to highlight as the main function of social theater.

Many cases of "representative theatricality" point to the basic (social, gender) contradictions, conflicts, and world-views that have been marked features of African societies since well before colonization. And it is mostly cultural performances such as rituals, festivals, etc. that have been called upon to lay bare, negotiate, and resolve those crises. They are often bewilderingly ambivalent events in terms of the potential of their mental and emotional and thus ideological efficacy. The same obtains for virtually all types of social formations, for more or less nonhierarchical structured entities (communities, households, village communities) as well as for highly complex societies based on social disparities and cleavages (kingdoms, empires).

Affirmative "representative theatricality" has often been highly contradictory itself. As forms of symbolic action, the respective performances affirm and uphold the actual, existing power structure. They display, and thus emphasize, the eternal, "natural" legitimacy of social hierarchy in empires, and above all the indisputable power of their leading functionaries (kings) by relating them to legendary history, creation myths, and kingly ancestors. Kings and paramount chiefs are presented or present themselves as the supreme or only agency (or individuals) who can effectively communicate with powerful gods and thus ensure the welfare of a given community. Cultural performances celebrating achievements such as successful harvests are intended to signify that any prosperity of and security for the people result from the very power embodied by the ruler who is considered to be the living successor of the (mythical) founding hero of the society in question. In his analyses of "representative theatricality" primarily in Central Africa, Pius Ngandu Nkashama comes to the conclusion that in any circumstance, the "play of the stage" (*le jeu de la scène*) becomes a most attractive factor that determines the "very existence of the social formation."[5] Everything is structured as if the despots seek to be exclusively both creators of the world and its dramaturges, and as if since its origin they had wanted to dominate the cosmos by images and the example of the stage (33). Just as symbolic actions signified that kings and chief were the privileged or the only agencies (groups, individuals) that could secure the prosperity and stability of society, the very performance implied, and thus connoted, that the respective society is based on essential differences and antagonistic disparities.

The performance honoring Ogun that John Pemberton III describes is a specific example of that ambivalence.[6] The main actors are the king and the most powerful chiefs. Their movements and attitudes (for example, parading to Ogun's shrine) define and dominate space, time (seven days), and the public activities of the festivities. Thus, the sym-

---

5. Pius Ngandu Nkshama, *Théâtres et scènes de spectacle: Etudes sur les dramaturgies et les arts gestuels* (Paris: L'Harmattan, 1993), 24–84.
6. John Pemberton III, "The Dreadful God and the Divine King," in *Africa's Ogun: Old World and New*, ed. Sandra T. Barnes (Bloomington: Indiana UP, 1989), 107–32.

bolic actions demonstrate the actual unquestionable power of ruling (royal) lineages and in particular the dominant agency, the king. On the other hand, significant parts of those performances consist of threatening confrontations between the king and the chiefs. The king and the leading warrior chief face each other with drawn swords: this signifies that there are discrepancies, conflicts, and tensions among the ruling groups themselves.

Other types of complex cultural performances that act out the real power structures and social hierarchies in order to demonstrate their legitimacy include components of symbolic actions that directly contest this legitimizing effort. They may throw the hierarchical structure into critical relief by constructing in performance an entirely different, "inverted reality." Social cleavages, conflicts, and tensions can thus be brought to the open and illuminated. A few examples of such "inversion" performances will be in place. The *odwira* Yam Festival of the ancient Ashanti empire is one such case. It was meant to perform the unquestionable legitimacy of the given social and political structure. It showed that the ancestors, the dead and their everlasting presence —embodied by the incumbent rulers and, above all, the current king as their rightful representative—guaranteed prosperity for all subjects. The performance was designed to literally impress in the minds of all individuals the notion that only the existing hierarchical system safeguarded their lives and, in particular, that their supreme ruler, the king himself, was the father, the Old Leader of all lineages, social groups, strata, families, and individuals—an indispensable, oversized being. The third day was most interesting. Slaves and lowly subjects were given the freedom to act as they wished and to behave as rulers of the city of Kumasi. According to T. Edward Bowdich, reporting on the activities in one such festival, the king had ordered "a large quantity of rum to be poured into brass pans, in various parts of the town." In less than an hour, "excepting the principal men" not a sober person was to be seen. The "commonest mechanics and slaves, furiously declaiming on state palavers; the most discordant music, the most obscene songs [. . .] all wore their handsomest cloths, which they trailed after them to a great length [. . .]." Bowdich called it a "drunken emulation of extravagance and dirtiness."[7] Toward the evening, however, the licence ended. A very different symbolic action then took place. Tributary chiefs "displayed their equipages in every direction," and there was a procession from the palace to the south end of the town and back with the king and dignitaries "carried in their hammocks," passing "through continued blaze of musketry" (279).

The Apo of Tekiman described by R. S. Rattray, and apparently hinted at by Willem Bosman already in the early eighteenth century,[8] is a second example of an inversion performance meant to invert power structures and, basically, contradictory social relations for a well-

---

7. T. Edward Bowdich, *Mission from Cape Coast Castle to Ashantee* (1824; rpt. London: Frank Cass, 1966), 278.
8. R. S. Rattray, *Ashanti* (Oxford: Clarendon, 1975), 158.

defined (circumscribed) period of time. On Tuesday, Rattray relates, the great local god, Ta Kese or Ta Mensa, and several other gods were carried upon the heads of their respective priests under gorgeous umbrellas of plush and velvet. The following day, however, the deferential attitude toward the existing social structure and dominating values was inverted: "That afternoon bands composed entirely of women ran up and down the long, wide streets, with a curious lolloping, skipping steps, singing apo songs." Later Rattray was able to record them into his phonograph. The English translation of some parts shows that they were mocking or even scathingly attacking him: "O King, you are a fool. / We are taking the victory from out your hands. / O King, you are impotent." The Ashanti people, they went on, may be children of slaves. The King of Ashanti might have bought them, but "he did not buy us." They knew that a Brong man ate rats but they maintained that they "never knew that one of royal blood eats rats." Today they had seen their master "eating rats" (55–157).

At least since Max Gluckman's first probings into inversion rituals in Zulu villages in the 1930s, attention has been directed to structural contradictions and tensions in stateless, apparently egalitarian communities. To overcome grave crises (scarcity, agricultural disaster, looming famine) that threaten the very existence of respective communities, Zulu village women, who normally occupied a disadvantaged, subordinate social and thus power position (patriarchal society), took over authority and could do things and "act out" social roles that normally were the prerogatives of men. For a limited period of time, they had the right, virtually the undisputed power, to mock scathingly and ridicule the males.[9] P. Rigby describes and analyzes a similar "inversion ritual" of the Gogo in Tanzania. In an existential crisis (cattle disease) that could wipe out the entire livestock, a basic means of subsistence, women took over the herding of cows and the "regimenting" not only of the households but of public life at large. Both functions were male prerogatives in "normal life." Taking action to avert disaster and end the crises, women dressed and behaved as men. They attacked the males, who were powerless for the period of the role-inverting practice and could only retaliate by verbally jeering at the women.[1] The intrinsic gender differences and tensions of Gogo reality could thus be brought to the open.

Seemingly indisputable moral and social norms have often been contested by the performance of a pair of masks that oppose and contradict each other. The "ugly masks" accompany and ridicule the beautiful, refined ones that embody the community's dominant concepts of beauty, moral behavior, and attitudes. They debunk or comment critically on governing values and norms by inverting the costumes and gestures of the beautiful, norm-setting ones. Latent con-

9. Max Gluckman, "Zulu Women in Hoecultural Ritual," *Bantu Studies* (Johannesburg) 9 (1935): 114–18.
1. P. Rigby, "Some Gogo Rituals of 'Purification': An Essay on Social and Moral Categories of the Gogo," in *Dialectic in Practical Religion*, ed. Edmond R. Leach (Cambridge: Cambridge UP, 1968), 160–67.

flicts, social rifts, differing views can be brought to the open. The *jowei*-mask is used as the embodiment of the highest moral and social values, and of the most secret forms of knowledge and dominant values of the female Sande Society of the Mendes of Sierra Leone. The beautiful Sande masker bears a variant of the name of the highest ranking member in the Society, *sowei*. Dances of the *jowei* constitute the apex of initiation activities and important sociopolitical events such as the enthronement of a king or paramount chief. The *jowei*, or the *sowei*, and the social value system or social structure they represent, have been, however, in most cases opposed, contradicted, and contested by the accompanying *gonde*-mask. The costume, make-up, shape, gestures, and movements of the *gonde*-mask are the very opposite of the solemnity, the gracious and idealized behavior, the refined costume, and facial mask of *j(s)owei*.[2] According to Ruth B. Philipps, *gonde* is "a clown-like figure which overturns all the conventions and decorum." Her costume

> is a pastiche of rags and tatters, and she is hung about with all sorts of junk—rusty tin cans, shells, and other discarded fragments. [. . .] *Gonde* is also shameless in going right up to people and asking for money despite her utter unworthiness, rather than waiting in a dignified manner for people to present whatever gifts they might want to give her. This angers *ndoli jowei* (who, people explain, wants all the money for herself) and, to the amusement of the crowd, she will try to chase the *gonde* away.[3]

The extent to which initiation rites can act out complex, contradictory, social positions and conceptions of the world may be best outlined by a cursory glance at a main component of the Bambara initiation cycle, that is, at the masks or performers *koré dugaw*. They are tricksters or clowns representing the inextricable intertwining of both viciousness and destructiveness, critical intelligence and creativity. According to Dominique Zahan's detailed description, the *koré dugaw* are, to their village spectators, the most appealing performers in initiation procedures that transform children into adults, and train them for leadership. *Koré* is the last or highest stage in the initiation cycle during which the initiated gain insight into the core values and secrets of their community. It is at this stage of the initiation that the *koré dugaw* intervene. Their function is to parody, satirize, mock, and ridicule everybody and everything held in highest esteem in society.[4] On the other hand, the clowns appear to embody the truly wise human being, the possessor of deepest knowledge (138–94). Additionally, their costume, speech, body movements, their whole appearance, seem

2. Ruth B. Philipps, "Masking in Mende Sande Society Initiation Rituals," *Africa* 48.3 (1978): 273–74.
3. Compare John Nunley (*Moving with the Face of the Devil: Art and Politics in Urban West Africa* [Urbana: U of Illinois P, 1987]) on Soweh or the female leader of the Western area Bundu Society in Freetown after the 1930s. Warren L. d'Azevedo touched on similar performances among the Gola ("Sources of Gola Artistry," in *The Traditional Artist in African Societies*, ed. Warren d' Azevedo [Bloomington, Indiana UP, 1973], 282–340).
4. Dominique Zahan, *Sociétés d'initiation Bambara: Le N'domo, le Ko* (Paris: Mouton, 1960), 20–83.

to criticize authority openly. Apparently "taking sides" with the dominated peasants, they scathingly ridicule in particular the dominant
values and deeds of the rulers—values praised by other types of performers.[5] The clowns fight the dreadful hyena-masks that signify the
king's instruments of control of the peasants. Engaging the dangerous,
much feared hyenas, the clowns appear to perform the underdogs'
critical attitude toward the oppressive power structure and its hegemonic value system. The *koré dugaw* wear a wooden sword, a parody
of the iron swords of the warriors and their policing guard (the hyenas). Grotesquely inverting the political and cultural hegemony of the
rulers, they call themselves "war chiefs" and claim to possess an artil-
lery called "tucking-in-the-cake."

Two related characteristics of perceiving and thinking and thus of
dealing with the world seem to have been at the basis of the performing or theatrical constructing of many domains of African societies
before and even during colonization. First, it is a noncompartmental-
izing conception that recognizes no rigid boundaries between different
classes of phenomena, between the visible and the invisible, between
earthly practices and supernatural forces. Taking the (imagined) communication with supernatural forces (worlds) as a constituent of real
life requires visualization (presentation, representation) of the invisible
agents. Intercourse with them must be rendered as a practice, or in
other words it must be performed. Symbolic action thus becomes a
major component (constituent) of social, political, and cultural life.
Cultural performance as signifying practice appears to be essential for
dealing with public matters in general and thus for constructing social
realities.[6]

Second, an all-encompassing pragmatism,[7] that is, pragmatic world-
views and their corresponding attitudes, seem to have made many African (oral) societies conduct "real life" as theatrical, even as playful
performing practices. Relating the performance of an "inverted reality," as described by Gluckman, as a practice for dealing with existential crises in Zulu villages, to what Axel-Ivor Berglund writes on the
Zulu may indicate the extent to which there may be a causal relationship, or at least a significant correspondence between African world-
views and pragmatic attitudes. Berglund emphasizes the complexity of
the pragmatic thought-patterns and symbolism: the Zulu think of oppositions as different sides of the same coin, and they handle practical
problems of everyday life accordingly. He avoids the term *ancestor*, for
instance, because "ancestor" suggests thinking along the lines of Western dichotomies and treating the dead as if they were totally separated
from the living. Quoting an informant—"Father is departed, but he

---

5. The villagers' approach to and their respective performing of war and warriors appear to be
   the direct opposite of the presentations ("representative theatricality") of royal warriors, war
   in general, in various versions of the Sunjata epic as, for instance, documented and interpreted by Gordon Innes, *Introduction to Sunjata: Three Mandinka Versions*, ed. Gordon Innes
   (London: School of Oriental and African Studies, U of London, 1974), 1–33.
6. Fiebach, *Die Toten*, 42–78.
7. John Miller Chernoff, *African Rhythm and African Sensibility* (Chicago: U of Chicago P,
   1979), 155–65; Fiebach, *Die Toten*, 80–81, 167–74.

is"—he claims that this expression should suggest the idea that the father is present and active although he is no longer living as the speaker is. Referring to a case in a customary court, Berglund points to the pragmatic flexibility of handling difficult-to-judge legal matters and other problems. Thus Zulu thought-patterns do not have a fixed code of laws that stipulate boundaries between the moral and immoral use of anger. Although the divisions are clear in theory, in practice there is room for manipulating the boundaries.[8] Focusing on Yoruba rituals and especially on Egungun/Apidan performances, Margaret Thompson Drewal stressed that ritual spectacles were plays but at the same time operated "as another mode of being," into and out of which people shifted, like other modes of being. Spectacle dwells, she claims, conceptually at the juncture of "two planes of existence—the world and the other world, at the nexus of the physical and the spiritual," and at the nexus of the "visible and invisible" (103–04).

Since the early twentieth century, African societies have undergone a fundamental transformation. New societal structures have been developing, determined and shaped by colonization, the emergence of peripheral capitalism, and the encroachment of modern consumerism. This process has been in particular propelled by a specific communication revolution that rests on the rapidly growing role of printed material and at the same time on a fast expanding network of audiovisual media, from phonograph, radio, and film, to television and video. Research must be done to determine to what extent, and how, these changes have remolded conceptions of theatricality as a factor in constructing realities, how they have altered performing practices, what new possibilities of "performing realities" they facilitate, and what different "theatrical practices" they have, and are generating. I can only hint at what should be more closely studied. There is the major role television has begun to play in Africa. So far, it has been the most powerful new "dramatic form" of this age, as Esslin put it. The frame of the television screens turns everything that happens on it "into a stage,"[9] not only or even primarily for the vast amount of fictional presentations (drama, film, series, music-videos) but above all for the specific constructions,[1] or for that matter the performative (theatrical) character of its entire program—in particular for news, documentaries, commercials. Concentrating on dramaturgies and "gestural arts" in francophone countries, Nkashama touches on television's power, on its almost violent all-pervasive impact on society. There are new types of theatricality to be found particularly in Congo-Kinshasa. Novel types of theater and theatricality have been transferred from former well-circumscribed performing places—for instance, educational institutions of the colonial period—to communal playing grounds,

8. Axel-Ivor Berglund, *Zulu Thought Patterns and Symbolism* (Bloomington: Indiana UP, 1976), 265.
9. Martin Esslin, *The Age of Television* (Stanford: Stanford Alumni Assoc., 1981), 27.
1. John Fiske, *Television Culture* (London: Routledge, 1989), 296–98; Stephen Heath, "Representing Television," in *Logics of Television,* ed. Patricia Mellenkamp (Bloomington: Indiana UP, 1990), 291–93.

amphitheaters in colleges, sport arenas, and to radio stations and television. He regards this process as an enormous extension of "the theatrical practice," whose essential function is to probe into and thus interpret "social story" (*la fable sociale*). One could observe that "public life in this country" changes along with the mode of permanent theatricalization.[2]

Further intensive comparative research is necessary into the history and the sociocultural mechanisms that have led to a comparatively new "mode of permanent theatricalization," which is essentially determined by the role of audiovisual media. At first glance it appears to be just another case of uncreative emulation of new trends in Western cultures resulting from the technological communications revolution. One should, however, approach those processes from a different angle. Here I can only hint at one line that future research could take. Turning to modern modes of theatricalization, such as described by Nkashama, seems to be just another instance of the "traditional" African pragmatism to cope with fundamentally new (modern) realities.

A case in point may be the complex, discrete history of the *egungun*-phenomenon and its close relationship with the emergence of the traditional, professional, itinerant Yoruba theater as a specific art form, and then, at least indirectly, with the development of the modern popular Yoruba traveling theater. The egungun-story, as I would like to call it, speaks of the astounding (pragmatic) mobility, the openness, the almost avid interest in new things and thus in innovation as essential characteristics of many African "traditional" cultures.[3]

Dancing the *egungun*, a kind of spirit of the dead, the performer's body is entirely disguised. The flesh of the performer's body, that is, a defining quality of the living, must be concealed. The reason is to present the *egungun* as a deadly, awe-inspiring force. It is, however, from the *egungun* masquerade that a professional mostly comic, funmaking theater originated. Death, or more precisely the dancing spirit of the dead, is a sensuous phenomenon, and a source of sensuous pleasure as well. Even those *egungun* who dance at funerals, awesome and dreadful guards of the deceased, terrifying manifestations of death (and the most powerful ancestors), are funmakers. *Egungun* are much open to change. They are curious about new things and embrace fragments from foreign cultures rapidly and avidly without giving up their original essential characteristics. Around the turn of the century, during the first stage of colonial penetration of Yorubaland, R. E. Dennett met an *egungun* who had performed at the funeral of an important

---

2. Nkshama, *Théâtre et scènes de spectacle*, 257–58.
3. Pondering on specific qualities and essential features of African religion(s), Wole Soyinka and Ulli Beier emphasized the openness and thus creativeness of received cultures. Beier claimed that both Christianity and Islam were conservative forces that actually retarded Nigeria's ability "to cope with the modern world," whereas traditional religions, Yoruba religion at least, were "much more open, and much capable of adaptation." Soyinka added succinctly: "Yes, and for that very reason liberating!" (Wole Soyinka, *Orisha Liberates the Mind: Wole Soyinka in Conversation with Ulli Beier on Yoruba Religion* [Bayreuth: Iwalewa, 1992], 4).

chief. Men and boys following the egungun were impressed when he cried out, "I am from heaven, therefore you must respect me." The *egungun* presented himself before Dennett's tent, saying that he was the father, that is, the deceased come from heaven, and at the same time he asked what Dennett was going to give him for his entertaining performance. The *egungun* not only wore proper Yoruba clothes but had top boots made by the Hausa and European pants.[4]

In Nigeria's much commodified cultural scene of the 1970s, egungun carried calling cards with them, always ready to serve spectators as paying customers. Cards would advertise the enjoyable play the respective egungun provided. Performances at funerals could be concluded with Sonny Ade's latest hit delivered "in the rough, guttural" voice meant to simulate that of the monkey with whom the *egungun* have been closely connected in Yoruba tradition. "Change has always been present in Yoruba cultural systems," says Marilyn Houlberg, "and those are just a few examples of how the more contemporary aspects of Yoruba life have been merged with the more traditional patterns in a mode consistent with Yoruba values."[5]

This (pragmatic) flexibility and openness to change seems also to have led to the Yoruba theater, the *alarinjo* or *apidan* that grew out from the complex of ritual egungun performances as a distinct art form. *Alarinjo* itself has been in some respects a forerunner of the modern traveling Yoruba theater that arose in the 1940s. Emphasizing *alarinjo*'s "innate dynamism" and "capability of infinite change," Joel Adedeji related the old traditional to the new modern form of a traveling popular theater. *Alarinjo*'s "undying influence," he claimed, was visible in the 1970s in the organizational and operational practice of the contemporary traveling theater led by Ogunde.[6] The modern Yoruba traveling theater's move into the home video business beginning in the late 1980s appears to be just another manifestation of this "innate dynamism," although it seems to have led to a virtual self-effacement as a major form of contemporary live performances. In early 1994, I found it almost dead as live theater. The actors and directors/producers, however, were much alive and active in doing home videos, at that time at an estimated production of some dozen video films a year. Since then the output has risen dramatically, up to more than 300 in 1997.[7] Abandoning live performance almost altogether, the practitioners have nevertheless not given up their identity as popular Nigerian artists. They have appropriated a new (technologized) medium to create their specific works of art and to communicate with their audience in the most suitable and probably only feasible way left

4. R. E. Dennett, *Nigerian Studies* (London: Macmillan, 1910), 29–30.
5. Marilyn Hammersley Houlberg, "Egungun Masquerades of the Remo Yoruba," *African Arts* (Los Angeles) 11.3 (1978): 26–27.
6. Joel Adedeji, "The Traditional Yoruba Travelling Theatre," in *Theatre in Africa,* ed. Oyin Ogunba and Abiola Irele (Ibadan UP, 1978), 78, 48–49.
7. Jonathan Haynes and Onookome Okome, "Evolving Popular Media: Nigerian Video Films," in *Nigerian Video Films,* ed. Jonathon Haynes (Jos: Nigerian Film Corp./Ibadan: Kraft, 1997), 22–29.

to them, thus considerably broadening the range of specific African cultural performances.[8]

DAVID KERR

Art as Tool, Weapon or Shield?:
Arts for Development Seminar, Harare†

This is a very personal account of a seminar on Arts and Development held in Harare between 4 and 8 March, 1997. My point of entry is to compare the seminar with other conferences and workshops which I attended in the late 1970s and early 1980s during the first flush of Southern Africa's Theatre for Development movement. In the intervening period I had refrained from attending international theatre seminars, so the contrast between my experiences might provide a useful indicator of the extent to which the Theatre for Development methodology/ideology has been established, and in what way it has changed. Naturally, these are also modified by alterations in my own theory and practice during the intervening years.

This is not the place to attempt a genealogy of Arts for Development, a task which would require tracing the various indigenous adaptations African cultures have made to the didactic elements within their own art forms. It would also entail describing the attempts made by colonial educators to mobilize African communities through a variety of imposed or transformed, indigenous arts.

Instead, I offer a much narrower historical framework—the 'conferencization' of arts for development in Southern Africa, interpreted from a very personal standpoint. For the sake of brevity I shall refer to the early Arts for Development seminars as 'pioneers', in order to contrast them with the Harare seminar. No normative value is intended by this choice of word.

---

8. The history(ies) of *Beni-Ngoma*, of masks like the central Malawian *nyau*, which originally represented the dead, and praise poems in Eastern and Southern Africa reveal similar or pertinent features. They corroborate "traditional" African societies' openness and flexibility. Their cultural performances permanently and eagerly integrate new components, thus creatively changing structures and functions in changing historical contexts (Terence O. Ranger, *Dance and Society in Eastern Africa 1890–1970: The Beni Ngoma* [Berkeley: U of California P, 1975], 7; Leroy Vail and Landeg White, *Power and Praise Poem: Southern African Voices in History* [Charlottesville: U of Virginia P, 1991], 198–230; Deborah Kaspin, "Chewa Visions and Revisions of Power: The Ritual Economy of the Nyau Dance in Central Malawi," in *Modernity and Its Malcontents: Ritual and Power in Postcolonial Africa,* ed. Jean and John Comaroff [Chicago: U of Chicago P, 1993], 35–55; Peter Probst, *Dancing AIDS: Moral Discourses and Ritual Authority in Central Malawi* [Berlin: Sozialanthropologische Arbeitsheft 66. FU Berlin Institut fur Ethnologie, 1995], 5–9). Those movements have not (yet) transformed into audiovisually mediated theatrical practices. Videotaping traditional performances such as weddings in Tanzania since the early 1990s shows, however, that the integration of modern state-of-the art technologies into received cultural productions and their innovative use are progressing on a rather large scale. The traditional *nanga* epics in Northern Tanzania are, for instance, presented today in modern performing modes. The performers began to do recordings on audio-cassettes in the 1990s, altering their art without abandoning it altogether. Technological mediation facilitates reaching a much broader audience.

† From *African Theatre in Development*, ed. Martin Banham et al. (London: James Currey, 1999) 79–86. Reprinted by permission of Indiana University Press and James Currey Publishers.

Perhaps the most influential workshop for launching the Theatre for Development movement was the one held at Chalimbana about 30 km east of Lusaka in Zambia in 1979. This provided a venue for the marriage between two types of activist—adult educators and social workers on one side (particularly the Botswana-based Laedza Batanani team of Ross Kidd, Martin Byram and Martha Maplanka) and the university-based artists with their roots in travelling theatre (such as Mapopa Mtonga, Dickson Mwansa and myself from Zambia, the Zimbabwean Stephen Chifunyise, and Tanzanians Amandina Lihamba and Eberhard Chambulikazi). The workshop linked the mobilization and social analysis skills of the adult educators to the drama and choreography skills of the theatre workers.

The Chalimbana workshop's main achievement was to develop the methodology initiated by the Laedza Batanani team:

1. Research into a community's problems;
2. Using a workshopped technique to create a play contextualizing those problems;
3. Presenting the play to the community;
4. Using the post-performance discussion as the basis for initiating action to solve the problems.

This methodology, with several variations, spread rapidly throughout Southern Africa (Swaziland, Lesotho, and Malawi, in addition to Botswana, Zambia, Tanzania and Zimbabwe).

The Chalimbana workshop, however, had several constraints, recognized even at the time. The main defects were:

1. The shortage of participants who spoke the language of the local Chalimbana village (the 'guinea pigs' of the experiment). Most of the Zambian participants spoke Nyanja, a widely understood lingua franca, but almost nobody spoke the minority Lenje language which was the first language of the local villagers.
2. The lack of genuine involvement by the local villages in the post-performance discussion;
3. The lack of meaningful follow-up programmes by the workshop organizers in addressing problems (such as illiteracy and poor roads) raised by the plays.

Theatre workers addressed these deficiencies at various international and regional workshops during the ensuing years, not only in Southern Africa, but in other regions too. The Malya project in Tanzania, the Kamiriithu experience in Kenya, the Morewa workshop in Zimbabwe and the Marotholi Travelling Theatre of Lesotho were all experiments which attempted to increase the participation of rural villagers, so they could build indigenous art forms as tools for social development or weapons in the class war.

The choice of metaphor here is important. Much of the debate in the pioneer workshops and seminars was about the extent to which theatre should be seen as a shield against colonial and neo-colonial indoctrination, or, even more controversially, as a weapon of class struggle. The metaphors need to be put into a historical context. The Chalimbana conference took place during the last and most aggressive phase of the Chimurenga war in Zimbabwe, and just a few months after Ngugi wa Thiong'o's release from the detention earned by his involvement in the Kamiriithu theatre.

There was a strong current among both academic and non-academic theatre workers of privileging art as a weapon/shield which could be used for the protection/mobilization of workers and peasants. There was also a strong interest in building a South/South network of popular/socialist artists in order to 'delink' African culture from Northern metropolitan control. This view emerged with particular strength at the 1982 Koitta workshop (Bangladesh), which brought together theatre workers from Asia, Africa, Latin America and the Caribbean. Among other activities the workshop helped launch the International Popular Theatre Alliance (IPTA), intended to provide a vehicle for South/South popular theatre networking.

At the 1984 Morewa workshop and conference (Zimbabwe), a pan-continental organization, UAPA (Union of African Performing Artists) was launched with considerable fanfare. The history of IPTA and UAPA is well known. IPTA, which was intended to have a rotating leadership, did manage to publish two issues of a newsletter from Lusaka, and it also mobilized, with some success, for the release of theatre workers detained for their political beliefs (one Philipino and four Malawians). Its demise, however, was fairly inevitable, given the funding crisis associated with scandals which rocked UAPA in the mid-1980s. The worst of these was a very public struggle for power between the chairman and secretary general, and an even more disgraceful theft by a senior committee member of funds intended to establish a school for the performing arts in Harare.

It was this betrayal of radical energy and solidarity which, more than anything else, made many popular theatre workers in Africa retreat from networking. In my own case, I concentrated on very local, unprestigious theatre work in support of Malawian village-based primary health care. It was with a once-bitten-twice-shy trepidation, therefore, that I attended the 1997 Arts for Development seminar in Harare, which many delegates, like myself, felt to be haunted by the ghost of UAPA.

The differences between the Harare seminar and the pioneering workshops were quite marked. There was a small rump of grizzled veterans, which included Stephen and Tisa Chifunyise, Mapopa Mtonga, Dickson Mwansa, Ngugi wa Mirii and myself. In addition, there was an extraordinarily varied assembly which included three South Africans, four Mozambicans, four Malawians, one Kenyan, several Britons and, of course, many Zimbabweans. As well as stage drama activists, there were fine and graphic artists, musicians, dancers, arts administrators and TV soap opera producers. Among these were young artists who had made their name in the late 1980s, such as the dynamic Zimbabwean, Cont Mhlanga of Amakhosi and Jayne Lungu of Television Zambia's *Play Circle*.

The large size of the British contingent was due to the sponsorship of the conference which was by the British Council. This in itself was a remarkable development. During the late 1970s and early 1980s the main sponsor for arts and development projects were the Scandinavian NGOs and donors such as the International Theatre Institute, the Gulbenkian Foundation and the International Council for Adult Education. In the eyes of many popular theatre workers at that time, the British Council, with its support for tours of the Royal Shakespeare Company or itinerant classical pianists, became associated with elitist 'neo-colonial' art. Several veterans at the seminar were not quite sure if the British Council's new interest in Arts for Development represented a genuine realignment towards popular culture, or an attempt to appropriate a radical movement.

The British group themselves was very varied. There was an eminent theatre academic, Martin Banham, who provided an amiable, avuncular chair for the meeting. There were several enthusiastic and conscientious arts administrators, such as Julia Rose, John Martin and Keith Lawrence and there were academics with wide experience of mobilization theatre, such as Jane Plastow (Zimbabwe and Eritrea) and Alex Mavrocordatos (Mali). Two of the British delegates were connected to post-graduation courses in Arts for Development at British universities, John Elsom at the City University, London, and Alex Mavrocordatos at King Alfred's College, Winchester. These courses seemed to be filling a gap left by the doomed UAPA Arts college in Harare.

The South African contingent, though small, made a major impact, especially as two of the delegates, Lebo Ramofoko, a television producer, and educator Masitha Hoeane, were perhaps the most articulate participants at the seminar. During the pioneer workshops, South African inputs were provided by ANC delegates, but, for security reasons, tended to be very low-key. Many of us expected the 1994 democratic elections to provide a radical shot-in-the-arm to the Arts for Development activities, similar to Zimbabwe's 1980 independence.

The actual situation is rather more complex. Scepticism about Arts for Development crystalized quite early in South Africa owing to the Sarafina II debacle. Many South African community art activists feel that Mbongeni Ngema's handling of Sarafina II has provided severe obstacles to the use of arts for development purposes (especially in the field of AIDS awareness). My impression from contacts with South African community theatre workers is that they would rather concentrate on small-scale community analysis and local skills development. This is needed in order for artists to break down the simplifications associated with 'theatre for struggle' and move towards the greater complexity required by a 'theatre of reconstruction'. For that reason, many South African community theatre workers seem unwilling to

participate in high profile regional or continental processes of networking, even if that means having to 'reinvent the wheel' of arts for
development strategies.

No such parochialism could be associated with the South African
delegates to the Harare Seminar. Masitha Hoeane proved an eloquent,
impromptu, keynote speaker on development, emphasizing its reliance
on human rather than material resources, and the need to encourage
humane disciplines. Lebo Ramafoko presented an energetic and enthusiastic case for artists to use the mass media of radio and television
in order to reach wide audiences. Her experience of incorporating
health education messages into a South African Broadcasting Corpo-
ration soap opera (*Soul City*) differed markedly from that of most veterans at the seminar.

During the pioneer workshops the participants tended to represent
face-to-face arts of theatre, music and dance. There was a feeling that
the macro-media of radio, television and commercial popular music
had a built-in cultural imperialism, due to the colonial origins of these
media in most of Africa, and to the way technological imperatives create a dependency on Western programming formats. This feeling led
to a perhaps rather romantic concentration on face-to-face arts and
an almost puritanical neglect of mediated arts.

At the Harare seminar, the role of mediated arts for development
was one of the most hotly debated issues. Cont Mhlanga presented a
model for breaking down the cultural imperialist tendencies of the
media. He described the way Amakhosi in Bulawayo used their existing
cultural facilities to encourage alternative distribution of locally made
programmes, documentaries, features and music through video and
audio cassette hire. Zambian cabaret singer, Maureen Lilanda, described the way commercial music could be used to break down gender stereotypes. Tisa Chifunyisa addressed the perennial problem of
feedback in mediated art forms. She described the 'Sara' project in
Zimbabwe, which used a variety of media—posters, radio jingles, face-
to-face drama and TV/radio drama in order to attack prejudices against
girls' education in Zimbabwe. The face-to-face media were able to
provide a context for feedback missing from the mediated performances.

The most radical case for using the media for developmentally oriented arts came from John Elsom who suggested that technological
innovations in the field of satellite communications and video record-
ing facilities made the whole concept of media imperialism obsolete.
He suggested that the cheapness and fluidity of the new millennial
media would make it impossible for the Northern metropoles to sustain their dominance of media systems. He envisaged a positive climate
for Third World filmmakers, musicians and actors to fulfil the insatiable appetite for cultural diversity in the global village. I found myself
playing devil's advocate to this vision, adopting a stronger media imperialism position than I would ideally have wanted to. I argued that
the vigour and subtlety of capitalism was strong enough and still sufficiently rooted in the Northern metropoles to frustrate any egalitarian

tendencies in the new technologies. The seminar could find no common voice on this issue.

A related, but much less hotly contested, issue was that of the relationship between popular theatre and arts theatre. During the pioneer workshops it became conventional wisdom to distinguish between a people's theatre (in African languages, using indigenous forms/stagecraft, and with themes geared to the 'masses') and 'elitist or 'art' theatre (in colonial languages using Western forms/stagecraft and bourgeois themes). This was a useful distinction at a time when many African national theatre associations were dominated by expatriate clubs and needed to decolonize themselves through the assertion of Afrocentric theatre modes.

At the Harare seminar the Mozambican delegation provided a useful corrective to this conventional binarism. Perhaps owing to the more popular position of Portuguese in Mozambique, compared to English in anglophone Africa, the Mozambican theatre workers, Candida Bila, Joao Chaque, Carlos Mende and Lucreca Paco, found it difficult to sustain distinctions between popular and elite theatre. They felt that conscientization of urban audiences (not excluding the bourgeoisie) was just as important as that of peasants and workers. Moreover, the skills and material resources associated with or generated by urban art theatre could be transferred to efforts in popular theatre.

Another important difference between the Harare seminar and the pioneer workshops was the role of arts other than drama. Participants in Harare not only looked at drama but also media entertainment, fine and applied arts, music, dance, and arts administration. In the pioneer workshops all these were considered, but tended to be subordinated to drama (for example, the way artistic skills were channelled into puppetry at the Chalimbana workshop). The Harare seminar explored the interdependence of the arts and the way they could support each other.

Underlying all these discussions was the wider issue of patronage. This crystalized around two closely related sub-issues:

1. The extent to which 'outsiders' could make contributions to community development programmes:
2. The role of NGOs (especially those funded by Northern agencies).

Some of the Zimbabwean delegates including Cont Mhlanga and ethnomusicologist Dumi Maraire took a quite strong 'indigenist' line, suggesting that only artists who were part of a local community could offer genuine and self-reliant support for development without imposing alien values or creating dependency on external resources. Not surprisingly, many of those whose work was in communities other than their own argued that the fluidity of modern migration patterns and the hybridity of even the most remote and rural cultures made the whole paradigm of 'insider' and 'outsider' meaningless. The latter group, perhaps because it was more numerous, seemed to win the day.

The issue of patronage was brought into sharp relief since the seminar was hosted by a single sponsor, the British Council. One whole session looked at the role of donor organizations, especially NGOs, as vehicles or patrons for arts for development strategies, particularly with respect to networking and the provision of training. Representatives from one government agency (ODA, Britain) and three NGOs (NORAD, Action Aid and Plan International) gave brief presentations.

The Arts for Development activists working in the field agreed that some agencies (e.g. NORAD) were far more sympathetic to art as a tool for transformation than others (e.g. ODA). Despite these differences the participants still felt able to raise common issues. The most serious of these was sustainability—how do NGOs encourage communities to become self-reliant and to avoid becoming dependent on external support?

It was in the lack of any meaningful response to this question that I found the most remarkable difference between the Harare seminar and the pioneer workshops. In the early 1980s, even if Arts for Development workers accepted NGO funding for seminars, they felt this was a temporary measure until indigenous South-based infrastructures and alliances became established. There was a strong spirit of repudiating the 'neo-colonialism' of NGO funding. At the Harare seminar it was only Ngugi Wa Mirii, veteran of the Kamiriithu experience, who used strong anti-imperialist rhetoric. He described NGOs as 'shock absorbers' of capitalism, mitigating the worst social effects of G7 domination of the Third World, without doing anything to change the structural imbalances in global economic systems.

That outburst produced a rather embarrassed silence, especially as many delegates wanted to encourage the British Council to support various projects. Most of the arts activists knew that they had been depending on donor funding for over twenty years, and to bite the feeding hand was not only imprudent, but also hypocritical. When African theatre workers attempted an autonomous alliance, greedy individuals destroyed it, while the honest and conscientious majority were too busy or naive to prevent the destruction of UAPA. Given that failure, networking organized by Northern-based agencies such as the Human Rights Forum or even the British Council seemed better than no networking at all.

As I flew back to Gaborone on my British Council–sponsored ticket, I tried to come to terms with the changes which the last fifteen years had brought. The barometer of the Harare seminar certainly seemed more finely calibrated than that of the pioneer seminars. The emphasis on media and other popular arts reflects popular culture much more accurately than the old 'Theatre for Development' paradigm. The incorporation of South Africa and Mozambique into the regional arts community provides more complexity in the relationship between national arts traditions and the policies/practice of cultural workers. The experience of earlier failed workshops has given a salutary sobriety to cultural workers' relationship with rural people's organizations.

This implies a more mature and patient appreciation of the need for institution-building.

The biggest change of all is the ambigious and less abrasive attitudes of cultural workers towards Northern funding for arts activities and training. This is no doubt based on a more realistic evaluation of North/South economic relationships than the rather simplistic polarities advocated during the pioneer workshops. Metaphorically, the weapons and shields of the early 1980s have been turned into ploughshares—tools of development, in recognition that the slogans of the liberation struggle are now too simple for the post-liberation tasks of reconstruction.

Yet . . . I think it is more than mere nostalgia which makes me feel some regret for the idealism and loin-girding optimism of those early workshops. Wa Mirii's comments on the neo-colonialism of NGOs, however tactless, need an answer. The control of the G7 countries over the Third World, and particularly Africa, has become even tighter with the collapse of the Soviet bloc and the widespread imposition of structural adjustment programmes. Many NGOs are doing very valuable work in reducing the social harm created by SAP programmes on people's health, education, agriculture, housing, employment prospects or water supplies. One cannot help feeling, however, that they are merely putting bandages on wounds which should never have been made in the first place.

At present, since almost all arts for development work is sponsored by NGOs with specific amelioration goals, it tends to be directed towards 'bandaging' strategies—namely plays, songs, dances, posters, radio jingles or soap operas advising people how to improve their lives within fairly narrow sectoral domains.

The major task of cultural workers still lies ahead—to create institutional solidarity and art forms with a holistic perspective, which can mobilize African communities to struggle against an iniquitous world system. The weapons and shields manufactured in the pioneer period of arts for development were undoubtedly crude (for example, in their relative neglect of gender issues), but the struggle for which they were designed is far from over.

I believe that the institutionalized instrumentality of arts for development as currently practised in Southern Africa needs to be transformed in ways which can help communities understand the macro-economic inequalities at the root of their major problems. In that task, there is still a need for art as weapon and shield, however improved and refashioned those artifacts may need to be.

Tawfik al-Hakim

PAUL STARKEY

[Trends in the Drama of Tawfik al-Hakim]†

* * *

Two main trends can be detected in al-Hakim's output in the twenty years between 1954 and 1974. First, though like most Egyptian writers he continued to produce regular articles for newspapers and magazines, his major works belonging to this period are, with a few exceptions, all plays. Indeed, the only publications of importance from these years in other than dramatic form are the autobiographical *Sijn al-'Umr,* a lively account of his family background and early years until his departure for France, and the philosophical *al-Ta'aduliyah,* an attempt to provide a comprehensive definition of his attitude to art and life; the latter, though a slight work in itself, is of some interest in that it provides an explicit statement of many of the ideas implicit in the author's imaginative works. Secondly, al-Hakim began during this period to show a new enthusiasm for technical experiment, with a view both to bridging the gap between the theatre and the general public, and to enriching the Egyptian stage by the importation of new ideas and techniques from the Western, avant-garde theatre. Thus in *al-Safqah* (1956) and *al-Wartah* (published ten years later) he attempted to solve the old dilemma of classical vs. colloquial Arabic by employing a new, simplified 'third language' which can be read either way; while in *Qalabuna al-Masrahi* he presented extracts from seven of the greatest European plays down the ages in a form which makes use of the traditional Arab storyteller. *Yā Tāli' al-Shajarah,* on the other hand, which appeared in 1962, makes no concessions to popular Egyptian taste: despite the reassuring presence of a dervish on stage and the derivation of the play's title from an old Egyptian peasant-song, the dramatic techniques employed are those of the 'Absurd' theatre of Beckett and Ionesco. This play marked an entirely new departure in the Arab theatre, prompting healthily varied interpretations from the critics, and the experiment has since been followed by further short plays in the 'Absurd' tradition, by the Brechtian *al-Ta'ām li-Kull Fam* (1963), and by the extraordinary *Bank*

† From *The Ivory Tower: A Critical Study of Tawfiq al-Hakim* (London: Ithaca Press, 1987) 33–35, 212–15. Reprinted by permission of Ithaca Press.

al-Qalaq (1966), an attempt to fuse the novel and the play in a hybrid form for which al-Ḥakīm coined the term *masriwāyah*.

Al-Ḥakīm's plays since *al-Aydī al-Nā'imah* present us with a bewildering variety of themes. In *Īzīs*, which appeared in 1955, for example, we find a discussion of the age-old philosophical question 'does the end justify the means?' set against the background of the ancient Egyptian myth of Isis and Osiris; a strong hint of contemporary relevance is, however, introduced in the play's final assertion that judgment in such matters belongs to the people alone. This note of relevance to contemporary Egyptian society is continued in *al-Safqah* (1956), the plot of which revolves around the attempt of a group of peasants to secure a land-deal in the face of almost insurmountable difficulties. As with *al-Aydī al-Nā'imah*, however, the tone of the play is generally conciliatory; al-Ḥakīm's social criticism has little in common with the more violent outbursts of the younger generation of Egyptian playwrights such as Yūsuf Idrīs and Nu'mān 'Āshūr, and he has tended since *al-Safqah* to revert to universal rather than specifically Egyptian themes. Thus in *Riḥlah ilā al-Ghad*, published in 1958, he again examines man's relation to time, using as background a science-fiction world of space-rockets and inter-stellar travel; while in *al-Sulṭān al-Ḥā'ir*, he poses the question which he regards as crucial for mankind today: 'are the problems of the world to be solved by law or by force?' This concern for the world peace also finds expression in *Ashwāk al-Salām*, a play marred however by a romantically idealistic outlook which takes small account of political reality. The same fault is apparent in *al-Ta'ām li-Kull Fam*, where what is promised as a plan for the abolition of world hunger turns out to be little more than a dream.

Al-Ḥakīm's plays in the 1960's and 1970's have tended to move back again from a direct consideration of national and international issues to a reappraisal of the situation of mankind in indirect terms. The message of *Ya Ṭāli' al-Shajarah*, if any, is obscure; but the two short pieces contained in *Riḥlat al-Kharīf* present us with a new vision of the human situation in which life is seen as a never-ending journey— a continuous struggle for progress to which the only alternative is death. This theme is echoed in *Masīr Sirsār*; while in *Bank al-Qalaq* al-Ḥakīm gives us at one and the same time a picture of modern man beset by anxiety and a critique of some of the problems of contemporary Egypt. Only in the three short pieces of *Majlis al-'Adl*, however, published in 1972, does he return to international affairs; and while two of these plays, inspired by man's recent achievements in space, are characterised by the same 'third world' idealism as we find in *al-Ta'ām li-Kull Fam*, the title-piece is a thinly-veiled, Brechtian allegory on the Palestinian problem, unique among al-Ḥakīm's works for its relevance to specific contemporary events.

*   *   *

A surprising feature of al-Ḥakīm's work is that, while it is easy to point to a number of common characteristics in the construction of his

plays, it is difficult to trace any obvious line or direction of
development in his dramatic technique until the publication of *Yā Tāli'
al-Shajarah* in 1962. The strengths and weaknesses of al-Hakīm's
earliest literary productions reappear almost unchanged in his plays
written in the 1950's; form and structure, though they vary, do not
evolve. Only in his use of the 'play within the play' is it possible to
point to a distinctive formal preference on his part during this period.

The publication of *Yā Tāli' al-Shajarah* thus represents a major new
departure in al-Hakīm's career as a dramatist. From this point on,
questions of form and structure assume an importance equal to, if not
greater than, questions of content or meaning for a study of al-Hakīm's
plays, as the author embarks on a remarkable series of technical and
formal experiments. As has already been shewn, the ideas explored in
Yā Tāli' al-Shajarah (though clearly owing much to the 'Theatre of the
Absurd') do not mark a complete break with his earlier work. In its
rejection of the established stage-conventions, however, al-Hakīm's
play owes everything to the new movement. Thus, *Yā Tāli' al-Shajarah*
has no sets and no 'props': when the play opens, we find the detective
himself bringing onto the stage his file and chair, while the maid
follows carrying the table on which he spreads his papers; later, when
the telephone rings, the maid leaves the stage and returns with the
'phone on a long lead. Nor are there any divisions of time or place in
the play: thus, the maid is able to show the detective how the old
couple lived simply by pointing to another part of the stage, and at
one point there are two Bahādirs on stage at once.

The freedom from the conventional limitations of time and place
which al-Hakīm discovered in the 'Theatre of the Absurd' allows him
to explore in *Yā Tāli' al-Shajarah* with a new directness the
psychological themes which had engaged him since the time of his
earliest work. It is from the 'Theatre of the Absurd' also that the two
short plays of *Rihlat al-Kharīf* derive their inspiration. *Al-Ta'ām li-Kull
Fam*, on the other hand, published in 1963, appears to owe more to
Brecht than to Ionesco; for despite the play's technical link with *Rihlat
Sayd* through the use of a screen, its tone is overtly didactic. The
audience are invited to identify themselves with Hamdī and Samīrah,
and to follow their experiences over a period of time—the two sections
of the final act being separated by an interlude representing the
passing of a whole year. This deliberately linear exposition of a
sequence of events is in sharp contrast to *Yā Tāli' al-Shajarah*, where
traditional concepts of time and place no longer apply. In other ways
also *al-Ta'ām li-Kull Fam*, despite its greater technical freedom, is
more reminiscent of the author's earlier plays than of *Yā Tāli' al-
Shajarah*; unlike *Yā Tāli' al-Shajarah*, for example—the tone of which
is consistent and well integrated throughout—*Al-Ta'ām li-Kull Fam*
suffers from a failure to integrate the various elements of the play. The
scenes between the couple and 'Atīyāt contain much brilliant writing;
but the vitality of these is offset by other, undramatic passages which
serve merely as the vehicle for the exposition of ideas. In short, *al-
Ta'ām li-Kull Fam*, though an interesting experiment, is a less

successful artistic creation than the more radical *Yā Tāli' al-Shajarah*.

Al-Hakīm's failure to integrate the constituent elements of his works is still more apparent in *Bank al-Qalaq*, published in 1967. Cast in a hybrid form, part novel, part play (to which al-Hakīm has given the name *masriwāyah*), *Bank al-Qalaq* is constructed in ten chapters and ten scenes, which follow one another alternately. The title is a reference to the bank set up by Adham and Sha'bān in the first scene to deal in 'anxiety' (*qalaq*)—'the malady of our modern age, from which the majority of mankind suffer'. The initial lack of response to their advertisements leads Adham to think that they are wasting their time; but eventually clients begin to arrive, each complaining of his own particular woe. A man whose son has failed his exams for love of a girl is followed by another who complains of the reactionary nature of the society in which he lives; a third is outraged by contemporary atheism; yet another by inflation. Against these afflictions, the efforts of Adham and Sha'bān are of little avail.

Meanwhile, however, the reader's interest has been held by the gradual progress of Sha'bān's relationship with a young woman, Mervat, and her aunt Fātimah, whose family, it soon becomes clear, harbours a terrible secret. There is a good deal of pathos (unusual for al-Hakīm) in his narration of Sha'bān's pursuit and seduction of Fātimah, which is quickly followed by an explanation of the mystery; for Fātimah, it appears, had had a year-long affair with 'Ādil, Mervat's father. When Mervat's mother found out about this liaison, she poured petrol over herself and her husband in bed and set light to it; but though 'Ādil died, he managed first to save his wife, who subsequently went mad. Since that time, Fātimah's life has been entirely devoted to her niece, who has no other relatives left. The work comes to an unexpected (and unconvincing) conclusion with a series of strange twists, apparently revealing a plot to compromise Adham.

In his discussion of the formal aspects of *Bank al-Qalaq*, al-Rā'ī suggests that the nearest parallel in Egyptian literature might be Najīb Mahfūz's *Thartharah fawqa al-Nīl*, and in world literature Shaw's *A Black Girl in Search of God*. It is clear that the dialogue portions of *Bank al-Qalaq* are not intended to be staged, for the narrative sections interposed between them are an integral part of the work, not merely extended stage-directions; moreover, the 'action' in the narrative passages moves forward to a large extent through reflections in the minds of the chief characters. Like the works just discussed, *Bank al-Qalaq* undoubtedly owes something to 'absurd' influences; but the symbolic aspects of al-Hakī's technique are never far from the surface; and the work also touches on social questions in the course of the interviews with the clients. Unfortunately, the basic silliness of the main idea makes it impossible to take any of it quite seriously, and the work can only be regarded as a rather confused piece of writing; the objectives which al-Hakīm hoped to achieve by the use of this curious form are likewise unclear.

To the year preceding *Bank al-Qalaq* belong two other plays, *Masīr Sirsār* and *Kull Shay' fī Mahallih*. The first of these is remarkable for

little other than for being one of the most blatant examples of the
tendency to lack of unity in al-Hakīm's plays; indeed, the work can
almost be regarded as two plays stitched together. The other work,
Kull Shay' fī Mahallih, though shorter, is more interesting, for it shows
al-Hakīm continuing to strive for the simplicity of presentation which
he had already attempted in *al-Safqah*; no props are required, and the
scene throughout is set in a village square. Unlike *al-Safqah* and
al-Wartah, however, it uses straightforward Egyptian colloquial,
suggesting that al-Hakīm had had second thoughts about his experimental 'third language'.

*   *   *

DENYS JOHNSON-DAVIES

Introduction to *"Fate of a Cockroach" and Other Plays*†

* * * Tawfik Al Hakim has occupied a central place in the Arab literary
scene since he first made a name for himself in the late 'twenties. He
is known primarily as a playwright, with an output of some seventy
plays, and one of Cairo's theatres has been named after him. He has
also produced several volumes of essays, a few short stories, and some
enjoyable volumes of autobiography; at least two of his novels are land-
marks in modern Arabic literature.

  Tawfik Al Hakim became interested in the theatre at an early age.
At that time, however, it offered neither a respectable nor a reliable
means of livelihood and it is not surprising that his upper middle class
parents showed no enthusiasm for his literary ambitions; in his autobiography he records how he did not allow his full name to appear on
one of his early plays for fear that the news that he was the author
might reach his parents. He was therefore persuaded to study law,
which he did initially in Cairo. Having taken his degree, he was sent
to Paris to complete his legal studies. He stayed in Paris from 1925
until 1928, where he spent the greater part of his time in the company
of writers and many of his evenings at the theatre; he also read widely
in French. On his return to Egypt he was appointed an attorney to the
Public Prosecutor in the provinces and his experiences there provided
the material for his novel *The Maze of Justice*. It was not long before he
resigned from government service and devoted himself wholly to creative writing. Since then he has held a number of official appointments,
including that of Director of the National Library in Cairo; he has also
been his country's permanent representative with UNESCO in Paris.

  While living through disturbed times, Tawfik Al Hakim's own life
has been comparatively free of dramatic incident; he himself is of a

† From *"Fate of a Cockroach" and Other Plays* by Tawfik Al Hakim, sel. and trans. Denys
Johnson-Davies (Washington, D.C.: Three Continents Press, 1973) vi–viii. Copyright © 1996
by Lynne Rienner Publishers, Inc. Reprinted by permission of the publisher.

retiring and reticent nature and though his face is as familiar in the Arab countries as, say, Bernard Shaw's was in the English-speaking world, few people know anything of his private life—that, for instance, despite the playful misogynism expressed in many of his plays (as for instance in *Fate of a Cockroach*) he married in 1946 and has a son and a daughter. Tawfik Al Hakim has never been interested in political creeds and 'isms'. No Egyptian, however, particularly a writer, can stand wholly aloof from politics and it is amusing to note that Tawfik Al Hakim recounts in his autobiography how his first full-length play, written in 1919 and since lost, dealt with the British occupation of his country and was entitled *The Unwanted Guest*. It remained unpublished and unproduced. Over the years Tawfik Al Hakim has shown great skill—not shared by many of his fellow authors—in keeping out of political trouble. The inevitable accusation of living in an ivory tower (he published a volume of essays under the title *From the Ivory Tower*) has been levelled against him; while he has never entered any political arena, he has none the less throughout his career shown himself deeply concerned with such fundamental and potentially dangerous issues as justice and truth, good and evil and, above all, freedom.

All four plays in the present volume[1] deal, directly or indirectly, with some aspect of freedom. In *The Sultan's Dilemma*, which takes place in the 'Thousand and One Nights' atmosphere of the rule of a Mameluke sultan, freedom and the choice faced by every absolute ruler are the themes. Those themes, incidentally, were as valid for the Egyptian reader in 1960, the year when the play was published, as for his forbears during the times of the Mamelukes. In *Fate of a Cockroach*, man's natural love of freedom, his refusal to despair in the face of adversity, are exemplified in the cockroach's strivings to climb out of the bath. *The Song of Death*, the earliest of the four plays and the most local, has as its central theme the conflict between traditional vengeance—as much a part of life in rural Egypt as in Sicily—and freedom through education from such deadening and destructive prejudice. *Not a Thing Out of Place* seems to suggest that while the ultimate in freedom, anarchy, can be fun, true freedom consists in pursuing a middle way. Tawfik Al Hakim's preoccupation with freedom can also be seen from the title of one of his volumes of autobiography, *The Prison of Life*, in which he discusses the individual's inability to escape from the imprisonment imposed upon him by the circumstances of his birth, by the fact that he is the child of two particular parents with particular attributes who in turn were brought into the world with inherited characteristics.

Tawfik Al Hakim is the undisputed pioneer of dramatic writing in Arabic. While Egypt has a theatrical tradition going back more than a hundred years, the plays produced were until recently either heavy melodrama adapted into cliché-ridden classical Arabic from the French or domestic farces, often with political overtones, written in

1. *Fate of a Cockroach, The Song of Death, The Sultan's Dilemma, Not a Thing Out of Place* [Editor].

the colloquial language. With his natural talent, his wide reading in French, his close study of the techniques of the European theatre (the dramatic form was unknown in classical Arabic literature), his interest in the problems of language—most pertinent in a culture where the written language differs so much from the spoken—with these attributes Tawfik Al Hakim gave to the Egyptian theatre the foundations of respectability it needed. That the theatre in Egypt today is both a serious and popular form of entertainment and that it is attracting some of the best talents among the younger writers is due in large part to the writer of the plays in this present volume.

RICHARD LONG

[Philosophical and Psychological Themes in *Fate of a Cockroach*]†

* * * *Fate of a Cockroach* (*Masir Sarsar*)[1] is unencumbered by experimentation and is Hakim's last great play. It is the brilliant and original tour de force which opened his *Troilus and Cressida* Period, brought about by an unexplained heartbreak, and is in three acts, the first of which appeared in *Al Ahram* before the publication of the complete work. Though Act One and Acts Two/Three are complete in themselves, the drama as a whole, though it has never been staged *in toto*, is in no way unsatisfactory. On the contrary, the cockroach King serves as an ample and ingenious bond between its two contrasting aspects.

If *Fate of a Cockroach* is an exercise in disillusion and bitterness, its chief protagonist nevertheless stems directly from Hakim's established psychological and philosophical attitudes. In *From Beyond,* the concluding item of *The Devil's Pact,* he refers to the wars of the ants and the cockroaches. In *From the Ivory Tower* he describes his 'frequent' contemplation, when a youth, of columns of ants bearing cockroach corpses; he used to scatter their ranks with cups of water, which he supposed they probably regarded as well-aimed acts of God and which prompted in him the by no means unprecedented thought that perhaps humans were 'ants', whose natural catastrophes were the deeds of 'ants' yet larger than them: 'Allah is greater than we can conceive, and our senses are more ignorant about this life than we imagine.' He returns to this train of thought in *Literature is Life.* In the preface to the play he declares again his interest in the insect world—one demonstrated in *Solomon the Wise*—which, he surmises, is the ancient Egyptian in him coming out: they 'used to link insects and man in one framework'. He says that he once saw a cockroach struggling to climb

---

† From *Tawfiq al-Hakim: Playwright of Egypt* (London: Ithaca Press, 1979) 99–105, 160. Copyright © Richard Long. Reprinted by permission of Ithaca Press.
1. This should be *Fate of a Cricket,* but Hakim is undoubtedly concerned here with cockroaches, though, as Adil and Samiyya found in Act Two, without lexicographical backing.

out of his bath and heralds one purpose of Act One of the play by continuing, 'How glorious is the sight of a determination to struggle without hope! . . . (it) is, as I understand it, the crux of tragedy . . . For me, sadness, catastrophes and the death of the hero are not properties of tragedy, but obligatory is (it) . . . that the hero's end comes as a result of his striving with a force over which he has no power'— as, he avers, is the case with Othello but not with Hamlet. 'Every human struggle lacks efficacy before that power against which man is powerless. Nevertheless he struggles, and that is the tragedy and greatness of man.' Having expounded his theory, he correctly dismisses the idea that *Fate of a Cockroach* is a tragedy—'it is merely a play and no more.' Containing much political criticism which is examined elsewhere, it is difficult to label.

Act One takes place in the bathroom of an Egyptian flat and is an account of an evening in the life of the Kingdom of the Cockroaches which flourishes there. The King, chosen for the length of his antennae, is alive to the threat posed to his rule, as to those of all his ancestors, by the traditional cockroach foe, the ants; also like his forebears, he is quick to evade pressure to do anything about them. His Queen constantly nags him about the problem, the non-solution of which inhibits her from walking abroad lest, should she be so unfortunate as to fall on her back, she be overrun by an enemy patrol. The King despises the ants but sees no reason why he should be picked on to force a confrontation. The regal pair have only three 'regular' subjects: the prime minister, who was unopposed for the position; the priest, enrolled on account of his habit of addressing incomprehensible remarks to the King; and the scientist, so dignified on the strength of his 'strange knowledge of things which exist only in his own head'. The King puts up with them only because they needed someone in whom to confide their tomfoolery and because he wanted to be called 'Your Majesty'. The ants' seizure of the upturned son of the prime minister brings matters to a crisis. The Queen urges action, the King—sure that he will have nothing sensible to propose—reluctantly asks the prime minister for his views, and the latter has the temerity to suggest that the cockroaches should try ant tactics and recruit a large army— of twenty—to fight them. The King scoffs at this notion—when in their long history have the cockroaches been able to muster a force of twenty?—and declares that the ants know about the organization of armies but the cockroaches are different and do not. The scientist is called in to advise but sees the question as a political one—if the King cannot solve it, what does his authority amount to? Pressed by the Queen he does, however, condescend to impart the information that, when he was very young, he did once witness ten cockroaches together, around a slice of tomato. He unbends sufficiently to state that cockroaches are conditioned against congregating because of the proven connection between their assemblies and catastrophes occasioned by such instruments of nature as moving hills and torrential downpours. The ants are too small to be targets for these perils and

can therefore do whatever they choose to. The others demand a solution from him and he recommends that, for a start, the cockroaches
get to know themselves and their environment.

The priest arrives and is similarly grilled. His answer is for sacrifices
to be offered to the gods more conscientiously than heretofore—a
response which attracts the mockery of the scientist, whom the others
think has gone too far. The passing of a phalanx of ants, holding triumphantly aloft the body of their victim and singing about their 'unity',
brings the quintet abruptly back to reality. The Queen scorns the
males for meekly standing by, but the scientist says they have no alternative because, unlike the ants, they are not warlike; they are superior to ants and, indeed, the most superior creatures on earth. The
prime minister, prolonging this self-deceiving line, adds that they have
never attacked a living soul or harmed anyone, and the King backs
him up enthusiastically with 'Are the ants more powerful than us?—
Never! Do they know we are thinking creatures?' Only the Queen
keeps her head during this hysteria, pointing out that the enemy they
so despise gives them rough treatment to which they must respond.
The King, closing the formal part of their meeting, sums up by concluding, to the Queen's disgust, that their only refuge is to avoid tumbling over.

The scientist proposes a tour of their surroundings, to look at the
view from the top of the bath. The King seconds this practical contribution to the debate, but the superstitious priest dislikes the suggestion and, with the Queen and the prime minister, elects to remain
behind. They seek to begin the enlistment of an army by soliciting the
services of a cockroach who wanders by, but he rejects their overtures
with contempt. The Queen and the priest criticize the King, the former
repeating earlier assertions that her character is stronger than her husband's and hinting that, by virtue of being female, she possesses un-
particularised special qualities.

The scientist appears up above to announce that the King has fallen
into the bath; it would be suicide for any of them to try and help him.
The priest, after a long delay while he reconciles his conscience to
participation by the atheistic scientist in their joint orations, leads
them in prayers for their master's safety.

At this point Act One closes. During the other two acts, while the
cockroach King's writhings are never overlooked, we come back to life-
size and find ourselves in an absurd, human world. The humans are
Adil and Samiyya, the young married couple who inhabit the flat whose
bathroom forms the territory of the Kingdom of the Cockroaches. She
wears the trousers and bullies her husband unbearably. Adil is defenceless against her and, while complaining that she has robbed him
of his identity, pretends that he always submits to her out of deference
to the weaker sex. On the day in question, Samiyya demands, and
secures, first use of the bathroom when the alarm clock rings (this,
though the human early morning, is the cockroach evening) and orders
Adil to start preparing breakfast. He telephones a friend, incoherently
enlisting his sympathy, and later tells his wife that it was a girl he had

spoken to. When Samiyya is about to run her bath, she sees her way barred by the beleaguered cockroach King. The self-pitying hysteria in which she consequently indulges, and her departure to fetch the insecticide, enable Adil to appropriate the bathroom, not so that he can get ready for work but to protect the cockroach. Samiyya can get no sense out of him as he parrots back to her everything she says through the door. She is convinced that he has gone mad (and says so to her cook, and to friends on the telephone), complains that he has never disobeyed her like this before and begins to feel sorry for herself for being, despite all her guidance, of, and support for, him, presented with so embarrassing a situation.

The doctor of the firm which employs them both arrives. Adil assumes that his mission is to kill the cockroach but, persuaded otherwise, is finally coaxed into opening the bathroom door. He will not come out but, after a violent battle with his wife, succeeds in pulling the doctor inside to observe the cause of his alleged illness. This done, having learned from Samiyya that her husband is writing a thesis after office hours, the doctor claims that he understands the case and prescribes rest and tranquillisers. This causes such an uproar from the couple—Adil insisting that the visit has been of no assistance to the cockroach, Samiyya protesting that she is still unable to bathe—that he flees their dual insanity.

At the beginning of Act Three he returns, impelled by his sense of duty. He decides, in another private talk with Samiyya, that her husband's concern to shield the cockroach stems from his identification of himself with it as a fellow-sufferer at her hands. The cure is to convince him that there is no resemblance between him and his insect protege and that he is not safeguarding his identity by defending it. They agree on a campaign to undeceive him but succeed only in making matters worse. They flatter him, Samiyya claims to believe that the cockroach's personality is more powerful than her own—a statement Adil dismisses as ludicrous—promises that everything will be different in future and finally voices the doctor's theory about his behaviour. He violently ejects her from the bathroom, into which she has stolen. The doctor puts to him the theory that his wife's character is stronger than his and elicits a denial which throws the medical man into disarray. He now retracts his diagnosis, and is shocked when Adil demonstrates its inaccuracy by saying that the cockroach is so superior to him that comparisons and identifications are irrelevant. All that matters, and concerns him, is its continuing efforts to get out of the bath. The doctor now becomes engrossed in the spectacle and gives sincere expression to a wish that he were its equal. Samiyya, certain that he is as mad as her husband, inveigles them out of the bathroom and orders her cook to run her bath.

Except for the down-to-earth final scene, the action ends here, with the arrival of the insensitive domestic in the centre of the stage. Samiyya, who vowed during her husband's cries never again to claim precedence over him in the matter of the bathroom, is now in repossession of it. What has the human episode told us? Principally, it is designed to show that everyday life is naturally absurd, that how people choose to spend their time is not the business of anyone else and that interpretations of their actions—as Pirandello said less colourfully in *Cosi e* (*se li vera*)—are as likely as not to be mistaken. Samiyya does not understand any of this and is scorned by Hakim for her treatment of Adil, who is to be seen not as unbalanced but as being merely intrigued by a sight which, admittedly unremarkable enough, affords him intellectual satisfaction. He is not interested in the cockroach's success or failure, as he reiterates several times ('I must leave him to his fate'), but simply fascinated by its unflagging persistence, which similarly enraptures the doctor. He is, in any case, precluded from giving it a helping hand because Samiyya might object, her finickiness makes it impossible for him to consider despatching it *in situ,* and no other answer occurs to him. He wishes the struggle to continue. The author makes it clear that he approves of Adil's attitude but regards it as undeserving of special note; he leaves us to infer that, if madness is really present in the flat, it resides in Samiyya.

The end comes quickly, and with it a perfect portrayal of the mindless callousness of one school of the Arab servant class. Umm Atiyya, the cook, unaffected by the drama of the cockroach or by knowledge of all that its heroism means to her employer, runs a bath according to her mistress's instructions, drowns the King and flings its carcass into a corner. Adil is upset, but soon recovers when the doctor reminds him of his indifference to its fate and when another spectacle is set before him: a column of ants marches up to bear the corpse away, and he and the doctor settle down to watch, absorbed. Both levels of action are, however, brought to a smart conclusion. Umm Atiyya's robot-like labours engulf both the ants and their trophy, and Adil, bereft now of any consuming diversion, receives a directive from his wife to spend the day in putting her wardrobe straight. We are back where we began. The wars of the cockroaches and the ants, and of Adil and Samiyya, are to be resumed at the point they had reached before greater issues temporarily supervened. Adil had the upper hand in his conflict as long as he retained the cockroach as a weapon against his wife. Once Umm Atiyya has done her work, the period of his sway is over and his normal lot is reimposed on him—a lot which, if Ar Raci's talk of heartbreaks is interpretable thus, may have reflected Hakim's own marital position at this time. * * *

Act Two of the play particularly contains some brilliant Absurdist dialogues between Adil and Samiyya. Acts Two and Three both make superb dramatic capital out of little concrete material and are extremely readable and tense. They show humans behaving in an even more purposeless and irrational fashion than the cockroaches of Act One. The play as a whole, far from being a tragedy, exhibits the futility and unimportance of life's petty details. Its enormous stage potential is readily apparent.

* * *

After *Shams an Nahar,* with all its faults and rambling confusions, Act One of *Fate of a Cockroach* comes as a shock. It puts before us the spectacle of a Kingdom which cannot raise an army (it could not, in any case, train one) and in which self-deluding propaganda masquerades as action; a despotic King, without self-respect or ideas, who is devoid of any sense of duty and scornful of the advice of his ruling clique; and a prime minister who cannot see plans through, a scientist who is unscientific, impractical, arrogant and uncooperative and a priest who is irreligious, hypocritical and haughty. Putting them all to shame is the Queen. Hakim's striking and vicious account of the Kingdom is so presented that the ordinary Arab spectator or reader ought to be able to assimilate the satire effortlessly. It is, nevertheless, doubtful whether the politically unaware Arab would grasp that it is not about cockroaches at all and, if coaxed into the theatre, would not be on the retreat within a short space of time. If he missed the satire he would, however, also be denied the humour and vivacity which make the act a continual joy. It is an anti-Egyptian (perhaps anti-Arab) parable: the Kingdom is Egypt, which has not studied its problems with the necessary seriousness and depth and substitutes slander and lies for the considered demarche; the King and his sensible Queen are respectively the Egyptian President and people, whom Hakim is not complimenting by dressing up as cockroaches; and the non-existent cockroach army is Egypt's.

It is remarkable that in *Fate of a Cockroach,* the product of a broken heart, the author should have so controlled his contempt and bitterness as to give us not only a drama, but also a political document, of value. The play is an inspired, thoughtful and vigorous denunciation of Egyptian (and Arab) politics and policies as he saw them in the years immediately prior to the June War and his last direct dramatic word on Abd an Nasir.

*   *   *

Kateb Yacine

BERNARD ARESU

[The Theatrical Carnivalesque in *Intelligence Powder*]†

* * *

It is easy to see how the mechanism of farcical representation allowed Kateb the kind of subversive liberation that carnival once provided from established norms. In particular, playful irreverence and gay satire furnished the playwright ideal weapons against political oppression. Bakhtin's description of the subversive and transformative function of carnival aptly summarizes the play of forces unmistakably at work here: "As opposed to the official feast, one might say that the carnival celebrated temporary liberation from the prevailing truth and from the established order; it marked the suspension of all hierarchical rank, privileges, norms, and prohibitions. Carnival was the true feast of time, the feast of becoming, change, and renewal. It was hostile to all that was immortalized and completed."[1] Making full use of the mechanisms of farce and parody, Kateb's comedies play havoc with easily identifiable social structures and with political injustice. At the same time, though, their Algerian reality invariably embodies the microcosm of a broader world view. An extreme example of his ferocious humor, "La poudre d'intelligence" [*Intelligence Powder*] foreshadows political plays whose humanitarian significance, from "Le luth et la valise" to "Le bourgeois sans-culotte," always transcended immediate geography.

Although farce and buffoonery pervade "La poudre d'intelligence," a striking feature of the play is its generic atopia. For pure comedy it is not. Toward the end of the play, for instance, Ali evokes his symbolic encounter with the tribal vulture in an abrupt tonal shift that barely disguises Kateb's didactic intentions and the play's attempt at mythic formulation. From a strictly formal perspective, however, the shift from farcical comedy to the incantation of free verse best represents the constant tension between didacticism and incantation, history and poetry, and invective and invocation characteristic of Kateb's larger literary project. Although Kateb's affinities with Baudelaire merit sep-

---

† From *Counterhegemonic Discourse from the Maghreb: The Poetics of Kateb's Fiction* (Tübingen: Gunter Narr Verlag, 1993) 6–8, 201–03. Copyright © 1993 Gunter Narr Verlag. Reprinted by permission of the publisher.
1. Mikhail Bakhtin, *Rabelais and His World* (Cambridge: The MIT Press, 1968), 10.

arate attention, it is not difficult to see how these tensions esthetically coincide with the French symbolist's dream of a "lyrical buffoonery" shrouded in the form of "a serious novel." In frequent instances throughout Kateb's work, the tone of comedy and satire interpenetrates lyrical evocation. * * *

* * *

The discussion of the carnivalesque elements in *La poudre d'intelligence* has pointed out the centrality of zoomorphic representations and, through Bakhtin's study of popular laughter, their ambivalent function. Bakhtin's insistence on the mythic, regenerative function of comic rituals aptly elucidates the striking intrusion of the grotesque and its zoomorphic representation in so many of Kateb's texts. Because of their frequency, animal images that clearly eschew the monstrous and theriomorphic allusiveness of the antithetic mode and that partake of a schema of ritual abasement and substitution are of special interest. As it stages a feigned acceptance of adversity provisionally transcended through a comical or even grotesque enactment of one's unenviable fate, such a schema paradoxically underwrites an abiding faith in ultimate personal renewal and political fulfillment. Two representative examples come to mind, the stream-of-consciousness, free verse poem in which Lakhdar[2] remembers the 1945 Sétif demonstration and the donkey sequence of Lakhdar's childhood.

In the first text, strategic ambiguity pervades Lakhdar's derisive use of entomological and bovine references. In the depiction of the political upheaval, "irascible" Algeria has become a domestic animal whose placidity can no longer be taken for granted. Suggesting a convulsive awakening from its political slumber, the animal's breathing seems at first sufficient to keep pestering flies at bay. In a text that would have to take into consideration, at the time it was published, the possibility of colonial censorship, the narrator strategically exploits the semantic ambiguity of the French "mouche," a fly, but also an unwelcome intruder and a stoolpigeon. A polysemic implication of victimization, aggression, and collaboration thus settles in, ostensibly complicated by the appearance of enigmatic red ants, which one can soon identify with the demonstrators having come to the rescue of their cohorts. Shortly thereafter, because of his political predicament and romantic failure Lakhdar envisions himself in the pathetic image of "a sentimental flea," and the pattern of self-derisive, zoographic caricature unfolds with quasi-predictable spontaneity. This is particularly noticeable in the use of ovine or bovine images, which stress, through a jocular pattern of substitution, an experience of utter abasement and sacrificial plight. Incarcerated in the police station's hayloft, Lakhdar and fellow demonstrators are tied together like cattle while a sheep freely gambols around, a conspicuous beneficiary of dubious favoritism. From his hayloft, Lakhdar refers twice to the "mugissement" of

---

2. One of the four protagonists of Kateb Yacine's celebrated novel *Nedjma*, a restless and irreverent activist [*Editor*].

the crowd. Observing Mustapha splashing around in a pool of black water, Lakhdar sticks his nose through the prison bars, "like a calf." Later in Bône, finally, Lakhdar strikes more than one pedestrian by "la fixité de ses prunelles de veau évadé" (the fixity of those calflike pupils) and "cet œil rapproché de l'oreille comme celui d'un taureau" (the oxlike closeness of eye to ear).

As it brings back to memory the buffooneries of *La poudre d'intelligence* and the donkey's many festive associations in the history of various folk cultures, the comedy of the donkey in Lakhdar's childhood is striking in the picturesque and incisive economy of its evocation. In its terse, automatic progression, mostly made up of extremely short, one-line paragraphs, it unfolds as a succession of snapshots that caricaturally frame the major participants' most revealing features. More precisely, the stubborn, wily and peevish donkey is personified as saboteur, slave, and soldier. Conversely, Lakhdar's and Mahmoud's attitudes evince much asinine pettiness and brutality. The intertwining of the "protagonists' " actions and the mechanical duplication of their behavior thus graphically establish again the emblematic interchangeability of man and animal that had been brought to farcical perfection in the satirical play. In their battle of the wills, the protagonists' actions and experiences are then mechanically mirrored (for instance, Lakhdar's brother, the donkey, and Mahmoud all "fall sick") to the point that a calculated degree of ambiguity surrounds the target of some of the satirical comments. This is particularly true of the sociological observation, pivotal in a colonial context, that "rien n'entame l'épaisse colère de l'opprimé" (nothing affects the heavy anger of the oppressed creature), which obviously applies to both the mount *and* its rider. It has been suggested that within the ludic context of a festive ritual and through the parodic, provisional reversing of its zoographic transformation, the figure of the donkey channels man's inferior impulses into an experience of controlled catharsis.[3] The cathartic pattern may not underlie Kateb's writing of the dialectical text, but given the uncannily Apuleian dimension of Lakhdar's donkey and the occurrence of prominent animal images throughout the works, it is easy to gauge the degree to which Kateb was indulging a circumventional mode of imagination that so readily nurtures feigning and elusion and favors the powerful lure of comic mythmaking as a primordial and regenerative form.[4]

---

3. Jean Chevalier, *Dictionnaire des symboles,* 4 vol. (Paris: Seghers, 1973), 1:65–66.
4. Bakhtin, 14, 17.

JACQUELINE KAYE and ABDELHAMID ZOUBIR

[Populist Aesthetics and Idioms in Kateb Yacine's Theatre]†

Since the publication of *Nedjma* in 1956, Kateb Yacine has been known as the most eloquent spokesman of Algerianness. We do not propose any new interpretation of this novel nor any comments on his successive publications. We are only concerned here with the fact that Kateb has deliberately ceased to publish in French and has devoted himself to vernacular Algerian in a way comparable with Dante's choice of the Florentine 'dialect' and his arguing for a selective language capable of grouping the best elements of all Italian 'dialects'. Although, unlike Boudjedra,[1] Kateb has not explicitly declared that he would not use French in the future, his use of vernacular Algerian in such plays as *Mohammed, prends ta valise, La Guerre de deux milles ans* or *Le Roi de l'Quest* is more convincing than Boudjedra's insistence on the fact that he writes in Arabic before translating into French:

> In so far as I am writing in French, it was obviously only for a peripheral group, the people who read this language. But they are not the Algerian people. The Algerian people had to be reached in their own language.[2]

This justification is consistent with his subversion of French in his written work and it has the benefit of revealing that what counts most for him is to draw his strength from his cultural reality, particularly in so far as the latter has no written language of its own and also because Kateb has an inkling of the dangers of a conversion to a classical form of Arabic. Unlike Boudjedra, who has opted for the challenge of translating Algerian culture through a personal use of Arabic, Kateb insists on the alienating implications of such a choice. Kateb's verbal reality has been maintained in a state of existence that has no clear ideological consecration and no political function beyond its instrumental character, because of the geopolitical and historico-religious compromises which led Algeria to put its nationalism under the auspices of Arabo-Islamism. Kateb's conversion to unwritten theatre much resembles that of Ngugi, not only because the latter turned to the Gikuyu language, but also because Ngugi shares the view that theatre is the best means of education in countries like Kenya and Algeria, where English and French have finally become the most visible stigma of an alienating educational system.

† From *The Ambiguous Compromise: Language, literature and national identity in Algeria and Morocco* (London and New York: Routledge, 1990) 113–21. Reprinted by permission of Taylor & Francis Books Ltd. The author's notes have been edited.
1. Rachid Boudjedra, Algerian novelist, playwright, and critic, a younger compatriot of Kateb Yacine's [*Editor*].
2. Hafid Gafaiti, *Kateb Yacine: un homme, une oeuvre, un pays* (Laphomic, Algiers, 1986), p. 10.

It could be said that Kateb's acceptance of Brecht's use of songs and his insistence on the fact that his own experience is 'en grande partie un théâtre chanté' (Gafaiti, 1986, pp. 31–2) reinforce his Africanness in terms of Ngugi's view that dance, mime and song have become more dominant than words in telling the African people's story of repression and resistance. Clearly, dance, mime and song are less alienating than either the colonial or local languages, for, unlike words, they communicate directly with people of all nationalities without forcing any of them to absorb the culture in which they are encoded. Not only does orature combine harmoniously with motions of the hand and facial expressions, it also remains exempt from ideological compliance with the establishment.

Kateb's mistrust of literary culture is also revealed in his understanding of the writers who use the language of the common people, who, he says, choose flesh and blood in exchange for Joycean cerebrality. Again and again Kateb condemns what Barthes calls the literary myth, especially Barthes's definition of French literature as a tabernacle of an awe-inspiring mystery; for, just like him, Kateb defines literature as 'la langue vivante' and not 'les belles phrases de l'Académie' (Gafaiti, 1986, p. 61). There is no doubt that Kateb's theatrical experience aims not only at reinstating the Algerian vernacular but also at questioning the validity of literary culture. It links up with the substance of Algerian culture through the most uneducated expressions instead of developing artificial symbols whose objectives are, as in the case of Boudjedra, whether in his Francophone or Arabophone works, to nationalize the language. Instead of using archetypes or allegories, which need the scrutiny of critics or well-read readers, Kateb prefers the stage where he has an immediate access to his audience, and he prepares his dialogues with actors who are as aware as he is of the complexity inherent in Algerian bilingualism.

The best evidence for the fact that Kateb's theatrical experience is meant for the common people and not just for the élite is that whenever it is considered academically it is impossible to quote anything; it is as if his drama cut itself off from intellectuals, whose respect for the written word conceals the fact that writing arose historically with the victory of bourgeois ideals. The difference between Kateb's theatre and any poetic 'dialect' is that, however inventive a written language seems to be, there is always the obstacle of what T. S. Eliot calls 'the imprecision of words'. Unlike poetry and novel writing, Kateb's experience draws its vitality from the versatility of spoken words, which depend not on orthography, nor tenses, nor on the length of vowels, but on the way people usually narrate events. Unlike poetry- and novel-writing, it seems to us that theatre is a unique occasion for the dramatist to reproduce conversational language, especially when, as in Kateb's case, the subject matter of the plays involves not only political, economic and ideological issues, but develops at the same time a linguistic procedure for writers who have decided to retrieve their freedom from the formal limits of literary culture.

Popular gnomic reasoning, proverbs, legends and songs are the elements on which Kateb prefers to rely when he attempts to denote the complexity of Algerian verbal reality because when they are combined with trilingual etymologies, from Algerian-Arabic, Kabylian and French, they create a mixture which defies attempts by Arabophone and Francophone writers to shift easily from one linguistic constituent of Algerian verbal reality to the other. Kateb's reliance on these elements emphasizes theatrical performance as the only adequate means for the Algerian artist today to recreate and to deepen a national culture which has always been confined to a transcription in an alien language. Although Kateb's characters are just characters, and not actual persons acting out their own tragedies as in therapeutic psychodrama, they are made to achieve a comparable catharsis. It should also be borne in mind that Kateb's political conception of catharsis makes his enterprise differ from such a literary manoeuvre as the *roman-à-clef* tradition for example, because his characters do not present real persons and real events under fictitious names. They do not indulge in any aesthetic or *savoir-vivre* mystifications; they are literal truths speaking the language of the people.

When the significance of Kateb's distinctive use of the chorus is properly interpreted, his mistrust of literary artifices is clear, because his chorus destroys the omniscient narrative voice to a point *ne plus ultra* which not even Joyce could attain. Indeed, while Joyce makes use of the stream-of-consciousness device and thus frees himself from traditional modes of writing, Kateb's chorus does not assume highly trained readers acquainted with literary techniques; while Joyce presents the flow of Irish experience through the inner lives of Leopold Bloom and Stephen Daedalus, the chorus of Kateb's plays presents the flow of political life through a group of actors who fit together like the limbs of a single body. While the stream-of-consciousness device acts on self-centred preoccupations pertaining to individual characters, Kateb's chorus develops broader political interests, more especially as every actor is enabled to request leave to speak. This explains why Kateb's theatrical improvisation is always welcomed and why, from one performance to another, Kateb's plays widen out; whereas, however versatile novels like *Ulysses* (1922) and *Nedjma* may be, their adopted modes of writing imply a mechanistic fixation actively antagonizing the dynamics of the living energies which spoken words, songs, mime and dance translate on the stage. Kateb's belief that Rabelais represents French culture much better than any of the Sorbonne-educated writers of his generation springs from the fact that Kateb has identified Rabelais's tactility as a reaction against the visual wall of print culture. Kateb's unwritten plays are not affected by the intrusion which writing imposes not only on accidence and syntax but also on the pronunciation of language and its social uses.

Unlike Ngugi's plays Kateb's theatrical experience might be regarded as a reaction against print culture, because none of his plays has as yet been pinned down to any written languages, local or alien. To the French language of his early career as a writer, Kateb now prefers the strength of non-print culture not only because Algerian culture has no written medium, but also because he is aware of the fact that print culture alters the dynamics of life. Kateb asserts his oral culture by transgressing the limits of a literary culture that has for a long time been the prerogative of Algerian intellectuals caught up in the wave of colonial hegemony, more especially as in post-1962 Algeria the rate of illiteracy was as high as 80 per cent. Kateb assumes that literacy does not contribute to the change from the notion of words as resonant, live, active, natural forces to the notion of words as having a purely intellectual force. His enterprise is not confined to the magical or liturgical intonations of non-literate cultures, even though he associates written words with the static elements of the visual wall of print culture and makes his art rest on spoken words which are related to the dynamism inherent in the oral and auditory world.

To paraphrase McLuhan,[3] if Kateb rejects literary culture by adopting spoken words to the detriment of seen words, it is out of his tendency to believe that literacy abstracts life and generates artificial forces. But this does not mean that his perspectives sacrifice what McLuhan calls 'meaning or significance for minds', because we cannot accept the idea that non-literate cultures do not burden their spoken words with meaning nor deprive them of spiritual intention. The spoken words of non-literature cultures would be no different from any instinctive animal-language if they were denied intellectual significance. McLuhan's partition of the linguistic sphere into an oral compartment on the one hand, and a visual compartment on the other is just an analytical illusion which is as ambiguous as the conflicting polarities of Algerian culture.

If Kateb's rejection of literacy may be regarded as reversing the process through which 'civilization' gives the tribal man an eye for an ear, this does not mean that Kateb's licensing of spoken words to the detriment of seen words truly dispenses with the eye. Kateb's artistic enterprise substantiates McLuhan's thesis that detribalized or 'civilized' man has emerged from the visual age of typography, resumed possession of 'uncivilized' man's oral peculiarity and is now confronting another medieval period in which technology has made simultaneity and oral expression keep pace with the complexity of man's *Gestalt*. After all, had it not been translated and written down, Si Mohand's poetry would have probably remained unknown to anyone beyond the compass of the poet's natural voice, whereas Kateb's theatrical experience is a form of communication which undoubtedly is superior to his literary work because, without any electronic help, it synchronizes dance, mime, song and words. Kateb's belief that art is life is an ideal which questions powerfully any linguistic mystifications. Indeed his theatre shows that the rejection of literacy is vindicated by a parallel decision to reject the means by which hegemonic cultures impose their will. It is a well-meaning kind of violence because it reveals itself as an act of self-assertion which intends to get rid of any abstract assumptions of universality behind which colonial powers have often concealed fierce

3. M. McLuhan, *The Gutenberg Galaxy* (Routledge & Kegan Paul, London, 1967).

economic exploitation. In other words his conversion to unwritten theatre is neither the resurrection of savage instincts nor the effect of
resentment but a violence intended to destroy the marks of violence.
Kateb's theatre augments this process of self-recreation because it does
not lend itself to any alien language encoded in cultures that might
pervert and inferiorize his Algerian traditions.

Kateb's conversion to unwritten theatre, in so far as it harmoniously
combines with man's silent forms of communication and because it
divests itself of the artificial rules of literary culture, not only recognizes the importance of non-verbal languages as well as the language
of forms implicitly, it also transcends the paradox of disclosing its identity in alien languages. *Nedjma*, despite its undisputed contribution to
the homogenization of the national consciousness, is unable to get rid
of its ontological hybridity. This is particularly true when one considers
the expletives that are meant to emphasize the Algerianness of the
dialogues. For example, although the onomatopoeia 'aouah' renders a
fairly acceptable account of the way in which Algerians express indecision, its French transcription does not indicate which vowel is long
and whether the final 'h' should be aspirated. Unlike the orthography
which Luther imposed through the sacred character of his German
version of the Bible, Algerian literature written in French cannot claim
any comparable references; the ambiguous spelling of a word like
'aouah' raises structural doubts. This onomatopoeia could in fact easily
be confused with 'aïouah', whose final 'h' is not aspirated as deeply
and which expresses approval, almost the contrary of indecision. The
context alone can determine whether the writer means indecision or
approval and, had the context not been a determining one, this ambiguity could have probably given a free rein to antithetical interpretations.

We are interested in looking at the demarcation between writers
who reproduced colonial stereotypes and those who found their
strength in their own culture. It is in this context that the contrast
between heteronomous and autonomous types is relevant, more especially as writers like Feraoun and Ould Cheikh exemplify the heteronomous types who partake of a cultural hybridity resulting from
colonial imperatives because they have failed to communicate properly
with the members of their original culture. A writer like Kateb belongs
to the stage of what David Riesman[4] calls 'inner-direction', as an autonomous type, because he calls into question the colonial group
which has substituted itself for his authentic identity and because he
attempts to recreate his particular Self. In a colonial situation a person's struggle against conformity focuses on a tangible power whose
administrative and military exactions designate nationalism as the saf-
est solution; in a non-colonial situation, a person's struggle against
conformity is not so simple to define because the exactions of the
dominant group imposing conformity are anonymous and spring from
the same nationality.

---

4. D. Reisman, *The Lonely Crowd* (Yale University Press, New Haven, 1960).

In the Algerian colonial context the struggle was often considered as corresponding to oppositions between races or nationalities, whereas in the Algerian post-colonial context it was considered as dependent on oppositions between social classes. In other words Kateb's subversive use of French may either be regarded as a nationalistic attitude or as the expression of his non-conformity with the dominant group, while his conversion to theatre, after independence, may just be regarded as the expression of his non-conformity with the dominant group that has replaced the colonial order and whose nationality is no different from his. This is why Kateb's disagreement with the choice of Arabic as the official language not only springs from his individual refusal to conform to the strategic imperatives of the dominant group, it also sets the problem in terms of the conflicts of social classes:

> [Literary Arabic is a danger in so far as it throws the intellectuals into the arms of the bourgeoisie. Popular Arabic is the best means of directing the cultural revolution towards the people, the folk who actually speak this language. And it seems to me that the true revolution would be to write books in this language, to ensure that it nourishes itself much more with popular content and resolutely gives up audacities and grammatical complexities by violating the form.]

> (Gafaiti, 1986, p. 59)

The linguistic allegiance of colonial literatures to tutelary cultures exhibits on an enlarged, transnational scale the subjections of so-called dialects with respect to the privileged language which the dominant group imposes as *the* national language. It also explains why a national language is indeed historically established by the tacit consent of the majority, but none the less compels official recognition to the detriment of so-called dialects only because it proceeds from the interests of the ruling class and aims at maintaining the social status quo. Literary culture should always be traced back to some economic class analysis which, we believe, would probably be a less prejudiced method of approach than any linguistic, religious or racial grounds of investigation, provided it does not in its turn nullify the intrinsic or aesthetic values of the work under discussion. When the linguistic factor is used either to define or to hold a culture together it engenders mystifications which are as poisonous as racial apriorisms, because it tends to falsify unity at the expense of refractory minorities by mistaking the attributes of the dominant class for national ones. The definition of national culture is further complicated in colonial backgrounds, because when one examines their literary cultures one finds out that linguistic allegiances reflect both colonial and class alienations.

Kateb's conversion from French to unwritten theatre and his rejection of the national language that has been adopted since 1962 reflect this awareness of both forms of alienation. The linguistic subjection of Algeria magnifies the identical plight of minority groups with respect to the dominant class within other non-colonial societies. Just as the colonial powers manipulate the colonized people's activities to their own ends, mainly through the implantation of educational systems designed to eradicate the colonized people's sense of their identity and through the monopoly of institutions like publishing houses and libraries, and central control of the economy, which secure the economic interest of the parent country and eliminate other forms of expression, so the dominant class of a non-colonial society rids itself of all forms of expression that might challenge or subvert its economic, political and cultural supremacy. * * *

KAMAL SALHI

The Pragmatics and Aesthetics of Kateb Yacine's Theatre Practice†

* * * Yacine's theatre depends almost completely on song and music, the dynamics of a circular performance space, word play, storytelling and the traditions surrounding a popular folk hero. In other words, it is based on authentic elements which are difficult to grasp and explain in another language and another culture.

The assertion that literary readings of Kateb Yacine's plays profit from a consideration of the requirements and effects of staging has become one of the recurrent commonplaces in the literature on his work. Even those critics unwilling to pursue a theatrical approach feel obliged to emphasise the 'incompleteness' of their readings. This recognition has not prompted, however, a proliferation of stage studies of Kateb Yacine's work. Even the few studies of his work on the stage that have been written fail, in my opinion, to address adequately the questions it raises. I argue that it is the stylistic and conceptual patterning of Kateb Yacine's theatre as a genre which has constituted, organised and maintained an authentic and popular form. The priority of text over performance in literary criticism can be seen as part of a larger manoeuvre within a shifting matrix of power relations, a manoeuvre which privileges academic discourse over the discourses of practitioners like Yacine and his actors, and privileges textual stability over the variety, nuances and power of performance.

Yacine's theatre does not use a written text in the sense of an established or final script. Scripts vary and great emphasis is placed on production techniques (the chorus, chanting, music, stage movements and improvisation). Kateb Yacine's repertoire was made up of 'scripted' performances rather than written plays. To identify the written script with his work is to subscribe to a limited view of the dramatist's artistic project as a whole. In point of fact, his themes allow for flexibility in the scripted material. In Yacine's own words:

† From *The Politics and Aesthetics of Kateb Yacine: From Francophone Literature to Popular Theatre in Algeria and Outside* (Lewiston, Queenston, and Lampeter: Edwin Mellen Press, 1999) 227–31, 244–45, 267–72, 286–87, 297–99. Reprinted by permission of Edwin Mellen Press.

The scripts we have worked out on the subject of emigration in *Mohamed prends ta valise, Palestine trahie* and *La Guerre de 2000 ans* are only rough texts, because the situation is changing and evolving. 'Political theatre' implies this ceaseless change. We do not know when or how things will end: every day the searing history of these problems takes place. While we study the situation, our vision is polished as we go along, and we are always finding that we need to change words. If a script is written down, it takes on an almost definite value, and [creativity] stops.[1]

It is doubtful whether any of the scripts which have been collected were ever seen as permanent by the actors, but were continually modified, rewritten, amended, lengthened and combined with other scripts both before a given performance and on stage during performance. Likewise, shorter or longer series of episodes could be presented as cohesive units.

Several 'fragments' have been published in different Reviews and Journals. These are either parts of the performance-scripts or shortened versions of the early published texts. * * * Sometimes sequences from one play or a group of plays are inserted or rearranged in another play. There are, for example, several sequences from *L'homme aux sandales de caoutchouc* which are developed in some performances of *Mohamed prends ta valise* and *La Guerre de 2000 ans*. (There are also many similarities between these two plays. However there are two exceptions which are relatively more stable textually. These are *Palestine trahie* and the recent version of *La Poudre d'intelligence*. *La Poudre d'intelligence* is still modified in performance, but the farcical and satirical episodes are kept in their original form.) A spectator at a performance of one of Yacine's works would not be surprised to see the sequence about 'Mohamed and Moses' in either play. * * *

The flexibility seen in these texts is also reflected in the way they are produced. The one exception to the rule is *La Poudre d'intelligence,* which is more stable in terms of stage directions and sets. Written and published before 1970, it is a regular part of the company's repertoire. It has preserved its textual integrity because of its use of the popular figure of Djeha and its impressive vernacular vigour. When performed in Berber areas the language is intensified by the addition of local phrases and humorous allusions. The quotations given in this chapter are from the published version of the play because the performance-script is a transliteration of the original. Sequences from this play are also used in *Mohamed prends ta valise,* especially those which show Djeha's farcical escapades. Indeed, it was a very conscious decision on Kateb Yacine's part to use these elements in other plays in order to maintain the satirical mode in his performances, and to play with the subtle political dimensions that this cunning character confers on his shows.

1. Interview with Jacques Alessandra. 'Le Theatre révolutionnaire algérien', *Travail Théâtral* (December 1979), p. 95.

* * *

Given the parameters within which he was operating, Kateb Yacine's achievement may be viewed as the creation of a convention of performance which combined and transcended the revival of tradition and modern naturalistic theatre. This mode of performance reproduced real life as faithfully and accessibly as possible; sets, props and costumes were designed to be comprehensible to an audience without any special previous knowledge. Most importantly, however, Yacine's theatre was designed to convey an ideological system to the audience, and to reinforce their understanding by engaging them in a pattern of active responses to the ideational content presented. The audience watch a performance which plays out their own situation as the victims of a repressive, exploitative, political system and, at the same time, because they are actively involved in that performance, they themselves take part in the act of representation. The hope is that, at the end of the performance, they will have come to a better understanding of socialism and also demonstrated their identification with it ideologically as it is represented by the characters in the performance. Some of the characters in these plays go through transformations from political agnosticism or hostility towards socialism to become advocates for it. The implication here is that if even enemies of the socialist revolution weep for it and defend it, how can the spectators refrain from demonstrating their commitment? Thus the performance offers a theatrical opportunity for the audience to demonstratively renew their commitment to an ideology in which they already believe.

In this way the performance invites the audience to share in an act of creation. The public is no longer a mere witness to the repetition of lifeless words and gestures: it shares in the adventure of creation. This is an innovative theatrical form of direct action, which has a wider symbolic function. It indicates that society is still in the process of formation and that it is each individual's duty to contribute to this process. Helping the audience to act creatively means, from this point of view, making the duration of the performance a time of creative renewal. The transformation of social and personal relationships is presented as a creative act. The audience and performers do not confine themselves only to acting. They also seek to go back to their roots and renew their relationship to history as they unite with the actors in recreating its defining moments.

* * *

The audience-performer relationship was the most important component in the structure of Kateb Yacine's work. The status of the audience as performer and spectator, existing within a dual time-scheme as part of the dramatic action, and also embedded within its own community against the background of public events, forms the central axis around which Yacine's principles of representation revolve. In order to bring the audience into the time-scheme of the performance, time needs to be represented in several ways. The first is 'real' time; for example, the time it takes for a piece of dialogue to be performed. The second is dramatic time: a conventional, compressed representation of time in which years pass in an instant. Another form of time on the stage is abstract time, a dimension which permits the coincidence of all sorts of characters and events that could not possibly have existed together at the same time. * * *

The audience experiences both literal time and dramatic time in the performance; but it is the dimension of abstract time which often moves the audience to action and enables the spectators to be simultaneously in the present and in the past. Space is represented in a similar way. Literal space is used on stage. Theatrical or representational space compresses or elongates actual space. 'Abstract space', or 'non-space', permits persons far removed from each other geographically as well as temporally to interact, making it possible for characters from outside the action to address the central character as the play unfolds.

The audience is placed in a strategic position, not only in terms of time and space, but in terms of their dramatic role within the performance as well. As participants in the performance, they are witnesses to the events, and contribute to the action. Performances in villages also bear a resemblance to many other familiar public activities, such as elections, demonstrations, political announcements and public meetings. Like these activities, Yacine's social and political plays were intended to bring about social change. They combine intimate communication with the public with the need to state beliefs and articulate national concerns. His work often represents an image of the country's public life in which the performers symbolise the ruling classes and the audience symbolise the ruled. Thus the form Kateb Yacine's performance took was ideologically distinct from all other Algerian drama as a committed form in which performance techniques are more important than the text which they are used to realise on stage.

Yacine never used scenery. At his outdoor performances the only backdrop was provided by the starry sky and the semi-darkness, maybe with a few trees or huts around the village square. At the TNA[2] the imposing set designs are expressions of a coherent aesthetic foreign to Algerian audiences. The aesthetics of Kateb Yacine's theatre are inextricably linked to communication. Scenery, all things considered, is only a visual representation of the text, while Algerians are more interested in expanding theatrical horizons and giving free rein to their imaginations. Flexible production is needed in order to involve the largest possible number of people and to present images and action which are popular in content and realisation, and from which people can draw lessons.

Yacine aimed to break away from romantic realism largely because

2. Algerian National Theatre, Algiers [Editor].

the identification between actor and role it promoted suggests that situations are inevitable. Kateb challenged this in a profound way. In drama the actor is a virtuoso performer able to distance himself from the role, never becoming totally immersed in it. An actor's performance becomes a criticism of the character played. Rather than representing the actions of an individual, the actor joins with a collective in creating discourse about society. Yacine always stressed the importance of team work for a group of actors. What Stanislavsky did for the art of the actor, Kateb Yacine did for the art of the theatrical collective.

Yacine's actors would work to find an objective set of actions and relationships in their rehearsals that, apart from anything they themselves might feel, would communicate to the audience the images, events and meanings they wanted to put across. This process took weeks or months as the group rejected more ideas than it accepted. Watched by Yacine, they would act out the associations particular events or ideas had for them. He helped them remove obstacles to understanding and confront the issues at hand. Finally, they would write a coherent script, which grew bit by bit, day by day, and included everything the audience would see. Such was the collective process by which these works were created.

By comparison with his early drama, Yacine's later work was straightforward in that it sought to communicate with a large public. One play touring the whole country was much more efficient than publishing a book in French which was only available to those who could read the language. This is perhaps the reason why Yacine gave up writing in French and publishing books after *L'Homme aux sandales de caoutchouc* came out in 1970.[3] Yacine's theatre spoke the people's language and addressed all those who were eager to learn about society and its problems. The dramatist emphasised this point:

> We could collect plays and leave them in a drawer or show them to hundreds of people. We do not think that this is our main job, but an exercise in depth. It is better to reach hundreds of thousands of people with a single play than collect plays which will only reach a few hundred intellectuals.[4]

Yacine's performance pieces consisted almost entirely of short speeches and very brief dialogues and songs. This is in sharp contrast to almost all other Algerian drama. This multiplication of technical devices was not an end in itself, as often seems to be the case at the National Theatre, but expressed a desire to release collective emotion. * * *

The chorus acts as a group, declaiming, singing, chanting and delivering statements about the action. At times it reinforces the voice of an individual actor or enhances the words of the storyteller by accom-

---

3. With the exception of *L'Oeuvre en fragments*, a collection of fragments and excerpts collected by Jacqueline Arnaud and published in book form in 1986.
4. Ibid.

panying them with other sounds and rhythms. The collective voice of the chorus is integral to, but must not be confused with, the individual voices of the characters. * * *

* * * It is important to note that in Yacine's drama the chorus is composed of actors who are already playing other roles. As Yacine's work depicts a world of injustice, exploitation, politics and history, the major characters are often peasants, workers and women. The actors playing these roles form the chorus. As a result, the chorus comes to speak as the voice of the principal social group around which a play revolves. For example, in *Mohamed prends ta valise*, the major characters are workers, so the chorus speaks for them every time it intervenes. In many of Yacine's plays women play an important role as a chorus performing songs or chanting comments, as in *Saout Ennissa* (*Voix des Femmes*). Kateb Yacine explained the function of the chorus as follows:

> Generally, the chorus is a group of people which speaks, chants and replies to the audience or to another group of actors on stage. One should not really make a mountain out of a molehill. The chorus is the idea of a group. Even one actor can be a chorus on his own. When I want to say that it is the people, the peasants or the workers, I make it clear by calling them 1st Peasant, 2nd Peasant, and so on. That is to avoid any confusion. Therefore if you see coryphaeus and chorus in my texts, for me that means two actors.[5]

The chorus (or coryphaeus) is an integral part of the action. It plays the role of articulating the aspirations of a social group which it represents. This notion of the group has an important place in every play not only in Kateb Yacine's theatre of later years but also in his early work. * * *

*   *   *

In the stage versions of *La Poudre d'intelligence*, the chorus does not just repeat sections of dialogue and speeches, as is the case in Yacine's early work. Now it takes part in the exchanges between other characters. The chorus and the coryphaeus address Nuage de Fumée [Puff of Smoke] directly:

Coryphaeus:
Hello *Philosophe*! Where are you going in such a hurry?

In another example the chorus takes on different roles at the same time:

Chorus:
What a scandal! Sultan you are witness of this act of violence.

---

5. Ammar Lemouchi and Ammar Tlili, interview with Kateb Yacine, *Bulletin de l'Ecole Primaire de Sedrata* (No. 8, October–November 1973), p. 20.

Chorus:
> It was predictable. The Sultan is covering up the Mer-
> chant's mistake. Those are the rules.

The chorus initiates dialogue, even if it only degenerates into an exchange of insults. In *La Poudre d'intelligence* the people are a single character with human qualities and failings. In the early plays the chorus had functioned more as a bridge between the text and the reader, communicating over the heads of the characters. In the satire of *La Poudre d'intelligence*, however, it does not submit to the action, it provokes it and judges it, sometimes harshly. The chorus assumes an active, dynamic role. Without the chorus, Nuage de Fumée on his own would have little effect as a character; his actions and gestures may awaken the audience's critical consciousness, but they do not encourage it to take action. The chorus provides a counterweight to his pronounced individuality and passivity, exemplifying a more active, collective approach to the same situations.

Yacine no doubt wanted his drama to be realistic and historical, a place where the stage action showed the great forces of life against which the people struggle. All his work was directed towards the aims of restoring a sense of purpose to the powerful aesthetic force of the theatre and recreating the emotions of a united mass of people around the important events in their history. The role of the chorus developed throughout his work as he pursued these aims, becoming more and more closely identified with the people. The chorus is made up of peasants when feudal society is being depicted; at other times it is composed of industrial workers when dealing with modern urban issues. Because these characters are not representative only of Algeria, but of all the post-colonial countries, Yacine's plays depict processes going on throughout the world. People everywhere want the same 'freedom' and 'independence' that the representative people on stage call for in the symbolic myth.

* * *

The audience for Yacine's work is usually a heterogeneous one made up of both sexes, all age groups and the various classes within a particular community. The group therefore has to structure its performances to appeal to a wide range of people, and so one finds that in any one performance they run through a varied repertoire of sequences, themes and tableaux. This explains the 'modular' format which allows different routines and episodes to be combined in a variety of ways. Before they decide on the running order of a specific performance, some of the actors will make advance inquiries in the area where they are to perform in order to identify topical issues.

The group draw their accompanying singers from among the audience. The musicians, however, are always professionals. They perform on the *Bendjou*, a trumpet-like instrument, and a drum. There is usually a choir made up of actors who sit or stand with the musicians in one part of the performing area, although not separated from the rest of the audience. This group does most of the choral singing during the performance, but the rest of the audience are free to join in and usually do so. Often the audience is encouraged to provide rhythmic accompaniment to the singing by clapping along to the music, which they do with gusto. Choral participation also makes it possible for the audience to intervene in the narrative flow by commenting on the action. In addition to these kinds of audience involvement, the group often assigns specific character roles to members of the audience. This is done in one of two ways. A volunteer may be asked to assist with a particular sequence. For example, during the performance of the scene about witchcraft (in *Kahena* or *La Poudre d'intelligence*), a member of the audience is persuaded to go to the centre of the performing area and play the role of the witch's or wizard's visitor. This spectator then engages in dialogue and action which successfully bring the story to life (though most of the burden of the performance rests on the actors). The second way in which the company assigns roles to members of the audience is by going right up to an individual and addressing him or her as a character in the drama. Although in most cases the individual does not respond verbally and is not expected to do so, in some instances they do respond, assuming the character thrust on them and engaging in dialogue with the actors. The audience is thus fully involved in the drama at every point, and the relationship between performer and audience is so intimate that the demarcation lines between the two become blurred. There are no spectators in the drama of Kateb Yacine: everybody is a participant. * * * The special relationship between Yacine's audience and his works has been noted by virtually all commentators. It contrasts particularly with the dominant Western/European theatrical tradition, because the spectators are both inside and outside the drama. They are simultaneously actors on the symbolic political stage which represents the forces of history and citizens of present-day Algeria with all its political and social conflicts. The purpose of Yacine's performances and the theatrical techniques employed identify his work as a form of drama unique in Algeria. It may make use of methods similar to traditional Arabic techniques, especially those of the storyteller and the folk hero Djeha, but these parallels in no way detract from its special status among the new and distinctive forms of authentic theatre in the third world.

Athol Fugard, John Kani, and Winston Ntshona

ATHOL FUGARD

Introduction to *Statements*†

Thirteen years ago, in an introductory note to a published extract from my play *The Blood Knot*, I put down a few thoughts about what I called 'the pure theatre experience'. I wrote:

> This experience belongs to the audience. He is my major concern as a playwright. The ingredients of this experience are already partially revealed in what I have said and are very simple—their very simplicity being the main justification for using the word 'pure' in the context of a form as open to adulteration as Theatre. They are: the actor and the stage, the actor *on* the stage. Around him is space, to be filled and defined by movement and gesture; around him is also silence to be filled with meaning, using words and sounds, and at moments when all else fails him, including the words, the silence itself.

I concluded:

> In other words the full and unique possibility of this experience needs nothing more than the actor and the stage, the actor in space and silence. Externals, and in a sense even the text can be one, will profit nothing if the actor has no soul.

There is obviously no credit attached to recognizing Theatre's fundamental dependence on the actor. What I do recognize now, however, in those few lines I wrote thirteen years ago, is the first formulation of an obsessional concern with the actor and his performance. This has been a major factor in my work, certainly to the extent that if it is categorized at all, then it must be as 'actors' theatre'. Without this primary involvement with the actor I would never have ended up 'making' theatre with them as I did thirteen years later with the three plays in this volume. It is partly for this reason also that I have directed most of my plays in their first productions; not because I felt that as the author I was in possession of *the* interpretation either of the play as a

---

† From *Statements* (New York: Theatre Communications Group, 1986). Copyright © 1974 by Athol Fugard. Reprinted by permission of Theatre Communications Group.

whole or the specific characters, but because I have always regarded the completed text as being only a half-way stage to my ultimate objective—the living performance and its particular definition of space and silence.

The next of the developments which led finally to the three plays in this volume came about as a result of my association with Serpent Players, the African drama group from New Brighton, Port Elizabeth. Seven years ago, after being in existence for four years (during which, among other plays, we performed *Antigone*) we decided to experiment with improvised theatre. Our reason for this was quite simply the desire to use the stage for a much more immediate and direct relationship with our audience than had been possible with the 'ready-made' plays we had been doing. Our first attempt was a sixty-minute exercise called *The Coat* and was based on an actual incident. The coat in question belonged to a New Brighton man, one of many, who had been found guilty of membership of a banned political organization and sentenced to five years imprisonment. It was all he had to send back to his wife. In an interview I have described the evolution of the exercise as follows:

> First we just wanted to see the moment when the coat was handed over. So we very crudely, using almost no words, improvised that one scene—the coat leaving Mabel's hands and ending up in the wife's. Nothing more. Just the coat being handed over. Then we asked: 'What do you do with the coat now that you've got it?' The wife, the actress playing the wife, said: 'Well, I'm in my house. I've now heard about my husband. I know I'm not going to see him for five years. I've got his coat in my hands. I'll hang it up, first of all, and then go on working. I want to think about him. And the coat.' She was a good actress and in the course of all this, something happened. It took a few exercises to fatten it. Know what I mean?
>
> I jotted down, very crudely, several of her attempts and at the end we compared notes. I said: 'This is how the last one came out, Nomhle.' The other actors joined in: 'Yes, that's right. You did. And remember that other thing she said when she was talking about the street? I thought that was rather good.' I made a few more notes and handed them over to her. 'Take these away. Come back next week. Same time, same place. Live with them. See if you can fill them out a bit.'
>
> She did. Next week we provoked her again and that little scene and its follow-up seemed intact. It had a shape, a life of its own. Then we provoked her still further, by questions and discussing, and in this way it all started to grow.
>
> I remember! At one stage we were trying to corner her. We felt that a certain edge of desperation in the wife's predicament was still eluding her. We said to Humphrey: 'Come on. We need a scene with the man at the Rent Office to whom she is going to appeal for a few days' grace. Will you take it on?' He did. The two of them discussed the 'geography' of the little encounter for a

second or so and then tried it out. That one almost worked completely the first time. In all of this I acted as scribe . . . you know, making my little notes and keeping an eye on the overall structure . . . .

The Coat was followed by many similar experiments over the next few years. I am enormously indebted to them, but equivalently I must admit that looking back now I am very conscious of them as being two-dimensional. Facts, and somehow we never managed to get beyond facts even though they were important facts, are flat and lacking in the density and ambiguity of truly dramatic images. The reason for this limitation was that I relied exclusively on improvisation in its shallowest sense. I had not yet thought seriously about alternative methods of releasing the creative potential of the actor. This came with my reading of Grotowski a few years later, an encounter which coincided with a crisis in relation to my own work. For several years, and particularly as a writer, I had become increasingly dissatisfied with the type of Theatre I was making. The content and personal significance of my response to Grotowski's ideas—I have never seen an actual performance—are indicated in the following extracts from an interview in London three years ago:

After the last run of *Boesman and Lena* in South Africa I decided to try and do something which had been on my mind for a long time. In a sense it involved turning my back on my securities as a writer. I regard my involvement in theatre as being total in the sense that I both direct and write, and sometimes even act. I am not yet addicted to the privacy of myself and blank paper to the exclusion of all else. I really do think I write plays because what I want ultimately is to be involved with actors and a living experience of the theatre. So, as I say, after that run of *Boesman and Lena* I decided to do something I had wanted to for a long time . . . turn my back on my securities, which is to write a play in total privacy, to go into a rehearsal room with a *completed* text which I would then take on as a director, and which the actors —under my direction—would go on to 'illustrate', to use Grotowski's phrase.

I mention Grotowski, because he was in every sense the *agent provocateur* at that moment in my career. His book *Towards a Poor Theatre* made me realize that there were other ways of doing theatre, other ways of creating a totally valid theatre experience . . . that it needn't be the orthodox experience I had been retailing for so many years since *The Blood Knot* . . . .

My work had been so conventional! It involved the *writing* of a play; it involved *setting* that play in terms of local specifics; it involved the actors *assuming* false identities . . . etc., etc. I wanted to turn my back on all that. Permanently or not I didn't know. I just knew I wanted to be free again. I had an idea involving an incident in our recent South African history . . . a young man took a bomb into the Johannesburg station concourse as an act of protest. It killed an old woman. He was eventually caught and hanged. I superimposed, almost in the sense of a palimpsest, this image on that of Clytemnestra and her two children, Orestes and Electra. There was no text. Not a single piece of paper passed between myself and the actors. Three of them. Anyway, after about twelve weeks of totally private rehearsals we got around to what we called our first 'exposure'. This was an experience that lasted for sixty minutes, had about 300 words, a lot of action—strange, almost somnambulistic action—and silence. It was called *Orestes.* . . .

What was so marvellous in working on this project, along lines suggested by Grotowski and my own experience, was just how pristine, what weight you gave to a line, a word, a gesture, if you set it in silence. . . .

The only fact I do not find reflected in the above quotations was my total response to Grotowski's sense of the actor as a 'creative' artist, not merely 'interpretive'.

Orestes was my first, and remains my most extreme excursion into a new type of theatre experience, in which we attempted to communicate with our audience on the basis of, for us at least, an entirely new vocabulary. It has defied translation onto paper in any conventional sense. I have tried. At the moment it is 'scored' in three large drawing-books. It is one of the most important experiences I have had in Theatre and I will be living with it, and using it, for as long as I continue to work. I can think of no aspect of my work, either as writer or director, that it has not influenced.

In relation to the three plays in this volume the importance of *Orestes* was to suggest techniques for releasing the creative potential of the actor. But I would just like to make one point clear: we did not jettison the writer. It was never a question of coming together with the actors on a 'let's make a play' basis. The starting-point to our work was always at least an image, sometimes an already structured complex of images about which I, as a writer, was obsessional. In all three of these plays the writer provided us with a mandate in terms of which the actors then went on to work. In the case of *Sizwe Bansi* our starting-point was my fascination with a studio photograph I had once seen of a man with a cigarette in one hand and a pipe in the other; *The Island* began with the notes and ideas I had accumulated over many years relating to Robben Island; *Statements* likewise started with my image of six police photographs of a White woman and a Coloured man caught in the act of love-making.

These initial mandates from the writer were also not his final contribution. He kept pace with us as fast as we discovered and explored . . . sometimes as no more than a scribe, but at other times in a much more decisive way. The final dramatic structure of each play, for example, was his responsibility. Looking back on the three experiences now, it was as if instead of first putting words on paper in order to arrive eventually at the stage and a live performance, I was able to write *directly* into its space and silence via the actor.

In this context my dependence on the actor (and his ability to rise

INTRODUCTION TO *STATEMENTS*

to the challenge involved) is even more fundamental than in the sense I showed at the beginning of these notes. I have made many attempts to formulate this challenge. A simple definition still eludes me, which I suppose is inevitable with an experience as obscure and at times as disturbing as those we have lived through in rehearsal rooms since *Orestes*. I do know, however, that it starts with—absolutely demands —a very special courage without which the actor cannot 'stake' his personal truth, and in the absence of words on paper that personal truth has been our only capital. I cannot stress this factor in strong enough terms. Pretence and deception are as fatal as they would be in a writer's private relationship with paper.

The basic device has been that of Challenge and Response. As writer-director I have challenged, and the actors have responded, not intellectually or merely verbally but with a totality of Being that at the risk of sounding pretentious I can only liken to a form of Zen spontaneity. As with the more obvious pitfalls of pretence and deception so too any element of calculation or premeditation in response has proved fatal. When, however, the response seemed meaningful in terms of the overall mandate provided by the writer, or to put it another way, when we thought it was of value and significance in terms of our intentions, we then applied ourselves to disciplining and structuring it so that the gesture, word, or event was capable of controlled repetition. I must stress this point. Spontaneous response and improvisation basically ended in the rehearsal room. Once the actor had created his text in the privacy of rehearsals, we then concerned ourselves with its performance in exactly the same way that we would have done with an independent text.

To arrive at an uninhibited release of Self is not easy. At times it has been painful. There have been harrowing experiences in rehearsal rooms. I say this without any sense of pride. It is just that in making these plays I have kept company with a group of remarkable actors. Their courage has at times frightened me. I have lived constantly with the fear of our work degenerating into a dangerous game with personalities. This might well be one of the reasons why at this point I feel that I have exhausted for myself personally the experience that started with *Orestes*, and that the time has now come to return to the privacy of blank paper.

I have included *Statements* in these notes although on the title page of this volume I claim sole authorship. The reason for this is that although I do regard myself as having *written* that play the production at the Royal Court Theatre, which this text partly reflects, was totally dependent on the methods I had evolved with *Orestes*.

Finally, one long overdue expression of gratitude. That is to Brian Astbury and his theatre The Space, in Cape Town. None of these plays would have happened if his vision and tenacity of purpose had not created that venue.

RUSSELL VANDENBROUCKE

"Robert Zwelinzima Is Alive"†

Sizwe Bansi is Dead and *The Island*, collaborative works devised by Athol Fugard, John Kani and Winston Ntshona, have received considerable praise, but the critics of the popular press have stressed the politics of these plays in a way that does them a disservice and that reveals much about prevailing (mis)conceptions about the relationship between 'politics' and art. These *are* political plays, but are not one-dimensional, undramatic or inartistic as is sometimes implied by the pejorative use of 'political' to imply a limitation in a work of art. The critic short-circuits his analytical function by simply naming a play 'political' and dismissing it out of hand, if its politics are 'bad', or damning it with faint praise for good intentions, if its politics are 'good.'

Following its American premiere, Allan Lewis wrote that *Sizwe Bansi* "would serve well as agitprop material." Clive Barnes observed that politics is never discussed in *The Island*, but could not resist mentioning Brecht and "didactic realism." Brendan Gill called *Sizwe Bansi* "an act of open . . . noble propaganda", but preferred *The Island*, "less a work of propaganda." John Simon denied that *Sizwe Bansi* was either drama or literature, and likened it to poster art.

It would be easy to dismiss these critics if they were not representative of a larger problem—the inability to recognize or accept the pervasive interconnection of politics, economics, education, values and art in their effect on daily life. The implication that 'politics' pertains only to government activities seems tacitly accepted. Rigid compartments are created as if there were only a single time and place for each activity, idea or belief. The inevitable result is the obfuscation of similarities and interrelations. Specialisation in a technocratic society refers to industries and the nature of work, but it has also permeated and distorted the ability to see lucidly and comprehend fully.

In the extreme is the attitude that presumes a work of art to be *sui generis*—produced in a vacuum, nourished on thin air, warranting analysis equally calm, lofty and remote. Such an attitude presumes that art is sacrosanct and that its purity and other-worldliness are beyond question. As a result, its inextricable relation to other realms is overlooked or discounted. Theatre, perhaps the most explicitly social and socially dependent of all art forms is, from such a perspective, especially misunderstood. An unwillingness to accept its societal context may be the reason poets and gentlemen critics have frequently preferred the drama of the study to the theatre of the playhouse.

Regardless of its purpose, medium or style, every work of art has a

---

† From *Athol Fugard*, ed. Stephen Gray (Johannesburg: McGraw-Hill, 1982) 190–97. Copyright © 1975 Russell Vandenbroucke. Reprinted by permission of the author.

multiple nature as a reflection of the culture from which it grew. Like the 'real' world, works of art are simultaneously religious, political, economic, historical and aesthetic. This is certainly obvious, but too often an artist is thought to have sold out his artistry and become a party hack or ideologist as soon as he adds the political dimension to his work, if only as a context rather than the subject itself. The avowed intentions of Shaw were so long assumed to be his practice that the quintessentially dialectical nature of his work was long ignored.

Because Athol Fugard speaks openly about the conditions in South Africa that he abhors, and because his plays are set in his homeland and confront the inhumanity spawned by its laws and values, it is facilely assumed that he is a propagandist and that his plays are mere devices. Art, dramatisation and suggestion are supposed to have been replaced by politics, explication and emotional marching orders. However, Fugard can no more ignore the conditions in which he lives than could Faulkner ignore slavery. Fugard's link to his homeland is complete. He cannot conceive of living or working elsewhere, and this intimate tie is evident in both his portrayal of blacks living under apartheid and his description of the exquisite mating of cobras.

Just as some naive Europeans still perceive America through the dusty myths of the Wild West and Al Capone, so we perceive South Africa solely in terms of its apartheid system, and even then ignore the complex basis of many of its laws and assumptions. The deceptions of first appearances, like the context of *Sizwe Bansi* and *The Island*, must be penetrated to find their underlying substance.

Fugard and his actor-collaborators implicity and profoundly understand that political values and processes permeate their lives and must, therefore, be reflected in their work. 'Politics' is not simply added on to a pre-existing work, nor is it an independent element solely intended from the start. Kani has said that "it is for the audience to call a play political, not for the artist to intend it so . . . . These plays are called political because they show our lives, not because we are politicians."

Kani and Ntshona are obviously not the didacticists they have sometimes been thought to be. It was not until after *Sizwe Bansi*'s American premiere (two years after it first appeared in Cape Town) that they spoke directly to a large audience about their country and work in the theatre. Even then their hesitancy was obvious. They prefer to have their artistry speak for them. Fugard admits he is politically naive and 'not good' at propaganda. Speaking of the Serpent Players, which he helped found in 1963, and around which his theatre work has centred, he has stated, "We want to use the theatre. For what? Here it gets a bit confused again. Some of us say to understand the world we live in but we also boast a few idealists who think that theatre might have something to do with changing it." The implication is clear—he is not one of those idealists. Like Ibsen, Fugard might claim, "I am less the social critic and more the poet than people seem generally inclined to believe." He is a kind of despairing pessimist, an agnostic whose faith resides in human beings and the making of theatre. He is not a writer with a political cause. Would any propagandist state, "I'd like to believe that a play can be a significant form of action but I've never been able to convince myself?"

Sizwe Bansi is Dead opens with a long monologue by Styles, a factory worker turned photographer, whose speech is finally interrupted by the visit of a customer who calls himself Robert Zwelinzima. In a flashback Robert, now called Sizwe Bansi, visits Buntu who, during a night of drunken revelling, discovers the body of a dead man. Sizwe's own identity book prohibits him from working or living in the city, and he is convinced by Buntu to switch books with the dead man, Robert Zwelinzima, whose book is in proper order. In *The Island,* John and Winston prepare *Antigone* for a concert at the prison where they are confined. John is called to the warden's office and informed that an appeal has been successful. He is to be released in three months. Ecstatic at first, the friends realise that their close relationship will soon end since Winston has been sentenced to life. They present *Antigone* nonetheless.

Sizwe Bansi has attracted more attention than *The Island* (and has been performed more frequently) but is marred in several ways. It is discursive at times, and some of its components are unassimilated. Yet the subject is powerful and suggestive, and the performance convincing. It is only in retrospection that one realises the accomplishment does not quite equal the potential of the material. The focus created by the opening monologue and Robert's visit to Styles's studio is dissipated in the second half of the play, particularly in the seemingly interminable carousal of Sizwe and Buntu.

The central image of a photograph—both the one snapped by Styles and the one on the identification card—is poignant. A photograph affords a kind of immortality, perhaps the only kind possible to a black South African. Styles calls his studio "A strong-room of dreams . . . . That's what I do, friends. Put down, in my way, on paper the dreams and hopes of my people so that even their children's children will remember a man."

In a society where the vast majority of people are treated as a uniform, faceless mass, a name must assume extraordinary importance. As Styles notes, "We own nothing but ourselves and when we die leave nothing but the memory of ourselves." Allowed no identity but that defined by his identification card, the man and card become one. To lose his name is to lose the only thing that is truly his own. Sizwe perceives his choice between his own card and name and that of the dead man as one between personal dignity and survival itself—unable to remain in the city because of the stamp on his own card, he cannot earn the money to support himself and his family. For them to survive, Sizwe pays out with his conception of his identity and sense of self, but he does not realise this at the time of his decision. Unfortunately, the photographic image is insufficiently sustained, underexposed by a torrent of words and emotion.

The play also suffers from some over-explanation and an inconsistency in the character of Sizwe. As a newcomer to the city from the government established 'homeland', Sizwe is unfamiliar with the difficulty of finding work or living quarters without the appropriate stamps in his book. Buntu tediously explains the bureaucracy of influx control, computerised records, permits, licences, Native Commissioners and government living quarters—but Sizwe's illiteracy can explain only a part of his innocence. It seems, finally, unbelievable, particularly when he is utterly confused by the opportunity of changing his name. While this underscores his association between name, identity, dignity and manhood it reaches a preposterous level when Sizwe becomes confused by the imagined effect a change of name will have on his relationship with his wife and children. Near the end of the play he states: "A black man stay out of trouble? Impossible, Buntu. Our skin is trouble." This rings a bit hollow coming from a man so naive and backward, one who has seemingly never before experienced the impact of the laws and regulations.

Sizwe Bansi is also somewhat formless and rambling at points: the improvisational monologue at the opening lasts anywhere from forty-five to seventy minutes, depending on the performance. At one time in its evolution in South Africa the play ran as long as four hours, and not until first performed in England was a text committed to paper.

While discursiveness might seem an inherent danger of the collaborative and improvisational process which resulted in these plays, *The Island* is structurally integrated, tightly controlled and sharply focused. This is a bit surprising for, while both plays are intensely personal, *The Island* especially reflects the experiences of the actors. The title refers to Robben Island, South Africa's maximum security prison for blacks political prisoners, which blacks refer to as The University, or The School of Man. Kani and Ntshona use their own names in *The Island* and refuse a curtain call. Throughout the play they refer to their wives and friends in their hometown, New Brighton. Also, the presentation of *Antigone* in the prison is based on fact: in 1964 the Serpent Players prepared a production of the play and on the day of its performance their Haemon was arrested and sent to Robben Island—where he later performed a one-man *Antigone*. These factors would seem to dispose the actors to excessive indulgence and emotion, but this is carefully avoided.

The Island is filled with action and details underscoring the inhumane conditions and treatment of the prisoners. Mere confinement and hard labour is insufficient punishment. Dressed in shorts, the inmates are made to look like the boys their keepers would make them. They wear no number that might give them even a semblance of individuality. When a guard enters their cell the prisoners immediately drop their shorts to the floor—standard humiliating procedure, one assumes. In the opening mime sequence each man fills a wheelbarrow with sand and empties it in front of his companion. Their futile task will never end. Pushing even an empty wheelbarrow demands a Sisyphusian triumph of determination over exhaustion. Winston counts the remaining days of John's sentence by tens and they fly past, in contrast to the numerous but finite days of imprisonment that define the rest of Winston's life. From the opening action at the sandpit to the closing mime in which John and Winston trot about the stage, hands and legs chained, the play has a contagious and accelerating rhythm.

Both plays contain aurally haunting moments: a siren blasts as John and Winston exit; Sizwe repeats again and again his new identification number and the repetition becomes an insistent chant, so earnest that one understands the daily significance of this number to the man. Both plays also use the audience. Styles's opening monologue is openly addressed to it and he is assisted at one point by a volunteer. While this is generally a self-indulgent device, there is none of the usual tension and anxiety when a spectator is startled from his voyeurism and asked to relinquish his anonymity. *Antigone* is presented to us, the audience of inmates and prison dignitaries. We are the citizens ruled by Creon and share in the responsibility for his sentencing of Antigone: "Take her to The Island."

The acting of Kani and Ntshona is energetic, sustained, and finally overwhelming. Their faces and heads are shaven: the spectator can follow the wrinkle of every smile, frown or twitch, literally, from ear to ear. In the mime scenes in each play the actors are precise and convincing, each action honed to its basic and graceful components. One never struggles to understand what it is they are doing, as so frequently happens with unskilled pantomimists. Playing both a factory worker and a foreman in *Sizwe Bansi*. Kani effects an instantaneous change and contrast between the two, comparable to that of Marcel Marceau's "David and Goliath." Here, however, one knows that Mr 'Baas' Bradley will be the ultimate victor despite the laughs Styles contrives at his expense.

Kani and Ntshona rely on their voices, faces and hands for expression. They also control and use every muscle in their bodies. They exhibit a kind of Grotowski malleability and one wonders about the extent of his influence on their work. While it was not until 1970 that Fugard received a copy of *Towards a Poor Theatre* and notes of Grotowski's New York lectures, nine years previously he had formulated "the pure theatre experience", which reveals his spirit kindred to that of the Polish director: "The actor and the stage, the actor on the stage. Around him is space, to be filled with meaning, using words and sounds, and at moments when all else fails him, including my words, the silence itself."

In both plays, but particularly in *Sizwe Bansi*, Kani is loquacious and has a flamboyant and urbane air about him. His characters are agile, quick-witted and sense the larger socio-political forces controlling their lives. Such insight does not make these characters even more frustrated, but gives them something with which to survive—a controlled outrage, a glimmer of sustaining hope. The characters played by Ntshona are less complex, more uncertain, direct and in immediate and overwhelming contact with their suffering. They are less able to understand their pain or intellectualise about its source. His characters are often inarticulate and rely on frequent and excited gestures to assist their speech. The differences between these two kinds of characters are similar to those between Morrie and Zach in Fugard's *The Blood Knot*—brothers differentiated by their psychological and intellectual make-up as well as the shade of their skin.

Fugard's characters are never the one-dimensional stick figures implied by those who see these plays as political tracts. *The Island* is the story of political prisoners, but also of the loving bond between two men. Styles's monologue in *Sizwe Bansi* on the Ford plant seems to imply an indictment of the capitalistic base, yet in his struggle for some degree of independence and integrity he turns to private enterprise. True, he has few alternatives, but he aggressively protects his investment from the curiosity and reach of a customer's children. His sales pitch is perfected, and his customers buy more photos than they really need or intend. Styles's favourite photo is the family portrait: "Good for business. Lot of people and they all want copies."

Fugard has stated that he is addicted to actors, who have been an obsession throughout his career. He implies that it is for the actor that he writes. In both these plays he has helped create original and full-bodied characters equal to those in his previous work. These collaborations also resemble Fugard's previous plays in at least two other ways—the characters, despite their plight, maintain an infectious and incisive sense of humour, and variations on the play-within-the-play technique are used.

Whatever the desperate conditions of their lives, Fugard's characters are able to laugh—at themselves and their surroundings. Sometimes it is the laugh that keeps one from the brink of insanity, but more often it is a simpler bemusement, an ability to see and embrace incongruities. John and Winston recount their confinement in a paddy wagon: cramped in the back of the van for hours, given no chance to rest or use a toilet, John eventually pisses in his pants. They now laugh at the incident, but it is yet another example of their inhumane treatment. During a furtive rehearsal, Winston dons Antigone's wig and breasts and John is wracked with paroxysms of laughter. The humour is stock, but it also serves another function. Winston demands that they switch roles, but he is unable to laugh when John dons the woman's dress: "Because behind all this rubbish is me, and you know it's me. You think those bastards out there won't know it's you?" As usual, Winston is slow to understand the meaning of this, but the audience is not. Man's dignity is transcendent. Appearances—shorts, shaven heads, white cloaks and smiling faces—do not define one's manhood.

Fugard's characters often engage in self-conscious play to escape themselves or their wretched environments, and their fantasies may lead to an epiphany of self-recognition. Indeed, in a pervasive and painful sense black South Africans are forced to play a role—that of the happy, contented and obeisant semi-human he is thought to be. Ntshona has stated, "Life is a game in South Africa." In *Sizwe Bansi* the visit of Henry Ford forces the white managers of the factory to play the kowtowing role which Styles had learned by rote, "I saw them play my role for life and I couldn't laugh."

In all of Fugard's plays the imagination is a certain road to an equitable and happy world of dreams. In *The Blood Knot*, Morrie and Zach relive their childhood in an escapist ride in an imaginary car. Milly and her lodgers in *People are Living There* give a party at which, she insists, they must have a good time (whether or not they actually do). Lena pretends to understand the words of the old African speaking a foreign language in *Boesman and Lena*. In *Statements after an Arrest under the Immorality Act* the lovers explain how they would spend their last forty-three cents on a day with no tomorrow.

Sometimes characters play by intentionally deceiving others: in *Hello and Goodbye* Johnnie leads Hester to believe their father is still alive; in *Sizwe Bansi* the foreman is dependent on Styles for the translation of his instructions to the "boys" and, by Styles's cunning, is made a dupe in the process. In the photography studio, Robert strolls down a make-believe avenue lined with imaginary office buildings, a cigarette in his hand, a pipe in his mouth. John and Winston have a nightly ritual of placing imaginary telephone calls from their cell to their friends back home.

The presentation of *Antigone*, however, is a return to the conventional use of a formal play-within-the-play and its use is more calculated than playful: insight and comprehension have preceded rather than followed the act of play. The parallel between Antigone, John and Winston is clear: whatever the higher law might be, each has contravened the inhuman, immoral and arbitrary law of the state and is held accountable. This use of a political play within a larger political play raises the question of the relationship between art and politics. Can art stimulate a plodding evolutionary process of change? Fugard, Kani and Ntshona have no answers; they can only reflect their lives. They have sometimes found themselves in large cities in foreign lands wondering why they left South Africa, suspecting, perhaps, that they should work only at home. In fact their instinct to tour these plays is correct; they have determined to share their work with others around the world for the simple reason that they are performing artists and have a provocative and sensitive statement to make.

Antigone is not saved, nor Creon deposed, but a statement is made—a dramatisation, not a call to arms. The mere ability and strength to make such a statement marks a change from the impotence of Fugard's previous plays. There is a clear shift from the complete powerlessness of *The Blood Knot* in which Zach has no choices and Morrie has some, but does not take them. Mary Benson, an exiled South African, has written, "the characters in Fugard's plays are vital metaphors of human survival." They endure, without self-pity. In *Sizwe Bansi* and *The Island*, however, survival is not simply the result of Promethean forbearance or saintly patience. The characters of these two plays begin to take an active hand, however tentative, in their own fate and future. Styles has opened a business and Sizwe breaks the law in order to support himself and his family. There is no call for revolutionary upheaval. For the time being at least, Sizwe uses the system for his own benefit; though somewhat dim-witted he is not impotent, nor as pathetic as Milly, Lena or Zach. In *The Blood Knot*, the brothers are passive, saved by fate from a confrontation with a white woman. In *The Island*, John and Winston openly present *Antigone* to the prison dignitaries. Characters have developed a sense of pride and are even willing to defy the laws—Winston was imprisoned for burning his passbook in front of a police station.

Since *Sizwe Bansi* and *The Island* are collaborations it is impossible to attribute changes from the earlier plays to a change in Fugard's perceptions. Indeed, this may suggest that the changes are not of his own making. He has been working with improvised theatre since 1967. Although useful, collaboration has been a stage of his development which he has now left to return to the privacy (and security?) of pencil and blank paper. He admits that collaboration does not always allow the opportunity to aver the personal statements he wants to make, "Yes, there is some difference between what I want to say and what we have said." *Sizwe Bansi* and *The Island* are more optimistic and hopeful than Fugard's own vision.

Some critics have complained that the material of *Sizwe Bansi* is well known by now and that nothing new has been added. It is true that we have heard before the plea for dignity, "I'm a man brother", and know, intellectually at least, the horror of prison life. However, *Sizwe Bansi* and *The Island* make us experience these deeply. They authenticate experience outside our own. The subjects are far from hackneyed within the context of these plays because they are so forcefully driven by felt experience. These plays *are* well known in one very important sense—they are human statements, not political treatises; we respond to them immediately.

The Island and *Sizwe Bansi is Dead* appear so pervasively political because the reality, the milieu, in which they are rooted, is so overtly political. Our society is equally political, though less obviously so because of its subtle (but perhaps more insidious) benign neglect, and protestations of normality, equality and legitimacy.

HILARY SEYMOUR

[Artistic Ambivalence in *Sizwe Bansi Is Dead*]†

* * *

There emerge two contradictory messages in the play: a cry of outraged human dignity stemming from the indignities of the urban situation confronting Sizwe Bansi (a cry echoed in Styles's earlier commentary on his work routine at the factory) and a plea for patient

† From *Race and Class* 21.3 (1980): 284–88. Reprinted by permission of the Institute of Race Relations, London.

endurance on the part of Styles the photographer, a plea which at moments does not escape the charge of complacency. The nature of these contradictions is inevitable, for they are embedded in the liberal position itself. The cries of outrage against the alienating conditions of the South African wage-labour system have to be balanced against the more persistent voices of accommodation. Contradictions also occur *within* the fragmented consciousness of individual characters such as Sizwe and Styles, who contain within themselves different and opposing voices.

Sizwe, in contrast to his customary tone of patient perplexity, does make one direct appeal to the audience for sympathetic understanding of his simple, indeed simplistic, plea: the right to urban employment and identity.

> What's happening in this world, good people? Who cares for who in this world? Who wants who?
> Who wants me, friend? What's wrong with me? I'm a man. I've got eyes to see. I've got ears to listen when people talk. I've got a head to think good things. What's wrong with me? (*Starts to tear off his clothes.*) Look at me! I'm a man. I've got legs. I can run with a wheelbarrow full of cement! I'm strong! I'm a man. Look I've got a wife, I've got four children. How many has he made, lady? (*The man sitting next to her.*) Is he a man? What has he got that I haven't . . . ?

The questions he puts to the audience are purely emotional appeals to 'man's better nature', a key concept in liberal philosophy, which at this point in the play manifests itself as an undefined existential assumption to be shared by actor and audience. Audiences are 'involved', to the extent that they are asked to 'feel' for the plight of Sizwe and participate in an emotional and abstract ritual of idealised liberal brotherhood.

At this point Sizwe shows himself to be a victim of acute alienation. Underlying the apparent simplicity of the Man's plea can be detected deep psychological malaise. First, Sizwe's or the Man's initial assertion is negative, self-deprecating, almost apologetic. The contrast in tone with Sipho Sepamla's 'At the dawn of another day' again springs to mind. Secondly, he sees himself through the eyes of others. Where the 'i' of Sepamla's poem is self-defining, the 'I' of Sizwe's appeal is defined for him by others. He is implicitly trapped in labels and categories that bear little relation to his experiences and perceptions of the world around him. It is only when he is drunk that a more authentic response surfaces, as I have already noted. There is a rupture between individual sensibility and its expression on the one hand, and societal norms and expectations on the other, where the former represent class interests fundamentally at odds with the latter. Liberal rhetoric and ritual appeals to universal brotherhood can only 'dodge' this issue. Thirdly, not only does Sizwe lament his degraded status in the eyes of the ruling white bourgeoisie, he also laments, though he does not understand, the state of alienation that reduces black urban workers to fragmented islands of defensive and exclusive material self-interest. The lesson of self-interest, as the best strategy for survival in a ruthless and reified world, is the one that Buntu attempts to teach his unwilling pupil; it is the same lesson that Leah preaches to Xuma in Peter Abrahams' *Mine Boy*, and it receives the same instinctively hostile reception.

Behind Sizwe's appeals and the dialogue that follows, we find a thinly-veiled indictment of the Pass System. But there is more at stake: Sizwe and Buntu are less than 'man', not simply because of their colour but because of their class. The problem of alienation is not simply a problem of colour. Replacing Baas Bradley and other 'bigger bosses' by black counterparts would not change the real face of capitalism.

In the closing lines of the play, Robert/Sizwe is asked to smile. Styles is in his position behind the camera, but the audience is left feeling uneasy about Robert Zwelinzima's precarious urban future and the long-term outcome of the false identity game Buntu persuades him to play. Styles's final message to Robert carried more than a literal meaning; for him 'smile' involves the adoption of a mask and identification with it. It also means accepting a split personality, torn between a public image and a suppressed private reality with which it is inevitably at odds. The devisers of the play have themselves exercised caution in the focus they give to the situations and characters they have chosen to sketch on to the silence of the stage. However, this may paradoxically explain the acclaim with which middle-class audiences in the West, and indeed elsewhere, have received the play. At times, the laughter is a little too light, the smiles a little too thin; for ultimately neither laughter nor smiles are adequate even if ambivalent responses to the painful realities of a strife-torn land.

The play belongs to a liberal tradition which is both international and national.

By way of conclusion, I wish to focus on certain ideological affinities 'Sizwe Bansi is Dead' shares with two earlier South African novels, namely Alan Paton's *Cry the beloved country* and Peter Abraham's *Mine Boy*. The perspective of these writers is that of the liberal visionary. (In this respect it is misleading to argue that *Mine Boy* is a proletarian novel whose plot displays a marxist perspective on life, just as it is misleading to discuss 'Sizwe Bansi is Dead' as though it carried a politically radical message.)

1   The humanitarian impulse is uppermost in the characters presented sympathetically to audience or reader. Characters like the Reverend Stephen Kumalo, Xuma, and Sizwe Bansi constantly appeal to the better side of human nature—an existential assumption never defined or contextually specified.

2   The message of the liberal visionary writer is reformist, often at odds with the reality described. It is a message which papers over cracks which in reality threaten the whole edifice. The vision of society, in this kind of literature, is static and pessimistic with regard to

material conditions and progress. Appeals are made to the emotions
at the expense of reason. Such appeals gloss over hard social realities
by a dubious process of sublimation and idealisation. Pessimism with
regard to material progress is offset by directing readers' and audiences' attention to spiritual or material fantasy worlds, in which problems miraculously disappear.

3   To carry the reformist message, everyman figures and ostensibly
universal types are frequently used. Thus, Sizwe Bansi is referred to
as 'the Man' and Xuma as 'the man' who comes 'from the north'. The
Reverend Stephen Kumalo is, par excellence, the suffering Christian
pilgrim and a direct descendant of John Bunyan's allegorical hero. The
novel, however, is not allegorical but borrows from the later traditions
of social realism. Social contexts, periods and places are all to a limited
extent particularised and specified, though they lack the vivid situa-
tional immediacy that characterises the work of such writers as Alex
La Guma. The reformist message produces a tension of modes and
methods in the three works cited for comparison.

4   Great emphasis is attached to the importance of individual morality. Characters held up for our approval are usually those who
accommodate themselves, in one way or another, to a status quo in-
herently inimical to their material interests.

Thus we meet the paradox of the cult of the individual given literary
expression in contexts clearly inimical to individual self-fulfilment.
Ndotsheni (Natal), Claremont (Johannesburg), Malay Camp (Johannesburg), and New Brighton (Port Elizabeth) are shown to be environments, in which the practice of a privatised or minority code of
liberal ethics becomes problematic to say the least. The treatment of
Ndotsheni in Alan Paton's *Cry the beloved country* is an interesting
example of the failure of the liberal position to connect the superstructure to the social and economic bases of society. Stephen Kumalo's
moral code, romantic pastoral attachment to the land and the 'tribe'
and his repeated lament over the rural exodus to the towns are typical
of the ahistorical notion that individual moral precept can change social conditions and that morals make men, rather than men morals.
Kumalo's, and by extension the author's moral vision, ignore: (a) the
historical background of the area. In Natal 'the use by the settlers of
state power to force the African peasantry to become workers', by de-
priving them of their land and liberty, had led to the Bambata Rebellion of 1906, in which 'some 4,000 Africans and 25 whites were killed
in the fighting'. (b) that the commercial success of John Jarvis and his
kind depends on the continuing exploitation and expropriation of rural
black labour, deprived of their ancestral farm lands and forced into
either a rural or an urban wage labour system. Thus, Stephen Kumalo's
moral injunctions have no historical or practical validity, except perhaps in heaven.

Kumalo, Xuma and Sizwe Bansi are models for the moral message
their creators use them to convey. They are long-suffering, passive and
accommodating by nature. At the same time, they often exhibit feelings of helpless moral anguish and intense loneliness. The authors'

literary pursuit of the cult of the individual tends to isolate characters from group experience. We see little of Xuma in his work situation, more attention being given to the romantic love theme. Sizwe and Xuma do assert the right to urban identity and residence, a position Alan Paton would appear to shy away from in *Cry the beloved country*. Nevertheless, Xuma offers himself as a sacrificial lamb to the legal and penal machinery of a system he has labelled unjust. Motivated by personal loyalty to his white liberal brother, he contemplates an act of futile heroism that can serve no social function. Ironically, considerations of colour override those of class. True sacrifice, argues Kihika, the freedom fighter in Ngugi's *A grain of wheat*, should have a practical objective and impact.

It is interesting to note that Athol Fugard has linked his political and artistic position and his responses to that position with those of Alan Paton, who, par excellence, represents South African liberalism:

> I think I can go on producing plays under segregation (mixed audiences are not allowed) even admitting some non-whites to private readings. But eventually I may have to take a stand like Paton's (i.e., a certain degree of political commitment). We are in a corner. And all we can do is dodge here and push there. And under it all there's a backwash of guilt.

No matter how well or effectively it is presented, the liberal position tends to be negative in its impact. It is a position caught in the web of its own contradictions. As a response to the South African situation it remains inadequate, characterised by 'dodges' and evasions. Kumalo performs a salvage operation for members of his family lost in urban iniquity and tries to hold family and 'tribe' together in a Christian, pastoral vision, which is blind to past and present realities. Xuma, like some latterday Don Quixote, dedicates his life to a personal crusade waged in the name of universal brotherly love. Sizwe/Robert smiles at a world that robs him of his 'manhood', and Styles asserts his manhood at the price of serving a system whose inhumanity he once deplored.

DENNIS WALDER

The *Statements* Plays†

Towards the end of *The Island*, the second of the three plays published in *Statements* (1974), a large, clumsy black man appears on stage in a wig of frayed rope, a necklace of nails, and a shirt stuffed with false breasts. He is pretending to be the ancient Greek princess Antigone. But we do not laugh. Nor do we laugh when he goes on to deliver Antigone's famous speech, defying the law which has condemned her. For what we are watching is a play-within-a-play: a two-man version of Sophocles's classic work performed by convicts before a prison au-

† From *Athol Fugard* (London: Macmillan, 1984) 75–88. Reprinted by permission of the author.

dience in South Africa's maximum security centre for political offenders, Robben Island. Moreover, our reactions have been anticipated by an earlier scene in the play, during which Winston's first assumption of Antigone's wig and padding has his cell mate John—and us—falling about with laughter. 'You call laughing at me Theatre?' the big man exclaims, resentfully. 'Who cares', comes the reply. 'As long as they' (John sweeps his arm to include both imaginary and real audiences), 'as long as they listen at the end!'

By listening, we may be said to 'witness' the 'statement' made by the play. It is a statement about the injustice of the law which sends men to Robben Island for defying apartheid. But it is also a statement about 'Theatre'. *The Island* makes explicit, and asks us to recognise, the function of drama in a society of struggle and oppression. The play suggests that men may survive the most intolerable conditions if they are able to discover and articulate a meaning for their suffering—a meaning here offered by *Antigone*. In *The Island* a tradition is reactivated (as it was by Anouilh in Nazi-occupied France) which defies the law in the name of the conscience and dignity of man.

Unlike the 'Port Elizabeth' plays, the three *Statements* plays—*Sizwe Bansi Is Dead*, *The Island* and *Statements after an Arrest under the Immorality Act*—all testify to the nature and effects of specific apartheid laws: the pass laws; the laws banning the black opposition, the ANC and PAC; and the so-called 'Immorality Act' (Prohibition of Mixed Marriages Act, 1949). Inevitably, this new explicitness aroused misunderstanding, even hostility, from critics accustomed to find in Fugard's work 'universal', 'spiritual' values: Stanley Kauffmann, who praised these qualities in *Boesman and Lena*, saw *Sizwe Bansi* as 'superficial' and 'only about the troubles of South African blacks'. The *Listener* noted that the first two *Statements* plays 'call for political change, if not for revolutionary action, but they also make us aware that better political systems ultimately depend upon changes of heart'.[1]

But, as George Orwell once remarked, calling for a change of heart rather than a change of structure is *the* alibi of people who do not wish to endanger the status quo. Is this all the *Statements* plays do? The answer is complicated, not least by the fact that the very process of creation behind the two plays, *Sizwe Bansi* and *The Island*, which were 'devised' by Fugard and the black actors John Kani and Winston Ntshona, was in defiance of the authorities, who, in turn, attempted to stifle performances. When *Sizwe Banzi* (original spelling) was first due to appear before an 'open', i.e. multiracial, audience at the Space in Cape Town in 1972, the police forced the management to cancel. And, when they reopened the next night as a (massively enlarged) 'club', two plain-clothes men attempted to intimidate the group, but without success. *The Island* could not be thus named for its early performances at the Space, where it appeared under the obscure but pointed (for those in the know) title, *Die Hodoshe Span*, i.e. 'Hodoshe's

---

1. Stanley Kauffmann, '*Sizwe Bansi* and *The Island*', *New Republic*, 21 Dec. 1974; John Elsom, 'The Condemned', *Listener*, 10 Jan. 1974.

work-team', so named after a Robben Island warder called 'Hodoshe' (literally, 'carrion-fly'). *Sizwe Bansi*, as well as the name of a character, is a Xhosa phrase meaning 'the people are strong'. To avoid censorship, neither play was written down until production—and the recognition which followed—abroad. It is illegal to publish material about conditions upon 'the island' in any case.

When all three *Statements* plays appeared at the Royal Court in London as a 'South African Season' (1973–4), Fugard was accused by the South African cultural attaché of creating 'hundreds of enemies' for his country every night. But by then the astonishing success and attendant publicity gained by the plays had become protection for the playwright and his co-creators, action against whom would then have been an embarrassment outweighing the supposed negative effects of the plays themselves—as was proved when an international outcry forced the authorities to release Kani and Ntshona after imprisonment in the Transkei for anti-Bantustan remarks expressed as part of their performance there.

The third play in the collection, *Statements after an Arrest*, created for, and to some extent with, Yvonne Bryceland, who performed with Fugard in the first version (provided as the opening production of the Space in May 1972), Fugard regards as his own. Certainly it reflects a more private, inward impulse than the other two, anticipating the direction he was to take subsequently, in *Dimetos*; yet it is also, as its title suggests, a 'statement'—of what it means to live within, and try to survive, apartheid. Less direct than *Sizwe Bansi* or *The Island* and, unlike them, dealing with interracial rather than the 'black' experience, it has been less vulnerable to outside pressure. But, again, like the other two plays, it is a radical, 'extreme' work: both in terms of what it says, and how it goes about doing so.

All three *Statements* plays involve extensive mime, narrative disruption, nudity or physical 'exposure', surreal lighting-effects and direct addresses to the audience. This reflects a shift in Fugard's conception of theatre. The 'Port Elizabeth' plays were written in the conventional modern way to show the absurdity of life, the senselessness of ideals and purpose, despite which humanity struggles to survive. But these plays had been, he thought, 'so conventional', involving 'the *writing* of a play . . . *setting* that play in terms of local specifics . . . the actors *assuming* false identities' (Introduction, *Statements*). The *Statements* plays challenge this orthodox procedure, in favour of involving the creative abilities of the performers—their history, experiences, the very shape of their bodies. They are, in Grotowski's terminology, to sacrifice themselves to the spectators so as to inspire in their audience a similar process of psychic discovery—the whole event to take on the intensity and significance of a religious ritual. In the *Statements* plays, Fugard was attempting to participate in the international search for a new theatrical language, initiated by, amongst others, Peter Brook and Jerzy Grotowski. What he achieved was the expression of an everyday experience of suffering and protest by others, which helped ensure the continuity and survival of that protest. Black South African theatre groups whose work began to flourish in the townships from the early seventies testify to this, even as they press for a theatre more explicit and revolutionary than anything Fugard or his co-creators were capable of. Fugard's intervention may have been partial and contradictory; nevertheless it represents a unique attempt to respond to the lives of those from whom his background, upbringing and education (not to mention the laws of the land) were supposed to have excluded him.

How did all this come about? The answer lies in a complex and stirring series of events, the details of which are not yet (if they ever will be) altogether clear. A brief account must suffice. As we have seen, the story began early in 1963, shortly after Fugard's return home from the *Blood Knot* tour—a tour which had made that play and, especially, Zakes Mokae's role in it, a byword in the townships. The playwright was approached by a group of amateur drama enthusiasts in New Brighton, Port Elizabeth, with 'the old, old request', as Fugard confided to his notebooks; 'actually it is hunger. A desperate hunger for meaningful activity—to do something that would make the hell of their daily existence meaningful.'[2] Fugard felt he could not refuse, and so, under his experienced direction, the group (which included a clerk, two teachers, a bus-driver and domestic servants) embarked upon a series of suitably adapted productions of 'classical' works—the first of which, Machiavelli's *The Mandrake*, was hailed locally as a masterpiece of improvisation.

Improvisation was the key to the Serpent Players' practice (their name derived from an abandoned snake pit in which they were offered a space to perform). Within two years, they had gone on to produce cheaply mounted 'township' versions of *Woyzeck*, *The Caucasian Chalk Circle*, *The Father* and *Antigone*, in venues such as St Stephen's church hall, without adequate lighting, seating, props or backstage facilities. Discussion–readings and rehearsals were held where possible after work—in a 'Coloured' kindergarten, or Fugard's own garage, to avoid the restrictions upon interracial activity. Rough working-conditions and the inevitable problems with the race laws were familiar to Fugard from his Sophiatown days. But this was not Johannesburg; and it was after Sharpeville, not before. Nelson Mandela had recently been arrested, and was soon to be convicted of sabotage and conspiracy to overthrow the government. The Players, their relatives and friends (including the Fugards) came under surveillance from the start. In December 1964, days before the opening of their Brecht play, Azdak (Welcome Duru) was arrested. Fugard took over the part, and the performance proceeded. But within months three more members were arrested, including Norman Ntshinga, who was about to play Haemon in *Antigone*. A purge of the Eastern Cape—with its long tradition of black militancy—had begun.

Astonishingly, the Serpent Players did not collapse. Instead, a new phase of 'playmaking', without texts or identifiable authors, began. Brecht's *Messingkauf Dialogues* provided particular inspiration. But it

2. Athol Fugard, *Notebooks, 1960–1972* (New York: Knopf, 1983), p. 81.

was the events of the time which bad overwhelming effect. When Fugard attended Ntshinga's trial (he was accused of belonging to one of the banned opposition movements), the playwright took the actor's wife, blues-singer Mabel Magada, along. She was recognised by an elderly man from New Brighton who had just been sentenced. He took off his coat (his only possession) and gave it to her saying, 'Go to my home. Give this to my wife. Tell her to use it.'[3] This became the Players' first attempt to improvise a play directly out of their own experiences. The whole process was made visible in *The Coat* (1967), 'An Acting Exercise from the Serpent Players of New Brighton', as it was presented to its first audience, a white 'theatre-appreciation group' who had asked to see a sample of their work. They were expecting a comedy. But, since permission for a performance in a 'white area' had only been given on condition that it was not public, that the black actors did not use the toilets in the hall, and that the cast returned home immediately afterwards, the Players decided to put on *The Coat*, using their own names, and a Brechtian actor–presenter who encouraged spectators to think about, and not merely sympathise with, the experiences they were witnessing. From then on, the Serpent Players alternated 'classic' productions with similar improvisations—*Friday's Bread on Monday*, *The Last Bus* and *Sell-out*.

Meanwhile, two new members began to show particular promise: John Kani, who replaced the arrested Ntshinga in *Antigone* in 1965; and Winston Ntshona, an old schoolfriend of Kani's from New Brighton, whom he introduced to the group two years later. Both in their mid twenties, Kani a janitor in the Ford plant, Ntshona a factory laboratory assistant, the men were to have an extraordinary effect upon the depleted Players, their director Fugard, and the theatre. By 1972 they were appearing in their first major production, Camus's *The Just*, retitled *The Terrorists*, at the Space—an experience which led to a remarkable decision. In a country without black drama schools, professional theatre, or the least encouragement to write, direct or act, they decided to become full-time. They had to be classified as Fugard's domestic servants. Within months, their joint commitment issued in the collaborative workshop productions *Sizwe Bansi* and *The Island*.

Fugard's involvement with the Serpent Players led him to recognise the importance of using the stage for a more immediate and direct relationship with the audience than had seemed possible with his own plays. Yet he felt that the 'facts', relevant as they were to the times, which formed the basis of the Players' work, lacked the 'density and ambiguity of truly dramatic images' (Introduction, *Statements*). After the South African tour of *Boesman and Lena*, and cut off from developments abroad by the withdrawal of his passport since 1967, he seemed to have reached an impasse. The arrival of Grotowski's *Towards a Poor Theatre*, along with notes taken at the Polish director's

---

3. As reported by John Kani in conversation with the author, Port Elizabeth, 17 Jan. 1982. See also *Fugard Notebooks*, p. 125. I have drawn on my interview with Kani for much of the information about the Serpent Players here.

New York lectures by Barney Simon and Mary Benson, provided the necessary 'provocation' to develop the more extreme form of improvised, actors' theatre which emerged, almost at once, in the scriptless experiment *Orestes* (1971).

Orestes was developed in collaboration with Yvonne Bryceland and two other white actors in a concentrated spell of private 'rehearsals.' It was based upon the Johannesburg-station bomb protest of 1964, an 'image' of which was 'superimposed' upon the 'image' of Clytemnestra and her two children, Orestes and Electra. In it, Fugard attempted to articulate the nature and effect of violence, encouraging the performers to use apparently trivial actions to suggest the deep, primitive roots of extreme events. A record of the experiment now rests in three large drawing-books, in the form of a 'score' and the developing 'exposures' of its limited, fringe run. The main significance of it lay in the opportunity it afforded Fugard of learning how to release the creative abilities of actors yet further than his work with the Serpent Players had so far permitted.

What Fugard did was to give his actors a 'mandate'—'at least an image, sometimes an already structured complex of images'—to create a performance which, disciplined and repeated until 'fixed' in broad dramatic terms, became the play. The role of writer was not jettisoned, it was transformed. Fugard was now writing '*directly*' into the 'space and silence' of the stage (Introduction, *Statements*). The element of control and discipline maintained by the 'scribe–director' in this process distinguishes Fugard's work from the loose, not to say wildly indulgent practice of other late sixties theatre groups abroad, such as Julian Beck's Living Theatre—whose version of *Antigone* signally failed to turn its white middle-class American audiences into permanent revolutionaries, as was claimed it would. Unlike such works, which exploit liberal uneasiness and make exaggerated claims about the imminent collapse of British or American society, Fugard's *Statements* plays invite understanding, even compassion, rather than facile anger or self-indulgent guilt, while making it quite clear that there is no escape from politics. This is not to deny their limitations, which are the limitations of liberal humanism in the South African situation; nevertheless, as 'statements', they still defy the status quo.

The Island is the most persuasive example of this. It takes us into the heart of the suppressed black opposition, languishing on Robben Island, to affirm brotherhood: '*Nyana we Sizwe!*' The Xhosa rallying-cry ('Son of the land' or, simply, 'People') is uttered by Winston (played by Winston Ntshona) at two critical moments: when the two men help tend each other's wounds at the beginning of the play; and, just before their joint performance of 'The Trial and Punishment of Antigone' at the prison concert, when Winston manages to overcome his resentment that John is to be released. The import is the same, and unmistakable: it is an expression of solidarity which will survive the disappearance of their oppressors. Fugard's continuing interest in the nature of the bonds which tie us one to another has never been more effectively politicized. This is what his collaboration with black actors has brought about. But it was *Sizwe Bansi Is Dead* which first revealed what the blend of creative talent, experience and responsiveness to the daily pains of ordinary black South Africans could provide in the theatre.

Sizwe Bansi began when Fugard came across a photograph of an African smiling broadly; Kani said no black South African would smile like that unless his passbook was in order; later, Ntshona noticed a studio photograph of a smiling man with a pipe in one hand and a cigarette in the other. These images became Fugard's 'mandate' to Kani and Ntshona, who added further details from their own lives, including what was to become the brilliant thirty-minute opening monologue from Kani as a photographer called Styles, who has (like Kani) worked in the Ford plant.

Sizwe Bansi consists of a complex web of monologues, played, as with the other *Statements* plays, entirely by two actors. Kani and Ntshona people their bare stage with what seems like the entire New Brighton community they know, in a *tour de force* of mime, improvised dialogue and remembered gesture. There are no conventional act or scene divisions; transitions are created by word, gesture and, most strikingly, lighting. A table, chair and simple props (camera, display board and a reversible map/city-scape) suggest Styles's studio. The play begins when the dapper young Styles enters his 'studio' and while waiting for business sits down to read his newspaper. He reads aloud from it, adding his own comments. The device defines his sagacity at the same time as it establishes contact with the audience. A news item about the Ford plant leads Styles to recall his days there, notably the preparations for a visit by 'Mr Henry Ford Junior number two'. The panic among the white bosses, the furious sweeping, washing and painting that ensues, and Styles's own role as 'translator' for the Afrikaans foreman, who urges the 'boys' to sing and smile while they work, are all re-enacted in graphic and hilarious detail. The climax of this sequence, which gives a very good idea of the dehumanising conditions of work in the plant, comes when 'Ford number two', the biggest boss of them all, walks in—and straight out again. Styles decides to leave and become his own boss: he has seen what it is like to fawn before others. So he sets up in business with his 'strong-room of dreams. The dreamers? My people. The simple people, who you never find mentioned in the history books'.

Just as we begin to wonder where all this is leading, Winston Ntshona enters. In contrast to Styles, he is hesitant, ill-at-ease. He has come for a 'snap' to send to his wife back in the Ciskei Bantustan. Styles prepares the man for entry into his 'dream' by seating him before the cityscape, a cigarette in one hand. Just as the photo is being taken, the man, beaming innocently, reaches into his pocket and produces his pipe—so that he seems to be smoking with both hands. The moment usually brings the house down. Like the greatest comedy, it is essentially simple—and sad, too: this rural illiterate will never realise his dream. Styles persuades him to have a 'movie' or action photograph; when the flash goes off, there is a blackout except for a single spot on 'Robert' (Ntshona), who dictates his letter to his wife, a device which reveals his history to us. His true name is Sizwe Bansi, and he recounts how he came to Port Elizabeth for the work unobtainable in the Bantustan. Lacking the necessary permit, he called on a man named Buntu for help. The play shifts yet again into a new dimension, and the scene in which Buntu (played by a sober, serious Kani) explains to Sizwe the consequences of not having a passbook in order.

This allows for a graphic account of the whole panoply of pass laws, labour permits, travel limitations, residence restrictions and so on which apply to black South Africans. 'Why is there so much trouble?' asks Sizwe, pathetically. Buntu's reply is to tell of the funeral of Outa Jacob, an itinerant farmworker left by his white employer to die: 'That's it brother. The only time we'll find peace is when they dig a hole for us and press our face to the earth.' Buntu then takes Sizwe to a 'shebeen' and, as they leave it, drunk, Buntu relieves himself on what he thinks is a pile of rubbish. But it is a dead man. He panics, but Sizwe cries out, 'Would you leave me lying there . . . ?' Buntu, who can read, notices that the dead man's passbook is valid; so they take it, abandoning the body. This is Sizwe's chance; he can take on the dead man's identity. But Sizwe, drunkenly self-righteous and stubborn, does not want to surrender his name. He is a man, not a ghost. In demonstration, he lowers his trousers and grasps his genitals. But Buntu persuades him that it is better to lose his identity and, implicitly, his manhood, to survive. With Sizwe's photo pasted in it, Robert Zwelinzima's passbook becomes his own, and—'Sizwe Bansi . . . is dead'. Buntu rehearses Sizwe in his new identity, taking on a variety of roles to ensure Sizwe can 'prove' he is Robert. The trick cannot keep him out of trouble for ever: 'Our skin is trouble.' But he will try it. The 'letter' comes to an end as 'Robert' returns to his 'movie' pose, Styles once again behind the camera, uttering the last words: 'Now smile, Robert. . . . Smile'. A camera flash and blackout fixes this final image in the audience's mind. But it is a deeply ironic image: we have been taken behind the black man's smiling face, and we now know what it hides.

John Kani reported that Fugard 'told us we need our art, not propaganda'.[4] There *is* propaganda in *Sizwe Bansi*: in the 'facts' of apartheid which are reported; in the assumption, plainly expressed, that only the blacks can help each other. Indeed, the liberal view that there is always another side to the question gets short shrift in these plays —as does a certain kind of liberal, when Styles mockingly refers to Buntu as someone always helping people: 'If that man was white they'd call him a liberal.' Of course Buntu *does* help; yet his help is no more than a temporary alleviation of the problem. *Sizwe Bansi* takes sides, suggesting that, even if survival is possible, life on these terms is questionable.

Nevertheless, any propaganda effect is subsumed within the art— which is primarily an art of performance. The actors and co-creators

4. *Guardian* (interview), 8 Jan. 1974.

earned the plaudits with which they were showered (*Sizwe Bansi* brought them, amongst other awards, a joint 'Tony'). Kani and Ntshona seemed inseparable from *Sizwe Bansi*, which thereby gained an authenticity absent from other 'political' drama of the time. Does this mean that the play can only operate successfully with the actors who helped create it and whose experiences it embodied? Time will tell, although it has already proved possible for others to perform the work. Moreover, the first, predominantly white-liberal audiences in South Africa and abroad, whose favourable responses perhaps ensured quick and widespread acceptance, have been succeeded by, for example, a New Brighton audience in which there was a near-riot as people reacted 'with disbelief, panic and fear that these things were actually being talked about out loud and then there was joy, that this was a celebration of small things in their lives'.[5]

'Celebration' is an important word in Fugard's vocabulary. It highlights the humour, the intense enjoyment of simple pleasures, which lifts *Sizwe Bansi* and its immediate successor out of the bleakness and pessimism they also suggest. If *Sizwe Bansi* shows what everyday life is like for black township people struggling to survive, *The Island* shows what happens when, as they must, they fall into trouble. 'Our skin is trouble.' In both plays, acting a part is a means for survival: the boundaries between life and art are redrawn. Like *Sizwe Bansi*, *The Island* evolved out of the experiences of its co-creators. Not that either Fugard (who once again provided the initial 'mandate' in the form of accumulated notes and ideas about Robben Island) or Kani or Ntshona had ever been to the notorious prison. But they were told about it by the Serpent Players, notably Welcome Duru and Norman Ntshinga, who served time there; and about a two-man version of *Antigone* (the play in which he was about to perform when arrested) which Ntshinga arranged.

*   *   *

5. *Observer Magazine* (interview), 4 Dec. 1983. A full account of this event is given in *A Night at the Theatre*, ed. Ronald Harwood (London: Methuen, 1983).

Wole Soyinka

WOLE SOYINKA

Author's Note to *Death and the King's Horseman*†

This play is based on events which took place in Oyo, ancient Yoruba city of Nigeria, in 1946. That year, the lives of Elesin (Olori Elesin), his son, and the Colonial District Officer intertwined with the disastrous results set out in the play. The changes I have made are in matters of detail, sequence and of course characterisation. The action has also been set back two or three years to while the war was still on, for minor reasons of dramaturgy.

The factual account still exists in the archives of the British Colonial Administration. It has already inspired a fine play in Yoruba (*Oba Wàjà*) by Duro Ladipo. It has also misbegotten a film by some German television company.

The bane of themes of this genre is that they are no sooner employed creatively than they acquire the facile tag of 'clash of cultures', a prejudicial label which, quite apart from its frequent misapplication, presupposes a potential equality *in every given situation* of the alien culture and the indigenous, on the actual soil of the latter. (In the area of misapplication, the overseas prize for illiteracy and mental conditioning undoubtedly goes to the blurb-writer for the American edition of my novel *Season of Anomy* who unblushingly declares that this work portrays the 'clash between old values and new ways, between western methods and African traditions'!) It is thanks to this kind of perverse mentality that I find it necessary to caution the would-be producer of this play against a sadly familiar reductionist tendency, and to direct his vision instead to the far more difficult and risky task of eliciting the play's threnodic essence.

One of the more obvious alternative structures of the play would be to make the District Officer the victim of a cruel dilemma. This is not to my taste and it is not by chance that I have avoided dialogue or situation which would encourage this. No attempt should be made in production to suggest it. The Colonial Factor is an incident, a catalytic incident merely. The confrontation in the play is largely metaphysical,

† From *Death and the King's Horseman* (London: Methuen, 1975) 3–4. Copyright © 1975 by Wole Soyinka. Reprinted by permission of W. W. Norton and Melanie Jackson Agency, L.L.C.

contained in the human vehicle which is Elesin and the universe of the Yoruba mind—the world of the living, the dead and the unborn, and the numinous passage which links all: transition. *Death and the King's Horseman* can be fully realised only through an evocation of music from the abyss of transition.

WOLE SOYINKA

Towards a True Theatre†

There were strange theatrical sights in Kampala. Two marvels essentially—a theatre (the structure), and a performance. That I elect to call attention to these two excruciating events is not because I wish to denigrate the efforts of an obviously prestige-conscious community, but to indicate the dangers of resigning the initial impetus for a creative institution to the death kiss of passionate amateurs. The building itself is an embodiment of the general misconception of the word 'theatre'. Theatre, and especially, a 'National Theatre', is never the lump of wood and mortar which architects splash on the landscape. We heard of the existence of a National Theatre and ran to it full of joy and anticipation. We discovered that there was no theatre, there was nothing beyond a precious, attractive building in the town centre. But even within that narrow definition of the word, we had expected an architectural adventurousness—Kampala is after all, a comsopolis— so we felt justified in expecting from the theatre, not only a sense of local, but of international developments in the theatrical field. What we found was a doll's house, twin-brother to our own National Museum. There were cushioned spring-back seats—I approved this, having nothing against comfort—but it was disconcerting to find a miniature replica of a British provincial theatre, fully closed in—another advantage this, extraneous noise at least was eliminated; there were vast corridors round the auditorium (for gin and the attendant small talk), the total corridors space was more than the auditorium; the toilets were sumptuous—there were good reasons for this we soon found, understanding for the first time the meaning of a wet performance. The stage? Well, no one could complain of the efficiency. And there were large rehearsal rooms located in the theatre whose constant utilization appeared to be classes in Ballroom Dancing, led by Indians in 22-inch bottom trousers.

There was one more sample of 'atmospherics'. Lining the walls of the foyer were posters (from *Look Back in Anger* and earlier) which made you think that the New Shakespeare Theatre Company was touring East Africa. A closer look reveals however that these posters were three years older than the completed theatre. And photographs of

† From *Art, Dialogue and Outrage: Essays on Literature and Culture* (Ibadan, Nigeria: New Horn Press, 1988) 3–6. Copyright © 1982, 1988, 1993 by Wole Soyinka. Used by permission of Pantheon Books, a division of Random House, Inc., and Melanie Jackson Agency, L.L.C.

Richardson, Olivier and others of the Old Brigade—tarnished slightly
from a long stand in the agents' shop-windows of Piccadilly, provided
the last word in imitativeness without the substance.

We were, however, fairly honest, and we soon fell to minding the
beam in our own eyes. There is the Arts Theatre of our University
College, Ibadan which possesses not even the outward deception of
the Kampala structure, and cannot boast practicalities such as venti-
lation or sound-proofing. As if the original crime was not enough, a
grant of some thousands of pounds was expended, as recently as a year
ago (1961) on new curtains and a few symbols of theatrical 'arrival'.
Interference from student radiograms and cross-balcony yells did not
activate the financial imagination into worthier ways of spending this
money. Motor-cars, indifferent to inadequate barriers, continue to
punctuate the actor's lines with roars. It did not matter that audience
enjoyment was, and still is, constantly punctured by arid saxophone
blasts from a competing highlife ball. No, not all these considerations
could persuade the controlling committee to spend the grant on erecting a barn somewhere beyond the depredations of college neighbour-
liness, disembowelling the present bulk entirely and transferring the
gadgets to the new, adaptable space where actor and audience may
liberate their imagination.

For it still astonishes me that those who planned the University had
the sense to isolate the chapels from the distractions of the ungodly,
but not the foresight to place the theatre beyond the raucousness of
student lungs.

And yet, there is the irony. There is a larger sense of theatre here,
even of a National Theatre, than we found in Kampala. Of the two
shows which we saw there, the less said the better. In Ibadan at least,
the students, in spite of frequent misguidedness, have at last taken
the theatre to the people. This has been due to the dedication of one
or two staff members especially. Conscious, one hopes, of the static
imposition of the Arts Theatre, they developed sufficient enthusiasm
among the student dramatic team to undertake two highly successful
tours of folk theatre. It is irrelevant that the plays from which the
shows were adapted came from European theatre, the success of transformation could be judged from each performance through Ilesha to
Enugu and Port Harcourt. This was some compensation for the long
tradition of formalism in university theatre.

Every event in the theatre, every genuine effort at creative communication, entertainment, escapism, is for me, entirely valid. It is very
easy to sniff for instance at the efforts of the Operatic Groups. What
one must regret is the atmosphere of sterility and truly pathetic pre-
ciosity that it seems to breed. For it must never be forgotten that the
opera was written for a certain society; recreating that society in Ibadan, causing an 'opera expectation' in attitudes is sheer retardation. I
am not of course trying to create a morality for theatrical selectiveness.
The Merry Widow has its place even on the Nigerian scene as a piece
of exoticism; the crime is that it is the forces of *The Merry Widow*
which have upheld what we may call the Arts Theatre mentality. In

the triumph of the Anouilh puff-ball tradition lies the perpetuation of the atrocity, lies the constriction of venturesome rarities like the musical *Lysistrata*—that show would, I contend, have been even more imaginative but for the symbolized tradition of the Arts Theatre. That medium of the arts proscribed true experiment—the result was a cheap English musical all over again, rescued however by genuine effort.

By all means, let us be accommodating—and I say this genuinely— there is room anywhere, and at any stage of development, for every sort of theatre. But when Anouilh and (for God's sake!) Christopher Fry—and Drew in true fusion of the Monolithic World—possess audience mentality and budding student talent in traps from which the British theatre is only slowly extricating itself, then it is probably time for a little intolerance against the octopine symbol of the Arts Theatre. If there appears to be some exaggeration in this, let me merely point out the theatrical age of the local critic, who, on seeing an example of simple space exploitation exclaims in disgust that it is very amateurish for actors to run in and out of the audience! This notice went on to say, '. . . admittedly the Museum grounds are not very suitable for a dramatic performance, in that case it would have been simpler for this group to find a hall in Lagos where their plays can be staged more conveniently'.

When the leading university proudly exhibits and reinforces the Perpendicular theatre, it is hardly surprising that the faithful twice-a-term weekend pilgrim will resent any invasion of his audience privacy!

There is the future, of course, which is what we are really talking about all the time. The only answer to the Perpendicularians was obvious to me from the start—construct an opposition plane. This has always proved more effective than bickering, and this of course still remains the only aim of tentative theatrical movements in the country. But it has become necessary to resort to words because, while the material facilities appear to elude the opposition, they practically beg to be abused at the hands of the inbreeders. One hears rumours of ambitious schemes for propagating—again that dirty word—culture! And the prestige symbol is again, as always, a 'National Theatre'. Since I saw the foundations, I have not dared to move near the completed theatre at Nsukka. Before the 'theatre' of the Nigerian College of Arts, Science and Technology was built, the designers pilgrimaged to the then University College Ibadan, to seek inspiration from Arts Theatre. In vain did a few harrowed producers plead with them to avoid repetition of existing crime—a replica was built and the 'Arts' was superseded in drabness and tawdry. J. K. Randle Hall now—the latest boil —would some imagination have cost it more? And these abortions will continue to rise all over the country, offensive to the eye and repressive of the imagination. It is surely because the structure controls, even manipulates the artist that it is more sensible to assist first of all the creative theatre, or at least—and since we are as in all other things, in a terrible rush and all steps must be taken together—at least look for architectural inspiration among countries with approximate traditions and a longer professional history—or simply use that common ordinary gift of sense and refrain from employing mud-mixers and carpenters to design media which must eventually control or influence the creative intellect.

This is no exaggeration. It has been proved for four years by an amateur group in Ibadan, *The Players of the Dawn*, who, in spite of the intelligence of the leaders, have consistently succumbed to the dictates of the British Council pre-historic structures and are incapable of seeing theatre as an activity which did not petrify with Galsworthy at the start of the century.

No one who is seriously interested in the theatre demands a playground for pushing buttons and operating gaily coloured panels. A university especially should refrain from such expensive pastimes. For this is not America where—to take one example, the Loeb Theatre in Cambridge, Massachussetts—a university theatre is built for five to six million dollars, a stupid amoral example of affluent patronage. Where, pray, is the university sense? But the tinny poor-cousins of this which, to judge from Kampala, Ibadan and Nsukka, will soon exert their calcifying influence over the continent should be stopped now, before Zaria and Ife, and even the National Five-Yearly Never-never Plans follow their example. For, as I have stressed from the beginning, we are not merely talking about the structure now, but of the dubious art to which it must give birth.

ANNEMARIE HEYWOOD

The Fox's Dance: The Staging of Soyinka's Plays†

The reputation of Wole Soyinka rests perhaps most firmly on his work for the theatre. His plays have proved themselves on the stages of three continents. Indeed it can be held that his gifts are essentially dramatic, and that even his poetry and fiction draw their vitality from a dramatizing imagination. His lyrical poetry usually suggests an incantatory voice, or the voice of a character in monologue. *Death in the Dawn*[1] *and Abiku*,[2] for instance, are voiced introspections, monologues, in which the poet's musings are distanced via a persona, an assumed mask and voice which is not entirely that of the poet himself. *Malediction*,[3] *Civilian and Soldier*,[4] and *Dedication*[5] suggest declamation or incantation within a given situation without which they would lack meaning.

† From *Critical Perspectives on Wole Soyinka*, ed. James Gibbs (Washington, D.C.: Three Continents Press, 1980) 130–38. Copyright © 1996 by Lynne Rienner Publishers, Inc. Reprinted by permission of the publisher.
1. *Idanre* (London, Methuen, 1967), p. 10.
2. ibid., p. 28.
3. ibid., p. 55.
4. ibid., p. 53.
5. ibid., p. 24.

Although it is cinematically rather than theatrically conceived, *The Interpreters* too has this dramatic rather than narrative quality.[6] Soyinka surrenders historical, sociological, or biographical sweep for a brisk succession of evocative scenes which range freely through past, present, and future. Sekoni's background, for instance, is established in a montage of brief snippets of dialogue, spanning many months, between two sections of interior monologue, followed by the slightly expanded scene of his return to Ijoha. Soyinka neglects the established techniques of introspection and authorial elucidation for establishing the inner life and the social attitudes of his characters. Instead we have episodes of almost pure dialogue interspersed with vivid evocations of setting rendered in the stylistic register of the character through whose mind they are experienced. Thus Sagoe provides the 'voice' for the satirical, irreverent, and frequently coprophiliac descriptions of the social milieu, whereas Egbo's style dominates the evocations of numinous nature and numinous woman. We find here a central strategy of contrastive characterization built up by the evocation of externals—dialogue, gesture, and mien; yet the characters, even though they are brilliantly defined and differentiated, are not given much depth; nor do they develop significantly. They are in fact masks or voices in an adventure of ideation, a dialectical exposition of possibilities. Like masks, they each represent one possibility only. This may be a complex and profound possibility, but it neither varies nor changes.

Put differently, Soyinka anatomizes the complex situation confronting his representative characters, idealistic and creative young graduates in post-independence Nigeria. They need to 'find new laws for living', and the complexities and ambiguities and choices are fully voiced through their personae. There is no resolution through conflict or action. The two main action set pieces are arranged around two catalytic characters, the Aladura Lazarus and Joe Golder, representing respectively the challenge of the unknowable, and the challenge of the unspeakable. They serve as tests of response. When the exposition is complete, the action stops abruptly in a tableau, each character frozen in an emblematic pose. The reader is left with an intolerable open paradox—'the choice of a man drowning'—a disequilibrium calling for commitment and action.

It is significant to note that the later plays end in this way too. In *A Dance of the Forests* Demoke had actually made a choice in seizing the Half-Child and giving it to the Woman:

> Darkness enveloped me, but piercing
> Through I came
> Night is the choice for the fox's dance.[7]

---

6. I am probably here leaning on the distinction drawn by James Joyce via the young Stephen in *Portrait of the Artist as a Young Man*, where he states that the dramatic writer effaces his own personality from his work, impersonalizes and distances his ideas and emotions in purely imaginary projections.

7. *A Dance of the Forests* (London, O.U.P., 1963), p. 85.

There is no such resolution in the later plays. *Kongi's Harvest* ends in a cacophonic re-statement of the conflict: 'A mixture of the royal music and the anthem rises loudly, plays for a short time, comes to an abrupt halt as the iron grating descends and hits the ground with a loud final clang.' The 'loud final clang', as well as the 'abrupt halt' also close *Madmen and Specialists* which ends with a revolver shot, followed by a brief passage in mime: the beggars' chant 'stops in mid-word and the lights snap out simultaneously'. In *The Road* the dying Professor's peroration adds no insight, merely re-states the enigma, whilst the spinning mask sinks lower and lower 'until it appears to be nothing beyond a heap of cloth and raffia'.

These endings leave us in the air, discomfited and unbalanced, uneasy. Important issues have been raised, yet they are not raised within the framework of a closed system which determines their resolution. The resolution of such issues is what customarily distinguishes tragic action from life. Soyinka, like the dramatists of the absurd, prefers to articulate in an ethical no man's land. The clowning and the paronomasiac dialogue too belong with this genre. Yet Soyinka does not chart private ontological anxiety. His writing remains communal, his concerns social, even political. In this he is, I think, most closely akin to Brecht whose 'sort of theatre, its liveliness and freedom, not so much his purpose or intentions' he was commending as early as 1962.[8]

It cannot be denied, however, that such an open-ended dialectical exposition creates problems for the audience. The critical response to Soyinka has of late been increasingly exasperated. His 'enigmatic obfuscations' have recently been forcefully attacked by Bernth Lindfors.[9] Such attacks are, I believe, demonstrably based on limited or mistaken expectations. Thus Lindfors praises the lucidity of earlier plays which are written in the realist idiom. *The Lion and the Jewel, Brother Jero, The Swamp Dwellers*, and *The Strong Breed* are localized in setting and illusionist in idiom. Here the greatest stylistic problem in staging is likely to be the relatively simple one of complete authenticity in the evocation of a West African locale.

The more weighty plays which take their shape from inner dialectic are sharply criticized by Lindfors. In the progression from *A Dance of the Forests* ('arty structure', 'plotless plot', 'incoherence') via *The Road* ('a defiantly difficult play which makes no compromises with instant intelligibility') to *Madmen and Specialists* ('a multi-faceted cryptograph') he diagnoses a growing 'tendency towards meaningless frivolity which robs his work of any serious implication' (about the very last thing to fault in this profoundly nihilistic exploration of the deadly follies of the political animal!) and wonders for whom these plays are written—'just for Westernized Yoruba eggheads . . . for a cosmopolitan international elite, or . . . simply for himself?'

Whilst attacking the 'histrionic razzle-dazzle' of the basic articula-

8. Dennis Duerden and Cosmo Pieterse, *African Writers Talking* (London, Heinemann, 1972), p. 173.
9. In a conference paper read to the Association for Commonwealth Literature and Language Studies, Makerere, 1974.

tion, Lindfors concedes that even the plays he condemns make brilliant theatre. Soyinka, he says, 'can apply a very slick surface to the roughest or least substantial of narrative foundations', and his 'plotless plots . . . could be enjoyed as a series of well-paced theatrical happenings' without making much sense. This is, surely, not quite good enough. The difficulty of the obscure plays arises from their idiom, or basic strategy, which is not well served by illusionist production and 'character'-acting inviting empathy. These plays are best plotted for production as masques or cabaret, with characters conceived as masks, dialogue as choral, movement and gesture as emblematic.

A Dance of the Forests appears incoherent only if one's expectations are geared to narrative articulation and character development. But this play is a spectacle and more closely akin to Comus, The Magic Flute, or Ravel's L'Enfant et les Sortilèges than to, say, A Midsummer Night's Dream, comparison with which it might invite. The mode in production should be surrealist and shun that leaden mimesis which can only stultify the poetic exposition of meaning.

Of all Soyinka's plays it is theatrically the most demanding. It requires a set and scenery which can effect the transition from one world to another by almost instantaneous transformations. A separately lit back scene is necessary for the transitions from forest to primeval glade, and from forest to the court of Mata Kharibu. The scenery must offer instant visual clues to the order of reality it evokes: drably 'natural' for the mundane forest with its sound-effects of 'beaters' and engine noise; supernatural and mysterious for timeless spirit-forest which is co-extensive with the former, but charged with mystery, power, and significance, particularly in the moist primeval glade which forms the setting for the ordeal; and lastly the barbaric splendour of Mata Kharibu's court in the past.

Similarly, the characters are drawn from four distinct levels of abstraction or 'reality', a number of them appearing as themselves, but in different forms, at two levels. Costume, make-up, and gesture therefore have to be contrived to make such crossers of the boundaries instantly recognizable, whilst at the same time suggesting the nature of their change.

Within the mundane forest we meet three orders of being: present-day humans; two revenants who must be instantly recognizable as such; and, in certain scenes, Murete the tree-imp who belongs to the spirit world. In the numinous forest we meet three of the humans; the same humans in a previous incarnation; the revenants as ghosts, and as incarnations; and a host of spirits, some of whom assume temporary disguises. The terrible Triplets, grotesque symbolic masks, are perhaps yet another category. The forest-dwellers should be symbolically garbed and masked or painted; their movements should be abstract and deliberate. The entire sequence needs to be carefully choreographed and scored so that the gravity and significance of the ordeal can be fully appreciated by the spectators as occurring at a deeper level of insight where human evolution over the centuries is on trial. It is further desirable to indicate degree in the masking: the hierarchy of authority and power should be reflected in the relative 'importance' of the masks. Ogun and Eshuoro are equal adversaries; Forest Head outranks them. Since his speeches, especially at first, are mild and he exerts no more power than a master of ceremonies, the spectators may suffer some perplexity which should be resolved by visual cues.

Forest Head is one of the boundary-crossers, in that he is first seen as Obaneji among the humans. Since he is masked in the forest scenes, it would be necessary to indicate his identity by a characteristic code of gesture, gait, and bearing, for voice and face will be modified. The second category of the boundary-crossers are the restless dead whom we meet first as ragged revenants, then as they were in life eight centuries back at Mata Kharibu's court, and lastly once again as ghosts. As ghosts they should not, of course, be masked, but costumed in cobwebby tatters and corroded remnants of armour. The third group are the humans who reappear at Mata Kharibu's court in a previous incarnation: Demoke, Rola, Adenebi, and Agboreko. They should be instantly recognizable, yet transformed to match the splendid and mannered mode of the historic world.

It is clear that the play makes considerable demands on the actors, particularly of versatility in projecting different modes of stylization in gesture and movement. The forest spirits should ideally be dancers and move with choreographed eloquence and precision. I like to imagine their style as characterized by kinetic distortions: a slightly slowed motion which in scenes of conflict bursts into formal movements of great speed and eloquence. Music and dance enrich the texture throughout, and should underline the passage of the action through levels of significance, as the folly of a generation is judged against an age-old history of 'cannibalism' and chosen individuals are offered insight into their repetitive destructiveness. From such insight alone might spring evolution, the only guidance to be offered by the guardians of the earth. As an argument the play is brilliantly articulated; but an audience which is confused about the levels of reality—timeless, past, and present: spirit, ghost, and human—is likely to remain confused. A highly disciplined and visually lavish production on a stage equipped for instant transformations is necessary for a realization that will translate this play fully on to the stage.

Whereas *A Dance of the Forests* demands sophisticated professionalism in stagecraft, costume, and make-up, as well as accomplished acting styles, *Kongi's Harvest* could be performed by amateurs, provided the direction stresses the patterns of similarity and contrast on which the satirical comedy largely rests. One could do much worse than follow Brecht's directives to actors and directors of the epic theatre. *Kongi's Harvest* is total theatre, brilliantly structured to articulate a dialectical confrontation of old and new, not so much through dramatic action, as by theatrical means. The 'meaning' is communicated by design, music, costume, style of gesture, and delivery over and above the dialogue within the plot.

Basically we are faced with a design in triptych form. The old and the new, Danlola and Kongi, facing each other across their synthesis, the club, Daodu and Segi's world whence originate the moves which activate both Kongi and Danlola towards the climax. The production demands a static set with three distinct acting areas, separately and characteristically lit and furnished. The final Harvest Festival will of course exuberantly occupy the entire acting area, although the various groups of characters may still be symbolically stationed on their previous locations.

Only thus can the central satirical pattern of similarities and contrasts, and the dialectical structure of the argument, be graphically conveyed and the importance of the Daodu/Segi section as the proposed synthesis be instantly recognized. The comic parallelism of Danlola and Kongi, which should come over almost like an inkblot picture, generates a bitterly ironical groundswell to the lyrical and farcical goings-on. They could be seen as static tableaux, each dominated by a central autocrat demanding superhuman status, given to histrionics, peevish rages, and behaving like a jealous prima donna. There is the same concern for image; the same preoccupation with protocol, dress, and emblems; the same claque of praisers and flatterers: the same static, self-perpetuating quality. Both are surrounded by a 'court' of dignitaries and functionaries, yet essentially isolated; both are guarded by the Carpenters' Brigade. There is even an attendant clown in each section: Dende and the Fifth Aweri. None of this is to deny that the audience will, and must, prefer Danlola to Kongi—but it should prefer him for reasons of style. Danlola's outmoded autocracy has a human, relaxed quality; it is also radiant with history, tradition, ritual, richly evocative: whereas Kongi's dictatorship is inhuman, grotesque. But Danlola's charm will overwhelm the play unless the parallels are underlined and Daodu's thematic importance stressed.

A naturalistic acting style is inappropriate. Danlola and Kongi are types; as simulated people they lack all depth and interest. Personal charm in Danlola or a psychologically credible form of megalomania for Kongi would be equally distracting. These characters demand to be 'narrated' in the epic style to use Brecht's terminology, rhetorically projected in the third person, so to speak. A similar stylization is required in the crucial Daodu/Segi exchange. When it is played as a 'love scene', that is, if an illusion of reality is attempted, actors and audience are equally ill at ease. This problem disappears if the scene is conceived as the emergence and development of a new motif to oppose directly the hitherto dominant Danlola/Kongi confrontation—the fullest statement, that is, of the positive values to set against their sterility. The dialogue should be spoken very formally 'as poetry'—perhaps best previously recorded on tape in a soft voice, and played back while the characters remain in an immobile tableau of Segi kneeling to the robed Spirit of Harvest. The break between heightened and normal dialogue is clearly discernible in the text. Similarly, Daodu's praises of Segi in the nightclub should not be spoken by him, but sung by the juju guitarist.

In the productions I have seen, Danlola elicited the audiences' sympathies, Kongi their derision; Daodu and Segi remained a romantic ornament. Yet they are thematically central. The play shows that there is little to choose between the two autocrats who have everything in common except style and the weight of tradition. Danlola is moribund, Kongi is a killer: Daodu is life. Kongi harvests death: Daodu, with his farmers' commune, harvests life. He is Danlola's rightful successor, but he is one with the common people too. (There are interesting parallels here with *Henry IV*). He challenges Kongi, not as the pretender, but as a revolutionary leader. If Daodu fails to emerge as the answer, the play loses much of its coherence and becomes a series of satirical sketches.

It may be worthwhile to indicate briefly how this stylized content might be reinforced in production. Music is all-important. The play could happily be expanded into a musical with a score as full of pointed contrast, grave nostalgia, and lyrical mockery as the text. Even a conservative realization demands versatility: traditional drumming and singing for Danlola; electronically amplified military march music for Kongi; amplified juju, with its synthesis of sounds and instruments, for Segi's Club. The movement of the actors on the stage is to some extent determined by the music, but should be pointedly choreographed to become another expressive instrument. In Danlola's area it should be static, or else engaged in the easy yet formal swirling of traditional dancing (In a student production we stressed the danced elements and dressed Oba Danlola's court in stiff *gbarye* dress which swirls out heavily: the dignified circling of Danlola's supporters in their gorgeous swelled-out robes suggested planetary analogies which were entirely apt). On Kongi's side movement is regimented, angular, machine-like. Drill and marches; leaping-up and sitting down. Kongi's own outbursts should suggest a robot out of control. In Segi's Club there should be constant swaying motion. The vegetation and snake imagery of the songs suggests the rhythm: sophisticated juju, and on-the-spot subtle swaying and rippling, cool.

Costume and colours also underline the contrasts: traditional robes for Danlola (exotic fantasies are out of place), a certain dusty splendour of colour, muted deep dyes. Kongi's adherents should all be uniformed, like himself: stark white and khaki; the Organizing Secretary in a grey suit, the New Aweri likewise in uniform (in Soyinka's own production they wore gown and mortarboard!). Costumes in Segi's Club should be stylish, but plainly cut; the colours electric, bright, but harmonious.

The lighting needs to be separately controlled for the rapid scene changes in the mid-section. It too should reflect the contrast with mellow warm light, suggesting oil lamps, for Danlola; a hard white brilliance, as of fluorescent strips, for Kongi; and fairy lights in Segi's Club. Gesture and delivery should be suited to the pattern: utterance in Danlola's section is rich, cadenced, modulated, humorous; gestures hieratic, yet relaxed. In Kongi's section a staccato quality prevails: tight angular gestures, 'pointlessly angry'; even the discordant chorus of the Reformed Aweri should have a shrill and peevish pattern. In Segi's

Club the voice rhythms are natural, even in the lyrical passages; movement relaxed, poised, cool.

Kongi's Harvest seen in this way has a very coherent and simple basic
articulation. The two most recent plays, *The Road* and *Madmen and
Specialists*, are more complex. In spite of their realistic surface and an
action which is for the greater part comic, even farcical, they are felt
to encode a disturbingly elusive oracular message. *The Road* is localized and must aim at verisimilitude in evoking Nigerian community
life around a motor park. *Madmen and Specialists* is not anchored to
any specific locale: it could be set in the hinterland of any modern
ideological war. The Earth Mothers, chorus of 'unformed minds in
deformed bodies', intelligence officer in search of power and control,
and Socratic teacher/therapist are modern archetypes and could be
translated into any location. Otherwise the two plays have much in
common. Both revolve around a central 'mad' guru with his band of
would-be initiates. The Professor of *The Road* is more eccentric, his
speeches oblique and cryptic; in *Madmen and Specialists* the Old
Man's drift is plainly towards sanity, scepticism, and humanism. But
the conception has become more nihilistic: the Old Man's followers
are also his tormentors, and his therapeutic exercises can be subverted
for propaganda and brainwashing purposes. Murano, the returned-
from-death vatic mute of *The Road*, has been replaced by the chorus
of the Earth Mothers. Both plays are substantial and serious, yet their
surface glitters with grotesque wit and comic invention.

The Road, by virtue of its local references, demands a stylized naturalism of staging and acting. The characters are partly recognizable
portraiture, partly symbolic; their speech cadences are specifically Nigerian and need to be sensitively reproduced, yet a 'dialect' naturalism
would be distracting. Say Tokyo Kid and Particulars Joe, for example,
are witty stylizations of familiar types—yet actors and director should
not be tempted into essaying a Stanislavskian verisimilitude. The pattern is still choric. The characters are still masks or mouthpieces in
an adventure of ideation. Every effort must be made to combine local
colour with pace, wit, and thematic phrasing. The flashback to the
masquerade should be clearly marked as occurring in a different dimension, through lighting change and by stylized, perhaps slowed, motion. The problem here is similar to that posed by *A Dance of the
Forests* with its multi-dimensional frame of reference. Yet *The Road* is
delightful quite simply as comedy, and this freshness must remain
dominant. We are in the world of absurd clowns where the laughter
is shot with the hysteria of chaos.

Madmen and Specialists is more abstract, the characteristic dialectic
at its tautest stretch yet. The prophet/sacrifice has evolved into a more
fully overt role of teacher/healer/sacrifice. Though the nature of his
dogma/therapy is only stated obliquely, it is plainly concerned with
self-knowledge, scepticism, and sanity. The paradoxical climax is po-
tently nihilistic, yet extraordinary energizing, more so than in any previous play. There is enough fun and 'business', movement and surprise,

to entertain any audience. It may be tempting because of this to treat the play as a vehicle for virtuoso character-acting and a plethora of illusionist 'business'. Inevitably the outcome would be an entertaining conundrum. I should like to see the play done in cabaret style, very rhythmical, tightly choreographed and scored, with stylized character-ization. The Mendicants and the Earth Mothers to be rehearsed as choral units, their speeches not so much dialogue addressed to one another (in the illusionist manner) as articulated themes addressed to the audience. Against these choric arbiters—humanity and the Earth —the conflict between son and father, cannibalism and humanism, political and individual sanity, should enact itself as a dialogue of prin-ciples. Again, as in Kongi's Harvest, a single set should be used with differentiated arenas (say, surgery, sanctum, and open place), so that the three interacting and conflicting interpretations of men's needs can be appreciated as co-existing without resolution. A monotonous yet relentless rock or West African drum rhythm might run on throughout, into which are woven characteristic themes for the Mendicants' chant and the Earth Mothers' utterances. Ideally the Mendicants would pro-vide their own percussion with crutches, beggar's bowl, hand-slapping on the floor, etc.

Two of the characters emerge as more than types, Aafaa and the Old Man, superb parts for skilled actors. Great tact is necessary in interpreting them. Even here a distancing stylization is essential: to invent a plausible history and convincing psychology for these char-acters would disrupt the pattern as a whole. It is sufficient that their rendering should be coherent, and consistent with their function within the action as a whole. They are not so much invented men as mouthpieces for arguments in the complex exposition of an ideological trap.

The easiest temptation in interpreting Soyinka's brilliant dramati-zations of ideas for the stage is to develop their surface realism; for actors to lose themselves in the vividly differentiated parts; for audi-ences to relish the rich evocations of the familiar and the sparkling fun of it all. That way perplexity about 'meaning' is inevitable. The remedy lies in interpreting the text like a musical score; in disciplined, stylized modes of acting; in alertness to the currents of ideation, as well as to the sparkle of recognition.

ADEBAYO WILLIAMS

[Cultural Death and the King's Horseman]†

* * *

Within Soyinka's distinguished corpus, *Death and the King's Horseman* has achieved the status of a classic. Critics have hailed its superb characterisation, its haunting beauty, and, above all, its lyrical grandeur. It is arguably the most intensely poetic of the 1986 Nobel laureate's plays. Written during a period of exile and existential anguish, the play derives its powerful dynamics from Soyinka's rather belated attempt to grapple directly with the "colonial question", a question which had exercised the mind of his literary peers for over two decades. For Soyinka, then, *Death and the King's Horseman* is the creative equivalent of the return of the repressed. In this play, Soyinka manages to capture the power and glory of the ancient Yoruba state in its dying moment, and at the same time to pose a serious intellectual challenge to those who would deny a conquered people its unique mode of apprehending and making sense of reality.

Death and the King's Horseman represents an attempt to confront on a creative level the arrogance and cultural chauvinism of Western imperialism. It must be stressed that Soyinka has taken umbrage at the "reductionist tendency" which sees the dramatic tension of his play as arising from "a clash of culture." According to him, this "prejudicial label . . . presupposes a potential equality *in every given situation* of the alien culture and the indigenous, on the actual soil of the latter" (author's note). The harsh polemical tone of this rebuttal shows the extent to which Soyinka's threnodic temperament is affronted by mundane cultural equations. Yet, by exploring the sacred terror of ritual suicide within the context of the cynicism and cultural dessications of the colonialists, Soyinka is engaged in nothing but a sublime cultural offensive. Indeed, by counterposing the notion of personal and public honour in the ancient Yoruba Kingdom as seen in the tragic career of its principal custodian of culture against the cynical presumptions of the colonial officers, Soyinka manages to expose the fundamental absurdity inherent in all assumptions of cultural superiority.

Death and the King's Horseman opens with a grand panorama of the Yoruba market place. Here, Soyinka deploys all his artistic power to paint a picture of grandeur and vitality. Apart from its obvious economic importance, the market occupies a signal cultural, political and spiritual position in the Yoruba cosmos. First, it is a site of political and cultural ferment. Second, it doubles as that numinous zone in which the distinction between the world of the dead and the living evaporates. Finally, it serves as a barometer for the spiritual well-being

† From *Soyinka: A Collection of Critical Essays*, ed. Oyin Ogunba (Ibadan, Nigeria: Syndicated Communications, 1994) 94–100. Bracketed page numbers refer to this Norton Critical Edition.

of the community. It is therefore a stroke of genius on the part of the playwright to have focused his artistic lens on the market place. But the profound irony of this choice hits us with the force of a gale as soon as we realise that what is going on between the indigenous culture and the alien culture runs counter to the natural logic of the market—a forum for buying and selling. Here, we are confronted with the bizarre phenomenon of a culture which insists on forcing its hardwares on another without a commensurate purchase.

The crisis in the play is thus predicated on what is known in economic parlance as trade imbalance between the culture of the conqueror and that of the conquered. The praise-singer, in a moving dialogue with Elesin, captures the angst and spiritual anguish of his people:

> Our world was never wrenched from its true course . . . if that world leaves its course and smashes on the boulders of the great void, whose world will give us shelter? [128]

It is easy to see behind the unease and anguish of this intensely poetic lamentation, the sympathies of the playwright himself. The very choice of images, "wrench", "boulders" and "void" betrays Soyinka's starkly apocalyptic mood.

It is against this turbulent background that one must situate the vexatious dynamics which transform Elesin, an otherwise minor cultural functionary of the ruling class, into the world historic role of deliverer of his people. For precisely because his suicide is now supposed to compel respect for the integrity and inviolability of a threatened culture, Elesin's routine function takes on a major historical and political burden. Hence for the people, the success or otherwise of the ritual becomes a matter of life and death. Here then is a classic example of a particular ritual going, under historical pressure, beyond its original cultural signification to assume a vaster political and spiritual importance.

Yet, if historical circumstances compel a particular ritual to serve purposes more complex than its original signification, it is hard to see how the same circumstances can transform a minor figure into a major historical personage. Indeed, the reverse is often the case. Marx's brilliant comparison of the two Bonapartes comes to mind: "(The French) have not only a caricature of the Old Napoleon, they have the Old Napoleon himself, caricatured as he must appear in the middle of the nineteenth century."[1]

So it is with Elesin. And this indeed is the source of the collective and individual tragedy in *Death and the King's Horseman*. Elesin's consciousness has been determined by the dialectic of his material and political circumstances. If he appears weak, vacillating, self-pitying and self-dramatising, it is because the old empire itself has run out of steam. If he is cynically preoccupied with pleasure and the spoils of

1. Terry Eagleton, *Walter Benjamin: Or Towards a Revolutionary Criticism* (London: NLB, 1981), 166.

office, if he is sceptical about the further credibility of his destiny, it is because the hegemony of the empire had long been fissured by internal contradictions as well as the antagonistic logic supplied by the conquering invaders. As evident in the play, the dying empire is already thoroughly infiltrated by the "other" empire and its various fetishes of political authority and cultural power: batons, bands, balls, cells gramophones, etc. In a rather resentful categorisation of the opulence of the Residency, Soyinka comes very close to the truth when he describes it as being "redolent of the tawdry decadence of a far-flung but key imperial frontier" [155].

Thus in its dying moment, the empire can only produce an Elesin who is a pathetic but ultimately subversive caricature of his illustrious forbears. In the light of this, one cannot agree with Jeyifo when he asserts that "the play never really dramatises either the force of Elesin's personality or the inevitability of his action."[2] The point is that there is no force to dramatise about Elesin's personality. Here, Jeyifo suffers a curious and paradoxical slippage into the bourgeois notion of history and literature as the study of the acts of great men. The character of Elesin is an actual reflection of the historical forces at play.

But to expect such a man to surmount the overwhelming historical and political forces ranged against him is to expect the impossible. That the playwright fails to recognise this fact shows to what extent his own imagination has been contained by the lingering efficacy of the ideological apparatuses of the old Yoruba state. Indeed, in an attempt to resist the mundane forces of concrete history, the playwright is compelled to look beyond Elesin to his son, Olunde. Olunde is perhaps the most sensitively drawn character in the play. It is easy to identify him as the playwright's ideological spokesman. As it were, Olunde's material and historical circumstances are quite different from his father's. Armed with immense personal courage and conviction, his considerable intellect honed by a sustained exposure to the foibles and contradictions of the alien culture, Olunde is a perfect match for the arrogance and chauvinism of the colonial administrators. As he tells Mrs. Pilkings: "You forget that I have now spent four years among your people, I discovered that you have no respect for what you do not understand" [158]. And yet in another cutting riposte: "You believe that everything which appears to make sense was learnt from you" [160].

Consumed by his contempt for the hypocrisy and cant of Western civilisation, bewildered by his father's tragic lack of honour, it is not surprising that Olunde chooses suicide to redeem the honour of the society and to expiate what must have seemed to him as his father's abominable act of cowardice and treachery. But rather than alleviate the burden of the people, Olunde's suicide only serves to compound their misery. The praise-singer again captures this moment of historic stress:

2. Biodun Jeyifo, *The Truthful Lie: Essays in a Sociology of African Drama* (London: New Beacon Books, 1985), 32.

What the end will be, we are not gods to tell. But this young shoot
has poured its sap into the parent stalk, and we know this is not
the way of life. Our world is tumbling in the void of strangers.
[176]

Yet, despite the enormous integrity of his self-sacrifice, one finds it
hard to pinpoint where his role as a great cultural hero ends and the
rearguard defender of a backward-looking political order takes over.
But the playwright does not leave us in doubt as to his conviction that
if suicide is the ultimate option available to Africa's revolutionary in-
telligentsia in the struggle for the cultural revalidation of the continent, it must be embraced without flinching.

This position engenders profound ideological difficulties. To start
with, it lays itself open to the charge of cultivating a cult of romantic
suicide. To left-wing critics, Olunde, by terminating his own life, has
succumbed to the whims of a reactionary culture, a flagrantly feudalistic ethos. Indeed, for critics of this persuasion, there may be something paradoxically progressive in Elesin's refusal to honour his bond.
Jeyifo is precise and uncompromising on this point: "The notion of
honour (and integrity and dignity) for which Soyinka provides a metaphysical rationalisation rests on the patriarchal, feudalist code of the
ancient Oyo Kingdom, a code built on class entrenchment and class
consolidation."[3]

It is necessary at this point to problematise these various antithetical
positions. The first step towards this will be to counterpose Jameson's
doctrine of the political unconscious[4] against Jeyifo's obviously instru-
mentalist marxist objection. As it is, the Elesin ritual is a projection of
a people's collective consciousness. Elesin's suicide is designed to facilitate the smooth transition of the departed king from the world of
the living to the world of the dead. Even for departing royalties, soli-
tude might be a terrifying prospect in what Soyinka himself often
sombrely refers to as "the abyss of transition". As the Iyaloja, the unwavering matriarch of culture and tradition, puts it:

> He knows the meaning of a king's passage; he was not born yes-
> terday. He knows the peril to the race when our dead father who
> goes as intermediary, waits and waits and knows he is betrayed
> . . . He knows he has condemned our king to wander in the void
> of evil with beings who are enemies of life. [173]

In Yoruba culture, a king never "dies". A king wandering "in the
void" is therefore an abomination, a serious threat to life and communal well-being. Thus, insofar as Elesin's suicide is conceived to
usher in the departed king into his new kingdom, it is a crucial ritual
of continuity, well-being and hope. Hence, the collective anxiety about
the dire consequences of its abortion.

Yet, as Jameson has advanced, a political unconscious always un-

---

3. Ibid., 34.
4. Fredric Jameson, *The Political Unconscious: Narrative as a Socially Symbolic* Act (Ithaca:
Cornell University Press, 1981).

easily coexists with even the most apparently innocent manifestation of a people's collective consciousness. The question then is: what is the political unconscious behind Elesin's ritual and Soyinka's fabulisation of this? In other words, what is the historical contradiction for which the Elesin ritual is supposed to be a symbolic resolution of?

It would seem that on one level, the ritual suicide of Elesin is supposed to take the sting out of the trauma of death through the drama of a privileged carrier who willingly and casually undertakes the journey to the unknown. This in itself may serve to assuage the people's collective anxiety about being forsaken as a result of the departure of the father of the "tribe". On another level, however, the ritual may well signify a symbolic conquest of death itself. For in the absence of viable oppositional forces in the community, Death becomes the distinguished scourge and ultimate terror of the ruling class: unconquerable, unanswerable; firm and unsmiling.

The Elesin ritual then magically transforms death into an ally of the rules. In death, the power and grandeur of the rulers remain. The transition of individual kings is thus immaterial; the kingdom remains unassailable. Auerbach, interestingly enough, sees the poetry of Homer as performing an analogous function for the ancient Greek aristocracy: "Thus rather than an impression of historical change, Homer evokes the illusion of an unchanging society, a basically stable order, in comparison with which the succession of individuals and changes in personal fortunes appear unimportant."[5]

It should be clear from the foregoing that the Elesin ritual is designed to reconcile the people of the ancient Oyo Empire to the supremacy, invincibility and the divine nature of what is essentially a feudal society. It is a socially symbolic act insofar as it negotiates the painful reality of death for the ruling class. Hence, the ritual suicide is one of those insidious strategies of survival and containment that Althusser has characterised as the ideological apparatuses of the state.[6] This is the political unconscious behind the Elesin ritual in *Death and the King's Horseman*.

It can now be seen that Jeyifo's objection is not without its merits. *Death and the King's Horseman* does provide metaphysical rationalisation for a patriarchal and feudalist code. The play's complicity with this order is obvious in as much as the playwright accepts the ritual as a communical necessity. But it is not just the dominant classes that fear death. The terror of death is a common denominator in all societies and hence a trans-class phenomenon. Hence, going back to Althusser's seminal definition of ideology, this particular manoeuvre of the ruling class is an essential mystification, ultimately beneficial to the entire society.

It is precisely this utopian dimension to the Elesin ritual that Soyinka's left-wing critics have failed to come to terms with. While recog-

5. Erich Auerbach, *Mimesis: The Representation of Reality in Western Literature* (New York: Doubleday, 1957), 142.
6. Louis Althusser, *Lenin and Philosophy and Other Essays* (London: NLB, 1971).

nising the power and urgency of negative hermeneutics for the marxist critical enterprise, the ultimate task of marxist criticism, according to Jameson, is to restore the utopian dimension to the work of arts, that is to view the work of art as an expression of some ultimate collective urge while not overlooking "the narrower limits of class privilege which informs its more immediate ideological vocation."[7]

* * *

MICHAEL ETHERTON

Tribute to Wole Soyinka†

* * * Wole Soyinka is one of the truly great dramatists of this century. Soyinka's plays are both the vehicle for his genius and the praxis of his revolutionary commitment. He is primarily a poet; but his poetic impulse is mediated by a need to give to others the means of recreating the understanding which comes from a poetic vision rather than merely to write down and record that vision. It is not simply a matter of the poet becoming a public performer, or story-teller in the mar-ketplace. Rather, I think, Soyinka finds himself compelled to flesh out the dialectic he perceives, through actors who can transform them-selves, transform their acting space, and so transform their audiences.

There have been great revolutionary poets in this turbulent century like Amilcar Cabral and there are analysts and philosophers whose prose works provide a basis for revolutionary action—Frantz Fanon, Walter Rodney, C.L.R. James. Sometimes it is the lives of people which become the poetic expression of their heroic commitment—Che Guevara. And sometimes poet, philosopher and politician are all com-bined in one person; Cabral is an outstanding example. Black Africa has been transformed during the last few decades by their deeds and by their words. They have inspired people and shaped the struggle.

On the other hand, and mainly within the European cultural tra-dition, the playwright as a craftsman rather than as a poet, has endeavoured to represent, upon the stage, the exploitation of the oppressed and the burden of the cultural legacy of still-powerful imperialist states. The British playwright Edward Bond, the French playwright Jean Genet and the German playwright Peter Weiss, are obvious examples.

However, in all these instances, the person or the work functions as an exemplar; an ideal, or a pattern, to be followed. Although we are inspired, and perhaps need to be inspired by noble example, we our-selves are ironically, paradoxically, diminished as originators and ini-tiators in our own right. If you and I feel less capable of our own

---

7. Jameson, 288.
† From *Before Our Very Eyes: Tribute to Wole Soyinka*, ed. Dapo Adelugba (Ibadan, Nigeria: Spectrum Books Limited, 1987) 33–37.

artistic abilities when confronted by the work of brilliant writers, or feel somehow reduced in our initiatives when in the presence of charismatic leaders, how much more inhibited must the oppressed masses feel who do not have the benefit of our middle class education and affluence?

This seems to me to be the central contradiction for the poet who is also a committed revolutionary. Some poets this century have embraced the dialectics of the social obligations of their genius and sought through the medium of drama to enable their audiences to remake the insights as their own. Four poets have done this in the twentieth century: Wole Soyinka, Bertolt Brecht, and John Arden and his wife Margaretta D'Arcy. They are the greatest dramatists of our time—though First World critics may not agree with this judgement. All of them are poets with a global vision and an unshakeable commitment to the world's most oppressed populations. However, rather than merely write down their vision, they have struggled to find ways to make people less gifted than themselves who are also persecuted, the actual makers of further insights and understanding. They have seen drama as the only medium to advance this artistic and committed process.

In all drama, each new performance remakes the original text; and through the passage of time the text accumulates meaning, for which we are all, performer or audience, collectively responsible. *Oedipus*, *Bacchae*, *Don Juan*, are play texts performed in a thousand different versions. Each age adds to or subtracts from the central vision of the piece. For revolutionary drama, however, the performance is more than just the remaking of meaning from one age to the next. It is the actual praxis of the ideology: the poetic vision embraces the contradictions within the ideal, within the social constraints and within our own passions. The subsequent drama then seeks to deconstruct its meaning, during the moments of a performance, so as to enable us as active audience to remake it ourselves.

Thus, the poet's revolutionary commitment is communicated through the drama to the ensemble of actors performing the play, who internalize the process of commitment through a restructuring of meaning—Brecht's *VerfremdungsEffekt*;[1] Soyinka "code of meaning . . . established through rhythm, movement and tonal-specific harmonies . . ."—and this commitment is transferred to the audience who are energized by the very process by which meaning is established. That the process is not always successful does not negate its wider intention of diminishing the gap between the revolutionary poet-dramatist and his potential revolutionary audience. Often the process cannot work because it is contradicted by a director who would seek to put the playwright on a pedestal and fail to wrest the meaning out of the text.

When the process does work, the art of performance becomes the paradigm of the revolutionary process itself. It is, as C.L.R. James observes, a combination of organization and its necessary opposite,

1. "Alienation Effect" [*Editor*].

spontaneity. Indeed Soyinka (and Brecht and the Ardens) are all part anarchist: it is an integral part of their vision. Soyinka's drama is anti-Aristotle: all the standard patterns of society and art in the second half of the twentieth century are disharmonious, and is a need to escape from history. The dramatist, through the actors, must engage with the audience and turn history from its set course. In his theory of drama, Soyinka describes the activation of the communal psyche in the moment of transition: the individual daring the abyss, on behalf of the whole community.

I talk about the praxis of Soyinka's drama from my own direct experience of its liberating force. *The Road* was published in 1965, and I confronted it as a text in Zambia at the beginning of 1966. As a white South African, I was at the time struggling against the whole economic and cultural thrust of my upbringing. The experience of living in Zambia in the first 24 months of its independence was a truly liberating one for me. The economic and political analyses were for a time radical; and the cultural discourse grounded in Kaunda's Zambian Humanism had a creative dynamic. All sorts of creative energies were released in people. Inevitably, I suppose, the revolution became bogged down in the harsh realities of the unliberated remainder of Southern Africa: the whites still retained hegemonic control throughout the area. To discover *The Road* in this context was suddenly to understand, as though one had thought it through oneself, the contradictions: in the technology, in political organization, in the structure of knowledge. The play was more than an analysis: it was a living-through of reality. I suddenly knew—though perhaps not as clearly as I do now—that the full cultural expression of a new world order would eventually come from the oppressed of the Third World. 'Art' would have to be redefined; and when the time came, those at the base of the society would take the initiative. I think that many people have found the poetry within *The Road* a powerful liberating force.

Largely on the strength of this experience I left Zambia to study African Literature—ironically and paradoxically at a British University. When I returned to Zambia a year later I was given the opportunity to direct some African plays for the Zambian Broadcasting Services. Together with my students we did, amongst other plays, a production of *The Strong Breed*. The productions for radio of the African plays were enjoyable; the production of *The Strong Breed* was riveting. Despite the stops and starts, and ad hoc production arrangements, I felt that the studio we were working in was invaded by the poetic energy of the play. Indeed, the stops and starts, reconstituting the play for radio, seemed to strengthen rather than dissipate the experience of the play. I still find *The Strong Breed* an extraordinarily powerful play. But the point perhaps is that Soyinka inspired us—not to do more of his plays (and to wait patiently for them to come as the printed text to Lusaka), but to set about doing our own plays. I have subsequently discovered that others who have worked on productions of Soyinka's plays have found a strong impetus to work through their own vision with actors and audiences in a similar way—Femi Osofisan is a notable example.

The global crisis deepens. Capitalism in the West increases its strangle-hold on Third World populations; Super Power rivalry bends the technological and material resources of the world to the manufacture of vast arsenals for global destruction—all this is said over and over again—and the present microprocessor and information technology is transforming our lives in ways which we could not imagine, but, certainly, to coerce the populations in the Third World more and more. At the same time the landless at the grass-roots are struggling to organize themselves, and are using popular drama as part of the process. Soyinka has moved into guerilla theatre, refocussing, perhaps, his response to the violence of the present time. Perhaps, too, if poets like Soyinka can find a way to merge their vision and their art with the political endeavours at the grass-roots, they may become a sounding-board for that revolutionary process initiated by the leaders, the scattered and the dispossessed of the Third World.

Tsegaye Gabre-Medhin

TSEGAYE GABRE-MEDHIN

Author's Note to *Collision of Altars*†

The play was written seven years ago[1] and is only now due for publication. Ours, Africa's in general, or, in this case, Ethiopia's in particular, is just another part of today's inquisitive generation that must be encouraged to come to terms with its historic past; even that historic past often torn and denied against him. And this, to a lesser or greater extent, may be achieved, by the process of re-interpreting to himself, the human events of his past, which in a way, is still responsible for his present conflicting awareness, if not for the shaping of his total future event. It is in this sense alone, that a historical play becomes an instrument of history and change. Yet, the position of the interpreter becomes even more difficult, when the material of historic documentation happens to be rather thin and sparse, sometimes handed down by unrealistic ancient spiritual mystics. The other difficulty is that of the dramatist: (a) How to condense, the rather widespread and complex machinery of the world Power inter-relationships. North East Ethiopian Axum's, Byzantium's, Persia's, and South Arabia's religious cultures and political state. (Considering of course that, what is a power struggle today behind the mask of ideological conflicts, was a power struggle then as now under the cover of religious cultures and political state. (Considering of course that, and the Kremlin palace at Red Square are now, the Temples of Altars in the cities of spiritual powers were then.)—(b) How to depict a story that took a lapse of over half a century, in a distant period as far removed from ours, occupied nearly twelve hundred years ago, into less than three hours of dramatic experience. It is because of these, and of course other less obvious contemporary difficulties, that this play should be considered as a play only based on history, and NOT a factual historic document. Besides, it is now accepted of any historical interpretation, that quite a considerable share of its body comes from legend, folk tales and proverbs, from its more recent research findings, and of course, from the humble interpreter's imagination.

Concerning the play's main body of history, my major reference

---

† From *Collision of Altars* (London: Rex Collings, 1977). Reprinted by permission of the author.
1. In 1970.

materials have been, Durnheim's *The Royal Cemeteries of Kush*, vols. I–V, the *Kibre Negest* or the Ethiopian Royal Chronicles, Book of the Ethiopian Saints Vol. I by Wallis Budge, also his *Bualam* and *Yewasef*, *L'Omilia di Yohannes* by C. Conti Rossini, *Il Gadla Arawi* by Giudi, *La vie de Saint Za Mikael Aragawi* by Marc Antoine Van de Oudenrigin, *Life of Mohammed* by Muar, *Mohammad at Mecca* by W. M. Watt, Ullendorff and Trimingham on the Ethiopian black Judaic 'Falashas' of the period, Byzantium and Persian history of Sixth Century, the fragments of the pre-Sabian legend of the North East nilotic 'Semri' people, the fragments of the ancient sun gods, Almugah, Astar, Mahrem, Beher etc., of the Saba Kingdom in South Arabia before the coming of the Sabeans and with them their influence of additional Greek gods; also *The Arabs and History* by Bernard Lewis, *Axum Expedition, India and Ethiopia* by Littman, and of course the Holy Bible, Old and New Testament, the Holy Koran and the Life and Religion of the Persian Zarathushtra.

Regarding set and production of this play, I would like merely to point out my preoccupation with the idea of an illustrative total theatre, functional dance, mime, incantation, incense burning, Ethiopian wigs and African type masks and rituals, old Ethiopian type Orthodox Church chant, music, praise singing and of course verse drama, which I hope will bring together that original sense of the theatre's craft, the dance-actor, director-designer and author relationship to a closer effort of combined imagination.

RICHARD PANKHURST

Collision of Altars: Notes on History†

Collision of Altars must be regarded as historical theatre, in the best sense of the term, rather than strict history, for the playwright has been inspired by history, which he in turn illuminates with poetic insight.

The play is set in the ancient Axumite empire in the late sixth and early seventh centuries—a period for which historical records are by no means rich, and this has enabled Tsegaye Gebre Medhin to give full scope to his artistic vision.

The principal characters are, however, almost entirely historical personages and the events they are made to refer to are largely ones with which the historian is familiar.

KALEB, one of the greatest emperors of Axum is said by Wallis Budge to have reigned from 514 to 542 AD, and is remembered for the victorious expedition which he despatched to South Arabia.

In this important event, as mentioned in the play, he is believed to have made use of elephants but was defeated by an outbreak of small-

† From *Collision of Altars* (London: Rex Collings, 1977) 77–80.

pox, plague in Tsegaye Gabre Medhin's account, as recorded in the Holy Koran. Shortly after his return to Axum, Kaleb sent his royal crown to Jerusalem to be suspended near the grave of our Lord, and, as in the play, retired from this world.

GABRE MASKEL was one of the two sons of Kaleb to succeed him as emperor, and, according to one traditional king list, is thought to have reigned for fourteen years.

BET ISRAEL is another of the sons of Kaleb who succeeded him as emperor, and the coins he struck have been found by archaeologists. Little is, however, known of either his life or that of Gabre Maskel.

ARMAH was the Emperor of Axum at the time of the rise of the prophet Mohamad. Arab tradition states that this ruler gave hospitality from 615 to 629 to some of the early followers of the Prophet, who were at that time being persecuted in Arabia. When asked by the then rulers of that country to return these refugees, which at one time numbered no less than 101, Armah is said to have refused, declaring. 'If you were to offer me a mountain of gold I will not give up these people who have taken refuge with me.' This act of generosity, or statesmanship, seems to have paid dividends, for on the death of Armah the Prophet is supposed to have prayed for his soul and to have commanded his followers to 'leave the Abyssinians in peace,' and thereby to have spared them the horrors of the Jihad or 'Holy War'.

DEGNA JAN, whom the playwright refers to as Araaya, appears in the Ethiopian king lists as Armah's immediate successor and thus was in all probability his son.

JAFFAR, or more fully Jaffar Bin Abu Talib, was the cousin of the Prophet Mohammad, the leader of the Muslim refugees in Axum. Arab tradition states that when the rulers of Arabia were demanding his repatriation Armah interrogated him on his faith, and Jaffar replied, more or less in the same words as in the play that the Arabs were 'a barbarous nation, worshipping idols, eating carrion, committing shameful deeds, killing our blood relations, forgetting our duty towards our neighbors, the strong among us devouring the weak. Such was our state until God sent us an apostle,' i.e. the Prophet Mohammed.

HABIBAH, or UMM HABIBAH, also known as Ramia, was an Arab woman who with other early Muslims found refuge at Axum where her first husband was converted to Christianity. Arab tradition states that the prophet later asked Armah to betroth her to him, and the Axumite sovereign sent her back to Arabia with a dowry of 400 dinars. She became Mohammad's ninth wife, and is said to have told her husband of the beauty of the Ethiopian Cathedral of St Mary at Axum.

ABA PANTELEON was one of the 'Nine Saints' who came to Ethiopia from Syria and played an important role in the evaluation of the Ethiopian Church. His sanctuary is still to be seen at Axum.

The historical Aba Panteleon was a contemporary of Kaleb's in the sixth century, but the playwright, presumably to extend the holy man's presence to later times, places on the stage a disciple of Panteleon's who takes his name and acts as the Royal Father Confessor.

ABBAS was Kaleb's governor of the Axumite port of Adulis and was known to the Egyptian monk Cosmas who mentions him in his book the *Christian Topography*. The playwright, again in order to prolong the character's presence into the Seventh Century, has given Abbas a son to take over in his name.

JULIAN, or JULIANUS, was yet another historical figure: the ambassador sent by the Emperor Justinian of the Eastern Roman Empire to Axum, to request joint action against the Persians.

DHU NUWAS was an Arab ruler at Negran in South Arabia who, according to tradition, had adopted the Jewish faith and massacred the Christian population of the city in 523, thus, as referred to in the play, prompting Kaleb's intervention.

The above brief notes on the DRAMATIS PERSONAE indicate that the great events referred to in the play, Kaleb's expedition to Arabia, his abdication, the epidemic, and the Muslim refugee's residence in Axum, are all historical events.

The names of places, such as Kasu and Tziamoe, and tribes, such as Agaw, Kasu, and Nubia, etc, are likewise known to have been employed at the time.

Tsegaye Gabre-Medhin's religious scene is, as far as we can tell, also broadly true to history. Several deeply engrained traditions emphasize the symbolic importance of the serpent in the age-old religious belief of the Ethiopians, while the influence of the Pagan gods Mohrem and Beher, who are mentioned in Emperor Ezana's earlier inscriptions of the fourth century, may well have continued, as the playwright suggests, to the time of Kaleb who, like his forebears for a couple of centuries, was, however, himself a devoted Christian.

At least one earlier Axumite inscription similarly makes reference to Zeus, as well as to other Greek gods, who are also referred to in the play. There is furthermore ample evidence of the long-established presence of Judaism in Ethiopia where people still follow the food prohibitions of the Jews and to this day number among the population, the Falashas or 'Black Jews.'

The playwright would thus appear fully justified in his use of the Serpent, the Star of David, the Cross and the Crescent as symbols of conflicting faiths.

Finally, we should recall that the Axumite empire held its own, as Tsegaye Gabre-Medhin indicates, besides the Eastern Roman Empire and Zoreastarian Persia, being with them one of the three great powers in the world in the period before the rise of Islam.

BIODUN JEYIFO

Art and Ideology in the Plays of Tsegaye Gabre-Medhin†

By reputation, the Ethiopian playwright Tsegaye Gabre-Medhin is a very active, prolific dramatist 'whose plays range from modern and historical works to Amharic translations of such plays as *Macbeth*'.[1] But only two of his works are available in published English texts and these are *Oda Oak Oracle* and *Collision of Altars*. Thus, it may very well be that the most important or successful works of this remarkable playwright are not accessible to us. Even so, the two texts mentioned here provide enough material for us to assert that in the dramas of Gabre-Medhin we see a rather unique instance of the sharp, contradictory interplay between art and ideology in contemporary African drama.

In explicit ideological intent, Gabre-Medhin is somewhat in the company of such other African writers as Chinua Achebe and Ayi Kwei Armah who have made it an important aspect of their work to go back to legends, folklore and history in order to identify what elements were negative and what positive in African pre-colonial traditions and experience so as to refurbish present attempts to overcome colonial and post-colonial alienation.[2] While this ideological intent is rather more muted in *Oda Oak Oracle*, it is quite explicitly stated in the playwright's prefatory remarks in *Collision of Altars*:

> Ours, Africa's in general, or, in this case, Ethiopia's in particular, is just another part of today's inquisitive generation that must be encouraged to come to terms with its historic past; even that historic past often torn and denied against him. And this, to a lesser or greater extent, may be achieved by the process of re-interpreting to himself, the human events of his past which, in a way, is still responsible for his present conflicting awareness, if not for the shaping of his total future event. It is in this sense alone that a historical play becomes an instrument of history and change.

Though more muted, the playwright's longish sub-title for *Oda Oak Oracle* also, in its own way, expresses this self-conscious burden of ideological purpose in the dramatic enactment: 'A legend of black peoples, told of gods and God, of hope and love, and of fears and sacrifices'. This mode of expressing his ideological intentions indeed points to an aspect of the texture of Gabre-Medhin's drama which again is more explicitly and fully expressed in both the prefatory remarks

---

† From *The Truthful Lie: Essays in a Sociology of African Drama* (London: New Beacon, 1985) 90–96. Reprinted by permission of the author. Page numbers in brackets refer to this Norton Critical Edition.
1. From the blurb on the dust-jacket of *Collision of Altars*, London, Rex Collings, 1977.
2. One thinks of Achebe's *Things Fall Apart* and *Arrow of God* and Armah's *The Healers* and *Two Thousand Seasons*. See also Achebe's important essay 'The Novelist as Teacher,' in his collection *Morning Yet on Creation Day*, Ibadan, Heinemann, 1975.

in *Collision of Altars* and the elaborate stage directions in the text, namely: an engrossing, even meticulous attention to finding the aesthetic, technical means of effectively achieving his ideological objectives. In Gabre-Medhin's drama, we encounter an even more pronounced manifestation of what we have come to associate with the dramaturgy of Wole Soyinka and Athol Fugard, the continent's greatest playwrights—as much attention to the *aesthetic means* of dramatic expression as its subject matter and social vision.

The subject matter of both *Oda Oak Oracle* and *Collision of Altars* are as deliberately *ideological* as any subject matter of drama can be, where ideology is understood to be the form and content of consciousness as it pertains to relations between individuals, groups, classes, nations and races. *Oda Oak Oracle* dramatises the tragedy which overtakes three young members of a clan—Goaa, Ukutee and Shanka— when the rationalist, altruistic outlook which they have imbibed from the 'ways of strangers' clashes with the iron-clad hold of ancient xenophobic, anti-rationalist sanctions in thought and behaviour on their elders and fellow clansmen. *Collisions of Altars* is even more starkly ideological in its dramatisation of the disintegrative effects of the competition of different religious faiths for ascendancy in a country—sixth century Axumite Ethiopia—undergoing relentless social decline. Thus, in their general outlines, these plays show Gabre-Medhin's intense concern with some of the important ideological issues of contemporary Africa.

It is of far greater significance for our exploration of Gabre-Medhin's dramatisation of ideological conflicts that our playwright takes great pains to show that his concern with ideology is itself ideological, that he takes sides and expresses definite views on the conflicts that arise from relations between men in society. Thus, between them, these two plays can be said to be exemplary in their passionate advocacy of the liberation of human consciousness from obscurantist, virulent and anti-human myths and modes of thought, especially those dressed in the garb of religion.

It can indeed be asserted with extensive textual supports from the two plays of Gabre-Medhin being discussed here that they are both sustained dramatic critiques of religious ideology and the phobias and alienations to which it often gives rise. In *Oda Oak Oracle* the dominant religious dispensation is the animist, ancestor-cult, magicoreligious tradition of an isolated clan; in the course of the drama it confronts an alien religion which is more universalistic, altruistic and man-centred. In *Collision of Altars* the dominant religious dispensation is the Ethiopian Orthodox Christian Sect under the theocratic manipulation of tyrannical emperors and cynical ecclesiastics, and at the point at which it begins to collapse before the rising star (or crescent) of Jihadist Islam.

The sharp focus on religion and the mutant ideological excrescences to which it gives rise, provides a specific context for Gabre-Medhin's ideological purview: this is Ethiopia before the 'secular revolution' initiated by the Revolution of 1974 and the policies of the new regime.

Oda Oak Oracle was published in 1965 and *Collision of Altars* in 1977, having in fact been written seven years earlier, according to the play-wright himself. This focus on religion and the different complex strands which it manifests is therefore a faithful reflection of the pre-revolutionary Ethiopia of the Emperor and the Ethiopian Orthodox Church and their domination of the Ethiopian state and society.

It does reflect Gabre-Medhin's immersion in the cultural and religious realities of his society that not only the dominant Ethiopian Orthodox Church, but other religious traditions both pre- and non-Christian are given adequate expression in both *Oda Oak Oracle* and *Collision of Altars*. More specifically, Gabre-Medhin, while he does not idealise the pagan, animist, pre-Christian religious traditions of many of Ethiopia's nationalities, he is somewhat partial to the warmth and reciprocity of these traditions. This attitude, barely expressed in *Oda Oak Oracle*, becomes one of the major themes of *Collision of Altars* where its ultimate affirmation against the inhuman, dogmatic, dualistic abstractions of Christian theology is given in the encounter between Queen Noba of the 'Southern Lake Region' of the 'Noble Serpent' religion and her son, the Crown Prince Armah:

> I am a Kush, and of this land of Ra
> On whose roots the first sun rose,
> My body living
> As my head is true.
> Mine is unlike your hybrid
> Devious, little Sabaean mind
> Where the quibbles of your Geez tongue
> Outlive the living body by far.
> With us, the body has a language
> The mind cannot speak.
> Both live. Without the one
> The other is dead: and
> The one cannot live
> The other's complete life. [230]

All told then, within the social context of pre-revolutionary Ethiopia of the Emperor, his ecclesiastical potentates and their aristocratic, anti-people pretentions, Gabre-Medhin's plays constitute an intense, passionate *ideological* contestation of the religious ideology which underpins and sustains the misrule of the oligarchy and the degradation of the governed. *Oda Oak Oracle* and *Collision of Altars* both depict dramatic heroes who, perhaps more than what we get in any other plays in contemporary African drama, not only totally refuse to compromise with oppressive and misanthropic misrule sanctioned and rationalised by custom, tradition or religion, but also give eloquent expression to a humanism built on true solicitude, reciprocity, human warmth and undogmatic rationalism. In *Oda Oak Oracle* this humanist will and consciousness are embodied in Shanka; in *Collision of Altars* they are incarnated in Armah, though quite often, as in the following bitter lament by the Royal Crier, the humanism finds a voice among those who have been misused by tyranny:

> For several long pitiless years
> Fear crawled in each night
> To hug this dying city of altars.
> Tempers rose in the ranks
> And grew horny each day.
> With each stab of pain
> Each ferment of deception
> The wooden hearts of god-makers
> Throbbed with contempt for each other.
> There is no measuring the walls
> That rose between
> Each interpreter of dreams.
> Each preached, ranted and collided
> In the minds of the strong
> And in the hearts
> Of the weakest of worshippers.
> In this lone city
> Where they never cease praying for man
> Men die most. [202–03]

By the evidence of these two plays alone, Gabre-Medhin must be one of the most self-conscious *aesthetes* working in the contemporary African theatre. These plays show that this dramatist pays as much attention to the dramatic *forms* and the *styles* of performance suitable for the social vision inherent in his strongly ideological views. Problematically, however, there seems to be a *displacement* between the progressive content of his plays and the possibly reactionary forms and styles of his theatre.

In the first place, the externalities of his dramatic form show features of a peculiar kind of verse tragedy. Both *Oda Oak Oracle* and *Collision of Altars* depict weak, ineffectual tragic heroes who, though they remain incorruptible and uncompromisable in their volitions, yet sink all too easily into romantic despair before the overwhelming forces of negation and alienation fostered by religious ideology. The effusive, poeticized language given these heroes at such crucial moments thus acts as both a refuge and an evasion. * * *

The displacement between form and content in *Oda Oak Oracle* and *Collision of Altars* works at an even more crucial level in the theatrical style of both plays. The two plays show a high degree of anti-naturalistic theatrical stylization, even though they do this with dissimilar methods. In *Oda Oak Oracle*, which is constructed as a ritualistic verse tragedy, the stylization takes the form of terseness in language, rapidity of pace and spareness of action: physical and emotional action are entirely subsumed in ritualistic verse dialogue (even a physical combat to the death between Goaa and Shanka is narrated by an individualised chorus which is present at the battle). In *Collision of Al-*

tars, on the other hand, the language becomes more ornate, the pace slower and more deliberate and the action more complex and many-layered, distributed as it is between silent mime, choreographed cult-dances and narrative declamatory chants. Thus, the stylizing impulse which seems to have been contained and more or less integrated with the imperative of communicating a social vision in *Oda Oak Oracle* becomes an end in itself in *Collision of Altars*. This play calls for the use of all the resources possible in the theatre as a meeting ground of diverse arts: sound effects, lighting effects, dance, music, mime, choral chants, cinematic projections, silence. In his prefatory notes, Gabre-Medhin places his performance idiom in this play in the tradition of the so-called 'total theatre'. Considering the meticulous attention to the interrelationships between the different units of performance and the modulations and precision which he advises in his generous stage directions in the playtext, it is not unfair to ascribe to Gabre-Medhin an aspiration to achieve the Wagnerian model of the 'Gesamt-kunstwerk', the 'unified, total art-work'.

Wagner, as is well known, represents one of the high points of Euro-pean bourgeois aestheticism in the theatre: this is aesthetic practice which draws attention away from the content or substance of drama to the splendid, dazzling mirror of enchantment in the spectacle and phenomenon of performance. This model of theatrical practice is an indulgence anywhere, but even more so in the contemporary African theatre. More pointedly, it works against the earnestness and relevance of dramatists like Gabre-Medhin whose social vision has much to con-tribute to the current ideological debates in Africa.

JANE PLASTOW

[Tsegaye Gabre-Medhin and Ethiopian Reformist Theatre]†

The New Drama

The radical change in the function of drama was initiated by a small group of young men, most of whom encountered drama via secondary or higher education, and who in some cases subsequently travelled abroad specifically to study drama techniques. The names that stand out in this group are those of Tsegaye Gabre-Medhin, Mengistu Lemma, Tesfaye Gessesse, Debebe Eshetu and Wogayehu Nigatu. With the exception of Tsegaye all were upper-class Amharas, and all were influenced in their work not only by an education in European dramatic forms but also by early experience of the traditions of clas-sical *qene*. Tesfaye, Debebe and Wogayehu all encountered drama for

---

† From *African Theatre and Politics: The Evolution of Theatre in Ethiopia, Tanzania and Zim-babwe* (Amsterdam and Atlanta, Ga.: Rodopi, 1996) 94–96, 98–99. Reprinted by permission of the publisher.

the first time as students at the University, became involved in acting, and so impressed audiences that they won scholarships—Tesfaye to the United States and the latter two to Hungary—to study the discipline further. Mengistu Lemma was the late starter of the group as far as theatre was concerned. He was first a poet, and became Ethiopia's most eminent satiric playwright in his thirties only after writing successfully in several other genres. However, it was Tsegaye Gabre-Medhin who was to become Ethiopia's most prolific and famous playwright, and the most powerful dramaturge in the country. The new reformist theatre must be dated from Tsegaye's return to Ethiopia in 1959, after spending a year in England and France studying drama on a UNESCO scholarship, and his subsequent appointment as Vice-Director of Arts at the Haile Selassie I Theatre.

Prior to 1959 the Haile Selassie Theatre had been run largely for the Emperor's pleasure. It opened in splendour for the 1955 Silver Jubilee, complete with imported electrical equipment and orchestral instruments, and with an Austrian director and technicians. The opening play was scheduled to be Makonnen Endalkachew's *Dawitna Orion*, but Haile Selassie ordered the actors off in mid-performance in order to bring on a French ballet company he had hired at enormous cost for the occasion. In the following four years only twelve short-running productions were mounted, often with costumes imported from abroad and lavish scenery. Since seats cost up to fifty Ethiopian dollars, few outside court circles attended; between sporadic bursts of imperial interest, the acting company, which had been moved wholesale from the old City Hall Theatre, languished in abject poverty.

With Tsegaye's appointment the theatre began to change. He and the new Director of Arts, Seyoum Sibhat, Ethiopianised the whole concern, and from 1959 until his resignation in 1970 Tsegaye effectively ran the Haile Selassie Theatre, using it primarily to mount a string of his own plays and his translations of Shakespeare and Molière. Such productions make up nearly half of the twenty-five plays for which I have been able to find records in this period. The plays cover a range of genres, from the historical to love stories, and vary from one-act pieces to epics which may take up to four hours of performance time. The most significant and popular were those which addressed the plight of both urban and rural masses, and the playwright's best-known work, *Tewodros*, which draws on the historical figure of Emperor Tewodros to question the role of a sovereign, and to cast doubt on the concept of divine right.

The greatest single innovation of Tsegaye's work was the placing of ordinary people at the centre of many of his plays. Ethiopian art traditionally sees the lower classes as of less value than the nobility, and had tended to concentrate on the glorification of God and the monarchy; the emblematic nature of this traditional art was also at odds with the move towards psychological realism in these new people's plays. Yet the people themselves responded by coming in growing numbers to a theatre which for the first time began to be representative of more than just the hegemonic group. Many of Tsegaye's plays were censored, and, even when a performance was allowed, permission for publication was frequently refused. His early works *Askeyami Ligagered* (The Ugly Girl) and *Kosho Cigara* (Cheap Cigarettes) were both subjected to cuts, while *Joro Dagif* (Mumps) earned Tsegaye a day in prison when the Chief of Police overheard what he considered to be inflammatory lines being quoted by an actor in a bar.

The most popular of the Sixties people's plays, and the one which perhaps most profoundly demonstrates the shift in drama to a concern for the masses, was *Ye Kermasow* (A Man of the People).[1] This is a sombre piece examining the degradation of city life among the poor and the aspiring petit bourgeoisie. The play centres on two brothers, Mogus and Tekola, who are living in poverty in Addis Ababa. Mogus is a clerk whose wife has left him, along with their only child, to go and live with a richer man. Mogus tries in vain to control his younger brother, Tekola, who, although nominally a student, has given himself up to a life of dissolution amongst the city's numerous bars. Into this scene of spiritual and material destitution comes the brothers' dying uncle, Abiye, who misguidedly seeks health in the sick atmosphere of the capital. However, this uncle has a further dream: to restore the brothers by persuading them to go back to their ancestral lands and seek salvation in the "pure" life of the countryside.

Ultimately Abiye dies, Mogus is left utterly demoralised, and Tekola finds himself in prison for attacking his former sister-in-law's second husband. Yet it is in Tekola that we see the possibility of salvation, for he alone retains his fighting spirit. Abiye's day of ultra-conservatism has passed, Mogus has been destroyed by his unending series of tribulations, but Tekola rejects traditional fatalistic acceptance of one's lot in life and at the end of the play is considering building a new future back on the family farm.

In all this there is a strong streak of the nostalgia common to many literary works coming out of Africa in the Sixties. The city is an evil, corrupting entity, and purity and hope lie in rejecting alien (i.e. Western) values and returning to true Ethiopian tradition. Yet it is not quite so simple. Abiye, who embodies tradition, is an anachronism and cannot survive in the new age. What Tsegaye would have us admire in Tekola is the spirit that rejects the traditional teaching of the church that the meek shall inherit the earth. Above all, the play raises questions about the future. If we cannot simply re-create the past, and the present is so hopeless for the urban masses, in what direction should youth look for the future? The implicit criticism of government in all this was sufficient to cause Haile Selassie to walk out of the play's premiere. In particular he could not tolerate the descent of Mogus's wife into prostitution, and the condition for performances to continue was that she and her small son should be cut from the script.

* * *

1. Tsegaye Gabre-Medhin, *Ye Kermasow* (Addis Ababa: Berhanena Selam Press, 1965/66).

Apart from plays about the social problems of the people, Tsegaye is notable for turning the tradition of historico-patriotic drama from an instrument of imperial glorification into a means of questioning the idea of the Solomonic divine right to rule. *Tewodros*, his best-known work, is on the surface a simple piece glorifying the imperial past. It tells the story of the rise of Tewodros, the great Christian-inspired unifier of previously divided Ethiopia, and portrays in almost biblical terms his downfall at the hands of the British.[2] Tewodros even dies with Christ's lament on his son's lips: *"Abbaba! Lemin Tewkegn?"* (Father! Why hast thou forsaken me?).[3]

However, the covert message is far more subversive. Throughout the play it is emphasised that Tewodros, who prefers to be known by his personal name of Kassa, is a man of the people. He comes from a simple peasant background, and his enemies are the selfish priesthood and the remnants of the Solomonic line, Empress Menen and Ras Ali, who care only for their rank and have allowed Ethiopia to fall into disarray. Tewodros is constantly tormented by the blood he is forced to spill in order to re-establish Ethiopia as a great Christian nation. His suicide occurs largely because he has been unable to convince the forces of reaction of the need to abandon selfish greed and unite in fulfilling his dream of modernising and re-uniting the Empire.

Tsegaye makes it clear that the traditional pillars of the Empire, the church and the aristocracy, are the very groups which prevent Ethiopia from advancing into a hopeful future. Bloodshed is inevitable:

> They make me do it! The petty, selfish lustful chiefs make me do it. They force me to shed the blood of the very people I would be more than willing to give my life for [. . .] The fools from within do not hesitate to make me sacrifice innocent souls to exploit their own wicked ends. Maybe they too are destined to make progress impossible, both for the people and themselves; these centuries old leeches! These stubborn powerful puppets! And, AND blaspheming monstrous priests! Those interwoven evil webs! Those eye-piercing, cheap candle-lights. They make me angry, my son. They make me do it to my beloved people.[4]

The criticism of the Solomonic empire here is barely veiled. Indeed, in his later historical works, *Oda Oak Oracle* and *Collision of Altars*, which are similarly anti-clerical and go further in preaching tolerance for Ethiopia's multiple religions and abhorrence for religious and state bigotry, Tsegaye turned to writing in English because he was so sure that the plays would be censored.[5]

---

2. Tewodros was originally called Kassa. It is the custom in Ethiopia for monarchs to take a crown name on assuming the throne. The choice of Tewodros was significant because legend had it that a messianic king called Tewodros would come to save Ethiopia in her moment of need.
3. Tsegaye Gabre-Medhin, "Tewodros," *Ethiopia Observer* (London, 1966): 93.
4. Tsegaye Gabre-Medhin, "Tewodros," *Ethiopia Observer*, 221.
5. Tsegaye Gabre-Medhin, *Oda Oak Oracle* (London: Oxford UP, 1965); *Collision of Altars* (London: Rex Collings, 1977).

Ama Ata Aidoo

LLOYD W. BROWN

[Oral Tradition in *Dilemma of a Ghost*]†

Among contemporary Ghanaian dramatists, male and female, only
Ama Ata Aidoo compares with Sutherland in exploiting oral literature,
especially folk drama, in modern theater. Like Efua Sutherland, Aidoo
has taught extensively in her field. She graduated from the University
of Ghana in 1964, and subsequently attended a creative writing program at Stanford University in the United States. Since then she has
taught as a research fellow at the Institute of African Studies in the
University of Ghana, and as visiting lecturer in other African universities and in American colleges. Both as writer and teacher she has
always demonstrated a special interest in the kind of oral literary
traditions that so strongly influence her own plays.

As Aidoo has remarked, her ideal form of theater is one that capi-
talizes on the dramatic art of storytelling. This kind of theater, she
feels, would actually be a complete environment in which the usual
amenities of eating and drinking would be combined with storytelling,
poetry-reading, and plays. In Aidoo one encounters a tremendous confidence in the integrity and inclusiveness of the oral tradition. She
perceives the tradition of storytelling as one that actually combines
techniques and conventions that are often separated into distinctive
genres, especially in the Western literary tradition. The storyteller's art
is therefore a synthesis of poetry, dramatic play-acting, and narrative
plot. This art is social in the most literal sense. The artist is physically
and morally located in the center of her, or his, audience, and the
story itself reflects and perpetuates the moral and cultural values of
the audience. Consequently when Aidoo talks of a theater that, ideally,
duplicates the oral tradition, she is emphasizing the inclusiveness of
that oral tradition—and the extent to which the art and function of
the storyteller's performance become direct extensions of the storyteller's society.

Aidoo's first play, *The Dilemma of a Ghost*, is a fairly obvious example of this ideal at work, for it is closely associated with a distinctive
storytelling tradition. This particular tradition is now known as the

† From *Women Writers in Black Africa* (Westport, Conn.: Greenwood Press, 1981) 84–90.
Reproduced with permission of Greenwood Publishing Group, Inc., Westport, CT. The author's notes have been edited. Page numbers in brackets refer to this Norton Critical Edition.

dilemma tale. The dilemma tale usually poses difficult questions of moral or legal significance. These questions are usually debated both by the narrator and the audience—and on this basis the dilemma is a good example of the highly functional nature of oral art in traditional Africa. * * *

* * * The raising of such questions and the debates that they provoke really function as a kind of intellectual exercise that develops and continually stimulates the audience's ability to discuss such dilemmas in everyday experience. It is therefore not difficult to see why such a storytelling tradition would attract someone like Aidoo with her strong interest in drama as an extension of the folktale heritage. The explicitly functional context of the dilemma folktale is compatible with her frank interest in the social setting of contemporary theater. The raising and debating of questions in the dilemma tradition is an example of the way in which her ideal theater would itself be an extension of the audience's society: that is, theater should raise issues that are of immediate and pressing relevance to the theater-goer's experience.

In *Dilemma of a Ghost* the central problem or issue is presented as a play-within-a-play. A boy and a girl play the game, "The Ghost," holding hands and skipping in circles as they sing the ghost's story. The story is a simple one: early in the morning, while the moon was still shining, the singers went to a crossroads, Elmina Junction. There they saw a "wretched ghost" debating with himself: he was trying to make up his mind which road he should take—the one leading to Elmina itself, or the one to the city of Cape Coast.

This vignette is presented as a dream by the boy, now grown into the young man, Ato. Ato, the play's main protagonist, is really the "ghost" of the play, for he is incapable of making firm choices in a society where fundamental changes often pose crucial questions. He himself represents some of those changes, having been sent to the United States for a university education. The circumstances under which he returns home are not easy. His family, having underwritten his education at great expense, has great expectations of the returning scholar. The black American bride with whom he returns is quite controversial because of cultural differences between Eulalie and her in-laws, and Ato contributes to the difficulties by not being frank to either side—by failing, for example, to explain to his family the nature of certain decisions (such as birth control) which he and Eulalie have made.

Eventually, it is Ato's family that demonstrates the ability to deal humanely and flexibly with a complete stranger whose ways are alien and whose ignorance is often compounded by arrogance. At the conclusion, Ato the scholar is literally deserted on stage, still unable to demonstrate any capacity for the complex choices and for the kind of compromise that are required by the conflicts between old and new ways—between the culture of an older generation of Ghanaians and the new modes that are represented by his own wife, his education, and his civil service job.

The tradition of the dilemma tale has been absorbed, not only into the play's themes by way of the dream-sequence, but also into Ato's personality. His character has been presented according to the basic principle in the art of the dilemma tale—the posing of ethical and sociopolitical choices and the individual's ability to weigh and make those choices. The audience's reaction to his character is therefore determined by the manner in which Ato fails to cope with the problems which have been formally presented by the play's dilemma-tale design. In assuming the ethical motives of the dilemma folk tradition, the dramatist's art has also adopted some of the characteristics of that design.

The ghost's dilemma is not only presented within Ato's conscious-ness (by way of his dream), thereby emphasizing the tale's immediate psychological pertinence. It is also presented in the communal context of the oral tradition to which it belongs (by way of the children's play-song), thereby juxtaposing Ato's dilemma as a contemporary Ghanaian with the communal customs which insist upon the need to deal with moral and social dilemmas. This kind of juxtaposition is as important to the play's structure as it is to the characterization of Ato himself, for the play brings together the distinctive literary conventions of dif-ferent cultural traditions (the Ghanaian and the European). The for-mal five-act structure incorporates the folk vignette of the ghost's tale upon which it draws for its central theme, and in the process the European convention of act divisions becomes the theatrical context for the the ethical viewpoint and communal mode of Aidoo's oral tra-dition. Similarly the familiar chorus assumes a double identity, recal-ling the interpretative functions of the standard Western chorus and revealing in its dialogue structure (between two women) the unmis-takable colloquial rhythms of living speech in Aidoo's Akan culture. The narrative embellishments and judgements of the chorus are of-fered from the vantage point of concerned neighbors, and they con-stitute the kind of communal perspective that is brought to bear on the alien individualism of both Ato and Eulalie.

Take, for example, the women's news of Eulalie's rumored preg-nancy:

2nd Woman:	As for you, my sister!
	She uses machines.
	This woman uses machines for doing everything . . .
1st Woman:	But this is too large for my head
	Or is the wife pregnant with a machine child?
2nd Woman:	Pregnant, with a machine child?
	How can she be?
	Does she know what it is to be pregnant
	Even with a child of flesh and blood?
1st Woman:	Has she not given birth to a child since they married?
2nd Woman:	No, my sister,
	It seems as if the stranger-woman is barren.
1st Woman:	Barren?
2nd Woman:	As an orange which has been scooped of all fruit [264–65].

The dramatic conventions upon which the play is structured reflect Aidoo's diverse cultural sources; and taken together these sources represent the multiple choices that are integral to Ato's dilemma and, by extension, to his changing society as a whole.

The role of women in one of these conventions, the chorus, is not unique, but it is appropriate here, for as women the chorus embodies and emphasizes the domestic or family context within which the play's dilemmas are located. More specifically, their role as commentators in the chorus and their identity as women bear directly upon the fact that the woman's situation is a focal point in the dilemma themes of the play. In describing Eulalie as the product of a machine-culture, the women speak out of a cultural tradition to which Eulalie is a complete stranger and from which she is progressively alienated when she is confronted with its expectations of a woman as wife and mother. On one hand, the rather brutal history which has often fragmented the black American family has given Eulalie a strong incentive to become part of the closely knit Odumna clan into which she has married. On the other hand, her American upbringing and the cultural habits which it represents, result in her being hostile and incomprehensible to Ato's family. In one sense, she is the outsider, amusingly naive at best and intolerably arrogant at her worst, but, in another sense, she is the archetypal New World black in search of West African roots and, through those roots, a coherent sense of her ethnic identity. In this cultural conflict, which is clearly analogous to Ato's dilemmas, her identity as a woman is of immediate significance. Her individualism scandalizes the communally oriented women of Ato's family just as much as her decision against childbearing for the time being. Her dilemmas as a woman (a sense of obligation to Ato's family versus her own egotistic preferences) are explained by the fact that she is a non-African woman as well as by her black American self-conflicts.

In keeping with the complexity of choices which she inherits from the tradition of the dilemma tale, Aidoo does not offer a simple contrast between a confused Eulalie and a simple, monolithic image of African womanhood. The Ghanaian women in the chorus demonstrate conflicts, or a sense of alternative possibilities, which are intrinsic to their own situation as African women—especially on the issues of childbearing and motherhood. The First Woman is childless, and she repeatedly bemoans the misfortunes of women like herself while recalling the wisdom of the ancestors in extolling the virtues of motherhood. The Second Woman, whose house is teeming with children, envies the childless woman's freedom from this "curse," as she describes childbearing.

The relative advantages of childlessness and childbearing are therefore as open to debate in the experiences of these women as they are in Eulalie's different cultural context. Of course, the parallel is not complete. Despite her complaints about her own fertility, the Second Woman does not really repudiate the maternal role as such. On the whole, one does not detect in her situation the kind of free choice Eulalie exercises in the matter—much to the scandalized amazement

of Ato's mother, Esi Kom: "I have not heard anything like this before.
. . . Human beings deciding when they must have children" [274].
Moreover, even in her most outrageously selfish moments Eulalie's
general image of untrammeled independence wins a reluctant admiration from Esi Kom herself, especially when Eulalie refuses to accompany her husband to a traditional thanksgiving festival. In Esi Kom's
words, "I would have refused too if I were her: I would have known
that I can always refuse to do things" [273].

Ultimately, the family crisis generated by Eulalie's presence is resolved, not by any clear-cut choice or pat solutions by Eulalie or Ato,
but by Esi Kom's recognition that Eulalie's failings have been due to
the natural errors of a stranger compounded by Ato's bungling and
indecisiveness. Just as she recognizes some enviable qualities in Eulalie's independence, Esi Kom also perceives that the women of the
community may have contributed to the conflict with Eulalie by virtue
of their ignorance of Eulalie's world. Esi Kom's real assistance to the
younger woman lies in the fact that the former recognizes Eulalie's
dilemmas as a displaced black American and as a woman caught between conflicting cultural assumptions about women. Neither Esi
Kom, nor the play as a whole, really claims to have solved the complex
dilemmas of Eulalie's identity and Ato's personality. In this regard, the
play is comparable with the dilemma tale, posing questions which are
not necessarily accessible to easy, straightforward solutions and which,
by their very complexity, ensure a crucial recognition of the complexities of social relationships and individual feelings. What is important
here is the fact that Esi Kom is able to offer the kind of compassionate
understanding that her son lacks, and that the older woman, unlike
Ato, has the perspicacity to recognize her own ignorance as well as
another's.

Much of the traditional wisdom which Esi Kom embodies and which
is inherent in the play's dilemma conventions is rooted in a frank self-
knowledge—the candor with which the women of the chorus reveal a
certain ambivalence towards childbearing and motherhood in a society
that prizes children, or in the honesty with which Esi Kom herself can
admire Eulalie's individualistic sense of choice even at the very moment that the older woman deplores the crude arrogance of that individualism. Ato and Eulalie, on their side, represent and experience
the dilemmas of a new generation of Africans and black Americans,
both in terms of broad cultural choices and with specific reference to
domestic relationships and sexual roles. On the other hand, Esi Kom
and her contemporaries represent the kind of wisdom traditionally demanded and nurtured by the convention of the dilemma folktale: as
the principal agent of reconciliation and compassion Esi Kom's personality integrates the traditional insights of the oral convention with
the moral perspectives of the play as a whole. At this point, in a per-
spectival as well as structural sense, Aidoo's theater literally becomes
an extension of the oral tradition.

* * *

C. L. INNES

[Motherhood in Ama Ata Aidoo's Plays]†

* * * From her earliest work * * * Aidoo has challenged the nostalgic image of 'African mother' as symbol with a series of mothers whose characters and roles as well as their very plurality prevent them from being seen either symbolically or nostalgically.

Her play, *The Dilemma of a Ghost*, first performed in 1964, makes motherhood a central issue, concerning three generations of women —Nana, the grandmother; Esi Kom, the mother; and Monka, the sister of a young Ghanaian man named Ato—he has just returned from America, after marrying Eulalie, an Afro-American. It is a cast very closely paralleled in Armah's novel *Fragments*, published four years later, although Armah's Afro-American outsider is a mistress rather than a wife. Unlike the frail, blind and unheard Nana of Armah's novel, however, Aidoo's grandmother is lively, imperious and very much at the centre of her family's life. And although she speaks as a member of the older generation, unable or unwilling to countenance change, she is also a 'character' in her own right and in all senses of the word. The impetus to symbolise comes not from the author or audience, but from Eulalie, the Afro-American wife, who seeks a lost homeland and a lost mother in Africa. The contrast between Eulalie's imagined caricature of her African 'homeland' and the actuality is central to this tragi-comic play.

The other central dilemma, which remains largely unresolved in Aidoo's earliest published work, is the choice between motherhood and childlessness, a dilemma shadowed in the debate between the two village women who act as a kind of secondary chorus, one of whom is burdened with the care of her many children and the other who is barren and longs for children. For them, and for Ato's family, the fact that Eulalie and Ato have *chosen* to remain childless is incomprehensible. It is a choice which, as in Armah's *Fragments*, is linked to materialism and western individualism as opposed to commitment to family and community, and to the view of marriage as a continuation of romance rather than as the continuation of family. It is interesting that Eulalie is less certain about this choice than her Ghanaian husband is. When she worries whether 'it won't matter at all', it is he who declares that they will 'create a paradise, with or without children', and insists:

> I love you, Eulalie, and that's what matters. Your own sweet self should be OK for any guy. And how can a first born child be difficult to please? Children, who wants them? In fact, they will

† From *Motherlands: Black Women's Writing from Africa, the Caribbean and South Asia*, ed. Susheila Nasta (New Brunswick, N.J.: Rutgers University Press, 1991) 133–38. Copyright © 1991 by Susheila Nasta. Reprinted by permission of Rutgers University Press and The Women's Press Ltd. Page numbers in brackets refer to this Norton Critical Edition.

make me jealous. I couldn't bear seeing you love someone else better than you do me. Not yet, darling, and not even my own children. [245]

The play ends abruptly and unexpectedly with a kind of reconciliation between Eulalie and her mother-in-law, in league against Ato after he has struck her for 'shaming' him in front of his family. Although this reconciliation seems imposed and is not altogether convincing, it nevertheless foreshadows a number of mother/daughter-in-law alliances in Aidoo's short stories, and also the failure of alliances between men and women of the younger generation for whom pregnancy or childbirth all too often bring disruption. Thus in an early story, 'Certain Winds from the South', a northern Ghanaian mother is left to tell her daughter-in-law that the son has decided he must go south to earn money for his wife and newborn child, and she remembers her own sorrow at the departure of her husband over 20 years previously to join the British army. In two stories, 'A Gift from Somewhere', and 'No Sweetness Here', a child for whom the mother bears special affection is the cause of marital anger and dissent. The husband in 'Two Sisters' is unfaithful to his wife because he finds her pregnant body repulsive. 'Something to Talk About on the Way to the Funeral' recounts the story of a mother who takes in the girl her son impregnates and deserts, and of the relationship between the two women: 'Some people said they were like mother and daughter. Others that they were like sisters. Still even more others said they were like friends.' 'The Message' humourously reveals the cultural distance between a rural grandmother and her urban granddaughter, but at the same time celebrates the grandmother's heroic journey to the city and her unwavering determination to do what is right for her grandchild—a journey that ends triumphantly with the discovery that the granddaughter has given birth to twins and that all are well. In this story, the husband appears only as the sender of a telegram; there is no further thought of him in either the grandmother's or the storyteller's mind.

Yet it is interesting to note that the alliances between women of differing generations are more often between mothers and daughters-in-law, than between mothers and their natural daughters. Between the latter friction is often the norm. Yaaba, the unruly young girl in the story 'The Late Bud', desperately longs for signs of affection from her mother, and is painfully beaten by her. Monka, the daughter in *The Dilemma of a Ghost*, resents the fact that all family resources have gone towards her brother's education while she has had to leave school early, and she rebels against the norms of 'feminine' behaviour. We are told:

But if Esi Kom bears a daughter
And the daughter finds no good man
Shall we say it is Esi Kom's fate in childbirth,
Or shall we say it is her daughter's trouble?
Is not Monka the sauciest girl

Born here for many years?
Has she not the hardest mouth in this town? [253]

Monka is the prototype for the title character in Aidoo's second play,
Anowa, who is condemned by her elders for 'behaving as though she
were the heroine in a story.' In both plays, the older women are seen
(at first sight anyway) as conservative supporters of a tradition which
restricts the roles of women and limits their choices. Anowa's mother,
Badua, laments her daughter's refusal to marry a suitor approved by
her parents, and resists the father's suggestion that she might be a
priestess who would have 'glory and dignity', because a priestess is 'not
an ordinary human being'. Badua declares:

> I want my child
> To be a human woman
> Marry a man,
> Tend a farm
> And be happy to see her
> Peppers and her onions grow.
> A woman like her
> Should bear children,
> Many children,
> So she can afford to have
> One or two die.
> Should she not take
> Her place at meetings
> Amongst the men and women of the clan?
> And sit on my chair when
> I am gone? And a captainship in the army
> Should not be beyond her
> When the time is ripe.

It is worth noting that Badua's concept of a normal 'human' life for a
woman differs from the future a traditional European mother might
have envisioned for her daughter 100 years ago, a future which was
unlikely to have included a captainship in the army or a place at meetings amongst the men and women of the clan. But such positions for
women are earned through fulfilling accepted roles, of which being a
wife and mother are primary. Such roles also assume a stable, agrarian
way of life, and a closely knit extended family which will provide support for the old and weak.

Anowa's assertion of her own choice of marriage partner entails
other unforeseen choices and assertions, beginning with the rejection
by and of her mother, and thus of a place in her own community. Her
refusal to be subservient as a daughter is in character with her refusal
to be subservient as a wife, and although it is clear that she is physically and intellectually more adventurous than Kofi, her husband, and
that this is what at first attracts him to her, these very same characteristics alienate him once he has become relatively wealthy (thanks
to her assistance).

In this play, Aidoo links Anowa's movement away from the restrictions of her mother's culture (or her motherculture) with the increasing impact of British colonisation (the play opens in 1874, the year that the British marched into the royal capital, Kumasi), a movement which is emphasised visually by the contrast between the opening scenes of village life and the closing scene in Kofi's sumptuous house, with its mixture of heavy Victorian furniture, animal skin rugs, and the self-glorifying portrait of Kofi Ako flanked by pictures of Queen Victoria and of the crow which is the totem bird of Kofi's clan.

In rebelling against her mother, Anowa finds that she has asserted her freedom only to lose it. Kofi cannot accept her as a comrade and equal; he wants a wife who will endorse his status, and who will bear him children. For Anowa, hierarchies of gender and class are clearly linked: she identifies with the slaves that Kofi has bought despite her bitter disapproval, and seeks desperately to disassociate herself from the privileged and ostentatious life that their labour brings for Kofi. Her determination to be true to herself and her principles, her vision, results in her becoming an outcast, rejected by her own family and branded as a witch by her husband, before he too casts her out. The ending of the play is a deeply pessimistic one, for in speaking out and telling the truth—that it is her husband rather than she who is infertile—she destroys him, the man for whom she gave up everything. The message seems to be that 'man cannot bear very much reality', and that women must either flatter their men and deny their own integrity; or speak out and destroy both themselves and those they love.

* * *

VINCENT O. ODAMTTEN

A Bird of the Wayside Sings†

Ama Ata Aidoo was twenty-two when her first major work, *The Dilemma of a Ghost*, was performed by the Student's Theatre, at Commonwealth Hall's Open-Air Theatre, University of Ghana, 12–14 March 1964. Aidoo arrived on the national and international scene as a promising young writer when the play was published the following year. As her literary debut, *The Dilemma* received mixed responses from critics and reviewers. Despite the popularity of the play in Accra, Lagos, Ibadan, and elsewhere in Africa, some of the critical authorities echoed C. J. Rea in tone: "It [*The Dilemma*] is less successful as a play, because Miss Aidoo lacked an experienced stage director to help

† From *The Art of Ama Ata Aidoo: Polyletics and Reading Against Neocolonialism* (Gainesville: University Press of Florida 1994), 14–15, 17–28, 41. Copyright © by Ama Ata Aidoo. Reprinted courtesy of the University Press of Florida and Ama Ata Aidoo. Page numbers in brackets refer to this Norton Critical Edition.

her work out a final version before publication. In this she suffers the same lack as all dramatists in West Africa, where there is no professional English-language theatre group."[1] * * *

More recent criticism seems divided. On the one hand, some still seems to echo many of the initial misgivings about the drama. On the other, the commentaries of a growing number of critics provide new and useful insights about *The Dilemma*.[2] What becomes apparent is that the highly critical responses came from those who still believed in the hegemony of a Western master narrative. Further, these critics did not or could not take into full account *the conflictual nature of the text at a presentational level* (that is, that of the characters themselves) as well as *the play's relation to the historical context that it narrates*, which is at a higher level of generalization.

*   *   *

That women's roles in the traditional society were more complementary than they are now speaks not so much to the "affirmation of African womanhood" as to the ravages of colonial oppression. It reveals how colonial domination can alter the precolonial social relations of many African societies. Only when we take this larger view of Aidoo's authorial project do her works in general, and this play in particular, make sense. As Aidoo herself has remarked, "You come to literature or things like that, and it's then that you really understand a term like neocolonialism. . . . Because of the colonial experience we still, unfortunately, are very much lacking in confidence in ourselves and what belongs to us. It is beautiful to have independence, but it's what has happened to our minds that is to me the most frightening thing about the colonial experience."[3] Aidoo is concerned with what happens to people under conditions of colonialism and neocolonialism, not just with the recognition of the African woman or mother as "the support and strength underlying the family." That she chooses women as a center should not be taken for an overriding feminist concern that subsumes all else. The literary and cultural context in which Aidoo was to make her debut as a writer was dominated by men. Quite often,

---

1. C. J. Rea, "The Culture Line: A Note on *The Dilemma of a Ghost*," *African Forum* 1, 1 (1966): 111–13.

2. These more open-minded critics, led by Eldred D. Jones, "Notes," *Bulletin of the Association for African Literature in English* 2 (1965): 33–34, were willing to engage Aidoo's first drama more or less on its own terms. Both Oyin Ogunba, "Modern Drama in West Africa," in *Perspectives on African Literature*, ed. Christopher Heywood (New York: Africana, 1971), 81–105, and John Nagenda, "Generations of Conflict: Ama Ata Aidoo, J. C. de Graft, and R. Sharif Easmon," in *Protest and Conflict in African Literature*, ed. Cosmo Pieterse and Ian Munro (New York: Africana, 1970), 101–8, comment favorably on Aidoo's "technical and verbal mastery" (Ogunba, 102) which is "so immediate and accurate" (Nagenda, 106). Mildred A. Hill-Lubin, in "The Relationship of African-Americans and Africans: A Recurring Theme in the Works of Ama Ata Aidoo," while pointing out the anachronisms in Aidoo's recreation of African-American speech patterns, stresses that Aidoo's "willingness to treat such a topic (the marriage between an African-American and an African) illustrates her curiosity, originality, individualism and perceptivity, qualities which characterize all her writings" *Présence Africaine* 124, 4th quarter (1982): 190–201.

3. Ama Ata Aidoo in *African Writers Talking*, ed. Cosmo Pieterse and Dennis Duerden (New York: Africana, 1972), 26.

592   Vincent O. Odamtten

the works of her contemporaries expressed a degree of ambivalence even as they attempted to unite a surfacing nationalism with aspects of Western bourgeois culture. It is partly in light of this literary inheritance that we begin to understand Biodun Jeyifo's characterization of *The Dilemma* as one among "certain plays [that] deal exclusively with the political, social and cultural problems of the emergent elites."[4]

In Aidoo's reaction to her literary inheritance she anchors her play in a fuller, more comprehensive context; by doing so, particularly in her use of the chorus of the two neighbors, she is able to focus attention on the major dilemmas of our age: gender, race, and class. Further, the play has been characterized as exhibiting "realism," which Jeyifo applies "to those plays that deal with 'real' people in 'typical' situations, with plots that seem credible or probable in relation to the daily rounds of life and the cycles and passages of time within a given human community" (Jeyifo, 56). The audience or reader is never allowed to forget that, although what is being seen or read is a fiction, it is rooted in a shared objective reality. Put another way, despite the obvious differences in terms of historical experience and geographical location, we, as social and political beings, must contend with the economic and ideological determinations and articulations of class, race, and gender.

Further, Aidoo's first play, though situated in modern Ghana just after the heady days of Independence (circa 1960), is both structurally and thematically related to the traditional dilemma tale, the pertinence of which is foregrounded in the title. Essentially, the dilemma tale is a narrative whose primary function is to stimulate serious, deep-probing discussion of social, political, and moral issues that confront human beings in their everyday lives. Aidoo uses the dilemma tale neither to satisfy the expatriate anthropological critic not to provide local color. The immediate task her drama confronts is the focusing of our regard, by means of the dilemma tale device, on contemporary Ghanaian and African problems. Although dilemma tales have been the object of inquiry by many Western anthropologists, their purportedly scientific investigations do not result in particularly insightful conclusions. For instance, William R. Bascom, who is more open than most anthropologists in the field, prefaces his documentation of these "riddle-cases of conscience" with this apologia:

> It is their intellectual function and their relevance to ethical standards, *rather than any literary merit,* that make the dilemma tales interesting. *No elaborate plot or surprising denouement is necessary to present a dilemma, and some examples barely qualify as prose narratives.* . . . It is perhaps in part because *many dilemma tales have little literary merit*—a shortcoming greatly exaggerated in my summaries which follow—that they have been relatively neglected by American folklorists; *this neglect also reflects the general indif-*

---

4. Biodun Jeyifo, *The Truthful Lie: Essays in a Sociology of African Drama* (London: New Beacon, 1985), 47.

*ference of American scholars to African folklore, of which dilemma
tales seem to be particularly characteristic.* (italics added)[5]

*   *   *

I suggest that this ploy achieves, among other ends, "a fidelity to the
oral, [so that] these texts can instead be 'heard' to declare the precedence of 'real' human—therefore essentially untextualizable—voices
and meanings over the putative political and historical hegemony of
the word." To this end, there is always an irresolution (on one or more
levels of signification) that creates a tension with the tale's formal
closure. Those present are compelled to resolve what is unresolved in
the performance outside the theater or text, in order to achieve a sense
of aesthetic-ideological satisfaction. In fact, the telling of dilemma
tales in particular, and of other oral narratives in general, affords excellent opportunities for raising issues that may be in unacknowledged
conflict with the dominant ideology.[6] It is in this regard that we should
begin our examination of *The Dilemma* and the rest of Aidoo's works.
Whether looking at "performance" or "text," *we must learn to read
against neocolonialism.*

It should be noted that the traditional raconteur has never been only
a creative artist or performer, but also one whose performance has
been *licensed*. That is to say, the nature of the performance (the choice
of material, genre, and so on) legitimized the criticism or challenging
of the status quo or perceived social and political injustices. The dilemma tale achieves a detachment from its fictive content, if handled
in a competent way, because it is a more critical mode of literary
discourse than, say, the traditional Kwaku Ananse folktale. This ability
to signify the "not-said" of its content—by way of self-reference to its
ideological determinations through its very structure—separates it
from the traditional oral folktale in the same way that literary criticism,
as a mode of discourse, is separate from the literary texts that are its
objects. As valid as is Terry Eagleton's critique of Pierre Macherey's
overdependence on the concept of "absence" and apparent negative
formulation of the relationship between the general ideology and the
text, in the case of the dilemma tale Eagleton's cautionary remarks
seem inappropriate.[7] When one considers the dilemma tale, it becomes
evident that the relationship between the general ideology and the
"whole text" *prevents* an uncritical reading, by simultaneously fore-
grounding and making unsatisfactory such critically negative repro-
ductions of the textual-ideological relationship. In the dilemma tale,
especially as it is deployed in Aidoo's play, the formal structure and
the significance of its content are inseparable. Thus, *The Dilemma*'s
performance value lies in the fact that, as a fixed and truncated part
of a larger whole, the dilemma is always extended out of the text and

5. William R. Bascom, *African Dilemma Tale* (The Hague: Mouton, 1975), 1–3.
6. See Leroy Vail and Landeg White, *Power and the Praise Poem* (Charlottesville, Va.: University
   Press of Virginia, 1991). Vail and White demonstrate how oral poetry is quite often used as
   a political tool to criticize perceived injustices against the people by their rulers.
7. Terry Eagleton, *Criticism and Ideology* (London: Verso, 1980), 96–97.

into the context of the audience. It can never remain within the "partial" text of the written form. This is what makes a polylectical materialist criticism of *The Dilemma* necessary for a full understanding of the text, one that avoids misreadings similar to those indicated earlier, which are characteristic of bourgeois criticism.

In the specific example of *The Dilemma*, which incorporates elements of a literary mode of production (a dilemma tale) rooted in precapitalist, precolonial African societies' general modes of production, we have a text. Having a text, however, indicates the influence of other determinations as well: namely, the emergent traditions of modern African literature that have been overdetermined by the realities of colonial and postindependent Ghana. This text belongs to a literary practice or tradition that is both Western *and* African. The multiple determinations that have produced its specifics throughout Africa are various; the particular form it assumed in the Ghanaian context, however, is our initial concern, although the discussion has significance for the rest of Africa. Lloyd Brown notes that "among contemporary Ghanaian dramatists, male and female, only Ama Ata Aidoo compares with Sutherland in exploiting oral literature, especially folk drama, in modern theater. Like Efua Sutherland, Aidoo has taught extensively in her field. . . . Both as a writer and teacher she has always demonstrated a special interest in the kind of oral literary traditions that so strongly influence her own plays."[8] Perhaps the demands of her activities as a teacher have made Aidoo more aware of the implications of her art. We see in her literary products a consistent effort to avoid those complications that her male precursors left only partially addressed; namely, the expression in their works of a bifocal vision, a complex cultural dualism that sought to unite a Romantic precolonial primitivism and a post-Romantic neocolonial existentialism. They undertook this partially realized effort toward unity to describe the historical division and trauma of the Western-educated African. Their ultimate objective was the amelioration of what has been called "cultural schizophrenia."[9]

The Dilemma is concerned with the return of Ato Yawson, a young Ghanaian who has been studying in the United States of America. This return is the cause of various conflicts that move the action, particularly because Ato has not informed his family of his marriage to an African-American, Eulalie Rush. His very traditional family, epitomized by his mother, Esi Kom, ignorant of this marriage, is naturally surprised and even antagonistic to Eulalie and all she represents.[1] They consider her a "wayfarer," "the offspring of slaves"; in other words, a person without history, a tree without roots. Eulalie

8. *Women Writers in Black Africa* (Westport, Conn.: Greenwood, 1981), 84.
9. oMolara Ogundipe-Leslie, "The Function of Radical Criticism in African Literature Today." Lecture at the Annual Ibadan African Literature Conference, Ibadan, Nigeria, 15–19 August 1981, 12–15.
1. Given that Aidoo had not yet been to the United States and was herself writing from Ghanaian ideological assumptions about African-Americans, the representation of Eulalie is slightly *de-centered* throughout the play.

comes to Ghana carrying the heritage of the "New World," its histories of invasion, slavery, and racism, its myths and misconceptions about the "Dark Continent."

More precisely, Aidoo's play has as its underlying concern the dilemma of a ghost. On one level it is the dilemma of the Ghanaian petit bourgeois intellectual who is confronted with the problem of what Chinua Achebe and others have called "the clash of cultures." The site of this fray occurs in perhaps the most immediate and intimate of contexts—marriage and family. On another level, the drama examines, through the formal elements of the dilemma tale, the reactions of the participant-audience to the confrontations at both the presentational level and the general ideological one.

A brief overview of the Ghanaian climate in which The Dilemma was written and produced will help further our appreciation of Aidoo's work. Under the leadership of Dr. Kwame Nkrumah, the former British colony of Gold Coast had become the independent "Black Star" of progressive African politics during the late fifties and early sixties. As a relatively wealthy nation Ghana had a significant educated elite, an aggressive agricultural cash-crop policy, and systematic exploitation of mineral resources, factors that contributed to the heightened optimism that marked the transition from colonial to independent status. Progressive intellectuals and activists from all over the globe were making trips to Accra.[2] Yet, even in those days, there was an inkling that things were going awry.

Partly because of Aidoo's authorial ideology and partly because the drama is structurally and thematically related to the traditional dilemma tale, the play is more able to reveal its own ideological determinations than, for instance, Wole Soyinka's The Lion and the Jewel or The Road.[3] Both Aidoo and Soyinka use material, whether formal-structural or mythological-religious, gleaned from the orature of the Akans and Yorubas, respectively. Mildred A. Hill-Lubin has observed, however, that Soyinka's works tend to be closer in design to the West-

2. It is ironic that during the four or five years immediately preceding the publication of The Dilemma, Ghana had a Republican constitution, formal press censorship was introduced, a Preventive Detention Act had come into effect, the nation became a one-party state, and the price of its major foreign exchange export, cocoa, was rapidly falling in the world markets controlled by the West. A further irony becomes evident when we realize that Nkrumah was both agent and victim of the same ideological and economic forces that then beset Ghana, and that he described in Neocolonialism: The Last Stage of Imperialism (1965; reprint, New York: International Publishers, 1972). It might be said that Ghana was a school for anticolonial and neocolonial struggles, with Nkrumah conducting the lessons. See Basil Davidson, Black Star (New York: Praeger, 1974).

3. Wole Soyinka, The Lion and the Jewel (London: Oxford University Press, 1965), and The Road (London: Three Crowns/Oxford University Press, 1965). See Abiola Irele's discussion of The Lion and the Jewel in The African Experience in Literature and Ideology (London: Heinemann, 1981), 189–93. Of particular significance is Irele's discussion of Soyinka's use of Yoruba orature as it turns upon the metaphysical, and the playwright's positing of the artist, represented by the character of the Professor, as outside history. Another revealing commentary is Biodun Jeyifo, "The Hidden Class War in The Road," in The Truthful Lie, 11–22. In a manner comparable to this study of Aidoo's work, Jeyifo applies a "materialist, dialectical reading of The Road, . . . [to rectify] the displacement, in dominant abstractionist and idealist criticism and scholarship on the play, of the concrete material passions and aspirations of the play's characters" (12) revealed in Irele's criticism, for instance.

ern literary tradition and relatively more accessible to the Western critic.[4] In *The Road*, Soyinka focuses on the dregs of Nigeria's urban population with the one exception of the character of the Professor. The Professor seems to have made the revolutionary leap that Ato Yawson, in *The Dilemma*, is incapable of making. Following the lead of Frantz Fanon, it is likely that Soyinka is actually echoing the old idea that society's urban dispossessed need guidance and leadership "from *without* by already revolutionized cadres" (Jeyifo, 19). The Professor, however, assumes this leading role because "he dominates, mystifies and bedazzles them with his torrential verbal salvoes and the brilliance of his talents" (Jeyifo, 20). His desire to be "a man of the people" originates from his hopes of gain and profit.

Despite what may appear to be a revolutionary step, or a mad Orphean descent into the hell of urban Africa, our reading discloses Soyinka's rejection of the possible transformative role of the revolutionized petit bourgeois intellectual. Perhaps Ngugi wa Thiong'o's assessment of Soyinka's artistic vision more precisely locates the problems:

> Confronted with the impotency of the elite . . . , Wole Soyinka does not know where to turn. Often the characters held up for our admiration are (apart from the artists) cynics, or sheer tribal reactionaries like Baroka. The cynicism is hidden in the language (the author seems to revel in his own linguistic mastery) and in occasional flights into metaphysics. . . . Although Soyinka exposes his society in breadth, the picture he draws lacks depth, it is static, for he fails to see the present in the historical perspective of conflict and struggle. It is not enough for the African artist, standing aloof, to view society and highlight its weaknesses. He must try to go beyond this, to seek out the sources, the causes and the trends.[5]

At variance with Soyinka's position, Aidoo's play dramatically challenges the assumption or rejection of this role by the Ghanaian intellectual. Aidoo's deliberate choice of traditional oral materials and forms, her authorial ideology, and the general radical ideological climate during Ghana's immediate pre- and post-Independence era seem to have enabled Aidoo to avoid a "static" depiction of her society.

Even when a critic like Lloyd Brown recognizes the influence of African orature in the works of Aidoo, he is unable to grasp the full significance of the traditional dilemma tale as it bears on the concerns of the play. (Brown, 84–121). A somewhat detailed analysis of the prelude, with reference to subsequent developments in the play, will show how Aidoo deploys an African orature within and beyond the drama. The play opens with a direct address to the audience:

4. Mildred A. Hill-Lubin, "Storyteller and Audience in the Works of Ama Ata Aidoo," *Neohelicon* 16, 2 (1989): 221–45.
5. Ngugi wa Thiong'o, *Homecoming* (1972; reprint, London: Verso, 1980), 65–66. Ngugi and Jeyifo arrive at similar conclusions in this respect, though Jeyifo may appear more understanding of Soyinka's predicament ("Hidden Class War," in *The Truthful Lie*, 21).

> I am the Bird of the Wayside—
> The sudden scampering in the undergrowth,
> Or the trunkless head
> Of the shadow in the corner.
> I am an asthmatic old hag
> Eternally breaking the nuts
> Whose soup, alas,
> Nourished a bundle of whitened bones—
> Or a pair of women, your neighbours
> Chattering their lives away. [242–43]

By calling herself the Bird of the Wayside the narrator is, in the traditional context of tale-telling, making a disclaimer, for this title suggests an outcast, a stranger to the community who, ignorant of the community's laws and customs (ideological practices), may inadvertently offend in the telling of the tale. At the same time, this characterization of the narrator, taken together with the self-descriptions that follow, foregrounds the mutual determinations that exist between the ghost of the title and the inability of the principal characters in the drama to resolve their conflicts. After her disclaimer, the narrator alludes to herself in the first three instances as immaterial: "the sudden scampering in the undergrowth," "the trunkless head," and "the shadow in the corner." These references to the intangibility of the narrator—who, as traditional raconteur, is all characters—suggest that the principal characters in the drama are unable or unwilling *to see* the ideological underpinnings of their own actions. As audience-critics to whom this is addressed, however, we are to be made aware of these determinations by the very structure of the dilemma tale. That is to say, the drama does not end with the choral singing of the children—

> Shall I go to Cape Coast
> Shall I go to Elmina?
> I can't tell
> Shall I?
> I can't tell
> I can't tell
> I can't tell
> I can't tell. [275]

—because, in the words of Louis-Vincent Thomas, their song, which poses a question, only serves as the point "of departure for interminable palavers between young and old." (Bascom, 3). The dilemmas that confront the characters are simultaneously seen and not seen, contained and not contained, within the performance.

In the context of bourgeois (dramatic) literary practice, the narrator is usually absent from the text, certainly from the drama's performance. In Aidoo's play, however, the narrator is not only present but, in the opening address to the audience, points to her absence (or potential absence). Although arising from different historical contexts, the consequence of this duality is similar to the Brechtian alienation

effect: "A representation that alienates is one which allows us to recognize its subject, but at the same time makes it seem unfamiliar.
. . . The new alienations are only designed to free socially-conditioned
phenomena from that stamp of familiarity which protects them against
our grasp today."⁶ Aidoo's use of the oral tradition in *The Dilemma*
allows us, indeed forces us, to be distanced from the dramatic action.
We are aware of it as performance; yet our "interminable palavers"
and the stark realities of our daily lives root the play in the now—our
historical present.

In contradistinction to the first self-descriptions, the next two place
the narrator, as an "asthmatic old hag," in the position of a transhis-
torical figure whose actions are unproductive: "Eternally breaking nuts
/ Whose soup, alas, / Nourished a bundle of whitened bones" [242].
In the next characterization, the narrator is placed within the same
historical moment as the audience—"a pair of women, your
neighbours"—whose actions are also unproductive: "Chattering their
lives away" [242]. The dilemma tale would have been useless if it gave
rise only to an "interminable palaver" over the choices to be made. As
audience and participants in the "whole performance," we cannot and
do not have all of eternity to make our choices; like the ghost at Elmina
Junction, mentioned in the children's choral song, we have only until
the dawn.

Having established the location of the play by means of the alienation
effect, Aidoo further heightens the situation by a series of juxtapositions
that illuminate the narrator's relationship with the audience:

> I can furnish you with reasons why
> This and that and the other things
> Happened. But stranger,
> What would you have me say
> About the Odumna Clan? . . .
> Look around you,
> For the mouth must not tell everything.
> Sometimes the eye can see
> And the ear should hear. [243]

The confidence of the narrator's assertion that "I can furnish you with
reasons why" speaks of the creative ability of the raconteur as well as
her knowledge of the neocolonial society. But the narrator undercuts
this confidence by asking the audience ("stranger"), "What would you
have me say / About the Odumna Clan?" The complexity of this utterance cannot be overemphasized, despite its apparent simplicity. In
keeping with the character of the traditional raconteur, the narrator is
assuming a posture of humility; in effect, she is asking the audience
to be patient with her telling of the story. After all, anything a Bird of
the Wayside's performance will speak of can only be hearsay; ironically, it is the narrator who is the stranger. But in the actual phrasing
of the question it is we, the audience-critics, who are now excluded

6. John Willet, trans. and ed., *Brecht on Theatre: The Development of an Aesthetic*, 2d ed. (New
York: Hill and Wang, 1979), 192.

and labeled the "stranger." This reversal of our position with respect to narrator and the play foregrounds the reversals that are to take place during the actual performance. We wish to be entertained, perhaps to escape the all too familiar dilemmas that confront us daily, but the narrator will not allow us such an easy way out:

> Look around you,
> For the mouth must not tell everything.
> Sometimes the eye can see
> And the ear should hear. [243]

We are enjoined to be attentive, critical, and distanced, because that is the only way we will truly understand *The Dilemma*.

The narrator-raconteur then proceeds to describe the locale of the play and its social background, situating the Odumna Clan house with respect to the town, and offering a brief historical overview of the events that lead up to the first act. The socioeconomic prominence of the Odumna Clan, the home of Esi Kom and her family, is referred to in the next few lines:

> Yonder house is larger than
> Any in the town—
> Old as the names
> Oburumankuma, Odapadjan, Osun.
> They multiply faster than fowls
> And they acquire gold
> As if it were corn grains—. [243]

The hegemonic position of the Odumna Clan within the semifeudal and semicapitalist society of Ato Yawson's hometown is emphasized by the clan's rapacious acquisition of wealth. The reference to "the Three Elders"—"Oburumankuma, Odapadjan, Osun"—legendary heroes of the Fanti, ironically accentuates the failure of leadership embodied in Ato Yawson's inaction.[7] The transition from a semifeudal aristocracy to a neocolonial capitalist ruling class is not easy, and the price is a heavy one. The emergent neocolonial social order demands leaders of a new type—"the making of / One Scholar"—who will solve the problems that are an inevitable result of that change. The superior individual is to lead the inheritors of the old colonial order to victory; for, as the clan's praise singer-historian chants, "We are the vanguard / We are running forward, forward, forward." But, one might ask, into what? Where will the new leaders, the Western-educated national bourgeoisie take us? Can we be sure that they will not be blinded, that "the twig shall not pierce [their] eyes"? Or that the masses—the peasants and the proletariat—will not take the struggle further, "the rivers prevail o'er us"? [242]. Set against this public dilemma are the private dilemmas of Ghanaian Ato Yawson, his African-American wife Eulalie Rush, and her in-laws, which are the immediate concerns of the play.

---

7. The micro-nation of the Fanti or "Fan-tse," which means "the breakaway part," journeyed southward until they reached the sea to escape their more ferocious kin, the Brongs and the Ashantis. They were led physically and spiritually on their journeys by "the Three Elders."

The central trope that concertizes the concerns outlined in the prelude is expressed in the song "The Ghost." We first hear this song in
act 3, which, like act 2, begins with what could be taken as the dramatic externalization of Ato's internal existential and ideological dilemmas. On the other hand, it can be a material happening, as Aidoo's
stage directions indicate. Either or both, the game the two children
are engaged in not only symbolizes Ato's predicament, and by extension
that of the Ghanaian petit bourgeois intellectual, but also signifies the
underlying philosophical assumption of the dilemma tale. This teasing
can be taken as Aidoo's scene setting, the authentication of the children's play activity, and the simultaneous underscoring of the importance of children in African societies. The question the children attempt to answer is: What is to be done? They decide on the
game of "Kwaakwaa"—hide-and-seek—but they cannot agree on who
should hide and who should seek. Their intransigence leads to an escalation of verbal insistence or hostility. Ultimately the boy resorts to
violence: he strikes the girl. As a result of the girl's crying, however,
the boy reconsiders: "Oh, I did not mean to hurt you. But you too! I
have told you I want to hide. . . . Let us play another game then. What
shall we do?" [257]. Significantly, the girl's next choice is to sing "The
Ghost," which involves holding hands and dancing, a communal act.
Seen in this way, not only does the childish banter become a paradigm
of the structural or formal rationale of the dilemma tale (that is, the
positing of a dilemma that leads to "interminable palaver" and, one
hopes, a consensus for action), but it also encapsulates the relationship between Ato and Eulalie up to this point. Ato and Eulalie wish
to return "home," to "play" in this new—relatively speaking—society
that is neocolonial Ghana; they cannot decide, however, who is to find
whom. Or what. And we must decide whose values are to guide them
in the context of shifting social, political, and ethical standards.

* * *

Aidoo's deployment of the dilemma tale convention vitally alters the
nature and experience of the drama itself; such use forces the audience
to eschew simple answers to the problems of gender, race, and class
as they come together in the public and private interstice of the social
relations of the major characters. So, even though the struggle seems
to be centered on Ato, the end of The Dilemma destroys that image.
Ato Yawson is unable to make a choice because he refuses to confront
his and our history honestly, to answer unequivocally the hailings of
both the antagonistic ideological material practices and the characters
within the drama. Aidoo in her first drama effectively uses the traditional dilemma tale to expose the problems that are symptomatic of
neocolonial Ghanaian society; at the same time, she forces the audience to adopt an engaged position vis-à-vis the issues raised by the
conflicts between and within the characters. The open-endedness
of the drama prevents the audience from remaining on the emotional or imaginary level of reconciliation. The uneasiness that most
audiences will experience forces a distancing and a recognition that

the ideological-material struggle is not over, as the first woman of the chorus observes in the final act: "And this is only the beginning" [273]. Yet the drama actually ends with the erasure of the petit bourgeois protagonist and the fading echo of the children singing the ghost's song of indecision.

Ngugi wa Thiong'o

NGUGI WA THIONG'O

Women in Cultural Work: The Fate of the Kamĩrĩĩthũ People's Theatre in Kenya†

In the Gĩkũyũ language play, *Ngaahika Ndeenda* [I Will Marry When I Want], a factory worker finds a peasant mother weeping over, among other things, the fact that her daughter is now employed as a barmaid: one of the most insecure, lowly paid and humiliating jobs in Kenya, into which hundreds of girls are forced in the modern Kenya of US military bases, the IMF, and World Bank. Working in a bar is, to the peasant, the same as becoming a whore.

The passage shows the double oppression of women. As suppliers of labour in colonies and neo-colonies, they are exploited; and as women they suffer under the weight of male prejudices in both feudalism and imperialism.

But the passage shows two other things: the need to look for both causes and solutions in the social system of how wealth is produced, controlled and shared out. This calls for the unity of the workers and peasants—without sexist prejudices—against imperialism and all its class allies in the colonies and neo-colonies.

In the specific case of Kenya, the passage pays tribute to the important role women have always played in our history. They have been at the forefront in all its crucial and decisive phases.

The wars against the British colonial occupation of Kenya, for instance, threw to the fore the leadership of Me Katilili. She was in her seventies when she organized the Giriama youth in the 1913–14 armed struggle against the British colonial administration. She was arrested and detained but she never gave in to her torturers.

The twenties also saw a great awakening among workers of all Kenyan nationalities and they united in a major workers' movement: demanding an end to forced labour, to carrying of identity papers, taxation, slave wages and all other oppressive features of the colonial system such as the beating of workers and the prostitution of teenage girls by the settler plantation owners. The British retaliated by arrest-

† From *Readings in African Popular Culture*, ed. Karin Barber (Bloomington: Indiana University Press, 1997) 132–38. Reprinted by permission of Indiana University Press and James Currey Publishers.

ing and detaining Harry Thuku, the leader of the workers' movement. The biggest demonstration of workers then ever seen in Kenya was led by Mary Mūthoni Nyanjirū and demanded his release. She was among the first to be shot dead by the British forces, followed by 150 others in what has now come to be known as the 1922 massacre.

The fifties saw the Mau Mau armed struggle. Kenyan women played a heroic role in the fighting in the forests and mountains, and in prisons and detention camps, and in the homes. They were everywhere.

This is the kind of history and struggle that the play *Ngaahika Ndeenda* (I will marry when I want) celebrates.

The play was performed by members of Kamĩrĩĩthũ Community Education and Culture Centre, Limuru, Kenya, in 1977. Over two-thirds of the members were women, ranging from children to those in their seventies. They were mostly poor peasants, plantation workers and unemployed school leavers. There was one office secretary. Together with the men—factory workers, poor peasants, the unemployed, primary school teachers and university lecturers—they had built an open-air theatre with a seating capacity of over 2,000. Although the script was drafted by Ngũgĩ wa Mĩrĩĩ and me, the peasants and workers added to it, making the end product a far cry from the original draft. Everything was collective, open and public, and it was fascinating to see a unity gradually emerge which virtually rubbed out distinctions of age, education, sex and nationality. The evolution of this community centre is described in my book *Detained: A Writer's Prison Diary*, and I cannot find better words with which to describe the transformation I experienced and witnessed with my own eyes:

The six months between June and November 1977 were the most exciting in my life and the true beginning of my education. I learnt my language anew. I rediscovered the creative nature and power of collective work.

Work, oh yes, work! Work, from each according to his ability for a collective vision, was the great democratic equalizer. Not money, not book education, but work. Not three-piece suits with carnations and gloves, not tongues of honey, but work. Not birth, not palaces, but work. Not globe-trotting, not the knowledge of foreign tongues and foreign lands, not dinners at foreign inns of court, but work. Not religions, not good intentions, but work. Work and yet more work, with collective democratic decisions on the basis of frank criticisms and self-criticism, was the organizing principle which gradually emerged to become the corner-stone of our activities.

Although the overall direction of the play was under Kĩmani Gecau, the whole project became a collective community effort with peasants and workers seizing more and more initiative in revising and adding to the script, in directing dance movements on the stage, and in the general organization.

I saw with my own eyes an incredible discipline emerge in keeping time and in cutting down negative social practices. Drinking alcohol, for instance. It was the women's group, led by Gaceeri wa Waigaanjo, who imposed on themselves a ban on drinking alcohol, even a glass, when coming to work at the centre. This spread to all the other groups including the audience. By the time we came to perform, it was generally understood and accepted that drunkenness was not allowed at the centre. For a village which was known for drunken brawls, it was a remarkable achievement of our collective self-discipline that we never had a single incident of fighting or a single drunken disruption for all the six months of public rehearsals and performances.

I saw with my own eyes peasants, some of whom had never once been inside a theatre in their lives, design and construct an open-air theatre complete with a raised stage, roofed dressing-rooms and stores, and an auditorium with a seating capacity of more than two thousand persons. Under a production team led by Gatoonye wa Mũgoiyo, an office messenger, they experimented with matchsticks on the ground before building a small working model on which they based the final complex.

The rehearsals, arranged to fit in with the working rhythms of the village, which meant mostly Saturday and Sunday afternoons, were all in the open, attracting an ever-increasing crowd of spectators and an equally great volume of running appreciative or critical commentaries. The whole process of play-acting and production had been demystified and the actors and the show were the gainers for it. The dress rehearsal on Sunday, 25 September 1977, attracted one of the biggest crowds I have ever seen for a similar occasion, and the same level of high attendance was maintained for the next four Saturdays and six Sundays.

Furthermore, the whole effort unleashed a torrent of talents hitherto unsuspected even by the owners. Thus before the play was over, we had already received three scripts of plays in the Gĩkũyũ language, two written by a worker and one by a primary school teacher. One unemployed youth, who had tried to commit suicide four times because he thought his life was useless, now suddenly discovered that he had a tremendous voice which, when raised in a song, kept its listeners on dramatic tenterhooks. None of the actors had ever been on stage before, yet they kept the audiences glued to their seats, even when it was raining. One of the most insulting compliments came from a critic who wrote that the orchestra was professional and had been hired from Nairobi. Another insulting compliment came from those who heatedly argued that simple villagers could never attain that excellence; that the actors were all university students dressed in the tattered clothes of peasants. Another equally insulting compliment came from a university lecturer in literature who argued that the apparent effortless ease of the acting was spontaneous: after all, the villagers were acting themselves. The fact was that all the actors and musicians, men, women and children, came from the village, and they put in more than four months of conscious disciplined work. Some of our university lecturers and those other critics, in their petty-bourgeois blindness, could never

conceive peasants as being capable of sustained disciplined intellectual efforts.

For myself, I learnt a lot. I had been delegated to the role of a
messenger and porter, running errands here and there. But I also
had time to observe things. I saw how the people had appropriated
the text, improving on the language and episodes and metaphors,
so that the play which was finally put on to a fee-paying audience
on Sunday, 2 October 1977, was a far cry from the tentative awkward efforts originally put together by Ngũgĩ and myself. I felt one
with the people. I shared in their rediscovery of their collective
strength and abilities, and in their joyous feeling that they could
accomplish anything—even even transform the whole village and
their lives without a single Harambee of charity—and I could feel
the way the actors were communicating their joyous sense of a
new power to their audience who too went home with gladdened
hearts.

Before long the centre received delegations from other peasant
communities who wanted similar cultural ventures in their areas. A
peasant/worker theatre movement was about to start.

But unfortunately the Kenya Government struck with a vengeance.
The public performances of the play were stopped on 16 November,
1977 and I was later arrested and detained for a year.

For the next three years or so, there were no theatre activities in
the centre. Adult literacy classes continued, and once again women
were the main participants.

Then, in November 1981, the group reassembled, ready to tackle
yet another play. This time it was a musical, *Maitũ Njugĩra* (Mother
sing for me), set in the twenties and thirties when Kenyan workers
were struggling against repressive labour conditions. The Kamĩrĩĩthũ
group was ready to put on the show at the Kenya National Theatre on
19 February, 1982, but the Kenyan authorities refused the group permission to publicly perform the play. In Kenya, a drama group has to
be registered: even then such a group has to get a licence for each
play they want to perform. The group retaliated by continuing with
rehearsals at Nairobi University but making them public. The rehearsals went on for seven days during which at least 10,000 people were
able to see the show. The government finally stopped the rehearsals.

The fate of the Kamĩrĩĩthũ Theatre is described in a statement I was
asked to make on 10 March, 1982. To understand the frustrations
faced by a progressive rural and community-based theatre movement
in neo-colonial Kenya, I reproduce the statement.

But there is another reason for reproducing it. Lately, and in response to widespread national and international criticism of the Kenya
Government's wilful destruction of Kamĩrĩĩthũ Theatre, the President
of the Republic has been making public speeches saying that Kamĩrĩĩthũ was teaching politics under the cover of culture. The statement
below is a detailed documented account of the group's tireless efforts
to get a response, in vain, from the government—and it shows the
total contempt the regime has for people's efforts. The statement was

released to both the Kenyan and international press for a conference in Nairobi.

> . . . , I have been asked by the management committee of Ka-mĩrĩĩthũ Theatre Group and those responsible for the production of our new play, *Maitũ Njugĩra*, to express the following observations regarding our efforts to obtain a government stage licence for the Kenya National Theatre.

First I must express our extreme disappointment and even much anger at the grossly irresponsible manner in which the authorities concerned chose to deal with our application for the licence, normally a quick routine administrative procedure, unnecessary in most countries, but introduced in most British colonies as a method of vetting and censoring native cultural expression.

Dutifully we applied for this licence, in writing, on 2 November, 1981 to the Nairobi Provincial Commissioner. We then followed this up with a reminder on 12 November, 1981. On 18 November, 1981 we got a letter from the Nairobi Provincial Commissioner's Office asking us to do something that no other theatre group has ever been asked to do, that is, to go back to the District Commissioner, Kiambu, to ask for a recommendation—this on the pretext that the physical address of our Group was in Kiambu. Still, we went ahead and on 23 November, 1981 we wrote to the District Commissioner, Kiambu, asking for a recommendation. We have never received a reply from the D.C., Kiambu, but throughout December 1981 and January 1982 the Chairman of our Group, Mr Ngũgĩ wa Mĩrĩĩ, kept running between Kiambu and Nairobi trying to get a reply and the result of our application. On 3 February, 1982 we wrote a second reminder to the Nairobi Provincial Commissioner. On 16 February 1982, three days before the scheduled opening of our performances at the Kenya National Theatre, we wrote a third reminder, which we even copied to the Chief Secretary.

To all these letters and reminders, the government, through the Nairobi Provincial Commissioner, never responded in writing. Instead the management of the Kenya National Theatre were given secret instructions not to allow our group into the theatre either for the technical rehearsals starting on 15 February or for the opening night of 19 February. The police must have also been given instructions to harass us for, on 19 February, they kept patrolling the grounds of the Kenya National Theatre where our Group sat singing, waiting for a last minute reply to our application for the stage licence.

After 19 February, our Group resumed rehearsals at the Theatre Two of the University of Nairobi where we had been rehearsing. But once again on 25 February, the University authorities were instructed by telephone not to allow us the use of their premises. I would like to make it clear that up to now the Government has not formally written to us about the fact of our application.

By so doing, the Government denied us one of the most elementary human and democratic rights: the right of every human community to cultural expression. The administration's handling of the matter showed total insensitivity to the sheer amount of labour, effort and money put up by a village group over a three month period. By refusing us a licence, the administration denied Kenyans the right to an entertainment of their choice. The fact that the rehearsals attracted over 10,000 people was an indication that they wanted the show. The play, which heavily drew from the songs and dances of different Kenyan nationalities, showed practical possibilities for the integration of Kenyan cultures. And, as brilliantly directed by Waigwa Wachira and Kimani Gecau, the play suggested a whole new basis for Kenyan theatre. It now looks as if Kenyans, especially peasants, are not supposed to dance, sing and act out their history of struggle against colonial oppression.

The play *Maitū Njugīra*, draft-written by myself and subsequently enriched by the cast, is what may be called a dramatized documentary on the forced labour and Kipande laws in the colonial Kenya of the twenties and thirties. It shows the attempts in one community to repulse these and other injustices and to survive as a unit despite tremendous official intrigue and brutality. It shows indirectly the genesis of some of our peoples' subsequent political movements and the seeds of their defeats and partial triumphs.

This play is unlike our earlier effort at communal drama, *Ngaahika Ndeenda*, whose staging was stopped without explanation by the government in 1977 after a highly acclaimed brief run and whose basic theme revolved around present-day Kenyan society. Understandably, the wealthy who control the government did not like the stark realities of their own social origins enacted on the stage by simple villagers. As a result, we were harassed, some of us even detained—as you know. We did not apologize. We still believe in and stand by the content of that play. The spirit of the Centre (that is, Kamīrīīthū Community Education and Cultural Centre) was not killed or even impaired.

Maitū Njugīra by contrast addresses itself to the rulers of a previous, albeit related, era and it seemed to us curious that the ghosts of the settler colonial regime of the thirties should, in 1982, come to haunt the same tiny circle of wealth that *Ngaahika Ndeenda* so terrified. It now seems, despite constitutional safeguards, that any public examination of Kenya's society, its history or future cannot be done without raising the nervousness of the authorities.

We consider this attitude undemocratic and extremely dangerous. It is our right to represent our art and culture from our own viewpoint so long as in the process no extant law is broken. We have sought to act strictly according to law and with complete legitimacy in all aspects of our work. We have followed the unnecessarily difficult and frustrating due process of registering ourselves, applying for permits and all the other now commonplace prerequisites of self-expression in Kenya. We have been very patient.

In return we have received official lies and ping-pong tactics: going from office to office, authority to authority, ministry to ministry, with never so much as a word of hard decision, only indirect instructions such as, for example, the administration's last minute letter to the National Theatre refusing us entry on 15 February, 1982. No department has had the courage to address itself decisively or conclusively to our countless communications over a period of three months. Instead we have encountered only monumental indecision and a farrago of verbal excuses to frustrate us.

The manner in which the refusal of permission to stage the play was carried out, reveals a very serious element in Kenya today. The fact that the government conducted their instructions verbally or by telephone without ever writing to us directly, so that no written record exists, reinforces a dangerous trend. Thus acts are carried out without any officials being held accountable. Under such an atmosphere, anything can be done to any Kenyan or group of Kenyans by officials without written documentation or accountability.

This is not just simple irresponsibility and heavyhanded use of authority. The government seems mortally terrified of peasants organizing themselves on their terms and their own initiative.

We wish to denounce in the strongest possible terms the government's increasing intolerance and repression of the Kenyan people's cultural initiatives. Secondly, we now question fundamentally the seriousness of the government's commitment to Kenyan culture. If, as we are told, the economy has slowed down for external factors of recession, inflation and petroleum prices, we ask is Kenyan culture to slow down or stagnate for the same reasons? If we had chosen to do often mindless and always irrelevant pieces as do the foreign groups, we probably might not have met with such official hostility. Foreign theatre can freely thrive on Kenyan soil. But there is no room for Kenyan theatre on Kenyan soil. During the Emergency, the British colonial regime introduced severe censorship of Kenyan theatre, particularly in detention camps like Athi River, and employed African rehabilitation officers to do their dirty work. Similar tactics are being used in Kenya today! We now call for an end to censorship of Kenyan people's cultural expression.

Finally, as you are now aware, we had secured independently a fully sponsored invitation from Zimbabwe to perform during the month of April as part of their rural cultural project. The invitation of the Zimbabwean Ministry of Education and Culture dated 2 December, 1981, and which we accepted on 21 December, 1981, was a tremendous boost to our morale and an important recognition of the contribution of the Kamĩrĩĩthũ Community Education and Cultural Centre to rural community-based theatre and was very much in the spirit of intra-African cultural exchange. In our letter of acceptance, we asked our prospective hosts to formalize this invitation, if only for simple protocol, through the relevant authorities in the Kenya Government. We believe this they did in writing. We, too, have written to the government through the Ministry of Culture about the visit but we have had no reply.

We now fear that the same forces which worked against our getting a stage licence to perform *Maitũ Njugĩra* at the Kenya National Theatre will now work to prevent the visit of our Group to Zimbabwe during April. . . .

I made this statement on Wednesday, 10 March, 1982 on behalf of Kamĩrĩĩthũ Community Education and Cultural Centre Theatre Group. On Thursday, 11 March, the government, through the Provincial Commissioner for Central Province, a Mr Musila, came to Kamĩrĩĩthũ and—dressed in the full regalia of his office (exactly the same uniform worn by British colonial provincial commissioners)—revoked the licence for Kamĩrĩĩthũ Community Education and Cultural Centre. He said that women were being misled into cultural activities that had nothing to do with development. He therefore banned all theatre activities in the area.

On Friday, 12 March, the District Officer for Limuru led three truckloads of heavily armed police and demolished Kamĩrĩĩthũ's people's open-air theatre.

The government never gave the group permission to go to Zimbabwe. Our letters to the Minister of Culture informing him about the invitation were never answered, not even acknowledged. We were unable to go to Zimbabwe.

In view of President Moi's recent public statements, attacking the theatre at Kamĩrĩĩthũ, one can now definitely say that the whole cultural repression was *not* an accident nor an isolated mistake by some over-zealous philistines in the provincial administration, but the deliberate, thought-out action of a nervous regime. The government ban on the public performance of other plays (*Muntu* by Joe de Graft, *Kilio* by students of Nairobi school, etc.) and the arrest and detention of university teachers, students, lawyers and left-wing politicians, and the general climate of terror, would confirm that the destruction of Kamĩrĩĩthũ was part and parcel of a programmed attempt to enforce conformity of thought on the entire population by rooting out critical elements and suspending the democratic process in politics, education and culture. But conformity to which thought?

It may be pointed out that during the same period that the Kenya Government was suppressing *Maitũ Njugĩra*, a musical depicting the worker and peasant resistance to colonial repression in a positive light, it had bought a TV film of Elspeth Huxley's autobiography *Flame Trees of Thika* and screened it in seven episodes over two months on Kenya Television. The film was made by a British television company and both it and the book, set in the twenties and thirties, show Kenyans as part and parcel of the animal and natural landscape. They are certainly not depicted as possessing any capacity for resistance.

What now? Is this the end of Kamĩrĩĩthũ? The Government's repressive measures were certainly a setback to the development of a people-based theatre in the countryside. For it means that, for the majority of women in the rural areas, the church on Sundays will remain their only venue for cultural expression—by way of religious hymns, prayers, sermons and bible readings. For the others, alcohol will be their only means of entertainment. But despite this, I am convinced that the Kamĩrĩĩthũ idea can never be killed. How do you kill the right and the determination of a people to have a cultural life?

Kamĩrĩĩthũ has shown what peasants and workers are capable of doing in modern theatre if left alone to organize on their own terms. In their participation in the peasant and worker-based theatre, the Kamĩrĩĩthũ women have joined a long line of others who have always stood for a free united Kenya, a Kenya in which if a bean falls to the ground, it is shared among the children. This is the vision that guided the Mau Mau anti-colonial movement and it is what today guides the Kenyan people in their anti-imperialist struggle against all forms of internal and external exploitation and oppression.

Gĩcaamba, the factory worker in the play Ngaahika Ndeenda (I will marry when I want), sums up the situation when talking to the other peasant and worker characters (both men and women) in the play.

Like Gĩcaamba, the people of Kenya—men, women and children—are looking out to see who their friends are. Anybody who would raise their voice against the current cultural and political repression in the land and against the denial to Kenyans of their democratic and human rights to organize, in whatever capacity, on their own terms, are friends of Kenyan people and of democracy.

'Everyone has the right to freedom of opinion and expression', says Article 19 of the Universal Declaration of Human Rights. All cultural and women's organizations throughout the world should raise their voices against what is happening in Kenya. Certainly, they should make their abhorrence of rule by terror known to the Kenyan authorities in every venue at every opportunity. No amount of material well-being (such as giving three sewing machines to a village of 10,000 people as the authorities have recently done at Kamĩrĩĩthũ!) can compensate for the loss of a people's right to determine their lives, or at least have a say in such determination.

Development should mean the release of the creative powers in men, women and children. The destruction of a cultural centre is an attempt to stifle creativity and says a lot about the spiritual and mental state of these regimes, which nervously reach out for the pistol at the mention of the phrase 'people's culture'. It is interesting that the authorities changed the name of Kamĩrĩĩthũ Community Education and Cultural Centre to Kamĩrĩĩthũ Polytechnic and Adult Literary Centre, while banning all theatre activities in the area. At the entrance of the open-air theatre (now destroyed) there stood a board with the inscriptions Mucit wa muingi in Gĩkũyũ, and Mji wa umma in Kiswahili. Both phrases meant the same thing: A People's Cultural Centre.

The board was the first object to be removed and destroyed in the police raid of Friday, 12 March, 1982. The regime can destroy people's centres and even abolish theatre: but can they destroy or abolish the people? That's why I say: KAMĪRĪĪTHŪ WILL COME BACK!

Ah, yes, may it come! But I'm still convinced that the biggest aid and gift to Kenyan people from their friends is a call and an insistence on Kenyan authorities to return to the democratic process by releasing the university lecturers and all the other political prisoners;[1] by lifting the ban on theatre among peasants and workers; and by allowing Kenyans their rights to organize for culture on their own terms.

OLIVER LOVESEY

I Will Marry When I Want†

Originally written from 1976 to 1977 in Gĩkũyũ, *I Will Marry When I Want* (*Ngaahika Ndeenda*) was published in English translation in 1982. The play was cowritten by Ngũgĩ wa Mĩriĩ, composer, playwright, educator, and director of the Kamĩrĩĩthũ Educational and Cultural Centre. After initial composition, the script was developed at Kamĩrĩĩthũ in close collaboration during workshops with the peasant, worker, student theater group and performed to great acclaim. Ngũgĩ's involvement with this group was one of the most important experiences of his career, merging his cultural and political interests and providing an opportunity to learn directly from the peasantry. The theater's site is significant. Kamĩrĩĩthũ is the place where Ngũgĩ was born, and its inhabitants are a cross section of Kenyan society: factory and industrial workers, shopkeepers, city workers, intellectuals, and peasants; it has a complex colonial and neocolonial history. Like *The Trial of Dedan Kimathi*, the play created there is a type of socialist folk opera, freely mingling both action and dialogue with ritual dramatizations, mime, and song. The play is written in a lively style, rich with earthy humor and proverbial sayings. This linguistic flair is most marked in act 1, which presents the domestic sphere of Kĩgũũnda and Wangeci comically, before the direct statement later of somewhat formulaic political binaries. *I Will Marry When I Want* is also an African morality play, targeting the alliance of capitalism and Christianity as the enemy of cultural integrity and national cooperation. In passing, the play criticizes a number of other social problems from drunkenness and divorce to fawning on material luxuries, and it also celebrates virtues from respect for women to neighborliness.

The play explores two conflicts. The first is the disagreement between Wangeci and Kĩgũũnda about how to respond to their daughter Gathoni's involvement with John Mũhũũni, the son of Kĩgũũnda's

---

1. The lecturers are: Alamin Mazrui, Kamoji Wachira, Edward Oyugi, Willy Mutunga, Mukaru Ng'ang'a and Maina wa Kinyatti—but there are many others currently languishing in prisons and detection camps.

† From *Ngũgĩ wa Thiong'o* (New York: Twayne, 2000) 94–97. Reprinted by permission of The Gale Group.

wealthy boss, Ahab Kīoi wa Kanoru (Kīoi). Wangeci and Kīgūūnda also disagree about whether they should sell their one-and-a-half-acre plot of land to Kīoi and Ikuua wa Nditika, rich African directors of a company planning to establish an insecticide factory on the site. Kīoi already owns most of Kīgūūnda's land, which was "given to home-guards," and Kīgūūnda labors for him. He cultivates and plants without enjoying the harvest, like the "pot that cooks without eating." Their neighbors Gīcaamba and Njooki, a worker and a peasant, who embody revolutionary ethics clothed in words of traditional wisdom, consistently advise them to avoid having anything to do with the devilish Kīoi. The play's second major conflict is between Kīgūūnda and Wangeci, and Kīoi and his party. The two groups are starkly contrasted onstage in terms of dress, language, manners, wealth, and even physical distance. Kīoi covets Kīgūūnda's land, but he also wants to introduce him into the church, regarding Kīgūūnda as an influential figure who will encourage other disgruntled factory activists to follow him into passive acceptance of all conditions, however unjust, as being divinely ordained. The point of entry into church membership for Kīoi is Christian marriage, hence the play's title, and incredibly Kīgūūnda and Wangeci readily accept this eventuality, though it requires expensive Western trappings. To finance the wedding dress and cake and other paraphernalia, Kīgūūnda takes a loan from Kīoi's bank using his cherished land title as collateral. Of course, the disastrous outcome is now inevitable, and the escalation of the first conflict—Gathoni's becoming pregnant and being abandoned by Kīoi's son—precipitates Kīgūūnda's confrontation with Kīoi, who refuses to sanction a marriage between Gathoni and his son. Kīgūūnda threatens Kīoi but backs down, a possibly fatal mistake. Kīgūūnda is fired from his job at the factory and becomes demoralized, and the play ends with his land being sold to pay the recalled bank loan. The four friends, Kīgūūnda and Wangeci, and Gīcaamba and Njooki, sing songs of resistance and unity.

As in *The Trial of Dedan Kimathi*, cultural and national solidarity is established through the reenactment of historical pageants within the play, dealing with significant moments in resistance history, such as, for example, the strike of 1948 and the Mau Mau war. The stark divisions between the patriots—Kīgūūnda and Wangeci, and Gīcaamba and Njooki—and their neocolonial exploiters are emphasized by their very different songs. The patriots sing resistance songs; the exploiters sing Christian hymns. The patriots' cultural cohesion also is demonstrated through proverbial sayings. Some of these are included for humorous effect or to foster the audience's recognition and identification. For example, Kīgūūnda repeats the backhanded boast: "A man brags about his penis however small" referring to his pride in his humble home. A number of proverbs relate homely folk wisdom. Some of these voice suspicions about Gathoni's courtship. Wangeci wonders if her daughter knows "that men have prickly needles," but Kīgūūnda begs for a qualification recognizing men's traditional code of honor: "You should have said that it is the modern men / Who have got prickly needles" Later, after Gathoni runs off with John for a romantic week in the beautiful coastal city of Mombasa, Wangeci reminds her annoyed husband that "a parent is never nauseated / By the mucus from his child's nose." Parents, she reminds him, must accept their children's faults. When the now pregnant Gathoni runs off again to be a barmaid (often synonymous with being a prostitute), Gĩcaamba warns her friend Wangeci not to abandon Gathoni, for although "a hyena is very greedy . . . she does not eat her young." Gathoni's actions, Gĩcaamba says, can be explained by another saying: "When a bird in flight gets very tired / It lands on the nearest tree."

Many other proverbial sayings in the play relate to its political theme and convey bitter truths, warnings of ominous events, and injunctions to solidarity. Gĩcaamba complains of his exploitation at the factory. He bitterly compares his factory salary, and more generally the gains of the poor after independence, to the peanuts "thrown to a monkey / When the baby it is holding is about to be stolen!" Referring to the fabulous wealth and arrogance of men like Kĩoi who exploit the poor's vulnerability, Wangeci comments that "a fool's walking stick supports the clever," and later Gĩcaamba says: "Haven't you heard it said that / A rich man's fart does not stink?" Stark observations on the inequalities of the present situation, however, do not forestall a warning of danger. Njooki, anxious about Kĩgũũnda and Wangeci's naive friendship with Kĩoi, warns that "a tooth smiles at a spear," the tooth, believing the spear is its comrade, overlooks its own danger. Kĩoi will not change his ways, just as the colonial church is the same as the neocolonial church: "Did the leopard ever change its spots?" asks Gĩcaamba. To counter the bedbug- and scorpion-like Kĩois of the world, vigilance and unity are necessary. The people must never renege on their oath to the nation and begin, like Kĩoi, to forget that only "a vulture eats alone." On the contrary, as the union leader intones, "if a bean falls to the ground / We split it amongst ourselves."

In contrast to the use of traditional lore to convey socialist messages, hypocritical Christian pieties convey the egotism and greed of the wealthy capitalists. The play does acknowledge, however, that some indigenous Christian churches provided shelter for oathing ceremonies during the Mau Mau period, and it equates a revival of revolutionary spirit with the Second Coming. By and large, however, Christian groups are portrayed as exploiting the poverty and desperation of the masses while using the communal rhetoric of *harambee*, for example, to raise funds at the local level, and then in some cases sending a portion of the monies collected to America. The very prolixity of Christian denominations in the area signals their scavenging nature. Gĩcaamba resents the way that passive resignation to social stasis is misconstrued as a humble Christian acknowledgment of God's sanction of the status quo. Such hypocrisy covers up the miseries of hazardous, underpaid factory shift work and industrial pollution, the export of profits, and the inadequacy of infrastructural improvements in transportation, health, and education. Self-described Christians such as Samuel and Helen Ndugĩre mix Christian humility with union busting. For them, material prosperity indicates spiritual favor. For example, Helen says it is necessary to "show the wicked that everybody's share comes from Heaven, / Be it poverty or riches." Similarly, such characters associate a blind mimicry of Western cultural traditions with spiritual purity, as in their insistence on the trappings of a Western wedding feast with Christian marriage. Patriotic peasants and workers must resist the drug of religion, remembering that earlier, "drunk with religion," their land was stolen. The deferred, otherwordly compensation of entry into the "Kingdom of God," instead of justice on earth, is mocked in song. This substitution is symbolically enacted when Kīgũũnda's title deed disappears from its prominent place on the wall and is replaced by the ubiquitous phrase: "CHRIST IS THE HEAD OF THIS HOUSE, THE UNSEEN GUEST AT EVERY MEAL, THE SILENT LISTENER TO EVERY CONVERSATION." Kīgũũnda's household, preparing for a Christian wedding, has become a poor parody of Kĩoi's. The play dismisses Christian/capitalist marriage in favor of a revolutionary union of "two patriots / Defending their home and nation."

By the end of the play, Kīgũũnda and Wangeci, through their experience of dispossession, have come to share the political opinions of Gĩcaamba and Njooki. They join the final dance and its songs, an affront to the historical colonial denial of such performances. These characters, unemployed and without shelter, will unite in a life-and-death revolutionary struggle, though their fortunes in the meantime are unclear. The play's ending is equally unclear about the fate of Gathoni, a pregnant barmaid. The play ends rather than concludes, though its message and even its outcome have been abundantly evident from the first scene, and any elaborate denouement or resolution would be superfluous. Audience members are enjoined to respond to the recital of exploitation and to perceive the only solution as lying in unified resistance to be undertaken whenever they want.

Femi Osofisan

FEMI OSOFISAN

[Formal Strategies and Social Commentary in the Plays]†

* * *

I have generally preferred an eclectic approach in the construction of my work, using whatever style or method I deem immediately apt, and dipping at will into the multiple matrix of a tradition inherited from western, Asian, and indigenous African sources. It was Pier Paolo Pasolini who reminded us after all, (in the memorable Epitaph to his 1974 film, *Il fiore delle mille e una motte*), that *"La verità non sta in un solo sagno, ma in molti sogni"* (One does not find truth in a single dream, but rather in many dreams). Thus scholars like Awodiya, Obafemi, Dunton and Richards have noted a rich diversity of approaches in my work: there are first the experimental plays inspired by the radical, avant-garde tradition of the west, such as *Another Raft* and *The Oriki of a Grasshopper*; then there are those which may be classified as parables, based as they are on the story-telling tradition of our raconteurs, plays such as *Once Upon Four Robbers, Farewell to A Cannibal Rage, Esu and the Vagabond Minstrels, Twingle-Twangle A-Twynning Tayle* and *Many Colors Make the Thunder-King.* (You can see where my preferences lie!) I have also written less adventurous plays in the popular-naturalist tradition, such as *Birthdays Are Not for Dying, Altine's Wrath*, and others. Then there are the political Epics, dealing with grand themes and grand historical figures, such as *Morountodun, Nkrumah-ni . . . Africa-ni!*, and *A Nightingale for Dr DuBois.* And perhaps the favourite with my actors are the satirical plays of the "Midnight Series", (of which perhaps the most famous is *Midnight Hotel*), in which I have tried to expose the foibles of our ruling classes, and sought through laughter to understand, and forgive them.

But as I have explained on other occasions, it is the topics themselves which choose me, and which then impose their own styles of articulation. In *Twingle-Twangle A Twynning Tayle*, for instance, it was the need to examine the tension between pacifism and militarism, between a politics of free choice, and one of coercion that spontane-

† From *Playing Dangerously: Drama at the Frontier of Terror in a 'Postcolonial' State* (Ibadan, Nigeria: University of Ibadan, 1997) 30–36.

ously invoked the familiar parable of the twins in our folk-tale. And lately, the concern about the failure of leadership in Africa, pushed me to embark on a political trilogy, in which I propose to explore some crucial moments in the lives of three radical and charismatic African leaders, namely Kwame Nkrumah, Sekou Toure, and Amilcar Cabral. For such a project, none but Brecht's Epic Theatre mechanics could evidently be as suitable. And the same form suggested itself when a play about the Pan-African ideal, woven around the ancestral figure of Dr WEB DuBois, began to take shape in my mind.

* * *

But these last considerations bring me back again to the question of form, which I regard as the kernel of all artistic creativity. * * * I have spoken above, of how I appropriate from all traditions for my own performative acts. But undoubtedly I need also to add that my borrowings are always with considerable modifications and re-readings— or, to put it in Okigbo's words, always with deliberate and provocative "errors in the rendering".

This approach is dictated not just by a gratuitous lust for invention, although there is a sense in which all artists heedlessly yearn for that. But in fact—and this should interest you particularly sir,—it is because the area of form constitutes the most visible site of the epistemological break I have made with the playwrights of the first generation.

Let me briefly explain. In response to Soyinka's Ogun model, which I discussed earlier on, I have substituted the *Opon Ifa* paradigm, in which you have a dialectical fusion of the Esu-Orunmila principles. (Esu of course has been much maligned by Christians and mistaken for Satan, and one can only hope that he will forgive them for this). But we know now that, far from being the repulsive devil of Christian mythology, he is in fact among the most important deities in the Yoruba pantheon, representing the principle of free choice and of revolution—the god who, with his prominent phallus, promiscuously incarnates the place of doubt and disjunction, but also of justice and accommodation, in our metaphysical cosmos.

Fused with Orunmila then, as you see on the divining tray (the "opon Ifa"), what you get is a combination which can produce the "anarchic conservatism" * * *. For Orunmila is the winnowing spirit which distils wisdom from chaos, prophecy from uncertainty, harmony from disjunction. Allied with Esu, the relationship leads dialectically to the doors of knowledge, justice, and compassion, the three principles exactly which my plays constantly promote.

And it is this advocacy which imposes naturally on dramatic form.

* * * I do not believe in methods which seek to push my convictions down the throat of my audience. On the contrary: what I reach for are dialogic climaxes, moments when, at the propulsion of the performance, the audience can commence a discussion with me and with itself, on the road to a dynamic relationship with the conflict the play enacts.

This is what authorises my constant interrogation of inherited forms. Thus, for instance, in borrowing the ancestral structure of the folktale for a play like *Esu and the Vagabond Minstrels*, I consciously set out to destabilise it, and so opened out its concluding scene, such that instead of an authorial dictation,—in the manner of state decrees—it is the audience itself that is called upon to determine the end of the play. Similarly, to take another example, the "Midnight Series" which I talked about earlier, have been conceived as *"songfarces"*, that is, farces in which the dramatic action is only of secondary import, and primary focus is given instead to the songs, projected onto a screen, which a standing orchestra accompanied by its complicit audience deliberately and conspicuously interjects into the play's process at selected moments. And I depart from Brecht's practice here, in that my preference is for melody, affective and stirring, in alliance with, and as a vehicle for, ideological meaning.

If therefore, as Harry Garuba rightly asserts, I am the most intertextual of all our contemporary dramatists; it is because I believe in this principle of exposition and debate, (which can only be initiated by the Esu spirit of healthy scepticism), to culminate and crystallise —at Orunmila's prompting—in an epiphanous light. For there is always a need to subject all categories and all relationships to the flame of constant questioning, constant revision; most especially the hierarchies of power, which are the most susceptible to sclerosis. Without such continual rituals of dissent, society will die in the embrace of Terror.

So, I write plays with open endings, with self-contradicting, self-referential plots. Plays which sometimes refuse in fact to be written, which continually signify on their own identities. I summon to the stage narrators who go in and out of the story at random, who, as it were, make the fables expose their own *fableness*. These ways, I establish the contingent nature of all experience, and hopefully, reveal through the process the fact that we are NOT programmed by any supernatural force for failure, or defeat; that society is always determined by the interventions we bring to it; that our present sorry predicament is not permanent or incapable of emendation.

Thus it is obvious, I hope, that in this deconstruction of inherited structures, I do draw my limits from the camp of post-modernism. I know that, as critics have pointed out, some of the methods I use have been claimed also by a school of post-modernist thought. But meaning, not meaningless-ness is what, for me, is vital to the purpose of art. My allegiance is with such writers as Thomas Mann, who maintained that "In our time, the destiny of man presents its meaning in political terms." Even far away and long ago, oriental philosophers had framed this need for engagement in an enigmatic question, when they asked: "Is there a sound in the forest, if a tree falls but there is no one around to hear it?" Without the impulse for justice, for compassion, for laughter, the lungs of artistic creativity will starve of oxygen, and atrophy, and usher in the death of our human civilisation. Let the postmodernists of the West celebrate, if they will, the End of History; for us,

History is still at its vibrant, challenging dawn. The song of our humanity, when I listen to it, is still full of stirring tunes. And it is in response to its music that I continue to write—because I believe in, and love my fellow men and women; because I care deeply about the well-being of my society, and cannot afford to remain indifferent to its destiny.

It is patent now that our nation committed a fundamental error when we allowed soldiers into the seat of power, and let them stain our land and our hands with blood. But it is not an ineradicable sin. As long as they remain in the saddle of course, our wounds cannot heal, and the land will not be able to commence the rites or cleansing that will end our nightmare. Thus they must be dislodged in order for Terror to cease. But not, in my opinion nevertheless, by adopting their own tactics of cruelty and intimidation. However strong the provocation we must resist that temptation to be equally corrupted into barbarity.

And it is not hard to wait, if you are an artist. Sheherezade taught us a lesson after all, from the pages of the *Arabian Nights*, that something as apparently harmless as stories can rescue us even from death. Indeed, the emperors, the Shahrayars of our times, can be likewise defeated, or purged, with the weapons fashioned from our imaginative spaces. The anguish they cause can be relieved with the fabulous tonic of metaphor and song.

SANDRA RICHARDS

Hegemony Rests with the Audience†

In *Esu and the Vagabond Minstrels* (1984/85) Femi Osofisan returns to the thematic terrain dramatized six years earlier in *Once Upon Four Robbers*. Compassion toward others is again at issue, but here it is conjoined with the scripted beginnings of a potentially open-ended, performer-audience discussion of the relationship between religious belief or art, political theory, and radical change. As might be expected, several distinct features of his dramaturgy are present in this script, so that to a certain extent, it represents a consolidation of the playwright's artistic form. The levity of *Who's Afraid of Solarin?* or *Altine's Wrath* is here combined effectively with the obvious seriousness of purpose found in *The Chattering and the Song* or *Morountodun*. Confidence in the capacity of theatrical spectacle to delight as well as critique, in evidence in a text like *Farewell to a Cannibal Rage*, is displayed here, too.

But unlike the other plays, here Esu is figured directly as well as

† From *Ancient Songs Set Ablaze: The Theatre of Femi Osofisan* (Washington, D.C.: Howard University Press, 1996) 132–45. Copyright © 1995 by Sandra L. Richards. Reprinted with the permission of The Permissions Company, P.O. Box 243, High Bridge, NJ 08829 USA on behalf of Howard University Press. The author's notes have been edited. Page numbers in brackets refer to this Norton Critical Edition.

structurally. That direct figuration has sparked considerable controversy with various protesters attacking the playwright's desacralization of the god or alleging a return to the mystification practices of his literary mentors. Highlighted by this debate, as well as by the play's scripted evolution, is the movement from the apparent order of a fixed text, shaped by the playwright, design team, and performers, to the undeniable diversity of reception or interpretive chaos on the part of viewers actively encouraged to voice their opinions. Though tension between a system of signifiers and its perceived signifieds is inherent in any artistic process, in the dramatic paradigm arising out of the Orunmila-Esu complex, the text's polysemic potential is greatly magnified.

Briefly stated, *Esu and the Vagabond Minstrels* concerns a group of starving musicians whom the god Esu, posing as a priest, promises wealth, provided they each bestow a magical cure on a truly needy recipient. As might be expected, all but one of the five choose to help those who clearly have the wherewithal to offer a handsome reward. The loner selects an impoverished, pregnant woman and a leprous couple, from whom he contracts the disease. The priest/god reappears to evaluate the musicians' choices, claims an inability to decide the leprous musician's case, and demands that the audience make known its opinions.

Even this abbreviated description suggests some of the ways in which *Esu* is similar to *Once Upon Four Robbers*. As in the earlier play, this script features a closely knit group of individuals or a pseudo-family bound together by a shared occupation and shared adversity. Gathered at a crossroads—this time the setting is an outdoor shrine to Esu, located en route to a grove sacred to Orunmila—this itinerant band of social and economic outcasts is given a miraculous gift that can temporarily bind others in pleasurable activity and bring profit to themselves, provided it is used wisely. For this group, too, the present occasions a betrayal. Not only do the musicians scorn their colleague's choice of the poor, pregnant woman, but also when Omele has dared to use the new power a second time in relieving the leprous couple of their suffering, they compound their self-centered choices by stoning and driving him from their midst. Once again, spectators are urged to articulate their evaluation of events.

Subtitled a morality play, *Esu*, however, possesses a unidirectional narrative in which opposing positions are distinctly demarcated at the outset and maintained throughout. As will become apparent in the discussion of the god's role in the text, Osofisan fashions here a dilemma tale in which a calculated innocence initially masks the complex moral alternatives the storyteller wants his listeners to consider.

The script's apparent lightness of tone is attributable to several factors. Primary among them are the presence of fantastic elements and the creation of spectacle. For example, the woman who has been pregnant with the same child for nine years is characteristic of the extraordinary events found in such beloved epics as D. O. Fagunwa's *Ogboju Ode Ninu Igbo Irunmole*, translated by Wole Soyinka as *The Forest of a Thousand Daemons*, or Amos Tutuola's *Palm-Wine Drinkard*. On six different occasions the minstrels effect their artistic cures, with the priest and his followers participating in the festivities yet unobserved by the others. Thus, there is considerable latitude for ingenious staging, lighting, and costuming devices that convey marvelous transformations, such as when the cult figures suddenly metamorphose from rocks, or the outcast husband and wife lose their deformities, transferring them to Omele instead. In addition, suspense regarding the technical execution of magic builds as the text progresses, for each remedy must be more theatrically unique and impressive than the preceding one. In the case of the impotent man and the pregnant woman, these situations allow for hilarious "low" comedy.

But not all the problems that these artists confront are of a fantastic, fairy-tale order. In the first place, they have been proscribed by a new military government, hostile to minstrels who, through their songs of praise, have helped make thieving politicians acceptable to the public. Wandering about begging for food, they discover that in Omele's hometown, the gracious hospitality customarily extended even to strangers is no longer operative. As he complains in bewilderment, "They taught us to always give, freely, like mother nature. They said God owned everything and that every man was a creature of God. . . . How could I have foreseen it, that a day would come when these same people, my own people, would see men in torment, and drive them back into the wind?"

Situations contemporaneous with an offstage reality intrude into the cures they are called on to effect. The fourth arrival at this fateful crossroads is a trio who can produce neither the import license with its accompanying, highly valued foreign currency authorization or the actual rice and fertilizer that the now vanished currency was supposed to have purchased. In contrast to their dubious allegations of victimization at the hands of a greedy manager is the fifth recipient's predicament. A young traditional ruler, who has tried to rid his people of superstition by killing a sacred python, sees suicide as the only solution to the fierce power struggle triggered by his radical actions. Clearly, both these situations, which the artists choose to ameliorate in narrowly defined terms benefiting a few, possess an immediate social referentiality. Equally clearly, were an ethic of interdependence and agency in the face of material constraints to gain the widespread acceptance of a symbolic order like religion, Nigeria would have taken a significant step toward achieving true liberation for its people.

Esu and the Vagabond Minstrels seeks to project such an ethic for community contemplation and possible absorption. The god as metaphor for a dialectical materiality is central to that articulation, but Osofisan is careful to characterize him at the outset of the play in terms of the belief system with which his audience is familiar. That is, the text offers an increasingly more complex portrayal of the god in a style that, given the playwright's status as a respected poet, is remarkably devoid of any sensuousness of phrasing. The written script must engage an intertext in which the very utterance of the god's name has the capacity to inspire in some hearers a Yoruba-derived sense of existential dread, compounded by a Christianized sensibility of cataclysmic evil. Hence, it seems as though the language is deliberately pitched in a register easily understood in English to counteract the intellectual resistance and emotional turmoil with which some may greet the god's representation onstage. * * *

Three differing views of Esu are presented. The first is perhaps closest to the popular imagination. It reflects the perspectives of someone informally schooled in Yoruba cosmology and hence frightfully aware of Esu's reputation as a vengeful trickster. When Epo Oyinbo learns that his colleague has brought them to Esu's shrine, he repeats the familiar lore of unfortunate male victims "suddenly losing their senses and beginning to bark!" or "of women turning into screaming monsters!" [367]. He contends that the plan to eat offerings made to Esu is an abomination that will be severely punished. In contrast, Omele advances a rationalist attitude. Regarding such reputed events simply as stories told to children, he contends that if this god, who is said to be kind to his favorites, allows vermin to eat his food, then surely he will forgive hungry humans.

Projected by Esu himself, the third characterization initially posits the god as an agent of justice. Suddenly appearing as an old man in response to a song of supplication, he sternly intones,

> The Owner of the World
> Has created balance
> Between the forces of Good
> And those of Evil. He appointed Eshu
> To watch over them, and I am his priest.
> But everywhere, Evil is in the ascendant!
> My ears fill daily
> With the woes of the afflicted. [373]

Dismissing the musicians' rhetoric of remorse, he upbraids them for having lived as parasites employed by the rich to rationalize misery. He challenges,

> Esu does not see into the hearts of men,
> Only their actions.
> Are you ready
> To help those among you, who are in distress?
> To bring redress to the wronged?
> And justice to the exploited? [374]

And accepting their promises, Esu makes one of his own, first warning that his gift is "a power, and it's a test" [375]. He then specifically instructs,

> . . . Sing and dance,
> Let the suffering man heal, and
> Afterwards, ask for anything. . . .
> . . . His gratitude

> Will make you rich, or make you poor,
> It depends on what you ask. [375]

But in a certain sense his very language is a trick. It possesses none of the density characteristic of Ifa divination poetry. Indeed, more than once he acknowledges the deceptive power of words, insinuating that beautifully crafted language can be deployed to mask negative conditions. Yet, his own unadorned rhetoric tends to hide or flatten complexity. That is, though he repeatedly advises the minstrels to choose carefully, he laces his speech with references to millionaires, hoardings, and targets, all seemingly calculated to stimulate their selfish impulses.

Thus, to the third characterization of Esu as dispenser of justice is added an emphasis on free choice or human control over destiny. Bewildered concerning their pact with the old man, Epo Oyinbo reasserts the typical opinion that Esu is not to be trusted, while Jigi reminds him of the god's position on the divination tray. Reflecting Yoruba philosophical discourse, the rationalist Omele says,

> Esu is not destiny, only the way to it. He is like a loom in the market of fate. But we each hold the shuttle, free to swing it the way we like. [376]

Having thereby established Esu's persona, the text is then free to chart the minstrels' adventures before bringing the god back onstage, this time as both character and structure.

As noted earlier, the old man reappears to assess the artists' choices and solicits spectators' aid in deciding whether Omele should be allowed to suffer leprosy as the inevitable consequence of an action freely (and generously) undertaken. In so doing, the priest/god functions as the structural sign of a passage of interpretive hegemony from artist to audience. His request, however, proves to be something of a trick on both the old couple and the audience itself. That is, in a ridiculously funny scene in which the husband and wife chase Omele about the stage in an attempt to recapture their disease, they finally demand that Esu exercise his authority. Recognizing presumably in their exasperated, imperious tone the divine presence of Yeye Osun and her husband Orunmila, Esu evades—or further fulfills—his responsibility by throwing the question into the auditorium and letting Omele's fellow humans decide.

Some more pragmatic individual may volunteer that in a context of severe austerity and pervasive materialism, such as Nigeria is presently experiencing, selfishness is the only viable reaction. Hence, the other musicians have acted reasonably. One imagines, however, that social conditioning prevails, and in fairly short order the audience decides that the afflicted man should be restored to health, and the selfish musicians should be made sick. But the audience's freedom to choose an ending appears counterfeit, given the discourse of the morality play that inculcates "proper" desire by dramatizing the rewards of righteousness and the punishment of wickedness.

Attempting yet another bit of mischief by claiming that he cannot determine which side has more proponents, Esu reluctantly responds to Orunmila's nudging,

> Let's end the play then old spoilsport. And yet so much fun still to be had! . . . Let the disease go to those who have won it, those who seek to be rich without working. Who have put their selfish greed first before everything, including their humanity! [408]

The drama concludes with magic and pomp, as the other minstrels are transformed by the god of disease and a restored Omele is hailed as "humanity's last remaining hero!"

But an epilogue punctures this fairy-tale ending and begins a genuine transition toward either a dynamic, collectively determined resolution of meaning or an articulation of multiple, contradictory interpretations. Stage directions indicate that two actors seated in the audience rise to question the relevance of songs and magic to current crises in Nigeria. Presumably voicing reactions shared by other observers, they launch into a freewheeling argument with actors onstage. "Complete mystification, as in all bourgeois art. Where are the dialectical forces of history?" complains one outraged observer. The director professes interest in presenting a light entertainment. Another spectator passionately urges the merger of progressive theory and praxis. And an actor defends their work with an acknowledgment of the common folk's belief in magic.

Although these objections have, in fact, been carefully scripted and rehearsed beforehand, the potential for audience intervention or self-assertion at this point is high because of several factors. Viewers have already been encouraged to voice their opinions; Nigerian spectators generally comment audibly on events as they are being enacted and thus can be expected at this juncture to participate fully; and the text has functioned in part as a critique of the Left, to which Osofisan himself belongs. Not only is the comment about dialectical forces a joking reference to a Marxist perspective, but also the text has been preceded by a prologue establishing the drama as a rehearsal presented to a community of workers, youth corps, or seminarists who share a set of values and assumptions. Consequently, its call for selflessness is likely to be interpreted as a critical comment on the absence of such generosity of spirit and vision within radical ranks.

But before relinquishing control and engaging the audience in a full-fledged discussion, the cast sings "Esu Does Not Exist." The song argues the need for compassion and asserts the materialist view that the gods do not exist. It also warns,

> And if evil does persist
> We must each search our soul. . . .
> If our ways seem so slick. . . .
> One day we'll come to reason. . . .
> Where Esu—or History—
> Waits in ambush with his noose! [411]

Now the audience has several questions before it. The playwright has functioned like a clever performer who, at the end of a storytelling session, innocently offers his listeners a possible solution. The overt assertion that "Eshu does not exist" is in fact a conundrum, for it does not bring clarity to the debate by shifting responsibility from the gods to human beings. In an atmosphere where traditional religions still find numerous adherents, such a declaration threatens to "derail" the discussion into an argument about the validity of specific religious beliefs. Furthermore, confidence in the ultimate operation of justice, whether it be called "Esu" or "History," does not confront directly the endemic materialism plaguing the nation now.

In fact, on the level of literal meaning, disavowal of Esu's existence has engendered seemingly peripheral audience debates. Although many theatre students in a 1984 post-performance discussion applauded the manipulation of mythology to confront pressing social issues, a vocal minority objected to the god's desacralization. Since that time Osofisan has revised the play and added the epilogue for reasons that seemingly relate to a love for theatrical spectacle and a willingness to seriously consider audience feedback.

Of course, neither of these reasons is without a theoretical dimension. The magic of theatrical spectacle signals in part the presence of the Other in the sense of the unexpected, the illogical, the disruptive embedded in the rational system represented by the drama. The spectacle's repeated eruption within a narrative pattern the viewers have been socialized to recognize resensitizes them to wonder if and to what extent phenomena elude their predictive analysis. When engineered by one character against others, the trick or magic places the latter in a position that approximates the one author, performer, and text occupy in relation to the audience's production of meaning. This activity, as I have pointed out earlier, is intensified in the Orunmila-Esu dramatic paradigm. That is, both these characters and the production team initially proceed based on a given, logical system. But the interplay of the unanticipated, of phenomena such as social events outside the theatre, the class character of a given audience, the rhetorical power and logical cogency of speaker-spectators, the nature of the performance facility, and even the atmospheric conditions generate an intertext out of which viewers produce meanings that may surprise, delight, or frustrate the team's totalizing desires.

By incorporating into the written script those audience concerns for which there are no easy solutions, the playwright actually shifts the story from a morality tale to a dilemma tale. What appeared simple has been rendered complex. Furthermore, the objective of the project changes. While the morality tale seeks to inculcate and reaffirm accepted social values, the dilemma tale strives to elicit an exchange of opinion among listeners. Disorder, or the interchange of potentially random viewpoints without any integrative resolution, is favored over the stately neatness of the scripted and rehearsed artistic process. The former encourages the active participation of the assembled community in attempting to articulate solutions to issues of great importance to that group. Art is thus conceptualized as a social process to which all are expected to contribute, both in its formal and informal components.

These theoretical implications notwithstanding, what seems apparent from these revisions is a certain authorial uneasiness with the open-ended structure dictated by the Orunmila-Esu complex. Though the text includes an epilogue that renders it fully vulnerable to the "tricks" of the Esu principle, it is preceded by dialogue in which Orunmila's identity is revealed, and he demands that Esu execute his duties. The result is an attempt to insinuate greater spectator focus on the issue of compassion, for Orunmila functions semiotically as the potential curb on Esu's subversive fun and as the guarantor of justice.

Ironically, these revisions have engendered further controversy. On the one hand, experts in Yoruba cosmology have charged evidence of inaccurate, Christianizing influences in the depiction of Esu and the selfless musician, while on the other, a group of university lecturers stormed out of a performance in disgust at the alleged move toward mystification. The first charge seems partially justified in that during Esu's inquiry, Omele rejects all opportunities to save himself, opting instead to suffer along with his colleagues because he did not use the gift as directed, namely as an antidote to poverty. In fact, he is so passive in the face of impending doom that even the god urges the musician to defend himself, that is, to attempt, as would any traditionalist, to find a mode of supplication and sacrifice that would at least lessen the consequences if not totally avert what is thought to be his destiny. For reasons that have more to do with plot than character consistency, the rationalist whose plan has engendered the narrative curiously lacks any activism in confronting this crisis.

The university dons' reactions reflect a narrow conception of the function of art. Nonetheless, as I will discuss in the following section, their position is indicative of an ongoing debate concerning definitions of the base and superstructure. More important to note now is that such occurrences underscore the fact that with the Orunmila-Esu dramatic paradigm, any interpretation is always provisional. It is subject to revision on later reflection and to being overturned by the interplay of dispositions and choices of another group of observers imposing its own consensual order. Thus the paradigm openly acknowledges that drama offers no eternal visions. Rather, its meanings remain intimately connected with the realities in which it appears, as represented by the people who debate its content.

ABIOLA IRELE

[Form, Content, and Context in
Femi Osofisan's Drama]†

Of the various art forms that have flourished in the especially fertile atmosphere in which cultural production has proceeded in Nigeria, drama has been, and remains, the most vibrant. More than any other form, drama, both in its literary/textual embodiments and as it manifests itself or inheres in other performance modes in the country, has exhibited most distinctly the dynamic interplay between the various factors that animate the manifold texture of life in contemporary Nigeria. The theatrical elements in the traditional performance modes— festivals, ceremonials, masquerades, rituals, and enactments of mythic narratives that constitute an integral part of social processes, cultural expression, and communal awareness of the various ethnic groups brought together within the framework of the modern nation-state and that have been carried over into its defining context of collective existence and awareness—these elements provide the background, indeed, a massive reference, for the more recent forms of dramatic expression that have been elaborated in this context.

For the playwrights and theatre practitioners involved in the two principal areas of this contemporary expression—the popular drama of the traveling theatres, and the literary drama in English and, increasingly, in the vernacular languages—the precolonial tradition defines a cultural and aesthetic resource that is vital to their creative endeavors. This implies not so much a question of reclaiming a heritage that has been obscured—of "going back to roots," as it were—as a natural extension and reformulation of the traditional forms in vigorous existence, in a continuous development that seeks to sustain the living principles of these forms under the changed circumstances of a new sociopolitical order and the conditions of a problematic modernity. The primary interest of these more recent elaborations of theatrical practice and dramatic art in Nigeria thus derives from their bearing the impress, in terms of their themes and expressive modes, of the extensive transformations provoked by the impact of British colonialism and its concomitant pressures of social and cultural change.

It is a commonplace of critical observation that modern African literature in the European languages has been distinguished largely by its engagement with the theme of transition, and no area of the corpus has illustrated this feature more than Nigerian literature. The theme determines the local inflection writers have sought to give to their

† From the Introduction to "The Oriki of a Grasshopper" and Other Plays by Femi Osofisan (Washington, D.C.: Howard University Press, 1995) ix–xii, xxxii–xxxvi. Copyright © 1995 by Howard University Press. Reprinted with the permission of The Permissions Company, P.O. Box 243, High Bridge, NJ 08829 USA on behalf of Howard University Press. All Rights Reserved. The author's notes have been edited.

expression, arising from the need to reflect as fully as possible their immediate environment in its unique quality. This need is all the more imperative in drama, which must incorporate an immediate sense of locale and cultural atmosphere to carry any conviction with the audience to which it is addressed in the first place. Nigerian dramatists writing in English have been especially responsive to this imperative, which has resulted in their producing perhaps the most substantial body of work for the theatre on the continent. This they have achieved largely through what one might call a process of osmosis, manifested at the level of form by their conscious infusion of the literary modes of Western drama along with the European language they employ, with the principles and mechanisms of the performance modes prevalent within their own environment. This convergence of thematic preoccupations and formal adaptation of medium has imprinted a distinctive character on English-language and university-based drama, pioneered in the late fifties and early sixties by Wole Soyinka, John Pepper Clark-Bekederemo, and Ola Rotimi.

To appreciate the significance of Femi Osofisan's plays, a selection of which is presented in this volume, they must be placed in this general perspective of the development of Nigerian drama in English. They confirm the dynamism of an evolving modern literary and theatrical tradition, while at the same time seeking to reverse its dominant trends and to redefine its areas of emphasis. Two related factors, one sociopolitical, and the other literary, account for this purposive reorientation of Nigerian drama, which has been the fundamental impulse behind Osofisan's work. The first has to do with the aftereffects of the Nigerian civil war, which has been, without question, the decisive event in the evolution of Nigerian history. Indeed, the war may be said to have marked the true beginning of this history, if by this is meant the taking up by Nigerians themselves, for good or ill, of the initiative for their own collective destiny. Osofisan belongs to the generation of writers and intellectuals that emerged in the aftermath of the war, and whose responses to its social implications have given a new direction and imparted a new temper to the artistic, cultural, and intellectual life of the country.

The second factor arises from this observation, which relates to the vigor with which these younger writers have sought to revitalize the established literature that preceded their own productions, a literature associated essentially with the coming into being of the national community. They had before them an antecedent body of works that had become more or less institutionalized, and while they acknowledged the achievement of their predecessors as a valuable national resource, it was obvious to them that they had to open up new perspectives in their own work, more in keeping with the changed circumstances that the trauma of the civil war and the subsequent emergence of new social forces had imposed as a compelling reference of imaginative expression, as indeed of intellectual reflection.

These younger writers, who began to emerge during the era of the so-called oil boom, which lasted through the early seventies into the mid-eighties, produced their work in a social atmosphere that had been radically transformed by a major national crisis, followed by the establishment of what they saw as an authoritarian and prebendary state. They wrote from their perception of a condition of systemic dysfunction into which the country was being locked by the policies of successive regimes. The primacy they have accorded to social and political themes stems directly from an initial focus on the civil war itself as a salient event of the national history and consciousness; this focus became expanded in the critical literature directed against the pattern of economic and social arrangements that were rapidly put in place in the immediate aftermath of the war. For these writers, a socially responsible literature seemed the only adequate response to what they saw as comprehensive, gross distortions in the national life, and to the range of human issues this situation presented to their minds and their imaginative sensibilities.

Although poetry and fiction have served as important means of expression for these writers in their effort to establish what the poet Funso Aiyejina has called an "alter/native" tradition, drama has, for obvious reasons, taken pride of place in their output. The determining consideration has been that drama provided the most direct artistic medium not only for articulating public concerns but also for communicating in a cultural milieu that continues to place a premium on the oral mode, more so where this is channeled through the gestural and specular protocols of theatre. Femi Osofisan is not only one of the most prominent members of this new generation of Nigerian writers but also, in the general estimation, the most accomplished among the dramatists.

*   *   *

Femi Osofisan's singular contribution to Nigerian drama in English has been to consolidate its development and practice as a viable form of cultural production in the modern context of a plural society. What I have called earlier the process of osmosis by which this drama has been constituted is in full evidence in his plays, in which heterogeneous elements from various sources are held in balance and marshaled to give dramatic effect to his thematic concerns and dramatic purpose. Such is the quality of their interanimation that it is often difficult to identify the precise provenance of a particular element in many of his plays. They collaborate to define an aesthetic of theatre that is both original and appropriate to their time and place.

The preoccupation with technique in these plays results in a virtuosity that occasionally verges on a mannered theatrical style. But the self-consciousness this implies bears witness to the self-reflexivity that is an essential function of drama. Osofisan's objective seems to be to remind us of the origins of drama in ritual, as an extension of the processes of communal life. This implies a process of *stylization*, centered on the need to reformulate experience in symbolic terms. Thus, his dramatic style emphasizes the reciprocity between drama and life, so well expressed in the phrase from Shakespeare's *As You Like It* ("All the world's a stage") with which every Nigerian school-child is familiar. As Osofisan himself has declared in an interview, Nigeria is "an intensely dramatic society." Theatre serves him, then, as a mode for the reenactment in significant form of the tensions at work in this society, of the predicaments with which it is beset.

It is in this respect that myth and ritual intervene as expressive resources for Osofisan's dramatic practice. It ought to be clear by now that the view sometimes expressed of his work as "mythopoeic" is mistaken. Myth functions in Osofisan's work primarily as an anchor in the communal sensibility for the thematic unfolding of the action and symbolic schemes of the plays rather than as substantive reference. In this sense, Osofisan's approach provides an instance of what I have called elsewhere an "aesthetic traditionalism" that is a means by which modern African literature has sought validation. This is borne out by Osofisan's constant striving to mark an intellectual and emotional distance to the belief system in which the mythical discourse itself is grounded. Thus, despite the frequent evocation of the supernatural, the constant reference of his plays is to the human world.

We have commented on the risk involved in this studied detachment from the appeal of myth and ritual in his work. Apart from this risk, it presents a problem that Soyinka has pointed out in this observation: "Fascinated with myth and history, clearly, is Osofisan. . . . But an ideological conviction and the aesthetic of theatre which he attaches to it places him, in company with a number of a new generation of writers, in a confused, ambivalent creative existence towards the past."

There is, it seems to me, a misapprehension involved in Soyinka's observation, which ignores the fact that the discourse of myth and of ritual (as well as of history, as we have seen) derives not from a concrete grasp of "essences" but is related to the fabric of existence. For Soyinka, as for those who have contributed to its systematization in the African context, myth is often presented as substantial, with ritual as its signifying text. In so doing, they disregard the mobility of myth as reference, and of ritual as a form of social practice, a condition of the intentionality with which they are invariably charged and which therefore constitutes them into social forces.

It needs to be stressed in this respect that within Yoruba, as indeed within other African cultures, myth and ritual have not always had the stable meanings assigned to them in their systematic ordering by academics and intellectuals. They are not the autonomous systems of apprehension and of signification they are made out to be. Ritual, in particular, although rooted in the deeply affective narrative of myth, is ultimately no more than a strategy of negotiation: between humans and gods and between social actors. Both myth and ritual involve a constant symbolic reshuffling of the cards, so to speak, according to the needs of the moment and of circumstance, and thus present themselves as forms of discourse that serve to position the motives and interests of collectivities, as a function of their modes of insertion in the scheme of things. They are thus, we might say, "relational" by definition and function.

This understanding of the critical, "deconstructive" function of myth and ritual informs Osofisan's dramatic practice. His conception of drama as a mode of communication extends to myth, one of the means by which it is regularly codified in the traditional culture, and to ritual its performative mode. The arbitrary nature of this code enables the playwright to mobilize its suggestive potential in the expressive strategy of his plays, as a comprehensive metaphor of human existence within which dramatic form itself has its operative life. But far from precluding a challenge of the belief system to which it is bound, this "second order" status of myth within the framework of drama calls attention to its contingency, to its lack of necessity, thus leaving open the possibility of its dissociation from any structure of belief. This sheds light on what Soyinka describes as "ambivalence" in Osofisan's deployment of myth and ritual: it assumes a *tropological* character as regards formal function and a *transgressive* one as regards ideological intent.

The more serious problem that arises from the plays is their constant didactic orientation, which is inseparable from their ideological inspiration. In the Preface to *Aringindin and the Nightwatchmen*, his latest published play (not included in this volume), Osofisan has restated the social purpose of his work, which brings this conjunction into direct view:

> This play is a mirror of what we do, and fail to do—deliberately magnified of course, but only in order to increase the shock, the awareness of the peril we continue to run, all of us, by preventable choice.

The problem here is one that haunts all forms of partisan literature (as distinct from what Barbara Harlow has called "resistance literature"), which cannot but openly manifest "its palpable design" on our responses. Too often, this leads to a rhetorical utopianism that disturbs the formal coherence of the work, as in the final scene of *The Chattering and the Song*. Here, as elsewhere in the work, the platform manner of Osofisan's insistence on his ideological message betrays him into a stridency out of tune with the artistic demands of his medium. But if Osofisan does not always avoid these pitfalls of committed literature, his plays are redeemed in the end by the overall sense of form and the fine artistic sensibility they display.

This observation prompts a final question concerning the relation between content and form in the plays. That Osofisan himself is conscious of the implications of this question is made clear in the following declaration by a character in another of his plays, *Farewell to a Cannibal Rage*:

> Revolutionaries come with every season
> The words of fire flare and fade to ashes
> Only the songs of the artist remain
> Yes! Only the works of beauty
> Are not quenched in the floods of time.

Osofisan seems to insist here on the primacy of the aesthetic dimension, even in committed art, and to discount the effectivity of such art as a practical proposition. Yet the whole tenor of his work demonstrates his rejection of art as merely a self-rewarding activity and his belief in its relevance to immediate social and moral concerns. This suggests that his work hovers between the imperatives of ideology and the appeal of the aesthetic. Sandra Richards has commented on this aspect of Osofisan's work: "The distancing or alienating devices . . . may work effectively, thereby stimulating audiences to reflect upon the explicit social critique. But there exists the alternate possibility that sensual delight in the ingeniousness of the theatrical spectacle overtakes a critical sensibility."

Yet, to pose these questions at all is to recognize the significance of Osofisan's work as a powerful statement of the social and existential dilemmas of his time and place, a preoccupation the new literature in Nigeria, and especially drama, has elected as its province. His best work illuminates with an especial intelligence and force of feeling his exploration of these dilemmas, and by taking this exploration to its furthest limits of moral interrogation, Osofisan's plays compel attention and achieve distinction.

CHRIS DUNTON

[The Theatre of Femi Osofisan]†

Osofisan's very large output—of about twenty-five plays to date—includes at least half a dozen of the most imaginative and powerful works in the Nigerian English language theatre. As yet rarely seen abroad, within his own country his plays are now amongst the most frequently staged of any Nigerian dramatist, and certainly hold pride of place for many university student groups.

Osofisan's work is characterized by two features that might appear mutually contradictory or whose relationship is at least problematic: an absorption in theatrical form that leads to the use of elaborate framing devices, multiple disjunctions in tone and in narrative flow, the use of role play and the play-within-the-play; and a commitment to the probing of social and economic injustice in Nigeria that consistently places the aspirations of the underprivileged as his drama's central reference point. At least one critic, Sandra L Richards, sees no ultimate contradiction here, but emphasizes Osofisan's acceptance that much of his work has, in practice, a largely bourgeois audience and his belief that an engagement with this audience is a necessary aspect of the struggle for a more equitable future:

† *Make Man Talk True: Nigerian Drama in English Since 1970* (London: Hans Zell, 1992) 67–70, 85–87. Reprinted by permission of the author. The author's notes have been edited. Page numbers in brackets refer to this Norton Critical Edition.

How may such people be expected to accept a vision of change which seemingly downplays the value of their education and raises the status of the lower classes? The task of awakening the consciousness of these elites is exactly the challenge Osofisan has taken upon himself, because he maintains that these groups have the most crucial roles to play in determining and implementing the course of development in Nigeria.

The dramatist and critic Tunde Lakoju to some extent agrees with Richards' assumptions, suggesting that, since the growing severity of conditions in Nigeria renders 'middle-class intellectuals' more receptive to a reappraisal of their objective conditions, a progressive literary drama has at least some political value. At the same time he argues 'there is a limit to which any playwright, however "revolutionary", can claim to be presenting the lives of the working-class or peasants in his drama. When he does, he does so without their consent and without their input'.

Osofisan has created a large body of plays that strive consistently, in Chidi Amuta's words, to find 'materialist explanations' for the contradictions in modern Nigerian society, and which do so through focusing on prominent features of the State's disarray: bureaucratic ineptitude, the prevalence of armed robbery, corruption, popular mass revolt. A particular concern is the insidiousness of corruption, the frequency with which a communal commitment is broken by betrayal, and this is a theme developed more effectively by Osofisan than by Sowande, who tends to scrutinize the betrayal of commitment at the level of an individual's failure to satisfy his own best potential. Generally, Osofisan addresses the need for social and political transformation far less rhetorically than do some other Nigerian dramatists. At the same time, perhaps especially because his project has yielded such impressive results, his work prompts questions about the potential of theatre as political activity, about the projection of political activism in the theatre, and—to return to Tunde Lakoju's point— about the seizure and use made by a literary drama of the experience of Nigeria's urban and rural masses.

In an interview with Ossie Enekwe, Osofisan speaks confidently of the corrective role of the dramatist:

> I want [the spectator] washed inside out, in the naked truth, and then I sew him back again a different man. I believe that, if we wound ourselves often and painfully enough with reality, with the reality all around us, if we refuse to bandage our sensitive spots away from the hurt of truth, that we can attain a new, and positive awareness.

Two years later, he is more cautious, expressing his role in terms closer to those of Akanji Nasiru, arguing 'it is not the writer who will correct Nigeria's . . . situation. The writer can help diagnose and increase awareness; he can protest, and move others to protest; he cannot cure or heal. . . .' But the idea of critique, of re-evaluation, of self-knowledge is present throughout. In his PhD thesis, Osofisan argues the modern playwright is no longer involved with 'the inculcation of communal faith or the celebration of customary ethos', but that his objective is 'the stimulation of active questioning, doubting and insurrection'. It is not surprising that, if Ogun is Soyinka's presiding god, for Osofisan the primary attraction is to Ifa, the 'symbol of knowledge, progress and hope for a better future'. The search for knowledge, for the understanding of a need for a commitment to the well being of society, is at the centre of Osofisan's work.

The imperative to stimulate question, debate, to elicit an audience response that is lively and critical, has led Osofisan to develop a range of techniques, of formal characteristics, that are present in the work of some other Nigerian dramatists but nowhere as fully developed as in his own. Some of these are closely influenced by Brechtian theatre: for example, the deliberate introduction, as the play proceeds, of disjunctions in style, tone, narrative flow; or the 'exposure' by the cast of their own status as actors (a device that threatens to become degraded to convention—though, seemingly aware of this, Osofisan pumps more life into it in later plays such as *Farewell to a Cannibal Rage*). The frequent use of role play episodes and their expansion into the play within the play, is a central characteristic of Soyinka's work (in *The Road* notably), but Osofisan employs the device even more extensively. Questioned about this, he gives a representational explanation, referring to the prevalence of role playing in Nigerian society ('People put on extraordinary masks; it's an intensely dramatic society'); but at the same time, and more significantly, the use of role play episodes throws into close focus the distinction between the representational and the presentational (again, Osofisan comments: 'I'm very much interested in the theatre as game, as metaphor. A play with levels, masks, role-playing, makes for a lively, provocative theatre'). Through the use of role play episodes Osofisan helps the audience to see how different ideological positions are projected by individuals, to be wary of a role that is false or impositional; to see how one thing stands in relation to another. That principle of the theatre as critique is carried forward, also, through a critical engagement with earlier theatre, the concept of a play as response to a preceding play. A process of adaptation may, it is true, be ideologically neutral: Osofisan has claimed he finds it difficult to write effective plots for comedy and gives this as a simple explanation for his borrowings from Gogol (*Who's Afraid of Solarin?*), Feydeau (*Midnight Hotel*) and Chekhov (*The Engagement*). But other plays can be seen as answers to existing works, refinements or rejections of their ideological burdens: *No More the Wasted Breed*, for instance, and *Another Raft*, which have as their starting points plays by Soyinka and Clark. Further, if the orthodox, most widely disseminated versions of history can be seen as texts, Osofisan's notion of theatre as critique takes on a wider dimension, challenging the validity for a reading of contemporary Nigerian realities of the accepted versions of the reign of Alafin Abiodun (*The Chattering and the Song*) or the status of Moremi (*Morountodun*). Behind this is Osofisan's insistence that any stated reading of the social world should be challenged, and these fixed, established readings include myth. In Osofisan's own words, 'I may use myth or ritual, but only from a subversive perspective. I borrow ancient forms specifically to unmask them'.

As Sandra L. Richards has pointed out, it is not the case that Osofisan simply opposes tradition; rather, 'he subjects tradition to scrutiny and reinterpretation, using its own modes of thought and structure'. The point is to offer the audience ways of exit from official history; to provide, in Dario Fo's phrase, 'counter-information on events in our social reality'. And beyond that there is a further objective (which brings us back to the principles of Ifa) that is, to stimulate in the audience an awareness of its own critical procedures. It is in this context that Richards argues that Osofisan's work seeks consistently to avoid the fixed form. Confirming the nature of Osofisan's drama as critique, she draws attention to the striving for open form in much of his work, to Osofisan's utilization of a whole range of theatrical devices to displace 'artistic hegemony' and to stimulate 'an explanation debated and articulated by [the audience itself]'. Again, however, questions arise as to how far this works in practice (a set of questions germane to questions about the political effectiveness of a literary drama); how far does Osofisan's striving for open ended form succeed in easing open the bounds of formal theatrical production, how far does his theatre remain entrapped—as production—within the material reality of Nigerian social experience?

* * *

Esu and the Vagabond Minstrels is one of the plays by Osofisan that has made the largest impact on its audience. Written in 1984, while Osofisan was at the University of Benin, it was revised and then produced at Ife in early 1986, when it was given a longer run than is usual for campus productions, and to packed houses. The play provoked some controversy over its apparent 'rehabilitation' of the god Esu—identified by conservative Christian groups on campus as none other than Satan.

Here again themes and motifs recur that are familiar from the earlier plays. While there is no systematic attempt to 'demystify' the process of performance (virtually the entire action constitutes a play within a play, but there are no intervening reminders of the actors' status), all the same, as in *Farewell*, the role of the artist is a critical concern, with Osofisan questioning again the social function of patronage of the arts by the elite. Thus the Old Man (Esu) reminds the group of minstrels:

> . . . . I know you:
> You used to eat in abundance, yes!
> At the feast of the wealthy, once,
> You sang the praise-songs,
> While their victims persished at the door. [374]

The most striking parallel with Osofisan's earlier work, though, is with *Once Upon Four Robbers*. In both plays, a group (there robbers, here itinerant singers) are granted a 'magic boon' enabling them to acquire wealth, in this case by solving the problems of a succession of individuals encountered at a crossroad. As in *Four Robbers*, in *Esu* the boon is granted with strict conditions: in this case that the art of healing should be used specifically to bring 'redress to the wronged / And justice to the exploited' [374].

During the early part of the play differences and similarities emerge between Osofisan's preoccupation here and in *Four Robbers*. Characterization of the minstrel group reveals again the fragility of solidarity amongst the socially marginalized. At the same time, the social setting is less realistic than in *Four Robbers*, with less specific detailing of the quality of life under the 'kleptocracy'. The fact, too, that the minstrels, while poverty stricken, are not stigmatized as a group in the way of the armed robbers, means that the tension that exists in *Four Robbers* between magic and realistic plot elements does not emerge here (nor the consequent pointing of the theme of natural as opposed to official justice). Overall, then, in terms of its thematic development, *Esu* stands at an angle to *Four Robbers*. Rather than the full frontal focusing in that play upon the venality, the injustice, of government and of its supporting structures, here Osofisan is more concerned with the quality of the conduct of each individual under such conditions, that is, with the question of individual choice.

While in *Four Robbers* the action is set in a market, in *Esu* the setting is a crossroad, a place of choice in a rather weak sense in European lore, but in Yoruba culture a much more resonant marker for individual will and for an individual's orientation towards the different forces his/her life intersects with, and towards destiny. At the crossroad waits Esu, and for a Yoruba audience, presumably, the whole action of this play is cast under the perspective of that god, the god who watches over the balance of good and evil and over the playing out of those principles through the sum total of human activity. With the magic boon granted to the minstrels (by Esu in disguise), there follows a series of encounters between the group and distressed individuals to whom they can choose to supply the healing dance ritual which Esu has taught them. Here Osofisan exploits parallelism—a major technique in Nigerian oral narrative (and one he draws upon again for a more recent play, *Twingle Twangle*)—in order to show how each of the suppliants represents a better or worse cause, and how each of the minstrels variously rises to the challenge of a self-denying use of the boon or succumbs to greed. By the end of this section, one of the minstrels, Omele, has exploited the boon so entirely selflessly, he has relieved a couple of leprosy, taking the disease on himself; the five variant healing episodes are capped by a powerful section [397–99] in which he is rejected by the other four—now wealthy—minstrels. Very much in the order of folk narrative, Esu then reveals himself, and there is a brief assessment of the quality of choice made by each of the minstrels. Finally Esu deals out punishment to those 'who have put their selfish greed first before everything, including their humanity' [408]. Though in its closing moments the play does extend—maybe not very convincingly—from the notion of individual humanity to the idea of communal action, in *Esu* Osofisan to an unexpected extent draws aside from a central focusing on actual social conditions, providing here a richly entertaining parable that has more to do with our response to individual suffering than with a confrontation with the forces that perpetuate this.

* * *

African Drama: A Chronology

1826	On Wednesday, April 22, a command performance is sponsored by the *alafin* (king) of Oyo by an Alarinjo theatre troupe for the entertainment of British explorers Hugh Clapperton and Richard Lander and their party.
1830	France annexes Algeria, inaugurating more than a century of colonial domination of North Africa.
1850s	A group of Syrian-born dramatists—Salim Khalil al-Naqqash, Yusuf Khayyat, and Sulayman al-Qardahi, among others—are active in Egypt by this period. Their theatrical fare is a medley of songs, dances, and dramatic sketches.
1878	Yusuf Khayyat produces a play, *al-Zalum* (*The Tyrant*), that puts him in trouble with the Khedive, leading to his banishment.
1880s	By this time in Lagos, Nigeria, European-style amateur dramatic activities by Afro-Brazilian returnees and other Europhile Lagosians are thriving.
1884–85	The Berlin Conference, at which Africa was partitioned according to the interests of European imperialist nations.
1899–1902	The Boer War.
1900	Around this time in the Belgian Congo, an Ekonda named Itetele reorganizes his people's songs, dances, and ceremonies into a new form of performance named the "Bobongo." Also around this time in Madagascar, an indigenous dramatic genre, the *kaonserita*, which is very much like music-hall performance, is well-developed and thriving. Prominent dramatists of this form are Alexis Rakotoba and Tsalatra Rajaonan, author of about sixty plays and numerous novels.
1912–16	In Ethiopia, the beginning of the modern theatre movement. In 1916, performance of a satire on the country's corrupt administration, Takla Hawaryat's *Fables and Animal Comedy,* based on La Fontaine's fables, leads to a ban on all theatrical performances.

Based partly on *The Drama of Black Africa* by Anthony Graham-White (New York: Samuel French, 1974).

1915   Kobina Sekyi's *The Blinkards* written and staged in the
             Gold Coast, later Ghana, after independence in 1957.
             It is based on the British comedy-of-manners form and
             uses dialogue that freely mixes English and Fanti to sat-
             irize the class pretensions and racial inferiority complex
             of the Anglophile Cape Coast elite.

1918   First West African concert party troupe founded by
             Master Yalley in the Gold Coast. Concert parties and
             trios are small acting and singing groups that present
             improvised comedies with a mass appeal in Akan lan-
             guages.

1923   Egypt gains independence from Britain and the Khedive
             becomes king.

1925   African students at Achimota College, the Gold Coast,
             one of the most prestigious high schools in British West
             Africa, are by this date writing and performing plays in
             English and, until 1933, in Akan languages.

1926   In Uganda, King's College, Budo, a prestigious boys'
             secondary school, is by this date performing plays in
             English and local languages.

1927   In South Africa, the first troupe of black actors, the
             Mtetwa Lucky Stars, is founded by a school teacher,
             Esau Mtetwa, presenting sketches in Zulu.

1930   British Drama League sponsors a conference on "Native
             African Drama"; at the end of the conference there is a
             formal declaration that there is no indigenous African
             drama.
             The ban on drama in Ethiopia imposed in 1916 is lifted
             upon the accession of Haile Selassie I; Yoftahe Neguse's
             Vain Entertainment, an allegory of the marriage of Faith
             and Fortune, is performed as part of the coronation
             celebrations.

1932   Charles Beart pioneers literary drama in French West
             Africa by encouraging African pupils at Bingerville to
             improvise and write plays. In 1933, he becomes prin-
             cipal of Ecole William Ponty, the most prestigious high
             school in French West Africa, and launches a tradition
             of playwriting by having pupils collect and transcribe
             oral sources.

1933   In South Africa, Bantu Dramatic Society is formed at
             the Bantu Men's Social Centre in Johannesburg with a
             first offering of *She Stoops to Conquer.*

1934   Ethiopia's first theatre is built, a zinc shed at the lycee
             Menelik 11.

1935   In Egypt, Ali Ahmed Ba-Kathir, born of Yemeni parents,
             is naturalized as an Egyptian; until his death in 1969
             he is active as one of North Africa's most influential dra-
             matists.

1936–41   Italian occupation of Ethiopia.

1937   A group from the Ecole William Ponty performs at the Exposition Internationale in Paris to great acclaim.

1938   Bernard Dadie, F. J. K. Amon d'Arby, and G. Coffi Gadeau, graduates of Ecole William Ponty, found the Theatre Indigene de Cote d'Ivoire; they write and direct plays for this group, which lasts until 1946.

1943   In the Gold Coast, the United Society for Christian Literature publishes the first two full-length plays in English by West Africans, J. B. Danquah's *The Third Woman* and F. K. Fiawoo's *The Fifth Landing Stage*.

1945   In Nigeria, Hubert Ogunde founds the Ogunde Concert Party, the first of the professional Yoruba-language "Traveling Theatre" troupes, modern Africa's most successful professional theatre movement.

1946   New French constitution includes deputies from the colonies in the metropolitan government and declares all residents of overseas territories French citizens.

1947   *Presence Africaine* is founded in Paris by Alioune Diop as the organ of the negritude movement. The journal has since become the leading and longest-surviving cultural journal of Francophone Africa, with a bilingual edition reaching out to Anglophone Africa and the English-speaking African diaspora.

1949   In Paris, Keita Fodeba founds Le Theatre Africaine, which moves to Guinea in 1959 to become Ballets Africaine.

1952   The Egyptian Revolution—Gamel Abdel Nasser and the "Young Officers" overthrow King Farouk.

1955   Haile Selassie 1 Theatre opens in Addis Ababa with a resident theatre company.

1956   Independence of Tunisia and Morocco from France.

              First World Congress of Negro Writers in Rome, co-sponsored by the Paris-based journal *Presence Africaine*.

              Compagnie des Griots is founded in Paris by African actors and stages premiere of Jean Genet's *Les Negres* (*The Blacks*).

1957   Independence of Ghana (formerly the Gold Coast), the first black African country to gain political freedom from European colonial rule.

              Ulli Beier founds *Black Orpheus*, the first cultural journal of Anglophone Africa, which reaches out to the writers and intellectuals of the English-speaking African diaspora.

1958   Referendum is held throughout French Africa on rela-
             tionship with France; only Guinea chooses to become
             independent.
             Kateb Yacine's play *Le Cadavre Encercle* (*The Encircled
             Corpse*) is produced in Paris, directed by Jean-Marie
             Serreau; the production generates a public riot on ac-
             count of its fierce attack on colonialism.
             Players of the Dawn founded by graduates of the Uni-
             versity of Ibadan, Nigeria.
             Efua Sutherland founds Experimental Theatre Players,
             which later becomes the Ghana Drama Studio. The
             group produces works in English and Akan languages.
1959   *Presence Africaine* sponsors Second World Congress of
             Negro Writers, held in Paris.
1960   Sixteen African countries gain political independence,
             including Nigeria. Wole Soyinka's first major full-length
             play, *A Dance of the Forests*, is staged as part of the
             independence celebrations.
             BBC African Service begins a monthly African Theatre
             radio series.
             Ghana Drama Studio building opens its courtyard the-
             atre, which is based on traditional performance areas; it
             is perhaps the first modern African theatre building to
             be based on an indigenous model.
             In Johannesburg, The Serpent Players, a group of black
             actors, is founded with the assistance of Athol Fugard.
1961   The University of Ibadan Traveling Theatre is created,
             taking adaptations of Moliere, Shakespeare, and other
             European playwrights to towns and villages throughout
             Nigeria.
             In Kampala, Rajat Neogy founds *Transition*, a lively cul-
             tural journal; it is suppressed by the Ugandan govern-
             ment in 1968 and in 1971 moves to Accra, Ghana,
             where Soyinka becomes its editor.
1962   Independence of Algeria after eight years of one of the
             most bitter anticolonial wars of national liberation in
             Africa.
             School of Music and Drama founded by the Ghana In-
             stitute of Arts and Culture and the University of Ghana.
             Duro Ladipo founds his traveling theatre company, the
             first to use Yoruba musical instruments. In 1964 his
             company appears in the Berlin Festival with his master-
             piece, *Oba Koso*, to great critical acclaim.
             School of Drama is founded at the University of Ibadan.
1963   Creative Arts Centre is founded at the Haile Selassie
             University, Addis Ababa, opening with Tsegaye Gabre-
             Medhin's first English-language play, *Tewodros*.
             Ugandan National Theatre starts a drama school.

1964	Chemchemi Theatre Company is founded in Nairobi by exiled South African writer Ezekiel Mphahlele and performs plays in English and Swahili.
1965	1500-seat Daniel Sorano Theatre opens in Dakar, Senegal.
	Theatre Arts Department is founded at the University of Dar es Salaam, Tanzania.
	University-based Makerere Free Traveling Theatre makes first tour of East Africa, presenting plays in English and several indigenous languages.
1966	World Festival of Negro Arts, Dakar.
1967–69	Nigerian civil war. Soyinka is detained in federal prison for his antiwar efforts for the duration of the war; most of the detention is in solitary confinement.
1967	BBC African Service drama competition. First prize is won by Guillaume Oyono-Mbia for his one-act play *Until Further Notice*. France's Office de Cooperation Radiophonique (OCORA), which is run by the Division des Affaires Exterieures et de la Cooperation, sponsors a competition of Francophone African drama; first prize is won by Guy Menga of Congo-Brazzaville for *L'Oracle*. The competition has since become an annual event.
	Nigerian Armchair Theatre, a weekly half-hour play series, begins on Western Nigeria TV.
1968	Robert Serumaga and others found Theatre Limited with the intention of making it the first fully professional theatre in East Africa.
1969	Festival of Pan-African Culture, Algiers.
	Oxford University Press (Nigeria) sponsors playwriting competition in English and some indigenous languages and Ola Rotimi wins English section.
	Soyinka's *Kongi's Harvest* is filmed, directed by Ossie Davis, with Soyinka himself playing the dictator Kongi.
1970	At the University of Zambia, Chikwakwa (Grass Roots) Theatre is founded by Michael Etherton; student members perform plays in a converted tobacco barn.
1977	World Festival of Black Arts and Culture (FESTAC), Lagos. At the end of the festival, the Center for Black and African Arts and Civilization (CBAAC) is established, with its permanent location in Lagos.

1986   In June, Wole Soyinka, as president of the International
            Theatre Institute (ITI), is embroiled in an international
            press and media controversy following the decision of
            the ITI to drop a dramatization of George Orwell's *An-
            imal Farm* by the National Theatre of Britain from the
            official program of the *Festival of Nations* in Baltimore,
            Maryland. The ITI decision is based on a petition by the
            Soviet Union that the *Animal Farm* production is a
            veiled cold war–inspired cultural assault on the Soviet
            state.
            In October, Soyinka wins the Nobel Prize for literature.

1994   *The Cambridge Guide to African and Caribbean Theatre*,
            edited by Martin Banham, Errol Hill, and George
            Woodyard, is published.

Selected Bibliography

• indicates works included or excerpted in this Norton Critical Edition

GENERAL: HISTORY, CULTURE, POLITICS

Boahen, Adu. *African Perspectives on Colonialism*. Baltimore: Johns Hopkins University Press, 1987.

Cabral, Amiicar. *Unity and Struggle*. London: Heinemann Educational Books, 1980.

Davidson, Basil. *The Black Man's Burden: Africa and the Curse of the Nation-state*. New York: Times Books, 1992.

de Braganza, Basil, and Immanuel Wallerstein, eds. *The African Liberation Reader*. 3 vols. London: Zed Press, 1982 [Vol. 1, *The Anatomy of Colonialism*; Vol. 2, *The National Liberation Movements*; Vol. 3, *The Strategy of Liberation*].

Fanon, Frantz. *A Dying Colonialism*. Trans. Haakon Chevalier. New York: Grove Press, 1967.

Josephy, Alvin M. Jr., ed. *Horizon History of Africa*. New York: American Heritage Publishers, 1971.

Langley, J. Ayo, ed. *Ideologies of Liberation in Black Africa, 1850–1970*. London: Rex Collings, 1979.

AFRICAN LITERARY HISTORY

Arnold, Stephen, ed. *African Literature Studies: The Present State*. Washington, D.C.: Three Continents Press, 1985.

Awoonor, Kofi. *The Breast of the Earth: A Survey of the History, Culture and Literature of Africa South of the Sahara*. Garden City, N.Y.: Anchor Press, 1976.

Cartey, Wilfred. *Whispers from a Continent: Writings from Contemporary Black Africa*. New York: Random House, 1969.

Cook, David. *African Literature: A Critical View*. London: Longman, 1977.

Duerden, Dennis. *African Art and Literature: The invisible Present*. London: Heinemann Educational Books, 1977.

Irele, Abiola. *The African Experience in Literature and Ideology*. London: Heinemann, 1981.

Klein, Leonard S., ed. *African Literatures in the Twentieth Century*. New York: Ungar Publishing Company, 1986.

Lindfors, Bernth, ed. *Black African Literatures in English*. Detroit: Gale Research Company, 1979.

Ngugi wa Thiong'o. *Homecoming: Essays on African and Caribbean Literature, Culture and Politics*. London: Heinemann, 1972.

Olney, James. *Tell Me Africa: An Approach to African Literature*. Princeton University Press, 1973.

Wauthier, Claude. *The Literature and Thought of Modern Africa*. London: Heinemann, 1978.

AFRICAN DRAMA

Al-Khozai, Mohamed Ali. *The Development of Early Arabic Drama, 1847–1900*. London: Longman, 1984.

Banham, Martin, and Clive Wake. *African Theatre Today*. London: Pitman, 1976.

———, Errol Hill, and George Woodyard, eds. *The Cambridge Guide to African and Caribbean Theatre*. Cambridge: Cambridge University Press, 1994.

Barber, Karin, Joachim Fiebach, and Alain Ricard, eds. *Drama and Theatre in Africa: Intercultural Perspectives*. Bayreuth, Germany: Eckhard Breitlinger and Reinhard Sander, 1986.

Bernard, M. *Le Theatre arabe*. Paris: Maspero, 1969 [a UNESCO publication].

"Drama in Africa." *African Literature Today* 8 (1976). Special issue.

Drama Review 32.2 (Summer 1988). Special issue on African theatre.

Etherton, Michael. *The Development of African Drama*. London: Hutchison University Library for Africa, 1982.

Graham-White, Anthony. *The Drama of Black Africa*. New York: Samuel French, 1974.

• Jeyifo, Biodun. "The Reinvention of Theatrical Tradition." In *The Intercultural Performance Reader*. Ed. Patrice Pavis. New York: Routledge, 1996. 149–61.

———. *The Yoruba Popular Travelling Theatre of Nigeria*. Lagos: Nigeria Magazine, 1984.

Kerr, David. *African Popular Theatre*. London: James Currey, 1995.

• ———. "Art as Tool, Weapon or Shield." In *African Theatre in Development*. Ed. Martin Banham et al. London: James Currey, 1999. 79–86.

Landau, Jacob S. *Studies in Arab Theatre and Cinema*. Philadelphia: University of Pennsylvania Press, 1958.

• Ngugi wa Thiong'o. *Penpoints, Gunpoints and Dreams: Towards a Critical Theory of the Arts and the State in Africa*. Oxford: Clarendon, 1998.

Ogunba, Oyin, and Abiola Irele, eds. *Theatre in Africa*. Ibadan, Nigeria: University of Ibadan Press, 1978.

Schipper, Mineke. *Theatre and Society in Africa*. Athens: Ohio University Press, 1982.

Soyinka, Wole. *Myth, Literature and the African World*. Cambridge: Cambridge University Press, 1976.

Theatre Research International 7 (Autumn 1982). Special issue on African theatre.

Traore, Bakary. *The Black African Theatre and Its Social Functions*. Trans. Dapo Adelugba. Ibadan, Nigeria: University of Ibadan Press, 1972.

Waters, Harold A. *Black Theatre in French: A Guide*. Sherbrooke, Canada: Editions Naaman, 1978.

AMA ATA AIDOO

Adelugba, Dapo. "Language and Drama: Ama Ata Aidoo." *African Literature Today*, no. 8. New York: Africana, 1976.

• Brown, Lloyd. *Women Writers of Black Africa*. Westport, Conn.: Greenwood Press, 1981.

Conde, Maryse. "Three Female Writers in Modern Africa: Flora Nwapa, Ama Ata Aidoo, and Grace Ogot." *Presence Africaine* 82 (1972).

Grant, Jane W. *Ama Ata Aidoo: The Dilemma of a Ghost—A Study Guide*. Harlow, U.K.: Longman, 1980.

Hill-Lubin, Mildred A. "The Relationship of African-Americans and Africans: A Recurring Theme in the Works of Ama Ata Aidoo." *Presence Africaine* 124 (1982).

Horne, Naana Bayinwa. "Ama Ata Aidoo." In *Twentieth-Century Caribbean and Black Writers*. Ed. Bernth Lindfors and Rienhard Sander. Detroit: Gale, 1992.

• Innes, C. L. "Mothers or Sisters?" In *Motherlands: Black Women's Writing from Africa, the Caribbean and South Asia*. Ed. Susheila Nasta. New Brunswick, N.J.: Rutgers University Press, 1991.

• Odamtten, Vincent O. *The Art of Ama Ata Aidoo: Polyletics and Reading Against Neocolonialism*. Gainesville: University Press of Florida, 1994.

Rea, C. J. "The Culture Line: A Note on *The Dilemma of a Ghost*." *African Forum* 1.1 (1966).

ATHOL FUGARD, JOHN KANI, AND WINSTON NTSHONA

• Fugard, Athol. Introduction to *Statements*. New York: Theatre Communications Group, 1986.

Hauptfleisch, Temple, Wilma Viljoen, and Celeste van Greuman. *Athol Fugard: A Source Guide*. Johannesburg: Donker, 1972.

Kavanagh, Robert. "Art and Revolution in South Africa: The Theatre of Athol Fugard." *The African Communist* (London), no. 88 (1981).

———. *Theatre and Cultural Struggle in South Africa*. London: Zed Press, 1985.

Read, John. *Athol Fugard: A Bibliography*. Grahamstown, South Africa: NELM, 1991.

• Seymour, Hilary. " 'Siswe Bansi Is Dead': A Study of Artistic Ambivalence." *Race and Class* 20.3 (1980): 283–88.

Vandenbroucke, Russell. *Athol Fugard: Bibliography, Biography, Playography*. London: TQ Publications, 1977.

• ———." 'Robert Zwelinzima Is Alive' " In *Athol Fugard*. Ed. Stephen Gray. Johannesburg: McGraw-Hill, 1982.

———. *Truths the Hand Can Touch: The Theatre of Athol Fugard*. New York: Theatre Communications Group, 1985.

• Walder, Dennis. *Athol Fugard*. London: Macmillan, 1984.

TSEGAYE GABRE-MEDHIN

Adera, Taddesse, and Ali Jamale Ahmed. *Silence Is Not Golden: A Critical Anthology of Ethiopian Literature*. Lawrence, N.J.: Red Sea Press, 1995.
• Gabre-Medhin, Tsegaye. Author's Note to *A Collision of Altars*. London: Rex Collings, 1977.
———. "Literature and the African Public." *Ethiopian Observer* (London) 2.1 (1967): 63–67.
Gessesse, Tesfaye. "Ethiopian Literature Before and After the Revolution." *Lotus: Afro-Asian Writings* (Cairo, 1978).
• Jeyifo, Biodun. *The Truthful Lie: Essays in a Sociology of African Drama*. London: New Beacon, 1985.
• Pankhurst, Richard. "*A Collision of Altars*: Notes on History." In *A Collision of Altars* by Tsegaye Gabre-Medhin. London: Rex Collings, 1977.
• Plastow, Jane. *African Theatre and Politics: The Evolution of Theatre in Ethiopia, Tanzania, and Zimbabwe*. Amsterdam and Atlanta, Ga.: Rodopi, 1996.
———. "Ethiopia: The Creation of a Theatre Culture." Master's thesis, Manchester University, 1989.

TAWFIK AL-HAKIM

Ali, Mohamed Hamed. *Philosophical Concepts in Five Published Plays by the Egyptian Dramatist Tawfiq al-Hakim*. Ph.D. diss., University of Denver, 1968.
Barbour, N. "The Arabic Theatre in Egypt." *Bulletin of the School of African and Oriental Studies* 111 (1935–37): 173–87, 991–1012.
Bar-Nassim, Nahman. *An Approach to Tawfiq al-Hakim, the Dramatist*. Ph.D. diss., University of Pennsylvania, 1967.
Long, Richard. "Tawfiq al-Hakim and the Arab Theatre." *Middle East Studies* 5 (1969).
• ———. *Tawfiq al-Hakim: Playwright of Egypt*. London: Ithaca Press, 1979.
• Johnson-Davies, Denys. Introduction to *The Fate of a Cockroach and Other Plays*. Washington, D.C.: Three Continents Press, 1973.
• Starkey, Paul. *From the Ivory Tower: A Critical Study of Tawfik al-Hakim*. London: Ithaca Press, 1987.

NGUGI WA THIONG'O

Brown, Nicholas. "Revolution and Recidivism: The Problem of History in the Plays of Ngugi wa Thiong'o." *Research in African Literatures* 30.4 (Winter 1999): 56–72.
Cantalupo, Charles, ed. *The World of Ngugi wa Thiong'o*. Trenton, N.J.: Africa World Press, 1995.
Cook, David, and Michael Okenimpe. *Ngugi wa Thiong'o: An Introduction to His Writing*. London: Heinemann, 1982.
Killam, G. D. *An Introduction to the Writings of Ngugi*. London: Heinemann, 1980.
———, ed. *Critical Perspectives on Ngugi wa Thiong'o*. Washington, D.C.: Three Continents Press, 1984.
• Lovesey, Oliver. *Ngugi wa Thiong'o*. New York: Twayne Publishers, 2000.
• Ngugi wa Thiong'o. "Women in Cultural Work: The Fate of the Kamiriithu Theatre in Kenya." In *Readings in African Popular Culture*. Ed. Karin Barber. Bloomington: Indiana University Press, 1997.
Robson, C. B. *Ngugi wa Thiong'o*. London: Macmillan, 1979.

FEMI OSOFISAN

Awodiya, Muyiwa, ed. *Extensions in Drama and Literature: Interviews with Femi Osofisan*. Ibadan, Nigeria: Kraft Books, 1993.
• Dunton, Chris. *Make Man Talk True: Nigerian Drama in English Since 1970*. London: Hans Zell, 1992.
• Irele, Abiola. Introduction to *The Oriki of a Grasshopper and Other Plays* by Femi Osofisan. Washington, D.C.: Howard University Press, 1995.
Jeyifo, Biodun. "Femi Osofisan as a Literary Critic and Theorist." *Matatu* 2.1 (1987): 47–51.
Obafemi, Olu. "Revolutionary Aesthetics in Recent Nigerian Theatre." *African Literature Today* 12 (1982): 118–36.
• Osofisan, Femi. *Playing Dangerously: Drama at the Frontier of Terror in a 'Postcolonial' State*. Ibadan, Nigeria: University of Ibadan, 1997.

Osundare, Niyi. "Social Message of a Nigerian Dramatist." *West Africa* 3262 (28 January 1980): 147–50.
• Richards, Sandra. *Ancient Songs Set Ablaze.* Washington, D.C.: Howard University Press, 1996.
———. "Femi Osofisan." In *Dictionary of Literary Biography: African and Caribbean Writers.* Vol. 125. Ed. Bernth Lindfors and Reinhard Sanders. Columbia, S.C.: Bruccoli Clark, Layman, 1993.

WOLE SOYINKA

Booth, James. *Writers and Politics in Nigeria.* London: Hodder and Stoughton, 1981.
• Etherton, Michael. "Tribute to Wole Soyinka." In *Before Our Very Eyes: Tribute to Wole Soyinka.* Ed. Dapo Adelugba. Ibadan, Nigeria: Spectrum Books, 1987.
Gibbs, James. *Wole Soyinka.* Modern Dramatists Series. London: Macmillan, 1986.
• Heywood, Annemarie. "The Fox's Dance: The Staging of Wole Soyinka's Plays." In *Critical Perspectives on Wole Soyinka.* Ed. James Gibbs. Washington, D.C.: Three Continents Press, 1980.
Jones, Eldred. *The Writing of Wole Soyinka.* London: Heinemann, 1973.
Katrak, Ketu. *Wole Soyinka and Modern Tragedy: A Study of Dramatic Theory and Practice.* Westport, Conn.: Greenwood Press, 1986.
Maduakor, Obi. *Wole Soyinka: An Introduction to His Writing.* New York: Garland Press, 1986.
Moore, Gerald. *Wole Soyinka.* Rev. ed. London: Evans, 1978.
Ogunba, Oyin. *The Movement of Transition: A Study of the Plays of Wole Soyinka.* Ibadan, Nigeria: University of Ibadan Press, 1975.
• Soyinka, Wole. "Author's Note." In *Death and the King's Horseman.* London: Methuen, 1975.
• ———. *Art, Dialogue and Outrage: Essays on Literature and Culture.* Ibadan, Nigeria: New Horn Press, 1988.
• Williams, Adebayo. "Ritual as Social Symbolism: Cultural Death and the King's Horseman." In *Soyinka: A Collection of Critical Essays.* Ed. Oyin Ogunba. Ibadan, Nigeria: Syndicated Communications, 1994.
Wright, Derek. *Wole Soyinka Revisited.* New York: Twayne, 1993.

KATEB YACINE

Abdoun, Mohamed Ismail. *Kateb Yacine.* Algiers: SNED, 1983.
• Aresu, Bernard. *Counterhegemonic Discourse from the Maghreb: The Poetics of Kateb's Fiction.* Tübingen: Gunter Narr Verlag, 1993.
Aziza, Mohamed. *Le Theatre et l'islam.* Tunis and Algiers: SNED, 1970.
———. *Regards sur le theatre arabe contemporain.* Tunis: Maison Tunisienne de l'Edition, 1962.
Baffet, Roselyne. *Tradition theatrale et modernite en Algerie.* Paris: l'Harmattan, 1985.
Dejoux, Jean. "Kateb Yacine, romancier, poete et dramaturge." *Presence Africaine,* no. 15 (Autumn 1977).
• Kaye, Jacqueline, and Abdelhamid Zoubir. *The Ambiguous Compromise.* London and New York: Routledge, 1990.
Roth, Arlette. *Le Theatre Algerie de langue dialectale.* Paris: Maspero, 1967.
• Salhi, Kamal. *The Politics and Aesthetics of Kateb Yacine: From Francophone Literature to Popular Theatre in Algeria and Outside.* Lewiston: Edwin Mellen Press, 1999.